Culturally Informed Approaches to Behavioral and Educational Assessment

Also Available

Handbook of Neurodevelopmental and Genetic Disorders in Adults
Edited by Sam Goldstein and Cecil R. Reynolds

Handbook of Psychological and Educational Assessment of Children, Second Edition: Personality, Behavior, and Context
Edited by Cecil R. Reynolds and Randy W. Kamphaus

Culturally Informed Approaches to Behavioral and Educational Assessment

edited by
Jennifer M. Twyford, Katie Eklund,
Erin Dowdy, Randy W. Kamphaus,
and Cecil R. Reynolds

THE GUILFORD PRESS
New York London

A Division of Guilford Publications, Inc.
www.guilford.com

Printed in the United States of America

This book is printed on acid-free paper.

For product and safety concerns within the EU, please contact *GPSR@taylorandfrancis.com*, Taylor & Francis Verlag GmbH, Kaufingerstraße 24, 80331 München, Germany.

Last digit is print number: 9 8 7 6 5 4 3 2 1

Library of Congress Cataloging-in-Publication Data is available from the publisher.

ISBN 978-1-4625-6128-5 (cloth)

About the Editors

Jennifer M. Twyford, PhD, NCSP, is Associate Professor in the School Psychology Program at Lewis & Clark College, where she serves as Co-Director of the Hybrid Track and as Assessment Coordinator. Dr. Twyford serves on the board of directors of the Oregon School Psychologists Association and on the editorial boards of several school psychology journals. She maintains a small private practice and has provided clinical services across the spectrum of school, juvenile justice, outpatient, and inpatient settings. Dr. Twyford's research interests include systemic response and culturally responsible identification and prevention of mental health disorders. She is passionate about the training of multilingual and culturally responsible school psychologists.

Katie Eklund, PhD, NCSP, is Professor in the Department of Educational Psychology at the University of Wisconsin–Madison. Prior to entering academia, Dr. Eklund worked in public education for 10 years as a school administrator, school psychologist, and school social worker. Her research focuses on school mental health, including universal screening and intervention for children with behavioral and social–emotional concerns, culturally responsive mental health interventions, social–emotional learning, and school safety. Dr. Eklund is Co-Director of the School Mental Health Collaborative, a research center focused on the social–emotional well-being of all youth.

Erin Dowdy, PhD, NCSP, is Professor in the Department of Counseling, Clinical, and School Psychology at the University of California, Santa Barbara. She previously worked as a school psychologist. Dr. Dowdy's research and publications have focused on assessment for social and emotional health and risk. She regularly supervises doctoral school psychology students in their clinical and research work and teaches courses in school-based mental health. Dr. Dowdy is committed to training the next generation of school psychologists and diversifying the school mental health care workforce.

Randy W. Kamphaus, PhD, is Professor Emeritus at the University of Oregon, where he previously served as Acting Executive Director of The Ballmer Institute for Children's Behavioral Health and Dean of the College of Education. His prior positions include Dean of the College of Education and Human Development at Georgia State University and Distinguished Research Professor at the University of Georgia. Dr. Kamphaus's research has focused on improving the measurement of psychological and educational constructs and advancing assessment practice. He has authored or coauthored books, scientific journal articles, and book chapters on these topics and has created psychological and educational tests. With Cecil R. Reynolds, Dr. Kamphaus developed the Behavior Assessment

System for Children (BASC). A Fellow of the American Psychological Association (APA), he has served as editor of *School Psychology*, as a member of the APA's Council of Representatives and Board of Professional Affairs, and as President of the APA Division of School Psychology.

Cecil R. Reynolds, PhD, ABN, ABPdN, is Emeritus Professor of Educational Psychology, Professor of Neuroscience, and Distinguished Research Scholar at Texas A&M University. Dr. Reynolds is the author of more than 300 scholarly publications and author or editor of over 50 books and more than 50 commercially published tests, including the Behavior Assessment System for Children (BASC; with Randy W. Kamphaus), the Reynolds Intellectual Assessment Scales, and the Test of Memory and Learning. For 25 years, Dr. Reynolds maintained a clinical practice treating trauma victims and also served as Chief of the Neuropsychology Service at Sandstone Psychiatric Hospital. He has held leadership roles in national professional organizations, and is currently editor of the *Journal of Pediatric Neuropsychology*. Dr. Reynolds is an elected Distinguished Practitioner and Fellow of the National Academies of Practice and a recipient of the Lightner Witmer Award and the Nadine Murphy Lambert Award from Division 16 (School Psychology) of the American Psychological Association (APA), the Samuel J. Messick Award for Distinguished Scientific Contributions from APA Division 5 (Quantitative and Qualitative Methods), and the President's Gold Medal Award from the National Academy of Neuropsychology. Dr. Reynolds continues to write and practice forensic neuroscience in Austin, Texas.

Contributors

Annmary S. Abdou, PhD, Attallah College of Educational Studies, Chapman University, Orange, California

Sarina H. Alavi, MA, Department of Health Studies and Applied Educational Psychology, Teachers College, Columbia University, New York, New York

Kizzy Albritton, PhD, Department of Educational Psychology, University of Texas at Austin, Austin, Texas

Ellen Anderson, EdS, Department of Educational Psychology, University of Wisconsin–Madison, Madison, Wisconsin

Christopher J. Anthony, PhD, School of Special Education, School Psychology, and Early Childhood Studies, College of Education, University of Florida, Gainesville, Florida

Staci C. Ballard, PhD, Department of Counseling and Educational Psychology, New Mexico State University, Las Cruces, New Mexico

Nicole M. Beadles, PhD, School Psychology Program, George Mason University, Fairfax, Virginia

Nneka Bonner, MEd, School of Human Services, University of Cincinnati, Cincinnati, Ohio

Nadia Bounoua, PhD, Department of Psychology, University of Maryland, College Park, Maryland

Bailey Braunstein, MS, Department of Education and Psychological Studies, University of South Florida, Tampa, Florida

Hong NT Bui, MS, Department of Psychology, University of Maryland, College Park, Maryland

Mei-ki Chan, PhD, Berkeley School of Education, University of California Berkeley, Berkeley, California

Andrea Chronis-Tuscano, PhD, Department of Psychology, University of Maryland, College Park, Maryland

Melissa A. Collier-Meek, PhD, BCBA, Department of Health Studies and Applied Educational Psychology, Teachers College, Columbia University, New York, New York

Tai A. Collins, PhD, School of Human Services, University of Cincinnati, Cincinnati, Ohio

Dewey Cornell, PhD, School of Education and Human Development, University of Virginia, Charlottesville, Virginia

Evan H. Dart, PhD, School Psychology Program, University of South Florida, Tampa, Florida

Bridget V. Dever, PhD, College of Education, Lehigh University, Bethlehem, Pennsylvania

James Clyde DiPerna, PhD, School Psychology Program, The Pennsylvania State University, University Park, Pennsylvania

Erin Dowdy, PhD, Department of Counseling, Clinical, and School Psychology, University of California, Santa Barbara, Santa Barbara, California

Katie Eklund, PhD, Department of Educational Psychology, University of Wisconsin–Madison, Madison, Wisconsin

Lindsay M. Fallon, PhD, BCBA-D, Department of Counseling, School Psychology and Sport, College of Education and Human Development, University of Massachusetts Boston, Boston, Massachusetts

Caleb D. Farley, MS, Department of Psychology, Utah State University, Logan, Utah

Zelda Fleming, MS, Department of Education and Psychological Studies, University of South Florida, Tampa, Florida

Paul J. Frick, PhD, Department of Psychology, Louisiana State University, Baton Rouge, Louisiana

Katherine E. Frye, PhD, Department of Educational, School, and Counseling Psychology, College of Education, University of Kentucky, Lexington, Kentucky

Jakayla Fulwood, MEd, School of Human Services, University of Cincinnati, West Chester, Ohio

Emily K. Gallagher, PhD, Devereux PA Children's Services, West Chester, Pennsylvania

Cody Gion, PhD, The Ballmer Institute for Children's Behavioral Health, University of Oregon, Portland, Oregon

Courtney M. Goetz, MA, Department of Psychology, Louisiana State University, Baton Rouge, Louisiana

Jon W. Goodwin, PhD, Department of Counseling, Clinical, and School Psychology, University of California, Santa Barbara, Santa Barbara, California

Kezia Gopaul-Knights, PhD, Department of Special Education and Counseling, California State University Los Angeles, Los Angeles, California

Amy Jane Griffiths, PhD, Attallah College of Educational Studies, Chapman University, Orange, California

Shelley R. Hart, PhD, Department of Child Development, California State University, Chico, Chico, California

Timothy C. Horn, MEd, School of Special Education, School Psychology, and Early Childhood Studies, College of Education, University of Florida, Gainesville, Florida

Jared T. Izumi, PhD, Attallah College of Educational Studies, Chapman University, Orange, California

Stacy-Ann A. January, PhD, Department of Educational and Psychological Studies, University of South Florida, Tampa, Florida

Janine Jones, PhD, University of California Santa Barbara, Santa Barbara, California

Julia Juechter, PhD, Children's Autism Assessment Center of Atlanta, Atlanta, Georgia

Randy W. Kamphaus, PhD, Professor Emeritus, University of Oregon, Eugene, Oregon

Aileen Kangavary, MA, School Psychology Program, University of South Florida, Tampa, Florida

Keri A. Keller, MS, College of Education, Health, and Human Sciences, The University of Tennessee Knoxville, Knoxville, Tennessee

Jordan Kerere, MEd, School of Education and Human Development, University of Virginia, Charlottesville, Virginia

Stephen Kilgus, PhD, Department of Educational Psychology, University of Wisconsin–Madison, Madison, Wisconsin

Nathan Kirk, MEd, College of Education, Lehigh University, Bethlehem, Pennsylvania

Anna Krasno, PhD, Koegel Autism Center, University of California, Santa Barbara, Santa Barbara, California

Matthew C. Lambert, PhD, Department of Special Education, University of Illinois Urbana–Champaign, Champaign, Illinois

Joseph Lampton, MEd, School of Human Services, University of Cincinnati, Cincinnati, Ohio

Jessica Lathrop, MEd, College of Education, Lehigh University, Bethlehem, Pennsylvania

Pui-Wa Lei, PhD, Department of Educational Psychology, Counseling, and Special Education, College of Education, The Pennsylvania State University, University Park, Pennsylvania

Temma Levis, MS, Department of Educational Psychology, University of Wisconsin–Madison, Madison, Wisconsin

Celeste Malone, PhD, Human Development and Psychoeducational Studies, Howard University, Washington, DC

Nicholas Marsh, MS, Department of Psychology, University of Maryland, College Park, Maryland

Lindsay M. McCary, PhD, Department of Psychology, University of South Carolina, Columbia, South Carolina

Taylor A. Miller, MA, Department of Psychology, Louisiana State University, Baton Rouge, Louisiana

Kelly N. Moore, PsyD, Department of Clinical Psychology, Graduate School of Applied and Professional Psychology, Rutgers University, New Brunswick, New Jersey

Stephanie A. Moore, PhD, School of Education, University of California Riverside, Riverside, California

Heather E. Ormiston, PhD, Department of Applied Psychology in Education and Research Methodology, Indiana University Bloomington, Bloomington, Indiana

Viviana E. Padilla, MA, School of Education, University of California, Riverside, Riverside, California

Danielle R. Palmer, PhD, School Psychology Program, George Mason University, Fairfax, Virginia

Leandra Parris, PhD, School of Education, William & Mary, Williamsburg, Virginia

Mary L. Phan, MS, Department of Psychology, Utah State University, Logan, Utah

Alexandra M. Pierce, PhD, Department of Health Studies and Applied Educational Psychology, Teachers College, Columbia University, New York, New York

Erik J. Reinbergs, PhD, Department of Psychology, Utah State University, Logan, Utah

Tyler L. Renshaw, PhD, Department of Psychology, Utah State University, Logan, Utah

Cecil R. Reynolds, PhD (Emeritus), Educational Psychology, Texas A&M University, Austin, Texas

Emily D. Romero, PhD candidate, Department of Counseling, School Psychology and Sport, College of Education and Human Development, University of Massachusetts Boston, Boston, Massachusetts

Ellen W. Rowe, PhD, School Psychology Program, George Mason University, Fairfax, Virginia

Kaylin Russell, PhD, University of Colorado School of Medicine, JFK Partners, Denver, Colorado

Katherine Schabilion, PhD, Belin-Blank Center, College of Education, University of Iowa, Iowa City, Iowa

Christopher H. Skinner, PhD, College of Education, Health, and Human Sciences, The University of Tennessee Knoxville, Knoxville, Tennessee

Kathryn Smith, PhD, Psychological Services Department, KGH Autism Services, Madison, Wisconsin

Kristen F. Stack, PhD, North Penn School District, Lansdale, Pennsylvania

Rachel Stein, PhD, School of Education and Human Development, University of Colorado Denver, Denver, Colorado

Daria Taubin, MS, Department of Psychology, University of Maryland, College Park, Maryland

Rachel Torres, EdS, Attallah College of Educational Studies, Chapman University, Orange, California

Jennifer M. Twyford, PhD, Department of Counseling, Therapy, and School Psychology, Lewis & Clark College, Portland, Oregon

Ishan Vengurlekar, MS, Department of Educational Psychology, University of Wisconsin–Madison, Madison, Wisconsin

Madeline Wadington, PhD, Department of Educational Psychology, University of Wisconsin–Madison, Madison, Wisconsin

Kirby L. Wycoff, PsyD, MPH, Department of Health Science and Clinical Practice, Thomas Jefferson University, Philadelphia, Pennsylvania

Brittany N. Zakszeski, PhD, School of Education, University of Delaware, Newark, Delaware

Kary Zarate, PhD, Department of Special Education, University of Illinois Urbana–Champaign, Champaign, Illinois

Preface

The intention of this text is to provide a current, culturally informed, and culturally responsible handbook that could be both a resource for training new child-focused assessors in clinical and school settings, as well as a reference for current practitioners. Each chapter addresses the ecological context and includes considerations for diversity, equity, inclusion, and social justice. In addition, each chapter highlights the relevance and implications of cultural factors on assessment practices, ensuring sensitivity and fairness in assessment procedures and interpretations. Although there are many terms to guide culturally informed work with youth to ensure equitable access to supports and services, we selected the term *culturally informed* in the title of the text to emphasize the responsibility on the clinician to approach services with cultural humility, self-reflection, empathy, and a sense of responsibility to provide these services to their client. However, throughout this text, we supported and invited each of the standout chapter authors to select their own terminology based in their areas of expertise.

The book is organized into four parts. Part I focuses on foundational considerations in the field and application of youth emotional and behavioral assessment across school and clinical contexts. Beginning with commentary from the editorial team, Chapter 1 includes both a rearview and forward look with reflections on major changes and trends in the field. This is followed by an overview from the editors with a review of historical milestones and current trends in assessment fairness (Chapter 2). The following chapters in Part I provide formative foundational considerations for culturally responsive assessment of behavior (Chapter 3), utilizing a public health paradigm (Chapter 4), with a dual-factor model framework (Chapter 5), considerations across clinical and school settings (Chapter 6), and from an ecological approach (Chapter 7).

Part II focuses on assessment strategies, methods, and measures. It provides details on specific methods, such as directly observing and recording behaviors (Chapter 9), having culturally informed interviewing practices in place (Chapter 10), and using comprehensive rating scales (Chapter 11). Strategies that align with a public health and multi-tiered approaches are also provided, specifically assessing implementation within multi-tiered systems of support (Chapter 8), using screening measures and methods (Chapter 12), and progress monitoring (Chapter 13).

Part III focuses on various mental health and intellectual disorders with the highest incidences to provide detailed culturally responsible overviews and assessment strategies for many of the youth that assessors are likely to collaborate with. These assessment chapters include a neuro-affirming approach to the assessment of autism spectrum disorder

(Chapter 14), attention-deficit/hyperactivity disorders (Chapter 15), intellectual disability (Chapter 16), the assessment of depression in school (Chapter 17), socially just assessment of anxiety and related disorders (Chapter 18), culturally contextual considerations for disruptive behavior assessments (Chapter 19), inclusive assessment of bipolar and related disorders (Chapter 20), and assessment of trauma-informed approaches for all youth (Chapter 21).

Part IV includes additional special considerations and topics within youth assessment. These special topics include an overview of assessment of twice-exceptionality (Chapter 22), functional behavioral assessment (Chapter 23), mindfulness (Chapter 24), social–emotional learning (Chapter 25), early childhood (Chapter 26), threat assessment (Chapter 27), suicide risk assessment (Chapter 28), and assessment for emotional and behavioral disturbance/disorder (Chapter 29).

We hope this text serves as a reference for assessment practitioners both new to the field and seasoned practitioners alike. Above all, we hope that the wisdom shared by each of the author teams improves upon each of our assessment practices in service to the wonderful children, youth, and families with whom we are all privileged to work.

Contents

III. Assessment of Various Disorders

PART I

FOUNDATIONAL CONSIDERATIONS

CHAPTER 1

Reflections on Changes, Trends, and Current Issues in the Psychological Assessment of Youth

Jennifer M. Twyford, Katie Eklund, and Erin Dowdy

According to a report of the U.S. Surgeon General, there is a mental health crisis among youth (U.S. Department of Health and Human Services, 2021). Many hypothesized reasons are cited in this report, including declining mental health, pandemic stressors, and shortages of school-based mental health providers. The need among youth in underserved schools and rural communities is even greater (Fontanella et al., 2015). For many youth, schools are the only place where they can access mental health resources, but unfortunately, only about half of U.S. public schools offer mental health assessments, and even fewer offer treatment services (National Center for Education Statistics, 2022). School-based mental health providers are now ramping up efforts to better equip schools to support student well-being onsite (Schaeffer, 2022), with schools being the most common location where children receive mental health services.

When challenges related to mental health and wellness arise, we hope youth and their caregivers can access culturally responsible mental health services. Psychological assessment for youth is an opportunity to provide insight, access, advocacy, and empowerment. This opportunity can only be actualized with an individualized approach to understand the whole child in their context, including their strengths. The psychological assessment process requires vulnerability from youth and their caregivers, and often plays a pivotal role in providing access to the appropriate support services. For psychological assessment to be helpful, it must be valid, accurate, and able to answer the referral questions. Moreover, the steps and methods of the assessment must be equitable, inclusive of diverse perspectives, and culturally responsible, and it must include socially just approaches.

Just as the language surrounding culturally responsible practice has evolved over time, so have psychological assessment methods and approaches. There is an expanding landscape of behavioral and social–emotional assessment in the fields of psychology and education. This introductory chapter will first explore major changes and trends in culturally responsible approaches to the psychological assessment of youth.

MAJOR CHANGES AND TRENDS IN THE FIELD

Although the field of education has been criticized for slow progress, some notable and exciting changes within the field of behavioral and psychological assessment have taken place in the last decade. As you will read about throughout this text, an impressive amount of conceptual thinking and applied research informs how to engage in assessment practices that will lead to effective interventions to best support children and youth. Similarly, scholars featured throughout this text have outlined needed directions for continued progress and research, all with the common aim of enhancing assessment services and related outcomes for children and youth.

We highlight five major areas of change impacting the evolving landscape of behavioral and social–emotional assessment of children and youth. First, we recognize the essential move toward providing culturally responsible and equity-focused assessments. This major emphasis is explicitly stressed in each chapter and is critical in considering how to improve our assessment practices with children and youth. Second, we describe the paradigm shift away from traditional categorical approaches to assessment toward dimensional and transdiagnostic approaches. This shift recognizes the need for more accurate classification systems that go beyond "all or nothing" categorizations and can better inform prevention, early intervention, and treatment decisions for children and youth. Third, we discuss the departure from an overreliance on deficit-focused approaches of psychological assessment to embrace a holistic approach to assessment through the inclusion of strengths-based assessment. The resulting framework emphasizes the need to employ more comprehensive approaches to assessment. Fourth, a shift toward school-based social and emotional competencies emphasizes the role of schools to support youth creating positive relationships and transferable skills. And finally, we highlight some technological and data analytic advances. Recent advances have provided an opportunity for innovation in the field of psychological assessment. Taken together, these five major changes provide examples of trends, current issues, and promise that the field of assessment can and does evolve as we learn more about how to best support children and youth.

CULTURALLY RESPONSIBLE AND EQUITY-FOCUSED ASSESSMENT

One of the significant challenges in assessment is addressing issues of fairness in testing. Significant ongoing efforts are underway, and they are continuing to develop to ensure that the assessment tools and approaches used are fair and responsive to the individuals being assessed within the testing contexts that are employed. The need for these efforts is emphasized in the jointly developed American Educational Research Association (AERA), American Psychological Association (APA), and National Council on Measurement Education (NCME) *Standards for Educational and Psychological Testing* (2014) test standards that describe fairness as encompassing:

> the multiple functions of testing in relation to its many goals, including the broad goal of achieving equality of opportunity in our society. It would consider the technical properties of tests, the ways in which test results are reported and used, the factors that affect the validity of score interpretations, and the consequences of test use. A comprehensive analysis of fairness in testing also would examine the regulations, statutes, and case law that govern test use and the remedies for harmful testing practices. (p. 49)

Although the *Standards* acknowledge the inability to adequately address each of these issues, the point is well-received that fairness is a critical matter to any psychological and educational assessment of children and youth. There is an ongoing need to develop, continually evaluate, and use assessment tools and practices that are fair and unbiased and that fully consider the diverse sociocultural and linguistic backgrounds of children and youth. This emphasis is present and emphasized explicitly and intentionally throughout this book.

For example, Chapter 3 describes an approach to engaging in culturally responsive behavioral assessment that centers youth voice. Complementing this culturally responsive approach to assessment, Chapter 5 describes a culturally responsible assessment approach that emphasizes the need for those engaged in any assessment practice to take *responsibility* to ensure fairness for the clients they are serving. This culturally responsible term is described as encompassing and extending upon culturally responsive, culturally relevant, and culturally sensitive practices (Moore et al., in press). Further, each of the subsequent chapters describes ongoing needs and specific efforts made to ensure that the assessment approaches and specific assessment tools for various disorders are used in ways that promote fairness and equity.

We are encouraged by the significant shift toward culturally responsible assessment practices, and we appreciate the continued push for equity-focused assessment practices. A few examples of current trends and progress being made with the goal of fairness in testing include the increased emphasis on context (see Chapter 7), the need for diverse representation in norm-referenced groups (see Chapter 11), examination of the differential item functioning in assessment tools (see Chapter 13), and inspection of the cultural loading of items (see Chapter 16). We anticipate that efforts to address bias, ensure fairness, and promote inclusivity in assessment tools, procedures, and interpretations will be ongoing and crucial to the field of psychological and educational assessment.

DIMENSIONAL TRANSDIAGNOSTIC APPROACHES

There is a growing paradigm shift away from the current use of taxonomies and toward transdiagnostic assessment. The current system for categorizing mental disorders, which utilizes the *Diagnostic and Statistical Manual of Mental Disorders* (DSM-5 TR; now in its 5th edition with a text revision; American Psychiatric Association, 2022) and the *International Classification of Diseases* (ICD; now in its 11th edition; World Health Organization, 2019), has been criticized for heterogeneity within diagnoses, poor symptom discrimination between disorders with overlap resulting in comorbid diagnosis as the rule not the exception, and lack of life course developmental considerations (Dalgleish et al., 2020; Lahey et al., 2022).

Dimensional assessment represents a departure from traditional categorical approaches using psychiatric nosology by considering behavior and social–emotional functioning along a continuum rather than assigning individuals to discrete diagnostic categories. Instead of viewing mental health or behavioral challenges as dichotomous (i.e., yielding a diagnosis as either present versus absent, or simply stated, diagnosis vs. no diagnosis), dimensional assessment acknowledges the multidimensional nature of psychological functioning and recognizes that individuals may exhibit varying degrees of symptoms or functioning across different domains and symptoms. This decreased emphasis on diagnosis highlights the impact of unitary symptoms on an individual's well-being and symptoms (e.g., suicide, anhedonia, impulsivity) that cut across diagnostic categories and disorders resulting in a "transdiagnostic" approach to assessment and treatment of behavioral and social–emotional functioning. By focusing on an individual within their ecological context, a personalized profile can inform culturally responsible supports. Moreover, school-based practitioners are already familiar with this type of assessment. School-based assessment is presently not provided for diagnostic purposes; rather, comprehensive assessment provides the opportunity to identify clinically significant symptoms across domains of functioning in order to create individualized support plans for students.

Dimensional assessment provides a framework that aligns with current research and advances in understanding mental health and behavioral functioning. It supports the integration of research findings into assessment practices and fosters collaborations between researchers and practitioners in refining assessment tools and interventions. For example, one such collaboration was created by the National Institute of Mental Health (NIMH) through Research Domain Criteria (RDoC) to offer a structure for investigating the biopsychosocial factors contributing to mental health challenges. However, few interventions and mostly cognitive behavioral therapies have come from RDoC. This attempt to translate dimensional approaches results in a "translational gap" demonstrating significant challenges in creating clinical interventions based on RDoC research findings (Dalgleish et al., 2020, p. 189). In another example, the Hierarchical Taxonomy of Psychopathology (HiToP; Kotov et al., 2017) is a consortium-based, research-driven effort to reduce problems with the current taxonomies (e.g., comorbidities, heterogeneity within diagnosis, diagnostic instability). HiToP uses a dimensional framework to further group symptoms into spectra. Although not yet fully mapped out, HiToP research is advancing quickly, has evidence of clinical utility in practice, and appears to be a promising model (Kotov et al., 2021).

Despite the current shortcomings and needs for further research, transdiagnostic approaches have a future potential to better capture the complex intricacies of behavior and social–emotional functioning, leading to improved identification of individual needs, targeted interventions, and a more personalized approach (Dalgleish et al., 2020) to support youth in their development and well-being. Before transitioning away from more common-place categorical systems to a dimensional model using a transdiagnostic approach, significant implementation challenges will need to be overcome. We look toward the future to better understand dimensional approaches through cultural responsiveness, shifting mindsets, transitioning existing systems, training implications, demonstrated reliability and validity of assessments, established norms and benchmarks, integration of assessment and intervention, ethical considerations, and managed healthcare limitations (e.g., time constraints, reimbursement, standardization vs. individualization, limited coverage for certain dimensions, challenges in explaining complexity to payers, managing treatment and intervention approvals, and balancing quality with cost efficiency). For further guidance on measurement selection for transdiagnostic approaches, see Stanton et al., 2020. For practitioners who would like to explore the use of HiToP in clinical practice, see the HiToP website (*https://hitop.unt.edu*).

STRENGTHS-BASED APPROACHES

Traditional psychological assessment practices often focus on the presence or absence of psychopathology, with diagnoses linked to behavioral symptoms and associated levels of impaired functioning. The last three decades have seen growing recognition in the field of psychological assessment of the importance of assessing children's strengths (e.g., positive qualities, dispositions) along with their challenges and needs. These strength-based approaches have focused on more holistic assessment procedures that can promote increased engagement from children and create interventions that build upon a child's strengths (Bozic, 2013; Furlong et al., 2014; Jimerson et al., 2004). For example, proponents of positive psychology have discussed new assessment models that integrate risk and pathology with aspects of human adaptation and development (Masten, 2001) and that are associated with optimal human functioning (Keyes, 2005).

An emerging trend in the field is the creation, use, and promotion of assessment measures that include factors that evaluate children's strengths and needs. The dual-factor or dual-continuum model has been proposed as a way to conceptualize factors that contribute to overall mental health functioning, which includes the co-occurrence of symptoms of mental illness paired with indicators of mental wellness. Several studies have used assessments of positive indicators of wellness with negative indicators of psychological functioning to demonstrate that some individuals with varying levels of low and high dysfunction also experience low and high levels of well-being; these studies have examined the impact that the combinations of positive and negative symptoms can have on behavioral and academic outcomes (e.g., Eklund et al., 2011; Keyes & Lopez, 2002; Suldo & Shaffer, 2008). Additionally, these studies have demonstrated that psychological flourishing is more than the absence of behavioral and emotional symptoms and that it also includes positive affective experiences and dispositions that contribute to the full range of human functioning. Chapter 5 provides an in-depth review of dual-factor assessment.

Unfortunately, the development and use of psychometrically sound and age-appropriate assessments of positive psychology constructs for children and youth lags far behind measures that assess psychopathology (Furlong et al., 2014). Schools in the United States often focus on identifying and remediating student weaknesses while often ignoring the identification of strengths and the integration of student competencies in the development of interventions and supports (Gordon, 2006). Additional work is needed to promote the idea that assessment measures that integrate a dual factor of human functioning can lead to more positive outcomes for children. Certainly, more information can be learned from the assessment of concepts such as mindfulness (see Chapter 24) and when assessing strengths in children with neurodevelopmental disabilities (see Chapter 14) that very clearly demonstrate the need for a more comprehensive understanding and perspective of student well-being and strengths.

FOCUS ON SOCIAL–EMOTIONAL COMPETENCIES

Aligned with a focus on strength-based approaches, assessing the social and emotional well-being of our youth is gaining increased attention. Psychologists and schools are recognizing the importance of evaluating not only academic achievements but also students' social skills, emotional regulation, and social–emotional competencies. Comprehensive assessment tools and practices that address these domains are needed. Social–emotional learning (SEL) is one term used to describe programs that many schools have implemented to help students build the necessary skills to effectively manage their emotions and navigate their social environments (Collaborative for Academic and Social Emotional Learning [CASEL], 2024). CASEL further defines SEL as "the process through which all young people and adults acquire and apply the knowledge, skills, and attitudes to develop healthy identities, manage emotions and achieve personal and collective goals, feel and show empathy for others, establish and maintain supportive relationships, and make responsible and caring decisions" (CASEL, 2021, p. 6). As the demand grows for future-ready skills, assessments will increasingly focus on evaluating transferable skills and competencies, such as critical thinking, creativity, collaboration, and problem-solving, rather than solely emphasizing content knowledge.

Emerging SEL programs are designed to teach youth how to recognize their own emotions and the emotions of others and develop the necessary social skills to establish positive relationships with peers and adults (Weissberg et al., 2015). SEL programs aim to create more positive school climates in which students feel supported and respected and where they can learn additional coping strategies to address adversity (Yeager, 2017). Although much has been done to advance SEL programs, policies, and state level standards that support the development of student competencies (Eklund et al., 2018), less research exists to support assessment tools and methods that assess student social and emotional competence (McKown, 2019). Chapter 25 provides a unique focus on culturally responsive assessment practices that include how fairness-related data may be considered in SEL assessments and provide future recommendations for culturally fair assessment practices. Additional lists of available SEL assessments, along with information about their psychometric properties, can be found at the CASEL assessment guide (*https://measuringsel.casel.org/assessment-guide*).

TECHNOLOGICAL AND DATA ANALYTIC ADVANCES

Another trend we are watching in the assessment field is related to advances in technological and data analytics. The rapid advancement of technology has created tremendous opportunities for innovative assessment methods. Online and computer-based assessments, adaptive testing, and data-driven approaches are being explored to enhance the efficiency, accessibility, and accuracy of assessment processes. For example, assessments of cognitive abilities (see Chapter 17 for description of their use in the assessment of Intellectual Disabilities), attention and neurological functioning (see Chapter 16 for description of continuous performance tasks for use in the assessment of attention-deficit/hyperactivity disorder), and behavioral and emotional functioning (see Chapter 12) are frequently completed online via computers or tablets.

Technology will continue to play a significant role in assessment. Utilizing artificial intelligence, machine learning, and data analytics can provide valuable insights into students' learning patterns, progress, and areas requiring intervention, enabling more data-informed decision-making. In a recent article describing the use of artificial intelligence (AI) in practice by health service psychologists, the potential benefits, limitations, and ethical and legal considerations were described (Farmer et al., 2024). Some of the notable benefits included reducing administrative burdens (e.g., integrating assessment data, generating explanations of complex concepts, providing interpretations of commonly used assessment tools, detailing recommendations aligned with assessment results) and enhancing service provision (e.g., having virtual therapists to provide low-level interventions based on assessment results; enhancing diagnostic capabilities); however, these benefits must be weighed with the potential risks including introducing bias (e.g., AI bots trained on datasets with societal biases; search engines reinforcing oppression), deskilling (e.g., loss of clinical skills due to overreliance on technology), and privacy concerns such as potential data breaches (Farmer et al., 2024).

Importantly, AI has also been described as an innovative tool uniquely capable of addressing health equity by facilitating the use of digital, population-level assessments of mental health and early interventions with an emphasis on culturally responsive care (Cerezo et al., 2024). The proliferation of AI tools specific to the roles of psychologists who are frequently engaged in the assessment process (e.g., SchoolPsychAI, Clickreport) is one of the many indicators that technological and data analytic advances are on the rise. As such, it is incumbent upon the professionals engaged in psychological and educational assessment to ensure that these tools are used wisely and to the benefit of the communities and clients we serve.

CONCLUSION

Herein, five trends, issues, and potential major changes are highlighted as ones to watch. It is imperative that practitioners remain committed to culturally responsible and equitable approaches as emerging practices are being adopted and evaluated. We are encouraged to see many trends emphasizing holistic frameworks, strengths, ecological variables and context, and the uniqueness of the individual. However, current practice remains largely focused on DSM-5 TR (American Psychiatric Association, 2022) and ICD-11 (World Health Organization, 2019), which emphasize diagnosis, with symptom counting, deficits, and categorical models. Researchers are investigating the shift toward dimensional models and the incorporation of technology into practice; we may possibly experience a large shift in the field during our lifetimes. These trends and changes reflect a growing recognition of the importance of cultural responsibility, equitable assessment practices, and cultural context in understanding and supporting youth, no matter where technology guides the field.

The increasing use of technology and data-driven assessment methods aimed at practitioners further indicates this emerging trend may become a major shift in the field. Although efficiency and accessibility are noble pursuits, new tools must be carefully examined for accuracy and bias and interpreted within the context of the individual. Practitioners must advocate for fair and inclusive assessment methods, many of which are detailed in the following chapters. If practitioners utilize a lens of cultural responsibility and equity, strengths-based assessment can be an important support tool for youth and their families.

REFERENCES

American Educational Research Association, American Psychological Association, & National Council on Measurement in Education. (2014). *Standards for educational and psychological testing.* American Educational Research Association.

American Psychiatric Association. (2022). *Diagnostic and statistical manual of mental disorders* (5th ed., text rev.). Author.

Bozic, N. (2013). Developing a strength-based approach to educational psychology practice: A multiple case study. *Educational and Child Psychology, 30*(4), 18–29.

Cerezo, A., Jackson, J., Nikiforova, K., & Lord, S.P. (under review, 2024). *Advancing mental health equity at scale: the potential of technology in psychological practice.*

Collaborative for Academic, Social, and Emotional Learning. (2021). *2011–2021: 10 years of social and emotional learning in U.S. school districts. Elements for Long-Term Sustainability of SEL.* Author. *https://casel.org/cdi-ten-year-report/?view=true*

Collaborative for Academic, Social, and Emotional Learning. (2024). *What is the CASEL framework?* Author. *https://casel.org/fundamentals-of-sel/what-is-the-casel-framework/#social-emotional-learning*

Dalgleish, T., Black, M., Johnston, D., & Bevan, A. (2020). Transdiagnostic approaches to mental health problems: Current status and future directions. *Journal of Consulting and Clinical Psychology, 88*(3), 179–195.

Eklund, K., Dowdy, E., Jones, C., & Furlong, M. (2011). Applicability of the dual-factor model of mental health for college students. *Journal of College Student Psychotherapy, 25*(1), 79–92.

Eklund, K., Kilpatrick, K., Haider, A., & Kilgus, S. (2018). A systematic review of state-level social–emotional learning standards: Implications for practice and research. *School Psychology Review, 47,* 316–326.

Farmer, R. L., Lockwood, A. B., Goforth, A., & Thomas, C. (under review, 2024). *Artificial intelligence in practice: opportunities, challenges, and ethical consideration.*

Fontanella, C. A., Hiance-Steelesmith, D. L., Phillips, G. S., Bridge, J. A., Lester, N., Sweeney, H. A., & Campo, J. V. (2015). Widening rural-urban disparities in youth suicides, United States, 1996–2010. *JAMA Pediatrics, 169*(5), 466–473.

Furlong, M. J., Gilman, R., & Huebner, E. S. (Eds.). (2014). *Handbook of positive psychology in schools.* Routledge.

Gordon, G. (2006). *Building engaged schools: Getting the most out of America's classrooms.* Simon and Schuster.

Jimerson, S. R., Shane, R., Sharkey, J. D., Nyborg, V., & Furlong, M. J. (2004). Strength-based assessment and school psychology: A summary and synthesis. *The California School Psychologist, 9*(1), 9–19.

Keyes, C. L. M. (2005). Mental health and/or mental illness? Investigating axioms of the complete state model of health. *Journal of Consulting and Clinical Psychology, 73*(3), 539–548.

Keyes, C. L. M., & Lopez, S. J. (2002). Toward a science of mental health: Positive directions in diagnosis and intervention. In C. R. Snyder & S. J. Lopez (Eds.), *Handbook of positive psychology* (pp. 45–59). Oxford University Press.

Kotov, R., Krueger, R. F., Watson, D., Achenbach, T. M., Althoff, R. R., Bagby, R. M., et al. (2017). The Hierarchical Taxonomy of Psychopathology (HiTOP): A dimensional alternative to traditional nosologies. *Journal of Abnormal Psychology, 126*(4), 454–477.

Kotov, R., Krueger, R. F., Watson, D., Cicero, D. C., Conway, C. C., DeYoung, C. G., et al. (2021). The Hierarchical Taxonomy of Psychopathology (HiTOP): A quantitative nosology based on consensus of evidence. *Annual Review of Clinical Psychology, 17,* 83–108.

Lahey, B. B., Tiemeier, H., & Krueger, R. F. (2022). Seven reasons why binary diagnostic categories should be replaced with empirically sounder and less stigmatizing dimensions. *JCPP Advances*, *2*(4), e12108.

Masten, A. S. (2001). Ordinary magic: Resilience processes in development. *American Psychologist*, *56*(3), 227–238.

McKown, C. (2019). Challenges and opportunities in the applied assessment of student social and emotional learning. *Educational Psychologist*, *54*(3), 205–221.

Moore, K. M., Sandeen, E., & Swanda, R. M. (in press). Reflective local practice: A pragmatic framework for improving culturally competent practice in psychology. *The Clinical Neuropsychologist*.

National Center for Education Statistics. (2022). *School pulse panel*. U.S. Department of Education, Institute of Education Sciences. *https://ies.ed.gov/schoolsurvey/spp*

Schaeffer, K. (2022, August 10). *Just over half of U.S. public schools offer mental health assessments for students; Fewer offer treatment*. Pew Research Center. *www.pewresearch.org/short-reads/2022/08/10/just-over-half-of-u-s-public-schools-offer-mental-health-assessments-for-students-fewer-offer-treatment*

Stanton, K., McDonnell, C. G., Hayden, E. P., & Watson, D. (2020). Transdiagnostic approaches to psychopathology measurement: Recommendations for measure selection, data analysis, and participant recruitment. *Journal of Abnormal Psychology*, *129*(1), 21–28.

Suldo, S. M., & Shaffer, E. J. (2008). Looking beyond psychopathology: The dual- factor model of mental health in youth. *School Psychology Review*, *37*(1), 52–68.

U.S. Department of Health and Human Services. (2021). *Protecting youth mental health: The U.S. Surgeon General's advisory on the mental health crisis facing youth* (HHS Publication No. HP-2021-01). Office of the Surgeon General. *www.hhs.gov/sites/default/files/surgeon-general-youth-mental-health-advisory.pdf*

Weissberg, R. P., Durlak, J. A., Domitrovich, C. E., & Gullotta, T. P. (2015). Social and emotional learning: Past, present, and future. In J. A. Durlak, C. E. Domitrovich, R. P. Weissberg, & T. P. Gullotta (Eds.), *Handbook of social and emotional learning: Research and practice* (pp. 3–19). Guilford Press.

World Health Organization. (2019). *International Statistical Classification of Diseases and Related Health Problems* (11th ed.). *https://icd.who.int*

Yeager, D. S. (2017). Social and emotional learning programs for adolescents. *The Future of Children*, *27*(1), 73–94.

CHAPTER 2

Test and Assessment Fairness in Historical Perspective

Randy W. Kamphaus and Cecil R. Reynolds

The development of current standards and standards of practice for achieving fairness in psychological, educational, and employment testing has evolved and improved over the course of at least a century. This history, however, has often been co-mingled and overshadowed by coverage of the highly publicized areas of intellectual assessment, test bias, and litigation related to disproportionate impacts of testing (French & Hale, 1990; Goodenough, 1949; Pintner, 1923; Reynolds & Brown, 1984; Reynolds & Suzuki, 2013). These histories have informed the 2014 edition of the current *Standards for Educational and Psychological Testing* (i.e., *Standards*; American Educational Research Association, American Psychological Association, & National Council on Measurement in Education [AERA, APA, & NCME], 2014), which devotes an entire chapter to developing a comprehensive set of standards for striving for fairness in testing. This publication also captures this history under "fairness," an overarching concept for assuring equitable opportunity for all examinees to demonstrate their knowledge, skills, and competencies during testing.

We use this chapter to explain the concept of fairness-focused assessment by tracing historical precedents and trends; summarizing the AERA, APA, and NCME professional standards; and providing examples of how the standards apply to routine child and adolescent psychological assessment practice. Assessment of "psychological" constructs will serve as our focus although we fully recognize, as do the *Standards*, that educational and employment testing, as well as psychological assessment, are rarely practiced in isolation from one another. In employment testing, selection and evaluation of employees often requires tests of educational knowledge, skills and competencies, personality and leadership, and screening for mental health status. In higher education, college students may be required to take an admission test, and in cases of suspected or history of educational or mental health disability, they may be required to complete a comprehensive psychological and educational assessment to determine eligibility for classroom modifications. In the interest of informing applied test development and assessment practice, we provide focused consideration of content validity and consequential validity associated with the long-term practice of intellectual assessment, which spurred concerns about test content and the emerging practice of behavioral health screening, which highlights questions about consequential validity.

HISTORY OF TEST STANDARDS

We are reminded that the *Standards* have been relying on leaders and experts in psychometrics, educational measurement, measurement science, and related academic disciplines to develop forward-looking principles for advancing the field of test development and test use for eight decades. The first APA committee promulgated a set of *Technical Recommendations for Psychological Tests and Diagnostic Techniques* in 1954 (Cronbach & Meehl, 1954). A second set of test standards, *Technical Recommendations for Achievement Tests*, was prepared by an independent committee of the AERA and the National Council on Measurement Used in Education (NCMUE; now the NCME) and published by the National Education Association in 1955. Subsequent versions of the modern *Standards* were prepared by joint committees of the APA, AERA, and NCME and published in 1966, 1974, 1985, 1999, and 2014. We think that the current fairness principles of the *Standards* are well-informed and wise because of the credibility and influence of three long-standing academic associations and the numerous eminent scholars who have contributed their scientific and applied practice expertise over many decades.

The 2014 edition introduced the term *fairness* as the preferred, encompassing term for long-standing testing topics, such as item bias, test bias, test adaptation for different nationalities and languages, and other related topics. *Fairness* thus became the term of choice for providing broad guidance for the development and use of tests for a wide range of applications, including educational, employment selection, and psychiatric. The fairness term is also recognized by members of the public and press (e.g., FairTest). For applied assessment purposes, we think that the fairness definition included in the 2014 edition of the test *Standards* is useful: "... fairness as responsiveness to individual characteristics and testing contexts so that test scores will yield valid interpretations for intended uses" (p. 50).

Furthermore, the *Standards* provide a compelling rationale for why fairness is important for studying assessment practices in a more comprehensive and less piecemeal way. For example:

> A full consideration of the topic would explore the multiple functions of testing in relation to its many goals, including the broad goal of achieving equality of opportunity. It would consider the technical properties of tests, the ways in which test results are reported and used, the factors that affect the validity of score interpretations, and the consequences of test use. (AERA, APA, & NCME, 2014, p. 49)

As much as the *Standards* serve as an important guide for test developers and publishers, they also have broad implications for how professionals practice their assessment craft. Adhering to the fairness standards of the AERA, APA, and NCME, for example, discourages practitioners from conceptually partitioning their work and decision making. Undue partitioning may lead to well-informed decisions in one area (e.g., test selection) without considering the potential downsides of another aspect of practice, such as unintended consequences of using that measure, which, regardless of its popularity and careful development, may ultimately still lead to poor outcomes for youth.

CURRENT TEST STANDARDS

The 2014 (current edition) *Standards* includes a Standards for Fairness chapter with 20 individual standards subsumed under four clusters as follows:

- Cluster 1. Test Design, Development, Administration, and Scoring Procedures that Minimize Barriers to Valid Score Interpretations for the Widest Possible Range of Individuals and Relevant Subgroups
- Cluster 2. Validity of Test Score Interpretations for Intended Uses for the Intended Examinee Population
- Cluster 3. Accommodations to Remove Construct-Irrelevant Barriers and Support Valid Interpretations of Scores for Their Intended Uses
- Cluster 4. Safeguards Against Inappropriate Score Interpretations for Intended Uses

We recommend that all test development and assessment practitioners become familiar with all 20 of the individual standards. The individual standards provide examples of how each standard applies to a real-world assessment issue. In fact, the details in the 20 standards provide enough examples of the application of fairness to assessment practice to serve as a helpful adjunct to any applied assessment coursework, whether the topic be behavioral, personality, observational, cognitive, or family assessment. Test development and assessment practice is required for virtually every topic in graduate programs for mental health professionals and allied disciplines, including psychiatric diagnosis. We provide a quick summary of some of the issues discussed under each cluster with the caveat that such a summary cannot substitute for the full reading of the 20 standards.

Cluster 1

The first cluster reads: "Test Design, Development, Administration, and Scoring Procedures that Minimize Barriers to Valid Score Interpretations for the Widest Possible Range of Individuals and Relevant Subgroups." Cluster 1 includes standards for test development practices that maximize the assessment of construct-relevant variance and minimize the likelihood that construct-irrelevant variance is being assessed. A test purporting to measure the social skills construct, for example, should be designed in a way to delimit the possibility of resultant test scores assessing construct-irrelevant demographic factors, such as socioeconomic, linguistic, or cultural background, and gender identity, ethnic, religion, ability status, age, physical capability, educational attainment, or other possible demographic characteristics. Test development procedures that enhance the assessment of construct-relevant variance might include creation of a content blueprint which includes social skills that are known to be relevant to the widest demographic range of potential examinees; conducting of interviews and focus groups with intended examinees; surveying of the research literature on item content that may be related to demographic characteristics; enlisting professional panels of experts to assess the relevance of item content for population subgroups; and articulating assessment settings and conditions that promote the full engagement of all potential examinees during the assessment. We interpret the language of the *Standards* as conveying that all test development processes are the responsibility of the test developers—not independent researchers, groups of test users, or other institutions, such as schools, community groups, or health care providers. We will revisit this topic later because it increases the responsibilities of test developers.

Cluster 2

This cluster is concerned with the "Validity of Test Score Interpretations for Intended Uses for the Intended Examinee Population." Essentially, this set of standards requires that test developers report information about score and validity evidence differences between population subgroups and take steps to address said differences. Test development steps might include actions such as explaining subgroup differences based on strong prior research evidence or theory and altering the item content or other test characteristics to address differences that suggest the presence of construct-irrelevant variance. In effect, this set of standards requires disaggregation of evidence to demonstrate the equivalency of score inferences across population subgroups. For example, providing reliability of validity evidence to support score inferences for a sample of children ranging in age from 5 to 11 years may mask significant differences in evidence between young children and those approaching adolescence. In these situations, it would be better to report reliability of validity evidence for individual age groups given the rapid development of children at younger ages.

Cluster 3

The standards subsumed under this cluster are concerned with "Accommodations to Remove Construct-Irrelevant Barriers and Support Valid Interpretations of Scores for Their Intended Uses." Collectively, these standards provide a variety of actions that can be taken for assuring that the obtained score inferences apply to a wide range of individuals. Guidance is provided for demonstrating the efficacy of assessment accommodations, interpretations, and modifications of tests for various nationalities and maximizing the match of the language of the test to examinees' linguistic competencies. A test that includes evidence in support of assessment of construct relevant variance for a limited age range, a single category of disability, or language will be of limited practical value for widespread adoption by clinicians, schools, pediatric practices, or other institutions.

Cluster 4

The final cluster offers "Safeguards Against Inappropriate Score Interpretations for Intended Uses." This set of standards requires test developers and publishers to proactively create a measure and set of supporting materials, such as manuals, that include protections from misuse. For example, a test manual should be clear about the conditions under which the test is most likely to assess construct-relevant variants (which Reynolds, 2016, has characterized as contextualized validity) and be equally clear about when, or how, a test might be misused.

For example, test authors may include a caution in their manual against using the test in isolation to make a high stakes diagnostic, special education eligibility, or forensic decision. Most diagnoses, for example, require assessing multiple domains to make a diagnostic decision, such as Intellectual Disability, which requires measures of both the intelligence/cognitive development and adaptive behavior domains. The failure to use information from the adaptive behavior domain, even when adaptive behavior tests had been administered, triggered the legal challenges to intelligence testing in the 1960s (Kamphaus, 2001; Kamphaus, 1987; Kamphaus & Walden, 2020a). The *Standards* require that test developers proactively take steps to prevent misuse of their measures by addressing well-documented potential misuses in the test's manual.

CONTENT VALIDITY

The issue of content validity of test items (or "indicators" of a construct) has been an enduring challenge for psychological assessments, especially when compared to other domains of assessment, such as educational or employment testing (Kamphaus, 2001). In educational assessment, for example, there is general agreement that the item "2 + 2 = ?" is an indicator of the mathematics knowledge construct. This is not the case in psychological assessment, whereby the same item has been used as an indicator of different constructs. Items about "worry," for example, may be included as indicators of anxiety, depression, or both anxiety and depression scales, leading to questions about the validity of all three scales. Confusion about the appropriateness of item content for measuring only construct-relevant variance leads to the creation of scales that are difficult for practitioners to interpret precisely because they include construct-irrelevant item content. Some examples of such scales from the history of psychological assessment, often developed via "empirical" means such as factor analysis, include a "Schizoid/Anxious" subscale/test, depression scales that include one or several anxiety items (e.g., worry) and two or more subtests that share overlapping item content. Although improvements are constantly being made in psychological test development, a full embrace of standards for content validity similar to those in educational or employment testing is yet to take hold. As a result, we think it is important to illuminate the history of the struggle of psychological assessment to embrace content validity and detail some of the progress made to date.

An overarching theme of the *Standards* is a focus on limiting the influence of construct-irrelevant variance on test scores. Per the *Standards*:

> On a test designed to measure anxiety, a response bias to underreport one's anxiety might be considered a source of construct-irrelevant variance. In the case of a mathematics test, it might include overreliance on reading comprehension skills that English language learners may be lacking. On a test designed to measure science knowledge, test-taker internalizing of gender-based stereotypes about women in the sciences might be a source of construct-irrelevant variance. (pp. 12–13)

The history of psychological test development is replete with examples of efforts, sometime successful, to improve the item content of tests to address concerns about unfair assessment practices due to the influence of construct-irrelevant influences. In the case of intelligence tests, both intelligence test developers and critics have targeted concerns about the potential influence of non-intellective/cognitive factors, including psychiatric condition, such as psychotic disorders, motor skills, prior academic achievement and access to schooling, culture, race/ethnicity, primary language, and speech/language skills. Although not obvious to the casual observer, efforts to limit the influence construct irrelevant factors date to the 19th century. For example, numerous historical accounts suggest that intelligence tests were created with item content intended to differentiate intellectual disability from psychosis in order to assure differentiated interventions/treatments for each condition (Kamphaus, 2001; Pintner, 1923). Itard and Sequin in France and Wilbur and Howe in the United States were among the pioneers who attempted to differentiate the assessment of intelligence from psychosis by developing the first tests recognized as measures of intelligence (Pintner, 1923).

The item content of these measures, however, was considered questionable because of the number of physical development (e.g., inclusion of a dental development item on a cognitive test), educational knowledge, and fine and gross motor items. The intelligence test created by Alfred Binet and Theophilius Simon (1905, 1916) in France was hailed as the first successful measure because it included item content that was considered better aligned with the construct of interest. Their measure was the first to assess the "higher-level" cognitive skills, and it further demonstrated evidence of criterion-related validity in the form of positive correlations with measures of academic achievement. Referring to the intelligence test development work of Sir Fancis Galton in the latter half of the 19th century (Kamphaus, 2001), Boring (1929) observed:

> Binet was seeking to measure the intellectual faculties, the complex mental processes, whereas Galton measured only simple capacities, hoping vainly that they might have some significance for the "intellect." Binet was right, Galton was wrong. . . . (p. 546)

In today's context, however, the Binet and Simon item content would be viewed as subject to the influence of construct-irrelevant factors. See, for example, the items for the 1905 scale:

1. Following a moving object with one's eyes
2. Grasping a small object which is seen
3. Finding and eating a square of chocolate wrapped in paper
4. Naming objects in pictures
5. Comparing two weights
6. Susceptibility to suggestion
7. Defining common words by function
8. Repeating a sentence of 15 words
9. Memory for pictures
10. Drawing a design from memory
11. Telling how two common objects are alike
12. Making rhymes
13. Using three words in a sentence
14. Reply to an abstract question
15. Defining abstract terms

We think that most observers would identify items 1, 2, 3, 5, 10 as susceptible to influences from motor skills and 12, 13, 14, and 15 may be cited by some observers as unduly influenced by first language, language development, academic achievement, and quality of schooling, versus assessment of developed cognitive abilities, or intelligence.

The *Standards* have created new interest in providing evidence of content validity. The *Standards* support the argument that content validity is central for limiting the unwanted influence of construct-irrelevant variance, which is the major threat to fairness. The *Standards* provide a useful definition of content validity to guiding test construction.

> *Content validity* is established by showing that the test items are a sample of a universe in which the investigator is interested. Content validity is ordinarily to be established deductively, by defining a universe of items and sampling systematically within this universe to establish the test. (p. 282)

Modern approaches for supporting the content validity of items, and the resulting improvement in assessment of the construct of interest, include:

- Defining the construct based on theoretical and research foundations and creating a "content blueprint"
- Creating items aligned with the blueprint, including engagement with the population (e.g., youth themselves, and including co-creation when feasible) for which the test is designed
- Ensuring "accessibility" of the items to the broadest range of examinees possible, including readability, language, age, and cultural considerations
- Expert and community panel review for item content acceptability
- Statistical studies of item bias for population subgroup of examinees, for example, gender and race/ethnicity
- Statistical studies of the degree to which items measure the construct of interest (e.g., item response theory analyses for assessing statistical "fit" of items with the remainder of the item pool)

We will address each of these considerations in turn.

Defining the Construct

Creating a defensible theoretical and research foundation to define the construct(s) of interest is a necessary step that should be thoroughly described in test manuals. Kane's (2013) concept of the "intended use argument" (IUA) is aligned with this work, in that the content validity of individual items/indicators is assessed for alignment with the eventual test inferences to be made, and "More-ambitious interpretations and uses require more backing (i.e., evidence) than less-ambitious interpretations and uses." This first test development step, in turn, has direct implications for the interpretability of test score inferences and thus for the utility of the test for practitioners.

Test developers commonly use science and theory to create a content blueprint. Using an example from our own experience, we chose to limit the assessment of general intelligence to verbal and spatial problem solving when creating the Reynolds Intellectual Assessment Scales (now RIAS-2; Reynolds & Kamphaus, 2015). We did not include memory and processing speed in the assessment of general intelligence per the long history of factor analytic findings demonstrating that verbal and spatial tasks accounted for most of the variance in intelligence test scores (Lubinski, 2004). We also chose to assess spatial problem solving without requiring the motor skills needed to construct spatial objects or figures in the interest of not introducing potential construct-irrelevant variance (i.e., motor skills). This is one of many examples of how test developers' hue to theory and science as sources for creating content blueprints and individual items.

Creating Items Aligned with the Content Blueprint

Creating aligned items can also support fairness by adopting inclusive test development practices, as opposed to the historical practices where the test developer, or team, creates all items with little involvement of others. Connell et al., (2018), provide an example of engaging community members and intended examinees in the process of creating items for the Recovering Quality of Life measure (ReQoL). Engagement with potential examinees allowed the developers to learn why some items were deemed acceptable versus others. Acceptable items ". . . should be relevant and meaningful, unambiguous, easy to answer particularly when distressed, do not cause further upset, and be non-judgmental." Items may also be created by surveying parents, teachers, and youth themselves to identify content that was potentially overlooked by the test developer and collaborators (Reynolds & Kamphaus, 2015). Collaborative and co-creative work with a variety of stakeholders with interests in the use of a test is facilitated by reference to well-conceived definitions of a construct and item content blueprint, and ultimately strengthening the blueprint.

Maximizing Accessibility of Items by a Wide Range of Examinees

Calculation of readability indexes is a relatively routine process for evaluating the accessibility of item content to the widest possible range of examinees. Eliminating words that have a low frequency of use in a language is another popular method. Language is constantly changing as new words come into usage across the generations. The numerous former terms for the diagnostic category of Intellectual Disability, for example, are no longer acceptable to mention.

Panel Review

Expert and community panel reviews of item content is also now de rigueur. The expertise of community members can be accessed to help identify items that may be susceptible to the influence of construct-irrelevant variance. For example, item content may be more unfamiliar to various socioeconomic groups, acceptable to the dominant culture, but offensive to one or more population subgroups, or the item content may underrepresent the experiences of some population subgroups. Although it is not a formal test of item bias per se, community members may be uniquely qualified to identify items that are simply in poor taste, and therefore, have the potential to contribute construct-irrelevant variance into the assessment process.

Item Bias Studies

Empirical methods also have an important role to play in the creation of items and ensuring that each is a good indicator of the construct of interest. In our experience, for example, statistical analyses of item bias produce different results than expert or community panel item reviews, and they typically identify far more items as problematic. On some occasions, the reason for gender, race/ethnicity, nationality, or other subgroup item bias is difficult to identify. If, for example, an item is found to be biased against boys at only 1 of 16 age groups for a test, the finding may be attributable to an anomaly such as sampling. Alternatively, if an item is found biased against boys at 12 of 16 age groups, the item will likely be discarded even if a rationale for biases cannot be identified by the test developers or expert or community panel members. Typical samples for assessing item bias include age/grade, gender, race, and ethnicity, although cross-national, geographic region, and socioeconomic group samples are also desirable.

Item Alignment with Hypothesized Construct

Statistical tests of the "fit" of items to the theoretical construct of interest provide another important test of the likelihood that a given item serves as a reasonable indicator. Simply put, item response theory (IRT) and structural equation modeling methods test the proposition that an item functions similarly to other items hypothesized to measure a construct. Our experience also shows that these statistical methods identify yet another unique set of items, not identified by either statistical item bias or panel review, that have the potential to contribute construct-irrelevant variance to the assessment.

It is increasingly apparent that principles and methods of supporting content validity apply to virtually all types of tests developed for use with youth. Historically, intelligence tests served as useful exemplars and content validity has been central to the development of academic achievement tests where content blueprints are the standard of practice. Now, tests of children's behavior, emotions, personality, and rating scales routinely use several methods for documenting content validity, including defining the construct or constructs clearly a priori, obtaining item review and co-development from community members, scientific experts, future examiners, and intended examinees, statistical methods of measurement invariance and item bias, item response theory or structural equation modeling methods, and readability indexes. We think that the *Test Standards* are having the intended effect of improving test fairness by improving test development practices and outcomes for youth across assessment domains.

This list of content validity methods is not exhaustive. Our intent is to provide an overview of popular methods, demonstrate the need for using multiple methods to make the case for content validity, and provide an example of the interplay of empirical, theoretical, and panel review procedures for reducing the unwanted influences of construct-irrelevant variance on the assessment of youth. Yet content validity is just one method for supporting test score inferences.

CONSEQUENTIAL VALIDITY

Consequential validity, as conceptualized by Samuel Messick (1988), represents an important consideration for evaluating test and assessment fairness because it extends the concept of validity beyond the internal properties of the test. Consequential validity refers to the actual impact of test use on populations and population subgroups. In Messick's (1980) words, "Questions of the appropriateness of test use in proposed applications are answerable on ethical grounds by appraising potential social consequences of the testing" (p. 1012). Messick's introduction of consequences of testing as a validity indicator has been incorporated fully into the test *Standards* as follows:

> Tests are commonly administered in the expectation that some benefit will be realized from the interpretation and use of the scores intended by the test developers. A few of the many possible benefits that might be claimed are selection of efficacious therapies, placement of workers in suitable jobs, prevention of unqualified individuals from entering a profession, or improvement of classroom instructional practices. A fundamental purpose of validation is to indicate whether these specific benefits are likely to be realized. (p. 19)

The field of universal behavioral health screening of youth serves as a timely example of the need to assess consequential validity. Although the practice of behavioral health screening has been nascent for 50 years, it is now expanding rapidly due to societal concern about the cascading mental health problems experienced by youth and the lack of service providers required to meet the demand for services. Adding further impetus to the practice, states including Illinois, Colorado, and New Jersey have recently passed legislation requiring universal behavioral health screening of students, and other states are actively considering such legislation. In 2022, the influential U.S. Preventive Services Task Force promulgated recommendations to pediatricians to expand depression and anxiety screening of youth (Viswanathan et al., 2022a, 2022b). This foundation for the expansion of screening practice, however, is decades old and can be traced to seminal work in the California Department of Education in the 1960s (Cowen, 1973).

Cowen introduced the case for universal screening as a public health prevention necessity as follows:

> There have been important shifts in the stance of the mental health fields during the past decade. Principal among these is a growing willingness to relinquish prior, near-exclusive emphases on repairing rooted dysfunction in favor of exploring programs designed to prevent disorder and to build health. (Cowen et al., 1973, p. 12)

The California Department of Education research team created a teacher-rated universal screener for use in kindergarten through 12th grades—the AML (Acting Out, Moody, Learning Problems). The content of the AML is described as follows:

> These 11 items, 5 "aggressive-outgoing" (A), 5 "moody-internalized" (M), and 1 "learning dis-ability" (L), comprise the scale. The teacher's task is to rate the frequency of occurrence of each of the 11 behaviors on 5-point scales, ranging from "seldom or never" (1) to "all of the time" (5). The measure is brief, objective, and concise, requiring only 30–60 sec. per child. An average-sized class can, thus, be rated in 20–30 min. (Cowen at al., 1973, p. 14)

Although this early screening movement did not result in significant expansion of the practice, the case for early detection of behavioral health problems received conceptual and scientific support in the 1990s and 2000s from the Institute of Medicine of the National Academies (O'Connell et al., 2009). The National Academies' most recent report also provided recommended content for universal screeners—"mild social, behavioral, and emotional problems" that set the stage for the development of a mental health disorder. This content recommendation is consistent with an emerging body of research documenting the transition from mild symptoms of mental health disorders in childhood to a much higher risk of development of a mental health disorder in adolescence or adulthood (Uchida et al., 2018). This definition is further supported by evidence that such a definition would capture a large number of children—from 15% to 30%—which constitutes a major public health burden worldwide (Balázs & Kereszteny, 2014; Bertha & Balázs, 2013; Roberts et al., 2015).

Research on the consequences of universal behavioral health screening is accelerating. Splett et al., (2023), for example, sought to assess the consequential validity of a screening program by following the services rendered to youth identified as possessing some heightened risk as measured by the presence of internalizing or externalizing problems and fewer adaptive behavior skills when compared to national norms. The results were, for us at least, disappointing. Approximately 900 students were identified as having overall risk at or above the 85th percentile rank. Of this number, 708 of these students were not receiving any type of school intervention or prevention services either before or after screening. The authors concluded, "insufficient use to provide intervention services at a rate that substantially reduced unaddressed SEB (social emotional behavioral) risk" (p. 137). In contrast, a large-scale randomized controlled trial (RCT) by Sekhar et al. (2021) found universal screening to be an effective tool for helping families address cases of depression by assessing treatment initiation. According to these authors, "In a large, statewide RCT (randomized control trial) of schools with a diverse student body, universal school-based depression screening successfully doubled student initiation of MDD treatments and services. . . ." (p. 7).

Two recent recommendations of the U.S. Preventive Services Task Force (2022) provide examples of how the consequences of screening (i.e., benefits) may be evaluated. The task force commissioned research syntheses, available on their website, to determine whether or not the benefits or screening for symptoms of depression and anxiety outweighed the risks and costs of conducting screening in pediatric settings (Viswanathan et al., 2022a, 2022b). The evidence synthesis included 39 randomized controlled trials. The overall summary statement for anxiety screening was as follows:

> Indirect evidence suggested that some screening instruments were reasonably accurate. CBT [cognitive-behavioral therapy] and pharmacotherapy were associated with benefits; no statistically significant association with harms was reported. (p. 1445)

Crucially, no studies that directly assessed the consequences of anxiety screening were found. Our interpretation is that the decision to recommend routine screening of youth for anxiety problems is based largely on evidence of a lack of evidence of harm associated with CBT and pharmacotherapy treatments. The results were similar for the depression screening research synthesis (29 RCTs). No direct evidence of the benefits or potential harms of universal screening for depression were identified as noted by the overall conclusion reached.

> The evidence for screening for suicide risk, anxiety, and depression in children and adolescents relies on indirect evidence on the accuracy of screening and the benefits and harms of treatment. Both pharmacotherapy and psychotherapy treatments have benefit for depression and anxiety (specifically, CBT for anxiety alone was reviewed); the evidence is limited for suicide risk interventions. The frequency of harms is greater for pharmacotherapy than placebo. (p. 68)

Thus, it is important to note that the screening for both anxiety and depression that is recommended by the task force appears to be based mainly on the absence of harm associated with the common treatments for these problems. Therefore, how might we evaluate the consequences of universal screening? Some proposals from the existing research base might include:

1. Developing screening tests yielding scores with strong evidence of reliability, which is necessary to support detection accuracy. We recommend the standard from the 1970s for making high stakes decisions about an individual of .90 or higher and .85 or higher as potentially acceptable (Kamphaus, 2001).
2. Engaging in adequate sampling to conduct disaggregated, by demographic characteristics, tests of sensitivity and specificity. The resulting values should meet or exceed those generally accepted for the field, although these could be evolving.
3. Tracking children identified through screening and making direct comparisons to those identified by parental, teacher, special education referral, and other methods for detecting risk and disorder.
4. Tracking and evaluating the results of prevention and intervention services provided in school, community, and pediatric settings.
5. Situating screening test findings in the context of societal needs for change, including prevention and intervention staffing models (see report of the Commonwealth Fund on alternative staffing around the world, reimbursement strategies, and needed legislative or regulatory action aimed at redressing access to services).

CONCLUSION

Ultimately, the *Standards* continue to increase the requirements and responsibilities of test developers and their financial sponsors, such as publishers, institutions of higher education, professional societies (e.g., credentialing examinations), state and federal research departments and institutes, and business and industry. We are far beyond the practices of a century ago, the time of David Wechsler and contemporaries, when an individual practitioner or researcher could develop and deploy a test and rely on a community of scholars to conduct reliability and validity studies. This limited test development process puts youth at risk of having major decisions, diagnostic or treatment, made about them before evidence or procedures are in place to maximize the accurate assessment of a construct. In addition, if the test developers and their sponsors are not conducting the necessary studies or engaging in standard-of-practice test development procedures, changes cannot be made to the test to mitigate the assessment of construct-irrelevant variance. For this reason, continuous improvement through revision and periodic updating of a measure, documented in a comprehensive test manual, is required to assure that a test is aligned with efforts to promote fairness. A useful framework evaluating scientific evidence to support testing fairness is provided in an article by Jonson et al. (2019).

The expansion of the *Standards* into the field of test fairness, the addition of consequential validity as a core consideration, and the complexity of testing programs such as universal behavioral health screening all reinforce redefining psychometric validity as the validity evidence available to support score inferences made from tests versus validity as a characteristic of a test per se. "It is the proposed interpretation/use that is validated, not the test itself or the test scores. Statements about validity should refer to particular interpretations for specified uses. It is incorrect to use the unqualified phrase 'the validity of the test'" (AERA, APA, & NCME, 2014, p. 11).

We think that these principles are at least as important as the ethical standards of professional societies that are commonly taught in graduate school preparation programs. We recommend that the *Standards* be required study in graduate programs in education, psychology, counseling, and related human service fields.

REFERENCES

American Educational Research Association, American Psychological Association, & National Council on Measurement in Education. (2014). *The standards for educational and psychological testing*. American Educational Research Association.

Balázs, J., & Keresztény, Á. (2014). Subthreshold attention deficit hyperactivity in children and adolescents: A systematic review. *European Child & Adolescent Psychiatry, 23*(6), 393–408.

Beck, C. T., & Gable, R. K. (2001). Ensuring content validity: an illustration of the process. *Journal of Nursing Measurement*, 9(2), 201–215.

Bertha, E. A., & Balázs, J. (2013). Subthreshold depression in adolescence: A systematic review. *European Child & Adolescent Psychiatry, 22*(10), 589–603.

Binet, A., & Simon, T. (1916). Application of the new methods to the diagnosis of the intellectual level among normal and subnormal children in institutions and in the primary schools (*L'Année Psych.*, 1905, pp. 245–336). In A. Binet, T. Simon & E. S.

Kite (Trans.), *The development of intelligence in children (The Binet-Simon Scale)* (pp. 91–181). Williams & Wilkins.

Boring, E. G. (1929). *A History of Experimental Psychology*. Century.

Connell, J., Carlton, J., Grundy, A., Taylor Buck, E., Keetharuth, A. D., Ricketts, T., et al. (2018). The importance of content and face validity in instrument development: lessons learnt from service users when developing the Recovering Quality of Life measure (ReQoL). *Quality of Life Research: An International Journal of Quality of Life Aspects of Treatment, Care and Rehabilitation, 27*(7), 1893–1902.

Cowen, E. L., Dorr, D., Clarfield, S. P., Kreling, B., McWilliams, S. A., Pokracki, F., et al. (1973). The AML: A quick screening device for early identification of school maladaption. *American Journal of Community Psychology, 1*(1), 12–35.

Cronbach, L. J., & Meehl, P. E. (1955). Construct validity in psychological tests. *Psychological Bulletin, 52*(4), 281–302.

French, J. L., & Hale, R. L. (1990). A history of the development of psychological and educational testing. In C. R. Reynolds & R. W. Kamphaus (Eds.), *Handbook of psychological and educational assessment of children* (pp. 3–28). Guilford Press.

Goodenough, F. L. (1949). *Mental testing: Its history, principles, and applications*. Rinehart.

Jonson, J. L., Trantham, P., & Usher-Tate, B. J. (2019). An evaluative framework for reviewing fairness standards and practices in educational tests. *Educational Measurement: Issues and Practice, 38*(3), 6–19.

Kane, M. T. (2013). Validating the interpretations and uses of test scores. *Journal of Educational Measurement, 50*(1), 1–73.

Kamphaus, R. W. (2001). *Clinical assessment of child and adolescent intelligence* (2nd ed.). Springer.

Kamphaus, R., & Walden, E. (2020a). Intellectual disability. In E. A. Youngstrom, M. J. Prinstein, E. J. Mash, & R. Barkley (Eds.), *Assessment of disorders in childhood and adolescence* (5th ed., pp. 358–373). Guilford Press.

Kamphaus, R. W. & Walden, E. (2020b). Behavioral and emotional risk screening at school. In P. J. Frick, C. Burns, & R. W. Kamphaus (Eds.). *Clinical assessment of child and adolescent personality and behavior* (3rd ed., pp. 263–278). Springer.

Kim, J., & Kamphaus, R. W. (2018). Investigation of factor structure and measurement invariance by gender for the Behavioral and Emotional Screening System among high school students. *Psychological Assessment, 30*(2), 231–240.

Lubinski, D. (2004). Introduction to the special section on cognitive abilities: 100 years after Spearman's (1904) "General Intelligence: Objectively Determined and Measured." *Journal of Personality and Social Psychology, 86*(1), 96–111.

Messick, S. (1980). Test validity and the ethics of assessment. *American Psychologist, 35*(11), 1012–1027.

Messick, S. (1988). The once and future issues of validity: Assessing the meaning and consequences of measurement. In H. Wainer & H. Braun (Eds.), *Test validity* (1st ed, pp. 33–45). Erlbaum.

O'Connell, M. E., Boat, T., & Warner, K. E. (Eds). (2009). *Preventing mental, emotional, and behavioral disorders among young people: Progress and possibilities*. National Academy Press.

Pintner, R. (1923). *Intelligence testing*. Henry Holt.

Reynolds, C. R. (2016). Contextualized evidence and empirically based testing and assessment. *Clinical Psychology: Science and Practice, 23*(4), 410–416.

Reynolds, C. R. & Brown, R. T. (Eds.). (1984). *Perspectives on bias in mental testing*. Plenum Press.

Reynolds, C. R., & Kamphaus, R. W. (2015). *Reynolds Intellectual Assessment Scales—Second Edition (RIAS-2)*. Psychological Assessment Resources.

Reynolds, C. R., & Suzuki, L. A. (2013). Bias in psychological assessment: An empirical review and recommendations. In J. R. Graham, J. A. Naglieri, & I. B. Weiner (Eds.), *Handbook of psychology: Assessment psychology* (2nd ed., pp. 82–113). Wiley.

Roberts, R. E., Fisher, P. W., Turner, J. B., & Tang, M. (2015). Estimating the burden of psychiatric disorders in adolescence: The impact of subthreshold disorders. *Social Psychiatry and Psychiatric Epidemiology: The International Journal for Research in Social and Genetic Epidemiology and Mental Health Services, 50*(3), 397–406.

Sekhar, D. L., Schaefer, E. W., Waxmonsky, J. G., Walker-Harding, L. R., Pattison, K. L., Molinari, A., et al. (2021). Screening in high schools to identify, evaluate, and lower depression among adolescents: A randomized clinical trial. *Journal of the American Medical Association, Network Open, 4*(11), e2131836.

Splett, J. W., Brann, K. L., Trainor, K. M., & Shen, Z. (2023). Examining utility and impact of social, emotional, and behavioral screening to identify and address needs. *School Psychology (Washington, D.C.), 38*(3), 137–147.

Uchida, M., Fitzgerald, M., Woodworth, H., Carrellas, N., Kelberman, C., & Biederman, J. (2018). Subsyndromal manifestations of depression in children predict the development of major depression. *The Journal of Pediatrics, 201*, 252–258.

Van Vleet, P., & Kannegieter, R. (1969). *Investments in prevention: The prevention of learning and behavior problems in young children*. PACE ID Center.

Viswanathan, M., Wallace, I., Middleton, J. C., Kennedy, S. M., McKeeman, J., Hudson, K., et al. (2022a). *Screening for depression, anxiety, and suicide risk in children and adolescents: An evidence review for the U.S. Preventive Services Task Force* (Evidence Synthesis No. 221; AHRQ Publication No. 22-05293-EF-1). Agency for Healthcare Research and Quality.

Viswanathan, M., Wallace, I., Middleton, J. C., Kennedy, S. M., McKeeman, J., Hudson, K., et al. (2022b). Screening for anxiety in children and adolescents: Evidence report and systematic review for the US Preventive Services Task Force. *JAMA, 328*(14), 1445–1455.

CHAPTER 3

Culturally Responsive Behavior Assessment

Janine Jones

Behavior assessment plays a critical role in the field of school psychology, serving as a foundational practice for understanding and addressing students' behavioral needs. At its core, behavior assessment involves the systematic collection and analysis of data to identify, describe, and understand students' behaviors within educational settings (Conroy & Stichter, 2003). This process is essential for developing effective interventions that support students' academic, social, and emotional well-being.

Behavior assessment encompasses a wide range of methods and tools designed to evaluate various aspects of student behavior. These can include direct observation, behavior rating scales, interviews, and functional behavior assessments (FBAs). The primary goal of behavior assessment is to gather comprehensive and accurate information that can inform decision-making and intervention planning. By understanding the antecedents, behaviors, and consequences (Hanley et al., 2003), school psychologists can develop tailored interventions to promote positive behaviors and mitigate challenging ones.

THE ROLE OF BEHAVIOR ASSESSMENT IN EDUCATIONAL SETTINGS

In educational settings, behavior assessment is vital because it helps to identify students who may require additional support due to the perceived behavioral challenges. Early identification is essential for preventing minor issues from escalating into more significant problems that could impact the student's academic performance and overall school experience. Behavior assessment also guides the process for the development of individualized behavior intervention plans (BIPs), ensuring that interventions are tailored to meet each student's unique needs. In schools, behavior assessment also provides a framework for monitoring and evaluating the effectiveness of interventions while allowing for adjustments as needed to achieve desired outcomes. Behavior assessment is a cornerstone of school psychologists' practice, as it provides essential insights into students' behaviors and informs the development of effective interventions. Its importance cannot be overstated, as it directly impacts students' academic success and overall well-being.

HISTORICAL CONTEXT AND EVOLUTION OF BEHAVIOR ASSESSMENT PRACTICES

Behavior assessment in schools initially focused primarily on observing and recording overt behaviors, with little consideration given to the underlying causes or environmental factors influencing those behaviors. Over time, advances in psychological theory and research have led to the development of more sophisticated measurement tools and methodologies for behavior assessment.

The introduction of FBA in the late 20th century marked a significant turning point in the field. FBA emphasizes understanding the function or purpose that a behavior serves for a student (Conroy & Stichter, 2003). This approach allows for more precise identification of the factors contributing to challenging behaviors and facilitates the design of interventions that address these root causes. In addition to the formalization of FBA, the increasing recognition of the importance of cultural factors in behavior assessment has further refined practices. Culturally responsive behavior assessment acknowledges that students' behaviors are influenced by their cultural backgrounds, values, and experiences (Fallon et al., 2012, Fallon et al., 2018; Jones et al., 2010). This perspective has led to the development of assessment tools and practices that are more inclusive and equitable, ensuring that all students receive fair and accurate evaluations. The evolution of behavior assessment practices reflects ongoing advancements in psychological research and a growing commitment to cultural responsiveness, ensuring that all students receive the support they need to thrive in educational settings.

THE NEED FOR CULTURALLY RESPONSIVE BEHAVIOR ASSESSMENT

In the diverse and dynamic environments of today's schools, the need for culturally responsive practices in behavior assessment has never been more critical. Cultural responsiveness in education involves recognizing, respecting, and responding to the diverse cultural backgrounds of students. It is essential for ensuring that behavior assessments are fair, accurate, and effective for all students, regardless of their racial or cultural backgrounds.

Cultural responsiveness in education means creating learning environments that acknowledge and embrace students' cultural identities. It involves understanding the cultural contexts in which students live and learn and incorporating this understanding into teaching, assessment, and intervention practices. Culturally responsive education goes beyond mere recognition of diversity; it actively seeks to validate and integrate students' cultural experiences into the educational process.

In the context of behavior assessment, cultural responsiveness means that school psychologists and educators are aware of and sensitive to the cultural influences that shape students' behaviors (Fallon & Mueller, 2017). It requires using assessment tools and methods that are appropriate for diverse populations and interpreting assessment data through a culturally informed lens. This approach helps minimize the impact of cultural biases that can lead to misinterpretation of behaviors and ensures that interventions are relevant and more likely to be effective.

Cultural factors significantly influence students' behaviors and how those behaviors are perceived and evaluated in school settings. Cultural norms and values shape students' communication styles, social interactions, and responses to authority, all of which can affect their behavior in the classroom. For instance, behaviors that are considered respectful and appropriate in one culture may be viewed differently in another. Thus, without applying a culturally responsive approach, school psychologists and educators might misinterpret these behaviors, leading to inaccurate interpretation of assessments and inappropriate interventions.

Moreover, cultural factors can impact the validity and reliability of behavior assessment tools. Many standardized assessment instruments are developed based on norms and values prevalent in the dominant culture, which may not accurately reflect the behaviors of students from diverse backgrounds. This can result in biased assessments that do not accurately capture the true nature of a student's behavior. Thus, clinicians should aim to conduct assessments that take into account student's background, including their cultural values and beliefs as they are strong contributors to one's behavior.

PRINCIPLES OF CULTURALLY RESPONSIVE ASSESSMENT

When aspiring to achieve optimal culturally responsive assessment, most clinicians are unsure of the best approaches to apply. A recent paper by Walker et al. (2023) provides five design principles for culturally responsive assessment, all of which emphasize the need to share power among all involved parties throughout the assessment process. By distributing decision-making power and involving stakeholders at every stage, assessments can better reflect diverse cultural perspectives and values, leading to more accurate and culturally sensitive outcomes. This collaborative approach to assessment fosters a sense of inclusivity and respect for diverse cultural backgrounds, enhancing the overall cultural responsiveness of the assessment process. Walker et al. (2023) principles include (1) sharing power among all parties, (2) fostering engagement and belonging, (3) holding high expectations, (4) maximizing flexibility, and (5) reflecting asset-based perspectives. These principles will be used as a foundation for a process framework that clinicians can use to complete culturally responsive behavior assessments.

Sharing Power

Sharing power is not simply the practice of including educators and caregivers in the assessment process, as it involves recognizing the value of all informants and ways in which authentic collaboration creates greater equity for students from diverse backgrounds. Most standardized assessment measures were developed based on a primary (or dominant) culture and place some students who do not represent that culture at a disadvantage (Sireci, 2020). As a result, intentional efforts are needed to minimize the bias created by the initial construction of measures and to understand a student's sociocultural characteristics that may impact the results of using such measures. Sharing power is an approach where clinicians can leverage relationships to create greater equity. For example, McCarthy and Wright (2015) named an approach called "experience-centered design" where participants simultaneously hold different levels of power while building trust and sharing ideas based on their experiences. Taking this approach during assessment means acknowledging the user experience with the assessment tools, as well as integrating their knowledge and experiences with the student being assessed. The shared power process may come in the form of having choice between assessment tools, choice in how to respond to assessment tools, and being empowered to co-interpret assessment tools.

Fostering Engagement

The principle of fostering engagement expands upon the previous principle of sharing power. Engagement includes having active participation and building trust so that all participants in the process feel connected to and accountable for the assessment outcomes. Engaging assessments are context-dependent and, in particular, have a positive impact on historically excluded students whose experiences are centered in the information collected. Engagement in the assessment process creates more motivation, a sense of autonomy, and opportunities for alignment with the identities, beliefs, and values of the student and their family.

All clinicians should keep in mind that many behavior rating scales are designed with a deficit perspective in mind. This deficit perspective is signaled through the wording of items (e.g., unable to regulate their emotions) or in the response options (e.g., "well below expected"). This deficit framing often feeds into deficit-centered expectations for behavior and outcomes. By fostering the engagement principle, the clinician can seek feedback from informants to reframe response options or interpret items through a growth mindset lens. This may include administering behavior rating scales interactively rather than asking the informant to complete them on their own. Engagement may also include initiating a dialogue about items that were rated the most negatively by asking related questions in an open-ended manner. For example, one could ask, "If you were to describe how well you regulate your emotions in your own words, what would you say?" Ultimately, the principle of engagement should be applied to every participant in the assessment process with the intention of generating context-rich data and foster greater equity in the assessment process.

Holding and Communicating High Expectations

Expecting all students to have the potential to perform at high levels is an important aspect of supporting historically marginalized students. For racialized and minoritized youth, negative stereotypes about their academic abilities may contribute directly to the reason for the referral—their behavior may be in response to others having low expectations for them and consequently the students having low expectations for themselves (Rojas & Liou, 2017). Intentional efforts are needed to counteract the negative stereotypes that some hold against such students.

Communicating high expectations can and should be part of the assessment and intervention process. Yeager et al. (2014) coined the term "wise feedback" to describe an effective strategy for educators to use when emphasizing that they not only have high standards but also to communicate their belief that a student can meet that high standard. By holding students to these high standards, their intervention reduced Black students' feelings of mistrust, improved grades, and even disrupted the fears associated with stereotype threat. These findings promote the need for clinicians to find ways during the assessment process to use asset-based language and communicate confidence with youth that a positive outcome will be achieved.

Maximizing Flexibility

Culturally responsive assessments allow clinicians to be flexible and to integrate individual characteristics such as cultural values, interests, preferences, and ethnic identity into the assessment process. Traditional assessments have long been criticized for being inflexible and non-adaptive for youth of color and multilingual learners (Walker et al., 2023). This is likely because we have assumed that assessments are only valid when strict standardized procedures are followed. However, the research on cultural adaptations in assessment and intervention has matured significantly over the past 10 years and has shown that appropriate adaptations enhance assessment rather than invalidate the results. In fact, Plake and Wise (2014) note that the 2014 version of the *Standards for Educational and Psychological Testing* includes an acknowledgment that adaptations to assessments can be substantial and integrate flexibility that is designed to reduce construct-irrelevant variance. Such flexible adaptations may include allowing for multiple ways of presenting assessment content (verbal, written, images, or video) and multiple ways for informants to respond (oral, written, nonverbal, multiple languages). Basically, the same information can be achieved through the most appropriate means for the person. By taking a flexible approach, it signals to the participant that all ways of knowing and communicating are equally valued, as well as limiting threats to validity and bias when only one modality is utilized for data collection.

Reflecting Asset-Based Perspectives

Culturally responsive assessments should measure what youth *can* do by using asset-based perspectives that disrupt deficit narratives (Walker et al., 2023). Assets include linguistic competency, cultural knowledge and experiences, social and community connections, and ways these diverse perspectives impact their learning in school. By seeing these unique characteristics as assets, the clinician automatically reframes behaviors as a foundation of strengths rather than challenges that need to be overcome (Ramasubramanian et al., 2021). Our assessment tools rarely give us the information we need to reflect an asset-based perspective of students and families. That means the clinician needs to intentionally learn about these assets through interviewing and connection. Assets to explore as part of a culturally responsive assessment can include personal characteristics, relationships with peers and family, acculturation styles, intersectional identities (e.g., gender, race, language, ability, sexual orientation), and collectivism (Jones et al., 2017; Zigarelli et al., 2016). Among these assets, clinicians should ask about the ways that a student's culture of origin impacts their interactions with their peers. For example, in spaces where their native culture is not dominant, they must learn to negotiate their self-identity artfully in order to belong. This process of negotiation can be complex and challenging, thereby causing behaviors that may be interpreted negatively instead of as a cultural strength. A clinician using an asset-based approach would recognize the behavior as a process of acculturation and an asset to the student's identity development. Using an asset-based perspective helps clinicians interpret assessment data in context and in ways that are likely to produce positive outcomes rather than harmful ones.

FOUNDATIONS OF BEHAVIOR ASSESSMENT

Traditional behavior assessment models have long been foundational in school psychology, providing essential tools and methodologies for understanding and addressing student behaviors. These methods are intended to systematically observe, measure, and analyze student behaviors in order to inform effective interventions. Two of the most prominent traditional behavior assessment models are the behavior rating scales and FBA.

Behavior Rating Scales

Behavior rating scales are standardized tools that gather information about a student's behavior from multiple informants, including teachers, parents, and the students themselves. These scales provide quantitative data that can be used to compare a student's behavior to normative samples. Common broadband behavior rating scales include the *Behavior Assessment System for Children*—Third Edition (BASC-3; Reynolds & Kamphaus, 2015) and the *Conners 4th Edition* (Conners, 2022). These instruments are considered broadband scales because they simultaneously measure a variety of dimensions of behavior, such as hyperactivity, aggression, anxiety, and social skills. Behavior rating scales are useful for providing quantitative data for screening, diagnosis, and monitoring the progress of interventions. They offer a broad perspective on a student's behavior across different settings by collecting data from multiple informants.

Behavior rating scales are strong tools for behavior assessment because they offer standardized methods for assessing behavior with normed samples as points of comparison which enhances reliability and validity of the assessment. They are also useful when designed for multi-informant input. When rating scales are available for multiple informants, they incorporate multiple perspectives of the same student and provide a more well-rounded view of the student's behavior. However, cultural bias can influence the results of rating scales since they are developed based on normative data that may not include a diverse norming sample or accurately reflect the behaviors of students from diverse backgrounds. In addition, ratings on behavior rating scales may not capture the dynamic and contextual nature of behavior over time.

Adapting behavior rating scales to be culturally responsive is essential for ensuring fair and accurate behavior assessments. Adapting behavior rating scales might include adjusting the language/terminology and/or offering culturally relevant examples. For the first adaptation, clinicians can adjust the language of behavior rating scales to ensure that the terms are culturally relevant and understandable to a variety of cultural groups. This involves looking for phrases that may be interpreted differently across cultures. For example, "expresses independence" may not represent a value of some cultural groups, so choosing terms that align better with cultural values such as "demonstrates confidence" might reflect language that is more universally understood. Offering culturally relevant examples is another way to adapt behavior rating scales. Items like "actively participates in class discussions" could be modified to incorporate culturally relevant examples of behavior and could ask if the student "contributes ideas in ways that feel comfortable to them." This is a supportive adaptation because some cultures prefer non-verbal forms of participation, and that preference is easily interpreted as disengagement. Adapting the items with culturally relevant examples opens the opportunity for the behavior to be interpreted appropriately. By modifying scales to reflect cultural diversity, conducting rigorous validation studies, and continuously evaluating their effectiveness, school psychologists and educators can provide more equitable and effective support for all students. These practices help to create an inclusive educational environment where every student's behavior is understood and addressed within their cultural context.

Functional Behavior Assessment

FBA is a systematic process for identifying the underlying causes or *functions* of challenging behaviors. It involves direct observation, data collection, and analysis to determine the antecedents (what happens before), behaviors (the actions themselves), and consequences (what happens after) of the target behavior (Hanley et al., 2003). FBA typically includes interviews with teachers and parents, direct observation of the student in various settings, and a review of academic and disciplinary records. The goal is to hypothesize the function that the behavior serves for the student, such as gaining attention, escaping a task, or accessing a tangible reward. FBA is used to develop BIPs that are tailored to address the specific functions of a student's behavior, with the goal of increasing the likelihood of successful intervention. The primary strength of the FBA is the comprehensive data collection, which provides detailed insights into the contextual factors influencing behavior, facilitating targeted interventions. However, conducting FBAs can be resource intensive since they are time consuming and require a trained skill set for recognizing the root cause of behavior. This trained skill set includes knowing how to explore and assess the influence of cultural factors on the behavior of youth. For example, a culturally appropriate response to experiencing frustration might be to seek support and guidance from an adult or peer; however, such behavior may not be appropriate in a classroom context when group instruction is occurring. The instructor may see the action of seeking support (i.e., talking) as disruptive to the learning context even though the behavior has an appropriate and adaptive "function." When FBAs are completed without consideration of the cultural context, the true function of the behavior may be overlooked, and school psychologists run the risk of pathologizing behaviors of youth and thereby contributing to problems of practice, including disproportionality in exclusionary discipline (Gregory et al., 2016; Vincent et al., 2013). Regardless of this potential limitation, including an FBA as part of behavior assessment has remained a part of the gold standard for behavior assessment in school psychology.

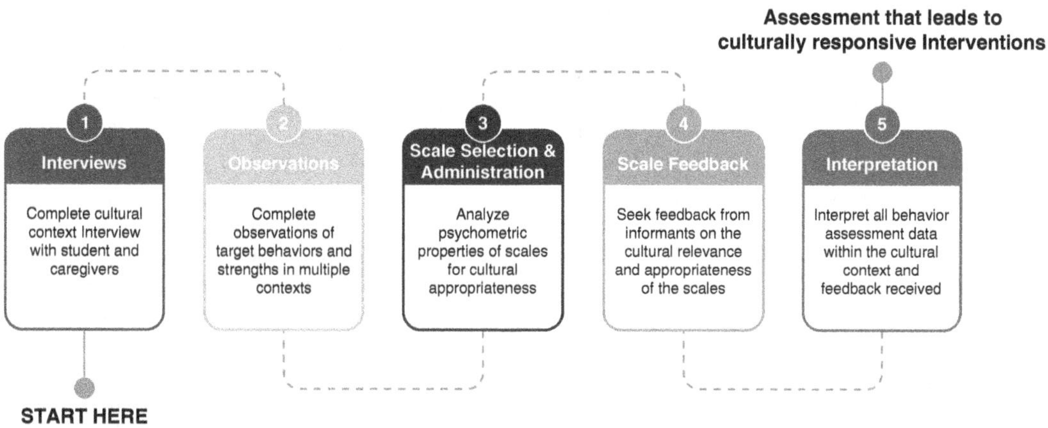

FIGURE 3.1. Culturally responsive behavior assessment (CR-BA): A process.

CULTURALLY RESPONSIVE BEHAVIOR ASSESSMENT: A PROCESS

To ensure equity and effectiveness, BAs and the integrated behavior rating scales need to be adapted for cultural responsiveness. Culturally responsive BA (CR-BA) involves understanding and respecting the cultural contexts that influence student behavior as well as choosing behavior rating scales that are representative of and appropriate for the population being served (Enders et al., 2022; Moreno et al., 2014). Traditional BA methods may not fully capture the nuances of behaviors shaped by different cultural experiences and values. Therefore, adapting these methods is crucial for accurate assessment and effective intervention.

In keeping with the principles of culturally responsive assessment (Walker et al., 2023) as a foundation, key adaptations for the CR-BA process include (1) sharing power and enhancing engagement by collaborating with educators, family, and community in the assessment process; (2) using interviews and observations to formulate high-quality sociocultural histories that are grounded in the cultural context; (3) selecting and flexibly administering culturally appropriate assessment measurement tools; (4) soliciting feedback from collaborators on the cultural appropriateness of the measurement tools; and (5) interpreting the behavior assessment data to create culturally appropriate interventions. Figure 3.1 outlines a process for completing culturally responsive behavior assessments.

Step 1: The Cultural Context Interview

Conceptualizing exactly how cultural variables should be considered by practitioners is somewhat elusive. Despite widespread recommendations for providing cultural adaptations, it is still challenging for many to envision how to apply these recommendations on a case-by-case basis and integrate into their own practice (Salend & Taylor, 2002). The most frequently used approach is to look for common problem behaviors and apply the best evidence-based practice for the target problem. This approach emphasizes starting with the problem behavior, then considering the specific characteristics of the targeted groups, and making adaptations with those characteristics in mind (Bradshaw et al., 2018; Castro-Olivo, 2014). However, an individualized approach where interventions are tailored to the student's specific needs and preferences is better for school psychologists to make the most appropriate adaptations to interventions (Castro et al., 2010; Dennison et al., 2019).

In behavior assessment, clinicians must recognize and account for cultural norms and values that may influence behavior. This involves understanding the student's cultural background, how it shapes their interactions with others, and how their responses to interactions manifest in their behavior. A CR-BA will consider differences in perspective and avoid misinterpretation of behaviors. In addition, the CR-BA will include analysis of the target behavior in other settings and consider variations in expectations depending on context.

When conducting an interview, school psychologists must explore the cultural context of the client and their family. This process should ideally be semi-structured, allowing for a natural flow of conversation while maintaining flexibility for follow-up questions and deeper understanding. Two prominent examples of semi-structured interviews include the Cultural Formulation Interview, which is embedded within *Diagnostic and Statistical Manual of Mental Disorders, Fifth Edition* (DSM-5-TR; American Psychiatric Association, 2022) and *Jones Intentional Multicultural Interview Schedule* (JIMIS; Jones, 2009). Both tools are designed to explore family values, such as communication styles, gender norms, socialization practices, religious beliefs, and coping mechanisms. Without integrating these questions into the structured interview, it is unlikely that families, children, or adolescents will volunteer this crucial information. Therefore, it is important to create a context that encourages clients to share different aspects of their identity as part of the behavior assessment.

Within this interview framework, school psychologists can learn about cultural and linguistic factors that impact learning and behavior. For instance, it is important to understand whether the client and family come from an individualistic or collectivistic culture, whether culture-bound syndromes may influence behavior, and whether their interactions with others rely on high-context interpretations of nonverbal communication. Additionally, school psychologists should consider family system variables, including the family constellation, primary caregiving responsibilities, and who plays a significant role in parenting, guidance, and discipline. This knowledge aids in interpreting behavior within different contexts.

The interview should also gather data on the student's acculturation styles when exposed to diverse cultural contexts. Acculturation refers to how an individual responds to interactions or exposure to a different culture (Berry, 2005). Understanding their acculturation style can provide insight into coping mechanisms and the ways in which behavior is influenced by other cultures. Moreover, understanding acculturation patterns and styles within the family can reveal whether acculturation conflicts contribute to additional stressors that may influence behavior. The following scenario demonstrates how a clinician might explore acculturation with a student.

CASE EXAMPLE

A school clinician is interviewing a student who recently immigrated to the United States and who exhibits signs of withdrawal in social settings. The clinician asks the student about their comfort with both their cultural traditions and practices in the new school. Questions might include "What aspects of your culture are most important to you in daily life?"; "How comfortable are you in participating in activities with classmates?"; "What activities do you enjoy that help you feel connected to home?"; "Are there things that you feel you need to do at school to make (and keep) friends that your family would not understand?" The student's responses will reveal the degree to which the student maintains strong ties to their home culture and might show that they feel disconnected from classmates. Understanding this helps the clinician integrate the student's acculturation style into their assessment and interpretation of behavior. This approach ultimately leads the clinician to tailor interventions that respect the student's acculturation style, potentially easing the student's transition and encouraging engagement without cultural compromise.

In summary, a culturally responsive interview involves a deeper exploration of how cultural context influences youth behavior. By addressing these issues during the interview, clinicians can model that culture is significant and profoundly influences how we think, behave, and interact with others. In addition, they can create powerful sociocultural histories that are grounded in the cultural context and that can inform contextual observations and subsequent interventions.

Step 2: Contextual Observations

Observations should be conducted in various settings and at different times to capture a comprehensive picture of the student's behavior. Clinicians must be trained to recognize and interpret behaviors within the appropriate cultural context. It is also important to involve observers who share or understand the student's cultural background to provide more accurate and culturally sensitive observations.

Most school psychologists are trained to conduct observations across multiple settings, which involves assessing a person's behavior in the classroom during various learning times, during unstructured academic periods, and during free time throughout the day. These observations can be influenced by preconceived notions about expected behaviors. Therefore, it is crucial for school psychologists to approach observations with a structured plan that includes identifying both challenging behaviors or the reasons for referral as well as recognizing strengths and positive behaviors exhibited throughout the day.

When clinicians have already conducted a cultural interview or cultural context interview, they are better equipped to observe with an understanding of culture-bound syndromes or culturally influenced interpretations or actions that may impact the client's behavior. Observations also involve analyzing the ABCs of behavior—antecedents, behavior, and consequences—which provides an opportunity to determine whether different behaviors manifest under similar antecedents in various contexts. When conducting these observations, school psychologists should ask themselves critical questions, such as "What strengths are evident that can be measured alongside the targeted behavior?" and "What is the core function of the target behavior?"

Step 3: Rating Scale Selection and Administration

One of the primary tools used in behavior assessment is the behavior rating scale. Before utilizing these scales, school psychologists should review the interview data collected during the exploration of the client's cultural context. By considering the most relevant cultural factors, the clinician can begin selecting potentially appropriate measures for the behavior assessment. Then, they should follow a multistep process for selecting the final rating scales that will be used in the assessment.

Review Psychometric Properties

When choosing these measures, it is crucial for school psychologists to assess how well the child's background is represented in the psychometric properties of the rating scales under consideration. This evaluation helps determine whether a particular rating scale is suitable for use with that specific population. For instance, psychologists should examine the percentage of the norming sample that includes the student's race, gender identity, and the region where the norming sample was developed. Additionally, they should consider whether the education level of the student's parents is adequately represented in the norming sample. Essentially, the psychometric properties of the rating scale must be inclusive of the student's identity characteristics.

If the measure meets these criteria, it can be selected as part of the behavior assessment. If not, alternative measures should be considered to minimize the risk of obtaining invalid assessment data. During the test selection process, school psychologists should also seek out behavior rating scales that identify not only the target behavior problem but also the student's strengths, particularly those that highlight cultural strengths, as evidenced by different informants. An example of a behavior rating scale that is designed to measure a student's strengths is the Behavioral and Emotional Rating Scale—3rd Edition (BERS-3; Epstein et al., 2022). The BERS-3 measures student strengths in the domains of Interpersonal Strength, Family Involvement, Intrapersonal Strength, School Functioning, and Affective Strengths. This measure empowers clinicians to collect data that provides the counter-narrative to the deficit approach to school psychological services.

Review for Cultural Relevance

Once behavior rating scales have tentatively been selected, clinicians should perform a cultural relevance review before administering the scales. This involves scanning for items that may not be culturally relevant or may be interpreted differently across cultures. This process is to ensure none appear unfamiliar, biased, or inappropriate for the student and their family. The skills for completing this review are acquired by experience with diverse cultures, by consulting with cultural experts, and by reviewing the literature on cultural behaviors and norms. The goal is to review items to determine if they have equivalent meaning and relevance across a range of cultures. This review can be conducted individually or with the assistance of a cultural broker to increase awareness of how cultural factors may influence informants' responses to the measure. A cultural broker is an individual who acts as a bridge between different cultures, facilitating understanding, communication, and collaboration. They help interpret cultural norms, values, and practices for both parties, reducing misunderstandings and promoting culturally sensitive interactions (Mortier et al., 2021). Such brokers can be community members, community agency professionals, tribal elders, teachers, friends, or family. Cultural brokers are often used in healthcare, education, and social services to support individuals navigating new cultural environments and ensuring their unique cultural perspectives are respected and integrated. Cultural brokers who review our tools for cultural relevance can be invaluable supports in the test selection process. If any items are identified as potentially biased or irrelevant, the clinician can replace the items with language that reflects culturally appropriate alternatives.

Rating Scale Administration Adaptation

After completing these various levels of screening, the behavior rating scale is ready for administration. A recommended administration adaptation is to invite informants to circle or annotate any item that they must think about (more than a few seconds) to answer. Additionally, clinicians should ask the person to consider whether the response options are inappropriate for their preferred answer, or whether they would likely respond "it depends." These responses are important clues that the item is context-dependent and requires more discussion than simply selecting a multiple-choice option. The clinician can invite them in advance to mark and skip such items and plan for further discussion after the remainder of the measure is completed.

Step 4: Feedback on Behavior Rating Scales

After informant's complete behavior rating scales, the clinician should seek their feedback about the tool—this includes educators, caregivers, family members, and even the student who completed self-report forms. It is essential to ask each informant about their experience with the rating scale and to obtain their perspective on whether the items accurately reflected the strengths and weaknesses of the student. This is the opportunity for clinicians to discuss the items that were not easily answered or were "context-dependent" (Walker et al., 2023). A collaborative discussion can occur about whether the response options for each item made sense to the informant and were inappropriate based on their experience with the student, and which items required the most deliberation before a response was selected. One method of assessing context-dependent items is to solicit a story or scenario to maximize engagement as well as gain insight into the social contexts of the student.

Specific questions to ask may include whether there were any items they perceived as inaccurate or inappropriate, and importantly, whether there were any items they did not perceive to be problematic but that others might interpret as a behavior problem. This question is crucial for identifying potential differences in perception regarding the interpretation of items on the behavior rating scales. Following this process is an informal assessment of validity of the instrument and helps determine how much weight should be given to the interpretation of the completed behavior rating scales. Table 3.1 provides a series of questions that can be used to generate feedback from each informant as well as to request a verbal rating to provide an estimate of the validity of the rating scale for that particular student.

Step 5: Contextual Interpretation of Assessment Data

A lack of cultural responsiveness in behavior assessment can perpetuate educational inequities. Students from marginalized cultural backgrounds are often disproportionately represented in disciplinary actions and special education programs. This overrepresentation can be partly attributed to culturally biased behavior assessments that fail to account for the cultural contexts of students' behaviors. By adopting culturally responsive practices, schools can reduce these disparities and provide more equitable support for all students.

Interpreting behavior assessment data within a cultural context is vital to ensuring that the conclusions drawn are accurate, fair, and relevant to the individual being assessed. Cultural factors significantly influence behavior, shaping norms, values, and expectations that differ across communities. Without considering these factors, assessments may lead to misinterpretations, such as labeling culturally normative behaviors as problematic or overlooking strengths that are culturally specific. By embedding cultural context into the interpretation of behavior assessment data, school psychologists and other clinicians can better understand the unique influences on an individual's behavior, leading to more informed, empathetic, and effective interventions that respect and support the client's identity and cultural background.

USING CR-BA TO INFORM BEHAVIOR INTERVENTIONS

In today's diverse educational landscape, the need for culturally responsive practices in behavior assessment is paramount. Cultural responsiveness ensures that behavior assessments are fair, accurate, and effective for all students, promoting equity and inclusivity. By acknowledging and

TABLE 3.1. Feedback Questions Regarding Behavior Rating Scales

Which items were hard to answer without thinking for a little while?
Were the response options appropriate for the items? How would you respond if you could choose your own answer?
Were there items that you answered that you do not perceive to be a problem, but other people might interpret differently?
Which items were the most representative of the student's strengths?
What are some of the student's strengths that these tools did not ask about?
What were the missed behaviors that you think may need some intervention?
Of the items that were hard to answer, please describe a scenario that reflects your perception of the student's behavior.
How accurate overall do they feel this measure is for the student?
As a final verbal rating, how well did this tool provide an indicator of the behavior of the youth in question? ■ Very well ■ Pretty well ■ Well ■ Okay ■ Not very well at all

incorporating the cultural contexts of students' behaviors, school psychologists and educators can develop more relevant and impactful interventions. This approach not only enhances the validity of behavior assessments but also fosters a more inclusive and supportive learning environment for all students (Vincent et al., 2011). The following sections offer a few examples of how findings from a culturally responsive behavior assessment can lead to culturally responsive behavior interventions.

Integrating Racial and Cultural Identity in Behavior Interventions

When providing culturally responsive services, cultural considerations should guide the intervention selection. Research has shown that integrating racial and cultural identity in behavior interventions enhances the efficacy of the treatment (Barrera et al., 2013; Jones et al., 2018; Soto et al., 2018). In fact, such integration is crucial for creating inclusive educational environments for youth of color in schools. This section explores the role of racial and cultural identity in student behavior, strategies for positive identity development, and collaborative approaches to identity-positive interventions.

Scores of studies show that a student's racial and cultural identity significantly influences students' behaviors and interactions within educational settings. Understanding these identities and their impact on behavior is essential for developing effective interventions that promote positive outcomes for all students. Social identity theory posits that students derive a sense of self based on their membership in social groups, including racial and cultural group status (Verkuyten et al., 2019).

The research shows that a strong positive racial and cultural identity can enhance self-esteem and resilience (Jones et al., 2018) while a negative or conflicted racial identity can contribute to behavioral and emotional challenges (Hughes et al., 2015). When students are experiencing racial discrimination and racism in their environments, there is undoubtedly a negative impact on their wellbeing and behavior. Positive racial identity development has been shown to buffer the negative effects of exposure to discrimination (Sellers et al., 2006). Students who have a strong, positive racial or cultural identity are more likely to exhibit resilience, academic motivation, and positive social behaviors. These students often feel a greater sense of belonging and engagement in school, whereas students who experience racial or cultural discrimination, or who struggle with their racial identity, may exhibit behaviors such as withdrawal, aggression, or disengagement from school. These behaviors can be misinterpreted as pathological (rather than a coping behavior) if not understood within the context of the student's identity. This is an example of the ways in which the root cause of a behavior needs to be identified to select the most appropriate intervention. In this case, the intervention should include a focus on racial socialization and positive racial identity development.

Identity-Positive Interventions

Fostering positive racial and cultural identity in students involves creating supportive environments that validate and celebrate their cultural backgrounds. Techniques such as implementing culturally relevant curricula in the classroom or in small group activities can be effective. Implementing a curriculum that reflects the diverse cultural backgrounds of students helps them see themselves represented in their education. This includes incorporating literature, history, and perspectives from various racial and cultural groups. Example of such curricula include *Jovenes Fuertes* (Castro-Olivo, 2014), *Sisters of Nia* (Belgrave et al., 2004), and *Brothers of Ujima* (Belgrave et al., 2011). These curricula include not only a foundational understanding of the cultural context but also activities that help students explore their cultural heritage and enhance pride in their identity.

Similarly, connecting students with mentors from similar racial or cultural backgrounds can provide role models who can reinforce positive racial identity development. Mentors can offer guidance, support, and a sense of belonging to a community of people with shared experiences. Peer mentoring programs can also be effective for fostering relationships and mutual support among students.

School-wide celebration and events can lead to greater positive racial and cultural identity. When schools organize, events that celebrate cultural diversity (e.g., heritage months, cultural fairs, assemblies), racialized and minoritized students can feel a sense of connection and belonging to their school environment. Such activities set the context for a positive school climate that values all identities. Thus, encouraging student participation in planning and leading these events fosters ownership and pride in their cultural identity.

In addition to planning schoolwide events, incorporating restorative practices into the everyday operations throughout the school year is another approach to creating an environment that supports positive identity development (Darling-Hammond, 2023; González & Epstein, 2022). Implementing restorative practices such as community circles and peer mediation can create inclusive spaces where student feel heard and respected. These experiences can help build a positive school culture that supports identity development, problem solving, and conflict resolution skills (Vincent et al., 2016).

Effective integration of identity-positive interventions requires collaboration with families, communities, and culturally specific organizations. Engaging families ensures that interventions are culturally relevant and supported. Engagement may include having family advisory boards, a routine practice of home-school two-way communication, and hosting workshops for families to foster strong relationships. Similarly, community organizations can be perfectly suited to serve as an additional source of support for students. Community organizations (e.g., Council on American–Islamic Relations, National Black Child Development Institute, Jewish Federations of North America, Asian Americans Advancing Justice, National Council of La Raza) may have local chapters that offer cultural enrichment programs, on-site afterschool activities, and/or mental health services to the youth and their families. Such organizations may offer professional development for school personnel on culturally responsive practices, including identity-positive interventions. Finally, some culture-specific organizations (e.g., Asian American Counseling Alliance) employ people who can serve as cultural liaisons (or cultural brokers). These are individual who understand the cultural backgrounds of some student groups and can bridge the gap between schools and communities. These liaisons can facilitate communication, provide cultural insights, and support the implementation of culturally responsive practices.

CONCLUSION

Educators, school psychologists, and policymakers must work together to ensure that behavior assessment and intervention practices are culturally responsive and equitable. Schools must commit to creating inclusive and equitable environments that support the diverse needs of all students. By embracing culturally responsive practices, adapting traditional models, and fostering positive identity development, we can create educational environments that support the success and well-being of all students. This commitment to cultural responsiveness is essential for promoting equity, inclusivity, and academic excellence in our schools.

REFERENCES

American Psychiatric Association. (2022). *Diagnostic and statistical manual of mental disorders* (5th ed., text rev.).

Barrera, M., Castro, F. G., Strycker, L. A., & Toobert, D. J. (2013). Cultural adaptations of behavioral health interventions: A progress report. *Journal of Consulting and Clinical Psychology, 81*(2), 196–205.

Belgrave, F. Z., Allison, K. W., Wilson, J., & Tademy, R. (2011). *Brothers of Ujima: A cultural enrichment program to empower adolescent African American males.* Research Press.

Belgrave, F. Z., Reed, M. C., Plybon, L., Butler, D. S., Allison, K. W., & Davis, T. (2004). An evaluation of Sisters of Nia: A cultural program for African American girls: *Journal of Black Psychology, 30*(3), 329–343.

Berry, J. W. (2005). Acculturation: Living successfully in two cultures. *International Journal of Intercultural Relations, 29*(6), 697–712.

Bradshaw, C. P., Pas, E. T., Bottiani, J. H., Debnam, K. J., Reinke, W. M., Herman, K. C., & Rosenberg, M. S. (2018). Promoting cultural responsivity and student engagement through double check coaching of classroom teachers: An efficacy study. *School Psychology Review, 47*(2), 118–134.

Castro, F. G., Barrera, M., & Steiker, L. K. H. (2010). Issues and challenges in the design of culturally adapted evidence-based interventions. *Annual Review of Clinical Psychology, 6*(1), 213–239.

Castro-Olivo, S. M. (2014). Promoting social-emotional learning in adolescent Latino ELLs: A study of the culturally adapted Strong Teens program. *School Psychology Quarterly, 29*(4), 567–577.

Conners, C. K. (2022). *Conners 4th Edition* (4th ed.). Multi-Health Systems.

Conroy, M. A., & Stichter, J. P. (2003). The application of antecedents in the functional assessment process: Existing research, issues, and recommendations. *Journal of Special Education, 37*(1), 15–25.

Darling-Hammond, S. (2023). *Fostering belonging, transforming schools: The impact of restorative practices.*

Dennison, A., Lund, E. M., Lund, E. M., Brodhead, M. T., Mejia, L., Armenta, A., & Leal, J. (2019). Delivering home-supported applied behavior analysis therapies to culturally and linguistically diverse families. *Behavior Analysis in Practice, 12*(4), 887–898.

Enders, O. G., Buonomo, K., & Robertson, R. (2022). Addressing race and implicit bias in the functional behavior assessment process: A pilot study of preservice teacher training modules. *Multiple Voices: Disability, Race, and Language Intersections in Special Education, 22*(1), 6–23.

Epstein, M. H., Pierce, C. D., Lambert, M. C. (2022). *BERS-3: Behavioral & Emotional Rating Scale* (3rd ed.). ProEd

Fallon, L. M., Cathcart, S. C., DeFouw, E. R., O'Keeffe, B. V., & Sugai, G. (2018). Promoting teachers' implementation of culturally and contextually relevant class-wide behavior plans. *Psychology in the Schools, 55*(3), 278–294.

Fallon, L. M., & Mueller, M. R. (2017). Culturally responsive wraparound supports: Collaborating with families to promote students' behavior regulation across settings. *Contemporary School Psychology, 21*(3), 201–210.

Fallon, L. M., O'Keeffe, B. V., & Sugai, G. (2012). Consideration of culture and context in school-wide positive behavior support: A review of current literature. *Journal of Positive Behavior Interventions, 14*(4), 209–219.

González, T., & Epstein, R. (2022). Critical race feminism, health, and restorative practices in schools: Centering the experiences of Black and Latina girls. *Michigan Journal of Gender & Law, 29*(2), 409–446.

Gregory, A., Clawson, K., Davis, A., & Gerewitz, J. (2016). The promise of restorative practices to transform teacher–student relationships and achieve equity in school discipline. *Journal of Educational and Psychological Consultation, 26*(4), 325–353.

Hanley, G. P., Iwata, B. A., & McCord, B. E. (2003). Functional analysis of problem behavior: A review. *Journal of Applied Behavior Analysis, 36*(2), 147–185.

Hughes, M., Hughes, M., Kiecolt, K. J., Keith, V. M., & Demo, D. H. (2015). Racial identity and well-being among African Americans: *Social Psychology Quarterly, 78*(1), 25–48.

Jones, C., Caravaca, L., Cizek, S., Horner, R. H., & Vincent, C. G. (2010). Culturally responsive schoolwide positive behavior support: A case study in one school with a high proportion of Native American students. *Multiple Voices for Ethnically Diverse Exceptional Learners, 9*(1), 108–119.

Jones, J. M. (2009). Counseling with multicultural intentionality: The process of counseling and integrating client cultural variables. In J. M. Jones (Ed.), *The psychology of multiculturalism in schools: A primer for practice, training, and research* (pp. 191–213). National Association of School Psychologists.

Jones, J. M., Lee, L. H., Matlack, A., & Zigarelli, J. C. (2018). Using sisterhood networks to cultivate ethnic identity and enhance school engagement. *Psychology in the Schools, 55*(1), 20–35.

Jones, J. M., Lee, L. H., Zigarelli, J. C., & Nakagawa, Y. (2017). Culturally responsive adaptations in evidence-based treatment: The impact on client satisfaction. *Contemporary School Psychology, 21*(3), 211–222.

McCarthy, J., & Wright, P. (2015). *Taking [a]part: The politics and aesthetics of participation in experience-centered design.* The MIT Press.

Moreno, G., Wong-Lo, M., Short, M., & Bullock, L. M. (2014). Implementing a culturally attuned functional behavioural assessment to understand and address challenging behaviours demonstrated by students from diverse backgrounds. *Emotional and Behavioural Difficulties, 19*(4), 343–355.

Mortier, K., Brown, I. C., & Aramburo, C. M. (2021). Cultural brokers in special education. *Research and Practice for Persons with Severe Disabilities, 46*(1), 3–17.

Plake, B. S., & Wise, L. L. (2014). What is the role and importance of the revised AERA, APA, NCME standards for educational and psychological testing? *Educational Measurement: Issues and Practice, 33*(4), 4–12.

Ramasubramanian, S., Riewestahl, E., & Landmark, S. (2021). The trauma-informed equity-minded asset-based model (TEAM): The six R's for social justice-oriented educators. *Journal of Media Literacy Education, 13*(2), 29–42.

Reynolds, C., & Kamphaus, R. (2015). *Behavior assessment system for children* (3rd ed.). Pearson.

Rojas, L., & Liou, D. D. (2017). Social justice teaching through the sympathetic touch of caring and high expectations for students of color. *Journal of Teacher Education*, 68(1), 28–40.

Salend, S. J., & Taylor, L. S. (2002). Cultural perspectives missing pieces in the functional assessment process. *Intervention in School and Clinic, 38*(2), 104–112.

Sellers, R. M., Copeland-Linder, N., Martin, P. P., & Lewis, R. L. (2006). Racial identity matters: The relationship between racial discrimination and psychological functioning in African American adolescents. *Journal of Research on Adolescence, 16*(2), 187–216.

Sireci, S. G. (2020). Standardization and "UNDERSTAND" ardization in educational assessment. *Educational Measurement: Issues and Practice, 39*(3), 100–105.

Soto, A., Smith, T. B., Griner, D., Rodríguez, M. M. D., & Bernal, G. (2018). Cultural adaptations and therapist multicultural competence: Two meta-analytic reviews. *Journal of Clinical Psychology, 74*(11), 1907–1923.

Verkuyten, M., Thijs, J., & Gharaei, N. (2019). Discrimination and academic (dis)engagement of ethnic-racial minority students: A social identity threat perspective. *Social Psychology of Education: An International Journal, 22*(2), 267–290.

Vincent, C. G., Inglish, J., Girvan, E. J., Sprague, J. R., & McCabe, T. M. (2016). School-wide positive and restorative discipline (SWPRD): Integrating school-wide positive behavior interventions and supports and restorative discipline. In R. J. Skiba, K. Mediratta, & M. K. Rausch (Eds.), *Inequality in school discipline* (pp. 115–134). Palgrave Macmillan.

Vincent, C. G., Randall, C., Cartledge, G., Tobin, T. J., & Swain-Bradway, J. (2011). Toward a conceptual integration of cultural responsiveness and schoolwide positive behavior support. *Journal of Positive Behavior Interventions, 13*(4), 219–229.

Vincent, C. G., Sprague, J. R., & Gau, J. M. (2013). *The effectiveness of school-wide positive behavior interventions and supports for reducing racially inequitable disciplinary exclusions in middle schools.* The Civil Rights Project.

Walker, M. E., Olivera-Aguilar, M., Lehman, B., Laitusis, C., Guzman-Orth, D., & Gholson, M. (2023). Culturally responsive assessment: Provisional principles. *ETS Research Report Series, 2023*(1), 1–24.

Yeager, D. S., Purdie-Vaughns, V., Garcia, J., Apfel, N., Brzustoski, P., Master, A., et al. (2014). Breaking the cycle of mistrust: Wise interventions to provide critical feedback across the racial divide. *Journal of Experimental Psychology: General, 143*(2), 804–824.

Zigarelli, J., Jones, J. M., Palomino, C. I., & Kawamura, R. (2016). Culturally responsive cognitive behavioral therapy making the case for integrating cultural factors in evidence-based treatment. *Clinical Case Studies, 15*(6), 427–442.

CHAPTER 4

Assessment within a Public Health Paradigm

Katie Eklund, Jennifer M. Twyford, Erin Dowdy, Jared T. Izumi, and Ellen Anderson

Historically, psychological assessment has primarily focused on individualized approaches to assessment for a variety of different problems and adaptive competencies. This is largely fitting within medical model service delivery frameworks, whereby individuals with significant mental health problems are referred for individualized assessment and treatment. However, continued recognition of the inadequacies of this service delivery model has led to a broader understanding of the need for more comprehensive, population-based approaches to psychological and educational assessment. Population-based approaches, which are designed to meet the needs of all students within a given population, require that service providers move beyond the traditional medical model of service delivery (Doll & Cummings, 2008).

Population-based service delivery approaches draw widely from the field of public health, which has long been concerned with protecting the health of entire populations. A central component of a public health model is the emphasis on society, as opposed to individuals, being the primary client (Mason & Linnenberg, 1999). Furthermore, public health models increasingly emphasize the promotion of health equity (e.g., Peterson et al., 2021) and the understanding that health and mental health outcomes and disparities are influenced by social determinants of health (Abraham & Walker-Harding, 2022; U.S. Centers for Disease Control and Prevention, 2022). Social determinants of health (SDH) are those nonmedical factors and systems that shape conditions of daily life, such as access to affordable health care, economic policies, education, food insecurity, social inclusion and discrimination, and structural conflict (World Health Organization, 2024). Public health professionals operate from a prevention-based framework to protect and improve the health of communities by monitoring health; detecting and investigating health problems and health disparities; conducting research to enhance prevention; implementing prevention strategies; promoting health care equity, quality, and accessibility; and fostering safe and healthy environments (Centers for Disease Control Foundation, 2024). Fortunately, there is an overlapping skill set among psychologists, educators, and public health professionals. Whereas public health professionals have a broader reach to all individuals across the lifespan within a wide range of environments, school psychologists and educators are primarily focused on improving the educational and psychological well-being of students in schools. In this chapter, we provide a framework for assessment within a public health paradigm. After describing the need to move service delivery from individual and reactionary to population-based and preventive models (Dowdy et al., 2010), we present a tiered approach to assessment consistent with a public health framework.

We provide examples of a public health approach to assessment within schools with an overarching goal of providing practitioners with a solid foundation upon which to conduct population-based assessment.

A PUBLIC HEALTH TIERED APPROACH TO ASSESSMENT IN SCHOOLS

With a focus on population-based service delivery and prevention, schools provide an ideal context for translating public health principles into practice. Schools are designed to serve the entire population of children, and they already systematically incorporate public health principles, such as vision and hearing screenings for all children, which may directly affect a student's ability to learn (Dowdy et al., 2010). Researchers are increasingly expanding screenings within schools to include a variety of areas, such as substance use, behavioral or emotional concerns, and social–emotional strengths due to the ability to provide a relatively cost-effective strategy by screening a large number of children (Furlong et al., 2014; Horowitz et al., 2009; Maslowsky et al., 2017). Additional research is currently underway to take an even broader approach to school-based screening by incorporating information on social determinants of mental health, including an examination of assets and barriers in school, home, and community environments (Koslouski et al., 2024). Overall, school-based practices align well with public health approaches due to their focus on multi-tiered approaches to assessment and intervention that aim to serve the entire population of students in schools.

The U.S. school system has traditionally focused on a single-case referral system for student behavioral and academic concerns, with follow-up individualized interventions. It has been suggested that this reliance on a refer-test-place model of service delivery has contributed to current failures present within mental health and educational systems, including the underidentification and undertreatment of students with mental health concerns within U.S. schools (Gutkin, 2012). In response, researchers and practitioners have shifted toward a public health model of assessment and service delivery (Berkeley et al., 2020; Dowdy et al., 2010). This approach to assessment provides an opportunity to overcome many of the traditional barriers to seeking care for individual students within schools by focusing on (1) social determinants of mental health; (2) the strengths and needs of populations of students rather than individuals; and (3) the consideration of prevention and early intervention services rather than remediation; and (4) by providing efficacious and equity-centered services at the micro-, meso-, exo-, and macro-environmental levels rather than solely at the micro level (Gutkin, 2012; Moore et al., 2023).

The public health model stems from the work of interdisciplinary collaboration and has been applied in an array of settings for prevention and intervention. Kumpfer and Baxley (1997) surveyed a wide variety of disciplines within the medical field to identify interdisciplinary approaches to prevent childhood substance abuse. Their findings highlighted a three-tier public health model championed by Gordon (1987) and adapted by the Institute of Medicine (1994), which outlined three levels of support: universal, targeted, and indicated tiers of prevention and treatment. The genesis of this tiered-model laid the foundation for the development of multiple educational models formed from the three-tier public health model, including response to intervention (RTI), positive behavioral interventions and supports (PBIS), and multi-tiered system of supports (MTSS), as well as models that schools have adopted for prevention, screening, intervention implementation, and progress monitoring (Fletcher & Vaughn, 2009; Vaughn et al., 2007). Although RTI and PBIS may be viewed as two distinct frameworks that independently address student behavioral and academic concerns, they have evolved into a comprehensive multi-tiered system of supports (MTSS) framework that is designed to concurrently address both the academic and social-emotional/behavioral needs of students (McIntosh & Goodman, 2016). A description of each model, and how it has helped move the field from an individual toward a population-based perspective, is provided below.

Response to Intervention

RTI is a data-driven systematic method for assessing, identifying, and responding to the needs of students who demonstrate academic and/or behavioral difficulties (Brown-Chidsey & Steege, 2005). In contrast to beginning with a student referral and identifying target variables and next steps, the defining quality of RTI is an approach to decision making using universal early screening and outcomes of intervention and progress monitoring sequences as the database for service delivery determination. Selecting targeted variables and students for intervention is based on objective criteria derived from data and research. At its core, RTI is a set of schoolwide procedures intended to promote successful school outcomes for an entire population of students.

Despite evidence that most students have the potential to attain basic academic skills in reading, writing, and mathematics, too many students do not receive differentiated instruction and support needed to master fundamental skills (VanDerHeyden & Burns, 2010). Although schools and school districts in the United States are held accountable for ensuring that all students meet challenging academic standards and attain core academic competencies (e.g., Every Student Succeeds Act [ESSA], 2015), only 32% of fourth-grade students are proficient in reading and only 35% are proficient in math (National Center for Education Statistics [NCES], 2022a, 2022b). Traditionally, students who fall behind or do not meet state standards are assessed for special education services. This aforementioned wait-to-fail paradigm, whereby students must demonstrate academic or behavioral failure prior to receiving interventions, steers quickly away from a prevention model and merely provides services to only the lowest performing students. Additionally, traditional standardized testing procedures, which are frequently used to determine eligibility for special education, are often minimally related to designing, implementing, or evaluating classroom instruction (Fuchs et al., 2005). Interest in RTI stemmed from the need for significant improvements in both general and special education systems.

Numerous national reports and meetings convened by experts in the field have demonstrated support for RTI as a model of prevention. Furthermore, RTI is now viewed as an alternative method for identifying a specific learning disability (Individuals with Disabilities Education Act [IDEA], 2004) as states can no longer require local education agencies (LEAs) to use a severe discrepancy between intellectual ability and achievement but must incorporate the use of a process based on the child's response to scientific research-based intervention (IDEA, 2004 §300.307). This model further supports the need for a tiered approach to assessment and intervention so that the needs of students can be adequately assessed and addressed. In this manner, RTI is seen as an effective instructional strategy because of its premise that schools can teach *all* students (e.g., Hattie, 2012). Tier 1 instruction, also known as universal or whole class instruction, consists of research-based classroom strategies that are known to be effective for most students. Universal interventions include scientifically sound core curriculum and instruction, a high-quality school and classroom environment, and evidence-based instructional practices (Graner et al., 2005). RTI's focus on universal services, followed by more targeted and intensive services, fits well within public health service delivery models.

Positive Behavioral Interventions and Supports

A popular example of multi-tiered models of prevention (Sprague & Horner, 2006), PBIS is a prevention-oriented approach focused on actively teaching and acknowledging students' prosocial behavior to support children's social, emotional, and behavioral competence and improve school climate (Benedict et al., 2007; Dunlap & Fox, 2009; Stormont et al., 2005; Sugai & Horner, 2020). The main focus is establishing an ecologically centered, program-wide plan for promoting prosocial behaviors and preventing challenging behavior across multiple levels of intervention delivery (universal, secondary, and tertiary; Stormont et al., 2005). Strategies include recognizing and rewarding positive student behavior through continual teaching in order to reduce unnecessary discipline; providing consistent, fair responses to behavior that does not align with expectations; and promoting a climate of greater learning and safety (Sprague & Horner, 2006; Sugai & Horner, 2020).

PBIS has been implemented in many schools across the country to help reduce disciplinary infractions and increase students' sense of safety at school. It has also been recognized as a viable alternative to the use of exclusionary discipline (e.g., suspensions, expulsions; Sugai & Horner, 2020). The goal of schoolwide PBIS is to build social competence across children and settings by developing instructional procedures for teaching the social and behavioral skills and tasks specifically related to a school's particular behavioral expectations (Fox & Little, 2001). These program-specific social skills and tasks that children need to exhibit are operationalized through program-wide expectations that include teaching behavioral expectations in the classroom (e.g., entering the classroom, transition periods, peer interactions) and reviewing a behavioral matrix, which details student behavioral expectations in each setting at school (e.g., hallway, lunchroom, bathroom).

In this manner, PBIS embraces a multi-tiered approach to prevention that identifies a universal schoolwide mission to guide schoolwide behavioral principles and also uses targeted and individualized interventions to support students and improve overall school climate.

Importantly, PBIS scholars and practitioners emphasize cultural responsiveness and equity within the framework. For instance, culturally responsive PBIS (CRPBIS; Bal, 2018) aims to transform school policy and practice by drawing upon the knowledge of local school and community members to collectively solve problems (e.g., racial disproportionality in exclusionary discipline) and create more equitable systems that align with the localized contexts in which they are situated. Scholars have further developed culturally responsive PBIS guidance and resource documents (i.e., Leverson et al., 2021) and provided recommendations for promoting racial equity within the context of PBIS (i.e., Fallon et al., 2021).

Multi-Tiered System of Supports

MTSS is an evidence-based framework for identifying needs and serving all students through a continuum of high-quality academic, behavioral, social, and emotional instruction, services, and supports (Burns et al., 2016). Whereas RTI models were initially focused on academic assessment, intervention, and progress monitoring, PBIS strategies used a similar multi-tiered framework to teach and reinforce positive behaviors in the school environment. MTSS models blend both frameworks to concurrently assess and address social–emotional skills, behavior, and academics, while also emphasizing a focus on interdisciplinary collaboration among educational professionals when developing plans for assessment and intervention implementation (Riley-Tillman et al., 2013). Although these frameworks look different across educational environments (e.g., elementary, secondary, alternative schools), many public health principles are embedded within these multi-tiered models.

Most often conceptualized as a three-tiered model, MTSS incorporates progressive tiers of support increasing in intensity and complexity to meet the needs of all students (Fabiano & Evans, 2019). Tier 1 refers to universal instruction and supports delivered across schools and classrooms; Tier 2 refers to targeted instruction and supports; and Tier 3 refers to intensive, individualized services. Core features include the use of universal screening, formative assessment, and progress monitoring to identify student needs and inform the use of high-quality, evidence-based curricular, instructional, and intervention supports (Loftus-Rattan et al., 2023). MTSS further incorporates data-based decision making; a problem-solving framework to inform services across tiers and a collaborative, team-based approach to plan, lead, and evaluate systematic implementation (Hawken et al., 2008; Lane et al., 2014; Reschly, 2014). Within MTSS, there is an emphasis on the importance of ecological systems and examining and changing contextual factors to facilitate student learning and development (Vaughn & Fuchs, 2003). As such, root causes for educational difficulties are examined within the child's learning context, as opposed to centering deficits within the child.

Given the prominence of universal evidence-based prevention in MTSS and the emphasis on changing ecological variables, it has been suggested that this framework has the potential to reduce educational disparities (Albritton et al., 2016). Researchers have emphasized the importance of centering equity within MTSS to ensure that its implementation achieves this goal and does not inadvertently perpetuate marginalization or existing disparities for students from minoritized backgrounds (Sullivan et al., 2022; Thorius & Maxcy, 2015). To do so, it is essential that MTSS processes elevate a focus on the whole child *within* context and embed culturally responsive principles throughout the framework (Malone et al., 2022; Miller et al., 2020). This includes the selection and implementation of assessments and interventions that center the localized and sociocultural contexts in which students learn and grow. Broad mechanisms through which to strengthen MTSS to promote equity include forming authentic family and community partnerships, engaging in holistic and systems-focused universal screening, disaggregating data to understand trends across student populations, conducting root cause analyses, and promoting inclusive and healing educational communities within classrooms and schools (Fallon et al., 2021; Garbacz, 2020; Malone et al., 2022; McIntosh et al., 2021; Moore et al., 2023).

In this chapter, we use the umbrella term of a public health tiered approach to assessment and intervention to discuss many of the strategies schools have employed to meet the needs of all students. In this model, assessment decisions about which students will receive interventions and which interventions to provide are intentional and based on carefully collected information about the functioning not only of individuals but also of all students in the school and a careful analysis of the strengths and needs of the school community (Doll & Cummings, 2008; Moore et al., 2023). This multi-tiered approach to prevention includes universal, targeted, and intensive levels of support that are described in further detail below.

UNIVERSAL ASSESSMENT AND INTERVENTION

Universal assessment can be used as a descriptive epidemiology technique to provide information about the nature and scope of a particular condition (Short & Strein, 2008). Descriptive epidemiology is used to define and count the number of students with a particular condition. From a descriptive epidemiological lens, it would also be important to examine the location of the condition to see if the system has any particular strengths or weaknesses (Short & Strein, 2008). An evaluation of schoolwide student data could include school climate assessment data, mental health screening outcomes, office disciplinary referrals, or academic benchmark data that could then be used to determine how to make systems-level change. The practice of disaggregating data to identify trends across student groups can help inform an awareness of inequities within these systems and guide these change efforts (Sullivan et al., 2020).

Within multi-tiered systems, Tier 1 generally includes universal assessment and intervention considerations, designed to influence the largest number of children and seen as a mechanism for widespread prevention of academic, behavioral, and social–emotional problems and promotion of student well-being. Within Tier 1, the primary prevention efforts intend to stop harm from occurring (Harrison et al., 2013; Kilgus et al., 2014). That is, they have the potential to operate long-term much like a vaccine or inoculation (Embry, 2002). Guidelines suggest that effective Tier 1 supports should meet the needs of about 80–90% of students in a given population (Mellard et al., 2011). These guidelines can be utilized to allocate resources or change prevention strategies for students at the school-, grade-, or classwide level.

The passages of ESSA (2015) and IDEA (2004) underscore the importance of early identification and intervention for children who exhibit difficulties in school (Fletcher & Vaughn, 2009). Based on research that shows positive outcomes may be achieved through early identification and intervention, educational policy and legislation place an increasing focus on data-based decision making and universal assessment in schools (ESSA, 2015; IDEA, 2004; Lane et al., 2010; Reschly, 2008). This includes the promotion of early identification and intervention considerations, including universal screening of all students for academic and social–emotional/behavioral difficulties (Fletcher & Vaughn, 2009; Seethaler & Fuchs, 2010) and the use of extant school assessment data to guide interventions. In addition, ESSA provides states and districts the ability to use various funds to support the implementation of MTSS at each level of intervention.

Evidence suggests that early screening, intervention, and prevention efforts have been found to reduce later academic difficulties as well as social–emotional and behavioral concerns among children and youth (e.g., McIntosh et al., 2006). For example, social–emotional and academic concerns that arise in early childhood are relatively stable throughout childhood and are predictive of negative social–emotional and academic outcomes (Turney & McLanahan, 2015). However, children who receive early intervention in social–emotional development display greater social–emotional competence than their peers whom did not receive services (Brophy-Herb et al., 2007). Early identification and intervention efforts are also critical to the academic development of children in both early literacy and math, demonstrating that specialized instruction and academic support in literacy and math interventions can prevent future reading and math difficulties (Foorman et al., 1997; Gersten et al., 2005).

Assessment practices in Tier 1 include conducting schoolwide screenings to gauge student performance in core academic (e.g., reading fluency) and social–emotional/behavioral (e.g., externalizing and internalizing behaviors) areas. Screening provides critical data about all students, gives schools the ability to identify systems-level areas of strength and need, and uncovers the existence of any disparities in outcomes based on student group membership (e.g., ethnicity, gender identity, language, race, sexual orientation, socioeconomic status). The data generated from screening serves as a needs assessment for a school to know where to quickly and efficiently allocate time and staff resources (Dowdy et al., 2010). These data can further inform short- and long-term reform efforts. Additionally, culturally responsive universal assessment practices may reduce the disproportionality of minoritized students in special education by allowing equal opportunity to receive intervention services (Raines et al., 2012).

As universal screening practices historically focused on the identification of individual at-risk students, current scholars recommend shifting to a systems- and holistic-focused approach to screening to enact socially just and equitable assessment practice (Moore et al., 2023). Within this approach, it is acknowledged that social determinants of health impact educational and mental health outcomes and inequities, and as such, gathering information regarding contextual factors is prioritized. Moore et al. (2023) provided a roadmap for equitable mental health screening, wherein they outlined guidance and recommendations for improving the universal screening process. Within this roadmap, they emphasized the importance of acknowledging and dismantling structural forms of oppression; identifying strengths, stressors, and needs within individuals, groups, and communities; and prioritizing positive mental health outcomes for minoritized students. This approach aims to disrupt deficit thinking and focuses on problems within school systems as opposed to within students.

This shift is particularly important because traditional psychological and psychoeducational assessments have followed a deficit-based model focused on assessing individual limitations and concerns (Epstein, 1999). A dual-factor model of mental health has been proposed in its place, integrating both the assessment of student psychopathology *and* subjective well-being to provide a more complete picture of mental health (Antaramian et al., 2010; Eklund et al., 2011; Suldo & Shaffer, 2008). Assessing for strengths and protective factors in addition to psychological distress or behavior problems provides a number of beneficial outcomes including (1) a more contextualized, effective prevention model of assessment; (2) a more holistic understanding of each student; (3) reduced stigma related to mental health; (4) reduced psychological distress; (5) improved academic outcomes; and (6) improved physical health (Dowdy et al., 2010; Greenberg et al., 2000; Moore et al., 2015; Proctor et al., 2009).

Conducting universal screening based on a dual-factor model of mental health has been identified as an important component of culturally responsive school mental health service delivery (Lazarus et al., 2021). As school-based teams prepare to engage in universal screening, it is important to select tools that (1) align with collaborators' goals for screening; (2) incorporate technical adequacy (see Jenkins et al., 2014) and usability; (3) have been evaluated on a demographically similar sample of students; and (4) incorporate options for obtaining information from multiple informants, including students themselves (Glover & Albers, 2007; Moore et al., 2023; von der Embse & De Los Reyes, 2024). Multidisciplinary teams comprised of school and community partners are encouraged to evaluate screening data in the context of individual, community, and cultural assets that contribute to students' well-being and seek to identify social determinants of health that serve as barriers to well-being. Problem-solving efforts can then be directed toward systems-level work that incorporates community strengths and seeks to overcome these challenges (Edyburn et al., 2023). These data can also be used to inform the delivery of evidence-based, culturally responsive instruction and interventions to support the student population (National Center for School Mental Health [NCSMH], 2020). Teams can apply the social–emotional and behavioral assessment framework (SEBA; Kilgus & Eklund, 2016), which uses base rates (i.e., prevalence) of risk to help teams identify how to allocate resources to equitably serve students at the school, classroom, and individual levels.

Universal academic, behavioral, and social–emotional assessment data can be a valuable resource in providing district-, school-, classroom-, and individual-level data to drive the implementation of evidence-based academic and social, emotional, and behavioral interventions within schools (e.g., Fuchs et al., 2005; Lane et al., 2010). Universal academic interventions and supports include scientifically sound, culturally relevant core curriculum and instruction as well as evidence-based instructional practices (Graner et al., 2005). Universal social–emotional and behavioral interventions include facilitating family and community partnerships; cultivating a culturally affirming and inclusive school climate; providing professional development to teachers related to creating culturally affirming and healing classrooms; collaboratively defining behavioral expectations with educators, families, and students; and implementing transformative social–emotional learning programming (Fallon et al., 2021; Jagers et al., 2019; Malone et al., 2022; Nganga et al., 2019; Sugai & Horner, 2020). The application of such supports allows for enhanced relationships, affirmation of strengths, and environmental modification in order to promote positive educational and mental health outcomes. In this manner, universal assessment data paired with the implementation of evidence-based supports use a prevention–orientation to consider the needs of all students within the broader school community.

TARGETED ASSESSMENT AND INTERVENTION

Individuals identified by systematic universal screening have access to *targeted* (or sometimes referred to as *selected*) assessment and intervention considerations at the secondary prevention level. Based on data gathered from universal assessment and intervention strategies, schools often use targeted assessment strategies to identify individuals who are at risk for clinically significant mental health problems or educational difficulties (Strein et al., 2003). Tier 2 also includes targeted academic and social, emotional, and behavioral supports for students for whom research-based universal interventions were not sufficient at Tier 1. Services are more intense and focused on small groups of students to address specific academic or social–emotional/behavioral needs.

Targeted assessment and intervention strategies are designed to meet anywhere from 5–10% (Sugai & Horner, 2020) to 15–25% (Severson et al., 2007) of students from the total population who require additional intervention or assessment at the targeted level. Targeted assessment and intervention strategies are designed to (1) identify specific student concerns, (2) use assessment data to develop appropriate interventions, and (3) engage in continuous assessment to monitor efficacious implementation of the interventions and also student response to the intended intervention. At this level, students are considered *subclinical*, that is not yet being identified as having an eligible educational impairment or a diagnosed psychological disorder. Instead, assessment and intervention data are used to prevent the development of more significant concerns.

Tier 2 assessment practices and interventions can be addressed through one of two methods: (1) a standard protocol/researcher approach or (2) the problem-solving/school practitioner approach (Fuchs et al., 2003). Optimally, both approaches can be integrated into the public health tiered approach to assessment. In a standard protocol approach, secondary prevention efforts are intended to address more serious academic or behavioral issues by reversing harm (e.g., identifying and supporting students who *might* be headed down an undesirable path; Severson et al., 2007). Namely, students who do not respond favorably to primary prevention efforts are offered secondary support programs to meet their specific acquisition needs. For example, students who have difficulty reading may be offered additional fluency or comprehension support, whereas students who demonstrate impulsivity or struggle with work completion may benefit from environmental accommodations or self-monitoring strategies. In this model, each level of prevention increases in intensity and magnitude, with a goal of providing more focused interventions in subsequent tiers for students in need of targeted assistance as determined by schoolwide data.

In the second problem-solving/school practitioner approach, students requiring additional supports are typically referred to a multi-disciplinary, schoolwide team that includes general and special education staff. These teams often utilize a problem-solving process to analyze student data in order to determine how to best match evidence-based, culturally responsive interventions with the referral concern. Both assessment and intervention activities increase in intensity, as more targeted and individualized services are warranted across tiers.

The first assessment consideration at the targeted level of intervention and assessment is to identify a targeted behavior for intervention. These assessment steps vary by individual, group, and contextual school and team considerations. Initial steps include a review of universal data (e.g., screening results, effectiveness of universal interventions). If universal screening results yield a non-specific positive screen, such as a student found to be experiencing elevated emotional or behavioral concerns, several steps may be used to assist with problem identification and conceptualization of the student's strengths and access to resources. Additional assessment strategies such as classroom observations, brief interviews with teachers, caregivers, and/or the student, or other extant data may provide additional insight that can be used to design targeted interventions that build upon students' strengths and are matched to student needs.

Students needing additional supports are served via short-term, empirically based targeted interventions. These Tier 2 services include targeted academic, social–emotional, and/or behavioral supports for students who have increased risk factors and who do not make adequate gains despite high-quality, evidence-based instruction, and for whom evidence-based approaches were not sufficient at Tier 1. Selecting specific targeted interventions in the school setting will vary by individual needs and the availability of school resources (Merrell & Buchanan, 2006). Thus, selection and implementation should consider internally valid, scientifically-based, and culturally-sensitive interventions tailored to meet the needs of the individual student and the school context. Generally speaking, targeted interventions could include individualized interventions (e.g., providing a student cognitive-behavioral training for test anxiety), group-based interventions (e.g., social skills training), or manipulation of the environment to influence student outcomes (e.g., classroom-wide strategies, group-based reinforcement for increased time on-task). Students should be provided access to culturally relevant interventions, and when existing interventions lack cultural responsiveness, school-based mental health providers can utilize content and procedural cultural adaptations (e.g., adjusting language and metaphors, incorporating local context) to increase the cultural congruence of these interventions (Brown et al., 2018, Malone et al., 2022). Several efficacious targeted Tier 2 interventions currently exist that address some of these needs, including Check-In/Check-Out (CICO; Filter et al., 2007), social skills training (Gresham et al., 2006), and programs designed to address academic skills (Wills et al., 2010). Many publicly available interventions can also serve as a starting point for targeted intervention implementation and subsequent progress monitoring. This includes the What Works Clearinghouse at *www.whatworks.ed.gov*; Intervention Central at *www.interventioncentral.org*; and the Center for Mental Health in Schools at *http://smhp.psych.ucla.edu*. A research review of Tier 2 interventions can also be found in Bruhn et al. (2014).

After a targeted intervention is selected and implemented, an assessment plan should include ways to monitor a student's response to the selected intervention (Gresham et al., 2013). Progress monitoring data are helpful in identifying learners who do not respond to targeted interventions by providing close monitoring and adjustment of instructional strategies based on analysis of frequent assessment data. In this model, each level of prevention increases in intensity and magnitude, with a goal of providing more focused interventions in subsequent tiers for students in need of targeted assistance. Progress monitoring traditionally includes regular formative assessment data designed to (1) assess student growth or performance in response to the intended intervention and (2) identify how to make the intervention more effective. Progress monitoring occurs at frequent time intervals (e.g., weekly, biweekly, or monthly) and can be collected through a variety of assessment methods, depending on the type of intervention and the specific aim of the targeted intervention. Methods for assessing targeted behaviors include student observations, simple functional behavior assessments (FBAs) paired with behavior intervention plans, direct behavior ratings, rating scales, self-monitoring strategies, and reinforcement plans. More specifically, classroom observations and brief FBAs may help to determine environmental contributors, antecedents, sustaining factors, frequency, and patterns across subjects, time of day, and/or task demands. Rating scales may help identify problem symptom changes in frequency, duration, and intensity. For example, targeted group interventions for social skills, test anxiety, or anger management may use weekly self-report rating scales to elicit student feedback on skill maintenance outside direct skill instruction. Progress monitoring data may be sensitive to time and implementation methods and is not recommended for use in isolation for eligibility or in diagnostic considerations (Ball & Christ, 2012).

Decision validity can help determine which individuals are appropriate for targeted intervention and assessment, as well as those who may require more intensive intervention or treatment. For some students, progress monitoring data may indicate successful progress that will either necessitate ongoing targeted intervention or a decrease and eventual withdrawal of interventions, eventually returning the student to universal level considerations. For youth who continue to demonstrate ongoing needs that cannot be met at the targeted level, assessment data should be used to help guide more intensive services at the highest level of support (see intensive assessment and intervention considerations in the next section). Assessment may include an evaluation of student progress monitoring data (e.g., self-monitoring data of times per week a de-escalation strategy was employed) or a more in-depth evaluation targeting the mastery of the skills that were the focus of the intervention (e.g., an intervention-linked posttest of the targeted skills). Intervention considerations should include what data constitute adequate progress from lack of progress or poor progress. Targeted assessment and intervention considerations should ultimately aim to help alleviate student academic or social–emotional/behavioral concerns, build protective factors that promote well-being, and prevent the development of more significant concerns that may warrant intensive interventions.

INTENSIVE ASSESSMENT AND INTERVENTION

For the approximately 1–5% of students who have not benefited from assessment and intervention strategies across Tiers 1 and 2, Tier 3 includes *indicated* or *intensive* assessment and intervention practices. Tier 3 interventions are necessary for students who continue to demonstrate the need for significant support even after being provided with high-intensity, evidence-based, and culturally responsive instruction and targeted interventions. The goal for intensive assessment is to gather and integrate data to understand the strengths and needs of the child in context and to identify the most appropriate interventions. Decision making at this level is considered "the ultimate application of the data obtained from our screening and progress-monitoring endeavors" (Ball & Christ, 2012, p. 233). Assessment should be culturally relevant and conducted by practitioners who demonstrate cultural humility—that is, those who are self-reflective and seek to understand the student's identity, culture, and context in relation to academic, behavioral, and social–emotional functioning (Hook et al., 2013; Malone et al., 2022). Practitioners engaging in assessment activities may use frameworks such as the ADDRESSING model (Hays, 2008) to understand a student's intersecting identities (Malone et al., 2022). The ADDRESSING model supports clinicians in connecting with students regarding the following nine identity dimensions: age, developmental or other disability, religion; ethnic/racial identity, sexual orientation, socioeconomic status, Indigenous group membership, nationality, and gender identity. To further promote culturally responsive assessment practice at Tier 3, scholars have recommended the use of clinical interviewing tools, such as the Jones Intentional Multicultural Interview Schedule (JIMIS; Jones, 2009), that intentionally attend to cultural and linguistic factors and their impact on student's functioning (Malone et al., 2022). See Chapter 3: Culturally Responsive Behavior Assessment.

Assessment at this tier may fall under the special education umbrella, although assessment for eligibility determination is not the purpose of a multitiered prevention framework. Due to the complex needs of youth referred for intensive services, professional and specially trained mental health staff are often needed to make these diagnoses to identify the most appropriate intervention (Bruns et al., 2016). Traditionally, this type of individualized assessment for eligibility or disorder could be provided by a school psychologist or other trained evaluator and represents historically how school psychologists have spent the majority of their professional efforts (Reschly, 2000). However, school psychological services based in a public health model would challenge that focus and instead advocate for an application of temporal resources at universal and targeted levels (Strein et al., 2003). Assessment practices within a prevention-oriented multi-tier model include having school psychologists and/or school teams analyze school, class, group, and individual contextual data at each tier to identify (1) what additional assessments are needed to supplement previously collected data, and (2) how these data can be used to guide the selection and implementation of evidence-based intervention(s).

Tier 3 individual diagnostic and assessment procedures could include a comprehensive, integrated psychological assessment conducted by an interdisciplinary team of specialists (e.g., school psychologist, child development specialist, behavior specialist, multilingual learner specialist, speech/language pathologist, occupational therapist, physical therapist, school nurse). As with Tier 1 and Tier 2, the use of multiple informant decision making is recommended to increase equitable student outcomes (von der Embse & De Los Reyes, 2024). Some of the same targeted assessment activities conducted at Tier 2 may be utilized with a different emphasis or purpose at Tier 3. For example, assessment methods such as classroom observations, interviews, or FBAs would be more complex and intensive at Tier 3, taking into consideration what interventions were successful and what modifications or changes are needed moving forward.

Specific psychological assessment measures will vary based on the individual student referral question, problem areas, strengths, identity, cultural, and linguistic background, as well as the need for differential diagnosis. The formal gathering of psychological data over the sole use of clinical judgment is also recommended to improve the accuracy of findings (Grove et al., 2000). In some cases, a comprehensive or omnibus measure may simultaneously provide data on a variety of domains of functioning and symptoms (Dowdy et al., 2013). In addition to rating scales, performance-based measures may be warranted to aid in assessment

(Psychology Assessment Work Group; Meyer et al., 2001). However, if assessment is focused on a specific syndrome or context, more narrow-band measures are recommended (Dowdy et al., 2013) and are highlighted throughout chapters elsewhere in this text.

This comprehensive data collection process includes ecological assessment to understand students' contexts, social determinants of mental health, and access to resources; observations of the student and classroom ecology; interviews with the student, family, and educators; data from testing, progress monitoring, and prevention programming; and findings from other professionals' evaluations. These data are integrated into a clinical understanding of the problems, strengths, and needs of the student. With a clear problem identified, intervention planning can be tailored to the individual. Those involved with the assessment can assist with decision-making, implementation of psychological interventions, monitor school-based interventions, and/or coordinate with community-based service providers.

Based on the aforementioned assessment process, intensive interventions can then be individualized, often addressing multiple issues simultaneously. Examples include behavior plans, counseling or therapy, and/or coordination of interventions and services across agencies or domains. Psychologists working in a public health model are ideally suited to coordinate school- and community-based services (Strein et al., 2003). Thus, referrals can be made for any individual, group, or family mental or physical health services that may be outside the purview of school-based practitioners. Linking youth and families to community-based mental health services is a critical step, as these services can support the child's growth across contexts (Atkins et al., 2015). This may include linkage to community-based mental health professionals that deliver culturally responsive services within the school or school district (e.g., such as within a school-based health center) or to agencies that provide counseling, behavioral plans, medication, or family therapy. Connecting students with mental health professionals based in schools may be particularly advantageous as evidence suggests students are more likely to access mental health care in schools than other settings (Duong et al., 2021).

Progress monitoring data should continue to guide the implementation and modification of intensive interventions. This could include an assessment of special education services that are subject to federal guidelines of periodic and frequent monitoring or may include formative assessment of intensive interventions. Due to the individual and intensive focus of targeted tertiary interventions, some individuals may only require brief Tier 3 interventions or support services, while other students may require longer-term supports or services. For more guidance on progress monitoring, see Chapter 13: Progress Monitoring Within a Culturally Responsive Evaluation Framework.

CONCLUSION

Conducting assessment and intervention within an equity-centered prevention framework is an important practice for advancing social justice in schools (Sullivan et al., 2020). Furthermore, this practice has effectively reduced economic and psychological costs to individuals, families, and society (Greenberg et al., 2000). Specifically, conducting psychological and educational assessments on an individual basis is costly, and existing literature suggests that a population-based approach may be a more effective and cost-efficient way to support the academic, behavioral, and social–emotional development of students (Dowdy et al., 2010). Research has demonstrated that positive outcomes can be achieved through early identification and intervention of student's social–emotional, behavioral, and academic functioning, including improvements in academic performance, school engagement, and student's commitment to learning (Catalano et al., 2003; Nelson et al., 2020). Relatedly, academic models that embrace early screening, formative assessments, the provision of evidence-based interventions, and ongoing instructional supports and services result in improved academic achievement and student success in school (Ball & Christ, 2012; Brown-Chidsey & Steege, 2005).

High-quality, culturally sensitive assessment data procedures within a multi-tiered prevention framework are needed to inform service delivery and intervention approaches while building the capacity to serve students with academic, social–emotional, and behavioral needs. School and community partners can continue to work together to provide more coordinated systems of care that are responsive to child, family, and community needs and incorporate child, family, and community assets and resources. However, a number of questions remain. Longitudinal research is needed to determine if these assessment and intervention practices will actually result in the reduction of short- and long-term negative outcomes, such as the diagnosis of mental health concerns, high school graduation rates, and other quality of life indicators (e.g., life satisfaction, employment, relationships). These data are necessary for supporting the aforementioned assessment and intervention considerations and ultimately support a more cost-effective approach to treating student barriers to learning. Research is also needed to determine the outcomes of the equity-centered assessment practices described. It will be important to determine if embedding these techniques within multi-tiered systems truly does reduce inequities in academic and mental health outcomes. Furthermore, research is needed regarding how to comprehensively implement recommended practices in optimal ways (Garbacz et al., 2024). Although ongoing research and continued evaluation of assessment practices is needed, it is hoped that the concepts and guidelines discussed in this chapter will help promote a socially just and prevention-oriented approach to assessment to aid in the prevention of future academic and behavioral concerns among students and to promote their educational success and wellness.

REFERENCES

Abraham, A., & Walker-Harding, L. (2022). The key social determinants of mental health: Their effects among children globally and strategies to address them: A narrative review. *Pediatric Medicine*, *5*(7).

Achenbach, T. M., & Rescorla, L. A. (2001). *Manual for the ASEBA school-age forms & profiles*. University of Vermont, Research Center for Children, Youth, & Families.

Albritton, K., Anhalt, K., & Terry, N. P. (2016). Promoting equity for our nation's youngest students: School psychologists as agents of social justice in early childhood settings. *School Psychology Forum*, *10*(3), 237–250.

American Psychological Association. (2017). *Ethical principles of psychologists and code of conduct* (2002, amended effective June 1, 2010 and January 1, 2017). *www.apa.org/ethics/code*

Antaramian, S. P., Huebner, S., Hills, K. J., & Valois, R. F. (2010). A dual-factor model of mental health: Toward a more comprehensive understanding of youth functioning. *American Journal of Orthopsychiatry*, *80*(4), 462–472.

Atkins, M. S., Shernoff, E. S., Frazier, S. L., Schoenwald, S. K., Cappella, E., Marinez-Lora, A., et al. (2015). Redesigning community mental health services for urban children: Supporting schooling to promote mental health. *Journal of Consulting and Clinical Psychology*, *83*(5), 839–852.

Bal, A. (2018). Culturally responsive positive behavioral interventions and supports: A process-oriented framework for systemic transformation. *Review of Education, Pedagogy & Cultural Studies*, *40*(2), 144–174.

Ball, C. R., & Christ, T. J. (2012). Supporting valid decision making: Uses and misuses of assessment data within the context of RTI. *Psychology in the Schools*, *49*(3), 231–244.

Benedict, E., Horner, R. H., & Squires, J. (2007). Assessment and implementation of positive behavior support in preschools. *Topics in Early Childhood Special Education*, *27*(3), 174–192.

Berkeley, S. B., Scanlon, D., Bailey, T. R., Sutton, J. C., & Sacco, D. M. (2020). A snapshot of RTI implementation a decade later: New picture, same story. *Journal of Learning Disabilities*, *53*(5), 332–342.

Brophy-Herb, H. E., Lee, R. E., Nievar, M. A., & Stollak, G. (2007). Preschoolers' social competence: Relations to family characteristics, teacher behaviors and classroom climate. *Journal of Applied Developmental Psychology*, *28*(2), 134–148.

Brown, C., Maggin, D. M., & Buren, M. (2018). Systematic review of cultural adaptations of school-based social, emotional, and behavioral interventions for students of color. *Education and Treatment of Children*, *41*(4), 431–456.

Brown-Chidsey, R., & Steege, M. W. (2005). *Response to intervention: Principles and methods for effective practice*. Guilford Press.

Brown Griffin, C., Metzger, I. W., Halliday-Boykins, C. A., & Salazar, C. A. (2020). Racial fairness, school engagement, and discipline outcomes in African American high school students: The important role of gender. *School Psychology Review*, *49*(3), 222–238.

Bruhn, A. L., Lane, K. L., & Hirsch, S. E. (2014). A review of Tier 2 interventions conducted within multitiered models of behavioral prevention. *Journal of Emotional and Behavioral Disorders*, *22*(3), 171–189.

Bruns, E. J., Duong, M. T., Lyon, A. R., Pullmann, M. D., Cook, C. R., Cheney, D., & McCauley, E. (2016). Fostering SMART partnerships to develop an effective continuum of behavioral health services and supports in schools. *American Journal of Orthopsychiatry*, 86(2), 156–170.

Burns, M. K., Jimerson, S. R., VanDerHeyden, A. M., & Deno, S. L. (2016). Toward a unified response-to-intervention model: Multi-tiered systems of support. In S. R. Jimerson, M. K. Burns, & A. M. VanDerHeyden (Eds.), *Handbook of response to intervention* (2nd ed., pp. 719–732). Springer.

Catalano, R. F., Mazza, J. J., Harachi, T. W., Abbott, R. D., Haggerty, K. P., & Fleming, C. B. (2003). Raising healthy children through enhancing social development in elementary school: Results after 1.5 years. *Journal of School Psychology*, *41*(2), 143–164.

Centers for Disease Control Foundation. (2024). What is public health? *www.cdcfoundation.org/content/what-public-health*.

Doll, B., & Cummings, J. (2008). Best practices in population-based school mental health services. In A. Thomas, & J. Grimes (Eds.), *Best practices in school psychology V* (pp. 1333–1347). National Association of School Psychologists.

Dowdy, E., Ritchey, K., & Kamphaus, R. W. (2010). School-based screening: A population-based approach to inform and monitor children's mental health needs. *School Mental Health, 2*, 166–176.

Dowdy, E. T., Twyford, J. M., & Sharkey, J. D. (2013). Methods of assessing behavior: Observation and rating scales. In D. H. Saklofske, C. R. Reynolds, & V. L. Schwean (Eds.), *The Oxford handbook of psychological assessment of children and adolescents* (pp. 623–650). Oxford University Press.

Dunlap, G., & Fox, L. (2009). Positive behavior support and early intervention. In *Handbook of positive behavior support* (pp. 49–71). Springer U.S.

Duong, M. T., Bruns, E. J., Lee, K., Cox, S., Coifman, J., Mayworm, A., & Lyon, A. R. (2021). Rates of mental health service utilization by children and adolescents in schools and other common service settings: A systematic review and meta-analysis. *Administration and Policy in Mental Health and Mental Health Services Research, 48*(3), 420–439.

Edyburn, K. L., Bertone, A., Raines, T. C., Hinton, T., Twyford, J., & Dowdy, E. (2023). Integrating intersectionality, social determinants of health, and healing: A new training framework for school-based mental health. *School Psychology Review, 52*(5), 563–585.

Eklund, K., Dowdy, E., Jones, C., & Furlong, M. (2011). Integrating a strengths-based approach to assessment: A dual-factor model of mental health. *Journal of College Student Psychotherapy, 25*(1), 79–92.

Embry, D. D. (2002). The Good Behavior Game: A best practice candidate as a universal behavioral vaccine. *Clinical Child and Family Psychology Review, 5*(4), 273–297.

Epstein, M. H. (1999). The development and validation of a scale to assess the emotional and behavioral strengths of children and adolescents. *Remedial and Special Education, 20*(5), 258–262.

Every Student Succeeds Act, 20 U.S.C. § 6301 (2015). *www.congress.gov/bill/114th-congress/senate-bill/1177*

Fabiano, G. A., & Evans, S. W. (2019). Introduction to the special issue of school mental health on best practices in effective multi-tiered intervention frameworks. *School Mental Health, 11*, 1–3.

Fallon, L. M., Veiga, M., & Sugai, G. (2021). Strengthening MTSS for behavior (MTSS-B) to promote racial equity. *School Psychology Review, 52*(5), 1–16.

Filter, K. J., McKenna, M. K., Benedict, E. A., Horner, R. H., Todd, A., & Watson, J. (2007). Check in/check out: A post-hoc evaluation of an efficient, secondary-level targeted intervention for reducing problem behaviors in schools. *Education and Treatment of Children, 30*(1), 69–84.

Fletcher, J. M., & Vaughn, S. (2009). Response to intervention: Preventing and remediating academic difficulties. *Child Development Perspectives, 3*(1), 30–37.

Foorman, B. R., Francis, D. J., Winikates, D., Mehta, P., Schatschneider, C., & Fletcher, J. M. (1997). Early interventions for children with reading disabilities. *Scientific Studies of Reading, 1*(3), 255–276.

Fox, L., & Little, N. (2001). Starting early: School-wide behavior support in a community preschool. *Journal of Positive Behavior Interventions, 3*(4), 251–254.

Fuchs, L. S. (2003). Assessing intervention responsiveness: Conceptual and technical issues. *Learning Disabilities Research & Practice, 18*(3), 172–186.

Fuchs, L. S., Compton, D. L., Fuchs, D., Paulsen, K., Bryant, J. D., & Hamlett, C. L. (2005). The prevention, identification, and cognitive determinants of math difficulty. *Journal of Educational Psychology, 97*(3), 493–513.

Furlong, M., Dowdy, E., Carnazzo, K., Bovery, B., & Kim, E. (2014). Covitality: Fostering the building blocks of complete mental health. *NASP Communiqué, 42*, 1–29.

Garbacz, S. A. (2020). *Establishing family–school partnerships in school psychology: Critical skills*. Routledge.

Garbacz, S. A., Eklund, E., Kilgus, S. P., & von der Embse, N. (2024). Promoting equity and justice in school mental health. *Journal of School Psychology, 104*, 101318.

Gersten, R., Jordan, N. C., & Flojo, J. R. (2005). Early identification and interventions for students with mathematics difficulties. *Journal of Learning Disabilities, 38*(4), 293–304.

Glover, T. A., & Albers, C. A. (2007). Considerations for evaluating universal screening assessments. *Journal of School Psychology, 45*(2), 117–135.

Gordon, R. S. (1987). An operational classification of disease prevention. In J. A. Steinberg, & M. M. Silverman (Eds.), *Preventing mental disorders: A research perspective* (pp. 20–26). National Institutes of Mental Health.

Graner, P. S., Faggella-Luby, M. N., & Fritschmann, N. S. (2005). An overview of responsiveness to intervention: What practitioners ought to know. *Topics in Language Disorders, 25*(2), 93–105.

Greenberg, M. T., Domitrovich, C., & Bumbarger, B. (2000). *Preventing mental disorders in school-age children: A review of the effectiveness of prevention programs*. Prevention Research Center for the Promotion of Human Development, College of Health and Human Development, Pennsylvania State University.

Gresham, F. M., Hunter, K. K., Corwin, E. P., & Fischer, A. J. (2013). Screening, assessment, treatment, and outcome evaluation of behavioral difficulties in an RTI model. *Exceptionality, 21*(1), 19–33.

Gresham, F. M., Van, M. B., & Cook, C. R. (2006). Social skills training for teaching replacement behaviors: Remediating acquisition deficits in at risk students. *Behavioral Disorders, 31*(4), 363–377.

Grove, W. M., Zald, D. H., Lebow, B. S., Snitz, B. E., & Nelson, C. (2000). Clinical versus mechanical prediction: A meta-analysis. *Psychological Assessment, 12*(1), 19–30.

Gutkin, T. B. (2012). Ecological psychology: Replacing the medical model paradigm for school-based psychological and psychoeducational services. *Journal of Education & Psychological Consultation, 22*(1–2), 1–20.

Harrison, J. R., Vannest, K. J., & Reynolds, C. R. (2013). Social acceptability of five screening instruments for social, emotional, and behavioral challenges. *Behavioral Disorders, 38*(3), 171–189.

Hattie, J. (2012). *Visible learning for teachers: Maximizing impact on learning.* Routledge/Taylor & Francis Group.

Hawken, L. S., Vincent, C. G., & Schumann, J. (2008). Response to intervention for social behavior: Challenges and opportunities. *Journal of Emotional and Behavioral Disorders, 16*(4), 213–225.

Hays, P. A. (2008). *Addressing cultural complexities in practice: Assessment, diagnosis, and therapy* (2nd ed.). American Psychological Association.

Hook, J. N., Davis, D. E., Owen, J., Worthington Jr., E. L., & Utsey, S. O. (2013). Cultural humility: Measuring openness to culturally diverse clients. *Journal of Counseling Psychology, 60*(3), 353–366.

Horowitz, L. M., Ballard, E. D., & Pao, M. (2009). Suicide screening in schools, primary care, and emergency departments. *Current Opinion in Pediatrics, 21*(5), 620–627.

Individuals with Disabilities Education Act, 20 U.S.C. § 1400 (2004).

Institute of Medicine. (1994). Reducing risks for mental disorders: Frontiers for preventive intervention research. National Academy Press.

Jagers, R. J., Rivas-Drake, D., & Williams, B. (2019). Transformative social and emotional learning (SEL): Toward SEL in service of educational equity and excellence. *Educational Psychologist, 54*(3), 162–184.

Jenkins, L. N., Demaray, M. K., Wren, N. S., Secord, S. M., Lyell, K. M., Magers, A. M., et al. (2014). A critical review of five commonly used social-emotional and behavioral screeners for elementary and secondary schools. *Contemporary School Psychology, 18*(4), 241–254.

Jones, J. M. (2009). Counseling with multicultural intentionality: The process of counseling and integrating client cultural variables. In J. M. Jones (Ed.), *The psychology of multiculturalism in the schools: A primer for practice, training, and research* (pp. 191–213). National Association of School Psychologists.

Keyes, C. L. M. (2005). Mental illness and/or mental health? Investigating axioms of the complete state model of health. *Journal of Consulting and Clinical Psychology, 73*(3), 539–548.

Kilgus, S., & Eklund, K. (2015). Consideration of base rates within universal screening for behavioral and emotional risk: A novel procedural framework. *School Psychology Forum, 10*(1), 120–130.

Kilgus, S. P., Methe, S. A., Maggin, D. M., & Tomasula, J. L. (2014). Curriculum-based measurement of oral reading (R-CBM): A diagnostic test accuracy meta-analysis of evidence supporting use in universal screening. *Journal of School Psychology, 52*(4), 377–405.

Koslouski, J. B., Chafouleas, S. M., Briesch, A., Caemmerer, J. M., & Melo, B. (2024). Developing a whole child school screening instrument: evaluating perceived usability as an initial step in planning for consequential validity. *School Mental Health, 16*, 370–386.

Kumpfer, K. L., & Baxley, G. B. (1997). *Drug abuse prevention: What works* (NIH Publication No. 97-4110). National Institutes of Health.

Lane, K. L., Oakes, W. P., & Menzies, H. M. (2014). Comprehensive, Integrated, Three-Tiered (CI3T) Models of Prevention: Why does my school—and district—need an integrated approach to meet students' academic, behavioral, and social needs? *Preventing School Failure*, 58, 121–128.

Lane, K. L., Kalberg, J. R., Lambert, E. W., Crnobori, M., & Bruhn, A. L. (2010). A comparison of systematic screening tools for emotional and behavioral disorders. *Journal of Emotional and Behavioral Disorders, 18*(2), 100–112.

La Salle, T. P., Wang, C., Wu, C., & Rocha Neves, J. (2020). Racial mismatch among minoritized students and white teachers: Implications and recommendations for moving forward. *Journal of Educational and Psychological Consultation, 30*(3), 314–343.

Lazarus, P. J., Doll, B., Song, S. Y., & Radliff, K. (2021). Transforming school mental health services based on a culturally responsible dual-factor model. *School Psychology Review, 51*(6), 755–770.

Leverson M., Smith K., McIntosh K., Rose J., & Pinkelman S. (2021). *PBIS cultural responsiveness field guide: Resources for trainers and coaches.* Center on PBIS. *https://assets-global.website-files.com/5d3725188825e071f1670246/6062383b3f8932b212e9c98b_PBIS%20Cultural%20Responsiveness%20Field%20Guide%20v2.pdf*

Loftus-Rattan, S. M., Wrightington, M., Furey, J., & Case, J. (2023). Multi-tiered system of supports: An ecological approach to school psychology service delivery. *Teaching of Psychology, 50*(1), 77–85.

Malone, C. M., Wycoff, K., & Turner, E. A. (2022). Applying a MTSS framework to address racism and promote mental health for racial/ethnic minoritized youth. *Psychology in the Schools, 59*(12), 2438–2452.

Maslowsky, J., Capell, J. W., Moberg, D. P., & Brown, R. L. (2017). Universal school-based implementation of screening brief intervention and referral to treatment to reduce and prevent alcohol, marijuana, tobacco, and other drug use: Process and feasibility. *Substance Use: Research and Treatment, 11*, 1–10.

Mason, M. J., & Linnenberg, D. M. (1999). Applying public health science to the counselling profession:

An initial examination. *British Journal of Guidance and Counselling, 27*(4), 527–537.

McIntosh, K., Chard, D. J., Boland, J. B., & Horner, R. H. (2006). Demonstration of combined efforts in school-wide academic and behavioral systems and incidence of reading and behavior challenges in early elementary grades. *Journal of Positive Behavior Interventions*, 8(3), 146–154.

McIntosh, K., Girvan, E. J., Fairbanks Falcon, S., McDaniel, S. C., Smolkowski, K., Bastable, E., et al. (2021). Equity-focused PBIS approach reduces racial inequities in school discipline: A randomized controlled trial. *School Psychology, 36*(6), 433–444.

McIntosh, K., & Goodman, S. (2016). *Integrated multi-tiered systems of support: Blending RTI and PBIS*. Guilford Press.

Mellard, D. F., Stern, A., & Woods, K. (2011). RTI school-based practices and evidence-based models. *Focus On Exceptional Children, 43*(6), 1–15.

Merrell, K. W., & Buchanan, R. (2006). Intervention selection in school-based practice: Using public health models to enhance systems capacity of schools. *School Psychology Review, 35*(2), 167–180.

Meyer, G. J., Finn, S. E., Eyde, L. D., Kay, G. G., Moreland, K. L., Dies, R. R., et al. (2001). Psychological testing and psychological assessment: A review of evidence and issues. *American Psychologist, 56*(2), 128–165.

Montague, M., Penfield, R. D., Enders, C., & Huang, J. (2010). Curriculum-based measurement of math problem solving: A methodology and rationale for establishing equivalence of scores. *Journal of School Psychology*, 48(1), 39–52.

Moore, S., Long, A. C., Coyle, S., Cooper, J. M., Mayworm, A. M., Amirazizi, S., et al. (2023). A roadmap to equitable school mental health screening. *Journal of School Psychology*, 96, 57–74.

Moore, S. A., Widales-Benitez, O., Carnazzo, K. W., Kim, E. K., Moffa, K., & Dowdy, E. (2015). Conducting universal complete mental health screening via student self-report. *Contemporary School Psychology, 19*(4), 253–267.

National Center for Education Statistics. (2022a). *National Assessment of Educational Progress (NAEP), 2022 reading assessment*. U.S. Department of Education, Institute of Education Sciences. *https://nces.ed.gov/nationsreportcard/reading*

National Center for Education Statistics. (2022b). *National Assessment of Educational Progress (NAEP), 2022 mathematics assessment*. U.S. Department of Education, Institute of Education Sciences. *https://nces.ed.gov/nationsreportcard/mathematics*

National Center for School Mental Health (NCSMH). (2020). *School mental health quality guide: Screening*. NCSMH, University of Maryland School of Medicine. *www.schoolmentalhealth.org/media/som/microsites/ncsmh/documents/quality-guides/Screening.pdf*

Nelson, R. B., Hemmy Asamsama, O., Jimerson, S. R., & Lam, S. F. (2020). The association between student wellness and student engagement in school. *Journal of Educational Research and Innovation*, 8(1), 5–26.

Nganga, L., Kambutu, J., & Han, K. T. (2019). Caring schools and educators a solution to disparities in academic performance: Learners of colors speak. SAGE *Open*, 9(2), 215824401984192.

Peterson, A., Charles, V., Yeung, D., & Coyle, K. (2021). The health equity framework: A science- and justice-based model for public health researchers and practitioners. *Health Promotion Practice, 22*(6), 741–746.

Proctor, C. L., Linley, P. A., & Maltby, J. (2009). Youth life satisfaction: A review of literature. *Journal of Happiness Studies: An Interdisciplinary Forum on Subjective Well-Being, 10*(5), 583–630.

Protection of Pupil Rights Amendment, 20 U.S.C. § 1232h (2002).

Raines, T. C., Dever, V. D., Kamphaus, R. W., & Roach, A. T. (2012). Universal screening for behavioral and emotional risk: A promising method for reducing disproportionate placement in special education. *The Journal of Negro Education, 81*(3), 283–296.

Reschly, D. J. (2000). The present and future status of school psychology in the United States. *School Psychology Review, 29*(4), 507– 522.

Reschly, D. J. (2008). School psychology paradigm shift and beyond. In A. Thomas, & J. Grimes (Eds.), *Best practices in school psychology* (5th ed., pp. 3–17). National Association of School Psychologists.

Reschly, D. J. (2014). Response to intervention and the identification of specific learning disabilities. *Topics in Language Disorders, 34*(1), 39–58.

Reynolds, C. R., & Kamphaus, R. W. (2015). *Behavior Assessment System for Children, Third Edition*. American Guidance Service.

Riley-Tillman, T. C., Burns, M. K., & Gibbons, K. (2013). *RTI applications: Vol. 2. Assessment, analysis, and decision making*. Guilford Press.

Seethaler, P. M., & Fuchs, L. S. (2010). The predictive validity of kindergarten screening for math difficulty. *Exceptional Children, 77*(1), 37–59.

Severson, H. H., Walker, H. M., Hope-Doolittle, J., Kratochwill, T. R., & Gresham, F. M. (2007). Proactive, early screening to detect behaviorally at-risk students: Issues, approaches, emerging innovations, and professional practices. *Journal of School Psychology, 45*(2), 193–223.

Short, R. J., & Strein, W. (2008). Behavioral and social epidemiology: Population-based problem identification and monitoring. In B. Doll & J. Cummings (Eds.), *Transforming school mental health services: Population-based approaches to promoting the competency and wellness of children* (pp. 23–42). Corwin Press.

Stormont, M., Lewis, T. J., & Beckner, B. (2005). Developmentally continuous positive behavior support systems: Applying key features in preschool settings. *Teaching Exceptional Children, 37*(6), 42–48.

Strein, W., Hoagwood, K., & Cohn, A. (2003). School psychology: A public health perspective: I. Prevention, populations, and systems change. *Journal of School Psychology, 41*(1), 23–38.

Sprague, J. R., & Horner, R. H. (2006). School-wide positive behavioral supports. In S. R. Jimerson, & M. J. Furlong (Eds.), *The handbook of school violence and school safety* (pp. 413–427). Erlbaum.

Sugai, G., & Horner, R. H. (2020). Sustaining and scaling positive behavioral interventions and supports: Implementation drivers, outcomes, and considerations. *Exceptional Children, 86*(2), 120–136.

Sugai, G., Sprague, J. R., Horner, R. H., & Walker, H. M. (2000). Preventing school violence: The use of office discipline referrals to assess and monitor school-wide discipline interventions. *Journal of Emotional and Behavioral Disorders, 8*(2), 94–101.

Suldo, S. M., & Shaffer, E. J. (2008). Looking beyond psychopathology: The dual factor model of mental health in youth. *School Psychology Review, 37*(1), 52–68.

Sullivan, A. L., Miller, F. G., McKevett, N. M., Muldrew, A., Hansen-Burke, A., & Weeks, M. (2020). Leveraging MTSS to advance, not suppress, COVID-related equity issues. *NASP Communiqué, 49*(1), 1, 26, 28–29.

Sullivan, A. L., Nguyen, T., & Shaver, E. (2022). *Foundations of equity-centered MTSS*. Midwest & Plains Equity Assistance Center (MAP EAC). *https://files.eric.ed.gov/fulltext/ED623069.pdf*

Thorius, K. A., & Maxcy, B. D. (2015). Critical practice analysis of special education policy: An RTI example. *Remedial and Special Education, 36*(2), 116–124.

Turney, K., & McLanahan, S. (2015). The academic consequences of early childhood problem behaviors. *Social Science Research, 54*, 131–145.

U.S. Centers for Disease Control and Prevention. (2022). *What is health equity?* U.S. Department of Health and Human Services.

VanDerHeyden, A. M., & Burns, M. K. (2010). *Essentials of response to intervention*. Wiley.

Vaughn, S., & Fuchs, L. S. (2003). Redefining learning disabilities as inadequate response to instruction: The promise and potential problems. *Learning Disabilities Research & Practice, 18*(3), 137–146.

Vaughn, S., Wanzek, J., & Fletcher, J. M. (2007). Multiple tiers of intervention: A framework for prevention and identification of students with reading/learning disabilities. In B. M. Taylor, & J. Ysseldyke (Eds.), *Educational interventions for struggling readers* (pp. 173–196). Teachers College Press.

von der Embse, N., & De Los Reyes, A. (2024). Advancing equity in access to school mental health through multiple informant decision-making. *Journal of School Psychology, 104*, 101310.

Wills, H., Kamps, D., Abbott, M., Bannister, H., & Kaufman, J. (2010). Classroom observations and effects of reading interventions for students at risk for emotional and behavioral disorders. *Behavioral Disorders, 35*(2), 103–119.

World Health Organization. (2024). *Social determinants of health. www.who.int/health-topics/social-determinants-of-health#tab=tab_*

CHAPTER 5

Assessment within a Dual-Factor Framework

Stephanie A. Moore, Brittany N. Zakszeski, Viviana E. Padilla, Kezia Gopaul-Knights, and Heather E. Ormiston

The mental health needs of children and adolescents continue to be a significant public health concern, and rates of diagnosable mental health concerns among children and adolescents are on the rise (Bitsko et al., 2022; Duong et al., 2021). Historically, the identification and treatment of youth mental health concerns have predominantly emphasized problem-focused symptomatology and distress (Suldo et al., 2016) rather than considering strengths-based well-being within the conceptualization of mental health (Suldo & Shaffer, 2008). In so doing, individuals experiencing mental distress at subclinical levels may be overlooked (Suldo et al., 2016). Further, focusing solely on a bipolar model of mental health (i.e., mental illness or mental health as the absence of mental illness; Iasiello et al., 2020) likely minimizes the influence of the structural, systemic, or social inequalities that contribute to or perpetuate mental health needs (Lazarus et al., 2022).

Traditional models of mental health have not typically conceptualized or measured psychological well-being as part of *mental health*. Instead, the assessment of mental health has been associated with the degree of problem behavior, mental distress, and maladjustment (i.e., psychopathology) demonstrated by an individual rather than perceptions of adjustment (i.e., well-being; Doll, 2008; Moore, Mayworm, et al., 2019). However, mental *health* is seen as more than just the absence of psychopathology. The World Health Organization (WHO) defines mental health as "a state of mental well-being that enables people to cope with the stresses of life, realize their abilities, learn well and work well, and contribute to their community" (WHO Newsroom, 2022, Concepts in Mental Health section, para. 1).

Through this lens, mental health has been broadly operationalized via three models: (1) the dual-factor model (DFM; Greenspoon & Saklofske, 2001; Suldo & Shaffer, 2008); (2) the two-continua model (Keyes, 2005); and (3) a cumulative assets-based model (Furlong et al., 2014). The DFM moves away from the unidimensional definition of mental health that emphasizes the presence or absence of psychopathology and instead looks at a more "complete state of being" including the presence of positive indicators of mental health and wellness (Greenspoon & Saklofske, 2001; Suldo & Shaffer, 2008, p. 53). The two-continua model (Keyes, 2005, 2006) similarly recognizes the complex continua of mental health beyond the absence of psychopathology. This model classifies mental health status as either *flourishing* or *languishing*. Defining mental health as *flourishing* reflects the inclusion of 13 different dimensions across the constructs of emotional, psychological, and social well-being, respectively, whereas *languishing* refers to low levels of subjective well-being in conjunction with low levels of social and psychological well-being (Keyes, 2005). Individuals who are neither flourishing nor languishing are considered to be *moderately mentally healthy* (Keyes, 2002, 2006). Compared to the dual-factor and two-continua models, the cumulative assets-based model more closely accounts for the positive indicators of mental health, such as an individual's collective strengths and assets that serve as protective factors (Furlong et al., 2014). Taken together, these models enable a comprehensive, that is, complete, view of child and adolescent mental health (Moore, Mayworm, et al., 2019).

The purpose of this chapter is to delineate a culturally responsible approach to dual-factor mental health assessment with children and adolescents. In this chapter, we use the term *dual factor* inclusively, encompassing conceptualizations and approaches that are consistent with the DFM (Greenspoon & Saklofske, 2001; Suldo & Shaffer, 2008), the two-continua model (Keyes, 2005), and the cumulative assets-based model (Furlong et al., 2014). We use the term *culturally responsible* to underscore that mental health service professionals (MHSPs) must take action to adapt their practice to the children, adolescents, and families with whom they work (Evans, 2021). Culturally responsible practice encompasses and extends "culturally sensitive" and "culturally relevant" practice as well as modifies the traditional term *culturally responsive* to reflect MHSPs' responsibility toward their clients (Evans, 2021; Lazarus et al., 2022). We begin by reviewing foundational theories that inform key principles to this approach. In doing so, we identify the utility and benefits of a culturally responsible dual-factor approach as well as practice considerations for MHSPs. We subsequently apply identified key principles to illustrate a culturally responsible dual-factor assessment approach, specifically, highlighting opportunities within multitiered system of support (MTSS) frameworks in educational settings. Finally, we articulate important future directions for research and practice.

THEORETICAL BACKGROUND

The traditional model of mental health, also known as the disease model, has focused primarily on the experience of psychopathology, which is defined as the presence of various psychological problems including behavioral and emotional disorders whose duration and severity are sufficient to cause functional impairment (Bansal & Barman, 2011). A critical limitation to assessment using the traditional model of mental health is that children and adolescents may be deemed "healthy" despite experiencing a poor quality of life (Suldo & Shaffer, 2008). In fact, several researchers (e.g., Keyes, 2005; Suldo & Shaffer, 2008) have demonstrated that an individual can experience low levels of psychopathology while still languishing (e.g., lacking motivation, feeling stuck, feeling empty), which may be a precursor to developing conditions such as major depressive disorder (Keyes, 2002). The disease model conflates psychopathology and well-being, treating them as the same construct on opposite ends of the same continuum (Lyons et al., 2012). Consequently, the predominating approach to assessment is focused on mental health problems while ignoring positive states (Myers & Diener, 1995). This approach is limited in its utility to identify and prescribe effective interventions and treatment options, especially for individuals who are experiencing low levels of both distress and positive states (Moore, Mayworm, et al., 2019).

Emergence of the Dual-Factor Approach

The historical focus on capturing the negative states of individuals while largely ignoring their positive states is well documented (Myers & Diner, 1995). The shift in attention to more positive states of functioning (e.g., "happiness," "well-being," "life satisfaction") began in the 1980s (Myers & Diener, 1995). Early such investigations attempted to identify those people who were happy, whereas subsequent studies focused on the processes underlying this happiness (Diener, 2000). In the 1990s, several paradigms emerged to shape and direct psychology and related fields toward a focus on the positive aspects of an individual's functioning. Positive psychology is one such framework. Positive psychology studies the optimization of an individual's functioning and includes three pillars: (1) the experience of positive emotions and experiences (e.g., happiness), (2) positive personality traits, and (3) positive institutions such as the family and school (Suldo et al., 2016). In contrast with the disease model, positive psychology advances a preventative approach and focuses on protective factors such as optimism, hope, and resilience (Terjesen et al., 2004), aligning with the movement to advance strengths-based assessment practice (Nickerson & Fishman, 2013). Positive psychologists posit that fostering positive assets are more effective safeguards for improving youth mental health than medication or therapy (Seligman, 1999).

The DFM was developed in response to the historical failure of the disease model to comprehensively address mental health and arose from the shift toward a more positive approach to conceptualizing it. Following an *American Psychologist* special issue (2000) highlighting the integration of positive and negative indicators of mental health, Greenspoon and Saklofske (2001) officially coined the term *dual-factor* to integrate the concepts of well-being and psychopathology to represent mental health. This era heralded a turning point in mental health service fields, from advocating for the inclusion of positive indicators of mental health to the conceptualization of well-being.

As a central tenet of positive psychology, well-being is defined as an all-encompassing construct that reflects aspects of a healthy and successful life, including physical, psychological, and financial domains, among others (Renshaw et al., 2015). Subjective well-being is a narrower construct that reflects high levels of positive mood and affect, low levels of negative mood and affect, and a general sense of high life satisfaction (Suldo & Shaffer 2008). Contemporary applications of the DFM operationalize well-being to include subjective well-being (e.g., Keyes, 2006; Suldo et al., 2016), as well as psychosocial strengths (e.g., Moore, Mayworm, et al., 2019).

Culturally Responsible Influences on the Dual-Factor Approach

As MHSPs engage in mental health assessment within a dual-factor framework, there is a need to infuse culturally responsible approaches into practice. Two theoretical perspectives applicable to this work are critical theory and intersectionality. Sabnis and Proctor (2021) identified three characteristics of critical theories. The first is that reality is continually changing, influenced by the historical landscape and solidified into hierarchal structures of capital, race, and gender. Second, existing knowledge reflects the beliefs, agendas, and interests of those who produce that knowledge. Third, it is necessary for individuals to evaluate how their beliefs, agendas, and interests influence their work and how they may have been accomplices to the oppression experienced by others. Within critical theory, intersectionality refers to the interaction of multiple dimensions of identity (e.g., race, gender, class) to establish unique structures of oppression and discrimination (Crenshaw, 1989). Attempting to understand the experiences of marginalized communities through a unidimensional focus on identity may fail to explain the complexity of experiences faced by these communities (Crenshaw, 1991). MHSPs must consider children and adolescents' multiple intersecting identities when attempting to fully understand their worlds (Proctor et al., 2018). In applying the DFM to mental health assessment in a culturally responsible manner, MHSPs must acknowledge and act on the realities of marginalized groups, the complexity of experiences, and the impact of oppression on youth mental health.

KEY PRINCIPLES OF DUAL-FACTOR FRAMEWORKS

Fundamentally, assessment within a dual-factor framework is characterized by (1) the distinction between well-being and psychopathology and (2) the integration of these two factors to classify mental health status to (3) inform intervention (Greenspoon & Saklofske, 2001; Suldo & Shaffer, 2008).

Assessment Distinguishes Well-Being and Psychopathology

Whereas psychopathology is the negative indicator of mental health that, traditionally, has served as the basis of assessment and diagnosis, well-being is the positive indicator of mental health that has emerged as a central construct within positive psychology (Keyes, 2005). These dual factors are understood to be inversely related but "not simply opposite poles of a single continuum" (Greenspoon & Saklofske, 2001, p. 81). Moreover, these factors are not entirely transactional; increases in one factor do not necessarily beget decreases in the other. Rather, well-being and psychopathology exist on separate continua and interact in dynamic and nuanced ways (Suldo & Doll, 2021). Integrative assessment of these dual factors provides a more comprehensive picture of psychological functioning than can assessment of either factor alone (Antaramian et al., 2010; Smith et al., 2020). This may occur using measures that capture both factors (i.e., assessing both well-being and psychopathology) or through the integration of data from separate measures (e.g., with one instrument assessing well-being and a second assessing psychopathology; Thayer et al., 2021).

Classification of Dual-Factor Mental Health

Assessment of both well-being and psychopathology is necessary for classifying an individual's dual-factor mental health. Classification involves assigning individuals, based on their relative degree of well-being and psychopathology, to a dual-factor mental health group or status. Whereas optimal mental health is generally understood to reflect high levels of well-being and low levels of psychopathology, dual-factor groups have been defined using varied methods.

The predominating approach applies cutoff- or criterion-based methods to define and classify individuals into mental health groups. Foundational DFM studies created groups using dichotomous classification schemes (Greenspoon & Saklofske, 2001; Suldo & Shaffer, 2008). This process involved first establishing and applying cut scores for "high" versus "low" well-being and psychopathology, resulting in two well-being and two psychopathology groups. Then, the resulting well-being and psychopathology groups were cross tabulated to form four groups comprising individuals with (1) high well-being and low psychopathology—*complete mental health*, (2) low well-being and high psychopathology—*troubled*, (3) low well-being and low psychopathology—*vulnerable* or *languishing*, and (4) high well-being and high psychopathology—*symptomatic but content* (Suldo & Shaffer, 2008; see Figure 5.1). Alternatively, Keyes's two-continua approach articulates diagnostic-like criteria to identify three states of well-being (i.e., flourishing, languishing, or moderately mentally healthy; Keyes, 2002, 2006). Mental health status is then similarly cross tabulated with groups reflecting varied degrees of psychopathology to form mental health groups.

The number of cut points and the resulting number of mental health groups may vary based on the approach and measure(s) used (Iasiello et al., 2020; Moore et al., 2015). Multiple instruments have been used to measure well-being, including the Positive and Negative Affect Schedule for Children (PANAS-C; Laurent et al., 1999), Student's Life Satisfaction Scale (SLSS; Huebner, 1991), Mental Health Continuum—Short Form (MHC-SF; Lamers et al., 2011), and the Social Emotional Health Survey (SEHS; Furlong et al., 2020), with cut points reflecting local or sample norms (e.g., *T*- or *z*-scores) or thresholds (e.g., top 70%). Instruments used to measure psychopathology have included the Behavior Assessment System for Children (BASC) student or teach-

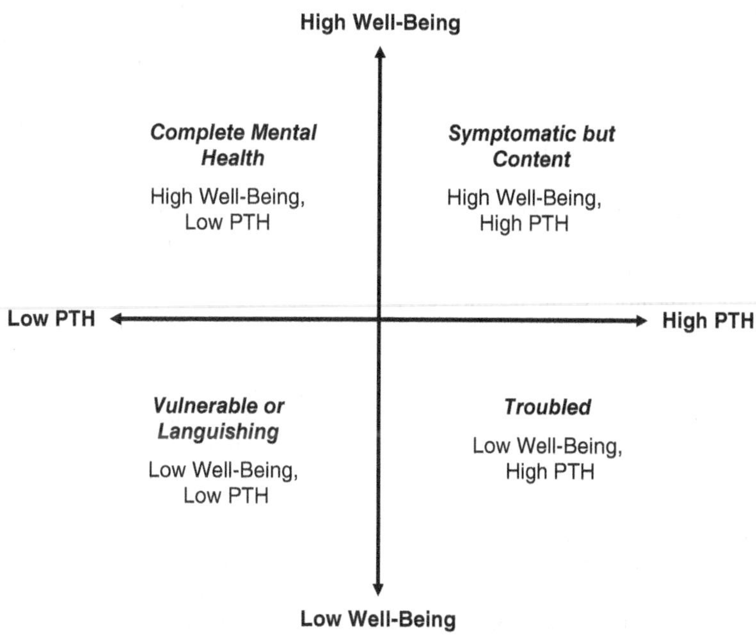

FIGURE 5.1. Visual depiction of the dual-factor model (DFM) of mental health. *Note*. PTH = Psychopathology

er report form (Reynolds & Kamphaus, 2015), Child Behavior Checklist—Youth Self Report (CBCL-YSR; Achenbach & Rescorla, 2001), and Depression Anxiety Stress Scales–21 (DASS-21; Iasiello et al., 2020; Kim et al., 2017; Lovibond & Lovibond, 1995). Some psychopathology measures yield standardized *T*-scores that are used to identify three levels of symptoms or risk (e.g., *normal, elevated, extremely elevated*). When more than two cut points are indicated, additional dual-factor groups are formed. For example, Furlong et al. (2022) identified nine dual-factor groups, consisting of three levels of psychopathology and four levels of well-being. Ultimately, the number of cut points appropriate for a given tool and context may be determined in consultation with a measure's manual, the measure developers, or the empirical literature (Moore et al., 2015).

Although widely applied, cut score classification approaches have recognized limitations. Most notably, the use of predetermined cut scores may "mask nuances" in well-being and psychopathology assessment results (Thayer et al., 2021, p. 4). This concern is most pronounced when classifying individuals on the threshold of a given group (e.g., scoring just above the cut point for "high" well-being; Kim et al., 2017). Although some instruments will have established population norms that inform cut points, many others will not have established criteria or guidance to determine appropriate cut points (Moore, Dowdy, et al., 2019). These limitations may contribute to creating groups that are not supported by data or classifying individuals into groups that incompletely represent their assessment results (Thayer et al., 2021).

Conversely, empirically driven classification methods use advanced statistical models to *identify*, rather than create, groups based on similarities in the pattern of scores on well-being and psychopathology indicators (Kim et al., 2017). Using this approach, researchers typically employ latent class analysis (LCA) or latent profile analysis (LPA) to identify groups and examine predictors or correlates of the groups (Thayer et al., 2021). The identified groups can vary in dimension and severity, and model information allows researchers to examine the extent to which individuals are accurately classified (Moore, Dowdy, et al., 2019). An empirical approach has been applied in research with children (e.g., Peterson et al., 2020) and adolescents (e.g., Clark & Malecki, 2022; Thayer et al., 2021) using various measures of well-being and psychopathology, typically identifying three or four mental health groups.

Data-driven classification methods are useful for evaluating if assessment data support theoretically identified dual-factor groups formed using cut score approaches (Thayer et al., 2021). Using LPA, researchers often identify the theoretically indicated complete mental health and troubled groups (e.g., Clark & Malecki, 2022; Moore, Dowdy, et al., 2019). However, groups consistent with the symptomatic but content and vulnerable statuses, respectively, are identified inconsistently (e.g., identified in Peterson et al., 2020; Thayer et al., 2021; not identified in Clark & Malecki, 2022; Moore, Dowdy, et al., 2019). Additionally, LPA studies have identified a group consistent with Keyes' (2006) moderately mentally healthy group (e.g., Moore, Dowdy, et al., 2019). Although results of LPA studies suggest that there may be more nuance in dual-factor mental health than what dichotomous cut score-formed groups capture, the methodological requirements of empirical classification approaches make them impractical. Nevertheless, findings from these studies suggest that using additional cut points to create more than four groups may better capture nuance in individuals' dual-factor mental health (Moore, Dowdy, et al., 2019).

Classification to Inform Intervention

Ultimately, assessment of well-being and psychopathology using a dual-factor approach and subsequent dual-factor mental health group classification can be used to inform intervention decisions. Although well-being and psychopathology are correlated, the predictors of wellness and mental illness are distinct (Kinderman et al., 2015; Lyons et al., 2012), suggesting interventions focused on promoting well-being and preventing or treating psychopathology "should be complementary but different" (Kinderman et al., 2015, p. 460). Thus, a dual-factor approach to intervention targets both the reduction of psychopathology and improvement in well-being (Iasiello et al., 2020) and recognizes that individuals in different dual-factor mental health groups may require different interventions (Suldo & Shaffer, 2008). For example, MHSPs working with children and adolescents with mental health characterized by low well-being and low psychopathology (vulnerable, languishing) may provide intervention that intends to build social-emotional competencies. However, youth with high well-being as well as high psychopathology (symptomatic but content) may receive interventions that primarily address psychopathology symptoms and build on existing competencies. Finally, youth with low well-being and high psychopathology (troubled) may require intervention that not only addresses their psychopathology symptoms but also builds social-emotional competencies and promotes well-being (Suldo & Shaffer, 2008). Necessarily, MHSPs who apply an approach to intervention that prioritizes efforts to enhance well-being and address psychopathology should also monitor the individual's progress and intervention outcomes using measures of both well-being and psychopathology.

EVIDENCE BASE FOR THE DUAL-FACTOR APPROACH

The DFM has been studied across developmental periods (e.g., children to adults), in clinical and non-clinical populations, as well as in the United States and internationally (see Iasiello et al., 2020, for a scoping review). Overall, research supports that well-being and psychopathology are distinct yet related constructs, and individuals across developmental periods can be placed into mental health groups reflecting well-being and psychopathology (Iasiello et al., 2020). Across studies investigating the validity of identified groups, group differences have been found for academic (e.g., grades, engagement; Antaramian et al., 2010), social-emotional (e.g., social adjustment, social support; Smith et al., 2020; Suldo et al., 2016), and behavioral (e.g., office discipline referrals; Suldo et al., 2011, 2016) outcomes. Consistent with the DFM, studies have generally supported that the absence of psychopathology is insufficient for supporting optimal outcomes (Iasiello et al., 2020). For example, research suggests youth with complete mental health (i.e., low psychopathology and high well-being) have better outcomes than those with vulnerable or languishing mental health (e.g., Antaramian et al., 2010; Suldo & Shaffer, 2008; Suldo et al., 2016), and among those with high levels of psychopathology (troubled or symptomatic but content), those with higher levels of well-being (symptomatic but content) experience better outcomes (e.g., Smith et al., 2020; Suldo et al., 2016).

Although a robust and increasing body of evidence supports the DFM, including in 20 Western and non-Western countries (Iasiello et al., 2020), scant research has explicitly examined the applicability of the DFM cross-culturally. The applicability of the DFM for individuals with different sociocultural identities and backgrounds may be understood, in part, by examining (1) who has been included in the research substantiating this approach and (2) whether the distribution of individuals across dual-factor mental health groups varies based on their sociocultural identity. The participant samples for DFM research conducted in the United States represent varied geographic regions, typically include boys and girls (although gender diverse youth were rarely captured), and have variable levels of racial and ethnic diversity. Whereas many studies included individuals identifying as White (non-Hispanic), Black or African American, and Hispanic or Latine, the largest racial or ethnic group was often White-identifying youth (e.g., Smith et al., 2020). Similarly, these studies less often included students with Asian American, Pacific Islander, or Indigenous identities. Researchers have also investigated whether an individual's sociocultural identity predicts the distribution of individuals across mental health groups. In several studies, the distribution of racial and ethnic identity was similar across groups (Antaramian et al., 2010; Suldo & Shaffer, 2008; Suldo et al., 2011); however, other research indicated that group membership may vary based on these characteristics (Clark & Malecki, 2022). Additionally, youth with fewer socioeconomic resources were overrepresented in the *vulnerable* or *troubled* groups and underrepresented in the complete mental health group (Suldo & Shaffer, 2008; Suldo et al., 2016). The limited nature of this available evidence underscores the importance of adopting a culturally responsible approach to dual-factor mental health assessment.

NECESSARY PRINCIPLES FOR A CULTURALLY RESPONSIBLE APPROACH

A culturally responsible dual-factor assessment approach has the potential to disrupt inequitable systems to promote mental health equity, thereby leading to positive outcomes for children and adolescents (Lazarus et al., 2022). Specifically, a culturally responsible approach (1) leverages a systems- and population-focused perspective that prioritizes equity and recognizes the impact of systemic oppression, (2) centers strengths and promotes healing, and (3) is grounded within cultural humility and cultural literacy.

Systems- and Population-Focused to Disrupt Inequities

Culturally responsible assessment practices are equity-centered and rooted in the acknowledgement that oppressive systems, policies, and practices contribute to inequity in dual-factor mental health outcomes for racial and ethnically minoritized (REM) populations (Moore et al., 2023). These systems, policies, and practices are understood as social determinants of health (i.e., socioeconomic and environmental factors including economic in/stability, housing or food in/security, trauma, racism, and discrimination) that impact and shape young people's development and mental health outcomes (e.g., Shim et al., 2014). Social determinants are inequitably distributed in U.S. society and create disparities that disproportionately impact historically marginalized populations (Compton & Shim, 2015). For example, racism, discrimination, and oppressive systems that limit socioeconomic resources are associated with lower well-being, greater psychological distress, and reduced access to mental health resources for REM youth (e.g., Astell-Burt et al., 2012). These discriminatory systems and actions simultaneously bolster White youth's outcomes while undermining REM youth's social, emotional, and academic development (La Salle et al., 2020). Ignorance to these social and environmental determinants can impact evaluations of children and adolescents' mental health and contribute to inappropriate or inaccurate identification, diagnosis, treatment, and placement decisions (e.g., Downey & Pribesh, 2004).

Therefore, culturally responsible dual-factor approaches recognize and proactively identify the impacts of social determinants on youth's dual-factor mental health. Furthermore, MHSPs applying this approach take intentional action to disrupt unjust or inequitable systems and practices and work toward mental health equity, for example, through systems-level advocacy and activism (Lazarus et al., 2022). In practice, this can include critically reviewing organizational policies and related data to examine whether there are subpopulation differences as well as seeking and amplifying the voices of REM groups (Sullivan et al., 2015). Additionally, a systems- and population-focused approach includes an emphasis on gathering and analyzing data at a population level (e.g., schoolwide; Doll & Cummings, 2008). Shifting from an individual-level to a community-oriented focus enables MHSPs to observe and identify population-level trends, including patterns among important subgroups (e.g., girls, Black children, LGBTQ+ youth), and encourages systems-level change to support mental health equity (Sullivan et al., 2023).

Strengths- and Healing-Centered

A culturally responsible dual-factor approach further centers on children's and adolescents' strengths as the foundation of their well-being (Lazarus et al., 2022), thereby promoting a holistic approach to understanding and building their mental health. Traditional mental health service delivery that applies the disease model is deficit-based, meaning it is focused on identifying and remediating individual problems or "weaknesses" (Naples & Tuckwiller, 2021). A deficit-based view of mental health fails to consider social determinants of health that maintain inequity and places responsibility on individuals to cope or become resilient (Edyburn et al., 2023). Instead, applying a strengths-based approach to assessment and service provision focuses on identifying and building upon skills, assets, and cultural values that promote well-being and may reduce mental health stigma (Dowdy et al., 2014). Although the integrative assessment of well-being and psychopathology is a fundamental component of dual-factor assessment, culturally responsible dual-factor assessment necessitates moving beyond a focus on individual well-being. MHSPs must also focus on identifying individual and community strengths, resilience-promoting factors (e.g., relationships with peers, family, teachers), and community cultural assets (Edyburn et al., 2023).

A strengths-based approach also supports moving toward *healing* as opposed to simply coping (Edyburn et al., 2023). French et al. (2020) developed a framework of radical healing for communities of color that centers justice and wellness and is grounded in collectivism, critical consciousness, radical hope, strength and resistance, and cultural authenticity and self-knowledge. In practice, radical healing works to promote thriving by helping individuals understand their mental health within the context of systemic oppression and collective trauma, building on community strengths and shared identities to promote health and well-being, and taking action to reduce oppression (French et al., 2020).

Grounded in Cultural Humility and Cultural Literacy

Despite an increasingly diverse population of children and adolescents, the majority of MHSPs (~4 out of 5) are White and monolingual in English (e.g., Goforth et al., 2021). This discrepancy contributes to an increasing cultural, racial, and linguistic mismatch between youth and the professionals who provide for their mental health needs (La Salle et al., 2020). Thus, as part of a culturally responsible dual-factor assessment approach, MHSPs must also work to practice with cultural humility and build their cultural literacy (Lazarus et al., 2022). Cultural humility involves "being aware of one's own assumptions about culture and value as well as the biases one holds toward others" (Lazarus et al., 2022, p. 6) and is developed through critical self-reflection on one's experiences of privilege and marginalization (Fisher-Borne et al., 2015). A culturally humble interpersonal stance reflects an other-orientation that emphasizes respect and understanding (Hook et al., 2013). Cultural literacy refers to actively and intentionally learning about the cultural norms and values of the youth and families served, including their cultural values or beliefs related to well-being and psychopathology (Sue et al., 2019).

Cultural humility and cultural literacy complement systems-focused and strengths-based approaches; together, they are essential in providing culturally responsible services and disrupting the status quo to build equitable systems of care (La Salle et al., 2020). For example, a culturally responsible, strengths-based approach recognizes that culture significantly influences conceptualizations of well-being (Moore et al., 2023), which has historically been conceptualized through a Western lens and may not represent the values held by individuals whose cultures prioritize varied dimensions of well-being (Krys et al., 2023). Asian cultures and other collective cultural structures, for instance, tend to place a greater emphasis on interdependent happiness, which values family and relationships, than do more individualistic cultures, which conceptualize life satisfaction and happiness in terms of achievement and success (Krys et al., 2023; Mathews & Izquierdo, 2008). Thus, a "one-size-fits-all" approach to measuring well-being may not be appropriate or accurate (Krys et al., 2023). When considering measures for dual-factor assessment, MHSPs must understand how well-being and psychopathology are understood in the youth or family's culture as well as what type of well-being is valued. As a starting point, MHSPs can use Hays's (2008) ADDRESSING model to critically reflect on privileged and marginalized aspects of their identity and to consider the identities of the youth they serve. The ADDRESSING model articulates nine primary cultural influences that MHSPs need to consider, with each influence corresponding to a letter in the acronym: age, developmental disability, religion, ethnicity, social status, sexual orientation, indigenous heritage, national origin, and gender (Hays, 2008). As part of their dual-factor assessment, MHSPs may also conduct multicultural interviews (e.g., using the Jones Intentional Multicultural Interview Schedule; Jones, 2009) with youth and families to further explore their identities and cultural values.

In practice, the principles of cultural humility and cultural literacy are realized through strong MHSP–family partnerships that guide assessment and resulting service delivery. When dual-factor assessment is conducted within collaborative partnerships, MHSPs can better identify individual *and* community strengths and needs (Moore et al., 2023). Moreover, through relationships with youth, their families, and their communities, MHSPs seek to understand different cultural perceptions of mental health, increase trust in systems for youth and their families, and receive feedback on how to engage in a culturally responsible assessment process that meets the needs of the community (Hook et al., 2013; Lazarus et al., 2022).

PRINCIPLES IN PRACTICE: EXAMPLE APPLICATIONS IN AN EDUCATIONAL SETTING

A case example is provided below to illustrate how the principles of culturally responsible dual-factor assessment may be applied in practice. In this example, we focus on the mental health service setting of schools and, more specifically, opportunities for culturally responsible dual-factor assessment in MTSS frameworks in schools. Within MTSS frameworks, multidisciplinary school teams use data collected at the levels of the school, classroom, and individual student to make decisions around the effectiveness of existing school-based supports; the need for systems improvement; and the need for supplemental student supports in academic, social, emotional, and behavioral domains, including mental health (McIntosh & Goodman, 2016). Across three tiers of services, supports are designed to address different levels of need: universal promotion and prevention supports are provided to all students at Tier 1; secondary prevention practices are delivered to students identified as at risk for challenges at Tier 2; and tertiary prevention practices are delivered to those students experiencing the most challenges at Tier 3 (McIntosh & Goodman, 2016).

In the sections that follow, we describe one school's mental health assessment practices at the universal promotion and prevention tier (Tier 1) as well as at advanced tiers of prevention (Tiers 2 and 3), with particular attention to elements that distinguish these practices as consistent with a culturally responsible dual-factor approach. The alignment of this school's practices with the principles for culturally responsible assessment, as delineated above, is highlighted in Table 5.1.

TABLE 5.1. Applications of Culturally Responsible Dual-Factor Assessment Principles within MTSS in Schools

Principle of culturally responsible dual-factor assessment	Tier 1 applications	Tiers 2 and 3 applications
Leverages a systems focus to disrupt inequities	• Data collected through Tier 1 MH assessments are used to describe MH statuses schoolwide, including subgroup analyses to detect MH disparities. • Tier 1 MH assessment results are conducted to evaluate (1) the effectiveness and equity of existing universal promotion and prevention initiatives and (2) the need for intensified or differentiated ecological supports.	• Universal and targeted MH screening results are interpreted within the context of societal and environmental risk factors as well as opportunities for systems-level intervention. • Progress monitoring data related to MH outcomes collected for groups of students and individual students are both synthesized and disaggregated by student characteristics of interest (e.g., race/ethnicity, primary language, disability status) to examine the equitable functioning of the advanced-tiers prevention system and opportunities for refinement.
Applies a strengths-based and healing-centered approach to assessment and intervention	• Schools select schoolwide MH general outcome measures that assess the protective and promotive factors that underlie the presence of well-being and absence of PTH, with attention to factors within the environment and at the population level. • Results of schoolwide strengths assessments are used to shape universal MH promotion and prevention initiatives.	• Assessment procedures for selecting and designing Tiers 2 and 3 MH interventions include the identification of strengths underlying the presence of well-being and absence of PTH to build upon within the intervention. • MH progress monitoring results are reviewed and interpreted within the context of students' strengths by members of multidisciplinary student support teams.
Exercises cultural humility and literacy in collaborative partnerships	• School leaders, faculty, and staff meaningfully engage families, moving beyond strategies for "involving" families and instead seeking to "partner" with families.	• Student support teams include students and families as critical members whose perspectives and values are centered in MH service decision-making.

(continued)

TABLE 5.1. *(continued)*

Principle of culturally responsible dual-factor assessment	Tier 1 applications	Tiers 2 and 3 applications
	• Multidisciplinary MTSS teams learn how students, their families, and their communities define and value MH (i.e., well-being and PTH), and they apply this understanding to select Tier 1 general outcome measures that assess culturally relevant constructs. • Multimethod, multisource Tier 1 assessment procedures are designed by MTSS teams in collaboration with students' families and, when indicated, community cultural brokers.	• Tiers 2 and 3 MH interventions are selected by student support teams with attention to the cultural relevance and responsiveness of needs-aligned approaches. • MH progress monitoring measures are selected, and procedures are designed to assess well-being and PTH as defined and valued by the student, their family, and their community.

Note. MH = Mental Health, PTH = Psychopathology

CASE EXAMPLE

Overview of Washington Middle School

Washington Middle School (WMS) is a Title I neighborhood school that serves approximately 800 students in grades 5–8. Much of its student population identifies as Latine (72% of students) or multiracial (19% of students), in stark contrast with the racial/ethnic composition of the school's faculty (81% White). Many students are considered English learners (28%) and/or first-generation-American students (45%).

When Ms. Ross first joined WMS as its principal, she realized she had much to learn about both the school and the community in which WMS resides, a community in which various Central American and Caribbean cultures are both represented and celebrated. Ms. Ross expanded the MTSS Leadership Team to be representative of the school's staff and to include family and student representatives. Ms. Ross then charged the expanded MTSS Leadership Team with (1) mapping the school's and community's existing resources and (2) identifying improvement needs prioritized by the faculty, staff, families, and students. Ultimately, the MTSS Leadership Team identified universal mental health promotion and prevention (i.e., promoting well-being and preventing psychopathology) as the school's most urgent improvement priority. Additionally, the MTSS Leadership Team recognized several aligned practices that were already in place (e.g., schoolwide social–emotional learning curriculum, psychoeducation embedded within health and wellness classes) but noted no formally adopted assessment practices to evaluate the impact of these supports or identify students in need of additional mental health support.

Accordingly, through a multi-year process, Ms. Ross, WMS's MHSPs (i.e., a school counselor, a school psychologist, and school social workers), and the broader MTSS Leadership Team ("WMS leadership") conducted a series of activities (e.g., listening sessions with faculty, staff, families, and students, respectively; having school policy drafts shared with parties for open comment) to develop and implement a multi-tiered system of mental health assessment. Driven by the goals of (1) measuring students' well-being and psychopathology as understood by and relevant to students and their families and (2) linking assessment results to culturally responsible and sustaining mental health promotion and prevention practices, they necessarily adopted *dual-factor* and *culturally responsible* approaches to assessment. The assessment practices implemented by WMS are described below, organized by (1) practices implemented schoolwide at Tier 1 and (2) practices implemented with selected groups and individual students at the advanced tiers (Tiers 2 and 3).

Dual-Factor Mental Health Assessment Practices at Tier 1

WMS leadership designed Tier 1 mental health assessment practices, or assessments administered to all students in the school, to answer the following questions:

1. *Strengths identification:* What are the current strengths of our school (e.g., environmental and population-based protective and promotive factors) in relation to mental health? How can these strengths be built upon in schoolwide promotion and prevention programming?

2. *Mental health status snapshot:* What is the status of our students' mental health (i.e., well-being and psychopathology at one point in time)? To what extent are current mental health outcomes equitable (i.e., similar across subgroups) in our student population?
3. *Tier 1 evaluation:* What is the impact of existing Tier 1 practices on students' mental health (i.e., changes in well-being and psychopathology across multiple points in time)? To what extent are existing Tier 1 practices similarly impacting students' mental health (i.e., equitably across student subgroups)?

WMS leadership's Tier 1 assessment approach centers the voices of students, their families, and the professionals who serve them in collecting information on both the school environment and individuals' perceived strengths and needs within the environment, which are aggregated to describe the student population. Three times per year (fall, winter, spring), WMS leadership invites each party to complete a survey, which includes one or more of the following elements: (1) a school climate questionnaire; (2) a brief rating scale assessing each student's well-being and protective factors; and (3) a brief rating scale assessing each student's psychopathology and risk factors. In selecting measures, WMS leadership considered measures' alignment with the school's assessment goals and existing support for their psychometric functioning (e.g., reliability, validity, sensitivity, specificity) in samples with similar characteristics to those of the WMS student population (e.g., grades, race/ethnicity, language, region; Glover & Albers, 2007; Moore et al., 2023).

Students, staff, and faculty complete surveys electronically during dedicated class time or administrator-provided preparation time on non-instructional days, respectively. All building staff complete the school climate questionnaire, whereas teachers also complete the additional rating scales (measuring well-being and protective factors as well as psychopathology and risk factors, respectively) for each student in one of their classes. Finally, students' guardians are invited to complete the school climate questionnaire and student rating scales in English, Spanish, or French and to contact the leadership team to request the survey in a different language. The survey may be completed by electronic questionnaire, by paper questionnaire, or through a confidential interview with a school professional. Although the family surveys take much more time to coordinate relative to the student, staff, and faculty surveys (all administered online), WMS leadership is committed to including families' voices in data for decision-making and have allocated staff's time (e.g., that of administrative assistants, community liaisons, translators, and MHSPs) to removing barriers to families' participation.

Survey results are synthesized by WMS leadership, who present summaries of survey results during all-staff meetings and through family newsletters. In using the data for decision-making, WMS leadership answers each of its three guiding questions and, in accordance with each question's answer, develops an action plan, which delineates next steps taken by the team to enhance the effectiveness and equity of schoolwide promotion and prevention programming. Data collected at Tier 1 are also used to identify students who may benefit from advanced-tier mental health services despite the implementation of effective and equitable Tier 1 support practices.

Dual-Factor Mental Health Assessment Practices at the Advanced Tiers

WMS leadership designed mental health assessment practices at Tiers 2 and 3 to answer the following questions:

1. *Screening:* Beyond the need for systems-level intervention, which students require more mental health support than they are current receiving?
2. *Strengths identification:* What are the current strengths of each student in relation to mental health? How can these strengths be built upon in mental health intervention?
3. *Intervention selection:* Given each student's current profile of well-being and psychopathology as well as their cultural values, what intervention approach is best suited to meet their needs?
4. *Progress monitoring:* How is the student responding to the intervention? How are the student's well-being and psychopathology changing across implementation?

At Tier 2, WMS leadership uses the survey administered for all students in the school to identify students in need of additional mental health support, considering opportunities for systemic changes prior to proceeding with a student-focused intervention. When student-focused intervention is pursued, WMS leadership collects additional information on students' strengths, well-being, psychopathology, cultural values, and preferences to evaluate the fit of potential interventions. Follow-up assessment at this stage commonly involves a review of students' records, conversations with students and guardians, and, in some cases, targeted rating scale administration. Once a culturally responsive intervention has been selected, student support teams, which include students and families, select an approach for monitoring students' progress that captures well-being and psychopathology, as defined and understood in the student's culture and context. At WMS, progress monitoring generally includes brief outcome rating scales, direct behavior ratings (Chafouleas et al., 2010), or a combination of these methods, completed weekly by students, educators, guardians, or a combination of informants. These data are reviewed by student support teams to evaluate both the effectiveness of the intervention with the individual student as well as the effectiveness of the intervention with the group of students receiving it, enabling the assessment of equity within the Tier 2 system. The categories of assessment practices described for Tier 2 are also implemented at Tier 3, but these practices may be further tailored to better capture the strengths and needs of individual students at Tier 3.

FUTURE DIRECTIONS

This chapter described a dual-factor framework for mental health assessment that is grounded in empirical research (Suldo & Doll, 2021) and holds potential for advancing culturally responsible assessment (Lazarus et al., 2022). It is generally recognized, however, that assessment within a single-factor framework—and, primarily, within a deficit-focused, disease model-based approach—remains the norm in mental health practice (e.g., Lazarus et al., 2022). For a dual-factor assessment framework to be adopted into practice in mental health service settings, additional work must be undertaken to translate proofs of concept into protocols for implementation—and, thereby, surmount the research-to-practice gap. In the sections that follow, we highlight three critical directions to take in research and practice to promote the adoption, sustained use, and utility of culturally responsible dual-factor assessment. These directions correspond with current barriers that, if unaddressed, are expected to limit the relevance and usability of the dual-factor framework. These directions include (1) refining measures for dual-factor applications in diverse populations; (2) developing systems for multimethod, multisource data-based decision-making; and (3) expanding dual-factor assessment applications beyond screening.

Refining Measures for Dual-Factor Applications in Diverse Populations

Despite the DFM's potential to reshape traditional assessment practice, use of the framework depends on the availability of instruments that have been optimized for this purpose and are appropriate for use in the intended population and setting (Glover & Albers, 2007). A plethora of instruments have been developed to assess children and/or adolescents' mental health, including indicators of well-being and symptoms of psychopathology, yet standard procedures for assessing, integrating, and classifying dual-factor mental health are lacking (Furlong et al., 2022). Despite the proliferation of measures, few were designed or validated for culturally responsible use (Brann et al., 2022). These limitations pose challenges for MHSPs in identifying appropriate instruments and interpreting assessment results. Future research is needed to investigate the technical properties (e.g., measurement invariance and differential item functioning) of available well-being- and psychopathology-focused instruments with REM youth and populations who have been underrepresented in DFM research (e.g., Latine, Asian American, Pacific Islander, Indigenous, Multiracial). In recognition of the dominant cultural values that underlie common well-being and psychopathology measures, research must also prioritize developing measures that are aligned with culturally bound conceptualizations of mental health and wellness (Krys et al., 2023; Moore et al., 2023).

Dual-factor research has historically prioritized measuring intra-individual factors—indicators of mental health that are "within" an individual or reflect internal states—including subjective well-being, life satisfaction, positive or negative affect, anxiety, depression, or distress. This focus on intra-individual characteristics lends itself to an individualistic approach to service provision that overlooks the impact of social determinants on mental health and may perpetuate mental health inequities (Edyburn et al., 2023). Social determinants of health can be assessed through screening or surveillance efforts, which prioritize collecting data to identify or monitor social, economic, and environmental strengths and needs of individuals or communities to inform intervention (Center for Health and Healthcare in Schools [CHHS] et al., 2021). Thus, in addition to refining measures of intra-individual indicators of well-being and psychopathology, research that develops and applies measures of social determinants of mental health to dual-factor assessment and classification is needed. It will also be important for this research to include a focus on developing measures of culturally specific strengths (e.g., familismo in Latine communities) and of community mental health (Edyburn et al., 2023).

Developing Systems for Multimethod, Multisource Data-Based Decision Making

For assessment results to provide actionable information, processes must be developed to both (1) integrate data across multiple methods and sources of data collection and (2) form mental health status classifications, when relevant and useful for the intended application.

With regards to the first point, the advantages of multimethod, multisource mental health assessment are well-recognized (De Los Reyes et al., 2019). Moreover, multimethod assessment is often required in dual-factor applications, as few existing measures (with limited applications) assess both well-being and psychopathology. Yet, making sense of data collected from multiple methods and sources—let alone using such data to make educational and treatment decisions—can be challenging for MHSPs (McIntosh & Goodman, 2016). For example, MHSPs lack automated methods of synthesizing data collected from multiple sources, such as behavior ratings provided by youth, their caregivers, and their teachers. In addition, the complexity of data integration is compounded by factors specific to dual-factor assessment, chief among them inconsistencies of cut-score approaches across measures combined within a dual-factor framework. These challenges underscore the importance of future research that develops and evaluates user-friendly procedures for integrating multimethod, multisource well-being and psychopathology data.

With regards to the second point, it is not enough to synthesize data; synthesized data must be interpreted in a way that drives educational and treatment-related decision-making (McIntosh & Goodman, 2016). In some assessment contexts, it may be desirable to analyze well-being and psychopathology data to classify youth's mental health status. For example, in educational settings, mental health status may be used as a general outcome criterion describing the "health" of the school or as one piece of information guiding the selection and design of targeted prevention practices (Doll et al., 2021; Moore, Mayworm, et al., 2019). In clinical settings, mental health status may be used to select intervention techniques or initiate the intensification, titration, or discontinuation of services. As previously noted, a variety of theoretically and empirically driven approaches to classification have been demonstrated in the research literature (Thayer et al., 2021); however, the literature is devoid of practical demonstrations of group classification in authentic mental health service settings. Research is needed to develop low-resource classification protocols and tools that demonstrate usability among MHSPs. It will be particularly valuable for such research to be conducted within a participatory action research approach, wherein researchers partner with MHSPs to iteratively develop such classification systems and evaluate these systems within naturalistic contexts.

Expanding Dual-Factor Assessment Applications Beyond Screening

Despite advances in the conceptualization of mental health (e.g., Diener, 2000; Greenspoon & Saklofske, 2001; Suldo & Shaffer, 2008), practical innovations in dual-factor mental health assessment remain in their infancy. To date, published demonstrations of dual-factor assessment with children and adolescents have primarily used lengthy outcome rating scales (e.g., Suldo et al., 2012, 2016) and/or universal screening measures (e.g., Moore, Dowdy, et al., 2019) to classify youths' mental health status, often with the stated objective of examining the DFM's utility within school-based universal screening systems. Beyond this screening application, however, limited attention has been paid to potential applications of dual-factor assessment.

Within schools, progress monitoring represents an important element of data-based decision-making systems (McIntosh & Goodman, 2016), enabling MHSPs to review routinely collected data and tailor supports according to youth's demonstrated responsiveness. Co-monitoring youths' well-being and psychopathology is a logical application of the dual-factor framework, and one with unique potential for guiding intervention adaptations. It is also an un(der)explored area within the dual-factor literature. Although published examples of progress monitoring approaches that align exist, generally, with a dual-factor approach, the studies using them have neither centered the development and evaluation of such an approach nor analyzed the benefits of a dual-factor approach relative to a traditional approach. For example, in one study (Zakszeski et al., 2024), high school students' responsiveness to a Tier 2 mental health intervention was monitored through both (1) students' ratings of the percentage of time, across each week, when they experienced an emotion they aimed to increase (e.g., "happy," "relaxed;" i.e., well-being) and (2) directly observed negative affect and social (dis)engagement (i.e., psychopathology). Thus, this study offers one example of how well-being and psychopathology can be co-monitored during intervention, but it offers no evidence of the advantages of this approach over one that only assesses well-being or psychopathology. Future research may explicitly contrast these approaches to offer additional rationale and potential examples of dual-factor progress monitoring applications.

CONCLUSION

A dual-factor approach transforms traditional assessment to emphasize the importance of well-being and psychopathology in understanding and supporting youths' complete mental health. Integral to the *culturally responsible* dual-factor approach we presented in this chapter is a focus on identifying the systems- and population-level factors that shape mental health and produce inequity, centering individual and community strengths and promoting healing, as well as applying cultural humility and cultural literacy to our work with youth and their families. We contend that integrating a culturally responsible dual-factor approach into routine mental health practice is critical for addressing disparities that result from standard service delivery. A coordinated effort among MHSPs, organizational and community leaders, policymakers, educators/trainers, and researchers—in community with children, adolescents, and their families—is needed to simultaneously redefine the scope of mental health service delivery (e.g., from individual- to community- and population-focused) in alignment with a culturally responsible dual-factor approach.

REFERENCES

Achenbach, T. M., & Rescorla, L. A. (2001). *Manual for the ASEBA school-age forms & profiles*. University of Vermont, Research Center for Children, Youth, & Families.

Antaramian, S. P., Huebner, E. S., Hills, K. J., & Valois, R. F. (2010). A dual-factor model of mental health: Toward a more comprehensive understanding of youth functioning. *American Journal of Orthopsychiatry, 80*(4), 462–472.

Astell-Burt, T., Maynard, M. J., Lenguerrand, E., & Harding, S. (2012). Racism, ethnic density and psychological well-being through adolescence: Evidence from the determinants of adolescent social well-being and health longitudinal study. *Ethnicity & Health, 17*(1–2), 71–87.

Bansal, P. D., & Barman, R. (2011). Psychopathology of school going children in the age group of 10–15 years. *International Journal of Applied and Basic Medical Research, 1*(1), 43–47.

Bitsko, R. H., Claussen, A. H., Lichstein, J., Black, L. I., Jones, S. E., Danielson, M. L., et al. (2022). Mental health surveillance among children—United States, 2013–2019. *Morbidity and Mortality Week Report Supplements, 71*(2), 1–42.

Brann, K. L., Daniels, B., Chafouleas, S. M., & DiOrio, C. (2022). Usability of social, emotional, and behavioral assessments in schools: A systematic review from 2009 to 2019. *School Psychology Review, 51*(1), 6–24.

Center for Health and Health Care in Schools, School-Based Health Alliance, & National Center for School Mental Health. (2021). *Assessing social influencers of health and education*. School Health Services National Quality Initiative. *www.schoolmentalhealth.org/media/som/microsites/ncsmh/documents/fliers-resources-misc-docs/resources/Assessing-Social-Influencers-of-Health-and-Education.pdf*

Chafouleas, S. M., Riley-Tillman, T. C., & Christ, T. J. (2010). *Directions for using a DBR form* [Manual]. University of Connecticut.

Clark, K. N., & Malecki, C. K. (2022). Adolescent mental health profiles through a latent dual-factor approach. *Journal of School Psychology, 91*, 112–128.

Compton, M. T., & Shim, R. S. (2015). The social determinants of mental health. *FOCUS, 13*(4), 419–425.

Crenshaw, K. (1989). Demarginalizing the intersection of race and sex: A Black feminist critique of antidiscrimination doctrine, feminist theory and antiracist politics. *University of Chicago Legal Forum, 1989*(1), 139–167.

Crenshaw, K. (1991). Mapping the margins: Intersectionality, identity politics, and violence against women of color. *Stanford Law Review, 43*(6), 1241–1299.

De Los Reyes, A., Cook, C. R., Gresham, F. M., Makol, B. A., & Wang, M. (2019). Informant discrepancies in assessments of psychosocial functioning in school-based services and research: Review and directions for future research. *Journal of School Psychology, 74*, 74–89.

Diener, E. (2000). Subjective well-being. The science of happiness and a proposal for a national index. *The American Psychologist, 55*(1), 34–43.

Doll, B. (2008). The dual-factor model of mental health in youth. *School Psychology Review, 37*(1), 69–73.

Doll, B., & Cummings, J. A. (2008). *Transforming school mental health services: Population-based approaches to promoting the competency and wellness of children.* Corwin Press.

Doll, B., Dart, E. H., Arora, P. G., & Collins, T. A. (2021). Framing school mental health services within a dual-factor model of mental health. In P. J. Lazarus, S. M. Suldo, & B. Doll (Eds.), *Fostering the emotional well-being of our youth: A school-based approach* (pp. 40–60). Oxford University Press.

Dowdy, E., Kamphaus, R. W., Twyford, J. M., Dever, B. V. (2014). Culturally competent behavioral and emotional screening. In M. Weist, N. Lever, C. Bradshaw, & J. Owens (Eds.), *Handbook of school mental health. Issues in clinical child psychology* (pp. 311–321).

Downey, D. B., & Pribesh, S. (2004). When race matters: Teachers' evaluations of students' classroom behavior. *Sociology of Education, 77*(4), 267–282.

Duong, M. T., Bruns, E. J., Lee, K., Cox, S., Coifman, J., Mayworm, A., & Lyon, A. R. (2021). Rates of mental health service utilization by children and adolescents in schools and other common service settings: A systematic review and meta-analysis. *Administration and Policy in Mental Health and Mental Health Services Research, 48*(3), 420–439.

Edyburn, K. L., Bertone, A., Raines, T. C., Hinton, T., Twyford, J., & Dowdy, E. (2023). Integrating intersectionality, social determinants of health, and healing: A new training framework for school-based mental health. *School Psychology Review, 52*(5), 563–585.

Evans, C. (2021, November 3). *Culturally sensitive, relevant, responsive, and sustaining assessment: Are there limits to making large-scale standardized testing culturally responsive?* The National Center for the Improvement of Educational Assessment, Inc. *www.nciea.org/blog/culturally-sensitive-relevant-responsive-and-sustaining-assessment*

Fisher-Borne, M., Cain, J. M., & Martin, S. L. (2015). From mastery to accountability: Cultural humility as an alternative to cultural competence. *Social Work Education, 34*(2), 165–181.

French, B. H., Lewis, J. A., Mosley, D. V., Adames, H. Y., Chavez-Dueñas, N. Y., Chen, G. A., & Neville, H. A. (2020). Toward a psychological framework of radical healing in communities of color. *The Counseling Psychologist, 48*(1), 14–46.

Furlong, M. J., Dowdy, E., Moore, S., & Kim, E. (2022). Adapting the dual-factor model for universal school-based mental health screening: Bridging the research to practice divide. In K-A. Allen, M. J. Furlong, D. Vella-Brodrick, & S. Suldo (Eds.), *Handbook of positive psychology in schools: In support of positive educational processes* (3rd ed., pp. 56–88). Routledge.

Furlong, M. J., Dowdy, E., Nylund-Gibson, K., Wagle, R., Carter, D., & Hinton, T. (2020). Enhancement and standardization of a universal social-emotional health measure for students' psychological strengths. *Journal of Well-Being Assessment, 4*, 245–267.

Furlong, M. J., You, S., Renshaw, T. L., Smith, D. C., & O'Malley, M. D. (2014). Preliminary development and validation of the Social and Emotional Health Survey for Secondary School Students. *Social Indicators Research, 117*(3), 1011–1032.

Glover, T. A., & Albers, C. A. (2007). Considerations for evaluating universal screening assessments. *Journal of School Psychology, 45*(2), 117–135.

Goforth, A. N., Farmer, R. L., Kim, S. Y., Naser, S. C., Lockwood, A. B., & Affrunti, N. (2021). Status of school psychology in 2020: Part 1 demographics of the NASP membership survey. *NASP Research Reports, 5*, 1–17.

Greenspoon, P. J., & Saklofske, D. H. (2001). Toward an integration of subjective well-being and psychopathology. *Social Indicators Research, 54*, 81–108.

Hays, P. A. (2008). *Addressing cultural complexities in practice: Assessment, diagnosis, and therapy* (2nd ed.). American Psychological Association.

Hook, J. N., Davis, D. E., Owen, J., Worthington, E. L., Jr., & Utsey, S. O. (2013). Cultural humility: Measuring openness to culturally diverse clients. *Journal of Counseling Psychology, 60*(3), 353–366.

Huebner, E. S. (1991). Initial development of the Student's Life Satisfaction Scale. *School Psychology International, 12*(3), 231–240.

Iasiello, M., van Agteren, J., & Cochrane, E. M. (2020). Mental health and/or mental illness: A scoping review of the evidence and implications of the dual-continua model of mental health. *Evidence Base: A Journal of Evidence Reviews in Key Policy Areas, 1*, 1–45.

Jones, J. M. (2009). Counseling with multicultural intentionality: The process of counseling and integrating client cultural variables. In J. M. Jones (Ed.), *The psychology of multiculturalism in schools: A primer for practice, training, and research* (pp. 191–213). National Association of School Psychologists.

Keyes, C. L. M. (2002). The mental health continuum: From languishing to flourishing in life. *Journal of Health and Social Behavior, 43*(2), 207–222.

Keyes, C. L. M. (2005). Mental illness and/or mental health? Investigating axioms of the complete state model of health. *Journal of Consulting and Clinical Psychology, 73*(3), 539–548.

Keyes, C. L. M. (2006). Mental health in adolescence: Is America's youth flourishing? *American Journal of Orthopsychiatry, 76(3)*, 395–402.

Kim, E. K., Dowdy, E., Furlong, M. J., & You, S. (2017). Mental health profiles and quality of life among Korean adolescents. *School Psychology International, 38*(1), 98–116.

Kinderman, P. Tai, S., Pontin, El., Schwannauer, M., Jarman, I., & Lisboa, P. (2015). Causal and mediating factors for anxiety, depression, and well-being. *The British Journal of Psychiatry, 206*(6), 456–460.

Krys, K., Haas, B. W., Igou, E. R., Kosiarczyk, A., Kocimska-Bortnowska, A., Kwiatkowska, A., et al. (2023). Introduction to a culturally sensitive measure of well-being: Combining life satisfaction and interdependent happiness across 49 different cultures. *Journal of Happiness Studies, 24*(2), 607–627.

Lamers, S. M. A., Westerhof, G. J., Bohlmeijer, E. T., ten Klooster, P. M., & Keyes, C. L. M. (2011). Evaluating the psychometric properties of the Mental Health Continuum-Short Form (MHC-SF). *Journal of Clinical Psychology, 67*(1), 99–110.

La Salle, T. P., Wang, C., Wu, C., & Rocha Neves, J. (2020). Racial mismatch among minoritized students and white teachers: Implications and recommendations for moving forward. *Journal of Educational and Psychological Consultation, 30*(3), 314–343.

Laurent, J., Catanzaro, S. J., Joiner, T. E., Jr., Rudolph, K. D., Potter, K. I., Lambert, S., et al. (1999). A measure of positive and negative affect for children: Scale development and preliminary validation. *Psychological Assessment, 11*(3), 326–338.

Lazarus, P. J., Doll, B., Song, S. Y., & Radliff, K. (2022). Transforming school mental health services based on a culturally responsible dual-factor model. *School Psychology Review, 51*(6), 755–770.

Lovibond, S. H., & Lovibond, P. F. (1995). *Manual for the Depression Anxiety Stress Scales*. Psychology Foundation.

Lyons, M. D., Huebner, E. S., & Hills, K. J. (2013). The dual-factor model of mental health: A short-term longitudinal study of school-related outcomes. *Social Indicators Research, 114*(2), 549–565.

Lyons, M. D., Huebner, E. S., Hills, K. J., & Shinkareva, S. V. (2012). The dual-factor model of mental health: Further study of the determinants of group differences. *Canadian Journal of School Psychology, 27*(2), 183–196.

Mathews, G., & Izquierdo, C. (2008). *Pursuits of happiness: Well-being in anthropological perspective*. Berghahn Books.

McIntosh, K., & Goodman, S. (2016). *Integrating multi-tiered systems of support: Blending RTI and PBIS*. Guilford Press.

Moore, S. A., Dowdy, E., Nylund-Gibson, K., & Furlong, M. J. (2019). An empirical approach to complete mental health classification in adolescents. *School Mental Health, 11*(3), 438–453.

Moore, S. A., Long, A. C., Coyle, S., Cooper, J. M., Mayworm, A. M., Amirazizi, S., et al. (2023). A roadmap to equitable school mental health screening. *Journal of School Psychology, 96*, 57–74.

Moore, S. A., Mayworm, A. M., Stein, R., Sharkey, J. D., & Dowdy, E. (2019). Languishing students: Linking complete mental health screening in schools to Tier II intervention. *Journal of Applied School Psychology, 35*(3), 257–289.

Moore, S. A., Widales-Benitez, O., Carnazzo, K. W., Kim, E. K., Moffa, K., & Dowdy, E. (2015). Conducting universal complete mental health screening via student self-report. *Contemporary School Psychology, 19*(4), 253–267.

Myers, D. G., & Diener, E. (1995). Who is happy? *Psychological Science, 6*(1), 10–19.

Naples, L. H., & Tuckwiller, E. D. (2021). Taking students on a strengths' safari: A multidimensional pilot study of school-based wellbeing for young neurodiverse children. *International Journal of Environmental Research and Public Health, 18*(13), 6947.

Nickerson, A. B., & Fishman, C. E. (2013). Promoting mental health and resilience through strengths-based assessment in US schools. *Educational & Child Psychology, 30*(4), 7–17.

Peterson, K. J., Humphrey, N., & Qualter, P. (2020). Latent class analysis of mental health in middle childhood: Evidence for the dual-factor model. *School Mental Health, 12*, 786–800.

Proctor, S. L., Kyle, J., Fefer, K., & Lau, C. (2018). Examining racial microaggressions, race/ethnicity, gender, and bilingual status with school psychology students: The role of intersectionality. *Contemporary School Psychology, 22*(3), 355–368.

Renshaw, T. L., Long, A. C. J., & Cook, C. R. (2015). Assessing adolescents' positive psychological functioning at school: Development and validation of the Student Subjective Wellbeing Questionnaire. *School Psychology Quarterly, 30*(4), 534–552.

Reynolds, C. R., & Kamphaus, R. W. (2015). *Behavior Assessment System for Children* (3rd ed.). Pearson.

Sabnis, S. V., & Proctor, S. L. (2021). Use of critical theory to develop a conceptual framework for critical school psychology. *School Psychology Review, 51*(6), 661–675.

Seligman, M. E. P. (1999). The president's address. *The American Psychologist, 54*(8), 559–562.

Shim, R., Koplan, C., Langheim, F. J. P., Manseau, M. W., Powers, R. A., & Compton, M. T. (2014). The social determinants of mental health: An overview and call to action. *Psychiatric Annals, 44*(1), 22–26.

Smith, N. D. W., Suldo, S., M., Hearon, B. V., & Ferron, J. M. (2020). An application of the dual-factor model of mental health in elementary school children: Examining academic and social outcomes. *Journal of Positive Psychology & Wellbeing, 4*(1), 49–68. *https://journalppw.com/index.php/jppw/article/view/61*

Sue, D. W., Sue, D., Neville, H. A., & Smith, L. (2019). *Counseling the culturally diverse: Theory and practice* (8th ed.). Wiley.

Suldo, S., & Doll, B. (2021). Conceptualizing youth mental health through a dual-factor model. In P. J. Lazarus, S. Suldo, & B. Doll (Eds.), *Fostering the emotional well-being of our nation's youth: A school-based approach* (pp. 20–39). Oxford University Press.

Suldo, S. M., McMahan, M. M., Chappel, A. M., & Loker, T. (2012). Relationships between perceived school climate and adolescent mental health across genders. *School Mental Health, 4*, 69–80.

Suldo, S. M., & Shaffer, E. J. (2008). Looking beyond psychopathology: The dual-factor model of mental health in youth. *School Psychology Review, 37*(1), 52–68.

Suldo, S., Thalji, A., & Ferron, J. (2011). Longitudinal academic outcomes predicted by early adolescents' subjective well-being, psychopathology, and mental health status yielded from a dual factor model. *The Journal of Positive Psychology*, 6(1), 17–30.

Suldo, S. M., Thalji-Raitano, A., Kiefer, S. M., & Ferron, J. M. (2016). Conceptualizing high school students' mental health through a dual-factor model. *School Psychology Review*, *45*(4), 434–457.

Sullivan, A. L., Artiles, A. J., & Hernandez-Saca, D. I. (2015). Addressing special education inequity through systemic change: Contributions of ecologically based organizational consultation. *Journal of Educational and Psychological Consultation*, *25*(2–3), 129–147.

Sullivan, A., Arora, P., Song, S. Y., & Jimerson, S. R. (2023). Theory, methods, and practice to advance equity and social justice in school psychology: Articulating a path forward. *School Psychology Review*, *52*(5), 493–503.

Terjesen, M. D., Jacofsky, M., Froh, J., & DiGiuseppe, R. (2004). Integrating positive psychology into schools: Implications for practice. *Psychology in the Schools*, *41*(1), 163–172.

Thayer, A. J., Weeks, M. R., & Cook, C. R. (2021). Dual factor mental health model: Validation through mixture modeling and cut scores. *Psychology in the Schools*, *58*(2), 286–306.

WHO Newsroom. (2022, June 17). *Mental health*. World Health Organization. *www.who.int/news-room/fact-sheets/detail/mental-health-strengthening-our-response*

Zakszeski, B. N., Cain, M., Eklund, K., Heurich, A., Friedman, R., Ward, A., & Zhou, J. (2024). Pilot evaluation of the POWER Program: Positive Outcomes with Emotion Regulation. *School Mental Health*, *16*, 387–402.

CHAPTER 6

Assessment for Schools and Clinical Settings

Ellen W. Rowe, Nicole M. Beadles, and Danielle R. Palmer

Practitioners work with a diverse array of individuals in both school and clinical settings. According to the National Center for Education Statistics (2023), in public schools, between 2010 and 2021 the percentage of White and Black children decreased, and the percentage of Latino, Asian, and those who identify as two or more races increased. This mirrored the changes from the 2010 to 2020 census, where nearly all groups saw population gains apart from the "White-alone" group, which dropped by 8.6% (U.S. Census Bureau, 2021). As our society continues to become increasingly diverse, with a multitude of cultures, ethnicities, and languages, the consideration of culture in the work of clinicians becomes vital. Furthermore, to be a competent practitioner, it is essential to understand culturally informed assessment practices (Sattler, 2022).

Despite our increasingly diverse population, education and health care in the United States have been and continue to be systems marked by bias, racism, and structural inequities (Grapin & Proctor, 2023). For instance, in the realm of mental health assessment, Liang et al. (2016) found evidence of misdiagnoses of emotional and behavioral issues for minoritized youth. In our current educational systems, students from marginalized backgrounds are more likely to attend schools with substantial numbers of students who live in poverty (Castillo & Abiola, 2023). Black students are more likely to receive exclusionary discipline than their White peers and are often perceived as less academically capable, more troublesome, and more defiant than other students. Moreover, Black students are significantly more likely to be found eligible for special education under the category of "emotional disturbance" (ED) than their White peers (U.S. Department of Education, 2021). Finally, opportunity gaps remain for many students from marginalized or intersectional backgrounds or identities, including students with disabilities (Castillo & Abiola, 2023).

The recognition of past and continuing inequity and injustices for minoritized youth in educational and healthcare settings has led to a significant increase in the focus, training, professional development, and research on culturally informed approaches to behavioral and educational assessments. Across schools and clinical settings, many similarities and differences exist in the use and application of culturally informed approaches, which are covered in depth elsewhere in this text (e.g., Chapter 3, this volume). Nonetheless, this chapter begins with a brief review of broad, culturally informed approaches to child and adolescent assessment that allow us to contextualize a comparison of school and clinical practices. Next, the chapter considers the general correspondence between the assessment processes and environments of schools versus clinical settings with specific attention to the degree to which the likenesses and differences may impact culturally informed approaches. We emphasize the word *general* in the previous sentence, as the use of culturally informed practices can vary from practitioner to practitioner, regardless of setting. The subsequent section will compare assessment practices with the *Diagnostic and Statistical Manual of Mental Disorders, Fifth Edition, Text Revision* (DSM-5-TR; American Psychiatric Association, 2022), which is typically used in clinical assessments, and the Individuals with Disabilities Education Improvement Act (IDEA, 2004), which sets forth standards for students' eligibility for special education and services in public schools. The DSM-5-TR and IDEA comparison emphasizes the degree to which the DSM and IDEA have or have not accounted for cultural considerations in diagnosis or special education eligibility. Following the discussion of the DSM and IDEA, we provide an example of an area of educational eligibility—ED—in which greater culturally informed approaches are warranted. The chapter concludes with ways in which clinical and school-based assessments and treatments have the potential for greater overlap.

CULTURALLY INFORMED ASSESSMENT APPROACHES

Regardless of setting, the first step in engaging in culturally informed assessment is an examination and consideration of the bias and marginalization that remain in our country and educational systems, as well as the bias that exits in our personal world views (Eklund & Jones, 2021; Goforth & Pham, 2023; Grapin & Proctor, 2023). Another fundamental component of culturally informed assessment is the development of an interpersonal, relational partnership with the student and the student's family or caregiver (Eklund & Jones, 2021; Goforth & Pham, 2023).

One consideration at the outset of all assessments regardless of setting is the question of "what is being asked" (Barrett et al., 2020). As Goforth and Pham (2023) point out, the goal of an assessment should always be to inform intervention or outcomes for students. One means of facilitating an assessment oriented toward intervention is by using a strengths-based approach. Assessing strengths allows the practitioner to consider protective factors or traits that can foster resiliency (Jimerson et al., 2004). A contrast to a strengths-based perspective is the tendency for educators to view student challenges from a medically oriented, deficit perspective. An example of this is when students who are learning English for the first time are viewed as having academic deficiencies instead of having the advantage of becoming bilingual (Castillo & Abiola, 2023). Strength-based reports that include opportunities for student growth, existing services that support the student's growth, and student assets can provide a broader understanding of the student (Climie & Henley, 2016). Additionally, strength-based approaches can examine contextual and environmental background factors, which may be critical in yielding valid assessments for students from marginalized backgrounds.

Interviews and conversations are one means for practitioners and related professionals to recognize and appreciate a family's and student's cultural identity and heritage, values, beliefs, adverse events, developmental history, views of health, family moves, and strengths (Barrett et al., 2020; Eklund & Jones, 2021; Goforth & Pham, 2023). It is worth noting that a "typical" interview is unlikely to provide the information needed for a culturally informed assessment (Eklund & Jones, 2021). For practitioners who do not have an established culturally responsive interview, many examples are available. For example, Goforth and Pham (2023) suggest a relational interview format for caregivers, and Jones (2009) published the Jones Intentional Multicultural Interview Schedule (JIMIS). The American Psychiatric Association (2013) provided the Cultural Formulation Interview (CFI) at no charge for use with individuals from diverse backgrounds. Further information regarding the CFI is presented in the DSM section of this chapter.

Second-Language Considerations

Given the role that background, culture, and language play in school functioning and assessment, an interview with the family/caregiver(s) and student is an essential, early component of engagement with students who are culturally and/or linguistically diverse (CLD; Barret et al. 2020; Goforth & Pham, 2023; Vega & Wolf, 2023). Some school systems have their own interviews or interview guidelines for CLD families (Barrett et al., 2020). Additionally, to practice in a culturally informed manner, practitioners must be knowledgeable about expected acculturation and second-language development, yet also cognizant of the fact that "typical" development in second-language acquisition and acculturation is broad and can be influenced by a multitude of factors (Barrett et al., 2020; Goforth & Pham, 2023; Ortiz, 2023). For acculturation, various scales or measures exist for specific cultural backgrounds, but as alluded to in the last sentence, acculturation is a complex and multifaceted concept (Goforth & Pham, 2023).

Likewise, information about language development is not straightforward. Even students who were born in this country or who arrived at the same time may have very different exposure to educational experiences and English language (Ortiz, 2023; Vega & Wolf, 2023). Another culturally informed practice for CLD students is a language assessment to determine the student's language proficiency (Barrett et al., 2020; Vega & Wolf, 2023). In 41 U.S. states, the World-Class Instructional Design and Assessment (WIDA; 2020) Assessing Comprehension and Communication in English State-to-State for English Language Learners (ACCESS) can be administered annually at school to students in first through twelfth grade to provide data on English proficiency. Other tests that yield a measure of language proficiency are the Woodcock–Johnson IV Tests of Oral Language (WJ IV OL; Mather & Wendling, 2014) and the Woodcock–Muñoz Language Survey (WMLS III; Woodcock et al., 2017). The WJ IV OL consists of nine subtests in English, three of which have parallel tests in Spanish. All four of the WMLS III subtests have English and Spanish forms. An ideal language assessment measures a student's proficiency both in their native language and in English (Sandberg & Reschly, 2011). Language assessments that integrate testing results, interview information, classroom products, observations, and multiple sources of information are best practice (Vega & Wolf, 2023). Knowledge of language proficiency in the student's native language is useful in thinking about language development generally and can determine the dominant language. In turn, this information allows practitioners to consider approaches to assessment that yield the most reliable and valid information (Barrett et al., 2019; Vega & Wolf, 2023). Furthermore, an understanding of proficiency in both languages may contribute to intervention strategies.

Trauma-Informed Approaches

Another dimension of culturally responsive assessment is a trauma-informed approach. There has been a growing realization that many students in the United States and throughout the world experience traumatizing events in childhood (Tishelman et al., 2010). In fact, Copeland et al. (2007) found that more than two-thirds of students acknowledged at least one traumatic incident by the age of 16. The rate of trauma among minoritized students is likely higher (Kisiel et al., 2021). Many students who undergo traumatic events go on to develop posttraumatic stress disorder (PTSD; Woolgar et al., 2022). Moreover, experiencing trauma in childhood may result in a myriad of other symptoms that resemble those of bipolar disorder, attention-deficit/hyperactivity disorder (ADHD), oppositional defiant disorder, learning problems, depression, anxiety, attachment disorder, and others (National Center on Safe Supportive Learning Environments, n.d.). Given the potential for exposure to trauma and the sequelae, attention to the possible role of trauma is critical for an accurate assessment.

As with most assessments, best practice in assessing trauma is an approach that includes various methods with multi-informants (Kisiel et al., 2021). In considering trauma, practitioners can review records, conduct interviews, and administer rating scales that assess trauma, PTSD, anxiety, or other symptom categories. All three methods have the potential to provide different types of information. As with other aspects of culturally informed assessment, the review of student records should focus on culture (Eklund & Jones, 2021; Goforth & Pham, 2023). Likewise, a culturally informed interview allows practitioners to gain knowledge of the traumatic incident(s), the student's emotional reactions and perspectives, as well as coping strategies the student has employed (Goforth & Pham, 2023). While a culturally informed interview can provide rich information, well-researched, standardized assessments allow practitioners to obtain data on similar questions across multiple individuals in the student's life. Kisiel et al. (2021) offer a list (pp. 91–93) and brief review (pp. 98–104) of trauma assessment measures for children and adolescents.

Performance- and Curriculum-Based Assessment

A final method of culturally informed assessment includes collecting data about students' skills or progress from sources other than standardized tests. Two approaches discussed in the literature are performance-based assessment and curriculum-based assessment (Goforth & Pham, 2023). With performance-based assessment, a teacher or practitioner evaluates the student's performance in a manner that can be more authentic than a standardized test. Common approaches to performance-based assessments include portfolios or project-based tasks. Both performance-based assessments and curriculum-based measures (CBMs) have the potential to confront some of the concerns with standardized assessments such as normative data that do not reflect the student being assessed (Sandberg & Reschly, 2011).

Furthermore, results from a series of CBMs administered over time allow the practitioner to consider growth as opposed to a single measure at one point in time (De Ramírez & Shapiro, 2006). In some instances, the rate and degree of skill growth may provide a better picture of the nature of student needs (Sandberg & Reschly, 2011). This type of ongoing measurement also allows for feedback on instructional effectiveness and fits well with a problem-solving, response to intervention (RTI), or multi-tiered systems of support (MTSS) model of education (Marcotte & McKenzie, 2023). As Barrett (2023) points out, RTI hybrid approaches are increasing in popularity and use for the identification of students with specific learning disabilities (SLD). One RTI hybrid approach proposed by Fletcher et al. (2019) recommends beginning with intervention. Only students who do not respond to intervention are considered for an assessment. Even then, Fletcher et al. advocate against the habitual use of IQ tests for identifying SLD. Barrett also highlights research that found that RTI models have the potential to reduce disproportionality in special education. At the same time, research on CBMs with CLD students is limited, and many questions remain. For example, do preliminary results hold for different languages, and how to capture the variety of educational experience and language exposure for CLD students? Moreover, the rate of growth in student skills must be compared with that of students who have similar educational experiences and general development, and finding this type of data can be a challenge (Ortiz, 2023).

COMPARISON OF CLINIC- AND SCHOOL-BASED ASSESSMENTS

Following this review of several culturally informed assessment practices, the chapter now turns to a comparison of school-based and clinical assessments. A foundational similarity among psychologists who conduct assessments, regardless of context, is a commitment to abide by a code of conduct or ethics. The two most common codes for practitioners engaged in assessment are the American Psychological Association's (APA) *Ethical Principles and Codes of Conduct* (APA, 2017) and the National Association of School Psychologists (NASP) *Principles for Professional Ethics* (NASP, 2020). Both codes address culturally informed practice. For example, the APA's *General Principles* explicitly admonish psychologists to consider and attempt to overcome their own biases, to acknowledge and accept individual differences in culture, and to acquire training or supervision regarding the impact of culture upon their work (APA, 2017). NASP includes the guiding principle of "fairness, equity, and justice" (NASP, 2020, p. 44). In abiding by NASP *Principles*, psychologists who work in schools are expected to promote schools "that are safe, welcoming, and equitable" (NASP, 2020, p. 44) to all students and their families. School psychologists are obligated to advocate against discriminatory activities or policies and to attempt to assure that all students have equal opportunities for school activities and services, including access to school psychologists.

In addition to the general principles, both codes of conduct address culturally informed approaches to assessment (APA, 2017; NASP, 2020). The APA *Ethical Standards* have specific guidelines on the use of interpreters in assessments, selections of tests and methods, as well as interpretation of assessment results (APA, 2017). Likewise, Section II.3 of the NASP *Professional Standards* (2020) includes recommendations on instrument selection, normative data, use of interpreters, as well as the validity and reliability of the tests and assessment methods for the student being assessed.

Another similarity among most practitioners, regardless of context, is employing a multimethod, multi-informant approach to assessment. In other words, practitioners typically consider information from various assessment techniques such as interviews, observations, standardized assessment measures, or samples of student schoolwork (multimethod) as well as collecting information from multiple individuals who know the student (multisource) (American Educational Research Association et al., 2014; see also NASP, 2020). This approach to assessment allows practitioners to obtain a clearer picture of all students. Given challenges of child and adolescent assessment generally, as well as the potential complexities for students from marginalized backgrounds, a multimethod, multi-informant approach seems mandatory for culturally informed assessment (Armistead & Clyne, 2023). In both clinics and schools, this comprehensive approach allows for trauma-informed and strengths-based assessments for students.

A difference that exists between clinical and school-based assessments is the availability in schools for broader methods and more adults who know the student. For example, almost all school-based assessments include classroom observations. School practitioners can observe the student in several classes, on several days, as well as during lunch or recess. All of these observations can provide distinct types of direct information about the student such as engagement with peers, antecedents and consequences of behavior, and language use. In contrast, clinic-based assessments tend to have mainly assessment observations during the testing. Although clinical assessments usually include information about the student from a teacher or the primary classroom teacher, school-based assessments can include information from multiple school personnel including a current teacher, teachers of different subjects, English as a second language (ESL) teachers, and even previous teachers. Having the input of multiple teachers allows school-based practitioners to consider students from many perspectives.

Additionally, school-based assessments have access to a broad array of educational data to inform the assessment. With the advent of RTI and MTSS, schools frequently deliver preventative or intervention services before a formal school assessment. School-based data from these prevention or intervention strategies are a vital component of the RTI or MTSS process (Castillo & Abiola, 2023). Data from these strategies and services can inform the assessment, and such data are often a determining factor of whether a school-based assessment is warranted. For most schools to conduct an assessment, the student concern must manifest with a noticeable educational impact. The impact need not be purely academic in nature, but assessing an effect on school performance is typically a consideration for school-based assessment.

It is worth pointing out that some student difficulties may not be obvious at school, and educators may not recognize the impact. An example may be a student with symptoms such as anxiety or depression. If these symptoms impact school functioning leading to school refusal or significant test anxiety, the school may consider an assessment to gather additional information. On the other hand, if the condition does not have a clear impact on the student at school, educators may not consider an assessment. In contrast, clinical assessments outside of schools usually occur with a simple referral from a caregiver, and preliminary attempts at intervention may or may not have been implemented. Furthermore, the requirement of educational impact is not a necessity for clinic-based assessment.

If a student's concern is academic, the prevention or intervention data often consist of CBMs. Many school-based practitioners also regularly administer CBMs as a component of their assessment. This allows school-based assessments to incorporate more authentic assessments and to interpret some assessment results without comparison to normative data that may not reflect the student being assessed. Of course, parents can always provide data from the school interventions or school-administered CBMs to clinical practitioners. Moreover, clinical practitioners have access to CBM materials on Lite Edition easyCBM (*www.easycbm.com*; Alonzo et al., 2006) or the University of Oregon's Dynamic Indicators of Basic Early Literacy Skills (DIBELS; *https://dibels.uoregon.edu*; University of Oregon, 2021) at no cost. Nonetheless, clinical practitioners tend to rely more on standardized assessment tests and less on CBMs or other more authentic or performance-based data.

Another source of data available to most school practitioners are the results from language assessments. As mentioned previously, Local Educational Agencies (LEAs) in over 80% of U.S. states can administer WIDA language assessment annually to students who are learning English as a second language. While each of the WIDA domains (listening, speaking, reading, and writing) have different scales, practitioners can compare scale scores within the domains over time to consider English language acquisition. At the same time, Barrett et al. (2020) remind practitioners to be careful about comparisons between students because many factors affect second-language development. In addition to WIDA, some LEAs provide an individualized dual language assessment at no cost (Barrett et al., 2020). If the school-based or clinical practitioner does not have access to dual language assessment results or WIDA scores, both the WJ IV OL (Mather & Wendling, 2014) and the WMLS III (Woodcock et al., 2017) provide information on English and Spanish proficiency. While information about English language can be obtained in interviews, concrete knowledge of English skills in different domains is essential for a valid assessment of an ESL student regardless of the setting.

Some of the most essential differences between school and clinical assessments relate to the school context. All students who demonstrate noticeable difficulties with school performance or whose parents have concerns can be considered for a school-based assessment at no cost. School assessments occur at school, so transportation is not a concern. However, clinical assessments typically occur with a fee (at times a considerable fee) and take place at a clinic or private practice setting. As a result, transportation must be arranged to and from the evaluation spot. Additionally, some clinical assessment settings have a waiting list for assessments, so the assessment cannot begin for weeks or months. Once the decision to evaluate the students has been made in a school, the assessment does not typically begin immediately, but most LEAs have state deadlines of approximately 45 to 60 days to complete the evaluation and provide feedback to the parents at a meeting to which parents are invited. The Individuals with Disabilities Education Improvement Act (2004) specifies a 60-day timeline for schools.

A further resource that LEAs or schools try to provide is an interpreter. While LEAs may not have access to interpreters in every language, they often have referral lists of trained interpreters. Likewise, bilingual school personnel can assist with interviews and even be trained to participate in some aspects of an assessment. Clinical practitioners too may have access to bilingual staff who can be trained as interpreters for interviews or parts of an assessment. In both settings, using an interpreter with a published assessment instrument represents a break in standardization and should be documented in the report.

Another important difference between clinical and school-based assessments is the role of the psychologist or practitioner. In school-based assessments, the school psychologist is the expert on assessment, and the approach is team-based. The team typically consists of an administrator, the school psychologist, and other school professionals such as the teacher, a special education teacher or intervention specialist, the school speech pathologist, and a school counselor and/or social worker. Different professionals from the team may also administer different components of the assessment for which they have training. For instance, a special education teacher might administer a standardized achievement test, and a social worker or counselor may conduct the caregiver/family interview. Moreover, various members of the team may contribute to the final assessment report, particularly if they were responsible for a component of the assessment. Just as the assessment process in schools is a team approach, so is the decision making about whether the student qualifies for special education. The decision is made by "the team."

While a team approach allows for different perspectives of the student and the potential for varied forms of input and data, there may be drawbacks in team functions and decisions. For example, individual team members can be affected by their own implicit biases regarding minoritized individuals or families, and all team members may not have engaged in challenging their assumptions (Barrett, 2023; Girvan et al., 2017). Likewise, team members may have a tendency toward deficit-based perspectives, where the problem resides within the student (Castillo & Abiola, 2023). Deficit-based models were present in schools for decades, and this perspective may be naturally engrained among educators, teams, and processes in schools. Finally, it can feel overwhelming and intimidating for families or caregivers to meet with many different individuals, particularly if the parents/caregivers are not familiar with U.S. school policies or had unpleasant experiences in schools themselves. Of course, all team members in a school-based setting may have a long-term, relational partnership with parents, but it can be easy to assume that the role of establishing that partnership rests with another team professional.

In clinical settings, the psychologist is often the expert on assessment. Although some clinical practitioners may have a psychometrist who conducts portions of the testing, in many settings, the psychologist conducts all the testing. Furthermore, the psychologist will almost always interview the family/caregivers and the student being assessed. Relatedly, after reviewing the data and writing the report, it is the psychologist who decides whether the student meets criteria for a diagnosis. For clinical psychologists who practice in a culturally informed manner, the one-on-one context of the assessment can lend itself to a trusting partnership and culturally informed practice. Naturally, the extent to which this happens rests with the psychologist. At the same time, psychologists in clinical and school settings may use continuing education as an opportunity to learn more about culturally informed approaches such as those described in this text.

A final difference between school- and clinic-based assessment is the immediate goal and outcome of the assessment. Although the overarching goal of all assessments, regardless of context, is to inform treatment, the criteria and mechanisms in the two settings are different. In clinical settings, psychologists determine whether the client meets criteria for a diagnosis, and the diagnostic criteria are established by DSM-5 TR. In turn, the diagnosis informs treatment. In schools, the criteria for access to services in the school setting are established via IDEA.

CULTURAL CONSIDERATIONS IN ASSESSMENT USING THE DSM AND IDEA

In this section of the chapter, two systems of classification in the fields of psychology and education will be discussed in relation to culture: DSM-5-TR and IDEA. DSM-5-TR is used by professionals across disciplines to diagnose specific mental health disorders in clinic settings. Criteria set forth in IDEA allow school-based professionals to determine whether school-age children qualify for special education services under 14 different categories of disability. While IDEA is solely used in public schools and DSM-5-TR is mainly used in clinics, the DSM can also be used in school settings by school psychologists (Tobin & House, 2016).

Through the process of assessment, either in schools or clinical settings, the practitioner strives to connect with the children and families who seek services to build rapport, understand their concerns, and accurately assess, categorize/diagnose, and develop interventions or treat the individuals he/she serves. Whether in schools or clinics, assessment is often done for classification (diagnosis or eligibility), enabling clients to obtain the proper services and treatment. Classification of disorders through assessment allows the provision of better-informed care, which can include special education services in the schools, therapy, or medication in clinic-based environments.

Throughout the early iterations of the DSM, the idea of culture was relatively absent, perhaps as it was not considered a relevant factor in diagnostic classification. Leading up to the passage of IDEA in 1975, schools were grappling with legislation regarding discrimination of minority students, misclassifying them as intellectually disabled or emotionally disturbed and providing unequal education. Given this, some safeguards were put in place within IDEA to recognize the importance of culture in the evaluation process (Jacob et al., 2022).

Brief Background of Cultural Considerations in the Development of the DSM

The discipline of psychiatry has not always considered the cultural aspect of an individual's presenting problems when applying criteria to formulate diagnoses. The DSM is the main referral source for psychiatric diagnoses (Kawa & Giordano, 2012), and only in the last two editions has it contained commentary and information on culturally relevant considerations for diagnostic categories (Good, 1996). Prior to the first edition of the DSM, the field of psychiatry was primarily working under a medical understanding of disease and disorder, and classification was primarily used in psychiatric hospitals and institutions with severely mentally ill patients (Kawa & Giordino, 2012). However, by the time the first DSM was published in 1952, the field of psychiatry was theoretically oriented toward psychodynamic understanding of disorders (Surís et al., 2016), and the DSM was being used with the general public who were presenting with less severe mental health concerns.

Neither the medical model nor the psychodynamic orientation of the early DSM editions was seen as culturally sensitive. In discussing the shift of DSM-III as it relates to cross-cultural application, Good (1992) critiques the medical model of diagnosis as being too reductionist with no consideration given for the social context or cultural meanings of disorder. Good also claims that the older psychoanalytic perspective was no better, being diagnostically unreliable and ethnocentrically aligned with middle class American culture. In stitching together an understanding, Good (1992) opined that while the biology of some illnesses may be more powerful than others, psychological patterns and factors like coping styles, inequities in access, and the meaning of illness attributed by a society and culture play a role in shaping the development of *all* forms of illness.

Early research on the use of the DSM with minoritized populations in clinic settings highlights the dangers of ignoring culture when making psychological diagnoses. Good (1992) summarized the literature documenting the misdiagnosis of Black and Hispanic patients using structured diagnostic interviewing for DSM-III and DSM-III-R. Major differences by race and ethnic group in rates and patterns of hospitalization and diagnoses were found, leading to ineffective psychotropic treatments, rehospitalizations, and negative impacts on life trajectories. For example, Good called attention to the overdiagnosis of schizophrenia and underdiagnosis of affective disorders in African Americans. Good made a call for more research to be conducted into the cross-cultural validity of diagnostic categories. In essence, his words suggest that if psychiatry is to be reliably practiced in a community setting with individuals who are not White, middle-upper class, and educated, the research that influences this practice should include all of society. In a later article, Good (1996) asserted that psychopathology is a social and cultural construct. When culture is not considered, what's at stake is "the care of the most disadvantaged members of American society" (p. 4).

Concerns regarding the use of the DSM with minoritized populations in clinic settings persisted. In their article on cultural, racial and ethnic competence in diagnosis, Bell et al. (2008) cite research indicating a higher percentage of Black individuals are diagnosed with paranoia when compared to White individuals, possibly due to cultural mistrust resulting from the Black experience in the United States. This would be in line with what Whaley and Geller (2003) describe as the sociocultural hypothesis of bias in diagnosis. In essence, paranoid symptoms are more prevalent among disadvantaged individuals due to their lived experiences. However, additional hypotheses explaining diagnostic bias include self-selection (certain groups of individuals wait until symptoms are severe before seeking treatment), social-selection bias (diagnosis is influenced by stereotypical perceptions of certain groups), and clinician bias (misdiagnosis is influenced by lack of familiarity or incorrect application of diagnostic criteria) (Whaley & Geller, 2003).

Similar findings have occurred in clinical work with young people. Liang et al. (2016) examined the literature regarding psychiatric misdiagnosis of racial/ethnic minority youth and the processes and cultural factors that could contribute to it, if present. Liang et al. (2016) concluded that diagnoses in treatment settings indicate racial/ethnic disparities. African American youth receive more diagnoses of psychotic and disruptive disorders and fewer mood and substance use disorder diagnoses. Latin American youth were more frequently diagnosed with substance use and disruptive disorders, and less often diagnosed with ADHD. Asian American/Pacific Islander youth had mixed patterns but seemed to receive more diagnoses of ADHD than other youth. Not enough research was available to study differences for Native American youth.

Liang et al. (2016) explain that while differences in diagnoses of youth across ethnic groups were noted, the presence of many variables affecting these patterns made it difficult to draw solid conclusions as to why this was occurring. The researchers mentioned that variability of results could have been due to variations in treatment settings where the research took place, the help seeking behaviors of the populations studied, the variety of and criteria used to make the diagnoses, and differences in control variables used in the studies. They further mentioned that prevalence rates of diagnoses are typically determined with rigorous diagnostic criteria and research protocols. With diagnostic decision making in clinic settings, many more sources of error exist, including less well-defined and more variable diagnostic criteria from setting to setting, bias in practitioner judgment, disagreement between multiple informants, and so forth. It would appear that many of the same issues plaguing diagnosis of culturally diverse adults impact work with adolescents, as well.

Given the early research highlighting discrepancies in diagnoses when working with culturally diverse individuals in clinic settings, an effort to enhance the cultural validity of DSM-IV started to take shape. In the 1990s, a scholarly independent workgroup convened with the aim of integrating the significance of culture into diagnostic practices (Mezzich et al., 1999). Spearheaded by the steering committee of the National Institute of Mental Health (NIMH) Group on Culture, Diagnosis, and Care, operating independently from the DSM workgroups, the committee sought to address the necessity of cultural sensitivity in diagnosis. As Mezzich et al. (1999) articulate, "Cultural sensitivity implies an understanding of the social and cultural context of the individual under examination to determine the applicability of diagnostic criteria and formulate a suitable differential diagnosis" (p. 6). The focus of the group was to enhance cultural relevance across various facets of the DSM, including its introduction, specific disorders, and the multiaxial framework utilized for diagnoses, with particular attention given to explaining culture-bound syndromes. Among the significant proposals was the introduction of a standard Outline for Cultural Formulation (OCF), which ultimately was embedded in the ninth appendix of DSM-IV. The OCF was aimed at facilitating person-centered diagnostic and treatment planning decisions for individuals from minoritized cultures.

The OCF comprised four domains: (1) cultural identity of the individual; (2) cultural explanation of illness; (3) cultural interpretation of psychosocial stressors, supports, and levels of functioning; and (4) the cultural elements of the patient-clinician relationship. These domains were intended to be integrated into the cultural formulation, made by the practitioner to better understand the individual, enhance rapport, and aid in diagnostic decision making. The OCF signaled a shift toward a more holistic and culturally informed approach to diagnosis. Although the cultural additions to DSM-IV were not as extensive as the group initially envisioned, the introduction of culturally sensitive diagnostic decision-making processes marked a significant milestone. It was hoped to have a far-reaching impact beyond isolated cases where cultural factors were prominent (Mezzich & Caracci, 2008). The OCF was a pivotal step in acknowledging and incorporating cultural diversity in psychiatric and psychological practice.

The OCF enhanced clinical practice in some ways but had its limitations. There is a large body of work that documents the use of the OCF in populations around the world in various clinical settings, noting its strengths and limitations (for a review, see Lewis-Fernández et al., 2014). The results of a handful of studies are provided here to elucidate some of the main points. Kirmayer et al. (2003) evaluated services provided by a cultural consultation service where cultural misunderstandings were common. These cultural misunderstandings led to incomplete assessments, incorrect diagnosis, inappropriate or inadequate treatment, and failed treatment alliances. Using the OCF led clinicians to reassess or change treatment, use an additional treatment, or change the diagnosis. Caballero (2009) documented strengths and limitations of using the OCF with 75 cases at a clinic in Spain. Its use reduced basic errors in diagnosis and treatment, improved communication between practitioners and clients, and improved adherence to treatment, among other things. Limitations included the time it took to administer, the lack of standardized administration procedures (and tendency to be influenced by the practitioner's theoretical orientation), and a lack of connection between the cultural formulation and other aspects of clinical assessment. More recently, Kirmayer et al. (2014) used the cultural formulation with 406 cases in a clinical setting, which resulted in a change of diagnosis in 61% of cases.

Though the OCF was an important step forward in applying cultural considerations to clinical work, the difficulties and limitations noted in its use were of concern. Consequently, the OCF was revised by the DSM-5 Cross Cultural Issues Subgroup (DCCIS) to prepare for publication in DSM-5 (Lewis-Fernández et al., 2014). The goal of the revision was "to create an assessment tool that promotes increased uptake among clinicians and can be administered in diverse clinical settings and countries by providers with a range of training and experience" (Aggarwal et al., 2020, p. 497). Consequently, the DCCIS revised the OCF and developed the Cultural Formulation Interview (CFI). The CFI included implementation instructions and standardized questions, which were intended to remedy some of the difficulties noted by those using the OCF (Aggarwal et al., 2020). The result was a 16-item semistructured assessment to be used by a practitioner with their client. The CFI was published in DSM-5 (American Psychiatric Association, 2013) and DSM-5 TR (American Psychiatric Association, 2022) and has been used successfully across the globe (see Jones-Lavallée et al., 2023).

The development and piloting of the OCF and the CFI was predominantly done with an adult population (Lewis-Fernández et al., 2014). Most research since its inception has been conducted in clinic-based settings with adult clients (Jones-Lavallée et al., 2023). For those practitioners who work with children or families, culture is no less important and should be considered when understanding presenting problems and symptoms.

Working with children (in schools or clinical settings) presents unique challenges, as they may not be able to understand or convey complex information such as cultural identity. Age, ability, developmental level, and language status are some of the factors that may make it difficult for clinicians to obtain direct information. When it is not possible to obtain direct report from clients, it becomes important to have collateral information provided by a trusted source, such as a spouse, parent, or caregiver (La Roche & Bloom, 2020). As the CFI is a direct measure administered to the client themselves, an informant version of the CFI (the CFI-I) was developed and published in DSM-5 (American Psychiatric Association, 2013). The CFI-I gathers culturally relevant data from informants other than the client. The CFI-I is primarily geared toward clinic-based work, but it could be used in various applied settings, including schools. In the case of school-age children, this could include parents, teachers, and other important figures in children's lives. An additional supplemental module to the CFI is available and provides interview prompts and questions that can be used directly with "adolescents and mature school-age children" (American Psychiatric Association, 2013) The School Age Children and Adolescent (SACA) supplementary module is free. Despite the benefits of the SACA, researchers have found that young children may not respond well to the questions. La Roche and Bloom (2020) documented the limitations of the CFI-I and the SACA in a case study with a 6-year-old boy. The standard questions were difficult for a young child to conceptualize; thus, they recommended the use of drawing, puppets, dollhouses, play dough, and other methods to elicit information from the child about their current situation, keeping in mind the use of culturally representative toys.

The challenges of integrating culture in clinical assessment and diagnosis are far from solved. As new understandings are discovered and improvements made in clinical application of the CFI, the world continues to turn and diagnosis, classification, or categorization remain necessary to access services like treatment, accommodations, and support. The use of the DSM, and the World Health Organization's *International Classification of Diseases, 11th Revision* (ICD-11), to label and categorize individuals' symptoms is part of a system of research and care worldwide. It provides a common language that professionals use to codify a client's symptoms and distress. Additionally, diagnosis cannot be avoided if one is utilizing insurance to pay for care, or a provider is seeking reimbursement from insurance companies.

Cultural Considerations in IDEA

In a parallel world, children who are diagnosed with a psychiatric disorder, among other conditions, may be eligible for specialized support and services in public schools. To access special services, a child must be identified as having a disability that significantly impacts their functioning and thus requires specialized instruction and supports. However, professionals in public schools do not use the DSM to categorize or diagnose children when considering their eligibility for services. Rather, school children may obtain special education services if they are determined to have a disability based on a certain set of criteria outlined in law by the federal government. The idea of special education, or any education at all, for children with disabilities originated in 1975 with the Educational for All Handicapped Children Act (EAHCA, Public Law 94-142). Briefly, this law was passed to guarantee that children with disabilities had access to free and appropriate public education.

Race, Culture, and Identification of Disability in Public Education

Any discussion about the history of the educational rights of children with disabilities cannot be held without acknowledging the fact that segregation by race in our nation's schools was the norm until its abolishment in 1954 with the Supreme Court ruling in *Brown v. Board of Education of Topeka, Kansas.* Although this ruling was a watershed moment for children of color in our nation, many localities continued segregation informally. President Johnson ultimately signed the Civil Rights Act of 1964 banning discrimination in employment and public places, as well as enforcing the Brown ruling more stringently.

Separately but relatedly, there is a long history of excluding children with disabilities from public education, starting in Europe in the 1800s and continuing through the mid-20th century (Woodill & Velche, 1995; Triano, 2000). Energized by the ruling of Brown, families of children with disabilities pushed to end the practice of exclusion and segregation. The fight for equal education for students with disabilities began with the court cases *Pennsylvania Association for Retarded Citizens (P.A.R.C.) v. The State of Pennsylvania* in 1972 and *Mills v. The District of Columbia* in 1972. Both focused on abolishing separate, unequal educational practices for children with disabilities. Notably, the plaintiffs in *Mills v. The District of Columbia* were Black families whose children were excluded from school due to intellectual functioning or behavioral problems.

Shortly after these rulings, there were early legislation efforts that attempted to meet the needs of students with disabilities, via antidiscrimination laws and amendments of federal education laws (Jacob et al., 2022). However, this piecemeal approach was not sufficient, and the need for federal action to provide education to students with disabilities was clear. In 1975, the EAHCA was passed, guaranteeing a free and appropriate public education to students with disabilities. The law was later replaced by the Individuals with Disabilities Education Act (IDEA, 1990). This law is intended to provide special education services to children with disabilities; children who do not have a disability but are underachieving due to other factors (e.g., poverty) are not the target. Social determinants of learning, a variation of the concept of social determinants of health, refer to outside negative experiences such as structural forces and access to resources that impact a child's learning (Levinson & Cohen, 2023). Disentangling these factors from learning and behavioral disorders and the need for special education can be a herculean task. It is difficult for educators to discern where one issue ends and the next begins. Children's difficulties do not fall in neat categories where etiology is easily discerned, and IDEA categories can be vague and difficult to interpret. Consequently, it is not surprising that the issue of race, culture, diversity, and IDEA/special education is fraught with discord and misunderstandings.

The identification of disabilities in special education has been plagued with many of the same cultural challenges as diagnostic, clinic-based assessment using the DSM. It should be noted that since its inception, IDEA built in language to reduce the influence of culture and socioeconomic status on eligibility decisions. For example, the original law states that evaluation materials and procedures "will be selected and administered so as not to be racially or culturally discriminatory" (EAHCA, 1975, p. 781). Additionally, EAHCA indicates that the term learning disability should not include children whose learning problems "are primarily the result of visual, hearing, or motor handicaps, of mental retardation, of emotional disturbance, or of environmental, cultural, or economic disadvantage" (EAHCA, 1975, p. 775)

Educators and researchers continue to grapple with the influence of race, culture, language, and ethnicity on the special education eligibility process. It is beyond the scope of this chapter to summarize the volume of literature studying the disproportionality of minorities in special education (both under and over identification). The issue continues to generate vigorous debate among scholars, with some arguing that minorities are underrepresented and others asserting that minorities are overrepresented (see Connor et al., 2019; Cruz & Rodl, 2018; Katsiyannis et al., 2023; Skiba et al., 2016).

The U.S. Office of Special Education Programs (OSEP) monitors the implementation and adherence to IDEA in school districts across the nation, gathering data each year. At a basic, numeric level, there are discrepancies between the national population statistics for many groups of minority youth ages 5 through 21 when compared to that group's percentage of students who are being served under IDEA (OSEP, 2021). During school year 2019–2020, OSEP reported the following percentages of students with disabilities receiving IDEA services by race/ethnicity as compared to their national population statistics: American Indian (1.3% in IDEA vs. .85% general population), Black (17.66% in IDEA vs. 13.9% general population), Hispanic/Latino (27.83% in IDEA vs. 24.87% general population), Native Hawaiian or Pacific Islander (.36% in IDEA vs. .20% general population), and two or more races (4.33% in IDEA vs. 4.04%). Two ethnic/racial groups showed the reverse: White (45.99% in IDEA vs. 51.09% general population) and Asian (2.52% in IDEA vs. 5.19% general population).

Examining the risk ratios provided by OSEP (2021) for specific race/ethnicities and disabilities gives a more detailed understanding of the probability of a student with a disability being identified with a specific disability. For example, Black children with disabilities were 1.3 times more likely to be identified with ED and 1.48 times more likely to be identified with intellectual disabilities when compared to all students with disabilities. They were less likely to be identified with autism (risk ratio = .85). Hispanic/Latine students with disabilities were 1.2 times more likely to be identified with a specific learning disability compared to all students with disabilities, but less likely to be identified with emotional disability (risk ratio = .69). Asian students with disabilities were 2.37 times more likely to be identified with autism compared to all students with disabilities but were less likely to be identified with "other health impairment" (risk ratio = .58) and specific learning disability (risk ratio = .60).

The complications inherent in disability identification increase when coupled with sociocultural factors that impact a child's development, learning, emotional adjustment, and behavior. Appreciating and acknowledging this confluence, intersectional approaches have more recently been applied to understand the complexities of race and disability in special education (Connor et al., 2019). Scholars in the field of disability studies and critical race theory (DisCrit) are knitting together various lines of inquiry and thought in order to shed new light on how disability, race, special education, policy, and research intertwine (Annamma et al., 2013; Artiles, 2011). It is hoped that future research includes interdisciplinary perspectives to better understand how to improve special education services to culturally diverse youth with disabilities.

Application of Diagnostic and Classification Systems with Culturally Diverse Youth

As discussed earlier in the chapter, the misdiagnosis and overrepresentation of ethnic minorities, including youth, in particular diagnostic categories are prevalent in the clinical setting (Good, 1996; Liang et al., 2016; Whaley & Geller, 2003). This phenomenon is also true in the school setting. Overrepresentation of ethnic marginalized youth is particularly prevalent in the assessment and diagnosis of ED. Data show African American and Native American youth are one to two times more likely to be identified as having ED in comparison to their White peers (U.S. Department of Education, 2021). Placement in special education under the classification of ED increases the risks of negative life outcomes, particularly for minoritized youth (Bal et al., 2019). IDEA defines ED as "a condition exhibiting one or more of the following characteristics over a long period of time and to a marked degree that adversely affects a child's educational performance." Characteristics of a student with ED are described as

A. an inability to learn that cannot be explained by intellectual, sensory, or health factors.
B. an inability to build or maintain satisfactory interpersonal relationships with peers and teachers.
C. inappropriate types of behavior or feelings under normal circumstances.
D. a general pervasive mood of unhappiness or depression.
E. a tendency to develop physical symptoms or fears associated with personal or school problems (IDEA, 2004).

According to the law, this classification includes students diagnosed with schizophrenia but excludes students who are deemed socially maladjusted, unless they are determined to have an ED. To qualify for special education services under ED, students are not required to have a clinical diagnosis. However, students with a clinical DSM diagnosis of major depressive disorder, anxiety disorders, conduct disorder, oppositional defiant disorder, and disruptive mood dysregulation disorder are often codified under the ED classification; students with schizophrenia and other psychotic disorders would qualify under ED as well (Forness, et al., 2012). The IDEA definition of ED has been criticized for many years. It has sparked controversy in both research and clinical practice due to the lack of clarity in the federal definition, antiquated terminology void of culturally responsive language, and the stigma and long-term implications for students serviced under this classification (Gresham, 2005; Hanchon & Allen, 2018; Wery & Cullinan, 2013).

Critiques of the ED Classification

Lack of clear, operationalized terms within the ED classification has made it challenging for school practitioners to identify students in a systematic way. Unlike other IDEA classifications, ED has many vague terms such as, "a long period of time," "marked degree," "inappropriate feelings," "normal circumstances," and "satisfactory interpersonal relationships" that allow for personal interpretation and increase the chances of personal biases influencing eligibility determination (Scardamalia et al., 2019). From a culturally responsive lens, this is important to consider given that research has shown school-based staff have an increased implicit bias toward minority youth, particularly African American students (Kunesh & Noltemeyer, 2015; Okonofua & Eberhardt 2015; Samuels, 2016). For example, teachers tend to view African American male students as aggressive and threatening (Wilson et al., 2017) and rate their physical appearance as older than their chronological age, starting as early as 10 years old (Goff et al., 2014). In addition, African American girls are also seen as older than their chronological age and have higher behavioral expectations than their non-African American peers, particularly between the ages of 5 and 14 (Epstein, 2017). This trend puts African American students in a particularly vulnerable position for increased discipline, suspension rates, and misinterpretation of behaviors and attitudes that often lead to lower academic aspirations and school disengagement (Cooper et al., 2022).

The ill-defined ED eligibility criteria has also led to inconsistent assessment practices among clinicians and influenced their interpretation of the federal law. Scardamalia et al. (2019) examined the reliability of the federal definition of ED to determine eligibility in the school setting. Researchers found that when given the same data and educational profile, only 56 school psychologists (out of 175 participants) determined the student met eligibility for ED. Although 56 agreed on the qualification, they varied on which student characteristics indicated the presence of ED, yielding 16 different combinations of the five criteria (Scardamalia et al., 2019). These research findings highlight a key problem of practice faced by school-based clinicians when assessing and determining eligibility in the school setting. In addition to contributing to the overrepresentation of specific populations, the unclear definition may also miss a population of students who are often under identified and whose needs are neglected in the school setting (e.g., students presenting with internalizing behaviors; Gage, 2013).

As previously noted, common DSM mental health diagnoses treated under the IDEA classification of ED include depression, anxiety, and conduct disorders. Research has found the DSM to be more inclusive in the diagnostic process, while IDEA is more exclusive (Brock, 2023). This means that there may be students diagnosed with significant emotional and behavioral disorders from a clinical setting unbeknownst to the school team, or, known to the school team but do not meet the classification of ED in the school setting. This may be particularly true for students who are diagnosed with mood disorders and display more internalizing symptoms versus their peers who display externalizing symptoms (Gage, 2013). ED continues to be one of the few eligibility classifications under IDEA that has not undergone revisions since its inception in the 1960s (Hanchon & Allen, 2018). The definition of ED was derived from a study of 207 children in the 1950s who were identified as students with "emotional disturbance" based on teacher report (Allen & Hanchon, 2013). The criteria used to make educational and lifelong decisions for children do not reflect the current research, practices, and understandings learned over time. In comparison, other IDEA classifications have been revised to reflect research and practices to reduce biases in assessment practices and minimize overrepresentation of certain populations in special education (Garwood & Carreo, 2023; Hanchon & Allen, 2013). In the clinical setting, diagnostic criteria for mental health disorders are often reviewed and revised to reflect current research and practice. Since the inception of the ED classification, the DSM has been revised five times and in the most recent revision includes the Cultural Formulation and Cultural Concepts of Distress scale to help integrate culture and social context into the diagnostic process and reduce biases in practice (American Psychiatric Association, 2022).

As discussed earlier in the chapter, experts in culture and diagnosis worked with the DMS-5 revision committee to address concerns of the mental health professional community regarding race, racism, and ethno-racial differences in understanding mental illness and diagnostic criteria within previous iterations of the DSM (Moran, 2022). Although not perfect, this level of effort and consideration to increase clarity and reduce biases in diagnostic assessment when using the DSM is best practice and should be mirrored for school-based evaluative and diagnostic systems such as IDEA. Making high-stakes decisions for students, such as mental health diagnoses or eligibility for special education, should not be based on criteria that do not reflect the current cultural and social climate in which children are developing. This is particularly important when marginalized student populations are overrepresented in these classifications, making them twice marginalized and at increased risks for negative life outcomes (Garwood & Carrero, 2023).

Marginalized youth face many inequities in society and the school environment. This population is particularly vulnerable to misdiagnosis of emotional and behavioral disorders and classifications (Garwood & Carrero, 2023; U.S. Department of Education, 2021), harsher punishments (Gage et al., 2019), lower academic and behavioral expectations, (Assari & Caldwell, 2018), school dropout (McKenna, 2013), and involvement with the criminal justice systems (Hanchon & Allen, 2018). The intersectionality between marginalized youth, ED classification, and poor life outcomes are not due to inherent inferiority, but are fueled by the sociocultural disadvantages and implicit biases experienced by this population of youth. Research has shown that students who qualify for ED, specifically African American students diagnosed with ED, are disproportionately placed in more restrictive settings with fewer educational opportunities than their peers (Bal et al., 2019; Garwood & Carrero, 2023). Research has documented the strong relationship between the academic achievement of students classified as ED and negative physical, psychological, and social outcomes. More specifically, poor school performance has been correlated with increased dropout rates, incarceration, poor cardiovascular health, and increased substance use (Hanchon & Allen, 2018; Vaughn et al., 2014). Understanding the trajectory of this vulnerable population makes it imperative that mental health practitioners consider the sociocultural factors contributing to the presenting problems and use assessment methods and instruments that focus on the whole child and ecological context in which they develop.

COMPREHENSIVE SYSTEMS OF CARE

School principals report supporting students with mental health needs is one of the greatest challenges in schools (Iachini, et al., 2015). Frameworks such as MTSS have been implemented in schools to support the strategic identification and support of students with a wide variety of needs in the school setting. When implemented with fidelity, MTSS has helped improve the over and under-identification of students who require additional emotional and behavioral supports (Barrett & Newman, 2018), as well as eradicate the notion that the only way to access school-based supports is through the special education process. In addition to MTSS, some school districts have also partnered with community-based agencies to provide mental health services in the school setting to reduce barriers to treatment.

Comprehensive school mental health systems (CSMHSs) are becoming increasingly popular to meet the growing mental health needs of school-age youth. CSMHSs are collaborative efforts between community-based mental health organizations and schools to provide comprehensive, multi-tiered supports to students in the school environment (McCance-Katz & Lynch, 2019). CSMHSs have been found to help prevent mental health crises and identify students who have mental health disorders and provide or refer students to the proper level of care needed for their well-being (McCance-Katz & Lynch, 2019). Substance Abuse and Mental Health Services Administration (SAMHSA) provides funding to school districts through their Project Advancing Wellness and Resilience in Education (AWARE) grants to allow schools to partner with communities to reduce delinquent behaviors and improve well-being. States awarded Project AWARE funding have reported decreased suspension and expulsion rates by half, reduced rates associated with depression by 51%, and reduced truancy by 37% (McCance-Katz & Lynch, 2019). CSMHSs are promising programs that help capture students with DSM diagnoses and make sure they are connected to supports in the school environment, even if they do not qualify for an IDEA special education classification. Other blended school–community models that have provided promising results for student mental and behavioral health are school-based health centers (SBHCs).

SBHCs help to support the physical and mental health of students by providing medical, dental, vision, and mental/behavioral health services in the school setting (Arenson et al., 2019). SBHCs are a collaboration between schools, health care organizations, and community-based organizations that originated as a method to reduce barriers to care, particularly for underserved communities who are at greater risk for negative physical and mental health outcomes (Arenson et al., 2019). In addition to reducing barriers to access care, these centers also maximize student learning because they do not have to leave the school environment to receive routine care. In 2022, there were 3,900 SCHCs across the United States (Soleimanpour et al., 2023). Research indicates a link between SBHCs and improved access to mental health care and services for underserved youth. Roughly 73% of SBHCs offer mental health services by licensed clinicians and service students with a variety of mental health needs (Soleimanpour et al., 2023). In 2016, an analysis of the utilization of SBHCs for mental health needs revealed that students across elementary, middle, and high school accessed their SBHC for mental health needs more than physical or medical needs (Bains & Diallo, 2016). SBHCs minimize barriers and maximize access to services for students who may typically be underserved. The integrated care provided in SBHCs allows medical professionals to seamlessly refer students for the support they need and provides access to a wide variety of data to allow for thorough assessment, referral, and treatment of student needs.

CULTURALLY RESPONSIVE PRACTICES ARE KEY

Culturally responsive assessment practices are key to reducing the overrepresentation of ethnic minority youth in the school and clinical based setting. Assessment practices and tools are one important consideration, but the importance of the evaluator's commitment to cultural reflexivity and cultural humility in their assessment and interpretation can really help reduce the biases in our diagnostic and classification systems. The inclusion of updated operationalized terms, culturally inclusive language, and cultural formulation and interview tools are only as useful as the dedicated mental health practitioners who utilize them. Psychologists in both school and clinical settings have an ethical responsibility to utilize assessment practices and diagnostic procedures that are current and reflect the population they serve (APA, 2017; NASP, 2020). The outcomes associated with mental health disorders and special education classifications are too dire, particularly for ethnic minority youth, to continue with the status quo.

REFERENCES

Aggarwal, N. K., Jarvis, G. E., Gómez-Carrillo, A., Kirmayer, L. J., & Lewis-Fernández, R. (2020). The Cultural Formulation Interview since DSM-5: Prospects for training, research, and clinical practice. *Transcultural Psychiatry, 57*(4), 496–514.

Allen, R. A., & Hanchon, T. A. (2013). What can we learn from school-based emotional disturbance assessment practices? Implications for practice and preparation in school psychology. *Psychology in the Schools, 50*(3), 290–299.

Alonzo, J., Tindal, G., Ulmer, K., & Glasgow, A. (2006). *easyCBM® Online Progress Monitoring Assessment System.* University of Oregon, Behavioral Research and Teaching. *http://easycbm.com*

American Educational Research Association, American Psychological Association, & National Council on Measurement in Education. (2014). *Standards for educational and psychological testing.* American Educational Research Association.

American Psychiatric Association. (2013). Cultural Formulation Interview. *www.psychiatry.org/File%20Library/Psychiatrists/Practice/DSM/APA_DSM5_Cultural-Formulation-Interview.pdf.*

American Psychological Association. (2017). *Ethical principles of psychologists and code of conduct* (2002, amended effective June 1, 2010, and January 1, 2017). *www.apa.org/ethics/code.*

American Psychiatric Association. (2022). *The Diagnostic and Statistical Manual of Mental Disorders, Fifth Edition, Text Revision.* American Psychiatric Association Publishing.

Annamma, S. A., Connor, D., & Ferri, B. (2013). Dis/ability critical race studies (DisCrit): Theorizing at the intersections of race and dis/ability. *Race, Ethnicity, and Education, 16*(1), 1–31.

Arenson, M., Hudson, P. J., Lee, N., & Lai, B. (2019). The evidence on school-based health centers: A review. *Global Pediatric Health,* 6, 1–10.

Armistead, R. J., & Clyne, A. (2023). The National Association of School Psychologists Model for Comprehensive and Integrated School Psychological Services; The NASP 2020 Practice Model. In P. L. Harrison, S. L. Proctor, & A. Thomas (Eds.), *Best practices in school psychology data-based and collaborative decision making* (7th ed., pp. 13–28). National Association of School Psychologists.

Artiles, A. J. (2011). Toward an interdisciplinary understanding of educational equity and difference: The case of the racialization of ability. *Educational Researcher,* 40(9), 431–445.

Assari S., & Caldwell, C. H. (2018). Teacher discrimination reduces school performance of African American youth: role of gender. *Brain Sciences,* 8(10), 183.

Bains, R. M., & Diallo, A. F. (2016). Mental health services in school-based health centers: Systematic review. *The Journal of School Nursing: The Official Publication of the National Association of School Nurses, 32*(1), 8–19.

Bal, A., Betters-Bubon, J., & Fish, R. E. (2019). A multilevel analysis of statewide disproportionality in exclusionary discipline and the identification of emotional disturbance. *Education and Urban Society, 51*(2), 247–268.

Barrett, C., Parent, A., Cajas-Laynez, L., & Salguero, S. (2020, spring). *Best practices in assessing culturally and linguistically diverse students.* Presentation at the Bilingual Assessment Leadership Group (BALG) of Texas via Virtual Format.

Barrett, C. A. (2023). Best practices in applying multiple models to assessment and identification of learning disabilities. In P. L. Harrison, S. L. Proctor, & A. Thomas (Eds.), *Best practices in school psychology data-based and collaborative decision making* (7th ed., pp. 227–239). National Association of School Psychologists.

Barrett, C. A., & Newman, D. S. (2018). Examining MTSS implementation across systems for SLD identification: A case study. *School Psychology Forum: Research in Practice, 12*(1), 30–43.

Bell, C., Williamson, J., & Chien, P. (2008). Cultural, racial and ethnic competence and psychiatric diagnosis. *Ethnicity and Inequalities in Health and Social Care, 1*(1), 34–41.

Brock, S. E. (Guest). (2023, February 7). *Navigating DSM-5-TRTM Diagnoses in Schools* [Audio Podcast]. *https://apps.nasponline.org/resources-and-publications/podcasts/player.aspx?id=350*

Brown v. Board of Education of Topeka, Kansas. 347 U.S. 483 (1954).

Castillo, J. M., & Abiola, I. (2023). Multitiered systems of supports: Principles for school psychologists. In P. L. Harrison, S. L. Proctor, & A. Thomas (Eds.), *Best practices in school psychology data-based and collaborative decision making* (7th ed., pp. 43–58). National Association of School Psychologists.

Climie, E., & Henley, L. (2016). A renewed focus on strengths-based assessment in schools. *British Journal of Special Education, 43*(2), 108–121.

Connor, D., Cavendish, W., González, T., & Jean-Pierre, P. (2019). Is a bridge even possible over troubled water? The field of special education negates the overrepresentation of minority students: A DisCrit analysis. *Race, Ethnicity and Education, 22*(6), 723–745.

Connor, D. J., & Ferri, B. A. (2005). Integration and inclusion—A troubling nexus: Race, disability, and special education. *The Journal of African American History, 90*(1–2), 107–127.

Cooper, S. M., Burnett, M., Golden, A., Butler-Barnes, S., & Inniss-Thompson, M. (2022). School discrimination, discipline inequities, and adjustment among black adolescent girls and boys: An intersectionality-informed approach. *Journal of Research on Adolescence, 32*(1), 170–190.

Copeland, W. E., Miller-Johnson, S., Keeler, G., Angold, A., & Costello, E. J. (2007). Childhood psychiatric disorders and young adult crime: A prospective, population-based study. *The American Journal of Psychiatry, 164*(11), 1668–1675.

Cruz, R. A., & Rodl, J. E. (2018). An integrative synthesis of literature on disproportionality in special education. *The Journal of Special Education, 52*(1), 50–63.

Cultural Formulation Interview—Informant (CFI-I). Supplementary modules. *www.psychiatry.org/psychiatrists/practice/dsm/educational-resources/assessment-measures#section_16*

De Ramírez, R. D., & Shapiro, E. S. (2006). Curriculum-based measurement and the evaluation of reading skills of Spanish-speaking English language learners in bilingual education classrooms. *School Psychology Review, 35*(3), 356–369.

Education for All Handicapped Children Act, Public Law No. 94-142, 89 Stat. 773 (1975). *www.govinfo.gov/content/pkg/STATUTE-89/pdf/STATUTE-89-Pg773.pdf*

Eklund, K., & Jones, J. (2021, May 27). Addressing implicit bias & disproportionality in social-emotional assessment and behavior assessment. *Illuminate Education. www.illuminateed.com/wp-content/uploads/2021/06/bias-in-seb-screening-presentation.pdf*

Epstein, R., Blake, J. J., & Gonzalez, T. (2017). *Girlhood interrupted: The erasure of Black girl childhood.* Georgetown Law Center on Poverty and Inequality.

Fletcher, J. M., Lyon, G. R., Fuchs, L. S., & Barnes, M. A. (2019). *Learning disabilities: From identification to intervention* (2nd ed.) Guilford Press.

Forness, S. R., Freeman, S. F. N., Paparella, T., Kauffman, J. M., & Walker, H. M. (2012). Special education implications of point and cumulative prevalence for children with emotional or behavioral disorders. *Journal of Emotional and Behavioral Disorders, 20*(1), 4–18.

Gage, N. A. (2013). Characteristics of students with emotional disturbance manifesting internalizing behaviors: A latent class analysis. *Education & Treatment of Children, 36*(4), 127–145.

Gage, N. A., Whitford, D. K., Katsiyannis, A., Adams, S., & Jasper, A. (2019). National analysis of the disciplinary exclusion of Black students with and without disabilities. *Journal of Child and Family Studies, 28*(7), 1754–1764.

Garwood, J. D., & Carrero, K. M. (2023). Lifting the voices of black students labeled with emotional disturbance: Calling all special education researchers. *Behavioral Disorders, 48*(2), 121–133.

Girvan, E. J., Gion, C., McIntosh, K., & Smolkowski, K. (2017). The relative contribution of subjective office referral to racial disproportionality in school discipline. *School Psychology Quarterly, 32*(3), 392–404.

Goforth, A. N., & Pham, A. V. (2023). *Culturally responsive school-based practices: Supporting mental health and learning of diverse students.* Oxford University Press.

Good, B. J. (1992). Culture, diagnosis, and comorbidity. *Culture, Medicine, and Psychiatry: An International Journal of Cross-Cultural Health Research, 16*(4), 427–446.

Good, B. J. (1996). Culture and DSM-IV: Culture, knowledge and power. *Culture, Medicine and Psychiatry, 20*(2), 127–132.

Goff, P. A., Jackson, M. C., Di Leone, B. A. L., Culotta, C. M., & DiTomasso, N. A. (2014). The essence of innocence: Consequences of dehumanizing Black children. *Journal of Personality and Social Psychology, 106*(4), 526–545.

Grapin, S. L., & Proctor, S. L. (2023). Equity and social justice: Foundations for school psychology. In P. L. Harrison, S. L. Proctor, & A. Thomas (Eds.), *Best practices in school psychology data-based and collaborative decision making* (7th ed., pp. 29–42). National Association of School Psychologists.

Gresham, F. M. (2005). Response to intervention: An alternative means of identifying students as emotionally disturbed. *Education & Treatment of Children, 28*(4), 328–344.

Hanchon, T. A., & Allen, R. A. (2013). Identifying students with emotional disturbance: School psychologists' practices and perceptions. *Psychology in the Schools, 50*(2), 193–208.

Hanchon, T. A., & Allen, R. A. (2018). The identification of students with emotional disturbance: Moving the field toward responsible assessment practices. *Psychology in the Schools, 55*(2), 176–189.

Iachini, A. L., Brown, E. L., Ball, A., Gibson, J. E., & Lize, S. E. (2015). School mental health early interventions and academic outcomes for at-risk high school students: A meta-analysis. *Advances in School Mental Health Promotion,* 8(3), 156–175.

Individuals with Disabilities Education Act, Public Law No. 101-476, 101 Stat. 1142 (1990).

Individuals with Disabilities Education Improvement Act, Public Law No. 108-446, Stat. 2647 (2004). *www.congress.gov/108/plaws/publ446/PLAW-108publ446.pdf.*

Jacob, S., Decker, D. M., Lugg, E. T., & Diamond, E. L. (2022). *Ethics and law for school psychologists.* Wiley.

Jimerson, S. R., Sharkey, J. D., Nyborg, V., & Furlong, M. J. (2004). Strength-based assessment and school psychology: A summary and synthesis. *California School Psychologist, 9,* 9–19.

Jones J. M. (2009). Counseling with multicultural intentionality: The process of counseling and integrating client cultural variables. In Jones J. M. (Ed.), *The psychology of multiculturalism in the schools: A primer for practice, training, and research* (pp. 191–213). National Association of School Psychologists.

Jones-Lavallée, A., Bernard, G., Taing, J., & Leanza, Y. (2023). The state of current knowledge on the Cultural Formulation Interview: A scoping review. *Journal of Psychopathology and Behavioral Assessment, 45*(1), 265–276.

Katsiyannis, A., Zhang, D., Ettekal, I., Chang, W. H., Li, P., Bigger, B., et al. (2023). Minority representation in special education: 5-year tends from 2016–2020. *Advances in Neurodevelopmental Disorders, 9*(1), 23–36.

Kawa, S., & Giordano, J. (2012). A brief historicity of the Diagnostic and Statistical Manual of Mental Disorders: Issues and implications for the future of psychiatric canon and practice. *Philosophy, Ethics, and Humanities in Medicine, 7*(2).

Kirmayer, L. J., Groleau, D., Guzder, J., Blake, C., & Jarvis, E. (2003). Cultural consultation: A model of mental health service for multicultural societies. *The Canadian Journal of Psychiatry, 48*(3), 145–153.

Kirmayer, L. J., Guzder, J., & Rousseau, C. (Eds.). (2014). *Cultural consultation encountering the other in mental health care* (1st ed.). Springer.

Kisiel, C., Fehrenbach, T., Conradi, L., & Weil, L. (2021). *Trauma-informed assessment with children and adolescents: Strategies to support clinicians*. American Psychological Association.

Kunesh, C. E., & Noltemeyer, A. (2015). Understanding disciplinary disproportionality: Stereotypes shape pre-service teachers' beliefs about black boys' behavior. *Urban Education, 54*(4), 471–498.

La Roche, M. J., & Bloom, J. B. (2020). Examining the effectiveness of the Cultural Formulation Interview with young children: A clinical illustration. *Transcultural Psychiatry, 57*(4), 515–524.

Levinson, M., & Cohen, A. K. (2023). Social determinants of learning: Implications for research, policy, and practice. *AERA Open, 9*.

Lewis-Fernández, R., Aggarwal, N. K., Bäärnhielm, S., Rohlof, H., Kirmayer, L. J., Weiss, M. G., et al. (2014). Culture and psychiatric evaluation: Operationalizing cultural formulation for DSM-5. *Psychiatry: Interpersonal and Biological Processes, 77*(2), 130–154.

Liang, J., Matheson, B. E., & Douglas, J. M. (2016). Mental health diagnostic considerations in racial/ethnic minority youth. *Journal of Child and Family Studies, 25*(6), 1926–1940.

Marcotte, A. M., & McKenzie, C. (2023). Best practices in curriculum-based measurement and data-based decision making for mathematics. In P. L. Harrison, S. L. Proctor, & A. Thomas (Eds.), *Best practices in school psychology data-based and collaborative decision making* (7th ed., pp. 121–135). National Association of School Psychologists.

Martínez, L. C. (2009). DSM-IV-TR cultural formulation of psychiatric cases: Two proposals for clinicians. *Transcultural Psychiatry, 46*(3), 506–523.

Mather, N., & Wendling, B. J. (2014). *Woodcock–Johnson IV Tests of Oral Language*. Riverside Insights.

McCance-Katz, E., & Lynch, C. (2019, July). *Guidance to states and school systems on addressing mental health and substance use issues in schools*. Substance Abuse and Mental Health Services Administration & Center for Medicare & Medicaid Services. *www.medicaid.gov/sites/default/files/Federal-Policy-Guidance/Downloads/cib20190701.pdf*

McKenna, J. (2013). The disproportionate representation of African Americans in programs for students with emotional and behavioral disorders. *Preventing School Failure: Alternative Education for Children and Youth, 57*(4), 206–211.

Mezzich, J. E., & Caracci, G. (Eds.). (2008). *Cultural formulation: A reader for psychiatric diagnosis*. Jason Aronson.

Mezzich, J. E., Kirmayer, L. J., Kleinman, A., Fabrega Jr., H., Parron, D. L., Good, B. J., et al. (1999). The place of culture in DSM-IV. *The Journal of Nervous and Mental Disease, 187*(8), 457–464.

Mills v. Board of Education of District of Columbia, 348 F. Supp. 866 (D.D.C. 1972). *https://law.justia.com/cases/federal/district-courts/FSupp/348/866/2010674*

Moran, M. (2022). Impact of culture, race, social determinants reflected throughout new DSM-5-TR. *Psychiatric News, 57*(3).

National Association of School Psychologists. (2020). *The professional standards of the National Association of School Psychologists. www.nasponline.org/standards-and-certification/professional-ethics*.

National Center for Education Statistics. (2023). *Racial/ethnic enrollment in public schools. Condition of education*. U.S. Department of Education, Institute of Education Sciences. *https://nces.ed.gov/programs/coe/indicator/cge*

National Center on Safe Supportive Learning Environments. (n.d.). Trauma-sensitive assessment and planning checklist. *https://safesupportivelearning.ed.gov/sites/default/files/Building_TSS_Handout_6assessment_and_planning.pdf*

Office of Special Education Programs. (2021). *OSEP fast facts: Race and ethnicity of children with disabilities served under IDEA Part B. https://sites.ed.gov/idea/osep-fast-facts-race-and-ethnicity-of-children-with-disabilities-served-under-idea-part-b*

Okonofua, J. A., & Eberhardt, J. L. (2015). Two strikes: Race and the disciplining of young students. *Psychological Science, 26*(5), 617–624.

Ortiz, S. O. (2023). Best practices in nondiscriminatory assessment. In P. L. Harrison, S. L. Proctor, & A. Thomas (Eds.), *Best practices in school psychology data-based and collaborative decision making* (7th ed., pp. 149–161). National Association of School Psychologists.

Pennsylvania Association of Retarded Children v. Commonwealth of Pennsylvania, 343 F. Supp. 279 (E.D. Pa. 1972). *https://law.justia.com/cases/federal/district-courts/FSupp/343/279/1691591*

Samuels, C. (2016). Early Childhood; Do early educators' implicit biases regarding sex and race relate to behavior expectations and recommendations of preschool expulsions and suspensions? *Education Week, 36*(8), 5.

Sandberg, K. L., & Reschly, A. L. (2011). English learners: Challenges in assessment and the promise of curriculum-based measurement. *Remedial and Special Education, 32*(2), 144–154.

Sattler, J. M. (2022). *Foundations of behavioral, social, and clinical assessment of children* (7th ed.). Jerome M. Sattler Publishing.

Scardamalia, K., Bentley-Edwards, K. L., & Grasty, K. (2019). Consistently inconsistent: An examination of the variability in the identification of emotional disturbance. *Psychology in the Schools, 56*(4), 569–581.

Skiba, R. J., Artiles, A. J., Kozleski, E. B., Losen, D. J., & Harry, E. G. (2016). Risks and consequences of oversimplifying educational inequities: A response to Morgan et al. (2015). *Educational Researcher, 45*(3), 221–225.

Soleimanpour, S., Cushing, K., Christensen, J., Ng, S., Yang, J., Saphir, M., et al. (2023). *Findings from the 2022 National Census of School-Based Health Centers.* School-Based Health Alliance.

Surís, A., Holliday, R., & North, C. (2016). The evolution of the classification of psychiatric disorders. *Behavioral Sciences, 6*(5), 1–10.

Tishelman, A. C., Haney, P., Greenwald O'Brien, J., & Blaustein, M. E. (2010). A framework for school-based psychological evaluations: Utilizing a "trauma lens." *Journal of Child & Adolescent Trauma, 3*(4), 279–302.

Tobin, R. M., & House, A. E. (2016). *DSM-5 diagnosis in the schools.* Guilford Press.

Triano, S. L. (2000). Categorical eligibility in special education: The enshrinement of the medical model in disability policy. *Disability Studies Quarterly, 20*(4).

University of Oregon (2021). *8th Edition of Dynamic Indicators of Basic Early Literacy Skills (DIBELS ®).* University of Oregon. *https://dibels.uoregon.edu*

U.S. Census Bureau. (2021). *Improved race and ethnicity measures reveal US population is much more multiracial. www.census.gov/library/stories/2021/08/improved-race-ethnicity-measures-reveal-united-states-population-much-more-multiracial.html*

U.S. Department of Education. (2021). *Forty-third annual report to Congress on implementation of the Individuals with Disabilities Education Act, 2021. https://sites.ed.gov/idea/files/43rd-arc-for-idea.pdf*

Vaughn, M. G., Salas-Wright, C.P., & Maynard, B.R. (2014) Dropping out of school and chronic disease in the United States. *Journal of Public Health, 22*(3), 265–270.

Vega, D., & Wolf, J. N. (2023). Best practices in assessment of bilingual learners in schools. In P. L. Harrison, S. L. Proctor, & A. Thomas (Eds.), *Best practices in school psychology data-based and collaborative decision making* (7th ed., pp. 163–173). National Association of School Psychologists.

Wery, J. J., & Cullinan, D. (2013). State definitions of emotional disturbance. *Journal of Emotional and Behavioral Disorders, 21*(1), 45–52.

Whaley, A. L., & Geller, P. A. (2003). Ethnic/racial differences in psychiatric disorders. *Ethnicity & Disease, 13*(4), 499–512.

WIDA. (2020) *English language development standards framework: The 2020 edition. https://wida.wisc.edu/sites/default/files/resource/WIDA-ELD-Standards-Framework-2020.pdf*

Wilson, J. P., Hugenberg, K., & Rule, N. O. (2017). Racial bias in judgments of physical size and formidability: From size to threat. *Journal of Personality and Social Psychology, 113*(1), 59–80.

Woodcock, R. W., Alvarado, C. G., Ruef, M. L., & Shrank, F. A. (2017). *Woodcock–Muñoz Language Survey III.* Houghton Mifflin Harcourt.

Woodill, G., & Velche, D. (1995). From charity and exclusion to emerging independence: An introduction to the history of disabilities. *Journal on Developmental Disabilities, 4*(1), 11–21.

Woolgar, F., Garfield, H., Dalgleish, T., & Meiser-Stedman, R. (2022). Systematic review and meta-analysis: Prevalence of posttraumatic stress disorder in trauma-exposed preschool-aged children. *Journal of the American Academy of Child & Adolescent Psychiatry, 61*(3), 366–377.

CHAPTER 7

Assessment from an Ecological Approach

Lindsay M. Fallon, Staci C. Ballard, and Emily D. Romero

In the 1970s, Urie Bronfenbrenner proposed *ecological systems theory*, positioning a child at the center of a series of nested circles representing the environment and contextual systems around them (Bronfenbrenner, 1979). Immediately surrounding the child is the *microsystem*, or places like their home, school, and neighborhood environment. In the *mesosystem*, Bronfenbrenner acknowledged interactions between multiple microsystems, indicating that each microsystem can impact others (e.g., home and school). The *exosystem* represents microsystems which may impact a child, but within which they may not be directly involved (e.g., a caregiver's work environment, local school committees). Finally, the *macrosystem* represents the values, cultures, and norms that may impact a child's surroundings (e.g., socioeconomic makeup of a neighborhood, dominant cultural or religious values in a community; Ettekal & Mahoney, 2017).

In 2006, Bronfenbrenner proposed a revised model called *bioecological systems theory* which centered the unique features of an individual (e.g., age, sex, race, ethnicity, health status) in a similar nested ecological structure, but with greater attention to child and human development as a process. Specifically, Bronfenbrenner (2006) named the *chronosystem* as the outermost layer of the model attributing importance to the chronosystem (or the patterns of events and transitions that occur over the lifespan) as well as *time* (or the sociocultural and historical conditions that may impact an individual's environment and development).

Calls for use of an ecological approach to assessment in school psychology have been made for several reasons. First, an ecological approach emphasizes a students' immediate (e.g., classroom, home) and distal (e.g., school district, region) environment. This may offer important information in the context of evaluating student concerns. Specifically, when a school psychologist receives a referral, use of an ecological approach might include consideration of not only a child's presenting concerns but also of the environmental variables that may be impacting the concern (such as what is occurring at home, in school, around the community, and how school policy impacts the child). Attention to environmental variables offers the school psychologist a more nuanced and contextual understanding of the referral issue.

For example, if a child is experiencing challenges with internalizing behavior (e.g., withdrawal, falling asleep in class) and is referred to the school psychologist for support, the school psychologist could include in their assessment environmental factors that might contextualize these behaviors. That is, rather than a school psychologist only assessing a students' internalizing symptoms (e.g., administering a depression inventory), they might also collect additional information using an ecological approach which could provide valuable information to guide the design and delivery of effective supports. This may include interviewing family members and teachers to gather additional information as well as conducting observations within home, school, and community environments. In this example, upon conducting interviews and observations, the school psychologist may learn that the student had recently experienced housing instability and an ill family member. This more complete picture as to why the student appears worried and tired in school might prompt the school psychologist to connect the family with needed resources and social services in addition to offering the student direct support at school. Essentially, an ecological approach to behavioral and emotional assessment can support school psychologists to get the complete picture when a referral concern is shared.

A second reason why there have been calls for an ecological approach is because it aligns well with the school psychologist's role. The National Association of School Psychologists (NASP) Practice Model conceptualizes 10 domains of practice including Family, School, and Community Collaboration (Domain 7; NASP, 2020). This collaboration is part of a school psychologist's indirect, systems-level support for youth. When collaborating with educators, families, and community members, an ecological approach will allow for multiple perspectives and systems to be considered. This is valuable for behavioral assessment as it can guide data collection to focus on environmental and systems variables in addition to individual-level factors. This also aligns with best practices in behavioral assessment (Achenbach, 2017). Specifically, researchers have emphasized the importance of a multimodal, multi-informant assessment process to support a comprehensive understanding of students' behavioral strengths and concerns, incorporating multiple perspectives and contexts in the assessment process.

A third reason for calls for an ecological approach to assessment is because it is important to consider the sociohistorical context of education and schools when it comes to evaluating and supporting student needs. In short, school has been a place that has largely valued White, English-speaking heternormative culture, making school less welcoming and affirming for those with marginalized and minoritized identities (La Salle et al., 2020). This context has laid the foundation for movements in education related to multicultural (Banks, 2015, Chapter 1), culturally responsive (Gay, 2018), culturally relevant (Ladson-Billings, 2023), and culturally sustaining (Paris & Alim, 2014) practice. An ecological approach includes consideration for sociohistorical context in a way other assessment approaches do not.

This chapter will present an introduction to behavioral and emotional assessment from an ecological perspective. Subsections will describe why an ecological approach is critical and propose how an ecological lens might be applied to the behavioral and emotional assessment process. We share culturally relevant practice considerations as well as future directions. To this end, the chapter begins with a brief overview of the sociohistorical context of education to frame the rest of the chapter.

SOCIOHISTORICAL CONTEXT

Youth exhibiting challenging externalizing behaviors in classroom and non-classroom school settings are often subject to exclusionary discipline practices (e.g., referrals to the office, suspensions, expulsions; Girvan et al., 2019). These practices have been used disproportionately with students who are Black, Native American, Latinx, and students identified with disabilities (Gage et al., 2019). There are many ways to assess discipline disproportionality (e.g., risk ratio, risk difference, discipline rate; see Girvan et al., 2019), but it is generally thought to be present when student characteristics (e.g., race/ethnicity, ability status, gender) are associated with discipline disparities (Fadus et al., 2021). Racial discipline disproportionality has been evident for decades (Children's Defense Fund, 1974) and has been linked to a host of negative outcomes including poor academic achievement (Morris & Perry, 2016), school dropout (Fadus et al., 2021), and contact with the juvenile justice system (Abrams et al., 2021).

For many years, results of quantitative analyses have indicated that children from certain racial and ethnic groups (particularly Black students) have been disproportionately identified as having *emotional disturbance* when evaluated to receive special education under the Individuals with Disabilities Education Act (2004; Tefera & Fischman, 2020). One explanation for this pattern pertains to the way students have typically been identified as requiring special education services. Specifically, critics contend that there is often a failure to consider the social context and any situational factors that may impact learning and behavior in the classroom (e.g., access to high-quality and evidence-based instruction, supportive student–teacher relationships; Fallon et al., 2023). Researchers and policymakers have called for a shift away from basing identification decisions on within-child deficits and instead advocate for the adoption of a multi-tiered system of support (MTSS) framework to focus on prevention and the consideration of environmental and ecological variables in the assessment process.

Modeled after the U.S. Public Health Service's multi-tiered pyramidal model of prevention, an MTSS framework emphasizes (1) high-quality instruction and behavioral supports; (2) universal screening and frequent progress monitoring to determine when intensive intervention is needed, and, when it is; and (3) maximizing resource efficiency by scaling intervention appropriately to the level of student need (Sugai & Horner, 2020). Data inform systems for successful staff implementation (e.g., training) and guide decision making about students' progress. When a student requires additional support, interventions are scaled according to that individual student's needs. That includes intensive interventions which may precede referral to special education.

Although MTSS has been widely adopted, educators may attribute a challenging or maladaptive behavior to be the result of student deficits (Chu, 2011) rather than structural challenges within school systems (e.g., systemic racism) or bias in teachers' perceptions and practices, both of which are evident in schools (see Shell et al., 2019). For instance, a recent research review of discrimination against children of immigrants in schools found that youth experience (1) inadequate educational resources; (2) low expectations for learning and intellect; (3) persistent, negative interactions with teachers; and (4) insufficient engagement between school staff and their families (Adair, 2015). This impacts students' social–emotional well-being and academic outcomes over time (Hughes et al., 2016). Teachers often enter the field with a lack of understanding of how bias impacts students and either engage in or not challenge discriminatory practices (Peters et al., 2016). For instance, teachers (who remain primarily White and female in the United States) may be biased in their ratings on screeners, consequently overidentifying students with marginalized identities as being at social or emotional risk (Fallon et al., 2022). Educators often assess students' social or emotional behavior given their own values, experiences, and expectations and may often be encouraged to consider "who is deciding what behaviors are appropriate, for whom, and under what conditions" (Utley et al., 2002, p. 197).

AN ECOLOGICAL APPROACH TO BEHAVIORAL AND EMOTIONAL ASSESSMENT OF YOUTH

Although there have been calls for use of an ecological approach to school-based behavioral and emotional assessment of youth, systems and policies in schools have historically relied on a medical model paradigm to guide evaluation processes (Gutkin, 2012). Within the medical model, it is often assumed that inherent deficits lie *within* a student and that they contribute to his/her inability to make adequate progress within the classroom. The goal of assessment is generally to arrive at an accurate diagnosis to inform potential interventions. This model often overlooks many other important factors, including students' strengths, the environmental context, and the complexities of learning and behavior, all of which are difficult to reduce into a diagnosis that links to a clear intervention (as may be the case when evaluating the presence of a physical disease).

In contrast, an ecological approach to behavioral and emotional assessment moves beyond conceptualizing behavior as occurring solely within the individual student and views the student's behavior as occurring within specific environmental contexts. A student's behavior is seen as a result of the interactive nature of the environment and the individual (McCurdy et al., 2015). An ecological approach assumes that (1) it is impossible to separate students (and their behavior) from the multiple environments in which they exist; (2) challenges are not located within the student, but rather occur as the result of a mismatch between the child and their environment; and (3) collaboration within environments is critical for addressing behavioral change. Of relevance for behavioral and emotional assessment is the "mental health environment," which encompasses the factors that facilitate or impede the development of social–emotional wellness, social skills, and life competences (Ysseldyke, 2012).

In moving beyond the individual level, this ecological approach is more consistent with NASP's current *Model for Comprehensive and Integrated School Psychological Services* (NASP, 2020). Within the first domain, data-based decision making, school psychologists are expected to conduct assessments within a multi-tiered framework that evaluates progress and outcomes. These assessment data can inform decisions at the individual level (e.g., intervention design), group levels (e.g., grade level planning), and systems levels (e.g., schoolwide decisions). Importantly, this framework explicitly calls for a consideration of ecological factors in assessing students' need for services, using a variety of assessment techniques and gathering data from a variety of sources (NASP, 2020). Although evaluations are traditionally associated with school psychologists assessing individual students for the purposes of special education eligibility, an ecological approach to behavioral and emotional assessment can take the form of gathering data to inform a problem-solving process at multiple levels.

An ecological approach offers many potential advantages over the traditional model of behavioral and emotional assessment. By broadening assessment to include the environment, an ecological approach has the potential to also broaden the provision of services to populations (versus individuals) to (1) focus on prevention, (2) be offered by a wider range of providers, and (3) have an impact across various environments potentially increasing the likelihood of effective treatment (Gutkin, 2012). Ultimately, the goal of an ecological approach to behavioral and emotional assessment moves away from a focus on accurate diagnosis (which may have limited utility in a school setting) toward identifying the mismatch between individuals and environments and redesigning environments to better support children, educators, and families (McCurdy, 2015).

CASE EXAMPLE

Toby is a kindergarten student who exhibits behaviors such as calling out during circle time, leaving the classroom without permission, and physically touching other students during a disagreement. Traditional approaches to assessment may involve a referral for behavioral assessment (e.g., teacher-report behavior checklist) and ultimately a comprehensive evaluation for a behavioral disorder. However, when taking an ecological approach, the school psychologist might consider factors such as (1) expectations and norms at home, (2) Toby's behavior in non-classroom settings (e.g., specials, cafeteria, bus), (3) whether this is Toby's first formal school experience, (4) the manner with which behavior was supported by former teachers in any previous school setting, (5) if current classroom instruction is meeting Toby's needs (i.e., instructional match), (6) the frequency with which Toby's current teacher taught expectations to all students in Toby's class, and (7) what Toby's family members identify as salient reinforcers to help Toby build the social skills necessary to be successful in school. An ecological approach gathers information not only about Toby but about their home, school, and community environment to guide a comprehensive understanding of the behavioral concern as well as information to guide an intervention approach that may be more supportive and successful than if informed by traditional assessment techniques. This could include support delivered to Toby's entire class (e.g., reteaching and reinforcing classwide expectations), potentially benefiting all students and the teacher instead of just Toby.

EQUITY AND CULTURAL CONSIDERATIONS

Using an ecological approach behavioral and emotional assessment has the potential to increase equity in school settings, which involves uplifting voices that have been traditionally marginalized, ensuring socially just outcomes, and challenging traditional balances of power and privilege (Great Schools Partnership, 2023). An ecological assessment allows for the assessment and recognition of students' and families' strengths in the environment (Ysseldyke, 2012). For instance, interviewing family members or observing students within their home may highlight support structures that work well at home and can be replicated in school. In addition, an ecological approach focuses on the role of systems and institutions, rather than centering problems within the student. As such, an ecological approach can help increase awareness and consideration of the many ways in which interdependent systems (including systems outside of the school) impact students' experiences and shape educational disparities (Sullivan et al., 2015). When advocacy and social justice are prioritized as part of an ecological approach to assessment, school psychologists can help interrogate school policies and practices that contribute to inequitable outcomes, moving systems toward promoting liberation and wellness (Hazel, 2017). Using an ecological approach, school psychologists can begin to assess and address the systemic and organizational factors that create inequities, rather than intervening only at the student level.

However, an ecological approach should not be assumed to inherently increase equity. Given that school and societal environments implicitly and explicitly center White heteronormative culture as dominant, school psychologists should be careful in considering intervention targets when a "mismatch" is found. If educators prioritize teaching students to "match" the environment without a thorough consideration of cultural factors (for instance, how "respect" or "academically engaged" are defined), they may contribute to maintaining the dominant White hegemony in education. Assessment and intervention within an MTSS framework have the potential to promote equitable outcomes if equity is truly at the center of the work. Enacting practices and systems that are void of equity considerations or are race and culture neutral may only perpetuate existing discipline and special education disproportionality rather than rectify them (Fallon et al., 2021).

In the following sections, we offer recommendations for using an ecological approach to behavioral and emotional assessment, proposing culturally relevant practice considerations. Structuring assessment to be considerate of students' micro-, meso-, exo-, macro-, and chronosystems will allow school psychologists to develop effective and affirming intervention targets at both individual and systems levels.

CULTURALLY RELEVANT PRACTICE CONSIDERATIONS

As we describe culturally relevant practice considerations across the various levels of an ecological model, we also integrate a focus on MTSS as it is the predominant assessment and intervention framework used in schools. For an overview of considerations at each level integrated within the MTSS model, see Table 7.1 and Figure 7.1.

Microsystems

School

Referral concerns often focus on students' behavioral functioning in the classroom, making it a natural setting in which to apply an ecological approach to assessment. However, it is difficult to understand an individual student's behavior without a broader understanding of the school

TABLE 7.1. Considerations for School Psychologists Using an Ecological Approach to Behavioral and Emotional Assessment in Their Work with Students, Educators, and Families

Ecological systems	Considerations and questions to ask
	When directly supporting students
Microsystem	• Consider asking students to share information about their behavior (when it happens, where, how often, why) either via a formal functional interview or informal semi-structured interview. • Consider asking students to share their experience as a learner in the classroom. Ask what makes it easier and harder for them. • Consider asking students to reflect on the support they feel from peers, teachers, and other school staff. • Consider asking students about their community, feelings of safety, and the general support they feel. • Consider asking students to reflect on the relationships they have with their peers, siblings, caregiver(s), and other close relatives. • Consider involving students in selecting assessment and intervention procedures.
Mesosystem	• Consider gathering information about how often teacher(s) and caregiver(s) communicate(s). Assess how communications occur, when and why communication typically takes place, and if both feel it is supportive. • Consider gathering information about emotional support and behavioral expectations in home and school settings. Assess how the two inform one another.
Exosystem	• Review policy (school, district, state, or federal level) that might impact students' behavioral health and emotional wellness. Consider how this might inform ways in which a challenging behavior is defined and supported. • Consider the ways in which you might advocate for policy change when you determine the current policy to be ineffective or harmful to students in your assessment processes.

(continued)

TABLE 7.1. *(continued)*

Ecological systems	Considerations and questions to ask
Macrosystem	• Assess for broader cultural and contextual factors (e.g., access to a local religious community for social support) that may influence a students' behavioral and emotional wellness.
Chronosystem	• Consider students' age and developmental stage when major societal or life events occurred (e.g., COVID-19 pandemic). Consider how these events may impact displays of the student's behavior. • Consider media messaging related to the identity (e.g., race, ethnicity, religion, gender). Assess for its impact on their social and emotional wellness.
	When supporting educators
Microsystem	• Tier 1: ○ Consider assessing school climate. ▪ Cultural: ecological model of school climate (CEMSC; La Salle et al., 2015) ○ Consider assessing teacher's perceptions of the cultural responsiveness of their classroom's curriculum and instruction. ▪ *Culturally Responsive Teacher Preparedness Scale* (CRTPS; Hsiao, 2015) ○ Consider assessing the impact of social-emotional curricula inclusive of and relevant to the identity of students. ▪ *Culturally Responsive Curriculum Scorecard* (Bryan-Gooden et al., 2019) ○ Consider assessing teachers' strengths and areas for growth related to culturally responsive practices. ▪ *Assessment of Culturally and Contextually Relevant Supports* (ACCReS; Fallon et al., 2023) ○ Consider assessing student-teacher relationships. ▪ *Teacher Relationship Interview* (Koenen et al., 2019) • Tier 2: ○ Consider what interventions teachers are trained and prepared to deliver to students who need more support. Consider what data were used to identify students in need of Tier 2 supports and if they are culturally biased. ○ Assess the impact of programs used for targeted intervention. ▪ The CASEL 5 Framework ○ Determine if targeted interventions used are culturally responsive. ▪ Culturally adapted Check-In/ Check-Out ▪ Affinity groups • Tier 3: ○ Consider the extent to which Tier 1 and 2 interventions have been implemented before assessment and intervention for Tier 3 supports. ○ Determine how progress monitoring data will be collected and used to make intervention adjustments. ○ Consider potential interventions to offer students. Determine how interventions will be selected and if they are culturally responsive. ▪ Culturally affirming individual therapy
Mesosystem	• Assess how and how often communication with families typically occurs (e.g., calls, texts, ClassDojo message). • Determine any power differential in the context of home-school collaboration. Are parents seen as experts? Do conversations about the student always occur at school? • Assess teachers' perceptions about their relationships with students' families.
Exosystem	• Consider if there are any policies (school, district, state, or federal level) that inform instructional and behavioral decisions in the classroom. Identify those to consider in the assessment process and engage in advocacy to change harmful practices, when possible. • Assess resource limitations to providing a culturally affirming environment (e.g., no access to training, financial support to buy intervention materials). • Assess how teachers have successfully overcome structural and systemic barriers to inform ways to identify and support emotional behavioral challenges.

(continued)

TABLE 7.1. *(continued)*

Ecological systems	Considerations and questions to ask
Macrosystem	• Assess whether teachers consider students cultural and religious values when identifying and supporting emotional or behavioral concerns.
Chronosystem	• Consider how major societal or life events (e.g., COVID-19 pandemic) impact educational systems and practices, specifically as they pertain to assessing emotional or behavioral concerns.
	When collaborating with families
Microsystem	• Ask how the family define the behavior concern of the student. ○ *Cultural Formulation Interview* (Veiga et al., 2025) • Ask the family about strengths, needs, values and expectations at home and in the community. ○ *Family-oriented, culturally sensitive* (FOCUS; Meller & Ohr, 2008)
Mesosystem	• Ask the family what communication looks like with teachers. Gather details about frequency, modality, topic, etc. • Ask the family what they believe their role is in their child's education.
Exosystem	• Ask the family if there are any policies (school, district, state, or federal level) that contribute to the child's concerns or strengths. • Ask the family if there are any policies (district, state, or federal level) that contribute to being discriminated against or marginalized. • Ask about life stressors (e.g., job loss, caregiving responsibilities for older relatives, mental health challenges). • Ask about changes that might alleviate stressors (e.g., job promotion, moved closer to social support, connected to community resources).
Macrosystem	• Ask the family to describe their cultural and religious values. ○ Ask the family if they believe school staff share and support these values. ○ Ask the family if school staff act in ways that align with these values.
Chronosystem	• Ask about the impact of societal or life events (COVID-19 pandemic) on family functioning. • Ask if media messaging related to identity (e.g., race, ethnicity, religion, gender) impacts social and emotional wellness.

environment. Thus, an ecological approach to behavioral and emotional assessment might include data collection at Tier 1, 2, and 3 within an MTSS framework.

TIER 1 (UNIVERSAL)

Within MTSS, Tier 1 pertains to the general classroom and school environment (e.g., assessment practices, supports delivered) for *all* students. It is important to collect and review data with at least an understanding of the cultural makeup of the school, including the racial, linguistic, and socioeconomic context of the student body. Understanding the schools' cultural makeup, particularly in relation to the identities of students and staff, can inform consideration of potential "mismatches" between the environment, staff, and students (La Salle et al., 2020). Within an MTSS framework, school psychologists should carefully consider if their assessment practices are culturally relevant to the student body, or if they serve to reinforce "racialized and gendered ideologies about what constitutes appropriate school behavior" (Irby, 2014, p. 517).

For more detailed information, school psychologists can collect or access schoolwide data that help illuminate broad patterns or factors related to students' behavioral and emotional wellness. For instance, school psychologists can assess dimensions of school climate (e.g., perceptions of safety, access to high-quality instruction, involvement in supportive relationships), which can facilitate behavioral and psychological functioning, to identify potential schoolwide needs (Wang & Degol, 2016). Given that students with marginalized

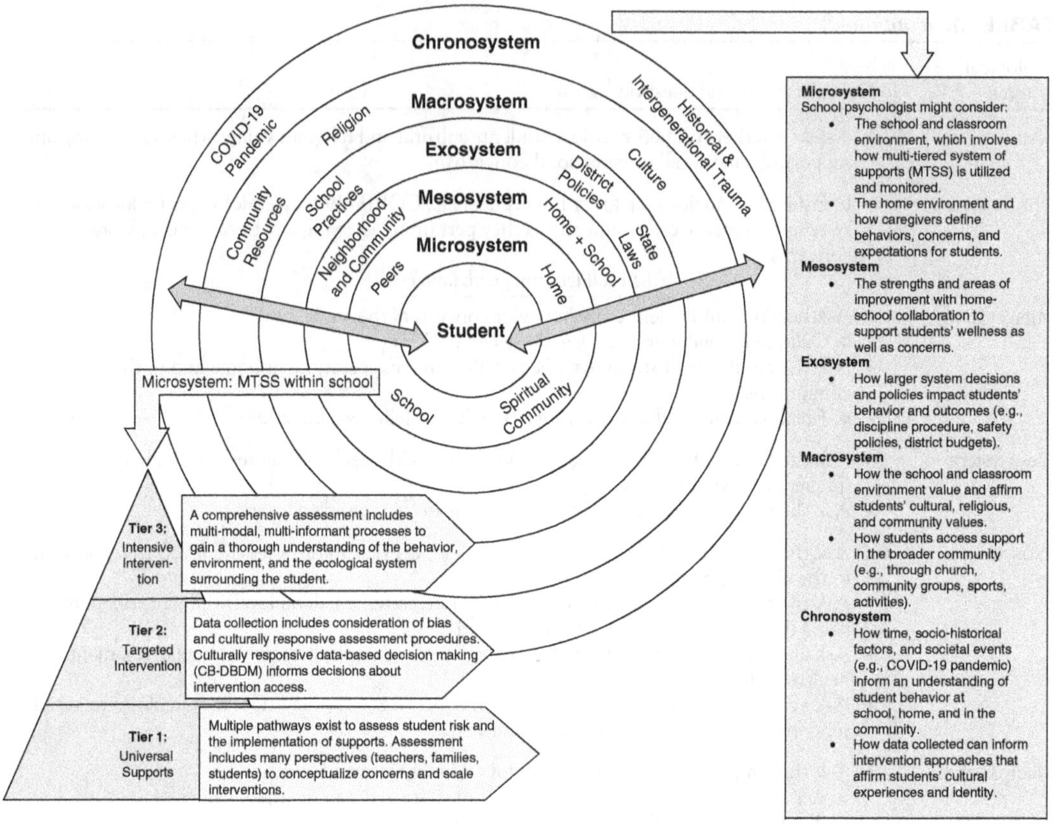

FIGURE 7.1. Consideration for behavioral and emotional assessment frames within an ecological model.

identities may experience school differently, an ecological framework for assessing school climate at multiple ecological levels, such as the *cultural–ecological model of school climate* (CEMSC; La Salle et al., 2015), is helpful to understand how individual, cultural, and contextual variables interact to shape students' experiences at school (La Salle et al., 2015).

School psychologists might also assess school racial climate. One way to do this is by surveying school personnel on relevant behaviors adapted from Learning for Justice (formerly Teaching Tolerance; 2013) in the domains of (1) adopting a social–emotional lens; (2) knowing students and developing cultural responsiveness; (3) moving discipline paradigms away from punishment toward teaching opportunities; (4) resisting the criminalization of school behavior; (5) maintaining an inclusive, cohesive, and nurturing work environment; and (6) addressing culture in school (Blitz et al., 2020). This may provide helpful insight to support both individual student and system needs related to behavioral and emotional functioning in schools, allowing educators to understand student behaviors within their environmental context.

In addition, universal screening for behavioral and emotional risk can highlight broad patterns of internalizing and externalizing concerns within the school environment, helping to identify who may benefit from additional support. Tools used for screening for behavioral and emotional concerns should be carefully assessed for cultural relevance (Fallon et al., 2022). School psychologists should spend time examining these data to determine if Tier 1 supports need to be strengthened schoolwide, disaggregating universal data to determine if perceptions of climate and behavior differ based on identity characteristics. If patterns in school climate or student behavior are noted to be related to marginalized identity characteristics, it may be paramount to design and deliver systems-level intervention to disrupt these disparities (Sullivan et al., 2020).

The instructional environment within the classroom also has an important impact on student behavior. In using an ecological approach, school psychologists can participate in assessing how curriculum and instruction are culturally appropriate for the classroom makeup (Lawson et al., 2024). For instance, administering the *Culturally Responsive Teacher Preparedness Scale* (CRTPS; Hsiao, 2015) will provide data related to teachers' perceptions of the cultural responsiveness of their classroom's curriculum and instruction, establishment of relationships and expectations, and group-belonging formation. School psychologists can evaluate whether social–emotional curricula are inclusive and relevant to the identities of their students using tools such as the *Culturally Responsive Curriculum Scorecard* (Bryan-Gooden et al., 2019). In addition, school psychologists can help teachers evaluate their own strengths and needs related to culturally responsive practices using tools like the *Assessment of Culturally and Contextually Relevant Supports* (ACCReS; Fallon et al., 2023), planning at a schoolwide level for professional development with resulting data. Finally, school psychologists can help assess the "mini-climate" of the classroom through tools that assess student-teacher relationships such as *Teacher Relationship Interview* (Koenen et al., 2019), which in turn predicts improved instruction and classroom behavior (Hasty et al., 2023; Li et al., 2022). By helping teachers self-assess their own practices and classroom environment, school psychologists can help increase the match between individual students and their learning environment.

ADVANCED TIERS

By having a proactive understanding of both the school and classwide ecological environment, school psychologists can begin to understand the behavior of students in context, identifying at which levels the "problem" exists and where intervention would be most beneficial (and equitable). In an ideal world, culturally responsive supports at the universal level would benefit all students in developing behavioral and emotional strengths that enable them to navigate their education successfully. However, regardless of the robustness of Tier 1, a certain percentage of students are likely to benefit from increased support provided at targeted and individual levels (i.e., Tiers 2 and 3). Importantly, it is critical that *culturally responsive data-based decision making* (CB-DBDM) is utilized in ruling out environmental factors (e.g., a lack of culturally responsive instruction) before deciding to refer a student for more intensive support (Kressler et al., 2020).

At Tier 2, students receive standardized, targeted interventions. This can consist of small groups providing manualized social–emotional instruction (e.g., culturally adapted *Strong Start*; Graves et al. 2017) or interventions such as Check-In/Check-Out (Simonsen et al., 2011). Gathering data to determine if students respond to these interventions is an important part of an ecological assessment approach. It allows school psychologists to understand and potentially rule out universal and environmental factors that contribute to the students' behavior by determining if they make progress when exposed to intervention (Loftus-Rattan et al., 2023). For instance, referring a student to a Tier 2 social skills group and examining progress monitoring data can help adults better understand the students' social skills in the context of a lack of exposure to culturally responsive social skills instruction and expectations rather than assuming an "inability" to socialize. At Tier 2, it is also critical to explore the degree of fit between the intervention and the students' cultural background. Otherwise, schools run the risk of further upholding dominant cultural norms and overlooking cultural strengths (Kressler et al., 2020).

Within Tier 3, students receive individualized interventions tailored specifically to their needs. Tier 3 supports are generally informed by more in-depth assessment procedures, frequent progress monitoring, and intensive intervention (Loftus-Rattan et al., 2023). Accordingly, school psychologists using an ecological approach assess the environment and the student more intensively within Tier 3. Often, this process involves conducting a functional behavior assessment (FBA), which examines the behavioral contingencies (e.g., antecedents and consequences) that reinforce and maintain a student's behavior within the context of the student's environment.

The FBA process should account for cultural factors, which can be done by incorporating a number of strategies (Veiga et al., 2025). As previously described, it is highly important to use multiple methods to gather information from multiple sources regarding the environmental correlates of behavior, particularly from caregivers. Methods should include direct observations on the frequency, duration, and intensity of behavior. In addition, information should be gathered from teachers through rating scales, interviews, and record review, all of which help understand behavioral patterns and the broader context of behavior. Including information from the student perspective is also important and may give the student an opportunity to share information about their behavior in the context of their particular culture (Johnson & Carpenter, 2022). This can help mitigate *some* bias that might come from a particular informant or method, although school psychologists should be continuously monitoring and be aware of the ways in which their own cultural background may impact the interpretation of the data and conceptualizations of which behaviors are "adaptive" (Leverson et al., 2019).

Home

Ecological assessment of students, particularly at the individual level, also necessitates gathering data from the multiple microsystems in which a student exists. Caregiver perspectives are the foundation of conducting a culturally relevant ecological assessment, as they have important insight on the student and family's cultural background, values, and norms (Veiga et al., 2025). Variables within the home environment, including structure and caregivers' discipline orientation, style of learning support, caregiver expectations, enrichment in the environment, and an affirming affective environment, have the potential to greatly impact a students' functioning at school (McCurdy et al., 2015). Functioning and expectations at home may differ from expectations at school to varying degrees, which can inform conclusions drawn as part of the assessment.

Several strategies and tools are available to help school psychologists consider culture when conducting assessment to inform intensive supports. For instance, Veiga et al. (2025) adapted the *Cultural Formulation Interview* for use within the context of conducting FBA with caregiver input. This interview process asked family members to define behavior and concerns, centering the family's perspective, expressing empathy, and using skills such as word matching to build trust. School psychologists trained in this approach reported high acceptability and moderate feasibility scores on a social validity assessment.

Similarly, Meller and Ohr (2008) outlined a *family-oriented, culturally sensitive* (FOCUS) model of assessment, which highlights the need to train personnel in culturally diverse assessment, evaluating both family and child strengths and needs, creating multidisciplinary interventions that emphasize both strengths and needs, and having an ongoing progress monitoring of interventions. By asking questions that help school psychologists gain an understanding of the family culture, school psychologists can better understand the function a behavior may be serving at school.

Mesosystems

A child's microsystems do not exist in isolation but rather interact and impact each other within the *mesosystem*, further influencing their behavior (Ettekal & Mahoney, 2017). Most relevant for behavior and emotional assessment, the mesosystem includes the ways in which caregivers and teachers interact and collaborate. Literature suggests that students are often more successful when home and school share consistent standards and expectations, have similar structure, offer cross-setting learning opportunities, provide mutual support, include positive and trusting relationships, and model desired behavior (McCurdy et al., 2015). Differences between a child's multiple environments (e.g., different expectations at home and school) are likely to impact their behavior as much as a mismatch between the immediate instructional environment and the child (Sheridan & Garbacz, 2022). In assessing social and emotional behavior, school psychologists should ask questions about these home–school interactions.

School psychologists should also assess what home–school interactions look like on a universal level. Wilson (2019) suggests that schools can form culturally responsive family–school partnerships by (1) rejecting deficit-based ideology, (2) understanding schools as contested cultural sites, (3) rejecting schools' legacies of racism and colonialism, and (4) validating familial and communicable knowledge; these domains can inform questions used to assess universal family–school relationships. Often, caregivers are blamed (implicitly or explicitly) for being "disengaged" or "resistant," which can alienate families from marginalized backgrounds, fails to account for White supremacy in education systems, and under-appreciates their cultural wealth. However, collaboration between home and school is bidirectional, and schools should take responsibility for creating opportunities for engagement that align more with the needs of caregivers and the community, accounting for the many cultural factors that impact school–home relationships (McWayne et al., 2019; Sheridan & Garbacz, 2022).

At the individual student level, school psychologists can ask all invested parties to share their perceptions of the home–school relationship. As part of an assessment process, school psychologists may ask teachers questions about how often they communicate with families, the methods they use to communicate, and the most frequent content of communications. They may ask caregivers how often they desire contact with the school, what they perceive their role to be in their child's education, and how they feel their relationship is with school personnel. Cultural values and expectations play a large role in families' expectations of what home–school collaboration means, making it important to understand how the family would like to be involved, as well as any potential barriers (Sheridan & Garbacz, 2022). School personnel's traditional expectations of family engagement may center dominant cultural norms (e.g., infrequent home/school contact, caregivers attending school events) and/or overlook barriers to engagement (e.g., timing of parent-teacher conferences, work schedules), necessitating a reframing of how caregiver engagement is conceptualized by educators (McWayne et al., 2019). By gathering this information, school psychologists can begin to understand the ways in which home–school relationships may be impacting a student's behavior and begin to work to strengthen systems and practices to benefit these relationships, as needed.

Exo-, Macro-, and Chronosystems

The ecological assessment literature within psychology and education often focusses on micro- and mesosystems with less emphasis on the exo-, macro-, and chronosystems in which a child exists. However, these larger systems are critical to account for in understanding how systems of advantage and disadvantage are formed and maintained, and in turn shape the educational experiences of students (Sullivan et al., 2015). Although perhaps harder to target with specific behavioral and emotional assessment practices, these broad systems remain crucial to assessing and understanding a child's behavior within a broad cultural context, particularly for students with marginalized identities. As such, an ecological approach to behavioral and emotional assessment should take steps to understand students' and families' perspectives on how factors at each level impact their functioning.

The *exosystem* involves systems and institutions in which students are not directly involved but have the potential to impact their emotions and behavior (Ettekal & Mahoney, 2017). This may include education policies, procedures, and laws decided at the district, school board, or even state level. These decisions can impact curriculum choices in schools, potentially limiting the degree of identity-affirming curricula students are exposed to and impacting their feelings of belonging (Covarrubias & Fryberg, 2015). Exosystem policies also have the potential to impact bullying and perceptions of support. For example, schools with specific protective policies regarding LGBTQ students were associated with less bullying and higher perceived support (Day et al., 2020). Laws passed that restrict gender affirming care and/or expression can impact students' access to care, in turn impacting their experiences of well-being, depression, and suicidality (Tordoff et al., 2022). Court decisions that uphold schools' racist and/or sexist dress code policies penalize students who do not meet typical standards of professionalism and appropriateness, most frequently marginalized students (Aghasaleh, 2018). These policies and procedures, which in turn impact the school environment, have direct impacts on students' behavioral and emotional well-being and on what is viewed as "a problem." An understanding of exosystem variables and their impact on well-being, perceptions of behavior, and environmental mismatch are important for school psychologists conducting assessment using an ecological approach.

Many institutions at the exosystem are influenced and informed by the larger *macrosystem*, which captures the values, cultures, and norms that impact a child's context. These may include factors such as dominant religions in the community, the socioeconomic structure of the students' environment, and values related to individualism (Ettekal & Mahoney, 2017). Importantly for the purposes of ecological assessment, macrosystem values often influence norms and expectations within the school. Given that the dominant culture within the United States is explicitly racialized and serves to uphold White, male, middle class, heterosexual norms, schools also function to uphold and perpetuate these macrosystem norms and thus contribute to disparities in healthcare, housing, education, and employment (Sanders & Molgaard, 2019). For many students holding marginalized identities, this creates an artificial "mismatch" between the student and their environment, perceived by many educators as a behavioral or emotional problem. If school staff fail to understand the differences between the current macrosystem and the students' cultural values, they risk pathologizing students' strengths and adaptive behaviors (Sheridan & Garbacz, 2022). Thus, school psychologists should carefully gather information on students' cultural values and norms, and the degree to which that is consistent with broader macrosystem norms in the United States when using an ecological approach to behavioral and emotional assessment.

At the broadest level, it is also important to consider the *chronosystem* and *time* as containing important sociohistorical factors that contribute to students' behavioral and emotional functioning (Ettekal & Mahoney, 2017). Many educators are acutely aware of the impact of the COVID-19 pandemic on students' social skills, anxiety, and behavioral functioning, which is likely to last for many years (Reuter et al., 2021). These impacts and others, including death and illness, disproportionately affected students from marginalized backgrounds (Sullivan et al., 2020). Less attention is often paid to other sociohistorical factors and the ways in which they continue to impact marginalized students. These events may include the broadcasting of racialized violence by the police; exposure to racialized war, violence, and oppression across the globe; and harmful, dismissive, and/or reductive narratives perpetuated via the media regarding these types of events (Howard et al., 2023; Staggers-Hakim, 2016). In addition, historical factors that continue into modern times, including schools' history of racial segregation, the racial underpinnings of psychoeducational assessment, and the legacy of race and gender-based oppression continue to impact the ways in which schools operate in modern day.

In drawing conclusions and developing intervention recommendations for students based on an ecological approach to behavioral and emotional assessment, it may not feel feasible or possible to address issues that occur or have occurred beyond the micro- and mesosystems. The long-term impacts of COVID-19, or of the country's history of racial oppression on school structures, are not likely to be eliminated at a social level in time to address an individual student's behavioral and emotional well-being. However, in incorporating an awareness of these impacts, their manifestations in schools, and concrete recommendations for addressing them when working with students, school psychologists can still incorporate multisystemic factors into an ecological assessment approach.

FUTURE DIRECTIONS

As mentioned throughout this chapter, traditional assessment of behavioral and emotional concerns may offer a limited understanding of the nuance and complexity of a student concern. An ecological approach to behavioral and emotional assessment allows one to expand their assessment beyond initial perspective of behavior to collect information about the systems surrounding a student or students (micro-, meso-, exo-, macro-, and chronosystem), gaining a more comprehensive understanding of not only a student's behavior but their life, culture, and experience both inside and outside of school. This can not only provide more information to guide decision making and hypotheses (e.g., determining behavioral function) but also lead to more culturally relevant and affirming intervention delivery.

As school psychologists navigate typical school systems, they can leverage an ecological approach to behavioral and emotional assessment. For instance, often when a referral for an intensive behavior concern arises, an FBA is conducted. During the FBA, a measurable definition of the behavior is developed, data are collected and reviewed (e.g., interviews, surveys, observations); a hypothesis of why the behavior occurs is created; a Behavior Intervention Plan (BIP) is formulated; and the implementation and evaluation of its effectiveness is measured. As shown in Figure 7.1, before defining and observing the student's behavior of concern, an ecological approach might involve a school psychologist evaluating

1. the *microsystem* of the student within the school (including the effectiveness of MTSS) and home environment
2. the strengths and areas of improvement in the school-to-home interaction within the student's *mesosystem*
3. the *exosystem* of the student and how larger systems, like school discipline policies and state laws, affect the student
4. the student's cultural and religious values and socioeconomic status that create their *macrosystem*
5. the *chronosystem*, where time and sociohistorical events, can impact the student based on their developmental stage

For example, the behavior of a Latinx male student who was referred for "aggression" can be conceptualized in two different ways depending on the approach. In both approaches to assessing the student's behavior, observations might indicate that a setting event is *absenteeism*; the antecedent is *teacher direction to do independent work*; the behavior is the *use of inappropriate language* and *physical altercations with peers*; and the consequence is *teacher reprimand* and an *office discipline referral*. A more traditional behavioral assessment approach may include generating a hypothesis about behavioral function (e.g., *escape from task demands*) via teacher interview, classroom observation, and review of past office discipline referrals. This approach largely centers the teacher's perspective and concerns about the child's behavior and may limit the school psychologist's understanding of the behavior to that specific classroom, teacher, and peers. In turn, the BIP reflects this lack of comprehensive understanding of the student's behavior by providing support only to the individual student within that specific classroom context. Specifically, the BIP instructs the classroom teacher to provide a break to the student when they use a break card appropriately, fading the number of breaks available to the student over time. This approach may work to improve classroom behavior, but it will likely not address any root cause of behavioral occurrences, potentially limiting its maintenance and generalizability outside of the immediate classroom context.

An ecological approach would involve data collection with multiple informants including the student (depending on their age) and others who are influential within the systems surrounding the student (see Table 7.1). There may also be observations within home, school, and community settings, comprehensive record review, and multiple perspectives offered via interview and on standardized rating forms. As a result of this process, the school psychologist may learn that this Latinx male student is frequently absent since there has been a change in his living situation due to his mother's incarceration. In talking with the student, the school psychologist also learns that he is bullied by his peers at lunch because of his mother's incarceration, and is sometimes targeted for speaking Spanish at school. This causes him to use inappropriate language and get into physical altercations in classes following the lunch period (*microsystem*). It is discovered that he is living with his aunt who is not connected to the school system and operations (*mesosystem*), often missing communications from school. In addition, the school did not inquire about the family's language preferences, communicating exclusively in English despite family members being bilingual Spanish and English speakers. Furthermore, the school's discipline policies (*exosystem*) are structured such that teachers are to send their students to the office for classroom disruption, causing students to frequently miss academic instruction. Moreover, in speaking to the student's aunt, the school psychologist learns the value of religion and community to the student and that the student volunteers with his neighbors in the local church every Sunday (*macrosystem*). His church leader is adept at breaking multi-step tasks down for the student, encourages teamwork among the student volunteers, and has a close relationship with the students' family. Lastly, when gathering data, the school psychologist considers the factors that contributed to the student's mother's incarceration (e.g., few economic resources and job opportunities, lack of access to a high-quality education; *chronosystem*) and the likelihood that intergenerational trauma (e.g., racism, oppression, immigration) impacts the student's lived experience in and outside of school. This informs the school psychologist's understanding of the student's environment; how his behavior is operationalized; and the types of support that may be most beneficial to him (e.g., affinity spaces, mentorship from an adult with similar identity characteristics, communication between church leaders, caregivers, and teachers, community groups for family members of incarcerated individuals). This type of assessment may not currently be typical in the field of school psychology, and we recognize that it requires additional steps, but systematically adopting an ecological approach to behavioral and emotional assessment is a viable future direction to advance culturally responsive practice in the field.

CONCLUSION

By using an ecological lens to approach behavioral and emotional assessment, school psychologists can begin to assess and address the systemic and organizational factors that contribute to inequities in education. This broadens the scope of impact from individual assessment and intervention to broader school communities and educational systems. An ecological approach often incorporates collaboration with educators, families, and students, gathering multiple perspectives across varied contexts, supporting a more comprehensive understanding of student concerns. Although adopting an ecological approach when engaging in behavioral and emotional assessment may not increase equitable outcomes inherently, it can serve as a valuable mechanism to shed light on potential inequities and begin the process toward systems change.

REFERENCES

Abrams, L. S., Mizel, M. L., & Barnert, E. S. (2021). The criminalization of young children and overrepresentation of Black youth in the juvenile justice system. *Race and Social Problems, 13*(1), 73–84.

Achenbach, T. M. (2017). Multi-informant and multicultural advances in evidence-based assessment of students' behavioral/emotional/social difficulties. *European Journal of Psychological Assessment, 34*(2), 127–140.

Adair, J. K. (2015). *The impact of discrimination on the early schooling experiences of children from immigrant families.* Migration Policy Institute.

Aghasaleh, R. (2018). Oppressive curriculum: Sexist, racist, classist, and homophobic practice of dress codes in schooling. *Journal of African American Studies, 22,* 94–108.

Banks, J. A. (2015). *Cultural diversity and education.* Routledge.

Blitz, L. V., Yull, D., & Clauhs, M. (2020). Bringing sanctuary to school: Assessing school climate as a foundation for culturally responsive trauma-informed approaches for urban schools. *Urban Education, 55*(1), 95–124.

Bronfenbrenner, U. (1979). *The ecology of human development: Experiments by nature and design.* Harvard University Press.

Bronfenbrenner, U., & Morris, P. A. (2006). The bioecological model of human development. In W. Damon, & R. M. Lerner (Eds.), *Handbook of child psychology: Vol. 1. Theoretical models of child development* (6th ed., pp. 793–828). Wiley.

Bryan-Gooden, J., Hester, M., & Peoples, L. Q. (2019). *Culturally responsive curriculum scorecard.* Metropolitan Center for Research on Equity and the Transformation of Schools New York University. *https://docs.steinhardt.nyu.edu/pdfs/metrocenter/atn293/ejroc/CRE-Rubric-2018-190211.pdf*

Children's Defense Fund. (1974). *Children out of school in America: A report by the Children's Defense Fund.* Washington Research Project.

Chu, S. (2011). Teacher perceptions of their efficacy for special education referral of students from culturally and linguistically diverse backgrounds. *Education, 132*(1), 3–14.

Covarrubias, R., & Fryberg, S. A. (2015). The impact of self-relevant representations on school belonging for Native American students. *Cultural Diversity and Ethnic Minority Psychology, 21*(1), 10–18.

Day, J. K., Fish, J. N., Grossman, A. H., & Russell, S. T. (2020). Gay–straight alliances, inclusive policy, and school climate: LGBTQ youths' experiences of social support and bullying. *Journal of Research on Adolescence, 30,* 418–430.

Ettekal, A. V., & Mahoney, J. L. (2017). Ecological systems theory. In K. Peppler (Ed.), *The SAGE encyclopedia of out-of-school learning* (pp. 230–241). SAGE.

Fadus, M. C., Valadez, E. A., Bryant, B. E., Garcia, A. M., Neelon, B., Tomko, R. L., et al. (2021). Racial disparities in elementary school disciplinary actions: Findings from the ABCD study. *Journal of the American Academy of Child & Adolescent Psychiatry, 60*(8), 998–1009.

Fallon, L. M., Cathcart, S. C., Johnson, A. H., Minami, T., O'Keeffe, B. V., DeFouw, E. R., et al. (2023). A teacher self-assessment of culturally relevant practice to inform educator professional development decisions in MTSS contexts. *Assessment for Effective Intervention, 48*(2), 100–112.

Fallon, L. M., Veiga, M., & Sugai, G. (2021). Strengthening MTSS for behavior (MTSS-B) to promote racial equity. *School Psychology Review, 52*(5), 518–533.

Fallon, L. M., Veiga, M., Susilo, A., Robinson-Link, P., Berkman, T., Minami, T., et al. (2022). Exploring the relationship between teachers' perceptions of cultural responsiveness, student risk, and classroom behavior. *Psychology in the Schools, 59*(10), 1948–1964.

Gage, N. A., Whitford, D. K., Katsiyannis, A., Adams, S., & Jasper, A. (2019). National analysis of the disciplinary exclusion of Black students with and without disabilities. *Journal of Child and Family Studies, 28*(7), 1754–1764.

Gay, G. (2018). *Culturally responsive teaching: Theory, research, and practice.* Teachers College Press.

Girvan, E. J., McIntosh, K., & Smolkowski, K. (2019). Tail, tusk, and trunk: What different metrics reveal about racial disproportionality in school discipline. *Educational Psychologist, 54*(1), 40–59.

Graves, S. L., Jr., Herndon-Sobalvarro, A., Nichols, K., Aston, C., Ryan, A., Blefari, A., et al. (2017). Examining the effectiveness of a culturally adapted social–emotional intervention for African American males in an urban setting. *School Psychology Quarterly, 32*(1), 62–74.

Great Schools Partnership. (2023). *Indicators of Educational Equity.* Great Schools Partnership. *www.greatschoolspartnership.org/resources/equitable-community-engagement/indicators-of-educational-equity*

Gutkin, T. B. (2012). Ecological psychology: Replacing the medical model paradigm for school-based psychological and psychoeducational services. *Journal of Educational and Psychological Consultation, 22*(1–2), 1–20.

Hasty, L. M., Quintero, M., Li, T., Song, S., & Wang, Z. (2023). The longitudinal associations among student externalizing behaviors, teacher-student relationships, and classroom engagement. *Journal of School Psychology, 100.*

Hazel, C. E. (2017). Ecological consultation as a means to promote child rights. In C. Hatzichristou & S. Rosenfield (Eds.), *The international handbook of consultation in educational settings* (pp. 264–288). Routledge.

Howard, L. C., Krueger, E. A., Barker, J. O., Cruz, T. B., Cwalina, S. N., Unger, J. B., et al. (2023). Young adults' distress about police brutality following the death of George Floyd. *Youth & Society, 55*(6), 1173–1190.

Hsiao, Y. J. (2015). The culturally responsive teacher preparedness scale: An exploratory study. *Contemporary Issues in Education Research*, 8(4), 241–250. *https://eric.ed.gov/?id=EJ1077322*

Hughes, D., Del Toro, J., Harding, J. F., Way, N., & Rarick, J. R. D. (2016). Trajectories of discrimination across adolescence: Associations with academic, psychological, and behavioral outcomes. *Child Development*, 87(5), 1337–1351.

Individuals With Disabilities Education Improvement Act (IDEA), 20 U.S.C. § 1400 *et seq.* (2004).

Irby, D. J. (2014). Trouble at school: Understanding school discipline systems as nets of social control. *Equity & Excellence in Education*, 47(4), 513–530.

Johnson, H. N., & Carpenter, M. E. (2022). Including student input as a critical component of functional behavior assessment. *Beyond Behavior*, 31(3), 175–184.

Koenen, A. K., Vervoort, E., Verschueren, K., & Spilt, J. L. (2019). Teacher–student relationships in special education: The value of the *Teacher Relationship Interview*. *Journal of Psychoeducational Assessment*, 37(7), 874–886.

Kressler, B., Chapman, L. A., Kunkel, A., & Hovey, K. A. (2020). Culturally responsive data-based decision making in high school settings. *Intervention in School and Clinic*, 55(4), 214–220.

Ladson-Billings, G. (2023). "Yes, but how do we do it?": Practicing culturally relevant pedagogy. In J. G. Landsman & C. W. Lewis (Eds.), *White teachers/diverse classrooms* (pp. 33–46). Routledge.

La Salle, T. P., Meyers, J., Varjas, K., & Roach, A. (2015). A cultural-ecological model of school climate. *International Journal of School & Educational Psychology*, 3(3), 157–166.

La Salle, T. P., Wang, C., Wu, C., & Rocha Neves, J. (2020). Racial mismatch among minoritized students and White teachers: Implications and recommendations for moving forward. *Journal of Educational and Psychological Consultation*, 30(3), 314–343.

Lawson, T., K., Knox, J., Romero, E., Palacios, A. M., & Fallon, L. M. (2024). Check yourself!: Exploring current culturally responsive teaching assessment measures. *Psychology in the Schools*, 61(6), 2649–2667.

Leverson, M., Smith, K., McIntosh, K., Rose, J., & Pinkelman, S. (2019). *PBIS culturally responsiveness field guide: Resources for trainers and coaches*. OSEP Technical Assistance Center on Positive Behavioral Interventions and Supports. *www.pbis.org*

Li, X., Bergin, C., & Olsen, A. A. (2022). Positive teacher-student relationships may lead to better teaching. *Learning and Instruction*, 80, 101581.

Loftus-Rattan, S. M., Wrightington, M., Furey, J., & Case, J. (2023). Multi-tiered system of supports: An ecological approach to school psychology service delivery. *Teaching of Psychology*, 50(1), 77–85.

McCurdy, M., Coutts, M. J., Sheridan, S. M., & Campbell, L. M. (2015). Ecological variables in school-based assessment and intervention planning. In R. Brown-Chidsey & K. J. Andren (Eds.), *Assessment for intervention: A problem-solving approach* (2nd ed., pp. 39–61). Guilford Press.

McWayne, C. M., Doucet, F., & Mistry, J. (2019). Family-school partnerships in ethnocultural communities: Reorienting conceptual frameworks, research methods, and intervention efforts by rotating our lens. In C. M. McWayne, F. Doucet, & S. M. Sheridan (Eds.), *Ethnocultural diversity and the home-to-school link* (pp. 1–18). Springer.

Meller, P. J., & Ohr, P. S. (2008). Family-Oriented, Culturally Sensitive (FOCUS) assessment of young children. In L. A. Suzuki, & J. G. Ponterotto (Eds.), *Handbook of multicultural assessment: Clinical, psychological, and educational applications* (pp. 565–593). Jossey-Bass/Wiley.

Morris, E. W., & Perry, B. L. (2016). The punishment gap: School suspension and racial disparities in achievement. *Social Problems*, 63(1), 68–86.

National Association of School Psychologists. (2020). *Model for comprehensive and integrated school psychological services. https://casponline.org/pdfs/pdfs/practice_model_brochure.pdf*

Paris, D., & Alim, H. S. (2014). What are we seeking to sustain through culturally sustaining pedagogy? A loving critique forward. *Harvard Educational Review*, 84(1), 85–100.

Peters, T., Margolin, M., Fragnoli, K., & Bloom, D. (2016). What's race got to do with it? Preservice teachers and White racial identity. *Current Issues in Education*, 19(1), 1–22. *https://cie.asu.edu/ojs/index.php/cieatasu/article/view/1661*

Reuter, P. R., Forster, B. L., & Kruger, B. J. (2021). A longitudinal study of the impact of COVID-19 restrictions on students' health behavior, mental health and emotional well-being. *PeerJ*, 9, e12528.

Sanders, K., & Molgaard, M. (2019). Considering race within early childhood education: A misunderstood and underexplored element of family-school partnerships in child care. In C. M. McWayne, F. Doucet, & S. M. Sheridan (Eds.) *Ethnocultural diversity and the home-to-school link* (pp. 19–36). Springer.

Shell, E. M., Johnson, L. V., & Getch, Y. Q. (2019). Good intentions, poor outcomes: Centering culture and language diversity within Response to Intervention. *Journal of School Counseling*, 17(24), 1–34. *http://www.jsc.montana.edu/articles/v17n24.pdf*

Sheridan, S. M., & Garbacz, S. A. (2022). Centering families: Advancing a new vision for school psychology. *School Psychology Review*, 51(6), 726–741.

Simonsen, B., Myers, D., & Briere, D. E., III. (2011). Comparing a behavioral check-in/check-out (CICO) intervention to standard practice in an urban middle school setting using an experimental group design. *Journal of Positive Behavior Interventions*, 13(1), 31–48.

Southern Poverty Law Center. (2013). *Toolkit for a "Teacher's Guide to Rerouting the Pipeline". Learning for Justice*, 43. *www.learningforjustice.org/magazine/spring-2013/toolkit-for-a-teachers-guide-to-rerouting-the-pipeline*

Staggers-Hakim, R. (2016). The nation's unprotected children and the ghost of Mike Brown, or the impact of national police killings on the health and social development of African American boys. *Journal of Human Behavior in the Social Environment*, *26*(3–4), 390–399.

Sugai, G., & Horner, R. H. (2020). Sustaining and scaling positive behavioral interventions and supports: Implementation drivers, outcomes, and considerations. *Exceptional Children*, *86*(2), 120–136.

Sullivan, A. L., Artiles, A. J., & Hernandez-Saca, D. I. (2015). Addressing special education inequity through systemic change: Contributions of ecologically based organizational consultation. *Journal of Educational and Psychological Consultation*, *25*(2–3), 129–147.

Sullivan, A. L., Miller, F. G., McKevett, N. M., Muldrew, A., Hansen-Burke, A., & Weeks, M. (2020). Leveraging MTSS to advance, not suppress, COVID-related equity issues. *NASP Communiqué*, *49*(1), 26, 28–29. *https://eric.ed.gov/?id=EJ1266121*

Tefera, A. A., & Fischman, G. E. (2020). How and why context matters in the study of racial disproportionality in special education: Toward a critical disability education policy approach. *Equity and Excellence in Education*, *53*(4), 434–449.

Tordoff, D. M., Wanta, J. W., Collin, A., Stepney, C., Inwards-Breland, D. J., & Ahrens, K. (2022). Mental health outcomes in transgender and nonbinary youths receiving gender-affirming care. *JAMA Network Open*, *5*(2), e220978–e220978.

Utley, C. A., Kozleski, E., Smith, A., & Draper, I. L. (2002). Positive behavior support: A proactive strategy for minimizing behavior problems in urban multicultural youth. *Journal of Positive Behavior Interventions*, *4*(4), 196–207.

Veiga, M. B., Fallon, L. M., Collier-Meek., M. A., Susilo, A., Ballard, S., & Sunda, R. (2025). Training school psychologists to conduct culturally-informed functional behavioral assessment interviews. *School Psychology*, *40*(2), 264–273.

Wang, M. T., & Degol, J. L. (2016). School climate: A review of the construct, measurement, and impact on student outcomes. *Educational Psychology Review*, *28*(2), 315–352.

Wilson, C. M. (2019). Volume 4 commentary: Insights for co-constructing transformative family–school partnerships that increase cultural responsiveness, justice, and care. In C. M. McWayne, F. Doucet, & S. M. Sheridan (Eds.), *Ethnocultural diversity and the home-to-school link* (pp. 145–160). Springer.

Ysseldyke, J., Lekwa, A. J., Klingbeil, D. A., & Cormier, D. C. (2012). Assessment of ecological factors as an integral part of academic and mental health consultation. *Journal of Educational and Psychological Consultation*, *22*(1–2), 21–43.

CHAPTER 8

Assessing Implementation Outcomes within Multi-Tiered Systems of Support

Melissa A. Collier-Meek, Alexandra M. Pierce, and Sarina H. Alavi

The recent Surgeon General's Advisory (2021) highlighted the stark increase in youth behavioral and emotional health challenges, rising to the level of a significant public health crisis. In 2021, 42% of high school students indicated persistent feelings of sadness and hopelessness with 22% seriously contemplating suicide (Centers for Disease Control and Prevention [CDC], 2023). Over 10% of children and youth ages 5–17 participate in counseling from a mental health professional (Zablotsky & Ng, 2023). Many more children are not able to access needed mental health treatment, with more barriers experienced by students from marginalized races/ethnicities and families with low socioeconomic status (Surgeon's General Advisory, 2021). Indeed, students who have had adverse childhood experiences (ACEs) and who come from marginalized backgrounds have higher rates of mental health conditions, such as depression and substance use disorders, and less access to high-quality care (CDC, 2023). To meet this public health crisis, children and youth need both proactive and responsive evidence-based support informed by empirically validated, culturally relevant assessment data (Sullivan et al., 2022).

Students in need of behavioral and emotional health support most often receive such support within schools (Surgeon's General Advisory, 2021). To systematically facilitate assessment and intervention, schools have adopted multi-tiered systems of support (MTSS; e.g., Algozzine et al., 2014; Schimke et al., 2022). Based on a public health model, MTSS includes Tier 1 universal supports for all students, Tier 2 targeted supports for students at-risk of social–emotional and behavioral difficulties, and Tier 3 intensive supports for students with more complex or severe needs (Jackson, 2021; Sullivan et al., 2022). To ensure appropriate, timely support, MTSS incorporates periodic assessment to inform Tier 1 practices and identify students who would benefit from additional intervention and, for those students, increasingly comprehensive assessment and progress monitoring to ensure appropriate interventions are provided and impactful. In this way, the goals of MTSS are to (1) improve all students' access to high-quality support, thus reducing the number of students who require intensive support and (2) provide responsive, timely intervention to remediate challenges, when appropriate (Jackson, 2021; Sullivan et al., 2022). For more foundational information on MTSS, see Chapter 4 (this volume), on assessment within a public health paradigm.

To realize these goals, school teams responsible for MTSS need to consider school and student data as well as implementation outcomes. Socio-emotional screening data, attendance/tardy data, grades, office discipline referrals, and other disciplinary outcome data can be used to inform student-level decisions as well as make decisions about the sufficiency of support from a whole school perspective (Jackson, 2021). However, extensive research spanning multiple disciplines demonstrates that interventions and practices, including those within school settings, are seldom executed as intended (i.e., not implemented as intended or at all), which leads to limited change or student improvement (Sanetti & Collier-Meek, 2019a). When student outcomes are evaluated without implementation data, school teams might unfairly attribute lack of progress to perceived student deficits rather than failures of implementation (Jackson, 2021; Sanetti & Collier-Meek, 2019b). Unfortunately, few schools implementing MTSS collect implementation data on the overall framework or implementation of interventions aligned with specific tiers, making direct measurements of student outcomes the primary gauge of effectiveness (Lendrum & Humphrey, 2012; Vekaria, 2017). Without implementation data, MTSS is unlikely to result in meaningful systems change and reach its purported goals.

IMPLEMENTATION OUTCOMES

Evaluating implementation outcomes enables MTSS teams to understand how well systems and interventions are being utilized in a school setting, shifting discussion and accountability away from individual students to the system itself (Fallon et al., 2021; Jackson, 2021). Implementation is a complex and multi-layered process of change (Sanetti & Collier-Meek, 2019a). Proctor et al. (2011) present a research-informed framework of implementation outcomes, which includes acceptability, adoption, appropriateness, costs, feasibility, fidelity, penetration, and sustainability as key variables to monitor and support. The assessment of MTSS implementation outcomes provides opportunities to pursue systemic changes that support equitable student outcomes, such as making culturally responsive adjustments to service delivery, curricula, or resource allocation. The purpose of this chapter is to introduce implementation outcomes and highlight their relevance for assessment within MTSS. In Table 8.1, we define implementation outcomes, associated measurement approaches, available tools, measurement timing, and considerations for advancing equity. Table 8.2 illustrates examples of implementation outcomes across tiers. The sections that follow provide detailed information about and recommendations to support schools' evaluation of these crucial implementation outcomes.

Adoption

Adoption, also referred to as uptake, can be conceptualized as initiating implementation and can incorporate the intention or actions associated with beginning to implement a new practice or intervention (Lloyd et al., 2023; Proctor et al., 2011, 2023). Adoption can encompass systemwide decisions (e.g., district adoption of screening

TABLE 8.1. Implementation Outcomes, Measurement Approaches, Tools, and Timing, and Equity Considerations

Implementation outcome	Measurement approach and considerations	Available tools	Measurement timing	Considerations for advancing equity
Adoption: the initial choice to implement or actions associated with implementing a practice, program, or intervention.	Validated scales, surveys, focus groups, and community advisory groups	Attitudes Toward Evidence-based Practice, Change Orientation Scale, Implementation Climate Scale	At the beginning of implementation	• Include community members in all aspects of adoption and its assessment to build trust. • Use focus groups, surveys, or interviews to assess the cultural appropriateness and cultural sensitivity of a new practice. • Make planned, proactive adaptations to improve fit.

(continued)

TABLE 8.1. *(continued)*

Implementation outcome	Measurement approach and considerations	Available tools	Measurement timing	Considerations for advancing equity
Fidelity: the extent to which a practice (e.g., tiered student intervention) is implemented as originally intended.	Three step process: (1) break down intervention into observable/measurable steps, (2) select measurement approach, and (3) select rating system. Use systematic direct observation, permanent product review, or self-report.	Treatment Integrity Measure for Early Childhood Settings (TIMECS), Tiered Fidelity Inventory, MTSS Fidelity Implementation Rubric	Throughout implementation	• Adjust fidelity measurement to incorporate cultural adaptation and ensure critical component delivery. • Use fidelity data to ensure that the student(s) is/are receiving the full extent of an intervention that they are intended to receive. • Ensure fidelity data inform systems changes, such as increasing feasibility and providing technical support.
Feasibility: the extent to which a program, initiative, or intervention can be carried out successfully in the implementation context.	Multi-informant, multi-method approach	Intervention Rating Profile–15 (IRP-15), Usage Rating Profile—Intervention Revised (URP-IR)	Before implementation, throughout implementation	• Incorporate feedback from educators about feasibility and make necessary adaptions. • Gather information about school-based implementation barriers and facilitators. • Consider cultural or linguistic barriers and make adaptations to enhance feasibility.
Acceptability: stakeholder perceptions of whether a given practice is appropriate, fair, reasonable, or satisfactory.	Use a combination of validated rating scales, surveys, focus groups, and interviews	Intervention Rating Profile (IRP), Children's Intervention Rating Profile (CIRP), Behavior Intervention Rating Scale (BIRS), Usage Rating Profile—Intervention Revised (URP-IR), Children's Usage Rating Profile (CURP), Kids Intervention Profile	Before implementation, throughout implementation	• Measure acceptability quantitatively and qualitatively. • Include interviews with community members, survey culturally diverse groups, and assess teacher and student perceptions of the intervention. • Keep in mind participants' reading level and language preferences. • Repeat acceptability measures throughout intervention implementation to inform changes and technical assistance.

(continued)

TABLE 8.1. *(continued)*

Implementation outcome	Measurement approach and considerations	Available tools	Measurement timing	Considerations for advancing equity
Cost: the overall resource requirements (financial or otherwise) of implementing a practice, program, or intervention.	Evaluate cost before adopting a new practice to ensure that adequate resources can be dedicated to its implementation and sustainment.	Ingredients method, cost-effectiveness analysis, cost feasibility analysis	Before implementation, throughout implementation, after implementation	• Take a mixed method approach, focusing on including diverse perspectives on cost at various levels, including community, district, school, and educators.
Reach: the extent to which a practice or intervention is integrated into a context, including the number of individuals who are willing to engage with a new intervention or practice.	Typically assessed as the proportion of individuals who are receiving an intervention to the total population who is intended to receive an intervention. Assess for differences between participants and non-participants. Use qualitative methods to gather more information about why an individual participates in or receives an intervention or why they do not.		Throughout implementation, after implementation	• Examine disproportionality across diverse groups and consider intersectional factors that might impede reach. Incorporate student and stakeholder expectations and perceptions of reach, gauged through methods like surveys, interviews, and focus groups. • Leverage a participatory approach to involve students, families, and community members who can provide information about cultural nuances, preferences, and barriers to reaching a specific student population.
Sustainability: the extent to which an intervention or practice is maintained over time.	Should be evaluated well into or after the implementation process. Can include focus groups, surveys, interviews, and classroom observations/walk-throughs	Schoolwide Universal Behavior Sustainability Index–School Teams (SUBSIST), Assessment of Barriers to Implementation and Sustainability in Schools (ABISS)	After implementation	• Utilize a multi-method approach to identify factors related to sustainment, including student and implementer culture/language, implementation challenges, and intervention effectiveness.

TABLE 8.2. Implementation Outcomes and Applied Examples in MTSS

Implementation outcome	Applied examples		
	Tier 1 (universal)	Tier 2 (targeted)	Tier 3 (intensive)
Adoption	A school team considers establishing a token economy system to reinforce desired schoolwide behaviors. Once implemented, the team sends a survey to staff to assess whether the system is being implemented and in what areas of the school; it includes open-ended questions about why the system is being used or not, as well as what changes could be made to the system. They use this information to make modifications.	An MTSS team considers implementing Check-In/Check-Out (CICO). A focus group is held with school staff and parents. The team asks staff about available time and the needed training and resources to implement CICO. They assess parents' interest in a home-school communication system and discuss with all participants whether CICO is a cultural and contextual fit. The team uses this information to guide adaptations.	A Tier 3 team receives a referral for a student who is struggling behaviorally and needs a brief behavior plan. The teacher and paraprofessional attend a meeting to identify needed resources and training and gain an understanding of their capacity to implement the plan. The teacher and paraprofessional attend monthly meetings with the team to assess and problem-solve the adoption of plan components.
Fidelity	An MTSS team recently implemented a social–emotional learning curriculum. To monitor fidelity, the team asks teachers to complete an online form after each lesson to indicate what percentage of components were delivered on a scale from 0 (*0%*) to 10 (*100%*), as well as how responsive students were to the lesson from 1 (*not engaged*) to 5 (*completely engaged*).	A school's MTSS team identifies seven students who require targeted social skills support and decides to implement small-group social–emotional skill instruction. The team monitors fidelity to the program by asking interventionists to provide permanent products in the form of lesson plans and copies of completed student worksheets. They review these data at regular monthly MTSS meetings.	A school team identifies a student requiring behavioral support and develops a behavior plan, defining specific goals, strategies, and progress monitoring measures. Fidelity data are collected through direct observations using a simple checklist. The team reviews data biweekly, discussing adaptations to improve cultural and contextual fit with the teacher.
Feasibility	An MTSS team is considering a Tier 1 intervention to reduce disruptive behavior. To their planning meeting, they invite grade-level lead teachers, paraeducators, the school psychologist, and the assistant principal. Together, they engage in resource mapping to identify available material resources, personnel, and time; this allows them to ameliorate barriers up-front. The team also sends out the URP-IR feasibility subscale to all teachers one month into implementation.	Several teachers have referred students to the Tier 2 team due to concerns about externalizing behaviors. The team reviews available programs, considering interventionist time, budget, and existing supports. The team invites staff to join their monthly meeting to solicit feedback on program feasibility, barriers, and suggestions for possible improvements. The team incorporates this feedback in planned adaptations and continues to engage with interventionists monthly.	At a monthly MTSS meeting, the team identifies three students who would benefit from individualized support for self-regulation skills. A meeting is scheduled with the BCBA, classroom teachers, and the principal. They identify and problem-solve barriers, including the BCBA's full schedule and the complexity of the program. The BCBA agrees to complete the IRP-15 after a few weeks of implementing to rate feasibility.

(continued)

TABLE 8.2. *(continued)*

Implementation outcome	Applied examples		
	Tier 1 (universal)	Tier 2 (targeted)	Tier 3 (intensive)
Acceptability	A middle school administrator is concerned about rising rates of referrals for bullying. The MTSS team suggests a program to promote prosocial behaviors. The team decides to conduct interviews with lead teachers and lunch/recess monitors to gain insight into whether they expect this program to work, how feasible it would be for them to use, and whether they have the resources needed to carry out the intervention. They also interview students from each grade to solicit their input on the intervention.	Reviewing progress monitoring data, an elementary team determines that a group of students would benefit from targeted social–emotional skill support. The team recommends the second step. During implementation, they assess acceptability among staff and students. They distribute two surveys: the URP-IR for teachers and the CURP for students. The teachers complete their surveys, as well as help their students to answer theirs. The team uses these data to adjust the intervention and its implementation.	Members of a middle school team have identified a student with persistent behavioral challenges. The team considers conducting an FBA and developing an evidence-based BSP. The team asks the classroom teacher and parents to complete the BIRS before implementation, after one month, and after three months to assess the acceptability of the behavior plan over time. The teacher also helps the student to complete the CURP to share their impressions of the plan across these three time points.
Cost	A high school team wants to implement a peer mentorship program overseen by the school psychologist and counselors to promote social-emotional development. The team analyzes the cost of their involvement (e.g., time, stipend), materials, space, etc. Staff weigh in on the costs of the program against the potential benefits. As a group, they discuss whether there is an undue cost burden on the student support services team involved in the intervention.	A group of students with externalizing behaviors in the classroom has been identified for Tier 2 support. The team considers a small group led by the behavior specialist, which would require physical materials (e.g., resources for a reinforcement system, curriculum, data collection tools) and staff time (i.e., behavior specialist's salary and benefits). The team conducts a cost-benefit analysis to weigh the potential student benefit with the anticipated cost.	A high school student on a 504 plan for ADHD struggles with disruptive behaviors. The MTSS team recommends weekly self-management support with the school psychologist and twice-weekly counseling with the school social worker. The team calculates potential costs, factoring in personnel time, material resources, and meeting time needed for collaboration with the student, family, and a community service provider.
Reach	An MTSS team at a primary school is implementing the Incredible Years SEL program to promote a positive school climate. The team asks teachers to record how often and for how long lessons are delivered and to provide a rationale for lessons not delivered and report student absences. The team estimates how many students received the intervention, how often, and for how long.	A first-grade team refers students for support with social skills. School counselors and the school psychologist implement the Social Thinking Superflex curriculum in small groups. They report how often sessions are held, what lesson(s) were completed, and how many students attended. Using these data, the team examines how much content reached the students and which students received the intervention consistently.	A high school's Tier 3 team is evaluating the extent to which students who should receive individualized counseling from the school psychologist utilize this support. The school psychologist reports attendance data, and the team evaluates which students have attended counseling regularly and which have not. They conduct brief interviews with each student to gather additional information.

(continued)

TABLE 8.2. *(continued)*

Implementation outcome	Applied examples		
	Tier 1 (universal)	Tier 2 (targeted)	Tier 3 (intensive)
Sustainability	A middle school MTSS team has implemented a token economy system. Students earn tickets for kindness, respect, and responsibility. The team monitors ticket delivery and surveys students about how often they've received tickets, assessing for systematic differences across groups. They meet with administrators about the availability of and willingness to dedicate needed resources to sustain the system.	A high school team of school counselors has implemented an intervention to support students' emotion regulation skills through weekly groups. The MTSS team uses the MTSS-SS to evaluate factors related to the sustainability of the intervention. Additionally, the team holds a feedback session with staff, asking questions about leadership support, availability of resources, and their need for ongoing training.	An elementary school psychologist implements Coping Cat to support a student with anxiety. To support consistent use over time, the MTSS team helps identify training needs, a plan to coordinate with staff and the student's family, and a progress monitoring plan. Data are collected on sustainability barriers through an open-ended survey completed by the school psychologist.

procedures, schoolwide adoption of Positive Behavior Interventions and Supports) as well as individual implementers' decisions (e.g., teacher adoption of the Good Behavior Game, school psychologist adoption of Second Step; Proctor et al., 2011). School administrators on the cusp of adopting MTSS report doing so given concerns about student behavior and the need to support their teachers and staff, among other reasons, while also indicating concerns about sustainability and gaining staff buy-in (Lloyd et al., 2023). Notably, school administrators' and teachers' readiness for adoption can differ and, as such, should be attended to and cultivated separately (Hustus & Owens, 2018). Better understanding adoption decisions can provide insight about motivation to implement, potential concerns, and hopeful outcomes (Lloyd et al., 2023) that can be incorporated into technical assistance and used to support implementation and sustainability (Merle et al., 2023). For example, if a school psychologist knows that classroom teachers are overwhelmed with behavior management, yet wary about new initiatives that change regularly, they might talk about adopting effective Tier 1 classroom management strategies to address their current student behavior challenges. In doing so, the school psychologist might highlight their alignment with current practices, share administrator commitment to this work (and, if possible, commitment to fend off other initiatives for a period of time), and potential to improve their classroom environment.

Approaches to assessing adoption include surveys, focus groups, or community advisory groups conducted within the scope of needs assessments (Castro-Olivio & Merrell, 2012; Kumpfer et al., 2017; see Table 8.1). Although assessing adoption can be as simple as a dichotomous item (e.g., Have you started implementing the Good Behavior Game?), consider including broader or related questions to understand implementer or systems characteristics and potential reasons for which a practice may or may not be adopted (e.g., self-efficacy, feasibility, knowledge, training). For example, Duong et al. (2020) used a combination of open-ended survey questions and focus groups with teachers and school administrators to understand adoption and related considerations to guide cultural and contextual adaptations for a Tier 1 intervention to improve student-teacher relationships. By collecting these data, researchers were able to gather general perceptions of the intervention, identify barriers to implementation, and incorporate recommendations from teachers and administrators to modify the intervention and sustain its implementation. Related measures include the Attitudes Toward Evidence-based Practice (Aarons et al., 2012), Change Orientation Scale (Hustus & Owens, 2018), or Implementation Climate Scale (Lyons et al., 2018). Indeed, adoption is a malleable outcome that can be monitored and used to inform systems-wide technical assistance or individual coaching to meaningfully improve fidelity (Merle et al., 2023).

Fidelity

Fidelity refers to the extent to which a practice (e.g., a tiered student intervention in MTSS) is implemented as it was originally intended. Fidelity has been conceptualized to include multiple dimensions, including adherence (i.e., to what extent components of the intervention are implemented as planned), quality (i.e., how well components of the intervention are delivered), and exposure (i.e., how often and for how long the intervention is delivered; Sanetti & Collier-Meek, 2019b). However, adherence is considered fundamental and has been conceptualized as a precursor to other dimensions of fidelity (Proctor et al., 2011); therefore, school teams should prioritize its measurement. Gathering fidelity data supports data-based decision making, as it can highlight whether a lack of desired student progress can be attributed to the intervention itself or insufficient exposure to an evidence-based practice (Sanetti & Collier-Meek, 2019b). For example, if a schoolwide data system indicates an increase in office discipline referrals for disruptive behavior, an administrator may review data on adherence to schoolwide behavior supports (e.g., school behavior expectations posted in each classroom and explicitly taught, schoolwide reinforcement system used regularly) to ensure that the current system is in place before assuming that the system is failing to meet student needs. Within an MTSS framework, the assessment of fidelity is often overlooked (Cochrane et al., 2019; Sanetti & Collier-Meek, 2019a). This is troubling, as evidence suggests that MTSS is often not implemented as intended (Serrato, 2023; Vekaria, 2017).

Unfortunately, few validated measures of fidelity are available to school teams seeking to assess intervention implementation (Cochrane et al., 2019; Sanetti & Collier-Meek, 2019b). Typically, this means that measuring fidelity involves the development of individualized tools. To do so, Sanetti and Collier-Meek (2019b) recommend (1) breaking down the intervention into observable and measurable steps, (2) selecting a suitable measurement strategy, and (3) establishing a rating system. When measuring the fidelity of MTSS interventions, typical measurement approaches include self-report, permanent product review, and direct observation (Sanetti & Collier-Meek, 2019). A recently developed multidimensional measure exists for evaluating fidelity to interventions to support students' social–emotional and behavioral functioning, and it is called the Treatment Integrity Measure for Early Childhood Settings (McLeod et al., 2022). There are also several tools that can be used to understand implementation of MTSS broadly, including the Tiered Fidelity Inventory (Algozzine et al., 2014) and MTSS Fidelity Implementation Rubric (American Institutes for Research, 2023).

Importantly, once a system for fidelity data collection has been established, MTSS teams should establish a plan for regularly reviewing, analyzing, and applying these data. Data can be evaluated across classrooms or grades to review for trends over time and examine differences across groups, or they can be summarized to provide an overall estimate of implementation throughout the school. Once data are reviewed and analyzed, they can be used to guide decision making. In the presence of inadequate fidelity, an MTSS team might explore various approaches to supporting educators' implementation of student interventions. Large-scale issues with implementation may be indicative of a need for additional high-quality training or professional development or may demonstrate issues with feasibility that warrant intervention adaptation (see Sanetti & Collier-Meek, 2019b for a detailed review). If acceptable levels of fidelity are present, teams may instead consider modifying or selecting a new practice to support the target student(s).

For example, teams measuring adherence to a Tier 1 token economy system might use a combination of approaches. MTSS team members might enter each classroom and indicate on a yes/no checklist whether the teacher has posted a visual of schoolwide expectations and whether tokens were readily available in the classroom; the team might review lesson plans developed by each teacher to ensure that students were taught how to earn tokens; and teachers may be asked to complete a brief weekly survey in which they indicate approximately what percentage of their students have earned rewards. The team can then summarize data across classrooms, indicating what percentage of teachers have posted a visual, have tokens available, and have developed lesson plans. They can also graph data on student rewards on an individual classroom basis to determine which teachers are regularly implementing this component of a token economy system. For teachers who indicate a low percentage of students earning rewards, additional data collection may be warranted to understand implementation barriers and ensure that, when delivered, rewards are being provided equitably. Fidelity is a crucial implementation outcome that should be measured regularly in schools to guide data-based decision making about student needs (Sanetti & Collier-Meek, 2019b).

Feasibility

Feasibility refers to the extent to which a program, initiative, or intervention can be carried out successfully in a given context (Proctor et al., 2011); it answers the question "Can this practice realistically be used in our setting?" (Gadke et al., 2021). Feasibility may be impacted at a systems level by factors such as availability of personnel and required resources, at the intervention level by factors such as intervention complexity, and at the implementer level by factors including time constraints and competing demands (Briesch et al., 2013). Attending to perspectives of feasibility across these levels can be informative. Proactive measurement of feasibility may highlight needed modifications or resources for MTSS implementation to be successful and may inform changes across levels to support implementers in their use of a novel practice. For example, prior to adopting Check-In/Check-Out (CICO) at the Tier 2 level, an MTSS team might seek input on the feasibility of the intervention from administrators to gain a systems perspective as well as from teachers responsible for implementing to understand feasibility at the implementer level. Throughout this process, the team might learn that additional personnel are needed for CICO to happen consistently and that teachers require additional training for it to be feasible within their classrooms. These data can be a catalyst for administrators to allocate more resources, like additional personnel and professional development opportunities, that will support the success of an intervention.

To evaluate feasibility, a multi-informant, multimethod approach to assessment is recommended (Gadke et al., 2021). Feasibility can be assessed through a combination of validated measures and open-ended surveys or interviews, which can offer quantitative and qualitative information about limitations on feasibility, respectively (Castro-Olivio & Merrell, 2012). In schools, this type of approach may include developing a survey for administrators and implementers about the feasibility of a new intervention or program that includes both items from a validated measure and open-ended questions (e.g., "What do you anticipate might prevent you from using this practice consistently?"), then conducting interviews with individuals who rate feasibility as low to gain an understanding of anticipated barriers. Two available validated methods for assessing feasibility include the Intervention Rating Profile–15 (IRP-15; Martens et al., 1985) and the Usage Rating Profile—Intervention, Revised (URP-IR; Chafouleas et al., 2011). These measures provide feasibility data that can be used to inform systemic changes or individual supports to promote implementation.

Acceptability

Acceptability encompasses perspectives of stakeholders on whether a given practice is appropriate, fair, or satisfactory (Proctor et al., 2011; Silva et al., 2019). Acceptability is distinct from feasibility; rather than relating to whether an intervention *can* realistically be used in practice, it concerns perspectives on whether the intervention *should* be used. Factors that have influenced acceptability include (1) perceptions of intervention effectiveness; (2) feasibility for educators to implement and fit with the educators' expertise and skills; (3) level of intrusiveness, restrictiveness, or disruptiveness of the intervention; and (4) time, effort, and skill requirements for implementation (Carter, 2007; Reimers et al., 1987; Miltenberger, 1990). Similar to other implementation outcomes, it is vital to evaluate the acceptability of an intervention across multiple levels. MTSS teams might consider assessing acceptability amongst administrators, implementers, and students. The acceptability of an intervention by the student receiving it is a critical component of social validity and has been identified as a crucial to intervention effectiveness (American Psychological Association, 2006; National Association of School Psychologists, 2020). Further, school leaders' perspectives of the acceptability of MTSS can influence other educators' attitudes toward a new practice during its implementation (Aarons et al., 2014) and acceptability by educators responsible for implementing MTSS can impact their use of an intervention (Briesch et al., 2013; Dart et al., 2012). For example, if a school principal believes that a new Tier 2 intervention program isn't appropriate or will not be effective for a particular group of students, interventionists may adopt a similar view and, ultimately, not implement the practice given the lack of buy-in.

When conducting an acceptability assessment, the perspectives of multiple key stakeholders should be considered, including administrators, teachers, interventionists, parents, and students, among others (Proctor et al., 2011). It is advised to assess acceptability before implementation of a practice and at various points throughout its implementation, recognizing that impressions of acceptability may fluctuate over time (Proctor et al., 2011). Common approaches to acceptability measurement include validated rating scales, surveys, and qualitative interviews or focus groups (Brann et al., 2022; Silva et al., 2019). Notable examples of acceptability measures for school-based interventions to be used with adults include the Intervention Rating Profile (IRP; Witt & Martens, 1983), Children's Intervention Rating Profile (CIRP; Witt & Elliott, 1985), Behavior Intervention Rating Scale (BIRS; Von Brock & Elliott, 1987), and URP-IR (Chafouleas et al., 2011). Student perceptions of acceptability can be assessed using the Children's Usage Rating Profile (CURP; Chafouleas et al., 2009) and the Kids Intervention Profile (Eckert et al., 2017). Incorporating both validated measures and interviews, school MTSS teams can gather useful acceptability data to inform necessary adaptations to improve contextual fit. For example, if a school team wants to implement a new Tier 1 social–emotional learning intervention, they might use the URP-IR with teachers and parents to assess their perceptions of the new program and its materials, as well as employ the CURP to assess acceptability among students. The team may then incorporate the use of interviews with individuals who rated acceptability as low to gain more information about the practice that was not perceived to be acceptable. Importantly, when employing scales or surveys like those referenced above, MTSS teams should evaluate whether there are systematic differences in acceptability across student groups (Brann et al., 2022); these data can inform cultural or linguistic adaptations. Overall, acceptability is a key implementation outcome that can be used to guide data-informed adaptations to improve intervention fit.

Cost

In the context of implementation, cost relates to the overall resource requirements (financial or otherwise) of implementing a practice, program, or intervention (Proctor et al., 2011). Implementation costs may vary based on the complexity of an intervention, how the practice is implemented, and the location(s) in which it is implemented (Proctor et al., 2011). In school settings and within the field of school psychology, costs of implementation are infrequently assessed or reported (Barrett et al., 2020; Baumann et al., 2015; Brann et al., 2022; Eisman et al., 2021). This is a significant oversight, as the costs associated with intervention implementation (e.g., MTSS) can include not only the cost of the intervention and its associated materials, but also personnel time, training, ongoing coaching, fidelity monitoring, and student progress monitoring (Barrett et al., 2020). Underestimation of the costs associated with an intervention may result in schools allocating insufficient resources to its implementation; this may ultimately contribute to poor implementation and a failure to realize the promise of an evidence-based intervention (U.S. Department of Education, 2012). Concerns about costs can pose a significant hurdle to the adoption and implementation of interventions such as MTSS (Brann et al., 2022; Eisner et al., 2021), an issue that is particularly pronounced in schools serving racially minoritized students that historically experience inequitable access to needed resources (The Education Trust–New York, 2022; Jackson, 2021).

The ingredients method is considered the gold standard for evaluating intervention implementation costs (Barrett et al., 2020). Using this approach, the following steps are taken to estimate cost: (1) resources needed for implementation (i.e., "ingredients") are identified; (2) for each resource, a unit of measurement is defined; (3) monetary values are specified for each unit; (4) the number of units is multiplied by the monetary value; and (5) a total sum of these costs is calculated (Barrett et al., 2020; Levin et al., 2018). In schools, one of the primary resources required for implementation is personnel time, which can include the time required for training as well as the time to implement; its measurement can include hourly wage plus benefits (Levin et al., 2018). Several recent studies have employed the ingredients method to evaluate the costs of positive behavioral interventions and supports (PBIS). Bradshaw et al. (2023) used this approach to calculate per school and average per pupil costs of PBIS by evaluating the cost of personnel (i.e., teachers and administrators), team meetings, training, implementation and monitoring, ongoing coaching, budgeting, and student referral management. Similarly, Lindstrom Johnson et al. (2020) used the ingredients method to determine school-, district-, and state-level costs of PBIS, dividing costs into fixed (e.g., initial trainings, materials cost) and variable (e.g., personnel time, ongoing training, fidelity assessment, technical assistance) costs. Pas et al. (2020) recently used the ingredients method to estimate the costs of a tiered social–emotional and behavioral intervention. The researchers included fixed costs, such as training, physical materials and equipment, facilities, and variable costs, including personnel costs calculated using time logs, salary data, and fringe benefit rates. By attending to MTSS costs using one of the methods defined above, school teams can determine whether an intervention is feasible to implement given existing resources and worthwhile to sustain given its impact on student outcomes.

Reach

Reach is a measure of the proportion of individuals in a particular population who are willing to engage with an intervention or practice (Proctor et al., 2011, 2023). As applied to schools, reach refers to the number of students who are the target of an intervention who actually receive or participate in that program or practice. Note that this differs from adoption, which relates to the number of *educators* who utilize a practice. In relation to MTSS, evaluation of reach allows school teams to determine whether evidence-based practices effectively extend to all individuals within the school community who could benefit from them regardless of sociodemographic factors. Identifying issues of reach can help teams to uncover unmet student needs or student groups that may be overlooked by existing supports. For example, attendance data can be used to determine the reach of a Tier 2 small-group intervention to target emotion regulation skills. If several students rarely participate, additional data collection may be warranted to identify barriers to participation. Such barriers may include poor acceptability, which could be addressed through intervention modifications to improve contextual, cultural, or linguistic fit.

Reach can be calculated as the ratio of actual recipients of an intervention to the number of potential recipients of that practice (Proctor et al., 2023). Within the MTSS framework, this may look like the number of students who are participating in an evidence-based program relative to the number who are expected to participate. Assessments of reach should be comprehensive and include the number or percentage of students who are excluded from an intervention, the ratio of participating students to non-participating students, and characteristics of participating students and of the target group (RE-AIM, 2023). Within MTSS, this might look like calculating the number of students who attend weekly counseling sessions with the school social worker as compared to the number of students intended to receive support from the social worker. A thorough evaluation of these Tier 3 supports should assess whether there are systematic differences in the students who attend or do not attend their counseling sessions. To prioritize a culturally informed approach to reach assessment within MTSS, teams should evaluate for disproportionality across diverse student groups. Once MTSS teams have identified participating and non-participating students, various qualitative methods can be used to gather more information about reasons for which students are not being reached by a particular program (RE-AIM, 2023). For example, McIntosh (2014) utilized a schoolwide teaming approach to involve administrators, teachers, support staff, parents, and members of the community to support the reach of PBIS to indigenous students. By engaging in active partnerships with families and community members, the school team was able to gather information about cultural nuances, preferences, and barriers to reaching the intended student population. Using quantitative and qualitative data, MTSS teams can identify and ameliorate barriers by adjusting an intervention or its implementation to achieve comprehensive reach.

Sustainability

Sustainability refers to the extent to which an intervention or practice is maintained over time (Proctor et al., 2011). Specific to MTSS, the following factors have been identified as contributors to sustainability: (1) administrator support at the district and school levels, (2) active staff participation, (3) educator buy-in and role flexibility, (4) comprehensive professional development, and (5) sufficient meeting time for coordination (Bahr et al., 2023; Hughes & Dexter, 2021). In the presence of insufficient support or resources for sustainability, educators' implementation of tiered interventions is likely to deteriorate over time (Noell et al., 2005). When implementation falls to low levels, the evidence-based programs selected by the MTSS team may not be delivered to students, who therefore cannot benefit from interventions not received. For example, at the beginning of a new school year, a middle school MTSS team decides to adopt a new Tier 1, universal social–emotional learning program. However, the team does not conduct a thorough cost analysis and, therefore, does not dedicate sufficient personnel or provide adequate training to sustain the program over time. Additionally, the team fails to evaluate acceptability and therefore does not learn that the school principal and several teachers are opposed to the selected program, as they believe that it is not culturally appropriate for their school. Although educators initially attempt to implement the curriculum, its use fades over time in favor of other school initiatives. that have more administrative support and buy-in, as well as sufficient allocation of resources. By the end of the first semester, students are no longer receiving social–emotional instruction at the Tier 1 level.

To assess sustainability, there are several validated measures available to schools. These include the School-Wide Universal Behavior Sustainability Index—School Teams (SUBSIST; McIntosh et al., 2011), the Assessment of Barriers to Implementation and Sustainability in Schools (ABISS; Turri et al., 2016), and the Multi-Tiered Systems of Support—Sustainability Scale (MTSS-SS; Bahr et al., 2023). Items on these scales measure leadership support, teacher buy-in, educator perceptions of the intervention and its effectiveness, progress monitoring and data-based decision making, availability of training, prioritization of the intervention, competing demands, and resource allocation. In addition to validated scales, researchers have incorporated other methods of sustainability assessment, including classroom observations, team meetings, and interviews. For example, Hoover et al. (2020) demonstrated a multimodal approach to assessing the sustainability of MTSS for culturally and linguistically diverse students. The researchers utilized classroom walk-throughs, observations of team meetings, and interviews with school leadership, as well as a teacher survey and sustainability checklist to collect both quantitative and qualitative data on the sustainability of MTSS. Hoover et al. (2020) were able to identify areas for improvement of MTSS, including incorporating native language into instruction, attending to family and community values during instructional decision making and referrals, and improving cultural and linguistic responsiveness. By attending to factors that may influence sustainability throughout implementation of MTSS, data can be used to guide teams in advocating for needed resources and supports to ensure that evidence-based programs can be maintained over time.

CULTURALLY RELEVANT PRACTICAL CONSIDERATIONS

MTSS has the potential to address persistent disparities in educational opportunities and promote equitable outcomes by incorporating culturally responsive practices, including data-based decision making and evidence-based tiered supports to prevent and address academic, social–emotional, and behavioral challenges (Fallon et al., 2022; Jackson, 2022). However, simply putting components of MTSS in place is insufficient (Sullivan et al., 2022). Rather, it is imperative that the delivery of MTSS is executed with a deliberate focus on equity and implementation (Collier-Meek et al., 2022; Fallon et al., 2022). The introduction to and assessment recommendations for implementation outcomes reviewed above are imbued with an equitable implementation perspective (DuMont et al., 2019), but some key actions critical to this perspective are highlighted below.

Building Trust through Cultural Humility

To build toward culturally responsive practices within MTSS, educators should attend to cultivating trust and forging partnerships with students, families, and community members (Awad et al., 2016; Collier-Meek et al., 2023; Baweja et al., 2016). Trust should not be assumed but rather be a continual area of focus and effort. Families of racially/ethnically, linguistically, and economically marginalized backgrounds are more likely to report a lack of trust with schools, which is reasonable given historically discriminatory treatment (e.g., Fisher et al., 2020). Further, student behavior or academic issues are related to decreases in family trust with school settings, which suggests that Tier 2 and 3 supports may often happen within the context of strained family–school relationships (Adams & Christenson, 2000; Santiago et al., 2016). To purposely build trust, educators and MTSS teams can begin with a perspective of cultural humility, an understanding of the ways in which one's culture influences their unique experiences and perspectives, including awareness of one's privilege and power (Fisher, 2020). From there, school messaging can emphasize the value of multiple perspectives and highlight a genuine investment in learning about diverse families and communities. Rejecting a narrow perspective of family involvement (e.g., volunteering during the typical workday), educators can prioritize engaging in responsive and flexible communication and actively seek feedback (Ingraham, 2000; Swanger-Gagne et al., 2009).

Continual Data Collection with Context-Defined Data

Although data-based decision making is a critical component of MTSS, data are often defined narrowly (e.g., office discipline referrals; Algozzine et al., 2014), which can limit the inclusion of diverse perspectives and implementation outcomes. Instead, more traditional data sources can be coupled with additional context-defined data that incorporate implementation outcomes and reflect the values of members of the school and surrounding community (DuMont et al., 2019). These efforts might include focus groups or advisory groups conducted in relevant languages to advance the understanding of cultural perspectives and variables related to values, implementation, and concerns (Duong et al., 2020). Gathering culture-specific conceptualizations of strengths, the problem(s) at hand, and social norms and beliefs can be used to enhance MTSS. At the schoolwide level, broader data related to topics such as the overall goals of schooling, communication preferences, acceptability, family engagement efforts, needs of the community, and school belonging can be collected (Fallon et al., 2022). When supporting specific students, educators can build a protocol for reaching out to families of students in need of more support in a manner that is culturally sensitive, respectful, engaging, and family-centered (Swanger-Gagne et al., 2009). In these efforts, educators should demonstrate genuine interest and an openness to learning and change. By broadening data collection, implementation outcomes and cultural dynamics can be better understood, and, consequently, practices can be sufficiently tailored within the MTSS framework to better meet the unique needs of diverse populations and the implementation context.

Cultural Adaptations

When interventions and practices are planfully adapted to be acceptable to key partners (e.g., students, implementers, families) and consistently implemented by educators, they can lead to improved student outcomes (Collier-Meek et al., 2019; Griner & Smith, 2006; Thier et al., 2020). Most school-based intervention research is conducted on a circumscribed student sample (e.g., White, middle class; Grant et al., 2022) and there is limited guidance about intervention adaption (Barrera et al., 2017). Instead, educators will need to understand their school population (e.g., demographics, culture, values) and review interventions to identify both core and adaptable components (Lee et al., 2023; Sengupta et al., 2020). Cultural adaption involves modifying an evidence-based practice "to consider the language, culture, and context in a way that is compatible with the client's cultural patterns, meanings, and values" (Bernal et al., 2009, p. 362). Likewise, implementation planning involves reviewing each intervention component and making modification to increase feasibility and fit while outlining the specific logistics (e.g., when, where, what resources; Sanetti & Collier-Meek, 2019b). In making modifications, educators can increase the relevance of their practices for the student population (e.g., language, values, materials) and implementation context while retaining core components (Barrera et al., 2017). To help maintain fidelity amid adaptions, a checklist of core and adapted intervention components can be developed and used to foster collaborative agreement and commitment to maintaining fidelity (Bernal et al., 2009). The impact of the adapted practice, as related to both implementation and student outcomes, should be continually assessed. In doing so, further modifications can be made as needed to continually improve fit and promote student and family engagement, while retaining core components (Kumpfer et al., 2017). With planful adaption, MTSS teams can assess the impact of tiered interventions on different populations, provide technical assistance to educators and community members, and facilitate the sustainability of programs (Baumann et al., 2015; Griner & Smith, 2006).

Ongoing Data-Based Decision Making to Advance Equity

To prioritize the effort to increase equitable access and reduce disparities through MTSS, school teams can explicitly name goal(s) related to improving equity (Fallon et al. 2022; Sullivan et al., 2022). For example, specific goals might include (1) incorporating cultural adaptations into the reading curriculum and evaluating the impact on Tier 1 outcomes for marginalized groups; (2) disaggregating Tier 2 and 3 data to critically review the sufficiency of educational practices; or (3) reviewing the classroom ecology (e.g., classroom environment, teaching practices, curriculum) and providing coaching as needed when more than two students are referred for Tier 2 or 3 support. The identification of equity goals should be based on context-defined data and incorporate perspectives from historically marginalized students and their families as well as the broader community (Collier-Meek et al., 2023; DuMont et al., 2019). Directly naming a goal related to improving equity is a matter of accountability for MTSS teams and can ensure dialogue and effort are sufficiently devoted to this work, reflecting changes in both discursive and material power (Stanton et al., 2022).

CONCLUSION

Educators can strengthen their MTSS by incorporating implementation outcomes into ongoing decision making to advance equity (Fallon et al., 2022; Proctor et al., 2011; Sullivan et al., 2022). Implementation science provides a framework for school-based practices; yet, additional research is needed within this context to articulate more specific and directive recommendations for educators (Sanetti & Collier-Meek, 2019a). Although our introduction to implementation outcomes highlights potential assessment methods, more research is needed to develop school-focused measurement tools that produce reliable and valid data; can be used feasibly by educators; and inform technical assistance (see Sanetti et al., 2024, for an example). Further, educators and researchers can contribute to better understanding the relation between implementation and student outcomes by taking care to measure and report these data (Sanetti & Collier-Meek, 2019a). Through this effort, researchers can (1) better understand how implementation outcomes moderate or mediate schoolwide and student-level outcomes in MTSS, and (2) provide data-driven guidance for educators (National Academies of Sciences, Engineering, and Medicine, 2022). In the meantime, MTSS teams can assess and consider implementation outcomes to ensure their efforts prioritize systems change and promote equitable student outcomes.

REFERENCES

Aarons, G. A., Cafri, G., Lugo, L., & Sawitzky, A. (2012). Expanding the domains of attitudes towards evidence-based practice: the evidence-based practice attitude scale-50. *Administration and Policy in Mental Health and Mental Health Services Research*, 39, 331–340.

Aarons, G. A., Ehrhart, M. G., Farahnak, L. R., & Sklar, M. (2014). Aligning leadership across systems and organizations to develop a strategic climate for evidence-based practice implementation. *Annual Review of Public Health*, 35, 255–274.

Adams, K. S., & Christenson, S. L. (2000). Trust and the family–school relationship examination of parent–teacher differences in elementary and secondary grades. *Journal of School Psychology*, 38(5), 477–497.

Algozzine, B., Barrett, S., Eber, L., George, H., Horner, R., Lewis, T., et al. (2014). *School-wide PBIS Tiered Fidelity Inventory*. OSEP Technical Assistance Center on Positive Behavioral Interventions and Supports. *www.pbis.org*

American Institutes for Research. (2023). *Multi-tiered systems of support fidelity of implementation rubric*. Author. *https://mtss4success.org*

Awad, G. H., Pattall, E. A., Rackley, K. R., & Reilly, E. D. (2016). Recommendations for culturally sensitive research methods. *Journal of Educational and Psychological Consultation*, 26(3), 283–303.

Bahr, M. W., Edwin, M., & Long, K. A. (2023). Development of a brief measure for multi-tiered systems of support sustainability. *Assessment for Effective Intervention*, 48(2), 90–99.

Barrera, M., Jr., Berkel, C., & Castro, F. G. (2017). Directions for the advancement of culturally adapted preventive interventions: Local adaptations, engagement, and sustainability. *Prevention Science*, 18, 640–648.

Barrett, C. A., Pas, E. T., & Lindstrom Johnson, S. (2020). A cost analysis of the innovation–decision process of an evidence-based practice in schools. *School Mental Health*, 12, 638–649.

Baumann, A. A., Powell, B. J., Kohl, P. L., Tabak, R. G., Penalba, V., Proctor, E. K., et al. (2015). Cultural adaptation and implementation of evidence-based parent-training: A systematic review and critique of guiding evidence. *Children and Youth Services Review*, 53, 113–120.

Baweja, S., Santiago, C. D., Vona, P., Pears, G., Langley, A., & Kataoka, S. (2016). Improving implementation of a school-based program for traumatized students: Identifying factors that promote teacher support and collaboration. *School Mental Health*, 8, 120–131.

Bradshaw, C. P., Debnam, K. J., Player, D., Bowden, B., & Lindstrom Johnson, S. (2023). A mixed-methods approach for embedding cost analysis within fidelity assessment in school-based programs. *Behavioral Disorders*, 48(3), 174–186.

Brann, K. L., Daniels, B., Chafouleas, S. M., & DiOrio, C. A. (2022). Usability of social, emotional, and behavioral assessments in schools: A systematic review from 2009 to 2019. *School Psychology Review*, 51(1), 6–24.

Briesch, A. M., & Chafouleas, S. M. (2009). *Children's Usage Rating Profile (Actual)*. University of Connecticut.

Briesch, A. M., Chafouleas, S. M., Neugebaur, S. R., & Riley-Tillman, T. C. (2013). Assessing influences on intervention implementation: Revision of the Usage Rating Profile-Intervention. *Journal of School Psychology*, 51(1), 81–96.

Carter, S. L. (2007). Review of recent treatment acceptability research. *Education and Training in Developmental Disabilities*, 42(3), 301–316. *www.jstor.org/stable/23879624*

Castro-Olivo, S. M., & Merrell, K. (2012). Validating cultural adaptations of a school-based social–emotional learning program for use with Latino immigrant adolescents. *Advances in School Mental Health Promotion*, *5*(2), 78–92.

Centers for Disease Control and Prevention. (2023). *Youth risk behavior survey: Data summary and trends report.* Author. *www.cdc.gov/yrbs/dstr/index.html*

Chafouleas, S. M., Briesch, A. M., Neugebauer, S. R., & Riley-Tillman, T. C. (2011). *Usage Rating Profile—Intervention (Revised).* University of Connecticut.

Cochrane, W., Sanetti, L. M. H., & Minster, M. (2019). School psychologists' beliefs and practices about treatment integrity in 2008 and 2017. *Psychology in the Schools*, *56*(3), 295–305.

Collier-Meek, M. A., Kratochwill, T. R., Luh, H. J., Sanetti, L. M. H., & Susilo, A. (2023). Reflections on consultation: Applying a DisCrit and equitable implementation lens to help school psychologists disrupt disparities. *Journal of Educational and Psychological Consultation*, *33*(1), 10–44.

Collier-Meek, M. A., Sanetti, L. M. H., Levin, J. R., Kratochwill, T. R., & Boyle, A. M. (2019). Evaluating implementation supports delivered within problem-solving consultation. *Journal of School Psychology*, *72*, 91–111.

Dane, A. V., & Schneider, B. H. (1998). Program integrity in primary and early secondary prevention: Are implementation effects out of control? *Clinical Psychology Review*, *18*(1), 23–45.

Dart, E. H., Cook, C. R., Collins, T. A., Gresham, F. M., & Chenier, J. S. (2012). Test driving interventions to increase treatment integrity and student outcomes. *School Psychology Review*, *41*(4), 467–481.

DuMont, K., Metz, A., & Woo, B. (2019, April 5). Five recommendations for how implementation science can better advance equity. *Academy Health* [blog post]. *https://academyhealth.org/blog/2019-04/five-recommendations-how-implementation-science-can-better-advance-equity*

Duong, M. T., Nguyen, L., Gaias, L., Benjamin, K. S., Lee, K., Buntain-Ricklefs, J., & Cook, C. R. (2020). Using stakeholder input to guide cultural and contextual adaptations for a universal school-based intervention. *The Urban Review*, *52*(5), 853–879.

Eckert, T. L., Hier, B. O., Hamsho, N. F., & Malandrino, R. D. (2017). Assessing children's perceptions of academic interventions: The Kids Intervention Profile. *School Psychology Quarterly*, *32*(2), 268–281.

Eisman, A. B., Quanbeck, A., Bounthavong, M., Panattoni, L., & Glasgow, R. E. (2021). Implementation science issues in understanding, collecting, and using cost estimates: A multi-stakeholder perspective. *Implementation Science*, *16*(75), 1–12.

Fallon, L. M., Veiga, M., & Sugai, G. (2021). Strengthening MTSS for behavior (MTSS-B) to promote racial equity. *School Psychology Review*, *52*(5), 518–533.

Fisher, E. S. (2020). Cultural humility as a form of social justice: Promising practices for global school psychology training. *School Psychology International*, *41*(1), 53–66.

Fisher, A. E., Fisher, B. W., & Railey, K. S. (2020). Disciplinary disparities by race and disability: Using DisCrit theory to examine the manifestation determination review process in special education in the United States. *Race Ethnicity and Education*, *24*(6), 755–769.

Gadke, D. L., Kratochwill, T. R., & Gettinger, M. (2021). Incorporating feasibility protocols in intervention research. *Journal of School Psychology*, *84*, 1–18.

Grant, S., Leverett, P., D'Costa, S., Anderson Amie, K., McCullough Campbell, S., & Wing, S. (2022). Decolonizing school psychology research: A systematic literature review. *Journal of Social Issues*, *78*(2), 346–365.

Gresham, F. M., Dart, E. H., & Collins, T. A. (2017). Generalizability of multiple measures of treatment integrity: Comparisons among direct observation, permanent products, and self-report. *School Psychology Review*, *46*(1), 108–121.

Griner, D., & Smith, T. B. (2006). Culturally adapted mental health interventions: A meta-analytic review. *Psychotherapy: Theory, Research, Practice, Training*, *43*(4), 531–548.

Hoover, J. J., Soltero-González, L., Wang, C., & Herron, S. (2020). Sustaining a multitiered system of supports for English learners in rural community elementary schools. *Rural Special Education Quarterly*, *39*(1), 4–16.

Hughes, C., & Dexter, D. D. (2021). Field studies of RTI programs, revised. RTI Action Network: A Program of the National Center for Learning Disabilities. *www.rtinetwork.org/learn/research/field-studies-rti-programs*

Hustus, C. L., & Owens, J. S. (2018). Assessing readiness for change among school professionals and its relationship with adoption and reported implementation of mental health initiatives. *Child & Youth Care Forum*, *47*(6), 829–844.

Ingraham, C. L. (2000). Consultation through a multicultural lens: Multicultural and cross-cultural consultation in schools. *School Psychology Review*, *29*(3), 320–343.

Jackson, D. (2021). *Leveraging MTSS to ensure equitable outcomes.* Center on Multi-Tiered Systems of Support at the American Institute for Research. *https://mtss4success.org/sites/default/files/2021-07/MTSS_Equity_Brief.pdf*

Kumpfer, K., Magalhães, C., & Xie, J. (2017). Cultural adaptation and implementation of family evidence-based interventions with diverse populations. *Prevention Science*, *18*(6), 649–659.

Lee, J. D., Meadan, H., Kang, V. Y., & Terol, A. K. (2023). Balancing fidelity and flexibility of manualized interventions in cultural adaptation: Issues to consider. *Education and Treatment of Children*, *46*(3), 263–273.

Lendrum, A., & Humphrey, N. (2012). The importance of studying the implementation of interventions in school settings. *Oxford Review of Education, 38*(5), 635–652. *www.jstor.org/stable/41702781*

Levin, H. M., McEwan, P. J., Belfield, C., Bowden, A. B., & Shand, R. (2018). *Economic evaluation in education: Cost-effectiveness and benefit–cost analysis.* SAGE.

Lindstrom Johnson, S., Alfonso, Y. N., Pas, E. T., Debnam, K. J., & Bradshaw, C. P. (2020). Scaling up positive behavioral interventions and supports: Costs and their distribution across state, districts, and schools. *School Psychology Review, 49*(4), 399–414.

Lloyd, B. P., Carter, E. W., Shuster, B. C., Axelroth, T. L., Davis, A. D., Hine, M. C., et al. (2023). Perspectives on the initial adoption of multitiered systems of support for behavior. *Journal of Positive Behavior Interventions, 25*(1), 3–15.

Lyon, A. R., Cook, C. R., Brown, E. C., Locke, J., Davis, C., Ehrhart, M., & Aarons, G. A. (2018). Assessing organizational implementation context in the education sector: Confirmatory factor analysis of measures of implementation leadership, climate, and citizenship. *Implementation Science, 13*(5), 1 –14.

Martens, B. K., Witt, J. C., Elliott, S. N., & Darveaux, D. X. (1985). Teacher judgments concerning the acceptability of school-based interventions. *Professional Psychology: Research and Practice, 16*(2), 191–198.

McIntosh, K., MacKay, L. D., Hume, A. E., Doolittle, J., Vincent, C. G., Horner, R., & Ervin, R. (2011). Development and initial validation of a measure to assess factors related to sustainability of school-wide positive behavior support. *Journal of Positive Behavior Interventions, 13*(4), 208–218.

McIntosh, K., Moniz, C., Craft, C. B., Risha, G., & Steinwant-Deschambeault, T. (2014). Implementing school-wide positive behaviour support to better meet the needs of indigenous students. *Canadian Journal of School Psychology, 29*(3), 236–257.

McIntosh, K., Mercer, S. H., Nese, R. N. T., Strickland-Cohen, M. K., Kittelman, A., Hoselton, R., & Horner, R. H. (2018). Factors predicting sustained implementation of a universal behavior support framework. *Educational Researcher, 47*(5), 307–316.

McLeod, B. D., Sutherland, K. S., Broda, M., Martinez-Lora, A. M., Cook, C. R., McCoach, D. B., & Snyder, P. A. (2022). Development and initial psychometrics of a generic treatment integrity measure designed to assess practice elements targeting social, emotional, and behavioral outcomes in early childhood settings. *Prevention Science, 23*, 488–501.

Merle, J. L., Cook, C. R., Pullmann, M. D., Larson, M. F., Hamlin, C. M., Hugh, M. L., et al. (2023). Longitudinal effects of a motivationally focused strategy to increase the yield of training and consultation on teachers' adoption and fidelity of a universal program. *School Mental Health, 15*(1), 105–122.

Miltenberger, R. G. (1990). Assessment of treatment acceptability: A review of the literature. *Topics in Early Childhood Special Education, 10*(3), 24–38.

National Academies of Sciences, Engineering, and Medicine. (2022). *A vision and roadmap for education statistics.* The National Academies Press. *https://nap.nationalacademies.org/catalog/26392/a-vision-and-roadmap-for-education-statistics*

Noell, G. H., Witt, J. C., Slider, N. J., Connell, J. E., Gatti, S. L., Williams, K. L., et al. (2005). Treatment implementation following behavioral consultation in schools: A comparison of three follow-up strategies. *School Psychology Review, 34*(1), 87–106.

Pas, E. T., Lindstrom Johnson, S., Alfonso, Y. N., & Bradshaw, C. P. (2020). Tracking time and resources associated with systems change and the adoption of evidence-based programs: The "hidden costs" of school-based coaching. *Administration and Policy in Mental Health and Mental Health Services Research, 47*(5), 720–734.

Proctor, E., Silmere, H., Raghavan, R., Hovmand, P., Aarons, G., Bunger, A., Griffey, R., & Hensley, M. (2011). Outcomes for implementation research: Conceptual distinctions, measurement challenges, and research agenda. *Administration and Policy in Mental Health, 38*(2), 65–76.

Proctor, E. K., Bunger, A. C., Lengnick-Hall, R., Gerke, D. R., Martin, J. K., Phillips, R. J., & Swanson, J. C. (2023). Ten years of implementation outcomes research: A scoping review. *Implementation Science, 18* (31), 1–19.

RE-AIM. (2023). *Assessing reach. https://re-aim.org/assessing-reach*

Reimers, T. M., Wacker, D. P., & Koeppl, G. (1987). Acceptability of behavioral interventions: A review of the literature. *School Psychology Review, 16*(2), 212–227.

Sanetti, L. M. H., & Collier-Meek, M. A. (2019a). Increasing implementation science literacy to address the research-to-practice gap in school psychology. *Journal of School Psychology, 76*, 33–47.

Sanetti, L. M. H., & Collier-Meek, M. A. (2019b). *Supporting successful interventions in schools: Tools to plan, evaluate, and sustain effective implementation.* Guilford Press.

Schimke, D., Krishnamoorthy, G., Ayre, K., Berger, E., Rees, B. (2022). Multi-tiered culturally responsive behavior support: A qualitative study of trauma-informed education in an Australian primary school. *Frontiers in Education, 7*, 866266.

Sengupta, K., Mahadik, S., & Kapoor, G. (2020). Glocalizing project ImPACT: Feasibility, acceptability and preliminary outcomes of a parent-mediated social communication intervention for autism adapted to the Indian context. *Research in Autism Spectrum Disorders, 76*, 101585.

Serrato, A. M. (2023). *The successes and challenges of implementing multi-tiered systems of support in urban elementary schools* (Publication No. 30567352) [Doctoral dissertation, Northeastern University]. ProQuest Dissertations & Theses Global. *www.proquest.com/dissertations-theses/successes-challenges-implementing-multi-tiered/docview/2833814343/se-2*

Silva, M. R., Collier-Meek, M. A., Codding, R. S., & DeFouw, E. R. (2019). Acceptability assessment of school psychology interventions from 2005 to 2017. *Psychology in the Schools, 57*(1), 62–77.

Stanton, M. C., & Ali, S. B., & the SUSTAIN Center. (2022). A typology of power in implementation: Building on the exploration, preparation, implementation, sustainment (EPIS) framework to advance mental health and HIV health equity. *Implementation Research and Practice, 3*, 1–16.

Sullivan, A. L., Nguyen, T., Shaver, E. (2022). *Equity by design: Foundations of equity-centered MTSS*. Midwest and Plains Equity Assistance Center. *https://eric.ed.gov/?id=ED623069*

Surgeon General's Advisory. (2021). *Protecting Youth Mental Health. www.hhs.gov/sites/default/files/surgeon-general-youth-mental-health-advisory.pdf*

Swanger-Gagne, M. S., Garbacz, A. S., & Sheridan, S. M. (2009). Intervention integrity within conjoint behavioral consultation: Strategies for working with families. *School Mental Health, 1*(3), 131–142.

The Education Trust–New York. (2022, July). *Our annual report 2022: Learning in a new normal*. Author. *https://newyork.edtrust.org/wp-content/uploads/2022/07/ETNY-Annual-Report_July-2022.pdf*

Thier, M., Martinez Jr, C. R., Alresheed, F., Storie, S., Sasaki, A., Meline, M., et al. (2020). Cultural adaptation of promising, evidence-based, and best practices: A scoping literature review. *Prevention Science, 21*, 53–64.

Turri, M. G., Mercer, S. H., McIntosh, K., Nese, R. N. T., Strickland-Cohen, M. K., & Hoselton, R. (2016). Examining barriers to sustained implementation of school-wide prevention practices. *Assessment for Effective Intervention, 42*(1), 6–17.

U.S. Department of Education (2012). *Prevalence and implementation fidelity of research-based prevention programs in public schools: Final report*. Author. *www.ed.gov/sites/ed/files/rschstat/eval/other/research-based-prevention.pdf*

Vekaria, H. (2017). Ask the administrators: Interviews provide guidance for MTSS implementation. *Perspectives on Language and Literacy, 43*(4), 37–39. *www.onlinedigeditions.com/publication/?i=445106&article_id=2908449&view=articleBrowser*

Von Brock, M. B., & Elliott, S. N. (1987). Influence of treatment effectiveness information on the acceptability of classroom interventions. *Journal of School Psychology, 25*(2), 131–144.

Witt, J. C., & Martens, B. K. (1983). Assessing the acceptability of behavioral interventions used in classrooms. *Psychology in the Schools, 20*(4), 510–517.

Zablotsky, B., & Ng, A. E. (2023, June). *Mental health treatment among children aged 5–17 years: United States, 2021* (NCHS Data Brief No. 472). National Center for Health Statistics.

CHAPTER 9

Directly Observing and Recording Behaviors

Christopher H. Skinner and Keri A. Keller

There are a variety of legal and professional reasons why those who work with children may need to apply and interpret direct observation data (Barnett et al., 1999; Jacob et al., 2022). In schools, educators are tasked with addressing the behavior challenges of students. As they develop and apply remediation procedures, they may use pre- and post-intervention data to evaluate the effects of their interventions (Steege et al., 2019). These evaluations may allow educators to make numerous decisions that can influence intervention effectiveness including whether to continue the intervention, alter the intervention, or try another intervention (Saecker et al., 2009; Skinner, 2013).

ASSUMPTIONS REGARDING CAUSES OF BEHAVIOR

Direct observation is often associated with behavioral theories and assessment procedures. Hartmann et al. (1979) provided a comprehensive overview that contrasts behavioral and traditional assessment. Many of these differences are related to assumptions regarding the causes of behavior. Almost all behavioral models recognize how various factors can influence behavior including physical and inherited factors. However, most applications of behavioral models focus on how behaviors are caused and/or maintained by current environmental conditions and past learning history. With more traditional models of psychology, behavior is often seen as caused by within-child traits, conditions, or mediating variables.

With most traditional models of assessment, overt behavior is measured and used to infer or diagnose these within-child variables (Hartmann et al., 1979). For example, a child's inappropriate behavior may be caused or influenced by their anxiety or attention-deficit disorder. Because these within-child factors are also seen as relatively stable, traditional models of assessment are often used to identify or diagnose problems and predict future behavior. Under a behavioral model, behavior is not seen as a mere symptom of some other underlying within-child problem. Rather, behaviors are viewed as legitimate problems in and of themselves.

Behavioral theory does not assume that a child's behavior is caused by some underlying construct. Instead, current behaviors are assumed to be maintained by current environmental events (e.g., antecedent and consequent stimuli). In many instances, these environmental events are also directly observable. Thus, under a behavioral model, both the behaviors of interest and the events thought to maintain behaviors can be assessed more directly, regardless of what procedures are used to measure the behavior and/or environmental events that may maintain the behaviors (Skinner, Freeland, et al., 2003).

In addition to lending themselves to direct assessment, environmental variables that are thought to maintain behaviors under a behavioral model are often mutable. For this reason, behaviorists do not focus all their assessment efforts on identifying and measuring problem behaviors. Instead, behavioral psychologists are equally, if not more, concerned with developing procedures for identifying and measuring environmental events that are thought to occasion and maintain these behaviors (Carr, 1993). Once variables that maintain problem behaviors are identified, interventions designed to alter target behaviors that are based on assessed causes of these behaviors can be developed (e.g., Steege et al., 2019).

When selecting a target behavior, it is important to consider its potential cultural significance. Within the United States education system, appropriate behavior is typically influenced by White, middle-class cultural norms (The IRIS Center, 2021). Selecting target behaviors simply because they are problematic within a school setting may not always be sensitive to behaviors that may be culturally appropriate for a student (Goldiamond, 1974). Obtaining the social validity of target behaviors from students and caregivers (e.g., parents) can give insight into the cultural significance of behaviors (Kauffman et al., 2008), which can help determine if the selection of these behaviors is influenced by bias and appropriate for intervention. Considering the potential influence of cultural, ethnic, gender, and religious stereotypes on target behavior selection occurs best when information is gathered from the student and their family (Kauffman et al., 2008).

RECORDING DIRECT OBSERVATION DATA

Behavioral assessment procedures have been characterized along a continuum from most to least direct (Shapiro & Browder, 1990). Many of the more indirect assessment procedures (e.g., checklists, rating scales, and interviews) are addressed in other chapters in this text. Direct behavioral assessment procedures include direct observation in natural settings and direct observation in analogue settings. Direct observation procedures can be conducted by professionals (e.g., psychologists), peers, parents, and the person being assessed, which is known as self-monitoring (Skinner, Rhymer et al., 2000). With each of these procedures, behaviors can be observed and recorded in real time as they occur. Furthermore, each of these direct assessment procedures can employ similar data collection procedures. The primary difference across procedures is who collects the data and under what conditions (natural vs. analogue or artificial environmental conditions).

Narrative Recording Procedures

Perhaps the least structured form of recording direct observation data merely requires an observer to write narrative descriptions of behaviors and sometimes events surrounding those behaviors (Skinner, 2019). Narrative recording procedures are often used to communicate general information about a child's behavior (e.g., "Johnny seemed anxious today") and can also be used in the initial stages of problem-solving to help (1) identify, validate, or confirm target or problem behaviors; (2) form a general idea of problem behaviors rates, intensity, and topography; and (3) begin to identify variables that may be serving to maintain target or problem behaviors (Skinner, Rhymer, et al., 2000). Although there are numerous narrative recording procedures and a variety of reasons to collect narrative recordings, daily communication logs, descriptive time sampling, and antecedent–behavior–consequence (ABC) analysis provide a broad overview of these procedures.

Daily communication logs can allow one to record data that can be used to track a child's general progress or to communicate with others. For example, a teacher working with students with autism may write a general description of a child's school behavior to be sent home to the child's parents. A parent of a child with social–emotional problems may be asked to make similar recordings for a child's teacher or therapist (e.g., Johnny appeared less anxious this week). These narrative descriptions are useful because individuals can provide flexible and rich descriptions of a child's behavior across settings and activities, and these descriptions may assist others who are working with that child.

If specific behaviors are of concern (e.g., self-injurious behavior during school), narrative recordings can provide data about the general topography (e.g., scratching oneself vs. oneslapping self), intensity (e.g., slapping oneself hard), rate (e.g., slapping oneself less frequently), or duration of a behavior. These data can prove useful when developing more systematic observation procedures. For example, descriptions of the topography of a behavior can be used to help develop operational definitions. Additionally, such data may provide some information that is useful for developing more systematic data recording procedures. For example, data on behavior rates and durations are useful when one is developing interval recording procedures.

Narrative recordings also can provide a general indication of behavior variability and the conditions when the target behavior is likely to occur (e.g., hitting oneself only during the first hour of school). These data can be used to determine when observers may be more likely to have the opportunity to directly observe target behaviors (Skinner, 2019). In addition, understanding behavioral variability may provide some initial information regarding conditions that may be serving to occasion or maintain target behaviors. For example, knowing that disruptive behavior occurs more during independent seatwork time than during small group activities could prove useful and may guide additional assessment activities that may assist with developing interventions.

Narrative recordings are often used to keep records of specific low-rate behaviors or events. Following unusual or dangerous events, teachers, parents, or staff often use narrative recording when completing "incident reports." When behaviors are obvious, discrete (i.e., clear beginning and end), and occur at low rates, incident reports can be converted to frequency counts of specific behaviors or events (e.g., number of times a child became physically aggressive). In this manner, narrative recordings can sometimes be used to determine whether students' behaviors are increasing, decreasing, or remaining stable.

Although narrative recordings can sometimes be translated into empirical data for low-rate behaviors or events, narrative time sampling may allow one to collect data on more typical and continuous behaviors and conditions. Narrative time sampling requires observers to write a narrative recording of a student's behavior at predetermined intervals. For example, every 20 minutes, an observer could look at a child and then write a description of the child's behavior and record other environmental conditions that were present at that time. This type of momentary time sampling can provide estimates of time students spend engaged in specific behaviors (Shapiro & Skinner, 1990).

ABC narrative recording requires observers to record narrative descriptions of both behaviors of interest and antecedent and consequent conditions that may be functionally related to those target behaviors (Steege et al., 2019). Typically, observers use the occurrence of target behaviors as a cue to record the occurrence of the target behavior that has already been defined or write a description of the target behavior. They also write a description of general antecedent conditions (e.g., class completing independent seatwork assignment involving punctuation) and specific antecedent events (e.g., a peer takes a student's pencil) that precede target behaviors. Additionally, they write a description of events that immediately followed the target behavior (Skinner, 2019). These events may allow observers to begin the process of identifying reinforcers of the behavior.

When collecting ABC data, observers must be careful to avoid letting their own learning histories or cultural influence have too much of an impact on what they record. For example, many people may not consider receiving a harsh rebuke from a teacher to be reinforcing. However, for some students, almost any type of attention may serve as a reinforcer. Considering cultural factors may help observers draw better conclusions regarding possible reinforcers (Kauffman et al., 2008). However, the best way to record ABC data may be merely recording what happens before and after behaviors and avoiding thinking about function or purpose until other data are collected, which may support or fail to support such hypotheses (Steege et al., 2019).

Limitations of Narrative Recording

Although narrative recording procedures can be useful for identifying or verifying behaviors and environmental variables that may be maintaining those behaviors, there are several limitations associated with narrative recording procedures (Skinner, 2019). Most narrative recordings involve nonsystematic data recording procedures. Although this method of recording may allow for rich, flexible data collection, narrative recordings often yield imprecise data. For example, an observer may spend some time with a family and write that Johnny disobeyed his parents often. Without more precise definitions of the words "disobey" and "often," it is difficult to use these data to determine what was actually occurring during the observation period.

The quality and quantity of narrative data are likely to be influenced by many variables, including the observer's writing skills (e.g., writing speed and vocabulary). Additionally, what observers write is influenced by their learning history, which includes both broad-based cultural influences and unique idiosyncratic influences, such as specific training in recognizing and recording environmental events that may be related to target behaviors (Johnston, 2014). For example, an observer with experience teaching mathematics may recognize that shifting from one type of mathematics problem to another may occasion escape–avoidance behaviors.

Because an observer's background, culture, and learning history can influence narrative recording, they are susceptible to observer biases. When behaviors or events of interest are obvious, obtrusive, discreet, uncomplicated, and occur at low rates, a second observer may be able to verify narrative recording data by simultaneously collecting their own narrative recording. However, because narrative recordings are influenced by so many different factors, it is often difficult to verify data collected via narrative recordings (Johnston, 2014; Skinner, 2019). Thus, few decisions should be based solely on narrative recordings.

Another limitation of narrative recording procedures is related to the time required to write narrative descriptions (Skinner, 2019). Because it takes considerable time to write narrative descriptions, observers cannot record all behaviors or events observed. Furthermore, narrative recording procedures often require discontinuous observation (i.e., observers halt observation in order to record data).

Discontinuous observation has several limitations (Skinner, Dittmer, et al., 2000). Because observation is not continuous (i.e., observers may pause to write out their narratives), they may miss the opportunity to observe and record important antecedent or consequent events that could lead to effective interventions. For example, while busy recording target behaviors (e.g., writing a narrative description of the behavior), observers may fail to observe an event that occurred after the target behavior that may be reinforcing it (Steege et al., 2019). Fortunately, a variety of empirical recording procedures that can address many of the limitations associated with narrative recordings have been developed.

Empirical Recording Procedures

Empirical recording procedures can yield more precise measures of behavior than narrative recording procedures (Skinner, 2019). This precision can allow for fine distinctions that may be necessary for measuring and detecting the effects of interventions over brief periods. In addition, empirical recording procedures yield data that can be independently verified. Verification is especially useful when (1) important decisions are being made (e.g., determining if the child's self-injurious behavior is getting worse or is severe enough to warrant alternative placement); (2) primary observers may be susceptible to biases (e.g., the residential staff member who has recently had a physical altercation with the student is collecting data); or (3) the behaviors being measured are difficult to observe and record.

Empirical recording systems typically require observers to record tally marks in appropriate columns or interval blocks when observing target behaviors. As this data recording procedure is often more time efficient than writing a narrative description, empirical recording allows observers to collect data in a more continuous manner and record observations across a greater array of behaviors or events. These advantages may make it easier to precisely measure target behaviors. In addition, efficient recording may increase the probability of observers being able to observe and record important antecedent and consequent events that may be maintaining these behaviors.

Operational Definitions

To record the presence of a target behavior, one must first define the behavior operationally (Steege et al., 2019). Operational definitions are typically based on the topography or shape of the behavior. In some instances, the intensity or duration of behaviors is also included in operational definitions. For example, "inappropriate voice" may include speaking too loud or too soft (intensity), and "passive–aggressive behavior" may include complying with mother's directions within 5 seconds of the direction being issued (duration). However, to avoid imprecise data collection, operational definitions rarely include inferred characteristics of the behavior, such as the intent, purpose, or function of the behavior (Skinner, Dittmer, et al., 2000).

Several procedures are useful for developing operational definitions of target behaviors. The typical procedure is to collect descriptive data from the referring agent. Thus, the first step may involve an intervention with a teacher or parent. Often, referrals are accompanied by broad, vague descriptions of problem behaviors (e.g., defiance), and interviews can be used to form more precise definitions of target behaviors (Bergan & Kratochwill, 1990). Including examples of behaviors that fit an operationally defined behavior and those that do not fit can help clarify operational definitions (see Saudargus, 1992).

When target behaviors are unusual or idiosyncratic (e.g., hand flapping), directly observing the behavior and making narrative recordings may allow one to develop operational definitions of the behavior (Skinner, 2019). This observation time may also help one obtain a clearer picture of the duration, rate, and continuity of the target behaviors, which is often necessary when developing direct observation recording procedures. It is not always necessary to construct a new operational definition for every referred problem. In many instances, it may be possible to find appropriate operational definitions in empirical intervention journal articles, behavioral psychology texts, and structured codes.

In some instances, direct observation data are collected when behaviors are operationally defined to include an entire class of behaviors. For example, physical aggression against peers could include any instance of biting, hitting, or kicking a peer. However, it is difficult and often not meaningful to record each particular hit or kick. Instead, aggressive instances could be defined as beginning when a child engages in any of the previously mentioned behaviors and ending with the absence of those behaviors over a 2-minute interval.

Developing operational definitions for a class of behaviors is often influenced by culture and context. Thus, it is important for observers to consider and confirm operational definitions of behaviors that would be placed into a class of antisocial verbal behaviors. For example, when collecting data on elementary students' inappropriate antisocial verbal behavior directed to other students (e.g., name-calling), it may be important to confirm with teachers or parents which specific terms fit this definition (Kirkpatrick et al., 2019). The meaning of verbal behavior can also change over time. For example, calling someone a *goat* was not a compliment 50 years ago, but today, a *goat* is often used to refer to the greatest of all time.

Another concern with operational definitions of behaviors or classes of behavior is related to how they are named or labeled, as people from different cultures and backgrounds may react to those labels. Thus, it is important to use culturally sensitive and specific language when referring to our target behaviors of behavior classes. For example, parents, professionals (e.g., teachers), and students from some cultures may object to terms like *defiance*, *non-compliance*, or *insubordination* (e.g., to teacher direction or instruction). In many instances, alternative terms that are more clearly aligned with operational definitions could be used. For example, failure to attend to and follow directions or instructions may be viewed more favorably than a behavior description of non-compliance or defiance.

In many cases, an even more acceptable strategy would be to operationally define and measure the desired replacement behavior (Lo & Cartledge, 2006; Reeves, 2014). For example, labeling a class of behavior as "stealing" may be more objectionable than using the term "taking objects without permission." An even more acceptable approach may be to identify and operationally define an appropriate replacement behavior for stealing. For example, rather than attempting to reduce taking objects without permission, educators could attempt to operationally define and attempt to increase an appropriate replacement behavior, such as asking for objects. Similarly, educators, parents, and students from across cultures may find it more acceptable to define and increase on-task and in-seat behavior as opposed to decreasing off-task and out-of-seat behavior.

Developing direct observation systems also requires developing data recording procedures. Successfully matching the data recording procedures to the target behavior can make data collection more reliable and enhance the social, educational, and clinical validity of the data collected.

Event Recording

Event recording requires an observer to record the number of times a behavior occurs during an observation session. Event recording is often used to collect data on discrete behaviors that have a clear beginning and end (e.g., failing to comply with directions within 5 seconds). However, because every instance of the behavior is recorded, it can be difficult to collect data on behaviors that occur at high rates (e.g., pencil tapping).

Event recording can also be used to collect data on instances of a behavior class. For example, tantrums or fighting may be operationally defined. However, it can be challenging to determine when this class of behaviors has ceased and a new class of behavior has begun. For example, two students may be engaged in a physical alteration that is scored as a fight. They may cease fighting for 30 seconds and then start again. The challenge becomes whether to score this as a new event. Thus, in order to count some events or classes of behavior, the operational definition often includes a duration component that indicates when an event is considered to have ended (e.g., no contact with each other for 5 minutes), which allows an observer to score a new event.

Event data can be reported as counts (e.g., Johnny did not comply with his father's directions on nine occasions, and Jane had six aggressive outbursts). However, converting such data to either rate or percentage data often provides more useful information. For example, knowing that Johnny eloped from school 11 times is not very useful. However, converting these data to rate data (e.g., 11 times in the last five school days or 11 times in the last 120 school days) provides useful information. Similarly, data can be converted to percent data by recording the occurrence divided by the opportunity for the behavior. An example would be that Johnny failed to complete any items on four of his math assignments. Converting these data to four of his last five math assignments (i.e., 80%) versus four of his last 40 math assignments (10%) provides more useful information. Converting counts to rate or percentage data allows one to compare data across observation sessions that are not equivalent and when opportunities to engage in behaviors are unequal. Thus, these types of conversions are extremely useful when repeated measures data are used to (1) analyze behavior trends, (2) analyze behavior variability, and/or (3) compare a child's behavior across conditions (e.g., baseline vs. treatment phases).

Duration Recording

Whereas event recording is often used for discrete behaviors that occur at moderate or low rates, duration recording can be used to collect data on more continuous behaviors (e.g., in-seat or on-task behavior), behaviors that occur at extremely high rates (e.g., pencil tapping), or behaviors without clear beginning or ends (e.g., hand flapping). An observer can use a stopwatch or electronic device to record the amount of time a child spends engaged in specific behaviors (e.g., in-seat behavior). However, it is often difficult to start and stop a timing device in a reliable manner. Furthermore, with continuous behaviors, it can be difficult to reliably determine when a behavior begins and ends. For example, if on-task were defined as a head oriented toward assignments or a speaker, an observer would be constantly starting and stopping the stopwatch every time the student reoriented (e.g., swiveled their head).

Time Sampling

Time-sampling procedures allow observers to collect duration estimates in a manner that addresses the limitations associated with collecting continuous duration data (Briesch et al., 2017; Lentz, 1982; Zakszeski et al., 2017). There are three types of time sampling (i.e., momentary, whole interval, and partial interval), and each requires observers to record behaviors on an interval-by-interval basis. Although observers can use a clock, stopwatch, or wristwatch to mark intervals, using audio recording to mark intervals may make it easier to observe and record student behavior. Marking intervals with audio may also make it easier to synchronize recording intervals when direct observation data are being verified by another observer (e.g., when collecting interobserver agreement data). Additionally, numerous applications have been developed for electronically scoring intervals using phones and related devices.

Momentary time sampling requires observers to record the presence of a target behavior if it is occurring at the moment the interval begins. When whole-interval time sampling is used, observers record the presence of a target behavior only if it occurs for the entire interval. With partial-interval time sampling, an interval is scored if the behavior occurs at any point during an interval. Momentary time sampling is often used when data collection systems are complex and require observers to record a variety of behaviors and events. Whole and partial-interval time sampling often requires more continuous observation (e.g., observation for entire intervals). Thus, these procedures can be challenging when observers are attempting to collect data on multiple behaviors and events or across multiple people (e.g., several peers of a child and the child's parents and siblings).

Time-sampling methods involve sampling and, therefore, are susceptible to sampling error. When using momentary time sampling, shorter intervals would increase the size of the sample collected during an observation session. Thus, shorter intervals tend to produce the most accurate and dependable duration estimates (Briesch et al., 2017; Zakszeski et al., 2017). Whole-interval time sampling tends to underestimate behavior durations, and partial-interval time-sampling procedures overestimate behavior durations (Lentz, 1982; Powell et al., 1977). The length of observation intervals can also affect the time-sampling estimates. Longer intervals tend to amplify overestimates of partial-interval time sampling, and shorter intervals tend to amplify underestimates provided by whole-interval time sampling (Lentz, 1982).

Because time sampling provides estimates of durations, when reporting data, in most instances, observers should not indicate the percentage of time the student was engaged in target behaviors. For example, it would be inaccurate to report that Jim was engaged in self-injurious behavior 80% of the time. Instead, one should report the length of the observation sessions (e.g., 10 minutes), the length of the intervals (e.g., 20 seconds), the type of time sampling recording being used (e.g., momentary time sampling), the number of intervals the behavior was recorded, the number of intervals the behavior was not recorded (e.g., self-injurious behavior was recorded for 24 of 30 intervals), and the percentage of intervals the behavior was recorded (e.g., self-injurious behavior was recorded for 80% of the observed intervals). Providing all the data allows readers to make judgments regarding the estimates (e.g., degree of over- or underestimation).

In some instances, partial-interval time sampling may provide a measure of the number of events. For example, Wright et al. (2022) measured student complimenting using partial-interval recording. Although it was possible to deliver multiple compliments in an interval, intervals were not scored unless a unique compliment was delivered. Hence, the number of intervals scored served as a minimum number of complements delivered.

Recording frequency data with time sampling is especially useful when observers collect data on target behaviors and variables thought to be maintaining those behaviors in natural environments. Recording events that occur during intervals provides a more precise record of the sequence of events. Thus, observers using interval recording can identify events that occurred immediately prior to and following target behaviors (see Saudargus, 1992). To the extent that these events serve to occasion and maintain target behaviors, this type of recording may provide data that lead to more effective interventions.

OBSERVERS

Several issues related to direct observation can affect the quality and clinical utility of direct observation data. These issues are affected by the individual who collects the data. Direct observations can be recorded by independent observers, participant observers, peer observers, and/or self-observers.

Independent Observer Collecting Data in Naturalistic Settings

Having an independent observer enter a child's natural setting (e.g., home or school) and record the child's behavior and environmental events surrounding those behaviors is the most direct and often considered the most desirable form of behavioral assessment (Cone, 1978; Hintze & Shapiro, 1995). However, there are major concerns with using independent observers to collect data in a child's natural environment. Perhaps the most important concern is that the process of data collection will affect the child's and others' (e.g., parent, teacher, and peers) behavior. This process is known as reactivity. A variety of variables, including (1) the obtrusiveness of the observer, (2) the perceived power or role of the observer, and (3) what the child is told about the observer's presence, may affect reactivity (Johnson & Bolstad, 1973). However, it is not possible to predict or measure the impact that reactivity is having on behavior(s) during any particular observation session (Shapiro & Skinner, 1990). Therefore, when the goal is to collect assessment data that most accurately reflects naturally occurring conditions, observers should make efforts to reduce reactivity (Skinner et al., 2003).

Efforts should be made to reduce the conspicuousness of the observer (Skinner, 2019). One-way mirrors are excellent devices that allow one to collect data in an inconspicuous manner. However, independent observers typically cannot conceal their presence in the child's natural environment. When this is the case, children are likely to ask questions about the observer (e.g., "Who is that guy in the back of the room?"). In these instances, teachers or other supervisors should not lie to the children, but they should avoid providing too much information. For example, informing a class of fourth-grade students that the observer is there to collect data on John because people are concerned about his inappropriate behavior could be unethical and illegal and is likely to cause reactivity. Not only is John's behavior likely to be affected, but John's peers are likely to interact differently with him. Thus, it may be best to provide vague, general statements about why the observer is present. For example, children could be told that Mrs. Smith is there to observe the teacher and learn more about fourth-grade classrooms (Skinner et al., 2003). Both comments are true but may also reduce reactivity.

Children often attempt to interact with independent observers (Johnson & Bolstad, 1973). Observers should keep responses to a minimum or avoid responding to students, as even quick social interactions may encourage children to continue initiating other interactions. These interactions with observers who would not be present if they were not collecting direct observation data are obvious examples of reactivity. Not all interactions are verbal. Children may engage in nonverbal behavior (e.g., writing on a piece of furniture) while they know that an independent observer is watching them in order to see if the observer reacts (e.g., tell their parents and take away their pen). If observers react, the child's future behavior is likely to be influenced by the presence of the observer. Of course, there are exceptions to this rule. If there is a clear and present danger (e.g., a child is leaning out of an open window), observers are legally and ethically obligated to react (Skinner et al., 2003).

Several other procedures can be used to reduce reactivity (Johnson & Bolstad, 1973; Kazdin, 1977; Skinner, Dittmer et al., 2000). Observers should not orient themselves directly toward the target child or children. Almost all of us have altered our behavior when someone is staring at us. Reactivity may be reduced when observers sit in an area of the room where they are less likely to be noticed (e.g., the back corner of the classroom). When possible, observers should attempt to enter the natural environment at unobtrusive times (e.g., enter a classroom before students do). To children, it can appear that observers are not busy and may increase the probability of children approaching the observer. Therefore, observers who appear extremely busy (e.g., constantly writing or quietly shuffling materials) may be less likely to occasion reactivity during observation periods (Skinner et al., 2003).

Timing related to other assessment activities may also affect reactivity. For example, psychologists may interview children as part of the assessment process. When the person who interviewed the specific child enters the classroom, that child is likely to behave differently because of the interview. In these instances, reactivity may be reduced by delaying the child interview until direct observation data are collected (Skinner et al., 2003). Another solution would be to have one person conduct the interview and another collect the direct observation data.

Although independent observers may occasion reactivity, this reactivity is likely to subside over time as children and others in the environment return to their typical behavior. Thus, initial observation sessions may yield less naturalistic data than subsequent sessions. Video cameras can also be used to record data that observers can record at a later date. As with the presence of an outside observer, the presence of a video camera is likely to occasion high levels of initial reactivity (e.g., mugging for the camera and saying, "Hi Mom!") that tend to subside as children become acclimated to the equipment.

Using independent observers to collect direct observation data has several advantages. Because external observers do not have a history of interacting with the child, they may be less susceptible to observer biases that could cause inaccurate or inconsistent data recording. Learning to collect direct observation data in a reliable manner can be time-consuming. It may be most efficient to train a few external observers and use them as direct observation specialists to collect data across environments (e.g., across classrooms or homes). One way to make this system even more efficient would be to train these observers to collect data using pre-established direct observation systems (for examples of classroom observation systems, see Alessi & Kaye, 1983; Saudargus, 1992; Shapiro & Clemens, 2023). These systems have been developed to allow observers to collect data on multiple behaviors, events, and conditions that may provide useful information for making decisions across problems and concerns. After becoming fluent with collecting data using these codes, observers can then make alterations in the system on a case-by-case basis (e.g., add a specific operational definition and recording procedure for a child's idiosyncratic behavior).

Although systematically recording (i.e., operational definitions scored using time sampling procedures) direct observations may provide objective data that is less susceptible to observer bias than anecdotal data or narrative recording procedures, individual observer biases may still affect the data collected. To combat this, interobserver agreement data can be collected. Interobserver agreement is conducted when two or more observers simultaneously collect data on the behavior of a student. Calculating interobserver agreement using the overall percent of agreement or occurrence and nonoccurrence percent of agreement can help determine if there are biases or issues with the operational definition (e.g., too vague) or data recording strategies (e.g., momentary versus whole-interval recording). Strong measures of interobserver agreement may enhance others' (e.g., parents, administrators, interventionists) confidence that had they been observing during this time, they would have seen the same events.

Teacher, Parent, or Other Internal Observers in Natural Settings

When target behaviors occur at low rates and/or unpredictable times, it may not be practical for external observers to record direct observation data. For example, a child may have a tantrum about once every three weeks where he throws and damages objects in their environment. Because this behavior occurs infrequently, it is difficult for an independent observer to schedule times when they can observe this behavior. In these instances, parents, teachers, or other adults who are part of the child's natural environment can record direct observation data.

When working with teachers, parents, or others who are working or supervising children in their natural environments, it may be important to construct relatively simple recording systems that require little time to record data. For example, a teacher could keep a daily count of a student's compliant and noncompliant behaviors by moving a penny from one pocket to another every time a student complied and moving a dime every time a student did not comply. At the end of each day, these data could be converted to percentage data.

When interval recording systems are being used, manipulating interval length can also make data collection easier. For example, it is much easier for a parent to record whether a child wet the bed during an entire night than it is to record whether a child wet the bed during a specific hour interval. Altering operational definitions can also make collecting data easier. For example, rather than measuring a student's in-seat behavior by determining if one or both buttocks are in contact with the chair seat, one could record whether or not any part of the student's body is in contact with their seat. Using naturally occurring intervals may reduce disruptions (e.g., intervals that last from waking to lunch, lunch to dinner, and dinner to bedtime or intervals that last an entire class period during schooldays). Furthermore, some procedures for marking intervals are likely to be less obtrusive and disruptive. For example, scheduling an electronic device to vibrate (e.g., phone in teacher's pocket) instead of beep may allow a teacher to mark intervals in a manner that is less likely to disrupt typical classroom behaviors and routines (Heering & Wilder, 2006).

When parents, teachers, or other adults who are part of a child's natural environment record observations, the process of data collection can have an impact on how they interact with the target child. Suppose a parent is collecting data on a child's compliant and noncompliant behavior by moving pennies and dimes from one pocket to another. While collecting these data, the parent may come to realize that the child is rarely complying and reduce the number of requests or demands made on the child. This reduction in the number of demands may increase or decrease the child's compliance rate. Thus, the reactivity occasioned by parents or other internal observers (e.g., teachers) collecting data can alter the child's natural environment and reduce the clinical utility of the data collection procedures.

Internal observers who have a history of interacting with a child may also be more susceptible to observer drift. For example, a parent who has listened to his/her child scream all day may be more (frustration) or less (habituation) likely to score a child's loud request as inappropriate verbal behavior. Finally, parents, teachers, or others who work with a child may have an interest in the decisions being made based on that data, which may influence their data recordings. Regardless, when this is the case, people who are making the decisions may be less likely to trust that data (e.g., a judge making a custody decision) when it is collected by an invested party (e.g., the father).

Peer Observation and Recording

Children can be used to collect direct observation data on the behavior of classmates, siblings, or peers. The reactivity associated with peer monitoring may occasion both desired and undesired behaviors, dependent on the behavior(s) being monitored. Within educational environments, tutoring programs often require peers to observe and record classmates' academic behaviors (e.g., Greenwood et al., 1984). Peer monitoring is an efficient procedure that can allow for immediate evaluation of academic responses. This immediate evaluation can cue immediate instant error correction procedures that prevent students from practicing inaccurate responding. In addition, immediate evaluation can serve as immediate reinforcement for accurate responding (McLaughlin & Skinner, 1996). Besides enhancing the tutee's academic performance, the process of observing, recording, and evaluating peers' responses has been shown to improve the tutor's or monitor's academic skills (e.g., Skinner et al., 1992). Serving as a peer tutor may also enhance a student's self-image and academic esteem (Henington & Skinner, 1998; Stern et al., 1988).

Children can also observe, record, and report peers' incidental social behaviors. In many environments, incidental antisocial behaviors are punished. In some instances, children learn to avoid punishment by not performing those behaviors. In other instances, children learn to avoid being punished by avoiding being caught or observed performing these behaviors. For example, it would be unusual for some children to forcefully take a toy from a peer when a parent or teacher was obviously watching. Thus, in some instances, peers may be the only people who observe a child's inappropriate behaviors (Skinner et al., 2002). When these behaviors are serious (e.g., bringing a gun to school or torturing an animal), it is essential that children who observe these behaviors also report these behaviors.

Children often learn to monitor and report their peers' incidental antisocial behavior (i.e., tattle) without any specific or programmed instruction (Skinner, Cashwell, et al., 2000). All methods of recording data described earlier could be used by students to record their peers' inappropriate behavior. However, peers may have difficulty recording behaviors that occur at high rates or accurately recording behaviors using complex observation systems. In addition, having children write narrative reports can be time-consuming, and the quality of these data may be compromised depending on students' writing (e.g., speed and vocabulary) and observation skills. Thus, in some instances, it may be best to train children to report peers' incidental inappropriate behavior and have adults record these behaviors (Henington & Skinner, 1998).

There are several limitations associated with using peers to collect data on antisocial behaviors (Skinner, Cashwell, et al., 2000). Observing peer behavior can distract children's attention from their own behavior (e.g., school work) or their teacher's, parent's, or supervisor's instructions or directions. Also, peers may intentionally or unintentionally provide inaccurate reports of their peers' behavior. Intentionally inaccurate reports can be used as a form of aggression to get other children in trouble. Such reports can also be used to shift the blame for a behavior to another peer. Peers may threaten their classmates to prevent them from reporting behaviors or physically assault them in retaliation for reporting those behaviors (Skinner et al., 2002).

Requiring children to monitor inappropriate behaviors may teach children to focus on their peers' inappropriate behaviors at the exclusion of their peers' appropriate behaviors (Cashwell et al., 2001). This may reduce children's awareness of their peers' incidental prosocial behaviors and cause children to form negative impressions of their peers (Kirkpatrick et al., 2019). Finally, it would be inappropriate to have peers collect data on the inappropriate behavior of a particular child, as this process would encourage peers to view this child as being deviant or bad and may increase the probability of children socially rejecting their peer (Cashwell et al., 1998; Ervin et al., 1996; Kirkpatrick et al., 2019).

Although there are some serious negative side effects associated with using children to collect data on peer's incidental inappropriate behaviors, having children observe, record, and report peers' incidental prosocial behaviors could have several positive side effects. Researchers have attempted to use peer observation and peer reporting to improve the social interactions and social status of socially rejected children and/or children who displayed high rates of inappropriate behaviors (Ervin et al., 1998; Jones et al., 2000). Results have shown that having groups of children publicly report peers' incidental prosocial behaviors at daily group meetings can improve the student's social status, increase interactions, and increase cooperative interactions among students.

Researchers used similar procedures classwide (i.e., tootling interventions) and found that reinforcing students for observing and reporting classmates' incidental prosocial behaviors (i.e., student-helping-student behavior) increased on-task behavior and decreased disruptive behaviors (Cihak et al., 2009; Lambert et al., 2015; Lum et al., 2017; McHugh et al., 2016). A similar procedure was shown to be effective in decreasing students' antisocial interactions (Kirkpatrick et al., 2019). Additionally, researchers have shown that after students receive social skills instruction, having peers observe and record their performance of those skills can enhance engagement in recently trained social skills in authentic social contexts (Crewdson et al., 2024; Wright et al., 2021).

Although there are positive side effects associated with having children observe and report peers' incidental prosocial and desired academic behaviors, these side effects represent reactivity. It is impossible to separate behavioral changes caused by reactivity versus behavioral changes caused by planned (e.g., interventions) or unplanned changes in the student's immediate or temporally distant environments. Furthermore, the process of peer monitoring can have a significant impact on the behavior of target children and peer monitors. This impact can be significant enough to cause broad changes within the child's natural environment that may alter how others (teachers and parents) interact with the child. Because this reactivity may be unpredictable, even when peer monitors collect accurate and reliable data, interpretation of these data must be tempered with the possibility that these data do not reflect natural environmental conditions.

Self-Monitoring

Self-monitoring requires children to observe and record their own behavior (Bruhn et al., 2015). There are several advantages to using self-monitoring over other direct observation procedures (Cole et al., 2000). Self-monitoring is an efficient procedure for collecting data when other data collectors are unavailable or too busy. In addition, self-monitoring may be the only procedure that allows one to collect data that are difficult for others to observe, such as (1) cognitive or emotional behaviors (e.g., fear or cognitive steps taken to solve mathematics problems), (2) behaviors that occur at low rates, (3) behaviors that occur at unpredictable times, and (4) behaviors that occur in settings that do not lend themselves to direct observation by others.

All previously described procedures for observing and recording data can be employed when self-monitoring is used. However, as with peer monitoring, several variables should be considered when structuring self-monitoring procedures. With young children and children with writing skills deficits, narrative recording may prove cumbersome and yield data that are difficult to interpret. It may also be difficult for children to observe and record several behaviors or events simultaneously (Nelson, 1977). Because children may find it time-consuming and difficult to consistently make subtle distinctions in behaviors, operational definitions should also be both clear and described in simple terms. In some instances, self-monitoring procedures can disrupt children who are engaged in desirable behaviors. For example, if a student is having problems maintaining her on-task behavior, interrupting that student at random intervals and requiring her to record whether she was reading silently could make it more difficult for this student to remain on task and finish assignments (Quillivan et al., 2011).

As with all other direct observation procedures, reactivity and accuracy are a concern when children self-monitor. The quantity and quality of training can have an impact on the accuracy of self-monitoring data (e.g., Shapiro et al., 1980). When children are told that someone else will also be monitoring and recording their behavior (e.g., checking their work or collecting interobserver agreement data), they may be more likely to self-record accurately (Santogrossi, 1975). Reinforcement for accurate self-monitoring also enhances accuracy (e.g., Lloyd & Hilliard, 1989). The valence of the behavior being monitored may also enhance self-monitoring accuracy. Researchers have shown that children may be more likely to accurately observe and record their own appropriate, as opposed to inappropriate, behaviors (Nelson et al., 1981).

The process of observing and recording one's own behavior often causes reactivity. Fortunately, the direction of the changes brought about via self-monitoring is generally in the desired direction. Thus, when children are trained to observe and record inappropriate behaviors, those behaviors tend to decrease. When they are trained to observe and record their appropriate behaviors, those behaviors tend to increase. A variety of other variables can affect the degree of reactivity that occurs when children observe and record their own behavior, including (1) training in self-monitoring, (2) obtrusiveness of self-recording devices, (3) timing of self-monitoring, and (4) accuracy of self-recording (Glynn & Thomas, 1974; Korotitsch & Nelson-Gray, 1999).

The reactivity caused by self-monitoring tends to make this a popular intervention. Not only is it efficient but self-monitoring is also seen as moving children away from external control and encouraging students to become more actively involved in programs designed to maintain or alter their own behaviors (Kern et al., 1997). However, as with all forms of reactivity, it is difficult to predict the degree of behavior change that occurs in reaction to self-monitoring. For example, some studies have shown that accurate self-recording results in higher levels of reactivity (Shapiro, 1984). Other studies have shown that accurate recording is not necessary for reactivity to occur. In fact, some students who were trained to self-record but failed to ever record data showed changes in their behavior (Hayes & Cavoir, 1977). Because the presence or absence of reactivity cannot be reliably predicted or measured, assessment data collected via self-monitoring must always be interpreted with an understanding that these data may be affected by reactivity (Korotitsch & Nelson-Gray, 1999; Skinner & Smith, 1992).

CONCLUSION

Even though the assessment procedures described and analyzed in this chapter are more direct than traditional procedures, these procedures can still yield data that do not accurately reflect a child's behavior in his or her natural environment. The process of data collection can cause changes in the behavior of the child being observed and of others in the environment including peers, teachers, and parents (i.e., reactivity). As with a child's behavior, data collectors' behavior can be influenced by their own learning history, culture, and biases. Although collecting interobserver agreement data can increase our confidence in direct observation recordings, these data do not control for reactivity.

Direct observation data can be influenced by observers, reactivity, and sampling error. Additionally, it is almost impossible to collect direct observation data continuously across environments. Even though direct observation data can prove useful, they present a limited sample of a child's behavior (e.g., a 20-minute period during independent seatwork in mathematics). Thus, direct observation data may not yield generalizable data. Consequently, high-stakes decisions should not be made solely based on direct observation data. When making high-stakes decisions, direct observation data should be supplemented with other data (e.g., teacher and/or parent interviews or rating scales).

When involved in all stages of the problem-solving process, it can be very useful to collect other data. For example, after recording narrative data for a 20 minute session, an observer may want to confirm that the behaviors they observed were what the teacher meant by hand flapping before constructing an operational definition and recording system (e.g., Skinner, 2019) Similarly, when collecting momentary time sampling data on in-seat behavior, observers may want to confirm that the behavior during the observation period was typical or representative.

Behavioral theorists assume target behaviors are variable, and identifying the context of when behaviors occur at higher and lower rates can be used to form hypotheses that can lead to effective interventions. Thus, direct observation data may need to be collected across contexts to assist with identifying these variables, including context where behaviors are likely to occur and unlikely to occur.

All the recording procedures described in this chapter can be used to identify conditions (e.g., broad context or specific antecedents or triggers) that precede behaviors and events that occur following a behavior that may be reinforcing it (e.g., attention from the teacher). However, operationally defining all conditions or events surrounding behaviors can be extremely challenging. Consequently, practitioners often rely on less systematic recording strategies (e.g., narrative ABC recordings) or informant reports (e.g., teacher interviews, checklists, and rating scales) to identify these environmental factors that may be occasioning and maintaining behaviors (Skinner, 2019). Once identified, researchers can develop interventions designed to alter behaviors in the natural environment (Steege et al., 2019). For these evaluations, the empirical data recording procedures described in this chapter allow for repeated measures of behavior that can be used to evaluate intervention effects (e.g., small effect, immediate effects, trends, variability) within the child's natural environment (Barnett et al., 1999).

ACKNOWLEDGMENTS

We would like to acknowledge Edward S. Shapiro, Jennifer T. Freeland, and Brooke Killin for their work on earlier drafts of this chapter.

REFERENCES

Alessi, G., & Kaye, J. H. (1983). *Behavior assessment for school psychologists*. National Association of School Psychologists.

Barnett, D. W., Daley, E. J., Hampshire, E. M., Hines, N. R., Maples, K. A., Ostron, J. K., et al. (1999). Meeting performance-based training demands: Accountability in an intervention-based practicum. *School Psychology Quarterly*, *14*(4), 357–379. *https://psycnet.apa.org/doi/10.1037/h0089014*

Bergan, J. R., & Kratochwill, T. R. (1990). *Behavioral consultation in applied settings*. Plenum Press.

Briesch, A., Ferguson, T., Daniels, B., Volpe, R., & Feinberg, A. (2017). Examining the influence of interval length on the dependability of observational estimates. *School Psychology Review, 46*(4), 426–432.

Bruhn, A., McDaniel, S., & Kreigh, C. (2015). Self-monitoring interventions for students with behavior problems: A systematic review of current research. *Behavioral Disorders, 40*(2), 102–121.

Carr, E. G. (1993). Behavior analysis is not ultimately about behavior. *The Behavior Analyst, 16*(1), 47–49.

Cashwell, C. S, Skinner, C. H., Dunn, M., & Lewis, J. (1998). Group reward programs: A humanistic approach. *Humanistic Education and Development, 37*(1), 47–53.

Cashwell, T. C., Skinner, C. H., & Smith, E. S. (2001). Increasing second-grade students' reports of peer's prosocial behaviors via direct instruction, group reinforcement, and progress feedback: A replication and extensions. *Education and Treatment of Children, 24*(2), 161–175. *www.jstor.org/stable/42899652*

Cihak, D. F., Kirk, E. R., & Boon, R. T. (2009). Effects of classwide positive peer "Tootling" to reduce the disruptive classroom behaviors of elementary students with and without disabilities. *Journal of Behavioral Education, 18*(4), 267–278.

Cole, C. L, Marder, T., & McCann, L. (2000). Self-monitoring. In E. S. Shapiro & T. R. Kratochwill (Eds.), *Conducting school-based assessment of child and adolescent behavior* (pp. 121–149). Guilford Press.

Cone, J. D. (1978). The behavioral assessment grid (BAG): A conceptual framework and a taxonomy. *Behavior Therapy, 9*(5), 882–888.

Crewdson, M., Richardson, R. D., Fowler, K., Skinner, C. H., Wright, S., & Cihak, D. (2024). Supplementing social skills training with Tootling to simultaneously enhance first-grade students' performance of two social skills. *School Psychology Review, 53*(3), 236–250.

Ervin, R. A., Johnston, E. S., & Friman, P. C. (1998). Positive peer reporting to improve the social interactions of a socially rejected girl. *Proven Practice: Prevention and Remediation Solutions for School Problems, 1*, 17–21.

Ervin, R. A., Miller, P. M., & Friman, P. C. (1996). Feed the hungry bee: Using positive peer reports to improve the social interactions and acceptance of a socially rejected girl in a residential placement. *Journal of Applied Behavior Analysis, 29*(2), 251–253.

Glynn, E. L., & Thomas, J. D. (1974). Effects of cueing on self-control of classroom behavior. *Journal of Applied Behavior Analysis, 7*(2), 299–306.

Goldiamond, I. (1974). Toward a constructional approach to social problems: Ethical and constitutional issues raised by applied behavior analysis. *Behaviorism, 2*(1), 1–84.

Greenwood, C. R., Dinwiddie, G., Terry, B., Wade, L., Stanely, S. O., Thibadeau, S., et al. (1984). Teacher versus peer-mediated instruction: An eco-behavioral analysis of achievement outcomes. *Journal of Applied Behavior Analysis, 17*(4), 521–538.

Hartmann, D. P., Roper, B. L., & Bradford, C. C. (1979). Some relationships between behavioral and traditional assessment. *Journal of Behavioral Assessment, 1*(1), 3–21.

Hayes, S. C., & Cavoir, N. (1977). Multiple tracking and the reactivity of self-monitoring: I. Negative behaviors. *Behavior Therapy, 8*(5), 819–831.

Heering, P. W., & Wilder, D. A. (2006). The use of dependent group contingencies to increase on-task behavior in two general education classrooms. *Education and Treatment of Children, 29*(3), 459–468. *www.jstor.org/stable/42899896*

Henington, C., & Skinner, C. H. (1998). Peer monitoring. In K. Toppings, & S. Ely (Eds.), *Peer assisted learning* (pp. 237–253). Routledge.

Hintze, J. M., & Shapiro, E. S. (1995). Best practices in systematic observation of classroom behavior. In A. Thomas, & J. Grimes (Eds.), *Best practices in school psychology III* (pp. 651–660). National Association of School Psychologists.

Jacob, S., Decker, D. M., Lugg, E. T., & Diamond, E. L. (2022). *Ethics and law for school psychologists*. Wiley.

Johnson, S. M., & Bolstad, O. D. (1973). Methodological issues in naturalistic observation: Some problems and solutions. In L. A. Hamerlynch, L. E. Handy, & E. J. Marsh (Eds.), *Behavior change: Methodology, concepts, and practices* (pp. 7–68). Research Press.

Johnston, J. M. (2014). *Radical behaviorism for ABA practitioners*. Sloan.

Jones, K. M., Young, M. M., & Friman, P. C. (2000). Increasing peer praise of socially rejected delinquent youth: Effects on cooperation and acceptance. *School Psychology Quarterly, 15*(1), 30–39. *https://psycnet.apa.org/doi/10.1037/h0088776*

Kauffman, J. M., Conroy, M., Gardner, R., III, & Oswald, D. (2008). Cultural sensitivity in the application of behavior principles to education. *Education and Treatment of Children, 31*(2), 239–262.

Kazdin, A. E. (1977). Artifact, bias, and complexity of assessment: The ABC's of reliability. *Journal of Applied Behavior Analysis, 10*(1), 141–150.

Kern, L., Marder, T. J., Boyajian, A. E., Elliot, C. M., & McElhattan, D. (1997). Augmenting the independence of self-management procedures by teaching self-initiation across settings and activities. *School Psychology Quarterly, 12*(1), 23–32. *https://psycnet.apa.org/doi/10.1037/h0088944*

Kirkpatrick, B. A., Gibbons, S, Daniels, S., Taylor, K. L. H., McCurdy, M., & Skinner, C. H. (2019). Tootling in a third-grade after-school classroom: Decreasing antisocial interactions in at-risk students. *Journal of Positive Behavior Interventions, 21*(4), 228–239.

Korotitsch, W. J., & Nelson-Gray, R. O. (1999). An overview of self-monitoring research in assessment and treatment. *Psychological Assessment, 11*(4), 415–425.

Lambert, A. M., Tingstrom, D. H., Sterling, H. E., Dufrene, B. A., & Lynne, S. (2015). Effects of tootling on classwide disruptive and appropriate behavior in upper-elementary students. *Behavior Modification, 39*(3), 413–430.

Lentz, F. E. (1982). *An empirical examination of the utility of partial interval and momentary time sampling as a measure of behavior* [Unpublished doctoral dissertation, The University of Tennessee].

Lloyd, M. E., & Hilliard, A. M. (1989). Accuracy of self-recording as a function of repeated experience with different self-control contingencies. *Child and Family Behavior Therapy, 11*(2), 1–14.

Lo, Y. & Cartledge, G. (2006). FBA and BIP: Increasing the behavior adjustment of African American boys in schools. *Behavioral Disorders, 31*(2), 147–161.

Lum, J. D. K., Tingstrom, D. H., Dufrene, B. A., Radley, K. C., & Lynne, S. (2017). Effects of tootling on classwide disruptive and academically engaged behavior or general-education high school students. *Psychology in the Schools, 54*(4), 370–384.

McHugh, M. B., Tingstrom, D. H., Radley, K.C., Barry, C. T., & Walker, K. M. (2016). Effects of tootling on classwide and individual disruptive and academically engaged behavior of lower-elementary students. *Behavioral Interventions, 31*(4) 332–354.

McLaughlin, T. F., & Skinner, C. H. (1996). Improving academic performance through self-management: Cover, Copy, and Compare. *Intervention in School and Clinic, 32*(2), 113–118.

Nelson, R. O. (1977). Methodological issues in assessment via self-monitoring. In J. D. Cone & R. P. Hawkins (Eds.), *Behavioral assessment: New directions in clinical psychology* (pp. 217–240). Brunner/Mazel.

Nelson, R. O., Hay, L. R., Devany, J., & Koslow-Green, L. (1981). The reactivity of children's self-monitoring: Three experiments. *Child Behavior Therapy, 2*(3), 1–24.

Powell, J., Martindale, B., Kulp, S., Martindale, A., & Bauman, R. (1977). Taking a closer look: Time sampling and measurement error. *Journal of Applied Behavior Analysis, 10*(2), 325–332.

Quillivan, C. C., Skinner, C. H., Hawthorn, M. L., Whited, D., & Ballard, D. (2011). Using a cell phone to prompt a kindergarten student to self-monitor off-task/disruptive behavior. *Journal of Evidence-Based Practices in the Schools, 12*(2), 131–146.

Reeves, L. M. (2014). *The role of the replacement behavior in function-based interventions*. University of Arizona.

Saecker, L., Skinner, C. H., Brown, K. S., & Roberts, A. (2009). Cover, Copy, and Compare to enhance number-writing accuracy: Linking responsiveness data to intervention modifications. *Journal of Evidence Based Practices in the Schools, 10,* 171–187.

Santogrossi, D. A. (1975). *Self-reinforcement and external monitoring of performance on an academic task* (doctoral dissertation). ProQuest Information & Learning.

Saudargus, R. A. (1992). *State-Event Classroom Observation system (SECOS)*. University of Tennessee, Department of Psychology.

Shapiro, E. S. (1984). Self-monitoring. In T. H. Ollendick & M. Hersen (Eds.), *Child behavior assessment: Principals and procedures* (pp. 148–165). Pergamon.

Shapiro, E. S., & Browder, D. M. (1990). Behavioral assessment: Applications for persons with mental retardation. In J. Matson (Ed.), *Handbook of behavior modification with persons with mental retardation* (2nd. ed., pp. 93–122). Plenum.

Shapiro, E. S. & Clemens, N. H. (2023). *Academic skills problems: Fifth edition workbook*. Guilford Press.

Shapiro, E. S., McGonigle, J. J., & Ollendick, T. H. (1980). An analysis of self-assessment and self-reinforcement in a self-managed token economy with mentally retarded children. *Applied Research in Mental Retardation, 1*(3–4), 227–240.

Shapiro, E. S., & Skinner, C. H. (1990). Best practices in observational/ecological assessment. In A. Thomas & J. Grimes (Eds.), *Best practices in school psychology II* (pp. 17–31). National Association of School Psychologists.

Skinner, C. H. (2013). Contextual validity: Knowing what works is necessary, but not sufficient. *The School Psychologist, 67*(1), 14–21.

Skinner, C. H. (2019). Narrative reports and recordings for behavioral problem solving in schools. In Akin-Little, K. A., Little, S. G., Bray, M., & Kehle, T. (Eds.), *Behavioral interventions in schools: Evidence-based positive strategies* (pp. 157–170). APA Press.

Skinner, C. H., Cashwell, T. H., & Skinner, A. L. (2000). Increasing tootling: The effects of a peer monitored group contingency program on students' reports of peers' prosocial behaviors. *Psychology in the Schools, 37*(3), 263–270.

Skinner, C. H., Dittmer, K. I., & Howell, L. A. (2000). Direct observation in school settings: Theoretical issues. In E. S. Shapiro, & T. R. Kratochwill (Eds.), *Behavioral assessment in schools: Theory research and practice* (2nd ed., pp. 19–45). Guilford Press.

Skinner, C. H., Freeland, J., & Shapiro, E. S. (2003). Procedural issues associated with the behavioral assessment of children. In C. R. Reynolds & R. W. Kamphaus (Eds.), *Handbook of educational and psychological assessment of children: Personality, behavior, and context* (2nd ed., pp. 30-47). Guilford Press.

Skinner, C. H., Neddenriep, C. E., Robinson, S. L., Ervin, R., & Jones, K. (2002). Altering educational environments through positive peer reporting: Prevention and remediation of social problems associated with behavior disorders. *Psychology in the Schools, 39*(2), 191–202.

Skinner, C. H., Rhymer, K. N., & McDaniel, E. C. (2000). Naturalistic direct observation in educational settings. In E. S. Shapiro & T. R. Kratochwill (Eds.), *Conducting school-based assessments of child and adolescent behavior* (pp. 21–54). Guilford Press.

Skinner, C. H., Shapiro, E. S., Turco, T. L., Cole, C. L., & Brown, D. K. (1992). A comparison of self and peer delivered immediate corrective feedback on multiplication performance. *Journal of School Psychology, 30*(2) 101–116.

Skinner, C. H., & Smith, E. S. (1992). Issues surrounding the use of self-management interventions for increasing academic performance. *School Psychology Review, 21*(2), 202–210.

Steege, M. W., Pratt, J. L., Wickerd, G., Guare, R., & Watson, T. S. (2019). *Conducting school-based functional behavioral assessments: A practitioner's guide.* Guilford Press.

Stern, G. W., Fowler, S. A., & Kohler, F. W. (1988). A comparison of two intervention roles: Peer monitor and point earner. *Journal of Applied Behavior Analysis, 21*(1), 103–109.

The IRIS Center. (2012, 2021). *Classroom behavior management (part 1): Key concepts and foundational practices. https://iris.peabody.vanderbilt.edu/module/beh1*

Wright, S., Skinner, C. H., Crewdson, M., Moore, T., McCurdy, M., Coleman, M. B., et al. (2022). Using a Tootling intervention to sequentially enhance and maintain at-risk elementary students' performance of multiple social skills. *School Psychology, 37*(3), 248–258.

Wright, S., Skinner, C. H., Kirkpatrick, B. A., Daniels, S., Moore, T., & Crewdson, M. (2021). Using Tootling to enhance first-grade students use of a social skill: Evaluating the Catching Compliments Game. *Education and Treatment of Children, 44*(2), 101–113.

Zakszeski, B. N., Hojnoski, R. L., & Wood, B. K. (2017). Considerations for time sampling interval durations in the measurement of young children's classroom engagement. *Topics in Early Childhood Special Education, 37*(1), 42–53.

PART II

ASSESSMENT STRATEGIES

CHAPTER 10

Culturally Informed Interviewing in the Psychological Assessment of Children and Adolescents

Taylor A. Miller, Paul J. Frick, and Courtney M. Goetz

GENERAL CONSIDERATIONS IN USING INTERVIEWS

Clinical interviews have a prominent place in the history of psychological assessment. The face-to-face verbal dialogue between assessor and client is the prototypical format for most clinical work. Historically, the most frequently used type of clinical interview is the unstructured interview. This interview format offers maximum flexibility to the clinician in developing questions based on the needs of the specific individual being assessed. This flexible format can also be very helpful in tailoring interviews to the educational, socioeconomic, racial, ethnic, and cultural background of the interviewee. Further, the interview content (e.g., how questions are worded) and format (e.g., who is being interviewed) can be tailored to the developmental level of the child. However, unstructured interviews rely heavily on the clinician's expertise to determine what questions are asked and how responses are to be interpreted. As a result, the flexibility of this format is counterbalanced by the unreliability often associated with unstructured assessment methods (McClellan & Werry, 2000). For these interviews to be appropriately tailored to unique cultural backgrounds and developmental level of the person being assessed, the clinician must have adequate training and experience to adjust interviews in an appropriate manner. Further, the unstructured and flexible format make these interviews susceptible to the influence of potential bias on the part of the interviewer.

Based on these limitations in the unstructured clinical interview, more structured approaches to interviewing were developed. Diagnostic interview schedules take away most, if not all, flexibility of the clinician. The questions to be asked are set; they must be asked in a certain way; and only certain answers are allowed and coded. Such interviews lead to highly reliable scores across clinicians that reduce potential biases in the assessment process (Frick et al., 2020). They are also typically closely tied to diagnostic criteria, ensuring that symptoms of common diagnoses are assessed, as well as important additional criteria, such as age of symptom onset, in which situations they are displayed, and their level of impairment. This reliability and comprehensive coverage of diagnostic criteria make them very useful in clinical research contexts (Walker et al., 2021). However, this increase in structure and subsequent increase in reliability comes at the cost of an inability to tailor interviews to the unique characteristics of the case. Further, the clinical usefulness of the resulting scores, as well as their potential validity for persons from diverse backgrounds, is dependent on the cross-cultural validity of the diagnoses being assessed.

The strengths and weaknesses of the various types of clinical interviews led to the development of an assessment strategy that attempts to blend these two approaches and capitalize on the strengths of each. A growing number of assessments use the structured professional judgment approach (SPJ; Lawing et al., 2017), which attempts to blend both structured and unstructured interviewing. Similar to the structured diagnostic interview, items to be scored are clearly specified, and only certain scores are allowed. However, like the unstructured clinical interview, the clinician is given great leeway in determining how the information is obtained to score the items. SPJ approaches require substantial training in assessment, including training in how to gather information from people from diverse backgrounds and developmental levels. However, the structured scoring has led to an increase in evidence for the reliability of scores in comparison to unstructured interviews (Childs et al., 2014). Unfortunately, most SPJ approaches were developed for the assessment of very specific psychological constructs, and no current SPJ assessments are available for many problem areas that need to be assessed when providing psychological evaluations to children and adolescents.

In this chapter, we describe each of these approaches to interviewing (i.e., unstructured interviews, structured interviews, SPJ). We give an example of each and provide guidance in their use in the psychological assessment of children and adolescents. This guidance focuses largely on three goals. First, this chapter provides an overview of the strengths and weaknesses to each approach to interviewing, as well as examples of each method supported by research. Second, specific considerations are provided for how each type of interview should be used in culturally informed assessments. That is, we provide guidance on how each approach should be used to provide clinically beneficial outcomes and avoid potentially harmful outcomes for persons from diverse cultural backgrounds. Third, we attempt to provide a useful guide for integrating interviews into clinical assessments that capitalize on the strengths of each approach and link children and adolescents from diverse backgrounds to effective clinical services.

GENERAL CONSIDERATIONS IN CULTURALLY INFORMED ASSESSMENTS

Before focusing specifically on the various types of interviews, it is important to introduce several general considerations that are important for any culturally informed assessment of children and adolescents. Most generally, it is important to clearly define the use of the term *culture*. We use the term *culture* to describe the set of "knowledge, concepts, rules, and practices that are learned and transmitted across generations" (American Psychiatric Association, 2022, p. 749). Culture can influence the interview process in several ways, as it involves the salient ecological contexts for an individual and the interaction of that individual's identity within those contexts. These interactions can be influenced by the individual's age, gender, race/ethnicity, language, socioeconomic status, disability, nationality, immigration, and sexual orientation. Culture also influences the individual's communication style, expression of mental health symptoms, perception and trust of authority figures (i.e., educational and mental health professionals), and perception of mental health services. More specifically, a person's intergenerational cultural experiences may influence a person's level of openness or perception of their own symptoms. For example, the individual or family may have a distrust of the medical and psychological profession due to previous individual or intergenerational negative experiences with members of the profession (American Psychological Association, 2021), which would make them reluctant to answer questions related to mental health.

In addition to these important interpersonal considerations, culture can also influence the structure of the interview process. Cultural considerations can help to determine who is included in the interview (e.g., grandparents, co-parents, family or community leaders, godparents). The assessment process should also consider practical and accessibility issues, such as the availability of insurance for mental services or transportation to clinics to receive these services. Thus, the assessment structure needs to be planned in consideration of potential barriers, such as minimizing the number of sessions required for the evaluation and remaining flexible by providing alternative means to conduct the interview (i.e., telehealth approaches, transportation services, time of the interview).

Up to this point, we have focused largely on the culture of the person being interviewed. However, culturally relevant practice also requires clinicians to be mindful of their own biases. Specifically, clinician bias in psychological assessment interviews may impact the rapport between the interviewer and interviewee, the selection of interview format, the types and content of questions asked in the interview, and how both verbal and nonverbal responses are interpreted. Research has provided examples of how clinician bias can influence diagnostic decisions for persons from different racial and ethnic groups, which has critically important treatment implications. For example, in a sample of 406 low-income children, African American youth were 2.6 times less likely to receive a diagnosis of autism spectrum disorder (ASD) than White children on their first specialty care visit and, as result, were more likely to have treatment delayed (Mandell et al., 2007). These authors also reported that African American youth were 2.4 times more likely to receive a diagnosis of conduct disorder than attention-deficit/hyperactivity disorder (ADHD) compared to White youth with similar symptoms. Fadus et al. (2020) suggest that this overdiagnosis of conduct disorder and underdiagnosis of ADHD could be the result of clinician bias (i.e., interpreting the behavior of youth of color as being more dangerous and disobedient and more worthy of punishment than treatment). As a result of this potential bias in diagnostic practice, children of color are less likely to receive stimulant medication for ADHD compared to non-Hispanic White children (Coker et al., 2016).

As we discuss below, certain types of interviewing can help reduce these potential biases and resulting problems in diagnosis. For example, using structured diagnostic interviews that ensure that all symptoms for multiple diagnoses are assessed during the interview can minimize the possibility of missing certain diagnoses. Also, matching clinicians and clients on their racial and ethnic backgrounds may possibly reduce biases. However, the results of research on such racial and ethnic matching are not entirely clear. In one study examining cultural matching with Black youth, attendance rates were unrelated to working with a Black clinician. However, Black youth were more likely to receive a developmental/learning/autism diagnosis during their first encounter when working with a Black clinician (Carroll et al., 2024). Further, in a large sample of 9,127 clients from several ethnic and racial groups who were evaluated by over 1,500 clinicians, there was a significant association between ethnic and racial matching and higher ratings of client functioning (Russell et al., 1996). Specifically, clinicians matched to clients of their own ethnic group reported less severe ratings of psychopathology and reported higher levels of positive psychological functioning in comparison to mismatched groups. Conversely, Ureche et al. (2016) did not find any differences in adolescents' self-disclosure of substance use when they were matched with a clinician of the same race and ethnicity. Clearly, more research is needed to clarify the influence of matching clinician and clients on their ethnic and racial backgrounds, as well as how intersectional cultural factors may impact assessment and treatment outcomes. However, it is important to note that currently, persons of color are substantially underrepresented among practicing psychologists. According to the U.S. Census Bureau (2015), 86% of psychologists in the United States workforce were White, with only 5% identifying as Hispanic and 4% identifying as Black. As a result, matching may not be currently possible for many children of color who are seeking a psychological evaluation.

A final consideration in a culturally informed approach to interviewing is the recognition that the method and content of the interviews themselves may be subject to bias. Like other forms of psychological assessment, interviews can be susceptible to test bias (Reynolds & Suzuki, 2013). Specifically, three types of bias can influence the interview process: method bias, construct bias, and item bias. With method bias, an interviewer does not adjust their questions, style or tone toward the interviewee, which can lead to invalid interpretations of an interviewee's responses. That is, the interviewer may not get accurate information from the interviewee due to their delivery of the interview questions. Construct bias refers to inconsistent rates of diagnoses and differential behaviors associated with the construct itself in relation to cultural groups (Van de Vijver & Poortinga, 1997; Van de Vijver & Tanzer, 2004). The previously described pattern for Black youth to be more likely to receive a diagnosis of conduct disorder, and less likely to receive diagnoses of ASD or ADHD, is an example of this type of bias. Finally, item bias (also known as differential item functioning; Van de Vijver & Tanzer, 2004) refers to misrepresentation at the item level, whereby a question asked by a clinician may have different meanings for persons across different cultural groups. Specifically, an item may have unintended connotative differences on an assessment that leads to different responses across various cultural groups. For example, an item that asks a child to report how "harsh" their maternal caregiver is may result in differential item functioning across cultural groups, as the term *harsh* may be interpreted and/or operationalized differently by children from certain cultural groups. Specifically, differences in interpretation of parenting practices have been found across European American and African American children (Jackson-Newsom et al., 2008; Kang et al., 2022).

In summary, there are many factors related to the culture of the person being assessed, the culture of the interviewer, and cultural influences on the content of the interview that are important to consider in the use of interviews in the psychological assessments of children and adolescents. The different types of interviews we review in this chapter not only have strengths and weaknesses in the quality of the diagnostic information they provide but they also vary in their susceptibility to certain biases and in their ability to contribute important information to a culturally informed assessment. In our description of the different methods for interviewing in the following sections, we attempt to highlight strengths and weaknesses of each method both overall and specifically in their use in culturally informed assessments. We then provide recommendations for their use in culturally informed psychological assessments that capitalize on their strengths to result in beneficial treatment recommendations for children and adolescents across a diversity of cultural backgrounds.

TYPES OF INTERVIEWS

Unstructured Clinical Interviews

The unstructured clinical interview involves the assessor asking questions that are completely tailored to the individual case of the person being assessed (or a knowledgeable informant). It is one of the few forms of assessment used widely by a variety of mental health professionals. In fact, unstructured diagnostic interviews may be the primary source of information for making diagnoses by psychiatrists (Hyman, 2010), and unstructured social histories are often the most critical piece of information used by clinical social workers in designing treatment plans (Sur et al., 2023). However, the lack of reliability of unstructured clinical interviews, the requirement of substantial training on the part of the interviewer, and the potential to be influenced by bias have also led some to suggest an over-reliance on their use (McClellan & Werry, 2000). These limitations clearly suggest that, like any assessment method, clinical interviews should not be used alone to make diagnoses and referrals for treatment. However, they do provide critical information to the assessment process.

As noted above, unstructured clinical interviews provide information tailored specifically to the individual case. While self-report questionnaires can indicate a child's overall level of anxiety and how severe it is relative to other children their age, the unstructured clinical interview allows for flexibility in identifying specific details and context. For example, an unstructured interview can ask questions to determine if a child's anxiety level is worse prior to weekends that the child is to be in the custody of their father and stepmother, or how the anxiety symptoms have manifested and developed over time for the child. Although other methods of assessment can help to chart the areas that may be causing problems for the child generally, the unstructured clinical interview can help to document what areas seem to be causing the most distress for the child and are of most concern to the parents. The unstructured clinical interview can also provide important information to aid in making a diagnosis, such as determining when the problems started for the child, how distressing and impairing the problems are, and whether there are family or community stressors contributing to a child's problems. Unstructured clinical interviews can provide content clarity as to how individual items on structured rating scales were interpreted. In addition, the clinical interview is an important method for determining what treatments have been tried in the past and how the child and the parents perceive the effectiveness of such treatments. This information could be critical for individualizing recommendations for future treatment. Finally, interviews can be an important method for ensuring that problems are not missed. Its open-ended format allows clinicians to briefly screen for a wide variety of problems that may not need further assessment, unless a concern is raised in the interview.

A number of guides for conducting clinical interviews are available (see Frick et al., 2020). Table 10.1 provides a summary of the key content areas that we recommend to be covered for most psychological assessments of children and adolescents. We provide the rationale and recommendations for each of these areas in the following sections. For children below the age of 9 years, these areas are primarily covered in an interview with a primary caretaker. For children and adolescents older than age 9, many of the areas can also be assessed from the child's point of view. However, it is usually best to conduct these interviews with the child and their parents separately, to allow each informant to be free to answer questions without concern about the reactions of others.

"What Is of Most Concern to You?"

We suggest that the clinician begin any unstructured clinical interview by asking the parent/caregiver what is currently concerning them most

TABLE 10.1. Content for Unstructured Clinical Interviews with Parents

Current problem causing the most concern.
- *What concerns you most about your child?*
- *What do you think led to your child's problems?*

Age of onset and duration of any problems.
- *At what age or in which grade did these problems start? Did your child have these problems in kindergarten? First grade?*

Level of impairment and distress associated with any problems.
- *What is the worst this problem has ever been?*
- *Does it affect them at home? School? With peers? During extracurricular activities? At church?*

What has been done for any problem area, both formal treatment and informal interventions tried by parents?
- *What have you tried to help your child with these problems?*
- *Has your child received any treatment or intervention for this problem? Do you think it was effective?*
- *Has your child received any tutoring? Has it been effective?*

Family/social context
- *Who lives at home with your child?*
- *Do any other adults help to take care of your child regularly?*
- *How has this changed since your child was born?*
- *Does your child have any friends? What do they do together?*

Family psychiatric history
- *Has anyone in your child's family experienced any mental health concerns? Learning difficulties?*

about their child or by asking the child about their main concerns. We recommend starting with this question because it conveys to interviewees that their concerns are important and helps to make them partners in the assessment process. Further, this information can begin to shed light on the level of distress and impairment any problems are causing for the child and the family. By asking this question of both the parent and child being assessed, the clinician can also uncover any disagreements as to what is of most concern. For example, a parent may report that a child's misbehavior at school is causing the most concern, whereas the child may report that it is the frequent arguments between the parents that are causing the most concern. Finally, how this question is answered can help provide the structure for the next sections of the unstructured clinical interview. If a parent states that the child's inattention and hyperactivity are of most concern, the next questions in the interview for the parent can be asked in relation to that problem area (i.e., when did these problems start; how severe and impairing are they; what interventions have been tried for them?). After these questions, the interviewer can then ask about other concerns (e.g., learning problems, anxiety) and repeat the process with similar questions about each area of concern.

Age of Onset and Duration of Problems

Age of onset is a crucial piece of information required for the diagnosis of many developmental disorders. For example, in the text revision of the fifth edition of the *Diagnostic Statistical Manual of Mental Disorders* (DSM-5 TR; American Psychiatric Association, 2022), the symptoms of disruptive mood dysregulation disorder must be present before age 10 years, and several of the symptoms of ADHD must have been present before age 12 years to make these diagnoses. Though DSM-5 TR (American Psychiatric Association, 2022) does not require an exact age of onset within the diagnostic criteria for ASD, it does require that "symptoms must be present in the early developmental period (but may not become fully manifest until social demands exceed limited capacities or may be masked by learned strategies later in life)" (p. 59). Duration of symptoms is also necessary for making many diagnoses and differentiating them from transient reactions to environmental stressors. For example, symptoms of oppositional defiant disorder (ODD) need to be present for at least six months to make the diagnosis.

Unfortunately, many other methods of assessment, such as behavior rating scales, self-report inventories, behavioral observations, and laboratory tests, do not provide this important information on onset and duration of symptoms. Thus, estimating the age of onset of any problems being experienced by the child is a very useful part and a strength of the unstructured clinical interview. Considering the importance of this information, it can be helpful to ask questions in several ways to ensure the most accurate information. Commonly, the age of symptom onset is much earlier than is initially reported by the child or parent/caregiver, who may be focusing on when problems started causing the most issues. For example, a parent may report that a child's inattention started in the sixth grade. However, after following up by asking if their child had any problems in kindergarten, the parent may report examples of inattention being displayed by the child at that time. By using the unstructured interview format to ask follow-up questions such as these, it can become apparent that what the parent meant in their initial response was that the problems onset much earlier, but they really didn't start having a clinically significant impact on the child's school performance until the sixth grade.

By charting the onset and duration of any problem areas, the unstructured interview helps to determine the role of any stressors that may be contributing to the child's difficulties. For example, if a child reports that they started feeling anxious at school in the fourth grade, the interviewer can follow up with questions about what was happening at that time. In this case, there may be relevant contextual influences, such as the child experiencing bullying from other students at this time. In addition, assessing age and duration of problem areas can help to determine if certain problems are secondary to other problem areas. For example, there is evidence that anxiety and depression can develop in children and adolescents who have shown behavior problems over an extended period. For these children, emotional distress can stem from problems in school and conflict with peers and family members (Robertson et al., 2023). Charting this progression of problems can help to determine the most important focus of treatment. Reducing the child's behavior problems and the impairments caused by such behavior problems is the most effective strategy for reducing the child's anxiety and depression. Finally, assessing the chronological progression of symptoms can also be important for determining if the problems are episodic or continuous. That is, it can be important to determine if symptoms represent a clear change in the child's emotions or behaviors, or if they represent a continuing pattern for the child. For example, adolescents who are going through a major depressive episode often experience a clear change from their normal mood when they are entering a depressive episode, whereas those with disruptive mood disorder show persistent irritability and anger throughout the day on most days, without long periods of relatively positive moods.

Level of Impairment and Distress

Another critical type of information that can be obtained in an unstructured clinical interview is the level of impairment experienced by the child due to their symptoms. Perhaps one of the main questions parents want answered in an evaluation is "Does my child need treatment?" This question is often best answered by determining whether any emotional, behavioral, or learning problems are affecting the child in important ways, such as whether the child's symptoms have resulted in missed opportunities (e.g., not being able to take tests or play in sports games due to anxiety; missing school due to depression), poor performance at school (e.g., making careless mistakes on assignments, getting detentions or suspensions), or problems with peers (e.g., avoidance of social activities due to anxiety; being rejected or bullied by peers). These potential consequences to the child are labeled "impairments." Often, the level of impairment associated with a child's emotional and behavioral problems is equated with the level of distress experienced due to the presenting problems. However, a child or adolescent could be substantially bothered by emotional or behavioral problems but manage to avoid serious impairment with great effort. Through individualized questions, unstructured clinical interviews can allow for the clinicians to better ascertain the amount of effort that the child needs to expend in order to maintain functioning despite symptoms.

Because the level of impairment and level of distress associated with problem areas may be critical for determining the need for treatment, most criteria in DSM-5-TR require documentation of substantial levels of impairment and distress to make a diagnosis. Sometimes, as in the case of ADHD, the diagnosis requires for the child to show impairment in multiple situations. For other diagnoses, the level of impairment is an important severity indicator. For example, in the diagnostic criteria for ODD, the number of situations in which the child is showing the oppositional and defiant behaviors is an indicator of the disorder's severity, with children showing impairment both inside and outside the home being at greater risk for future problems than children showing only impairment at home (Frick & Nigg, 2012).

It is important to note that other methods of assessments can provide information on a child's level of impairment and distress. For example, some rating scales were designed specifically to assess the child's level of impairment in various settings (see Lewandowski et al., 2009, for a review). However, the unstructured interview allows these assessments to be tailored to the exact symptoms being shown by the child, which helps to determine what problems are most severe and in most need of treatment. One question that can help in assessing level of impairment and distress is to ask the question "What is the worse this has ever been?" For example, if a parent is describing temper tantrums by the child, it can help to ask them to describe the worst tantrum the child has ever displayed. It can be very helpful to determine if the worse tantrum described involves the child "showing an angry face and sulking off," as opposed to a tantrum that led to a child hurting someone else or punching a hole in the wall. Similarly, if a child describes getting very nervous before tests, it can help to ask about the worse this has ever been. It can be very helpful to know if the worse is described by the child as a little knot in the stomach, as opposed to a child staying up all night worrying and not being able to go to school to take the test.

Previous Treatment

Another important area to assess with the unstructured interview involves past attempts to address any problems. These can be informal attempts made by the parent or child without professional help (e.g., being more structured at homework time) or more formal interventions (e.g., special education classes, mental health counseling, medication). This information is important for several reasons. First, it is sometimes necessary to know about previous treatment in order to make a diagnosis. Many school systems require documentation of a lack of response to intervention before a diagnosis of a learning disability can be made (Fletcher & Miciak, 2024). Second, knowing what has been tried before can help to determine the level of severity of the problem. That is, a child who has asked to see a counselor due to anxiety is providing a clear indication of the high level of distress being caused by their emotions. Third, documenting past treatments can also help to determine the duration of the problems. If a parent states that they requested a developmental assessment of a child at three years of age, this information provides a clear indication that there were concerns about the child's adjustment very early in development. Fourth, knowing past treatments can help tailor recommendations. For example, knowing that a child has not responded to previous interventions may lead to recommendations for different types of treatment. If past treatments have not been those that research supports as being most effective for a child's specific problems, this can also be used to provide a strong justification for the parent and child to try a different approach to treatment.

Family/Social Context

A critically important aspect of the unstructured interview is an assessment of the child's family and other social contexts. This assessment is critical because many other aspects of a psychological evaluation, such as their intelligence, their learning, their behavior, and their emotions, focus largely on the child. However, to adequately interpret all of this information and use it to make recommendations for treatment, it is important to place these findings within the child's larger social ecology. This part of the interview could start with questions related to who lives in the home with the child and who is involved in caretaking duties for the child. Additionally, the clinician should ascertain whether the child shares time at different homes and determine how has this living situation changed over the child's life. In addition to these structural aspects of a child's family context, the clinical interview should consider various aspects of family functioning that could be critical for interpreting other assessment information. For example, it could be important to determine how different caretakers view the child's behavior and how they each respond to it. Such differences could help in interpreting very different scores from the two caretakers on a behavioral rating scale and to give clues about possible maintaining factors for a child's behavioral difficulties (e.g., inconsistent responses from caretakers). Another example of an important area of family functioning to assess is the level of conflict between caretakers that is evident to the child. Such conflict, whether the parents live in the same home or different ones, can be critical for explaining a child's emotional and behavioral difficulties (van Eldik et al., 2020). When discussing past conflict, a helpful question can be "What is the worse fight that your child has ever seen between you and the child's father?" These questions are particularly important for families that have gone through a divorce and have had to negotiate custody arrangements for the child.

It is also important to note potential reasons that may lead to different views of the child's behavior or make it difficult for the caretakers to appropriately respond to a child's difficulties. One such reason may be mental health difficulties in the parents themselves, which is why we recommend assessing for a history of mental illness in the family as part of the unstructured interview. However, it is also important to assess the degree of support the family has in terms of extended family and other community resources, such as support from a church group or other neighborhood and community resources, as well as the financial resources of the family. This information is not only helpful for determining possible factors contributing the child's difficulties but also will be important for how treatment recommendations are made so that these recommendations can capitalize on supports that exist in the family and are realistic for the family, considering the resources available to them.

In addition to gathering information on the child's family context, it is critical to also gather information on the child's peer relationships. For some disorders, the quality of a child's peer relationships can be critical for determining the presence of a diagnosis, such in assessing the symptoms of ASD or social anxiety disorder. Further, having close and supportive relationship with peers is a critical source of social support that buffers the effects of potential stressors on a child and provides the child with an important source of socialization that promotes healthy social development (e.g., development of appropriate levels of concern toward others; Boele et al., 2019). On the other hand, social rejection and bullying can have dramatic, immediate, and long-lasting effects on a child's emotional and behavioral health (Barlett et al., 2024). Thus, it is important to determine if a child's emotional, behavioral, and learning problems are having a detrimental impact on their peer relationships.

Family Psychiatric History

Another important area to assess in an unstructured interview is whether there is a history of mental health or learning problems in the child's biological relatives. Many disorders have some genetic component. As a result, knowing if a child is at risk for certain types of problems can help guide assessments (i.e., point to specific areas to assess) and help to make differential diagnoses (e.g., help to determine what might be causing a child's emotional or behavioral difficulties). Given the differences in diagnostic and treatment rates across various sociocultural groups, it is important to note family history of problems regardless of whether a formal diagnosis or treatment was obtained. In addition, current psychiatric problems in the child's caregivers and sibling(s) may help explain certain stressors that a child is experiencing in the home and should be considered when planning the appropriate intervention strategies for a child. This screening can be as simple as asking a parent if anyone in the child's family has experienced any mental health concerns or learning problems, even if a formal diagnosis has not been made.

Additional Concerns

The clinical interview can often serve as a screening tool. That is, it can provide a way of assessing a wide variety of issues that could be important to help the clinician determine if any potential problem area should be pursued further with additional questions or even with additional methods of assessment. Thus, it is very helpful to end the clinical interview with both the parent and child using the question "Do you have any other concerns that we have not talked about?" This not only reduces the chance that major problem areas are missed, but it also conveys to both the parent and child how important their perspective is to the assessment process and that addressing their concerns is a primary goal of the assessment.

Positive Interviewing Techniques

Our recommendations for the content of the unstructured interview are problem-focused. We feel that this is important because caregivers have sought services for their child due to concerns about potential emotional, behavioral, or learning problems. Their primary concern is to determine what might be leading to these problems and to get recommendations for ways to help their child. However, it is important that the interview is conducted in a way that encourages optimism, promotes hope for positive change, and enhances both the parents and child's self-concept. We have found several helpful strategies for creating this framework during the interview process.

First, parents often feel responsible or blameworthy for their child's difficulties. It is therefore critical to change this perception. This can be done within the interview by frequently commenting on how lucky the child is to have caretakers who want to provide as much support as possible for them. This should be communicated early and often during the interview. For example, during the discussion of what problem areas for a young girl are of most concern for the parent, the interviewer could state, "I can see that you are really worried about her behavior; she is so lucky to have a parent who doesn't just let these problems go on but wants to help her to be successful." When asking about past treatment for an adolescent boy, the interviewer could state, "You have really worked extremely hard to try to get help for him; he is very lucky to have you as an advocate." These are just two examples of how an interviewer can use the unstructured interview to shift a caregiver's perspective from feeling like their help-seeking is a sign of parental failure to it being evidence of them being a loving and caring parent.

Second, part of positive interviewing is to acknowledge the strengths of the child throughout the interview. We have found that this rarely requires that the interviewer specifically asks for strengths. Instead, it typically involves commenting on strengths, no matter how small, that are brought up during the interview. Such comments are important to include in unstructured interviews with both the parent and the child or adolescent, although it is particularly important for the latter. As an example, a middle school boy may be describing to you the fights he gets into at school, saying, "My buddies keep telling me to just let it go, but I can't." You could then say, "It sounds like you have some good friends who really care about you," before asking other questions about the fighting. However, if these opportunities don't arise naturally, the interviewer can specifically ask for strengths. For example, if an adolescent girl has described having difficulties in all subjects at school and doesn't give any areas in which she does well, the interviewer can ask, "It sounds like school has been really challenging for you. Have you had *any* positive experiences at school?"

Third, another way to use positive interviewing to enhance optimism about the child's future is by emphasizing the child's potential. For example, when a parent is clearly frustrated about their young son and is describing him very negatively, we find it is helpful to reframe this frustration as a sign of caring. The interviewer can say, "I know that seeing him get into trouble is really frustrating because you see such potential in him." It can also be helpful to reframe problems as "potential," like describing a boy who is oppositional and defiant as being "strong-willed, which can really serve him well if he learns to channel it." The hyperactivity in a young girl could be reframed as showing that she is "highly energetic, and just think how successful she will be if she just learns to harness this energy!" Anxiety can be described as a sign that an adolescent boy is "a highly sensitive and caring person."

The Role of Unstructured Interviews in Culturally Informed Assessments

Given the potential for bias, one may assume that unstructured interviews should be used sparingly in culturally informed assessment. This is not the case. In fact, such interviews are essential for a culturally informed assessment. By starting the interview with a question about what concerns the parent or child the most, it helps to build rapport with people from diverse cultural backgrounds by conveying that their opinion and concerns are important and that the interviewer wants to meet their needs with the evaluation. Further, by allowing the parent and child to describe their concerns in their own words, the interviewer can determine what words and expressions they are using to describe a child's difficulties. For example, people can describe anxiety in many different ways (e.g., worry, unease, the willies, wound up, uptight, etc.) or even through somatic symptoms (e.g., headaches, stomachaches). Listening to and matching the client's language can facilitate the interviewer in obtaining needed information about the child's anxiety (e.g., finding out how severe and impairing it is for the child). As part of this qualitative information gathering, the interviewer can begin to assess the parent and child's perceptions of the causes of the problems, which can be highly related to a person's cultural background. For example, culture can influence how persons vary in their perceptions of mental health problems as medical problems, familial failures, spiritual weakness, or societal problems (e.g., due to discrimination and racism; Raglin et al., 2015). Further there may be stigma related to educational, social, emotional, or behavioral health problems, or symptoms may be exacerbated based on experiences of racism and discrimination.

Perhaps most importantly, the unstructured interview allows the interviewer to place the child's or adolescent's emotional and behavioral functioning into each the family's unique cultural context. This can start with determining the child's primary caretakers, which can range greatly across families, and how the caretaking duties are shared across caretakers. Even beyond the primary caretakers, the interview can help determine the level of support provided to the caretakers by extended family members, neighbors, and others (e.g., church members). In addition to these potential sources of support within a child's ecological context, the unstructured interview can also help to identify unique stressors being faced by the child and their family, such as the number of people living in the home, the parents' work schedule, the child's role in the family, access to transportation, financial stressors, and the level of social support and presence of stressors within the local community where the family resides.

DSM-5 TR provides a cultural formulation interview (CFI) that can be used to assist with a conducting a culturally informed interview (American Psychiatric Association, 2022). The CFI consists of several recommendations for structuring the interview to be culturally informed and these recommendations fit well within the problem domains outlined above and provided in Table 10.1. These include:

- *Cultural definition of problem*: determine how the individual views the problem, how the individual frames the problem to individuals in their social context, and the aspects of the problem that matters most to the individual.
- *Cultural perceptions of causes, context, and support*: determine the meaning of the problem for the individual, stressors and degree of social support for the individual, and the role of cultural identity (e.g., how discrimination and non-acceptance may play a role in problems).
- *Cultural factors affecting self-coping and past help-seeking*: determine both formal and informal ways that the person has tried to address the problem, how effective the individual views these attempts, and barriers experienced in past methods for coping or seeking help.
- *Cultural factors affecting current help-seeking*: determine what led to current help-seeking and consider possible concerns about setting (e.g., hours, degree of travel required for client) and clinician (e.g., cultural background of clinician, language barriers) that may influence quality of care.

Structured Diagnostic Interviews

Structured interviews are also called diagnostic interview schedules. In this approach to interviewing, the clinician has little flexibility in the questions asked or what responses to code. As a result, information obtained from these interviews tends to be highly reliable. Due to this reliability, most of these instruments were designed for use in research with adults. However, in recent years, several structured diagnostic interviews have been developed for use with children and adolescents in many types of clinical settings, not just for clinical research (see Frick et al., 2020).

These interview schedules give very clear and explicit guidance on what questions should be asked, what follow-up questions should be asked based on the person's response, and what responses are allowed. Interview questions generally start with a stem question (e.g., "Have you been involved in many physical fights?"). If the stem is answered affirmatively, then follow-up questions are asked to determine other relevant parameters such as frequency (e.g., "How many fights have you been in the past year?"), severity (e.g., "Have you ever used a weapon in a fight?"), onset (e.g., "When was the first time you got in a fight?"), and impairment (e.g., "Has fighting caused problems for you at school, home, or with kids your age?"). Given this format, the length of time to complete these interviews can vary greatly, depending on how many stem questions are answered affirmatively.

There are several common features across these interview schedules. First, most interviews are designed to assess disorders according to DSM criteria. As a result, most interviews organize questions by diagnosis. Which DSM disorders are assessed by youth interview schedules are generally similar across the different interview schedules, with most assessing the disruptive behavior disorders, affective disorders, and anxiety disorders. Most interviews also allow for some tailoring of what diagnostic criteria are included in the assessment, allowing the clinician to include some but not all diagnoses. Second, to promote multi-informant assessments, most interviews contain parallel forms to ask identical questions of both the child and a caregiver. This format allows for easy comparison of the child's symptoms as reported by each informant. Third, most current structured interviews allow administration via computer either to be administered by the examiner or to be self-administered by the interviewee. The computer format was designed to enhance the reliability of the interviews by increasing the ease of administration and data collection. The computer quickly stores responses, selects the appropriate follow-up questions, and skips out of diagnostic sections when the respondent fails to endorse a minimum number of symptoms. Computer-administered interviews have programs that quickly score the interview and provide various summary scores (e.g., symptom indexes, number of diagnostic thresholds met) that aid in the interpretation of the results.

There are also some differences across the various structured diagnostic interviews that are currently available for use with children and adolescents. First, while interview schedules all provide some degree of structure in their format for asking questions, they can differ in the degree of structure. For example, the *Schedule for Affective Disorders and Schizophrenia for School-Age Children* (KSADS-PL; Kaufman et al., 2016) is one of the least structured interviews. Typically, the interviewer is encouraged to begin by building rapport in an unstructured format. Then, the clinician is instructed to "move the conversation towards more focused questions, such as 'Do you feel sad?' and 'Do you cry?'" In contrast, the *Diagnostic Interview Schedule for Children* (DISC; Fisher et al., 1992) was designed to have a high degree of structure in administration. The manual for its administration includes the following instructions:

> The DISC symptom questions are designed to be read *exactly* as written. There is very limited scope for independent questioning. DO NOT deviate from the prescribed question sequence. DO NOT make up your own questions because you think you have a better way of getting at the same information, or because you think the question is poorly worded. (Fisher et al., 1992, p. 31)

The tradeoff between leeway and structure is obvious. Less structure allows the assessor to tailor the interview according to the language and developmental needs of the individual client. However, these interviews generally require a greater degree of experience to administer and often have lower levels of reliability.

Another major source of variation among the structured interviews for children is the time frame used to assess symptoms and diagnoses. Most interviews assess whether symptoms of the disorders are currently evident. This is called a *present episode* frame of reference. Most interviews consider present episodes to be within the previous six months. However, the DISC considers the present episode to be as long as within the last year for the symptoms of conduct disorder. The Child and Adolescent Psychiatric Assessment (CAPA; Angold & Costello, 2000) restricts the assessment of symptoms to the previous three months due to concerns with the reliability of memory in children over longer time intervals. An increasing number of interviews provide for the assessment of both present and *lifetime* diagnoses. For example, the DISC includes a whole-life module, which assesses whether or not a child has exhibited symptoms of diagnoses at any time in their life.

Another source of variation within the interview schedules is the answer format. For many structured interviews, the responses are coded into a categorical format (*yes/no*). This categorical format is consistent with the DSM orientation in which symptoms are considered either present or absent. In contrast, the CAPA and K-SADS have answer formats that can be placed on a Likert-type scale that allows one to rate the severity of a symptom. Although this format makes it more difficult to translate responses into DSM diagnoses, it does not create an artificial dichotomy between the presence or absence of a symptom by allowing symptom scores to reflect gradations in severity.

Strengths and Weaknesses of Diagnostic Interviews

As noted above, structured interviews lead to very reliable assessments of major diagnostic criteria. Further, they assess for some very important parameters of a child or adolescent's emotions and behaviors that are not typically assessed by other assessment sources. Specifically, most interview schedules provide questions that obtain information on the duration of a child's behavioral difficulties and the age at which the problems began to emerge. This temporal information allows one to take a developmental perspective in understanding a case and helps to determine temporal sequencing of a child's emotional or behavioral problems, which could be very important clinical information. For example, it is important to determine whether periods of sadness occurred contiguously with other symptoms of depression (e.g., thoughts of death and dying, changes in sleep or appetite) in order to determine if a person being assessed has shown a major depressive episode (Klein et al., 2005). In addition, most structured interviews assess the level of impairment associated with any emotional and behavioral problems behaviors being reported. Specifically, most interviews have questions that elicit information on the degree to which a child's difficulties are affecting their functioning in major life areas (e.g., at home, at school, and with peers). This could be important for determining if a child's level of anxiety has led to significant impairment in their life or if a child's problems of inattention—disorganization and impulsivity—hyperactivity are causing problems in multiple situations.

Because they are based on diagnostic criteria, the diagnostic interviews enhance the correspondence between the assessment information collected and diagnostic criteria. For example, another way of assessing a child's emotional and behavioral adjustment is through behavior ratings scale; however, the items on most of these ratings scales do not correspond to the actual symptoms used in the DSM (Frick et al., 2020). The correspondence with diagnostic criteria on structured interviews is also helpful for training professionals in psychological assessment. As assessors are developing their competence in interviewing, it is often helpful to have an explicit format for conducting the interview. It gives the assessor a good way to learn the basic characteristics of childhood emotional and behavioral disorders and to learn good ways to ask about these characteristics. After being trained in administration procedures and after conducting several interviews with actual clients, assessors often begin to internalize the diagnostic criteria for the most common disorders of childhood. This knowledge can then be applied in situations in which a structured interview is not possible.

Diagnostic interviews also have several weaknesses which limit their use in many assessments. Of most importance is their time-consuming nature. If a child or adolescent does not show many symptoms and does not endorse many of the stem questions, interviews can be as short as 45 minutes. However, interviews with children and adolescents with many different types of emotional and behavioral symptoms can take as long as 2 to 3 hours. This lengthy format has led to problems for diagnoses assessed later in the interview. Symptoms assessed earlier in the interview are more likely to be endorsed as present because respondents learn that not endorsing symptoms shortens the interview (i.e., fewer follow-up questions; Edelbrock et al., 1999). In addition, structured diagnostic interviews don't allow one to make norm-referenced interpretations of a child's emotional and behavioral difficulties. Clinically significant levels of symptoms are often based on diagnostic criteria (e.g., four symptoms of ODD) rather than based on a comparison with a representative normative sample. Therefore, the appropriateness of clinical elevations for a given age depends on the appropriateness of the diagnostic criteria for that age (Frick & Nigg, 2012). Although diagnostic interviews typically have versions of questions to get information from both the child and a caretaker, the reliability and validity of these interviews with young children (prior to the age of 9) is questionable (Edelbrock et al., 1985). Lastly, diagnostic interviews typically do not provide a format for obtaining information from a child's teacher. As a result, information from teachers must be obtained by some other method.

NetDISC-5

One example of a diagnostic interview schedule for use with children and adolescents is the NetDISC-5, which is an internet administered version of the DISC-5 (Bitsko et al., 2024), an updated version of the DISC-IV (Shaffer et al., 2000). Licenses for the NetDISC-5 are commercially available through TeleSage (*www.telesage.com*). The DISC-5 can also be administered without NetDISC-5 administration format (*prudence.fisher@nyspi.columbia.edu*). The DISC-5 and NetDISC-5 administration formats are compatible with both DSM-5 (American Psychiatric Association, 2013) and the ICD-11 (World Health Organization, 2018). Like the earlier versions of the DISC, DISC-5 was designed to be highly structured. As a result, it can be given by lay interviewers who are trained in administration procedures but who do not have advanced degrees and are not licensed. In addition to the interviewer version in which the interviewer asks the questions to the person being assessed, there is also a self-report version of the NetDISC-5 in which the person being assessed can take the interview themselves on a computer, tablet, or smartphone. For both administration types, there is a parent version available for youth ages 6 to 17 years old and a youth report version for youth ages 10 to 17 years old.

With the NetDISC-5 and DISC-5, not all diagnostic modules need to be administered, and the clinician can choose the desired modules to administer. The NetDISC-5 generally assesses for current diagnoses—typically whether symptoms have been shown to be present within the past year. If symptoms have been present within the past year, follow-up questions determine the age at which symptoms were first shown and whether they are currently being shown (i.e., within the past four weeks). Prior to assessing diagnostic criteria, the timeline of events is established with the respondent. That is, the person being assessed is asked if "anything important happened" a year ago, six months ago, and four weeks ago. These events are then integrated into the interview questions. For example, if the parent says that the child changed school 12 months ago, the questions related to depression would be worded as such: "In the last year, that is since he changed schools, has your child) seemed sad or depressed?"

As is typical of structured interviews, the NetDISC5 and the DISC-5 use a stem question format, in which certain questions are asked initially and follow-up questions are only asked if the stem question is answered affirmatively. For example, in the ADHD module of the parental report, the interviewer may ask, "In the last year, has your child often forgotten what he is supposed to be doing or forgotten to do things that he needed to get done?" If the parent answers "yes," the following questions are asked:

- "Has (he/she/they) been forgetful like this for six months or longer?"
- "At home, has he often forgotten what he is supposed to be doing or what he had planned to do?"
- "How about at school or other places?"

Once all symptoms are assessed, the NetDISC5 and DISC-5 determine if enough symptoms (half required by DSM) were endorsed to indicate a potential disorder. If so, the following questions are asked:

- "You said in the last year he often (NAME SYMPTOMS ENDORSED). Now what about the last four weeks? In the last four weeks, has he often had trouble paying attention or keeping his mind on things like this?"
- "How old was he the first time he stated to have trouble paying attention or keeping his mind on things"
- "How old was he when having trouble paying attention or keeping his mind on things began to cause problem for him?"
- "Did having trouble paying attention or keeping his mind on things cause problems back when he was in first grade or kindergarten?"
- "Now I'd like you to think back to the time in the last year when having trouble paying attention or keeping his mind on things caused the most problems." "At that time, did you (or his OTHER CARETAKERS) seem annoyed or upset with him because he had trouble paying attention or keeping his mind on things?"
- "At that time, did having trouble paying attention or keeping his mind on things keep him from doing things or going places with you or his family"
- "When the problem was worst, did having trouble paying attention or keeping his mind on things keep him from doing things or going place with other [children/people his age]?"
- "At that time, did having trouble paying attention or keeping his mind on things make it difficult for him to do his school work or cause problems with his grades?"
- "When the problem was worst, did having trouble paying attention or keeping his mind on things cause his teacher to be annoyed or upset with him?"
- "At that time, did having trouble paying attention of keeping mind on this make him feel bad or make him feel upset"

After the interviews are complete, the NetDISC5 provides a clinical report that can be downloaded. This report provides a summary of key diagnostic information. For each interview administered, it lists which diagnoses were endorsed with sufficient number of symptoms to be of clinical concern within the past year, whether they were present within the past 4 weeks, and the degree of impairment associated with that diagnosis. Then, for each diagnostic module that was administered, the NetDISC5 report lists the symptoms that were endorsed, even if they were not sufficient to meet diagnostic criteria. These reports are kept in each user's account for future reference. Finally, the NetDISC5 also allows users to download the raw responses provided on the interview, which can be helpful to clinicians who want to review responses to help in interpreting the resulting diagnoses and can be helpful for researchers who want to code individual responses from the interview.

Use of Structured Interviews in Culturally Informed Assessments

Use of structured interviews can play an important role in culturally informed assessments. The structured format can reduce several types of biases in the assessment process. For example, because of the cultural variations in language used to discuss mental health symptoms, sufficient information may not be collected to make diagnoses consistent with DSM-5 from the unstructured interview. The clear and simple questions provided by structured diagnostic interviews can help to obtain information about the types of symptoms being displayed by the child, how long they have been going on, and how impairing they are for the child. Such information can be critical for determining appropriate treatment recommendations. Further, use of structured interviews can help to ensure that certain diagnoses are not missed due to potential attributions by the interviewer, such as the tendency to attribute hyperactive behavior as being indicative of conduct problems in children of color (Fadus et al., 2020). Structured interviews can ensure that the child's hyperactive behavior is assessed accurately and appropriate referrals for treatment are made.

However, the standardization that comes with the diagnostic interview comes at a cost. The set questions provided by structured interviews can be difficult to understand by persons from diverse cultural and educational backgrounds. Further, limited response options (e.g., the requirement to answer "yes" or "no") can be difficult and frustrating to some parents. Perhaps most importantly, the content of these interviews largely focuses on assessing DSM-5 TR criteria and provides little help in placing the problems within a cultural context. Structured interviews typically provide little information on how the problems are viewed by the child and their family, the causes of the child's problems, and how the child's social context can reduce or enhance the impact of a diagnosis on a child's functioning. Finally, the structured format does not allow the interviewer to use the positive interviewing techniques that can help provide an optimistic frame on a child's difficulties and allow the interviewer to focus on a child's strengths and potential. In short, the structured interview provides a reliable way to assess a child's emotional and behavioral functioning in way that corresponds to diagnostic criteria but provides limited help in placing any problems being experienced by the child into a social and cultural context.

Structured Professional Judgment

As a result of weaknesses in both the unstructured (i.e., low reliability, potential for bias) and structured (i.e., inability to tailor interview to needs and characteristics of the person being assessed) interviews, there recently have been attempts to use an approach to interviewing that tries to capitalize on the strengths of each approach. This approach has been labeled "structured professional judgment" (SPJ; Lawing et al., 2017). Like structured diagnostic interviews, SPJs have very clear and explicit definitions for how the interview is to be scored. The symptoms that need to be scored are clearly defined, and how they should be scored is clearly specified. However, like the unstructured interview, the clinician is given great flexibility in how to obtain the information needed to make the scores. Thus, the questions that are asked to obtain information needed to make scores can be tailored to the age, culture, and education of the person being assessed. Further, the clinician can utilize whatever information is available to make the scores, and this information can vary greatly across settings. In some settings, persons being assessed can have extensive medical, psychiatric, educational, and/or legal records available that can be used to determine scores. In other settings, scores may depend on the information gathered by the assessor through semi-structured interviews.

The area in which SPJ has been used most is in risk assessment, where this approach has been used to determine a person's risk for later violence, either to themselves (Gray et al., 2021) or to others (Douglas, 2019). These SPJ approaches have proven to result in reliable scores (Vincent et al., 2011), which is a critical psychometric property given the degree of flexibility that is allowed by the interviewer. Further, SPJ approaches seem to predict later risk better than unstructured clinical interviews (Borum et al., 2010). Thus, the SPJ approach seems to provide flexibility in assessment while still maintaining an adequate level of reliability and validity. However, the SPJ approach also has some weaknesses. Given the flexibility of the assessment format, it requires a high level of training for administration. Further, most SPJ assessments focus on a limited number of constructs to assess, such as assessing risk for violence or suicide (Douglas, 2019; Gray et al., 2021) or psychopathic traits (Hare, 2003). Thus, the level of training and time required to administer SPJs that assess only a limited number of constructs make them unfeasible in many clinical settings. Even more limiting is the fact that there are not SPJ approaches available for assessing many constructs that need to be assessed in psychological evaluations of children and adolescents.

Clinical Assessment of Prosocial Emotions

One example of the SPJ approach to assessment is the Clinical Assessment of Prosocial Emotions (CAPE 1.1; Frick, 2013). In the most recent editions of the both the DSM (i.e., DSM-5; American Psychiatric Association, 2013) and the ICD (ICD 11; World Health Organization, 2018), a specifier was added to the diagnosis of conduct disorder (DSM-5) or the diagnoses of conduct–dissocial disorder and oppositional defiant disorder (ICD-11) to designate a subgroup of persons with the disorder who show elevated levels of callous–unemotional (CU) traits. These traits are defined by a lack of guilt, callous lack of empathy, failure to put forth effort in important activities, and a constricted level of emotional expression. These traits have proven to designate a subgroup of children who have serious conduct problems and who who show more severe and chronic behavior problems, show different emotional and cognitive characteristics (which could suggest distinct causes to their behavior problems), and are more difficult to treat effectively (Frick, 2022). When children with the relevant diagnoses show these CU traits, they can be diagnosed with the specifier "with limited prosocial emotions (LPE)."

The research that led to this change in diagnostic classification was largely based on rating scales (Frick, 2022). However, with the inclusion in classification systems used in clinical settings around the world, more extensive methods of assessment were needed to make diagnoses in many mental health and forensic settings. As a result, the CAPE was developed using the SPJ approach. The CAPE was developed to assess the four symptoms of the LPE specifier for children and adolescents ages 3–21 years old. Like most SPJ approaches, the CAPE must be administered by experienced clinicians who have been trained in both the psychological assessment of children and adolescents and in the specific administration procedures of the CAPE.

Again, like most SPJ approaches, the CAPE provides comprehensive descriptions of characteristics associated with each of the four LPE symptoms and the clinician rates the person being assessed on each symptom using a 0 (Not Descriptive or Mildly Descriptive), 1 (Moderately Descriptive), and 2 (Highly Descriptive) scale. To help the clinician make this rating, semi-structured interviews are provided. These interviews are to be administered to the person being assessed and at least one additional informant who knows the person being assessed well (e.g., parent, teacher, case manager). These interviews provide questions that help the clinician gain information needed to make the ratings for each symptom but allow for substantial leeway for the clinician to follow up with questions designed to determine why the informant answered the question in the way they did. This format allows the clinician to adjust the follow-up questions to the educational and developmental level of the person being assessed and to their sociocultural background. The interviews also provide standard prompts to assess the duration and pervasiveness of each symptom. This is critical information, since the symptoms of the LPE specifier must be considered to be "typical" of the child being assessed and not just characteristics that are temporary or shown in only certain situations or with certain people. The clinician then considers information from these interviews, as well any additional clinical information that is available, to make the ratings on the four LPE symptoms.

It is important to note that here have been only limited tests of the reliability and validity of the CAPE. However, it has proven to lead to reliable scores in young children (Neo et al. 2023), older children (Goetz et al. 2024), and adolescents (Molinuevo et al., 2019). Again, showing adequate inter-rater reliability is critical for an SPJ approach to assessment given the flexibility that is provided to the assessor in obtaining information to make scores. Also, the SPJ has proven to predict important outcomes (e.g., aggression) in children and adolescents with serious conduct problems, even when controlling for behavior ratings of CU traits (Goetz et al., 2024; Hawes et al., 2020; Neo et al., 2023). Further, the CAPE has proven to identify a more severe subgroup of children with a conduct problem diagnosis (Goetz et al., 2024). However, the CAPE also illustrates one of the major limitations in the SPJ approach to interviewing. The CAPE must be administered by highly trained clinicians and takes between 30 minutes to an hour to administer and score. This is quite costly for assessing only one part of only one potential diagnosis for the child (i.e., the LPE specifier of conduct disorder).

As a result of these limitations, the CAPE likely could not be administered to all referrals to a mental health clinic. However, Goetz et al. (2024) suggest that more time efficient behavior rating scales could be administered as a screening method. The CAPE would then only be administered when a possible diagnosis with the LPE specifier is likely based on scores from the rating scales. This would substantially limit the number of youth who require the CAPE and, as a result, the number of clinicians who need to be trained in its administration. However, the validity of such a multiple-gating diagnostic procedure has not been tested.

Use of SPJ in Culturally Informed Assessment

Use of structured professional judgment techniques have great potential for enhancing a culturally informed assessment. This method of interviewing leads to reliable coding of key diagnostic criteria that reduces bias but still allows the interviewer to tailor how the information is obtained based on a person's cultural and educational background and developmental level. The potential importance of this approach can be seen in the use of risk assessment in the juvenile justice system. Specifically, there is clear evidence that unstructured approaches to risk assessment can lead to youth of color being judged as being at greater risk for reoffending or violence and, as a result, being more likely to receive harsher sentences and more restrictive placements (Padgaonkar et al., 2021). Ensuring that more objective criteria are used to assess risk can reduce these biased assessments of risk with important beneficial consequences for many youth of color.

However, to use these techniques appropriately, interviewers must be trained in multicultural assessments and in appropriate interviewing techniques across developmental levels in order to obtain information in a way that is appropriate for the individual being assessed. Further, such techniques also require extensive training in the assessment of mental health problems for children and adolescents in order to appropriately weigh information across different sources of often conflicting information (Frick et al., 2020). Interviews that use structured professional judgment are time consuming. They often assess a single problem area, and, for most assessment of children and adolescents, a child needs an assessment of multiple types of emotional and behavioral problems to ensure an appropriate diagnosis. Finally, there are only a few areas of functioning for which well-validated structured professional judgment methods are available.

RECOMMENDATIONS FOR CULTURALLY INFORMED INTERVIEWING

In this chapter, we provide an overview of the different interviewing formats that can be used in the psychological assessment of children. It is clear from this summary that each format has its strengths and weaknesses in the information obtained for making appropriate diagnoses of the child or adolescent overall and in their ability to aid in a culturally informed assessment specifically. These strengths and weaknesses lead to several recommendations for their use in assessments.

- Assessments should always include an unstructured clinical interview. These interviews are critical for building rapport with clients across a range of cultural backgrounds, and they provide the best way for obtaining information that is unique to each person's sociocultural context, including using language in a way that is culturally appropriate and by allowing consideration of important cultural influences that should influence diagnostic decisions and treatment recommendations. Recommendations for the content for such interviews is provided in Table 10.1.

- *Assessments should always include standardized assessments of a person's emotional and behavioral functioning.* It is equally important that assessments do not rely only on information gathered during the unstructured clinical interview. Even clinicians well-trained in multicultural assessments can be susceptible to biases, and it is important that the critical information that can lead to appropriate diagnosis and beneficial treatment recommendation be assessed in a standardized manner. In this chapter, we reviewed one way of doing this through structured diagnostic interviews. However, such interviewers are quite time consuming to administer. Other chapters in this volume provide alternative methods (e.g., behavior rating scales, behavioral observations) that can be used for this standardized assessment as well, when structured diagnostic interviews are not feasible.

- *Assessments should include structured professional judgment when needed and when validated assessments are available.* Use of structured professional judgments provide a reliable and valid method of assessment that allows for best practice in culturally informed interviewing. They allow clinicians to obtain information that is sensitive to cultural background of the person being assessed but also provides a method for the clinician to translate this information into reliable scores. However, they typically are focused on very specific types of problem areas and are time consuming. Thus, this approach to interviewing is typically most feasible as part of a multiple-gating approach to assessment in which they are only used for persons who are screened and, based on this screening, would benefit from this more intensive and focused assessment of a single problem area. Further, currently there are many problem areas for which no structured professional judgments are available. Given their potential, this situation will hopefully change in the coming years but as of now, these assessments can be used for only a limited number of mental health problems experienced by children and adolescents.

REFERENCES

American Psychiatric Association. (2022). *Diagnostic and statistical manual of mental disorders* (5th ed., text rev.; DSM-5-TR). American Psychiatric Publishing.

American Psychological Association. (2021). *Apology to people of color for APA's role in promoting, perpetuating, and failing to challenge racism, racial discrimination, and human hierarchy in U.S.* Author. *www.apa.org/about/policy/racism-apology*

Angold, A., & Costello, J. (2000). The Child and Adolescent Psychiatric Assessment (CAPA). *Journal of the American Academy of Child and Adolescent Psychiatry, 39*(1), 39–48.

Barlett, C. P., Kowalski, R. M., & Wilson A. M. (2024). Meta-analysis of the predictors and outcomes of cyberbullying perpetration and victimization while controlling for traditional bullying perpetration and victimization. *Aggression and Violent Behavior, 74*, 1–31.

Bitsko, R. H., Smith, A. J., & Jones, M. K. (2024). Development and validation of the NetDISC-5: An internet-administered diagnostic interview for children and adolescents. *Journal of Child and Adolescent Psychology, 52*(3), 245–258.

Boele, S., Graaff, J., Wied, M., Valk, I. E., Crocetti, E. & Branje, S. (2019). Linking parent-child and peer relationship quality to empathy in adolescence: A multilevel meta-analysis. *Journal of Youth and Adolescence, 48*(6), 1033–1055.

Borum, R., Lodewikjs, H., Bartel, P., & Forth, A. (2010). Structured Assessment of Violence Risk in Youth (SAVRY). In K. Douglas, & R. Otto (Eds.), *Handbook of violence risk assessment* (pp. 63–80). Routledge.

Carroll, I. C., Senior, C. J., Davenport, M. A., Foster, C.S., Carmelita, S., Diaz-LePage, A. K., et al. (2024). Racial match: Black youth and pediatric integrated primary care. *Clinical Practice in Pediatric Psychology*, Advance online publication.

Childs, K., Frick, P. J., Ryals, J. S., Lingonblad, A., & Villio, M. J. (2014). A comparison of empirically based and structured professional judgment estimation of risk using the Structured Assessment of Violence Risk in Youth (SAVRY). *Youth Violence and Juvenile Justice, 12*(1), 40–57.

Coker, T. R. Elliott, M. N., Toomey, S. L., Schwebel, D. C., Cuccaro, P., Emery, S.T., et al. (2016). Racial and ethnic disparities in ADHD diagnosis and treatment. *Pediatrics, 138*(3), e20160407.

Douglas, K. S (2019). Evaluating and managing risk for violence using structured professional judgement. In D. L. L. Polaschek, A. Day, & C. Hollin (Eds.), *The Wiley international handbook of correctional psychology* (pp. 429–445). Wiley Blackwell.

Edelbrock, C., Costello, A. J., Dulcan, M. K., Kalas, R., & Conover, N. C. (1985). Age differences in the reliability of the psychiatric interview of the child. *Child Development, 56*(1), 265–275.

Edelbrock, C., Crnic, K., & Bohnert, A. (1999). Interviewing as communication: An alternative way of administering the Diagnostic Interview Schedule for Children. *Journal of Abnormal Child Psychology, 27*(6), 447–453.

Fadus, M. C., Ginsburg, K. R., Sobowale, K., Halliday-Boykins, C. A., Bryan, B. E., Gray, K. M., & Squeglia, L. M. (2020). Unconscious bias and the diagnosis of disruptive behavior disorders and ADHD in African-American and Hispanic youth. *Academic Psychiatry, 44*(1), 95–102.

Fisher, P., Wicks, J., Shaffer, D., Piacentini, J., & Lapkin, J. (1992). *NIMH Diagnostic Interview Schedule for Children: User's manual*. New York State Psychiatric Institute.

Fletcher, J. M. & Miciak, J. (2024). Assessment of specific learning disabilities and intellectual abilities. *Assessment, 31*(1), 53–74.

Frick, P. J. (2013). Clinical assessment of prosocial emotions: Version 1.1 (CAPE 1.1). Author. *https://faculty.lsu.edu/pfricklab/pdfs/cape-manual.pdf*

Frick, P. J. (2022). Some critical considerations in applying the construct of psychopathy to research and classification of childhood disruptive behavior disorders. *Clinical Psychology Review*, 96, 102188.

Frick, P. J., Barry, C. T., & Kamphaus, R. W. (2020). *Clinical assessment of children's personality and behavior* (4th ed.). Springer.

Frick, P. J., & Nigg, J. T. (2012). Current issues in the diagnosis of attention-deficit hyperactivity disorder, oppositional defiant disorder, and conduct disorder. *Annual Review of Clinical Psychology*, 8, 77–107.

Goetz, C. M., Miller, T. A., & Frick, P. J. (2024). The Clinical Assessment of Prosocial Emotions (CAPE): Initial tests of reliability and validity in a clinic-referred sample of children and adolescents. *Psychological Assessment, 36*(8), 452–461.

Gray, N. S., John, A., McKinnon, A. Raybould, S., Knowles, J., & Snowden, R. J. (2021). Structured professional judgement to assist the evaluation and safety planning of suicide risk: The Risk of Suicide Protocol (RoSP). *Frontiers in Psychiatry, 12*, 607120.

Hare, R. D. (2003). *The Hare Psychopathy Checklist—Revised* (2nd ed.). Multi-Health Systems.

Hawes, D. J., Kimonis, E. R., Mendoza Diaz, A., Frick, P. J., & Dadds, M. R. (2020). The Clinical Assessment of Prosocial Emotions (CAPE 1.1): A multi-informant validation study. *Psychological Assessment, 32*(4), 348–357.

Hyman, S.E. (2010). The diagnosis of mental disorders: The problem of reification. *Annual Review of Clinical Psychology*, 6, 155–179.

Jackson-Newsom, J., Buchanan, C. M., & McDonald, R. M. (2008). Parenting and perceived maternal warmth in European American and African American adolescents. *Journal of Marriage and Family, 70*(1), 62–75.

Kang, S., Gair, S. L., Paton, M. J., & Harvey, E. A. (2022). Racial and ethnic differences in the relation between parenting and preschoolers' externalizing behaviors. *Early Education and Development, 34*(4), 823–841.

Kaufman, J., Birmaher, B., Axelson, D., Perepletchikova, F., Brent, D., & Ryan, N. (2016). *Schedule for affective and disorders and schizophrenia for school aged children (6–18 years): Kiddie-SADS-lifetime version*

(K-SADS-PL DSM 5). Western Psychiatric Institute and Clinic.

Klein, D. N., Dougherty, L. R., & Olino, T. M. (2005). Toward guidelines for evidence-based assessment of depression in children and adolescents. *Journal of Clinical Child and Adolescent Psychology, 34*(3), 412–432.

Lawing, K., Childs, K. K., Frick, P. J., & Vincent, G. (2017). Use of structured professional judgement by probation officers to assess risk for recidivism in adolescent offenders. *Psychological Assessment, 29*(6), 652–663.

Lewandowski, L. J., Lovett, B. J., & Gordon, M. (2009). Measurement of symptom severity and impairment. In S. Goldstein, & J.A. Naglieri (Eds), *Assessing impairment: From theory to practice* (pp. 5–14). Springer.

Mandell, D. S., Ittenbach, R. F., Levy, S. E., & Pinto-Martin, J. A. (2007). Disparities in diagnoses received prior to a diagnosis of autism spectrum disorder. *Journal of Autism and Developmental Disabilities, 37*(9), 1795–1802.

McClellan, J., & Werry, J. S. (2000). Introduction to special section: Research psychiatric diagnostic interviews for children and adolescents. *Journal of the American Academy of Child and Adolescent Psychiatry, 39*(1), 19–27.

Molinuevo, B., Martínez-Membrives, E., Pera-Guardiola, V., Requena, A., Torrent, N., Bonillo, A., et al. (2020). Psychometric properties of the Clinical Assessment of Prosocial Emotions: Version 1.1 (CAPE 1.1) in young males who were incarcerated. *Criminal Justice and Behavior, 47*(5), 547–563.

Neo, B., Fleming, G. E., Kauoar, S., Chan, M. E., Huang, N. N., Hawes, D. J., et al. (2023). Clinical utility of diagnosing limited prosocial emotions in young children using the Clinical Assessment of Prosocial Emotions (CAPE). *Psychological Assessment, 35*(12), 1085–1097.

Padgaonkar, N. T., Baker, A., Dapetto, M., Galvan, A., Frick, P. J., Steinberg, L., & Cauffman, E. (2021). Exploring disproportionate minority contact in the juvenile justice system over the year following first arrest. *Journal of Research on Adolescence, 31*(2), 317–334.

Raglin, W. J. B., Jacquez, F., & Vaughn, L. M. (2015). Attributions of mental illness: An ethnically diverse community perspective. *Community Mental Health, 51*, 540–545.

Reynolds, C. R., & Suzuki, L. A. (2013). Bias in psychological assessment: An empirical review and recommendations. In J. R. Graham, J. A. Naglieri, & I. B. Weiner (Eds.), *Handbook of psychology: Vol. 10. Assessment psychology* (2nd ed., pp. 82–113). Wiley.

Robertson, E. L., Ray, J. V., Frick. P. J., Vaughan, E. P., Thornton, L. C., Wall Myers, T. D., et al. (2023). The bidirectional effects of antisocial behavior, anxiety, and trauma exposure: Implications for our understanding of the development of callous-unemotional traits. *Journal of Psychopathology and Clinical Science, 132*(4), 445–460.

Russell, G. L., Fujino, D. C., Sue, S., Cheung, M.-K., & Snowden, L. R. (1996). The effects of therapist-client ethnic match in the assessment of mental health functioning. *Journal of Cross-Cultural Psychology, 27*(5), 598–615.

Shaffer, D., Fisher, P., Lucas, C. P., Dulcan, M. K., & Schwab-Stone, M. E. (2000). NIMH Diagnostic Interview Schedule for Children Version IV (NIMH DISC-IV): Description, differences from previous versions, and reliability of some common diagnoses. *Journal of the American Academy of Child & Adolescent Psychiatry, 39*(1), 28–38.

Sur, D., Ashcroft, R., Adamson, K., Nailisa, T., Webb, J., Mohamud, F., & Shamsi, H. (2023). Examining diagnosis as a component of social workers' scope of practice: A scoping review. *Clinical Social Work Journal, 51*, 12–23.

TeleSage. (n.d.). *Home*. Author. *www.telesage.com*

Ureche, D. J., Smith, D. C., Davis, J. P. & Tabb, K. M. (2016). Racial matching and adolescent self-disclosure of substance use and mental health symptoms. *Journal of Ethnicity in Substance Abuse, 15*(2), 176–188.

U.S. Census Bureau. (2015). *American Community Survey 1-Year PUMS file*. Author. *www.census.gov/programs-surveys/acs/data/pums.html*

van de Vijver, F. J. R., & Poortinga, Y. H. (1997). Towards an integrated analysis of bias in cross-cultural assessment. *European Journal of Psychological Assessment, 13*(1), 29–37.

van de Vijver, F., & Tanzer, N. K. (2004). Bias and equivalence in cross-cultural assessment: An overview. *European Review of Applied Psychology / Revue Européenne de Psychologie Appliquée, 54*(2), 119–135.

Van Eldik, W., de Haan, A. D., Parry, L. Q., Davies, P. T. Luijk, M. P. C. M., Arends, L., et al. (2020). The interparental relationship: Meta-analytic associations with children's maladjustment and responses to interparental conflict. *Psychological Bulletin, 146*(7), 553–594.

Vincent, G. M., Chapman, J., & Cook, N. E. (2011). Risk-needs assessment in juvenile justice: Predictive validity of the SAVRY, racial differences, and the contribution of needs factors. *Criminal Justice & Behavior, 38*(1), 42–62.

Walker, T. M., Frick, P. J., Matlasz, T. M., Robertson, E. L., Mikolajewski, A. J., Mitchell, C., et al. (2021). Psychometric properties of a semi-structured interview to assess limited prosocial emotions. *Assessment, 28*(7), 1755–1764.

World Health Organization. (2018). *The ICD-11 classification of mental and behavioural disorders: diagnostic criteria for research*. Author.

CHAPTER 11

Comprehensive Rating Scales

Annmary S. Abdou, Amy Jane Griffiths, Jared T. Izumi, and Rachel Torres

CASE EXAMPLE

Three months into her tenth-grade year at Southlake High School, Nathaly's individualized education plan (IEP) team convened to discuss some pressing concerns regarding her social–emotional and behavioral functioning and recent academic difficulties. Nathaly is an autistic, tenth-grade female student who was adopted at six months old by her maternal aunt. She and her family have not had contact with her biological mother since her adoption, leaving her family with limited information regarding early developmental milestones and prenatal care. Nathaly and her aunt are of Latin American descent and predominatly speak Spanish at home; however, Nathaly's dominant language is English.

Although the transition to high school was difficult, Nathaly performed successfully in her classes during her first year and responded well to the differentiated supports and services outlined in her IEP. However, over the past three months, Nathaly has exhibited significant difficulties related to anxiety and engaging with peers. Nathaly regularly perseverates on her grades and academic performance. She exhibits anxiety-related symptoms, sometimes requiring her to leave the classroom to regulate herself. Simultaneously, Nathaly has also been engaging in and, at times, initiating peer conflict.

Nathaly's aunt shared that in addition to autism, Nathaly has a diagnosis of attention-deficit/hyperactivity disorder (ADHD) and generalized anxiety disorder. Her aunt is requesting a re-evaluation as she is concerned about Nathaly's anxiety and social difficulties and is wondering how the IEP team can better support her at school.

Whether practicing in clinical or school-based settings, psychologists must gather information from various sources in multifaceted ways to conduct culturally responsive and comprehensive assessments. This process includes collecting data on the perceptions of student's social, emotional, and behavioral (SEB) functioning. Even though there are many ways psychologists gather data, comprehensive rating scales serve as one method to collect information systematically and efficiently on students' strengths and needs across diverse settings from multiple individuals. Rating scales are essential to most educational and clinical psychologists' assessment practices. They are particularly appealing because of the wide range of data they gather with seemingly minimal effort compared to other assessment activities. School psychologists, in particular, rated the Behavior Assessment System for Children—Third Edition Teacher and Parent Rating Scales (Reynolds & Kamphaus, 2015) within the top five most frequently used tools out of 150 instruments (Benson et al., 2019).

Chapter authors contributed equally and are in listed in alphabetical order.

Comprehensive rating scales are a category of assessment tools that allow the student or client and informants (e.g., parent or caregiver, teacher, or service provider) to report their experience and perception of the SEB dimensions of the referred individual's functioning (Wodrich, n.d.). Typically, respondents read and rate each objective item on a Likert-type scale (e.g., *Never*, *Sometimes*, *Often*, and *Almost Always*) based on their experience with and observation of the client or student. Each answer choice is assigned a raw score value. The assessor then combines each item's raw score values from the same scale and/or composite to generate a score for a particular area of interest (e.g., internalizing problems and adaptive functioning). Technical manuals and scoring software allow practitioners to assemble and convert this raw data into a standard score. Through data interpretation, assessors can identify how the student or client compares with relevant normative groups (e.g., gender, age, and diagnosable condition). Based on these results in the context of other data collected, practitioners can identify specific strengths and targetable areas of need for their students or clients.

In this chapter, we will discuss the following:

- The role of comprehensive rating scales within a culturally responsive and ecological framework for assessment
- Types of comprehensive rating scales and their use from a dual-factor perspective
- Culturally responsive considerations for selecting, administering, and interpreting comprehensive assessments
- The future of comprehensive assessment

AN ECOLOGICAL LENS FOR CULTURALLY RESPONSIVE ASSESSMENT

Culturally responsive use of comprehensive rating scales for SEB assessment requires evaluators to develop an ecologically informed lens. Bronfenbrenner's ecological systems model (1977) provides a comprehensive framework for understanding the complex interactions between individuals and their environments and has been used to advance equity perspectives in educational practice (Edwards, 2021). Adopting an ecological lens to guide assessment practices allows for a more holistic examination and interpretation of the multifaceted environmental and cultural influences that may impact SEB functioning. In addition to illuminating the cultural, linguistic, and socioeconomic factors that influence student development, strengths, and difficulties, an ecological lens and approach can help to shift evaluators from a deficit perspective of student functioning to one that considers structural variables that may impact SEB health on a broader scale. When examining these variables within the individual and across systems, one must consider a complete view of mental health, as described in the dual-factor model of mental health.

DUAL-FACTOR MODEL OF MENTAL HEALTH

SEB is increasingly understood as a complete state of being, which is not merely related to the presence (or absence) of symptoms of distress or a disorder but also to the presence (or absence) of psychological well-being variables, such as life satisfaction, optimism, and hope. In a dual-factor model of mental health, assessments of positive indicators of wellness (i.e., subjective well-being [SWB]) are included with indicators of distress (e.g., depression or anxiety symptoms) to measure mental health comprehensively (Greenspoon & Saklofske, 2001). When holistically evaluating a student's SEB needs, practitioners must consider "both sides of the coin" by evaluating individual and systemic distress markers and indicators of well-being and thriving. Figure 11.1 depicts how the student in the case study is conceptualized within an ecological systems model, focusing on strengths and struggles.

Several widely recognized and tangible frameworks facilitate an ecological approach for assessment and can be adapted to include measures of distress and well-being. A beneficial tool that encourages data collection from a wide range of sources and supports consideration of all likely explanations for SEB concerns is the RIOT (review, interview, observe, test)/ICEL (instruction, curriculum, environment, learner) matrix. This approach allows practitioners to efficiently decide what relevant data to collect and how to organize that information to identify why a student may be struggling. The RIOT/ICEL material is not an assessment instrument but a framework that practitioners use to manage and understand data from a more holistic perspective (Hosp, 2006, May).

The acronym RIOT helps us guide an assessment process. It can put the assessment process

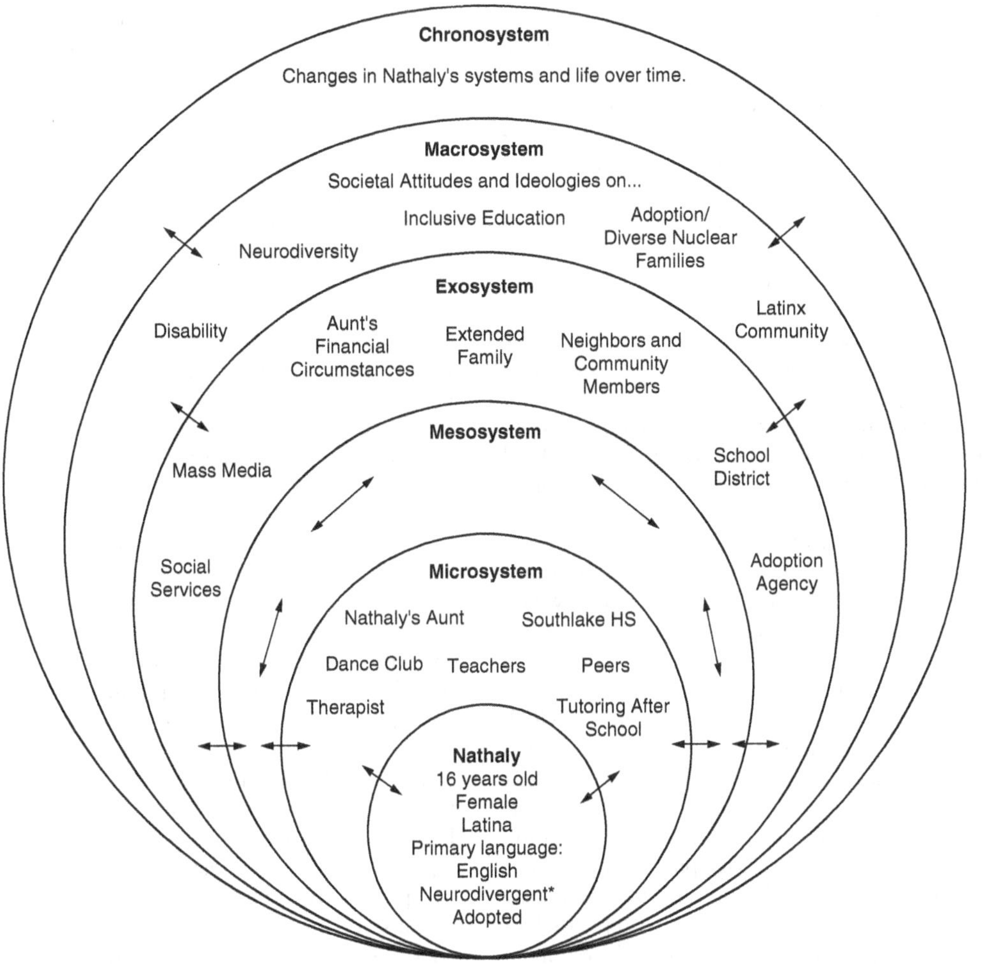

FIGURE 11.1. Nathaly's Ecological Systems Map. *Note.* For Nathaly, when we indicate "Neurodivergence" we are referencing her diagnoses of Autism, Attention-Deficit/ Hyperactivity Disorder (ADHD), and Generalized Anxiety Disorder (GAD)

Adapted from Bronfenbrenner (1977)

into an interconnected sequence of activities and direct the sources and approaches for gathering data in the assessment process (Leung, 1993). This model is perhaps most easily understood concerning an individual assessment, but we can also apply RIOT when thinking about larger contexts such as classwide or schoolwide assessments. When collecting data using this framework, practitioners engage in the following tasks: review, interview, observation, and test. For each component, practitioners would collect data from various sources and settings to control for potential bias from any source. Based on the referral question, practitioners collect data through a review of records, interviews with multiple team members (including the child and caregivers), and observations across settings and compared to peers. The practitioner uses these data to decide what assessment instruments should be used to improve the understanding of the concerns and illuminate student strengths.

At the "test" stage, practitioners may consider the referral question and all data collected from relevant parties and add comprehensive rating scales to the process. These rating scales should be directly related to the referral question, consider the concerns identified during initial data collection, be normed for the target audience, and consider the responses in the context of the relationship between the raters and the child.

Understanding these relationships can assist the practitioners in data interpretation (e.g., if we ask teachers to complete rating scales, we must also ask questions to understand their relationship and perspectives toward the student). Behavioral observations are also vital data to collect during any direct testing session. A savvy assessor will track how students interact and engage with the assessor and the testing materials. This data can be vitally important when developing a culturally responsive intervention plan. (See Chapter 9, this volume, on directly observing and recording behaviors, for foundational considerations on assessment strategies.)

In addition to individual student information, gathering information related to the child's school functioning is imperative, as this impacts all areas of SEB functioning. Assessors should focus on the child and consider the learning environment (e.g., curriculum demands, instructional strategies, and task difficulty) and its impact. When assessing academic impacts on SEB functioning, practitioners consider four critical learning domains: instruction, curriculum, environment, and learner. Using the combination of RIOT and ICEL, practitioners can get a well-rounded perspective and possible explanations for student strengths and struggles. The assessment process is iterative and responsive, resulting in an ongoing and flexible approach. This approach implies that information obtained during the assessment may require the assessor to revisit prior steps, including gathering additional information, before making diagnostic or intervention decisions. This assessment process often occurs within the context of a larger system of approaches to identify youth needing additional support. "Multiple gating" is one term that describes a systematic approach to identification.

MULTIPLE GATING

Rating scales serve several potential purposes across different levels within a community or school context. Practitioners often use rating scales, in some form, as the primary method to facilitate multiple gating procedures, a cost-effective and systematic way to screen and identify students with or who may be at risk of learning, behavioral, and/or social–emotional challenges. Multiple gating is a general procedure in which a school or community sets up sequential gates or levels of assessment and then uses assessment data to link groups and individuals to relevant supports, interventions, and more comprehensive assessments (Walker et al., 2014).

Typically, universal screening serves as the foundation for multiple gating processes and for implementing a multi-tiered system of support. This process begins by collecting data from an entire community with a uniform measure to identify individuals needing intervention and further assessment (Romer et al., 2020). Through a series of more intensive and specific data collection at each gate, practitioners are then able to narrow down a larger population to a small number of students, for example, in need of classroom or small group interventions (i.e., Tier 2) or a multidisciplinary assessment for special education services (i.e., Tier 3). Practitioners and invested persons regularly use various broadband and narrowband rating scales at each gate to assist in considering all students' potential risks and challenges. When considering scenarios in which various challenges disproportionately impact specific populations, employing universal screeners and methods of multiple gating should take a structural versus deficit perspective. In other words, population-based issues should be framed to uncover structural deficits rather than population-specific deficits (e.g., Palma et al., 2023). Upon identifying systemic issues and specific groups needing additional support through universal screening, teams then employ more targeted forms of measurement, often through diagnostic tools or narrowband measures, to develop and tailor interventions based on the unique needs of individual clients or students. (See Chapter 12, this volume, on screening measures and methods, for more information.)

Diagnostic tools are specific assessment tools that, in conjunction with other data sources, assist a clinician in establishing a diagnosis or presence of a condition or disorder based on commonly used classification systems, such as the *Diagnostic and Statistical Manual of Mental Disorders, Fifth Edition, Text Revision* (DSM-5-TR) (American Psychiatric Association, 2022). For school-based professionals, diagnostic tools can also assist in determining eligibility for special education services by allowing the assessor to gather specific data on a suspected condition or potential diagnosis. Screeners are frequently based on one respondent (e.g., student or teacher), whereas diagnostic tools include opportunities for multiple respondents across settings. The selection of a specific diagnostic tool may be based on a screener, but it yields information that extends beyond identifying the presence of an issue. Diagnostic tools often provide information on the severity level, presence, and degree of specific symptomology. In both clinical and school settings, the specificity of diagnostic tools may provide insights into potential interventions and evidence-based practices designed to address a student's needs based on a specific condition, diagnosis, or special education eligibility.

Considering individual assessment practices, practitioners often employ measures capable of detecting a wide range of challenges and adaptive skills in the early phases of the process. They then use this information, in conjunction with other data sources, to further individualize the assessment process to the strengths and challenges of that student or client. Broadband measures help us understand the presence and degree of symptoms across a wide range of areas, allowing us to make data-based decisions on the direction of the assessment and potential areas of need.

BROADBAND AND GENERAL MEASURES

Broadband, also called *general measures*, are designed to measure perceptions of various emotional, behavioral, and social difficulties, as well as assets. For many clinical and school psychologists, broadband measures are a fundamental aspect of SEB assessment, as they can provide data directly related to a referral question or suspected eligibility. The results of a broadband measure also inform subsequent choices regarding further data collection in the assessment process. Often, issues will come to light through the results of broadband measures, prompting practitioners to conduct further observations and interviews or administer additional rating scales to better understand the needs and strengths of a client or student.

Broadband measures yield wide-ranging information on the SEB functioning of an individual and, as mentioned earlier, produce results related to specific areas of interest (e.g., externalizing problems or internalizing problems). Many broadband measures also include scales and subscales that measure adaptive behaviors and characteristics (Whitcomb, 2019). Most broadband measures include forms for teachers, parents/caregivers, and self-report measures, depending on the age of the client. As emphasized in this chapter, a broadband measure serves as one data source within the context of a comprehensive assessment, so selecting an appropriate measure is highly dependent upon one's referral questions. There are several examples of well-constructed, widely researched broadband measures, which we have included in the subsequent sections and summarized in Table 11.1 to provide a sense of what is available to professionals based on suggestions by Whitcomb (2019) and Wodrich (n.d.).

Behavior Assessment System for Children—Third Edition

The Behavior Assessment System for Children—Third Edition (BASC-3) (Reynolds & Kamphaus, 2015) is one of the most widely used broadband measures among practitioners (Benson et al., 2019). This multidimensional assessment system includes Teacher Rating Scales (TRS), Parent Rating Scales (PRS), and the Self-Report of Personality (SRP). Evaluators use the BASC-3 to assess the strengths and needs of individuals ranging from ages 2 to 25, with the TRS and PRS available for preschoolers (ages 2–5), children (ages 6–11), and adolescents (ages 12–21). The SRP is available for children (ages 8–11), adolescents (ages 12–18), and college-age individuals (ages 18–25). The primary function of the BASC-3 is to assess SEB problems in children and adolescents within a school or clinical setting. This measure also includes an adaptive composite, allowing users to gather information about strengths such as activities in daily living, leadership, functional communication, and social skills. The BASC-3 is currently available in English and Spanish.

At the same time, there is some emerging research regarding multicultural assessment and the psychometric properties of adapted or translated versions of the BASC-3 for linguistically diverse populations (Ahn et al., 2014; Garcia-Barrera et al., 2015; Tan et al., 2021). Ahn and colleagues evaluated the psychometric properties of the BASC-SRP Child Form translated in Korean (n = 1,100) and found adequate psychometric properties across composites (alpha = 0.84–0.94). Three subscales yielded low reliability: Self-Esteem (alpha = 0.31), Locus of Control (alpha = 0.60), and Self-Reliance (alpha = 0.68).

Regarding cross-cultural use, results of another recent study validated the use of the Spanish BASC

TABLE 11.1. Broadband Rating Scales

Measure	Available forms	Standardized based on national sample	Available languages	Additional features	Limitations
Achenbach System of Empirically Based Assessment (ASEBA) (Achenbach & Rescorla, 2001)	Preschool Children Behavior Checklist for Ages 1.5–5 (CBCL), Caregiver–Teacher Report Form (C-TRF); CBCL for Ages 6–18, Teacher's Report Form (TRF), Youth Self-Report (YSR) for Ages 11–18	Yes	Available in over 110 languages	Gender-inclusive designations and scale scores are available; *Multi-Cultural Supplement to the Manual* is available for all forms—includes research from over 30–50 societies, depending on the tool; multicultural norm options; multicultural case illustrations across settings and research applications; includes Language Development Survey (LDS) that can be used as a screener for language delays	Norms have not been updated since 2001
Behavior Assessment System for Children—Third Edition (BASC-3; Reynolds & Kamphaus, 2015)	Teacher Rating Scale (TRS) and Parent Rating Scale (PRS) are available for ages 2–21; Self-Report of Personality (SRP) is available for ages 8–25	Yes	English, Spanish	TRS and PRS are available for preschool and children/adolescents; available norm groups include general combined, general gender-specific, clinical combined, clinical gender-specific, ADHD combined, ADHD gender-specific. Produces results relevant to clinical diagnoses and establishing special education eligibility	Has not yet been adapted for use in other languages or in other countries
Conners Comprehensive Behavior Rating Scale (Conners CBRS) (Conners, 2008)	Conners CBRS–Parent and Conners CBRS–Teacher for Ages 6–18; Conners CBRS–Self-Report for Ages 8–18	Yes	English, Spanish	Identifies challenges across 9 content areas and 11 diagnostic areas (e.g., ADHD and autism spectrum disorder, disruptive behavior, mood, and anxiety disorders). Produces results relevant to clinical diagnoses and establishing special education eligibility	Has not yet been adapted for use in other languages or in other countries

Devereux Student Strengths Assessment (DESSA) (LeBuffe et al., 2009)	Parents/guardians, teachers, school staff, or staff serving in after-school, social service, and mental health programs. (grades K–8)	Yes	English, Spanish	Strengths-based assessment measures students' abilities across three constructs, which include eight social and emotional competencies. Researchers have validated use of DESSA with low-income kindergarten students (Doromal et al., 2017), low-income, school-age Black students (Anderson, 2018), and American Indian and Alaskan Native students (Chain et al., 2017)	Only applicable for students in K–8; limited to adult respondents; has not yet been adapted for use in other languages or in other countries
Social Emotional Health Survey (SEHS) (Furlong et al., 2014)	Student Response Form for primary (SEHS-P), secondary (SEHS-S), and higher education (SEHS-HE) students	No	English, Spanish	Strengths-based assessment provides an overall CoVitality score and 12 subscores that comprise four domains (i.e., belief-in-self, belief-in-others, emotional competence, and engaged living); emerging research on use in Japan (Ito et al., 2015), Korea (Lee et al., 2016), Turkey (Telef & Furlong, 2017), and China (Xie et al., 2018). SEHS-S (Furlong et al., 2021; Furlong et al., 2022) normed with large samples from California. There is also available recent research validating the use of Spanish and English forms with Latinx students (Hinton et al., 2021).	Limited to student respondents; normative studies primarily focus on the school setting

executive functioning screener with Colombian children with (n = 155) and without ADHD (n = 848). While not designed as a diagnostic tool, the study found strong psychometric properties regarding the identification of executive functioning challenges in the clinical setting based on teacher reports (Garcia-Barrera et al., 2015). Additionally, based on a sample of 716 Australian children, Tan and colleagues (2021) found acceptable cross-cultural validity of the BASC-PRS-C and TRS-C. Though these results are promising, more research is needed regarding translated versions and cross-cultural use of the BASC-3.

Achenbach System of Empirically Based Assessment

The Achenbach System of Empirically Based Assessment (ASEBA) is an assessment system designed to measure SEB and thought difficulties, adaptive functioning, and personal strengths for individuals across the lifespan (ages 1.5–90 years). Available forms include the Preschool Children Behavior Checklist for ages 1.5–5 years (CBCL), Caregiver–Teacher Report Form (C-TRF), CBCL for ages 6–18 years, Teacher's Report Form (TRF), and the Youth Self-Report (YSR) for ages 11–18 years. The ASEBA is supported by international research and is available in over 110 languages (Achenbach, 2019). A Multicultural Supplement is available for each form that includes a variety of resources for working with diverse populations, detailed in Table 11.1; however, more research is needed regarding the validity and utility of using supplemental materials with culturally and linguistically diverse populations.

Conners Comprehensive Behavior Rating Scale

The Conners Comprehensive Behavior Rating Scale (Conners CBRS) (Conners, 2008) is an assessment and diagnostic tool intended to provide information on a broad range of clinical and SEB conditions. Available forms include the Conners CBRS–Parent form and Conners CBRS–Teacher form for individuals ages 6–18 and the Conners CBRS–Self-Report for ages 8–18, intended for use across clinical and school settings. The Conners CBRS produces scores according to DSM-5 (American Psychiatric Association, 2013) or DSM-5-TR (American Psychiatric Association, 2022) symptom scales, which include several different diagnoses: Validity Scales, Rational Scales, and Empirical Scales. The most recent version is based on a large, diverse sample and is particularly useful for school-based evaluations as the results align with the Individuals with Disabilities Education Act (IDEA, 2004) criteria and feature subscales regarding bullying (Whitcomb, 2019). Currently, the Conners CBRS is available in English and Spanish, with minimal recent research evaluating its use across culturally and linguistically diverse populations (Mattar et al., 2020). More research is needed in this area.

As stated earlier, one way to disrupt deficit-centric assessment practices and maintain a culturally responsive and ecological lens is by considering an individual's strengths, assets, and protective systems (Perez-Brena et al., 2018). Below are two broadband measures that provide information regarding an individual's strengths, resilience, and adaptive functioning, allowing for a more comprehensive integrative assessment.

Devereux Student Strengths Assessment

The Devereux Student Strengths Assessment (DESSA) (LeBuffe et al., 2009) is a strengths-based broadband measure for kindergarten through eighth-grade students. This form measures eight social-emotional competencies (i.e., self-awareness, social awareness, self-management, goal-directed behavior, relationship skills, personal responsibility, decision making, and optimistic thinking). It is designed for parents/caregivers, school-based professionals (e.g., teachers and afterschool staff members), and those working in other childcare settings (e.g., mental health professionals and social services practitioners) to complete. Researchers used a national sample reflective of the U.S. census to produce national norms (Lebuffe et al., 2014). The DESSA has demonstrated convergent results with the BASC-2 (Reynolds & Kamphaus, 2004).

Current research indicates promising results regarding the validity of using the DESSA with low-income kindergarten students (Doromal et al., 2017), low-income, school-age Black students (Anderson, 2018), and American Indian and Alaskan Native students in third through eighth grades (Chain et al., 2017). Although some studies have explored the use of translated versions of the DESSA (Sepanta et al., 2017), research in this area is limited.

Social and Emotional Health Survey

The Social and Emotional Health Survey (SEHS) (Furlong et al., 2014) is a module within the California Healthy Kids Survey that measures the strengths associated with success in school, higher education, and career. There are three versions of this self-report measure available for students in primary (SEHS–Primary), secondary school (SEHS–Secondary), and higher education (SEHS–Higher Education). The SEHS-P contains 16 items that assess persistence, zest, optimism, and gratitude. The SEHS-S yields an overall score and 12 subscale scores in self-awareness, self-efficacy, persistence, family coherence, peer support, school support, gratitude, zest, optimism, behavioral control, self-control, and empathy. For students in higher education, the SEHS-HE comprises 36 items and measures the same constructs as the SEHS-S (i.e., belief-in-self, belief-in-other, emotional competence, or engaged living), with slightly modified subscales to align with the post-secondary population. Instead of school support, the SEHS-HE measures institutional support, and the emotional competence construct is comprised of subscales measuring cognitive reappraisal, empathy, and self-regulation (Dowdy et al., n.d.). Recent studies with large sample sizes have assessed the use of translated versions of the SEHS in Japan (Ito et al., 2015), Korea (Lee et al., 2016), Turkey (Telef & Furlong, 2017), and China (Xie et al., 2018), as well as with linguistically and culturally diverse samples in the United States (Furlong et al., 2014; You et al., 2015).

Practice Considerations

Reviewing the results of a broadband measure from multiple informants often provides further insights into the specific needs and challenges a student or client may face and adaptive skills and assets that were not apparent through other forms of data collection. In these instances, it may be beneficial to administer an additional narrowband measure to gather more in-depth information on a specific problem or adaptive behavior. The focus of available narrowband scales includes depression, anxiety, antisocial behavior, school-based behaviors, social skills, and attention, among others. Although an in-depth description of narrowband measures is outside the scope of this chapter, as with any other assessment procedure, practitioners should use these tools in a purposeful manner that assists them in answering the referral question(s) relevant to a student or client.

Although professionals across settings widely use several of these broadband measures, it is recommended that practitioners thoroughly familiarize themselves with the testing manual to understand test construction, administration, interpretation, reliability, validity, relevance, and efficacy for specific populations (Wodrich, n.d.). With broadband data, practitioners can identify student needs and strengths more effectively, establish diagnoses or eligibility for special education services, set relevant goals, and recommend appropriate services.

CULTURALLY RESPONSIVE CONSIDERATIONS FOR SELECTING MEASURES

As the assessor selects measures based on the referral question and available data, they must investigate norming samples of the standardized measures and tools to ensure an appropriate representation of subgroups of interest. Specifically, practitioners should evaluate the norming samples to determine if the tool is appropriate for the individual being assessed and will provide data related to answering the referral question. Similarly, the assessor must consider the student's primary language, basic interpersonal communication skills, and cognitive academic language proficiency and select assessment tools accordingly. Practitioners must also consider caregiver communication and language when selecting comprehensive assessment tools for caregiver completion. When collecting assessment information and integrating it into the report, practitioners can look to understand the student's culture and acculturation, experience in school systems, and social, emotional, behavioral, and academic history (Diamond et al., 2023). Practitioners should only use an assessment tool once they understand the features of the assessment and have evaluated their use for the population being assessed. They can begin to select appropriate rating scales by evaluating the data available to them.

Approaches to Identifying Appropriate Comprehensive Rating Scales

Information about rating scales can be found in the publisher's manual, in reference books such as the *Mental Measurements Yearbook* (Carlson et al., 2021), and through test critiques published by peer-reviewed journals. Individuals are encouraged to search for sources outside of the publisher's manual. However, manuals are the first place to look for information and will likely contain answers to most, if not all, questions related to adopting a rating scale for practice. The information and stringency of the information needed depends on the proposed use of the rating scale. For example, rating scales may be used to screen students, identify progress on an intervention, allocate resources, evaluate programs, or diagnose students. The individual interpreting the obtained scores from a rating scale is ultimately responsible for the appropriate and accurate interpretation. The first step in reviewing a rating scale for adoption is to examine the publisher's manual and to evaluate test purpose, norms, reliability, and validity. The practitioner will then use these data to decide which comprehensive rating scale is most appropriate.

Test Purpose

The test publishers should clearly state the intended purpose of the rating scale. For example, the BASC-3 (Reynolds & Kamphaus, 2015) is intended to aid clinical diagnosis, educational classification, individualized education plan (IEP) development, manifestation determinations, and intervention planning. If one or more of the intended purposes outlined by the test publishers match the purpose of the current assessment, the assessor would move to the next step of identifying evidence to support the purpose. For example, after reviewing Nathaly's (in the case that opened this chapter) records and discussing how the school year has gone with her, her teachers, and her aunt, the school psychologist decided to administer the BASC-3 and the SEHS to gather more information on specific social–emotional needs, as well as potential strengths that the team could integrate into intervention development.

Norms

Scores are interpreted relative to the performance of other individuals, also called the reference population, from which a normative sample is developed. Test users should consider the impact on the intended user who may be insufficiently included in the normative sample. Test developers should describe the normative sample, and if the intended examinee(s) background or demographics are not included in the normative sample, then inappropriate or inaccurate score interpretation may occur. However, even if the intended examinee's background is included in the norm sample, the number of individuals from the intended examinee's background should be examined. The number of individuals from the intended examinee's background should be of sufficient size for accurate interpretations of scores. Lastly, the usefulness of norms should be relative to the recency with which they were collected. Test publishers are generally responsible for updating norms; however, test users are ultimately responsible for the interpretations resulting from outdated tests.

When we consider Nathaly's identity and needs along with normative information on the BASC-3, the testing manual and available research indicate that the teacher, parent, and self-report measures were standardized using a large national sample (TRS n = 1,700; PRS n = 1,800; SRP n = 900), reflective of U.S. census data from 2013 and includes general gender-specific norms and gender-specific norms for clinical groups (Reynolds & Kamphaus, 2015). Recent research with large national samples on the SEHS shows acceptable validity for female students of Latin American descent (You et al., 2014; You et al., 2015) and students with disabilities (Furlong et al., 2014; Kim et al., 2014). These data indicate validity for use with the case study of Nathaly.

Reliability

Reliability generally refers to the consistency of a score, and a reliability metric should be available for each score that is intended to be interpreted (American Educational Research Association et al., 2014). Adequate reliability is required for all tests; however, the standard for adequate differs depending on the consequences of the decision. Decisions that occur less frequently and are irreversible require a higher standard of reliability than decisions that occur more frequently and are easily reversible. For example, test scores that are used for important decisions such as clinical diagnosis or special education eligibility should have minimum reliability metrics of .90 (Salvia et al., 2017). In contrast, decisions made from screening measures should have a minimum reliability of .80. Types of reliability that should be considered include internal consistency (i.e., alpha or omega), interobserver agreement, test–retest, and alternate form.

The reliability of a measure may be evaluated before validity because unreliable measures are inherently invalid. That is, an accurate interpretation of scores cannot be made with an unreliable test. Another way to evaluate the reliability of a test is by examining the average error in obtained scores (i.e., the standard error of measurement. [SEM]). Larger SEMs will lead to larger confidence intervals, indicating less precision. One thing to note is that the SEM is assumed to be the same across the distribution of scores. For example, the score for an individual at the middle of the distribution has the same SEM as someone at the very top end of the distribution. Instead, test users may consider the conditional SEM (cSEM), which describes the SEM for a particular score. This can be especially important when decisions are made at the extremes of the distribution because the cSEM is larger at the extremes.

For Nathaly's assessment, initially, it was not clear which behaviors and social–emotional challenges were impacting her across classes. To gather a more holistic picture of her needs and establish reliability between raters, the assessor provided the BASC-3 to her algebra teacher and English teacher. While scores varied slightly, the results indicated that Nathaly displayed difficulties with anxiety and social skills across both classes. The anxiety and social skills subscales on the BASC-3 have high internal consistency for females ages 15–18 (i.e., above .90), indicating that the subscales measure a single construct. However, interrater reliability scores between teachers on the anxiety and social skills subscales are relatively low (i.e., correlation r is below .70). The team should follow up with each teacher to provide context to their rating to ensure concerns in those areas. This information helped the team establish interventions to address her needs across academic settings.

Validity

Validity is the degree to which a test measures what it was intended to measure. This is a more complex matter to evaluate; however, the argument-based approach to validity (Kane, 2013) provides a simple two-step process to assist individuals in determining whether a rating scale should be adopted for practice. The two steps are (1) the proposed claims for the interpretation and use of the rating scale (the interpretation and use argument) and (2) the claim's plausibility, either inherently plausible or supported by data (the validity argument). The two steps evaluate whether the conclusions drawn from an observed score can be stated confidently. In the first part, the test user identifies the proposed interpretation of the test (e.g., diagnosis, treatment identification, and current or future performance). In the second step, the test user identifies the evidence supporting the claim in step one. The type of analysis and information needed will differ depending on the claim. For example, rating scales that are used for diagnostic purposes require some combination of criterion validity, predictive validity, concurrent validity, and classification accuracy. A claim that a tool can be used for a special population would require information about measurement invariance, similar reliability, and similar validity between groups. For example, when reviewing recent research and the testing manual of the BASC-3 (Reynolds & Kamphaus, 2015), this measure is designed to detect symptoms related to autism, ADHD, and anxiety and has been shown to be effective in distinguishing symptoms related to autism and ADHD (Zhou et al., 2020). In the case of Nathaly, she has several diagnoses and presents with various symptoms in the school setting. Understanding to what degree difficulties associated with each diagnosis impact her will allow for more strategic choices regarding further assessment, goals, and services.

Making a Decision

Test developers are responsible for providing information for test users to adopt a test; however, once a test has been adopted, test users are responsible for the interpretations made from test scores. Tests should meet the norming, reliability, and validity requirements for appropriate and accurate decisions to be made. The inferences can only be trusted if all of these are present. For more information, individuals may also benefit from referencing the Standards for Educational and Psychological Testing during the review process as a more comprehensive framework for evaluating tests (American Education Research Association et al., 2014). Once a decision is made about comprehensive rating scales, the practitioner should continue incorporating culturally relevant practices in the administration and interpretation processes.

CULTURAL CONSIDERATIONS IN COMPREHENSIVE RATING SCALE ADMINISTRATION AND INTERPRETATION

Cognitive Processes in Rating Scale Completion

As assessors consider and use comprehensive rating scales, individuals must recognize that biases exist within the tests themselves, and practitioners should interpret results accordingly. For example, before using a rating scale that was not developed for a special population, it is essential to consider if the cognitive process that the rater goes through is the same as the intention of the rating scale developer. Individuals undergo four main cognitive processes (described below) when completing rating scales (Tourangeau & Rasinski, 1998). These steps may result in confusion on the rater's end, which may lead to additional sources of error. This confusion can be particularly problematic for culturally and linguistically diverse populations, in which mismatches between the rating scale developer's intent for the item and the interpretation of the rater are more likely to occur (Townsend, 2000).

A hypothetical survey item, "The student plays appropriately with others," and the possible cognitive processes errors are described as an example. In the first step, the individual *comprehends* the rating scale item. Is the rating scale developer's definition and/or topography of plays appropriately the same as the rater's definition? In the second step, the rater *retrieves* memories relevant to the item. Here, the rater accesses memories or a general evaluation related to the rating scale item. If there are differences in definition, then different memories will be accessed. Next, the rater makes a *judgment* from the set of retrieved memories. In this step, the individual combines their memories by placing weight on individual instances or using another heuristic to make a determination. In the final step, the rater places their judgment on the available *response* options. Response options typically follow a frequency distribution (e.g., Never to Almost Always), and the rater's cultural background may have different frequencies of behaviors than the normative sample. Lastly, the rater response style might also be susceptible to extreme response bias, where some individuals may be more likely to endorse extreme ends of a response choice (Baumgartner & Weijters, 2015; Chumney & Hayes, 2021; Kemmelmeier, 2016).

Measurement Invariance

Rating differences between groups may be examined mathematically with measurement invariance or differential functioning studies. A rating scale may have strong psychometric properties when examined as a whole. However, it may show differential functioning when examined for different subgroups of the normative sample (e.g., native vs. non-native English speakers). Measurement invariance can be evaluated with item response theory and multiple-group confirmatory factor analysis. Fairness and equity within rating scale use cannot be empirically supported without measurement invariance studies. From a measurement standpoint, fairness has been defined as equal conditional distribution of predictors given the true criterion and equity as equal conditional distribution of the criterion given the true predictor (Meredith, 1993). In each of these definitions, other factors such as race/ethnicity, gender, language, and age are independent of observed scores, and only the underlying latent variable influences variability in the observed scores.

In addition to items functioning similarly across groups, the rating scale should lead to similar score interpretations across groups. Rating scales should be examined for differential reliability and validity. Manuals may not provide reliability and validity data disaggregated by subgroups (e.g., race/ethnicity and gender). Users may need to search for peer-reviewed articles to support the use of a rating scale tool for a special population. For example, a rating scale may have differential predictive validity for diagnosing a mental health disorder or have larger standard errors for specific subgroups. This information may be found outside of the publisher's manual (e.g., in published articles). Examining these data would provide empirical data suggesting using the rating scale for special populations.

Culturally Relevant Practice Considerations

In addition to developing strong technical SEB assessment knowledge and skills, the ability to apply those skills in culturally responsive and equitable ways requires several considerations. As outlined in prior sections of this chapter, an ecological lens is critical to ensure that structural and cultural factors are adequately considered within any assessment process. Beyond the development of an ecologically informed lens, there are several practical applications to consider in a culturally responsive evaluation.

Cultural Humility

Researchers define cultural humility as a lifelong and evolving practice of developing a reflective and critical awareness of how culture, power, privilege, and oppression shape all individual experiences and perspectives (Fisher, 2020). Closely related to the concepts of cultural competence and social justice, the practice of cultural humility can help practitioners more deeply understand experiences and perspectives that differ from their own and develop stronger relationships with the youth and families they serve. Critical attributes of cultural humility include openness, self-awareness, egolessness, supportive interaction, and self-reflection and critique (for definitions, see Foronda et al., 2016).

Culturally Affirming Relationship Building

Given the time and energy-consuming nature of comprehensive assessments in the context of large caseloads and responsibilities, the process can often be experienced as transactional and even disempowering to culturally and linguistically diverse (CLD) youth and families. Comprehensive SEB rating scales typically comprise deeply personal questions that often reflect stigmatized behaviors and experiences across different cultures. CLD youth and families often enter assessment processes with varying degrees of mistrust toward educators and systems from which they may have experienced marginalization and other relational harms. Understanding and acknowledging these realities with cultural humility, using clear and direct communication, is crucial for evaluators as they develop new relationships with youth and families during the assessment process.

Effective collaboration is associated with positive student outcomes and is a key component of equitable educational opportunities. Griffiths et al. (2020) developed a framework that includes eight key common constructs that are critical to collaboration: (1) open communication, (2) trust, (3) mutual respect, (4) shared goals, (5) common understanding, (6) shared responsibility, (7) active participation, and (8) shared decision making. The model indicates that communication, trust, and mutual respect are critical to relationship building, particularly for CLD youth and their families.

Prioritizing trust, communication, and mutual respect and focusing on relationship building may allow for higher-quality assessment and provide a healing experience for youth and families needing culturally affirming support. In the case example referenced above, when working with Nathaly and her family, the case carrier and school psychologist reached out to her aunt at the start of the school year to introduce themselves and learn more about Nathaly's strengths, familial background, and pressing concerns for this school year. Upon starting the assessment, the school psychologist was in regular contact with Nathaly's aunt, gathering information regarding her concerns and goals to formulate an appropriate assessment plan, conducting a comprehensive interview with Nathaly and her aunt, and discussing the purpose and directions for each rating scale. The practitioner intentionally used jargon-free language and tailored the information to the family. By spending time with Nathaly and her aunt throughout the assessment, building rapport and trust, and reviewing preliminary results of rating scales together, Nathaly and her aunt could actively participate in the IEP meeting and thoughtfully contribute to the formulation of Nathaly's goals and services.

Treating Linguistic Diversity as an Asset

As over 80% of SEB assessment practitioners in school and clinical settings identify as White (American Psychological Association, 2022; Goforth et al., 2021), communication with and perceptions of linguistically diverse clients is another significant consideration for culturally responsive practices. It is essential first to recognize and acknowledge that non-English speaking or multilingual learners have historically and continued to be treated using deficit-centered perspectives rooted in White supremacy within psychological and educational systems. Language barriers are perpetuated by structural deficiencies that have failed to recruit and retain CLD practitioners. In addition, systems have struggled to build adequate interpreter services. Despite these challenges, linguistic diversity is often viewed as a problem and inconvenience within the assessment process.

Reframing the ability to speak or navigate multiple languages as *linguistic capital*, a type of community wealth (Yosso, 2005), can support practitioners in moving away from deficit-centered perspectives and toward more strength-based and culturally responsive perspectives. Ensuring the availability of comprehensive rating forms in multiple languages is also crucial to ensure the accessibility of SEB assessments. Further, advocating for strong recruitment and retention of CLD practitioners and better access to high-quality interpretation and translation services may address the structural barriers to communication with CLD youth and families.

Culturally Responsive Assessment Interpretation

As previously described, the foundations of a culturally responsive assessment begin long before the interpretation of results and require proactive steps in developing an ecologically informed assessment plan, strong technical competencies, and relational and culturally humble administration strategies. By cultivating a culturally responsive assessment foundation, the interpretation of comprehensive rating scales should utilize consistent strategies to ensure that the interpretation of results accurately reflects the individual's contextualized experience and clarifies cultural definitions of the problem (Hass & Abdou, 2019). During the interpretation process, evaluators should confirm that raters understand and rate scale items as developers intended. This confirmation is critical when analyzing critical items and elevated scales.

Assuming that the assessor has established trust with the rater, follow-up interviews can be critical to clarify responses to critical items and gather more cultural context for those ratings. For example, when Nathaly expressed that she "heard voices" on one of the comprehensive rating scales, the practitioner followed up to further understand what she was experiencing. Through this follow-up interview, the practitioner learned that Nathaly's family holds strong spiritual beliefs about the afterlife. Nathaly expressed that she heard her grandmother's voice guiding her throughout her life. Nathaly's aunt confirmed that they often discussed using their ancestors as spiritual guides, which was a common practice in their family. Had the practitioner not followed up or discussed this further with Nathaly and her aunt, there may have been concerns about more significant psychopathology. Follow-up interviews to review and clarify results with the rater allow for a deeper understanding of cultural nuances, perspectives, and assets, leading to more accurate interpretations and more effective and culturally affirming intervention recommendations.

Another essential practice for interpreting comprehensive rating scale results is to triangulate findings with other sources of data (e.g., record reviews, interviews, and observations) for a richer and culturally nuanced context (Hass & Carriere, 2014). Item responses and scale scores from comprehensive rating scales can provide valuable information about SEB strengths and challenges that can inform intervention recommendations. Further, assessors must interpret assessment results within the ecological context to determine the extent to which environmental factors may harm or support SEB functioning. This approach is critical when rating scale scores differ by rater and setting, as this can often indicate differences in environmental deficits or support structures.

The RIOT/ICEL framework is a helpful tool to investigate and interpret comprehensive rating scale results. For example, when interpreting Nathaly's anxiety scores related to her academic performance, the assessor should investigate how grades are discussed, valued, and reinforced across different environments. Rather than just reporting her comprehensive rating scale scores without context, her scores should be described and integrated with interview and observational data throughout the report. The perspectives of Nathaly, her teachers, caregivers, and the assessor can be tied together to provide a well-rounded picture of Nathaly's experiences and needs.

THE FUTURE OF COMPREHENSIVE ASSESSMENT

One of the primary issues with rating scales is that responses are mediated by perception, either an outside rater (e.g., teacher or parent) or self-report, which produces error in scores. The differences in how people understand the item, recall memories related to the item, make a judgment about an item, and provide a response to an item are all potential sources of error. In the future, technologies may be applied to provide information on constructs in new ways. The term "digital health" has described these technological advances.

Digital health is an overarching term for categories of information and communication technologies related to healthcare, such as mobile health, health information technology, wearable devices, telehealth, and personalized medicine (U.S. Food and Drug Administration, 2020). For example, heart rate variability, the length of time between heartbeats, may be used as an indicator of psychological stress (Kim et al., 2018). These data may be collected with wearable technologies, like smartwatches. The information would provide empirical data on an individual's personal experience.

Another way technology may play a role in how we use rating scales is by connecting rating scale results to other information systems. Data on adults and children have already been collected for various medical and educational purposes. Artificial intelligence (AI) advances may identify new ways of interpreting data. For example, a rating scale that is completed for a child may be compared with every digital document in the school's student information systems and other data collection systems (e.g., report cards, office discipline referrals, attendance, intervention progress, screening data, and medical file). The AI system could consider millions of data points simultaneously when interpreting scores.

Lastly, computer vision with embedded AI may complement behavioral rating scales. For example, a clinician may want to collect information about a child's social skills. The two primary data collection methods are rating scales and direct observation. Systematic direct observation is the gold standard for behavioral assessment; however, this assessment method can be resource-intensive (e.g., time and training requirements) (Riley-Tillman et al., 2008). Alternatively, the child could be monitored during social interactions. A computer could watch the interactions to evaluate skills such as initiating social interaction, expected social responses, and other social skills. Beyond the ethical issue of recording individuals, the time needed to obtain reliable information may be extremely long. Alternatively, the child could be placed in extended reality (XR). XR includes augmented reality, mixed reality, and virtual reality. The benefit of XR is that the child could be placed in a controlled setting (i.e., the setting is the same for each individual), the setting can prompt social interactions to occur, and the naturalistic setting of XR may promote similar responses as in reality. Computer vision could be used to evaluate the child's behavioral responses in XR in a way that is similar to how it would be in reality.

Technology can change the way data are collected. This may include using rating scales in new ways or removing rating scales completely. Although the possibilities are fascinating, additional research is needed on these emerging technologies to determine the best way to integrate them ethically and effectively into practice.

CONCLUSION

Comprehensive rating scales are an effective and efficient category of assessment tools. These tools allow practitioners to investigate their clients' SEB experiences through their own perspectives and those of caregivers, teachers, and service providers involved in the youth's life. As practitioners, we are responsible for making culturally informed decisions when selecting, administering, and interpreting data gathered from these tools. Culturally informed and responsive use of these tools begins during problem identification and assessment planning, including carefully selecting measures that accurately reflect our clients' experiences. Using an ecologically informed and culturally humble lens, practitioners can leverage comprehensive rating scales to enhance assessments with measurable data to strengthen clinical conceptualization and intervention planning. Although the future of comprehensive rating scales holds promise, we must continue to engage in ethical and culturally responsive approaches to data interpretation and application.

REFERENCES

Achenbach, T. M. (2019). International findings with the Achenbach System of Empirically Based Assessment (ASEBA): Applications to clinical services, research, and training. *Child and Adolescent Psychiatry and Mental Health, 13*(30).

Achenbach, T. M., & Rescorla, L. A. (2001). *Manual for the ASEBA school-age forms and profiles*. Research Center for Children Youth and Families.

Ahn, C. M., Ebesutani, C., & Kamphaus, R. (2014). A psychometric analysis and standardization of the Behavior Assessment System for Children–2, Self-Report of Personality, Child Version among a Korean sample. *School Psychology Quarterly, 29*(2), 198–212.

American Educational Research Association, American Psychological Association, & National Council on Measurement in Education. (2014). *Standards for psychological and educational testing.* American Educational Research Association.

American Psychological Association. (2022). *Demographics of U.S. Psychology Workforce* [Interactive data tool]. *www.apa.org/workforce/data-tools/demographics*

American Psychiatric Association. (2013). *Diagnostic and statistical manual of mental disorders* (5th ed.).

American Psychiatric Association. (2022). *Diagnostic and statistical manual of mental disorders* (5th ed., text rev.).

Anderson, R. E. (2018). And still WE rise: Parent–child relationships, resilience, and school readiness in low-income urban Black families. *Journal of Family Psychology, 32*(1), 60–70.

Baumgartner, H., & Weijters, B. (2015). Response biases in cross-cultural measurement. In S. Ng & A. Y. Lee (Eds.), *Handbook of culture and consumer behavior* (pp. 150–180). Oxford University Press.

Benson, N. F., Floyd, R. G., Kranzler, J. H., Eckert, T. L., Fefer, S. A., & Morgan, G. B. (2019). Test use and assessment practices of school psychologists in the United States: Findings from the 2017 National Survey. *Journal of School Psychology, 72*, 29–48. *https://doi.org/10.1016/j.jsp.2018.12.004*

Bronfenbrenner, U. (1977). Toward an experimental ecology of human development. *American Psychologist, 32*(7), 513–531.

Carlson, J. F., Geisinger, K. F., & Jonson, J. L. (Eds.). (2021). *The twenty-first mental measurements yearbook*. Buros Center for Testing.

Chain, J., Shapiro, V. B., LeBuffe, P. A., & Bryson, A. M. (2017). Academic achievement of American Indian and Alaska Native students: Does social–emotional competence reduce the impact of poverty? *American Indian & Alaska Native Mental Health Research: The Journal of the National Center, 24*(1), 1–29.

Chumney, F. & Hayes, M. (2021). *The definitive series: Response scales across countries*. ADP Research Institute. *www.adpri.org/wp-content/uploads/2021/04/R0140_0421_v1_RSAC_ResearchReport.pdf*

Conners, C. K. (2008). *Conners comprehensive behavior rating scale*. Multi-Health Systems.

Diamond, E., Hart, S. R., Griffiths, A. J., & Brock, S. E. (2023). *Psychology in the schools: Addressing the learning, behavior, and mental health needs of students*. Taylor & Francis.

Edwards, E. C. (2021). Centering race to move towards an intersectional ecological framework for defining school safety for Black students. *School Psychology Review*, 1–20.

Doromal, J. B., Cottone, E. A., & Kim, H. (2017). Preliminary validation of the teacher-rated DESSA in a low-income, kindergarten sample. *Journal of Psychoeducational Assessment, 37*(1), 40–54.

Dowdy, E., Furlong, M., Nylund-Gibson, & K. (n.d.). *Project covitality. www.covitalityucsb.info/sehs-surveys.html*

Furlong, M. J., You, S., Renshaw, T. L., Smith, D. C., & O'Malley, M. D. (2014). Preliminary development and validation of the Social and Emotional Health Survey for secondary students. *Social Indicators Research, 117*, 1011–1032.

Garcia-Barrera, M. A., Karr, J. E., Duran, V., Direnfeld, E., & Pineda, D. A. (2015). Cross-cultural validation of a behavioral screener for executive functions: Guidelines for clinical use among Colombian children with and without ADHD. *Psychological Assessment, 27*(4), 1349–1363.

Greenspoon, P. J., & Saklofske, D. H. (2001). Toward an integration of subjective well-being and psychopathology. *Social Indicators Research, 54*(1), 81–108.

Griffiths, A.J., Alsip, J., Hart, S. R., Round, R. L., & Brady, J. (2020). Together we can do so much: A systematic review and conceptual framework of collaboration in schools. *Canadian Journal of School Psychology, 36*(1), 59–85.

Hass, M. R., & Abdou, A. S. (2019). Culturally responsive interviewing practices. *Contemporary School Psychology, 23*(1), 47–56.

Hass, M. R., & Carriere, J. A. (2014). *Writing useful, accessible, and legally defensible psychoeducational reports*. Wiley.

Hosp, J. L. (2006, May) Implementing RTI: Assessment practices and response to intervention. *NASP Communiqué, 34*(7), 7–8.

Individuals with Disabilities Education Act, 20 U.S.C. § 1400-1414 § (2004).

Ito, A., Smith, D. C., You, S., Shimoda, Y., & Furlong, M. J. (2015). Validation of the Social Emotional Health Survey-Secondary for Japanese students. *Contemporary School Psychology, 19*, 243–252.

Kane, M. (2013). The argument-based approach to validity. *School Psychology Review, 42*(4), 448–457.

Kemmelmeier, M. (2016). Cultural differences in survey responding: Issues and insights in the study of response biases. *International Journal of Psychology, 51*(6), 439–444.

Kim, E. K., Dowdy, E., & Furlong, M. J. (2014). Exploring the relative contributions of the strength and distress components of dual-factor complete mental health screening. *Canadian Journal of School Psychology, 29*, 127–140.

Kim, H. G., Cheon, E. J., Bai, D. S., Lee, Y. H., & Koo, B. H. (2018). Stress and heart rate variability: A meta-analysis and review of the literature. *Psychiatry Investigation, 15*(3), 235–245.

LeBuffe, P. A., Shapiro, V. B., & Naglieri, J. A. (2009). *The Devereux Student Strengths Assessment (DESSA): Assessment, technical manual, and user's guide*. Apperson.

LeBuffe, P. A., Shapiro, V. B., & Naglieri, J. A. (2014). *The Devereux Student Strengths Assessment (DESSA): Assessment, technical manual, and user's guide*. Apperson.

Lee, S., You, S., & Furlong, M. J. (2016). Validation of the Social Emotional Health Survey for Korean school students. *Child Indicators Research, 9*, 73–92.

Leung, B. (1993). Back to basics: Evaluation is a RIOT! *NASP Communiqué, 22*(3), 1–6.

Mattar, J., Hamaidi, D., & Al Anati, J. (2020). Emotion regulation and its relationship to academic difficulties among Jordanian first grade students. *Early Child Development and Care, 190*(8), 1313–1322.

Meredith, W. (1993). Measurement invariance, factor analysis, and factorial invariance. *Psychometrika, 58*(4), 525–543.

Palma, C., Abdou, A., Danforth, S., & Griffiths, A. J. (2023). Are deficit perspectives thriving in trauma-informed schools? A historical and anti-racist reflection. *Equity & Excellence in Education, 24*(2), 23–45.

Perez-Brena, N. J., Rivas-Drake, D., Toomey, R. B., & Umaña-Taylor, A. J. (2018). Contributions of the integrative model for the study of developmental competencies in minority children: What have we learned about adaptive culture? *American Psychologist, 73*(6), 713–726.

Reynolds, C. R., & Kamphaus, R. W. (2004). *Behavior Assessment System for Children—Third Edition*. AGS.

Reynolds, C. R., & Kamphaus, R. W. (2015). *Behavior Assessment System for Children—Third Edition*. Pearson.

Romer, N., von der Embse, N., Eklund, K., Kilgus, S., Perales, K., Splett, J. W., Suldo, S., & Wheeler, D. (2020). *Best practices in social, emotional, and behavioral screening: An implementation guide. Version 2.0. smhcollaborative.org/universalscreening*

Riley-Tillman, T. C., Chafouleas, S. M., Sassu, K. A., Chanese, J. A., & Glazer, A. D. (2008). Examining the agreement of direct behavior ratings and systematic direct observation data for on-task and disruptive behavior. *Journal of Positive Behavior Interventions, 10*(2), 136–143.

Salvia, J., Ysseldyke, J. E., & Witmer, S. (2017). *Assessment in special and inclusive education* (13th ed.). Cengage Learning.

Sepanta, M., Juzdani, M.H., & Ahmad, A. (2017). Psychometric properties of Persian version of the Devereux Student Strengths Assessment Scale. *Developmental Psychology: Journal of Iranian Psychologists, 14*(53), 63–73.

Tan, T. X., Yi, Z., Li, Z., Cheng, K., & Li, J. (2021). Comparing Chinese youth with American youth on adjustment: An illustration of measurement issues in cross-cultural research. *International Journal of Psychology*, 56(2), 286–295.

Telef, B. B., & Furlong, M. J. (2017). Adaptation and validation of the Social Emotional Health Survey-Secondary into Turkish culture. *International Journal of School & Educational Psychology*, 5, 255–265.

Tourangeau, R., & Rasinski, K. A. (1998). Cognitive processes underlying context effects in attitude measurement. *Psychological Bulletin, 103*(3), 299–314.

Townsend, B. L. (2000). The disproportionate discipline of African American learners: Reducing school suspensions and expulsions. *Exceptional Children*, 66(3), 381–391.

U.S. Food and Drug Administration. (2020, September 22). What is Digital Health? *www.fda.gov/medical-devices/digital-health-center-excellence/what-digital-health*

Walker, H. M., Small, J. W., Severson, H. H., Seeley, J. R., & Feil, E. G. (2014). Multiple-gating approaches in universal screening within school and community settings. In R. J. Kettler, T. A. Glover, C. A. Albers, & K. A. Feeney-Kettler (Eds.), *Universal screening in educational settings: Evidence-based decision making for schools* (pp. 47–75). American Psychological Association.

Whitcomb, S. A. (2019). *Behavioral, social, and emotional assessment of children and adolescents* (5th ed.). Routledge.

Wodrich, D. L. (n.d.). *Social–emotional assessment in the schools: concepts and cases*. University of Arizona. *https://opentextbooks.library.arizona.edu/wodrichseas*

Xie, J., Liu, S., Yang, C., & Furlong, M. J. (2018). Chinese version of Social and Emotional Health Survey–Secondary. *Chinese Journal of Clinical Psychology, 25*(6), 1012–1026.

Yosso, T. J. (2005). Whose culture has capital? A critical race theory discussion of community cultural wealth. *Race Ethnicity and Education*, 8(1), 69–91.

You, S., Dowdy, E., Furlong, M. J., Renshaw, T., Smith, D. C., & O'Malley, M. D. (2014). Further validation of the Social and Emotional Health Survey for high school students. *Applied Quality of Life Research*, 9, 997–1015.

You, S., Furlong, M. J., Felix, E., & O'Malley, M. D. (2015). Validation of the Social and Emotional Health Survey for five sociocultural groups: Multigroup invariance and latent mean analyses. *Psychology in the Schools*, 52, 349–362.

Zhou, A., Reynolds, C., Zhu, J., & Kamphaus, R. W. (2020). Differentiating autism from ADHD in children and adolescents using BASC-3. *Journal of Pediatric Neuropsychology*, 6, 61–65.

CHAPTER 12

Screening Measures and Methods

Bridget V. Dever, Emily K. Gallagher, Kristen F. Stack, Jessica Lathrop, and Nathan Kirk

Screening is a critical step in the prevention of deleterious outcomes among children, including academic difficulties, social problems, and mental disorders. Universal screening for social, emotional, and behavioral (SEB) risk involves screening all youth in a given setting for risk for potential difficulties in these domains (Stiffler & Dever, 2015). Screening tools are meant to detect risk for disorder(s), rather than the presence of a disorder, and are therefore not diagnostic tools. Screening instruments typically take only a few minutes to administer, making them feasible for universal use in a population. Although such screening has been conducted in health care settings, schools are most often the setting for SEB screening programs among children and adolescents (e.g., O'Connell et al., 2009). Due to mandatory educational enrollment regulations, schools provide a unique context for universal screening in which it becomes possible to screen every child in a classroom, school, or district for risk for SEB difficulties. Although universal screening programs have become more common in schools during the past decade, currently less than 20% of schools have a mechanism in place for screening for SEB risk (Herman et al., 2020).

Universal screening fits well within multi-tiered systems of support (MTSS) models of identification and intervention. Universal screening serves as an initial step in the data-based decision-making process for identifying SEB risk within MTSS and is an alternative to traditional teacher referral and nomination methods for such identification (Dever et al., 2012). Given that all students in a school typically participate in universal screening, such data can be used to inform schoolwide or classroomwide prevention efforts at Tier 1 of MTSS based on areas of need. Schools can also use individual-level data to identify students who may be at risk of SEB difficulties, such that follow-up assessments can be administered to determine whether at-risk students could benefit from interventions at Tier 2 (e.g., small group interventions) or Tier 3 (e.g., more intensive individual interventions or special education services).

Presently, there are a variety of measures and methods available to schools, health care providers, and others to detect early risk for SEB problems. Although these educational and health care service providers are invested in the well-being of the children whom they serve, navigating the multitude of instruments that are available can be a challenge that prevents the adoption of a universal screening program (Dever et al., 2012). However, there is research evidence that schoolwide and districtwide screening programs can be successful and that such screening data can be used within MTSS models to inform data-based decision making at the student, classroom, school, and district levels (e.g., Dever et al., 2013).

One of the first steps in a successful screening program is the choice of an appropriate instrument or methodology. Glover and Albers (2007) suggested that those interested in screening should consider the (1) appropriateness for intended use, (2) psychometric adequacy, and (3) usability of the available instruments before making a selection. In terms of appropriateness, it is important for service delivery providers to decide the goal(s) of screening procedures. For example, does a school want to assess students for risk across the SEB domains broadly? Or is the school more interested in risk more narrowly defined, such as risk for a depressive disorder? In this chapter, we review both broadband and narrowband screening tools in order to provide the reader with options that might best match their unique goals for screening. In addition, we provide information about the psychometric properties of each screening instrument, including evidence of reliability and validity for its intended use. Finally, details concerning the cost, time, informant choices, and use of each screening measure are provided in order to help the reader make a determination regarding the feasibility of using the measure for a particular purpose in the context of interest. We acknowledge that this is not a comprehensive review of all available instruments, but rather an attempt to summarize some of the most widely used measures that are available for screening for SEB risk. Throughout our review of the instruments, we highlight information relevant to culturally informed approaches to assessment, including research regarding measurement equivalence, potential differential item functioning, the availability of forms in multiple languages, and other available evidence to support screening in diverse populations of students.

BROADBAND SCREENING MEASURES

In this section, we review available screening methods and measures that include content that cuts across the SEB domains. In doing so, broadband screening measures must strike a balance between coverage of a range of symptoms and brevity of the instrument. One of the benefits of broadband screening measures is the potential to detect risk in any one of multiple domains, which could lead to identification of children with a variety of difficulties who would otherwise go undetected. However, most of the available broadband measurement tools to date have been longer and more comprehensive and, therefore, would not qualify as screening instruments due to the time requirements. In this section, we include assessments that typically only take a few minutes to administer in order to adhere to the purposes of screening. Below is a review of commonly used broadband screening measures and methods, presented in alphabetical order.

Behavioral and Emotional Screening System

The Behavioral and Emotional Screening System (BASC-3 BESS) (Kamphaus & Reynolds, 2015) is a broadband screening measure that assesses risk across multiple domains. The BASC-3 BESS was developed to reflect the content of the Behavior Assessment System for Children—Third Edition (BASC-3) (Reynolds & Kamphaus, 2015). The BASC-3 BESS includes two age-related choices for the parent and teacher forms (preschool: ages 3–5, school age: grade K–12), with 25–30 items on each form. Parent and teacher forms provide risk indices for internalizing, externalizing, adaptive skills, and overall risk. There is also a 28-item self-report measure appropriate for children and adolescents in grades 3–12, which provides risk indices for internalizing, self-regulation, personal adjustment, and overall risk. Parent and self-report forms are available in both English and Spanish. The BASC-3 BESS has been updated to allow the user to produce either single- or multi-informant reports in order to compare results across informants. The typical administration time is between 5 and 10 minutes per form. Scoring can be done by hand, using scoring software, or via online scoring.

Items on all versions of the BASC-3 BESS are rated on a four-point Likert scale (i.e. *never*, *sometimes*, *often*, and *almost always*). Based on the raw score, a Behavioral and Emotional Risk Index is generated, which includes both a *T*-score and a percentile for overall risk. This *T*-score is then categorized as either normal risk (0–60), elevated risk (61–70), or extremely elevated risk (71+) for behavioral and emotional problems. A risk category is generated for overall risk and for each of the domains listed above for a given informant. The BASC-3 BESS was developed to broadly represent the domains included on the BASC-3 (Reynolds & Kamphaus, 2015).

The BASC-3 BESS was normed in the United States using a nationally representative sample. Overall, the BESS has adequate reliability and validity evidence to support its use across forms (Kamphaus & Reynolds, 2015). Split-half reliability estimates range from .72 to .96, with lower reliability evident specifically for the self-regulation index of the self-report form. Test–retest reliability ranged from .76 to .93, and interrater reliability ranged from .52 to .85, with higher estimates for the parent measure. Sensitivity of the parent form in predicting relevant BASC-3 composite scores ranged from .69 to .82 and .95 to .98 in terms of specificity. Sensitivity on the teacher form ranged from .49 to .83, and specificity estimates were from .94 to .99. Sensitivity on the self-report was found to be .69 to .71, and specificity was .95 to .98. The cost of the BESS screener is approximately $1.50 per student; this instrument is also available to schools via a subscription through Pearson clinical assessments.

Prior research with the BASC-2 BESS (Kamphaus & Reynolds, 2007) provided further evidence of its validity, with scores predictive of later mental health and academic outcomes (e.g., Dowdy et al., 2016; Juechter et al., 2012). In addition, the factor structure of the BASC-3 BESS has demonstrated measurement equivalence across diverse groups of children and adolescents (e.g., Basting et al., 2022; Dever & Gaier, 2021; Edyburn, 2020). The BESS can be used in multiple contexts and can be used by schools to assist with behavioral–emotional response to intervention and MTSS (Dever et al., 2013).

Pediatric Symptom Checklist

The Pediatric Symptom Checklist (PSC) (Jellinek et al., 1986) is a 35-item parent report measure of cognitive, emotional, and behavioral problems for children ages 4–16 that is available online at no cost. A youth self-report form (Y-PSC) (Pagano et al., 2000) is also available for adolescents (ages 11 and older). Items are rated on a three-point scale (*never*, *sometimes*, and *often*); different cut scores have been established for preschool (ages 4–5) and school-age (6–16) children. The PSC has adequate sensitivity (.77 to .95) and specificity (.68 to 1.00) (e.g., Boothroyd & Armstrong, 2010; Simonian & Tarnowski, 2001; Stoppelbein et al., 2005). Data support the use of the PSC across diverse samples, with evidence of internal consistency, test–retest stability, interrater reliability, measurement invariance across gender, and validity for identifying children in need of intervention (Bergmann et al., 2018; DiStefano et al., 2017; Jellinek et al., 1986; Simonian & Tarnowski, 2001; Stoppelbein et al., 2005). The PSC is available in over 30 languages and dialects.

This tool has typically been used in primary health care settings, which distinguishes it from most of the available behavioral and emotional screening measures. However, scores of the PSC have been found to correlate with academic problems and teacher rating scales of behavior. The PSC has also been useful for finding students whose behavioral and emotional difficulties were previously unidentified in the school setting; therefore, data from the PSC may be of utility to schools as well (Murphy et al., 1989). For example, the PSC-Y has been implemented successfully within the context of a school-based health center (Gall et al., 2000). In addition, the PSC-Y identified adolescents with internalizing symptoms who were not identified using the parent report form, supporting the use of the self-report form specifically among those at risk for symptomology related to anxiety or depression.

Social, Academic, and Emotional Behavior Risk Screener

The Social, Academic, and Emotional Behavior Risk Screener (SAEBRS) (Kilgus & von der Embse, 2014; von der Embse et al., 2016) is a measure that assesses both risk and well-being across three domains: social behavior, academic behavior, and emotional behavior. The scores for these subscales are combined to represent total behavior, with higher scores representing more adaptive behavior. There are two forms, a teacher report (grades K–12) and a student report (grades 2–12). The teacher-reported SAEBRS consists of 19 items, with each domain consisting of 6 (social and academic) and 7 (emotional) items. The student-reported mySAEBRS consists of 20 items, with each domain consisting of 7 (social and emotional) and 6 (academic) items; the student report is available in English and Spanish. The items for both informants are rated on a four-point Likert scale (*never*, *sometimes*, *often*, and *almost always*). The SAEBRS/mySAEBRS can be completed in 1–3 minutes per student and is available through FastBridge. The typical cost is $6/administration; however, lower rates may be available for larger subscription plans.

Recent research with the teacher SAEBRS found internal consistency coefficients ranging from .59 to .88 for each of the domains as well as for total behavior among a sample of elementary school students (Whitley & Cuenca-Carlino,

2020). In addition, evidence supports the bifactor structure of the SAEBRS, with social, academic, and emotional factors that all load onto one general factor (von der Embse et al., 2016). It was noted that the general factor accounted for the majority of the variance; therefore, the total behavior score may demonstrate more utility than the individual subscales.

Multiple studies have been conducted to establish diagnostic accuracy in elementary samples (e.g., Kilgus et al., 2018) for the SAEBRS Teacher Rating Scale. Results differ based on the type of criterion measure used (Kilgus et al., 2018). Izumi and Eklund (2023) evaluated differential item functioning (DIF) across race/ethnicity and gender for the teacher rating scale and found that teachers differentially rated Black students and male students higher in SEB risk. Teachers with higher scores on a cultural responsiveness measure generally rated students lower in risk on the SAEBRS (Fallon et al., 2023). Interestingly, Eklund and colleagues (2023) found that diagnostic accuracy of the SAEBRS did not differ by race or ethnicity for 730 students across 54 teachers.

The SAEBRS Student Rating Scale, also referred to as mySAEBRS, has a similar bifactor structure to the teacher version with three subscales (social, academic, and emotional risk) and one general risk score (von der Embse et al., 2017). Kilgus and colleagues (2021) found that the mySAEBRS demonstrated adequate omega reliability coefficients (.73–.82) for the general index and the three subscales in a large sample of students in grades K–12. Jenkins and colleagues (2021) investigated the stability of mySAEBRS scores over time. The researchers used latent class analysis to establish three risk groups (low, moderate, and high). The percentages of students in each of these groups remained the same across one academic year (Jenkins et al., 2021). von der Embse and colleagues (2017) established convergent validity with the Strengths and Difficulties Questionnaire (SDQ) (Goodman, 1997) and also established scalar measurement invariance across gender in a sample of 1,102 middle school students.

Research has provided evidence that the SAEBRS may be used within MTSS as a screening instrument to help inform the data-based decision-making process (Kilgus et al., 2016). Eklund and colleagues (2017) found that the SAEBRS was predictive of academic achievement (reading), office disciplinary referrals, and student attendance, further supporting its use for screening in the school setting. The SAEBRS was created and validated using a racially and ethnically diverse U.S. sample, and multiple studies have assessed measurement invariance across gender and race/ethnicity (Eklund et al., 2023; von der Embse et al., 2017; Whitley & Cuenca-Carlino, 2020).

Strengths and Difficulties Questionnaire

The Strengths and Difficulties Questionnaire (SDQ) (Goodman, 1997) is available online for no cost in 60 languages. This measure includes various forms that are appropriate for children ranging in age from 2–17 years. There are different parent- and teacher-report forms for children ages 2–4 years, 4–10 years, and 11–17 years. In addition, there is a self-report form for children and adolescents between 11–17 years of age. Scoring can be completed by hand based on guidelines provided online or through an online scoring system.

All versions of the SDQ include 25 questions, which assess behavioral and emotional resources and challenges. Responses are reported on a three-point scale (*not true*, *somewhat true*, and *certainly true*). The items are divided into five subscales: emotional symptoms (five items), conduct problems (five items), hyperactivity/inattention (five items), peer problems (five items), and prosocial behavior (five items). The emotional symptoms, conduct problems, hyperactivity/inattention, and peer relationship problems subscales are combined to generate a total difficulties score. The categories and items on the SDQ were developed based on theory using the fourth edition of the *Diagnostic and Statistical Manual of Mental Disorders* (DSM-IV) (American Psychiatric Association, 1994), as well as factor-analytic work.

Overall, the measure has adequate reliability and validity to support score inferences; however, the reliability of specific subscales has been questionable historically. The total score has been found to have internal consistency coefficients between .66 and .82 (Brann et al., 2018; Goodman et al., 2003) and test–retest reliability of .96; however, the Peer Problems subscale has reported internal consistencies between .51 and .81 (Goodman & Scott, 1999; Mellor, 2004; Speyer et al., 2023). Hall and colleagues (2019) reported high specificity (.84) but low sensitivity (.45) for the hyperactivity subscale in a randomized controlled trial for children ages 6–17 with attention-deficit/hyperactivity disorder (ADHD).

With consideration of language and culture, Vugteveen and colleagues (2022) established new norms for a Dutch population after the British cutoff scores classified fewer than the expected 10% of the sample as at risk. Across cultures, the SDQ has been shown to possess favorable psychometric properties when used with Chinese and Japanese samples (Lai et al., 2010; Liu et al., 2013; Matsuishi et al., 2008), although the Conduct and Peer Problems subscales demonstrated poor internal consistency across Nigerian (Akpa & Bamgboye, 2005), Chinese and Hong Kong (Du et al., 2008; Lai et al., 2010), and Iranian samples (Ghanizadeh, 2007). The factor structures of the parent and child forms have been confirmed using samples from the United Kingdom, Germany, Honduras, and the Netherlands in their respective languages (Harry et al., 2019; Keller & Langmeyer, 2019; Vugteveen et al., 2020). Measurement invariance has also been established across age and setting (Smits et al., 2018; Speyer et al., 2023).

Taken in sum, although the SDQ is intended to identify specific domains of problem behavior, it may be best to use the total difficulties score to identify general symptomology (Goodman et al., 2003). In support of its use, when compared to a semi-structured interview, the SDQ was significantly better at detecting hyperactivity/inattention than the Child Behavior Checklist (CBCL) (Achenbach, 2009) and as good at detecting internalizing and externalizing problems (Goodman & Scott, 1999). The SDQ has been used in research as a screening measure to detect untreated mental health problems in a community setting (Goodman et al., 2000), as well as in mental health clinics (Goodman et al., 2000). In addition, there is research to suggest that the SDQ can be used in schools to inform prevention and intervention for culturally and linguistically diverse students as early as preschool (Downs et al., 2012).

Student Risk Screening Scale

The Student Risk Screening Scale (SRSS) (Drummond, 1994) is a teacher report measure originally designed to detect risk for externalizing behavior problems among students in grades K–6. However, evidence suggests that its use can be extended to those in grades K–12 (Lane et al., 2008). The original measure included seven items, rated on a four-point scale (*never*, *occasionally*, *sometimes*, and *frequently*), and the responses are summed to arrive at a total score. Based on their total scores, students are classified as low (0–3), moderate (4–8), or high (9–21) risk.

The revised SRSS-IE (Internalizing/Externalizing) (Lane et al., 2013) includes an additional five or six items addressing internalizing concerns, with an additional item included for ratings of middle/high school students as compared with elementary school students. The original 7 items for externalizing concerns are also included on the updated version, for a total of 12–13 items. The response options for the SRSS-IE are the same as described above. For the internalizing items on the elementary school form, cut scores have been established such that scores of 0–1 indicate low risk, 2–3 indicate moderate risk, and 4–15 indicate high risk. For the internalizing items on the secondary school form, cut scores have been established such that scores of 0–3 indicate low risk, 4–5 indicate moderate risk, and 6–18 indicate high risk.

The SRSS-IE has been validated in a sample of 12,141 sixth- through twelfth-grade students from 13 schools in 3 states, establishing adequate internal consistency (.83–.86) (Lane et al., 2016). Lane and colleagues (2019) compared the results of the SRSS-IE and the BASC-2 BESS in a sample of 624 middle school students and found a strong positive correlation, supporting convergent validity. Moulton and Young (2020) found three items that functioned differently based on student gender and recommended gender-specific cut scores. Moulton and colleagues (2019) also found that the four response options may not adequately discriminate the frequency of the problem behaviors addressed. Based on results from 93 teachers' ratings of 2,122 middle school students, reducing the category response options to two or three, depending on the item, increased category and item information for all 12 items (Moulton et al., 2019). In many cases, teachers were able to determine if the behavior was occurring, but they were unable to differentiate the frequency of the behavior. If response options are adjusted in the future, cut scores would need to be reconsidered as well.

Menzies and Lane (2012) found that the original SRSS scores predicted the number of office disciplinary referrals a child would receive during an academic year. For the SRSS-IE, only the externalizing scale predicted office disciplinary referrals (Gregory et al., 2021). Interestingly, student self-report externalizing problem scores on the SDQ shared a small positive correlation (r = .24) with teacher ratings of externalizing problems on the SRSS in a majority Black female sample (Jones et al., 2020). Due to its brevity, teachers can complete the assessment for an entire classroom in 15–20 minutes, which increases the feasibility of the screening process for schools or districts interested in conducting universal screening for all students. In addition, the SRSS is available at no cost online.

Systematic Screening for Behavior Disorders

The Systematic Screening for Behavior Disorders (SSBD) (Walker & Severson, 1992) is a multiple-gated procedure for screening, which involves a process of screening steps that increase in intensity as a student progresses through each step. The purpose of this process is to potentially overidentify students in the first gate and then narrow down the pool of focal students as they move through each gate in order to devote time and resources to "true positive" cases. The SSBD identifies students in preschool through grade 9 who are at risk for either externalizing or internalizing disorders. The second edition of the SSBD (SSBD-2) (Walker et al., 2014) was updated for norming purposes.

The SSBD-2 procedure consists of two steps. At stage 1, teachers are asked to identify (1) the 10 students with the most internalizing problems and (2) the 10 students with the most externalizing problems. Teachers are instructed that no student can appear on both lists. Only the top three students on each list (six in total) proceed to the next stage. During stage 2, teachers complete two rating scales for each of these six students, which assess the frequency and intensity of the internalizing and externalizing behaviors of each student. These two rating scales are called the Critical Events Index and the Combined Frequency Index. The system is available through Ancora Publishing for $243, which includes the manual and screening materials for 2 preschool/kindergarten classrooms and 10 classrooms in grades 1–9. Classroom packets can also be purchased individually for an additional cost.

Overall, there is evidence for the reliability of the original SSBD. For example, researchers reported internal consistency coefficients ranging from .88–.90 for the adaptive and maladaptive subscales (Richardson et al., 2009). The internalizing and externalizing critical events indices had lower reliability coefficients when examined separately from the combined frequency indices, .54 and .73, respectively (Richardson et al., 2009). Additionally, the SSBD-2 correlates with similar screening measures such as the SRSS (Lane et al., 2014) and the Achenbach System of Empirically Based Assessment (Richardson et al., 2009). Richardson and colleagues (2009) provided criterion validity evidence for the SSBD-2, with the SSBD-2 predicting student behavioral records in school and grade point averages. Alkherainej and Alebrahim (2019) published a study validating an Arabic version of the SSBD-2 that they developed in a sample of 77 teachers and 346 students in grades 1–9 in Kuwait. While teacher nomination procedures have become less popular due to their subjectivity in referring students with pronounced externalizing symptoms while neglecting those with less-noticeable behavioral or emotional problems (Loades & Mastroyannopoulou, 2010; Pearcy et al., 1993), there is support for the use of the SSBD-2 as a screening tool within the school setting.

NARROWBAND SCREENING MEASURES

In this section, we review available screening methods and measures that include content specific to either the social, emotional, or behavioral domain of child strengths and challenges. In some instances, these narrowband measures focus on a singular disorder (e.g., depression), whereas others focus on a single domain (e.g., externalizing problems). One of the benefits of narrowband screening measures is the ability to maintain brevity and focus on one risk area that might be of most interest for a particular purpose. Below is a review of some of the more commonly used narrowband screening measures and methods, presented in alphabetical order.

Children's Depression Inventory, Second Edition

The second edition of the Children's Depression Inventory (CDI 2) (Kovacs, 2011) is a set of tools for assessing depressive symptoms among youth ages 7–17 years. The CDI 2 assesses both emotional and functional problems. Because the full-length CDI 2 self-report (CDI 2:SR) requires 15 minutes to administer, a short form of the measure was developed specifically for screening purposes. The short self-report form (CDI 2:SR(S)) consists of 12 items written at the grade 1.5 reading level and takes approximately 5 minutes to complete. Parent- and teacher-report forms are also available for use. The teacher report form is structured similarly to the short self-report form (12 items, 5 minutes to complete). The parent report is a 17-item form that can be completed in 10 minutes. Both of these forms are written at the grade 2 reading level.

The standardization sample for the CDI 2:SR short form consisted of 1,100 children and adolescents ages 7–17 years from 28 U.S. states (Kovacs, 2011). The sample was selected to contain an equal number of boys and girls and to closely match (within 1%) the 2000 U.S. Census figures regarding race/ethnicity. For the parent (CDI 2:P) and teacher (CDI 2:T) forms, standardization samples from the original CDI were updated to include a greater number of children from racial/ethnic minority groups. As a result, the final norming samples for both the CDI 2:P and CDI 2:T were approximately representative (within 5%) of the 2000 U.S. Census figures. In terms of the internal consistency of the measure, alpha values for the total scores on the CDI 2:SR(S) ranged from .77 to .85, the CDI 2:T ranged from .86 to .91, and the CDI 2:P ranged from .85 to .91. Test–retest reliability for the CDI 2:SR(S) ranged from .77 to .92 across a 2- to 4-week time frame; test–retest data for the CDI 2:T and CDI 2:P were not available. The correlation between the teacher and parent forms on the total score and subscales ranged from .40–.61. Evidence of interrater reliability was not presented for the short form of the self-report, but the full form correlations with the teacher and parent forms ranged from .18 to .53. Detullio and colleagues (2022) found a medium correlation (r = .36) between CDI/CDI 2 scores and suicidality.

The original version of the CDI short form also has validity evidence for use with youth with physical disabilities (De la Vega et al., 2016). However, measurement invariance studies have identified DIF based on gender and structural differences for African American, White, and Hispanic subsamples (Gonzales-Backen et al., 2020; Jelinek et al., 2021). Therefore, more research is necessary to establish psychometric evidence for use across diverse populations. The CDI 2 costs approximately $4/administration and is available in English only through Pearson clinical assessments.

Conners, Fourth Edition

The Conners 4th Edition (CRS-4) (Conners, 2022) is a series of rating scales that assesses externalizing behavior problems such as oppositional behaviors and hyperactivity. There are parent- and teacher-report forms of the scales for children and adolescents ages 6–18 and a self-report form for children ages 8–18. The CRS-4 includes both long forms (109–118 items) that take approximately 12–15 minutes to complete and short forms (49–53 items) for each informant that require about 5–7 minutes to complete. Although the long forms are too cumbersome for use as screening tools, the short forms may be appropriate for these purposes. In addition, there is a 12-item ADHD index scale and four brief *Diagnostic and Statistical Manual of Mental Disorders, Fifth Edition* (DSM-5) (American Psychiatric Association, 2013) Symptom Scales that screen for ADHD, inattentive type; ADHD, hyperactive–impulsive type; conduct disorder; and oppositional defiant disorder. The CRS-4 can be administered on paper or online and is scored digitally. It can be purchased online for $5.50 for a single use in any of the available languages (English, Spanish, and French Canadian).

The CRS-4 was normed based on a representative sample of children and adolescents ages 6–18 from U.S. and Canadian census figures, stratified based on age, gender, race/ethnicity, parental education level, and geographic region. The CRS-4 has demonstrated excellent internal consistency with a median omega coefficient of .94 across subscales and raters. Test–retest reliabilities had a median value of .89, and values for interrater reliabilities had a median of .84 for the parent form and a median of .52 for the teacher form (Conners, 2022).

The CRS-4 is often used as a diagnostic aid or for treatment monitoring, as well as a research tool. The authors of the CRS-4 also suggest that the instrument can be effectively used as a screening measure to screen for children and adolescents with ADHD, learning problems, or externalizing behavior problems (Conners, 2022).

Multidimensional Anxiety Scale for Children, Second Edition

The Multidimensional Anxiety Scale for Children (MASC 2) (March, 2013) is a 50-item screener designed to assess dimensions of anxiety in children and adolescents ages 8–19 years. Both a self-report form (MASC 2-SR) and a parent-rating form (MASC 2-P) are available. The six subscales include separation anxiety/phobias, generalized anxiety disorder index, social anxiety, obsessions and compulsions, physical symptoms, and harm avoidance. In addition, an anxiety probability score can be computed. The MASC 2 is written at the second-grade reading level, making it suitable for use with most children ages 8 and up and their parents. For children between the ages of 8 and 9 and those with reading difficulties, it is appropriate to read the items aloud. Although the MASC 2 is suitable for screening large groups, it should be noted that administration takes approximately 15 minutes. The MASC 2 is available in English only through Pearson clinical assessments for about $4 per administration.

The normative sample included 1,800 self-report ratings and 1,600 parent ratings, most of which were completed by mothers (March, 2013). The sample was weighted to match U.S. and Canadian census data, such that children and adolescents in North America were considered to be the reference group. It was noted that anxiety scores tended to be higher for females and younger children. According to the technical manual, the MASC 2-SR and the MASC-2 P have adequate internal consistency (.89–.92). Interrater reliability for both forms ranges from .43 to .48, and test–retest reliability estimates range from .90 to .94. It should be noted that these psychometric properties might not hold for special populations. For example, Kaat and Lecavalier (2015) found that internal consistency and test–retest reliability for the self- and parent-report forms were acceptable among children with autism spectrum disorder (ASD), but interrater reliability was poor, especially for younger children with more severe ASD symptoms. The structure of the self-report was investigated and confirmed in a sample of 676 Latinx adolescents (Rapp et al., 2022). The same researchers established convergent validity between the MASC-2 and the Youth Self-Report.

Reynolds Adolescent Depression Scale, Second Edition

The Reynolds Adolescent Depression Scale, Second Edition (RADS-2) (Reynolds, 2002), was designed to assess adolescent depressive symptoms in school, community, and clinical settings. The RADS-2 is a self-report tool that is recommended for use with adolescents ages 11–20 years to estimate risk for clinical levels of depression by assessing the following symptom areas: dysphoric mood (e.g., sadness), anhedonia/negative affect, negative self-evaluation, and somatic complaints (e.g., fatigue). The RADS-2 consists of 30 items written on average at the grade 2 level and is available in both English and Spanish. It can be administered in approximately 5 minutes to an individual or a group. In addition, there is a short-form version (RADS-2:SF) that takes only 2–3 minutes to administer. Either form could be feasible as a screener for depression. According to the Psychological Assessment Resources website, test booklets for the RADS-2 cost approximately $4 per administration, and the RADS-2:SF is approximately $3 per administration. The decision to use either the RADS-2:SF or the full version is likely to be a trade-off between practical considerations, such as cost or ease of administration, and the psychometric properties of the measures.

The RADS-2 was normed based on a re-standardization sample (N = 3,300) that was collected to resemble the 2000 U.S. census figures. Most students identified as Caucasian (70.5%) and were living with both parents (54.5%). It is worth noting that female adolescents endorsed a greater severity of depressive symptoms than males, a finding that is thought to reflect gender differences in this population. Internal consistency values were high, ranging from .91–.96. Vassar and Bradley (2012) reported alpha values ranging from .70 to .97 in school, community, and clinical settings. The test–retest reliability coefficient for scores taken approximately 2 weeks apart was .84 for the total depression score and .77–.84 for the subscales. In terms of validity evidence, the total score and subscale scores on the RADS-2 are correlated with several other internalizing measures (e.g., the total depression score is correlated .77 with the Revised Children's Manifest Anxiety Scale). The RADS-2:SF is less widely used but also appears to have acceptable psychometric properties. One study suggested that the 10-item RADS-2:SF demonstrated psychometric equivalence across age, gender, and ethnic groups among a sample of adolescents in New Zealand (Szabo et al., 2014). Research supports the use of the RADS-2 in clinical and inpatient settings (Gutierrez & Osman, 2009; Osman et al., 2010).

Screen for Child Anxiety Related Emotional Disorders

The Screen for Child Anxiety Related Emotional Disorders (SCARED) (Birmaher et al., 1999) is a 41-item screener that is meant to identify youth at risk for anxiety disorders. Items are rated on a three-point response scale. The estimated administration time is approximately 10 minutes, and the measure is free and available online in child and parent report versions. The five factors include panic/somatic, generalized anxiety, separation anxiety, social phobia, and school phobia. Risk scores are calculated for overall anxiety and for each of the factors. The intended audience for this measure includes psychiatrists and clinicians; however, the SCARED has also been found to be useful in school settings (e.g., Hale et al., 2005). It should be noted that this screener may function differently among minoritized populations in that a five-factor structure has been found to apply to predominantly White samples, but a three-factor structure (panic/somatic, social phobia, and generalized anxiety) emerged among a sample of African American adolescents (Boyd et al., 2003).

The research involved in developing the SCARED indicated that internal consistency for the total score on the full version is approximately .90. Intraclass correlation coefficients describing parent–child agreement on the total score and subscales ranged from .14–.19, with higher agreement among anxious children than nonanxious children (Behrens et al., 2019). Test–retest reliability was found to be .59 for the youth report and .74 for the parent form (Behrens et al., 2019). It has also been suggested that the SCARED is useful in discriminating between anxiety disorders and depression, as well as between different diagnoses of anxiety disorders. Recently, two studies evaluated and demonstrated adequate reliability and validity in two specialized samples: children with ASD and Native American children (Carruthers et al., 2020; Runyon et al., 2020).

In addition to the full version, a five-item short form of the SCARED is available. The five-item short form has similar psychometric properties to the full version (Birmaher et al., 1999) and has been tested as a mental health screener implemented by nurses in secondary school settings (Allison et al., 2014). Scores range from 0–10 on the short form, with scores from 3–10 indicating risk for anxiety. The short form is also available for free online.

Social Skills Improvement System

The Social Skills Improvement System (SSIS) (Gresham & Elliott, 2008) is a set of tools targeted for use in screening and classifying students who may be experiencing difficulties related to social functioning. The Social Skills Improvement System-Rating Scales (SSIS-RS) can be used to assess the following domains: social skills, problem behaviors, and academic competence. Teacher and parent forms are available for students ages 3–18, and separate student forms are available for ages 8–12 and 13–18. Because the SSIS-RS can take between 15–25 minutes to complete, it may have limited usefulness as a screener.

The SSIS Performance Screening Guide (SSIS-PSG) (Elliott & Gresham, 2008) offers a more efficient option targeted toward school-based universal screening efforts. The SSIS-PSG was developed for use in screening of social, behavioral, and academic skills for students from preschool through high school. Three packets are available for different age ranges: preschool, elementary, and secondary. The SSIS-PSG offers teachers the opportunity to rate students on a five-point scale in each of four performance areas (prosocial behavior, motivation to learn, math skills, and reading skills) based on expectations for each of the three developmental ranges. Because teachers complete only four items per student, the brevity of this measure increases its value as a screener. The manual suggests that, on average, it takes approximately 30 minutes to complete the screening information for a classroom of students.

The SSIS-PSG was developed with 138 teachers in the United States (Elliott & Gresham, 2008). The majority of the participants were female teachers at the elementary level, and the norming sample was most representative of the South and North Central regions of the country. Test–retest reliability coefficients ranged from .53 to .74 and were higher at the elementary and secondary levels than at the preschool level across all domains. Intraclass correlation coefficients between raters ranged from .37 to .73, with agreement higher among preschool staff than elementary or secondary personnel. Data gathered to assess convergent validity with the teacher form of the SSIS Rating Scales indicated correlations of .63–70 between the prosocial behavior ratings on the SSIS-PSG and the social skills scale of the SSIS and correlations of .60–.70 between reading/math skills on the SSIS-PSG and academic competence on the SSIS. In addition, among the elementary student population, there is evidence of convergent validity with the SRSS-IE (Lane et al., 2015). At the elementary level, there is evidence of predictive validity of the SSIS-PSG with regard to academic subject grades and, to a lesser extent, conduct grades (Krach et al., 2017). Teachers generally provided high ratings of social validity and utility of the screening measure (Oakes et al., 2016).

The SSIS manual does not provide cut scores for the SSIS-PSG. Two studies have completed analyses to establish cut scores (Kettler et al., 2012; Krach et al., 2017). Kettler and colleagues (2012) established cut scores in an Australian elementary sample using a national achievement test, while Krach et al. (2017) completed a receiver operating characteristic curve analysis with a sample of African American elementary school students to establish discriminant power for the three subscales: reading skills, math skills, and prosocial skills. They found that teacher ratings on the SSIS-PSG reading and math scales predicted reading and math grades, while the prosocial ratings were no better at predicting conduct grades than chance (Krach et al., 2017).

One of the main limitations of the SSIS is the lack of a student or parent report form. In addition, the norming samples used to develop the SSIS screener were fairly small and not fully representative of teachers in the Northeast or Western regions of the country, as well as those working outside of the elementary school level. Given that the majority of the focus in development and research on the SSIS-PSG has been placed on elementary-age students, additional research is needed to explore the usefulness of the SSIS-PSG as a screener for students at other grade levels. SSIS-PSG forms are currently sold in kits of 4 for preschool and kits of 10 for elementary and secondary classrooms, at the cost of approximately $7 per kit. Each kit can be used to screen one classroom, consisting of a maximum of 25 students.

CONCLUSION

Screening for SEB risk has gained increasing attention as a proactive and cost-efficient practice for addressing a wide range of SEB challenges in youth (Dowdy et al., 2010; Humphrey & Wigelsworth, 2016; Severson et al., 2007). To address these challenges most effectively, it is crucial to understand the population of interest. As schools have become increasingly diverse, it is imperative to expand the scope of screening to include cultural considerations, providing a more inclusive and holistic view of each student's social, emotional, and behavioral symptoms (Dowdy et al., 2014). Many of the available screeners were developed using WEIRD (White, educated, industrialized, rich, and democratic) samples, and the applicability of some screeners has revealed varying levels of effectiveness when implemented across cultural contexts (Du et al., 2008; Ghanizadeh et al., 2007; Kersten et al., 2016; Samad et al., 2008). In order to best serve a multicultural population of students, culturally robust screening is necessary.

Prior to the screening process, ethical issues for universal screening with socioculturally and linguistically diverse students are important to consider. This is particularly important when addressing aspects such as community acceptance, family rights, the identification of individuals eligible for services, and the delivery of those services (Chafouleas et al., 2010). Attitudes about behavioral and emotional issues and the usefulness of screening and intervention will vary across individual families and cultural groups (Dowdy et al., 2014). In order to effectively reach these families, psychologists and practitioners should collaborate with families and trusted members of the community throughout the entire screening process to gain trust and rapport.

Language plays a major role throughout the entire screening process. Before screening, school psychologists and practitioners must consider the dominant language of the students they aim to serve. Language considerations should be individualized, collecting information about student language proficiency, history, and administration preference (i.e., speaking vs. reading) to accommodate each student's needs. Psychologists and practitioners can offer students multiple language versions of the screener or face-to-face delivery to reduce language barriers during implementation (e.g., Kersten et al., 2016). Language equivalence for the screener items must be demonstrated before administering a translated version of a screener to ensure constructs are measured as intended (Frick et al., 2020). It is important to note that simply translating a screener is insufficient; failing to have screening assessments vetted by diverse experts from the population of interest could lead to the inclusion of items that are culturally or linguistically bound, limiting the capability to draw meaningful conclusions from screening data with socioculturally diverse youth (American Educational Research Association et al., 1999).

As screening measures continue to be updated and developed, it is crucial for both researchers and practitioners to keep up to date on the available SEB screening instruments, their uses, and their properties. The science of behavioral and emotional screening is still in its early years of development and optimization, and there are unanswered questions regarding how to best implement universal screening practices to maximize validity and effectiveness of the screeners within a diverse population of students. With the increasing globalization of behavioral and mental health service delivery, further research is needed to continue providing evidence for the use of SEB screeners among socioculturally and linguistically diverse populations, including understanding when and how to develop screening instruments designed specifically for use with diverse samples as opposed to adapting existing measures. Moreover, research should consider additional factors in the decision-making process, including optimal screening schedules and procedures, in order to assist practitioners with implementing a screening program in alignment with best practices. Only through continued collaboration will researchers and practitioners be able to design evidence-based practices in screening using instruments that are both psychometrically sound and feasible for use in applied settings.

REFERENCES

Achenbach, T. M. (2009). *The Achenbach System of Empirically Based Assessment (ASEBA): Development, findings, theory, and applications.* University of Vermont Research Center for Children, Youth, & Families.

Akpa, O. M., & Bamgboye, E. A. (2015). Correlates of the quality of life of adolescents in families affected by HIV/AIDS in Benue State, Nigeria. *Vulnerable Children and Youth Studies, 10*(3), 225–242.

Alkherainej, K., & Alebrahim, S. (2019). Preliminary psychometric findings on the Arabic Systematic Screening for Behavior Disorders. *Assessment for Effective Intervention, 44*(3), 184–196.

Allison, V. L., Nativio, D. G., Mitchell, A. M., Ren, D., & Yuhasz, J. (2014). Identifying symptoms of depression and anxiety in students in the school setting. *The Journal of School Nursing, 30*(3), 165–172.

American Educational Research Association, American Psychological Association, & National Council on Measurement Education. (1999). *The standards for educational and psychological testing.*

American Psychiatric Association. (1994). *Diagnostic and statistical manual of mental disorders* (4th ed.).

American Psychiatric Association. (2013). *Diagnostic and statistical manual of mental disorders* (5th ed.).

Basting, E. J., Naser, S., & Goncy, E. A. (2022). Assessing the factor structure and measurement invariance of the BASC-3 Behavioral and Emotional Screening System student form across race/ethnicity and gender. *Assessment for Effective Intervention, 48*(1), 43–51.

Behrens, B., Swetlitz, C., Pine, D. S., & Pagliaccio, D. (2019). The Screen for Child Anxiety Related Emotional Disorders (SCARED): Informant discrepancy, measurement invariance, and test-retest reliability. *Child Psychiatry & Human Development, 50,* 473–482.

Bergmann, P., Lucke, C., Nguyen, T., Jellinek, M., & Murphy, J. M. (2018). Identification and utility of a short form of the Pediatric Symptom Checklist—Youth Self-Report (PSC-17-Y). *European Journal of Psychological Assessment, 36*(1), 56–64.

Birmaher, B., Brent, D. A., Chiappetta, L., Bridge, J., Monga, S., & Baugher, M. (1999). Psychometric properties of the Screen for Child Anxiety Related Emotional Disorders (SCARED): A replication study. *Journal of the American Academy of Child & Adolescent Psychiatry, 38*(10), 1230–1236.

Boothroyd, R. A., & Armstrong, M. (2010). An examination of the psychometric properties of the Pediatric Symptom Checklist with children enrolled in Medicaid. *Journal of Emotional and Behavioral Disorders, 18*(2), 113–126. *https://psycnet.apa.org/doi/10.1177/1063426609337604*

Boyd, R. C., Ginsburg, G. S., Lambert, S. F., Cooley, M. R., & Campbell, K. D. M. (2003). Screen for Child Anxiety Related Emotional Disorders (SCARED): Psychometric properties in an African-American parochial high school sample. *Journal of the American Academy of Child & Adolescent Psychiatry, 42*(10), 1188–1196.

Brann, P., Lethbridge, M. J., & Mildred, H. (2018). The young adult Strengths and Difficulties Questionnaire (SDQ) in routine clinical practice. *Psychiatry Research, 264,* 340–345.

Carruthers, S., Kent, R., Hollocks, M. J., & Simonoff, E. (2020). Brief report: Testing the psychometric properties of the Spence Children's Anxiety Scale (SCAS) and the Screen for Child Anxiety Related Emotional Disorders (SCARED) in Autism Spectrum Disorder. *Journal of Autism and Developmental Disorders, 50,* 2625–2632.

Chafouleas, S. M., Kilgus, S. P., & Wallach, N. (2010). Ethical dilemmas in school-based behavioral screening. *Assessment for Effective Intervention, 35*(4), 245–252.

Conners, C. K. (2022). *Conners 4th Edition.* Multi-Health Systems.

De la Vega, R., Racine, M., Sánchez-Rodríguez, E., Solé, E., Castarlenas, E., Jensen, M. P., & Miró, J. (2016). Psychometric properties of the short form of the Children's Depression Inventory (CDI-S) in young people with physical disabilities. *Journal of Psychosomatic Research, 90,* 57–61.

Detullio, D., Millen, D. H., & Kennedy, T. D. (2022). A meta-analysis of the association between the Children's Depression Inventory (CDI) and suicidality. *Aggression and Violent Behavior, 64,* 1–11.

Dever, B. V., & Gaier, K. (2021). Psychometric properties of the Behavior Assessment System for Children–3 Behavioral and Emotional Screening System student-report form among a predominantly Latinx elementary school sample. *Journal of Psychoeducational Assessment, 39*(1), 128–133.

Dever, B. V., Kamphaus, R. W., Dowdy, E., Raines, T. C., & DiStefano, C. (2013). Surveillance of middle and high school mental health risk by student self-report screener. *Western Journal of Emergency Medicine, 14*(4), 384–390.

Dever, B. V., Raines, T. C., & Barclay, C. M. (2012). Chasing the unicorn: Practical implementation of universal screening for behavioral and emotional risk. *School Psychology Forum*, 6(4), 108–118.

DiStefano, C., Liu, J., & Burgess, Y. (2017). Investigating the structure of the Pediatric Symptoms Checklist in the preschool setting. *Journal of Psychoeducational Assessment*, *35*(5), 494–505.

Dowdy, E., Harrell-Williams, L., Dever, B. V., Furlong, M. J., Moore, S., Raines, T., & Kamphaus, R. W. (2016). Predictive validity of a student self-report screener of behavioral and emotional risk in an urban high school. *School Psychology Review*, *45*(4), 458–476.

Dowdy, E., Kamphaus, R. W., Twyford, J. M., & Dever, B. V. (2014). Culturally competent behavioral and emotional screening. In M. Weist, N. Lever, C. Bradshaw, & J. Owens (Eds.), *Handbook of school mental health* (pp. 311–321). Springer.

Dowdy, E., Ritchey, K., & Kamphaus, R. W. (2010). School-based screening: A population-based approach to inform and monitor children's mental health needs. *School Mental Health*, *2*, 166–176.

Downs, A., Strand, P. S., Heinrichs, N., & S. Cerna (2012). Use of the teacher version of the Strengths and Difficulties Questionnaire with German and American preschoolers. *Early Education and Development*, *23*(4), 493–516.

Drummond, T. (1994). *Student Risk Screening Scale (SRSS)* [Database record]. APA PsycTests.

Du, Y., Kou, J., & Coghill, D. (2008). The validity, reliability and normative scores of the parent, teacher and self-report versions of the Strengths and Difficulties Questionnaire in China. *Child and Adolescent Psychiatry and Mental Health*, *2*, 8.

Edyburn, K. L., Dowdy, E., DiStefano, C., Bertone, A., & Greer, F. (2020). Measurement invariance of the English and Spanish BASC-3 behavioral and emotional screening system parent preschool forms. *Early Childhood Research Quarterly*, *51*, 307–316.

Eklund, K., Kilgus, S. P., Barber, A., Dubose, K., Collins, B., & Eikenmeyer, M. (2023). The effect of student race/ethnicity on the diagnostic accuracy of the Social, Academic, and Emotional Behavior Risk Screener (SAEBRS). *Psychology in the Schools*, *60*(10), 3878–3895.

Eklund, K., Kilgus, S., von der Embse, N., Beardmore, M., & Tanner, N. (2017). Use of universal screening scores to predict distal academic and behavioral outcomes: A multilevel approach. *Psychological Assessment*, *29*(5), 486–499.

Elliot, S. N., & Gresham, F. M. (2008). *Social Skills Improvement System—Performance Screening Guide*. Pearson.

Fallon, L. M., Veiga, M. B., Susilo, A., & Kilgus, S. P. (2023). Do teachers' perceptions of high cultural responsiveness predict better behavioral outcomes for students? *Behavioral Disorders*, *48*(2), 97–105.

Frick, P. J., Barry, C. T., & Kamphaus, R. W. (2020). *Clinical assessment of child and adolescent personality and behavior* (4th ed.). Springer.

Gall, G., Pagano, M. E., Desmond, M. S., Perrin, J. M., & Murphy, J. M. (2000). Utility of psychosocial screening at a school-based health center. *Journal of School Health*, *70*(7), 292–298.

Ghanizadeh, A., Izadpanah, A., & Abdollahi, G. (2007). Scale validation of the Strengths and Difficulties Questionnaire in Iranian children. *Iran Journal of Psychiatry*, *1*(2), 65–71.

Glover, T. A., & Albers, C. A. (2007). Considerations for evaluating universal screening assessments. *Journal of School Psychology*, *45*(2), 117–135.

Gonzales-Bracken, M. A., Holcomb, J. E., & McWey, L. M. (2020). Cross-ethnic measurement equivalence of the Children's Depression Inventory among youth in foster care. *Journal of Emotional and Behavioral Disorders*, *28*(3), 144–155.

Goodman, R. (1997). The Strengths and Difficulties Questionnaire: A research note. *Journal of Child Psychology and Psychiatry*, *38*(5), 581–586.

Goodman, R., Ford, T., Simmons, H., Gatward, R., & Meltzer, H. (2000). Using the Strengths and Difficulties Questionnaire (SDQ) to screen for child psychiatric disorders in a community sample. *British Journal of Psychiatry*, *17*(7), 534–539.

Goodman, R., Meltzer, H., & Bailey, V. (2003). The Strengths and Difficulties Questionnaire: A pilot study on the validity of the self-report version. *International Review of Psychiatry*, *15*, 173–177.

Goodman, R., Renfrew, D., & Mullick, M. (2000). Predicting type of psychiatric disorder from Strengths and Difficulties Questionnaire (SDQ) scores in child mental health clinics in London and Dhaka. *European Child and Adolescent Psychiatry*, 9(2), 129–134.

Goodman, R., & Scott, S. (1999). Comparing the Strengths and Difficulties Questionnaire and the Child Behavior Checklist: Is small beautiful? *Journal of Abnormal Child Psychology*, *27*(1), 17–24.

Gregory, C., Graybill, E. C., Barger, B., Roach, A. T., & Lane, K. (2021). Predictive validity of the Student Risk Screening Scale—Internalizing and Externalizing (SRSS-IE) scores. *Journal of Emotional and Behavioral Disorders*, *29*(2), 105–112.

Gresham, F. M., & Elliott, S. N. (2008). *Social Skills Improvement System (SSIS) rating scales manual*. Pearson.

Gutierrez, P. M., & Osman, A. (2009). Getting the best return on your screening investment: An analysis of the Suicidal Ideation Questionnaire and Reynolds Adolescent Depression Scale. *School Psychology Review*, *38*(2), 200–217.

Hale, W. I., Raaijmakers, Q., Muris, P., & Meeus, W. (2005). Psychometric properties of the Screen for Child Anxiety Related Emotional Disorders (SCARED) in the general adolescent population. *Journal of The American Academy of Child & Adolescent Psychiatry*, *44*(3), 283–290.

Hall, C. L., Guo, B., Valentine, A. Z., Groom, M. J., Daley, D., Sayal, K., & Hollis, C. (2019). The validity of the Strengths and Difficulties Questionnaire

(SDQ) for children with ADHD symptoms. *PLOS One, 14*(6).

Harry, M. L., Acevedo, J., & Crea, T. M. (2019). Assessing the factor structure of the Spanish language parent Strengths and Difficulties Questionnaire (SDQ) in Honduras. *PLOS One, 14*(3), e0214394.

Herman, K. C., Reinke, W. M., Thompson, A. M., Hawley, K., Wallis, K., Stormont, M., & Peters, C. (2020). A public health approach to reducing the societal prevalence and burden of youth mental health problems: Introduction to the special issue. *School Psychology Review, 50*(1), 8–16.

Humphrey, N., & Wigelsworth, M. (2016). Making the case for universal school-based mental health screening. *Emotional and Behavioural Difficulties, 21(1)*, 22–42.

Izumi, J. T., & Eklund, K. (2023). Universal screening for social-emotional and behavioral risk: Differential item functioning on the SAEBRS. *School Psychology, 38*(4), 238–246.

Jelínek, M., Květon, P., Buresova, I., & Klimusova, H. (2021) Measuring depression in adolescence: Evaluation of a hierarchical factor model of the Children's Depression Inventory and measurement invariance across boys and girls. *PLOS One, 16*(4), e0249943.

Jellinek, M. S., Murphy, J. M., & Burns, B. J. (1986). Brief psychosocial screening in outpatient pediatric practice. *The Journal of Pediatrics, 109*(2), 371–378.

Jenkins, A., Thoman, S., Wang, Y., von der Embse, N., Kilgus, S., & Reynolds, F. (2021). Identifying type and evaluating stability of behavioral risk. *Psychology in the Schools, 58*, 2225–2237.

Jones, C., Graybill, E., Barger, B., & Roach, A. T. (2020). Examining the predictive validity of behavior screeners across measures and respondents. *Psychology in the Schools, 57*, 923–936.

Juechter, J., Dever, B., & Kamphaus, R. (2012). Mental health screening and academic outcomes in elementary school. *School Psychology Forum: Research in Practice*, 6(4), 137–147.

Kaat, A. J., & Lecavalier, L. (2015). Reliability and validity of parent- and child-rated anxiety measures in Autism Spectrum Disorder. *Journal of Autism and Developmental Disorders*, 45(10), 3219–3231.

Kamphaus, R. W., & Reynolds, C. R. (2007). *Behavior Assessment System for Children—Second Edition (BASC-2): Behavioral and Emotional Screening System (BESS)*. Pearson.

Kamphaus, R. W., & Reynolds, C. R. (2015). *Behavior Assessment System for Children—Third Edition (BASC-3): Behavioral and Emotional Screening System (BESS)*. Pearson.

Keller, F., & Langmeyer, A. N. (2019). An item response theory analysis of the Strengths and Difficulties Questionnaire (SDQ). *European Journal of Psychological Assessment, 35*(2), 266–279.

Kersten, P., Dudley, M., Nayar, S., et al. (2016). Cross-cultural acceptability and utility of the Strengths and Difficulties Questionnaire: Views of families. *BMC Psychiatry, 16*(1), 347.

Kettler, R. J., Elliott, S. N., Davies, M., & Griffin, P. (2012). Testing a multi-stage screening system: Predicting performance on Australia's national achievement test using teachers' ratings of academic and social behaviors. *School Psychology International, 33*, 93–111.

Kilgus, S. P., Eklund, K., Nathaniel, P., Taylor, C. N., & Sims, W. A. (2016). Psychometric defensibility of the Social, Academic, and Emotional Behavior Risk Screener (SAEBRS) Teacher Rating Scale and multiple gating procedure within elementary and middle school samples. *Journal of School Psychology*, 5(8), 21–39.

Kilgus, S. P., Eklund, K., von der Embse, N. P., Weist, M., Barber, A. J., Kaul, M., & Dodge, S. (2021). Structural validity and reliability of Social, Academic, and Emotional Behavior Risk Screener–Student rating scale scores: A replication study. *Assessment for Effective Intervention*, 46(4), 259–269.

Kilgus, S. P., & von der Embse, N. P. (2014). *Social, academic, and emotional behavior risk screener*. FastBridge.

Kilgus, S. P., von der Embse, N. P., Taylor, C. N., Van Wie, M. P., & Sims, W. A. (2018). Diagnostic accuracy of a universal screening multiple gating procedure: A replication study. *School Psychology Quarterly, 33*(4), 582–589.

Kovacs, M. (2011). *Children's Depression Inventory 2nd edition (CDI 2): Technical manual*. Multi-Health Systems.

Krach, S. K., McCreery, M. P., Wang, Y., Mohammadiamin, H., & Cirks, C. K. (2017). Diagnostic utility of the Social Skills Improvement System Performance Screening Guide. *Journal of Psychoeducational Assessment, 35*(4), 391–409.

Lai, K. Y. C., Luk, E. S. L., Leung, P. W. L., Wong, A.S., Law, L., & Ho, K. (2010). Validation of the Chinese version of the Strengths and Difficulties Questionnaire in Hong Kong. *Social Psychiatry and Psychiatric Epidemiology*, 45(12), 1179–1186.

Lane, K. L., Kalberg, J. R., Parks, R. J., & Carter, E. W. (2008). Student risk screening scale initial evidence for score reliability and validity at the high school level. *Journal of Emotional and Behavioral Disorders, 16*(3), 178–190.

Lane, K. L., Oakes, W. P., Cantwell, E. D., Menzies, H. M., Schatschneider, C., Lambert, W., & Common, E. A. (2016). Psychometric evidence of SRSS-IE scores in middle and high schools. *Journal of Emotional and Behavioral Disorders, 25*(4), 233–245.

Lane, K. L., Oakes, W., Carter, E. W., Lambert, W. E., & Jenkins, A. B. (2013). Initial evidence for the reliability and validity of the Student Risk Screening Scale for internalizing and externalizing behaviors at the middle school level. *Assessment for Effective Intervention, 39*(1), 24–38.

Lane, K. L., Oakes, W. P., Common, E. A., Brunsting, N., Zorigian, K., Hicks, T., & Lane, N. A. (2019).

A comparison between SRSS-IE and BASC-2 BESS scores at the middle school level. *Behavioral Disorders, 44*(3), 162–174.

Lane, K. L., Oakes, W. P., Ennis, R. P., & Royer, D. J. (2015). Additional evidence of convergent validity between SSRS-IE and SSIS-PSG scores. *Behavioral Disorders, 40*, 213–229.

Lane, K. L., Richards-Tutor, C., Oakes, W. P., & Connor, K. (2014). Initial evidence for the reliability and validity of the Student Risk Screening Scale with elementary age English learners. *Assessment for Effective Intervention, 39*(4), 219–232.

Liu, S.-K., Chien, Y.-L., Shang, C.-Y., Lin, C.-H., Liu, Y.-C., & Gau, S. S.-F. (2013). Psychometric properties of the Chinese version of the Strength and Difficulties Questionnaire. *Comprehensive Psychiatry, 54*(6), 720–730.

Loades, M. E., & Mastroyannopoulou K. (2010). Teachers' recognition of children's mental health problems. *Child and Adolescent Mental Health, 15*, 150–156.

March, J. S. (2013). *Multidimensional Anxiety Scale for Children 2nd edition (MASC 2): Technical manual.* Multi-Health Systems.

Matsuishi, T., Nagano, M., Araki, Y., Tanaka, Y., Iwasaki, M., & Yamashita, Y., (2008). Scale properties of the Japanese version of the Strengths and Difficulties Questionnaire (SDQ): A study of infant and school children in community samples. *Brain & Development, 30*(6), 410–415.

Mellor, D. (2004). Furthering the use of the Strengths and Difficulties Questionnaire: Reliability with younger child respondents. *Psychological Assessment, 16*(4), 396–401.

Menzies, H. M., & Lane, K. L. (2012). Validity of the Student Risk Screening Scale: Evidence of predictive validity in a diverse, suburban elementary setting. *Journal of Emotional and Behavioral Disorders, 20*(2), 82–91.

Moulton, S. E., Young, E. L., & Sudweeks, R. R. (2019). Examining the psychometric properties of the SRSS-IE with the nominal response model within a middle school sample. *Assessment for Effective Intervention, 44*(4), 227–240.

Moulton, S. E., & Young, E. L. (2020). An item analysis of gender differences on the SRSS-IE in middle school. *Psychology in the Schools, 58*, 789–803.

Murphy, J. M., Jellinek, M., & Milinsky, S. (1989). The Pediatric Symptom Checklist: Validation in the real world of middle school. *Journal of Pediatric Psychology, 14*(4), 629–639.

Oakes, W. P., Lane, K. L., & Ennis, R. P. (2016). Systematic screening at the elementary level: Considerations for exploring and installing universal behavior screening. *Journal of Applied School Psychology, 32*(3), 215–233.

O'Connell, M. E., Boat, T., & Warner, K. (2009). *Preventing mental, emotional, and behavioral disorders among young people: Progress and possibilities.* The National Academies Press.

Osman, A., Gutierrez, P. M., Bagge, C. L., Fang, Q., & Emmerich, A. (2010). Reynolds Adolescent Depression Scale- Second Edition: A reliable and useful instrument. *Journal of Clinical Psychology* 66(12), 1324–1345.

Pagano, M. E., Cassidy, L. J., Little, M., Murphy, J. M., & Jellinek, M. S. (2000). Identifying psychosocial dysfunction in school-age children: The Pediatric Symptom Checklist as a self-report measure. *Psychology in the Schools, 37*(2), 91.

Pearcy M. T., Clopton J. R., & Pope A. W. (1993). Influences on teacher referral of children to mental health services: Gender, severity, and internalizing versus externalizing problems. *Journal of Emotional and Behavioral Disorders, 1*, 165–169.

Rapp, A. M., Dixon De Silva, L. E., Escovar, E., & Chavira, D. A. (2022). Psychometrics of the Multidimensional Anxiety Scale for Children in Latinx adolescents. *Journal of Latinx Psychology, 10*(1), 71–79.

Reynolds, C. R., & Kamphaus, R. W. (2015). *Behavior Assessment System for Children—Third Edition (BASC-3).* Pearson.

Reynolds, W. M. (2002). *RADS-2: Reynolds Adolescent Depression Scale: Professional manual.* Psychological Assessment Resources.

Richardson, M. J., Caldarella, P., Young, B. J., Young, E. L., & Young, K. R. (2009). Further validation of the Systematic Screening for Behavioral Disorders in middle and junior high school. *Psychology in the Schools, 46*(7), 605–615.

Runyon, K., Barnard-Brak, L., Stevens, T., & Lan, W. (2020). The psychometric properties of the Screen for Child Anxiety Related Emotional Disorders (SCARED) in a Native American child and adolescent population. *Measurement and Evaluation in Counseling and Development, 53*(4), 264–278.

Samad, L., Hollis, C., Prince, M., & Goodman, R. (2005). Child and adolescent psychopathology in a developing country: Testing the validity of the Strengths and Difficulties Questionnaire (Urdu version). *International Journal of Methods in Psychiatric Research, 14*(3), 158–166.

Severson, H. H., Walker, H. M., Hope-Doolittle, J., Kratochwill, T. R., & Gresham, F. M. (2007). Proactive, early screening to detect behaviorally at-risk students: Issues, approaches, emerging innovations, and professional practices. *Journal of School Psychology, 45*(2), 193–223.

Simonian, S. J., & Tarnowski, K. J. (2001). Utility of the Pediatric Symptom Checklist for behavioral screening of disadvantaged children. *Child Psychiatry and Human Development, 31*(4), 269–278.

Smits, I. A. M., Theunissen, M. H. C., Reijneveld, S. A., Nauta, M. H., & Timmerman, M. E. (2018). Measurement invariance of the parent version of the Strengths and Difficulties Questionnaire (SDQ) across community and clinical populations. *European Journal of Psychological Assessment, 34*(4), 238–246.

Speyer, L. G., Auyeung, B., & Murray, A. L. (2023).

Longitudinal invariance of the Strengths and Difficulties Questionnaire across ages 4 to 16 in the ALSPAC sample. *Assessment, 30*(6), 1884–1894.

Stiffler, M. C., & Dever B. V. (2015). *Mental health screening at school: Instrumentation, implementation, and critical issues.* Springer.

Stoppelbein, L., Greening, L., Jordan, S. S., Elkin, T. D., Moll, G., & Pullen, J. (2005). Factor analysis of the Pediatric Symptom Checklist with a chronically ill pediatric population. *Journal of Developmental & Behavioral Pediatrics, 26*(5), 349–355.

Szabo, A., Milfont, R. L., Merry, S. N., Robinson, E. M., Crengle, S., Ameratunga, S. N., & Denny, S. J. (2014). Equivalence of the short form of the Reynolds Adolescent Depression Scale across groups. *Journal of Clinical Child and Adolescent Psychology, 43*(4), 592–600.

Vassar, M., & Bradley, G. (2012). A reliability generalization meta-analysis of coefficient alpha for the Reynolds Adolescent Depression Scale. *Clinical Child Psychology and Psychiatry, 17*(4), 519–527.

von der Embse, N. P., Iaccarino, S., Mankin, A., Kilgus, S. A., & Magen, E. (2017). Development and validation of the Social, Academic, and Emotional Behavior Risk Screener-Student Rating Scale. *Assessment for Effective Intervention, 42*(3), 186–192.

von der Embse, N. P., Kilgus, S. P., Iaccarino, S., & Levi-Nielsen, S. (2017). Screening for student mental health risk: Diagnostic measurement invariance, predictive validity of the Social, Academic, and Emotional Behavior Risk Screener—Student Rating Scale SAEBRS-SRS). *School Mental Health, 9*, 273–283.

von der Embse, N. P., Pendergast, L. L., Kilgus, S. P., & Eklund, K. R. (2016). Evaluating the applied use of a mental health screener: Structural validity of the Social, Academic, and Emotional Behavior Risk Screener. *Psychological Assessment, 28*(10), 1265–1275.

Vugteveen, J., de Bildt, A., Serra, M., de Wolff, M. S., & Timmerman, M. E. (2020). Psychometric properties of the Dutch Strengths and Difficulties Questionnaire (SDQ) in adolescent community and clinical populations. *Assessment, 27*(7), 1476–1489.

Vugteveen, J., de Bildt, A., & Timmerman, M. E. (2022). Normative data for the self-reported and parent-reported Strengths and Difficulties Questionnaire (SDQ) for ages 12–17. *Child and Adolescent Psychiatry and Mental Health, 16*(5).

Walker, H. M., & Severson, H. H. (1992). *Systematic Screening for Behavior Disorders (SSBD)*. Sopris West.

Walker, H. M., Severson, H., & Feil, E. (2014). *Systematic screening for behavior disorders* (2nd ed.). Pacific Northwest.

Whitley, S. F., & Cuenca-Carlino, Y. (2020). Examining the technical adequacy of the Social, Academic, and Emotional Behavior Risk Screener. *Assessment for Effective Intervention, 46*(1), 67–75.

CHAPTER 13

Progress Monitoring within a Culturally Responsive Evaluation Framework

Stephen Kilgus, Evan H. Dart, Ishan Vengurlekar, and Aileen Kangavary

Monitoring of student progress and growth is a pivotal component of the multi-tiered systems of supports (MTSS) model. The purpose of progress monitoring is to evaluate changes in student functioning (e.g., academic, social–emotional, and behavioral [SEB]) in response to an intervention (Pentimonti et al., 2017; Vannest, 2012). More specifically, progress monitoring aims to make data-based decisions about (1) student growth; (2) the effectiveness of the chosen intervention; and (3) when to discontinue, change the intensity of, or adapt interventions (Bruhn et al., 2018). To achieve these aims, progress monitoring employs a multifaceted approach with specialized attention to several components of its implementation (e.g., design, tools, procedure, and analysis; Kilgus et al., 2014). Importantly, data are collected continuously and involve multiple personnel (e.g., teachers and behavioral specialists) to ensure student outcomes are properly assessed (von der Embse et al., 2022). The continuity of data collection is a boon, as it yields multiple data points to enhance accuracy regarding decision making (Kilgus et al., 2016), as well as in-depth information about student functioning throughout intervention implementation. Similarly, various informants boost the validity of assessment and provide multiple perspectives on student functioning.

Typically, the importance of progress monitoring is emphasized in the targeted and intensive domains of the MTSS model (i.e., Tier 2 and Tier 3, respectively). In these tiers, interventions are matched to student challenges to meet their needs. Students may be placed in small-group or individualized interventions that address their presenting difficulties. For instance, a student at risk for behavioral challenges may be placed in Check In/Check Out (CICO), an evidence-based Tier 2 intervention (Drevon et al., 2019). Coupled with placement in an intervention, progress monitoring serves as a crucial way of determining student changes throughout its implementation. Consequently, robust decisions can be made about its effectiveness.

Many tools and methodologies have been utilized to assess student changes in response to an intervention. For example, curriculum-based measurement (CBM) is a widely used and evidence-based tool to monitor academic growth and evaluate instructional interventions (Shinn, 2008; Stecker et al., 2005). Externalizing concerns (e.g., aggression, disruptive behavior, and rule breaking) also possess respective evidence-based assessment methods such as systematic direct observations (SDOs) (Hill et al., 2023) and direct behavior ratings (DBRs) (Matta et al., 2020). Though there is a paucity of validated tools available for assessing internalizing symptoms (Dart et al., 2019, 2020), researchers have opined the importance of self-reporting mechanisms (Heck et al., 2022), which is especially salient considering the recent intensification of youth mental health (Elharake et al., 2022; Kauhanen et al., 2023; Weist et al., 2023). Furthermore, monitoring SEB concerns is particularly challenging, as there is no standard growth rate for improvement (Bruhn et al., 2018). This complicates the already difficult process of monitoring concerns, as practitioners must develop their own criteria for a given construct or behavior of interest.

Despite the complexities surrounding the progress monitoring process, researchers have provided guidelines to address these concerns. SEB progress monitoring can be viewed as a multistep process (Bruhn et al., 2018; von der Embse et al., 2022). After a student is identified for supplemental support—which can be accomplished through the use of universal screening—a necessary next step is to identify the behaviors or constructs that warrant monitoring (e.g., aggression or rule breaking). This should be done in collaboration with parents, teachers, or other relevant personnel. Next, practitioners must select the tool that most corresponds with the target behavior or construct of interest. As mentioned, various tools have been proposed to monitor SEB difficulties. After this step, practitioners must solidify the logistics of data collection. This includes deciding who the informants will be, when and where data collection will occur, as well as how often. Following logistical planning, progress monitoring teams decide the structure of data collection (e.g., reversal or multiple baseline designs). After these steps are completed, data collection and analyses can commence, and school personnel can eventually reach conclusions about student growth (e.g., continue, fade, or intensify the intervention).

The remainder of this chapter provides a detailed overview of these progress monitoring guidelines with recommendations for (1) identifying students for monitoring, (2) selecting a progress monitoring tool, (3) administrative procedures, (4) goal setting, and (5) data analysis. We begin with an overview of the theoretical foundations of progress monitoring grounded in cultural responsivity. Later, we detail a culturally responsive evaluation (CRE) framework that can guide educators toward a more responsive and equitable approach to evaluating student performance.

THEORETICAL FOUNDATIONS

Some communities face underservice, underrepresentation, and/or marginalization within educational systems. Consequently, educators are called upon to serve as advocates for social justice and ensure equitable treatment for every student. Progress monitoring provides a valuable opportunity to integrate cultural humility into evaluation and assessment, fostering inclusive and responsive educational decision making. Incorporating culturally responsive and equity-driven strategies and frameworks can allow the tailoring of assessment strategies to better align with the unique needs and experiences of students from various cultural backgrounds. Therefore, this chapter will outline culturally responsive positive behavioral interventions and supports (CRPBIS) and CRE as pertinent frameworks for progress monitoring and guiding equitable educational decision making.

CRPBIS is an adaptation of positive behavioral interventions and supports (PBIS) (Bal, 2011), an evidence-based three-tiered framework to promote positive student culture and individualized behavior support through a whole-school context. PBIS is a widespread evidence-based framework reported to decrease office discipline referrals, suspensions, and expulsions in schools across the United States (Sugai & Horner, 2020). Although instrumental in providing a solid framework for improving school climate and student behavior due to its ability to create tailored behavioral goals and reward systems, Bal (2018) adapted PBIS to incorporate cultural responsiveness to promote student, family, and community involvement and to address racial disproportionality. CRPBIS provides a holistic framework designed to intervene in school culture, facilitating the inclusion of decision-making and problem-solving processes for traditionally marginalized families and communities. Because progress monitoring is a central component of an effective PBIS framework, components from this framework should be applied when engaging in progress monitoring.

CRPBIS shifts away from a cultural deterministic approach, which acknowledges the role of culture in behavior, and moves toward a cultural instrumentalist approach, which underscores the use of culture to achieve specific goals, emphasizing the applied aspects of culture within numerous contexts. A cultural deterministic approach is insufficient, as it assumes that the cultural characteristics associated with culturally and linguistically diverse students (e.g., explicit behaviors, values, or cognitive processes) differ from the majority (e.g., White or middle class). Students comprise diverse cultures and activity systems, including their families, school districts, after-school programs, and sports. Students' distinct identities play a crucial role in shaping their learning and development, both within and outside the school environment, emphasizing the importance of acknowledging, addressing, and celebrating these multidimensional influences.

In alignment with this ecological perspective, CRPBIS delves into the intricate layers of school systems and culture, drawing from Bronfenbrenner's (1977) ecological systems theory. CRPBIS provides a comprehensive framework to foster inclusivity and cultural responsiveness within educational environments by recognizing and addressing individual, institutional, interpersonal, and systematic infrastructural factors. CRPBIS emphasizes four layers within school systems and culture: (1) individual factors (i.e., the culture and linguistics brought to the school by students and staff); (2) institutional factors (i.e., the structure of the school that exists, such as rules, privileged behavioral practices, and narrative styles); (3) interpersonal/interactional factors (i.e., the overlapping social environments that are created outside of schools); and (4) systematic infrastructural (i.e., structures that bring the school system together). The theoretical underpinnings of CRPBIS can be applied to the progress monitoring process in several ways. For instance, educator, caregiver, student, and community member voices can drive the selection of targets for progress monitoring (e.g., critical behaviors and skills) and the tools to assess those targets. Caregiver and student perspectives can also inform goal setting, ensuring chosen goals are rigorous but realistic and student-centered.

STUDENT IDENTIFICATION

An essential step before progress monitoring is identifying students who should be monitored. Typically, these individuals would include students receiving intervention at an advanced tier (e.g., Tiers 2 or 3) or students whom educators suspect need intervention, which they wish to verify through additional data collection. Students can be identified via several means. The most traditional identification method is parent, teacher, or student self-referral. Many schools also monitor student record data to determine need. For example, a school might conduct weekly or monthly evaluations of student data and provide interventions to students who are frequently absent, repeatedly referred to the office for behavioral infractions, or commonly visit the nurse's office (e.g., due to somatic complaints associated with internalizing concerns; Lane et al., 2019).

Unfortunately, monitoring referrals and record data is a largely reactive approach, which requires students to demonstrate a pattern of heightened concerns for them to be identified (Eklund & Dowdy, 2014). Accordingly, many schools have begun to apply more proactive methods, such as universal screening at Tier 1, which can support more timely student identification (Briesch et al., 2022). Research has repeatedly pointed to universal screening as an effective means by which to more accurately and equitably identify students needing support (Eklund et al., 2023). Recent work has examined the extent to which screening drives fair and equitable decision making (Eklund et al., 2023), with researchers also publishing guidelines for centering equity-screening models (e.g., Moore et al., 2023). Readers are encouraged to see Chapter 12 in this volume for a comprehensive overview of universal screening and how it can be used to identify students who need support, as well as those may subsequently be progress monitored.

SELECTING A PROGRESS MONITORING TOOL

Once a student has been identified, the next step is to select the tool that will be used to monitor their progress. Within any given school, students will demonstrate a variety of needs that can be addressed via intervention. The nature of each student's needs will determine which progress monitoring approach is relevant to them, as each progress monitoring tool addresses different targets. Some tools can be used to evaluate behaviors and skills we seek to increase through intervention (e.g., social skills, academic engagement, and prosocial behavior). Other tools can be used to evaluate behaviors we seek to decrease (e.g., aggression, disruption, and off-task behavior). Some tools can be used to examine behaviors we are explicitly targeting through intervention (e.g., coping skills). Other tools correspond to correlates that should change along with target behaviors (e.g., internalizing concerns). It can be helpful to examine the information that drove the student identification decision (e.g., referrals, record data, and universal screening scores) to determine student needs, thus informing progress monitoring tool selection. See Table 13.1 for an overview of progress monitoring methods that have been researched and are commonly used in schools.

TABLE 13.1. Common Progress Monitoring Methods

Method	Description	Examples	Availability
Systematic direct observation (SDO)	Method using systematic procedures to collect data regarding operationally defined behaviors within predetermined times and settings (e.g., math instruction on Mondays and Fridays).	1. Behavioral Observation of Students in Schools (BOSS)	Academic Skills Problems: Direct Assessment and Intervention (Shapiro & Clemens, 2023)
		2. Internalizing Behavior Observation Protocol (IBOP)	*https://smhcollaborative.org/rep*
Direct Behavior Rating (DBR)	Method for collecting brief ratings of students within predetermined times and settings (e.g., science and reading instruction each day of the week).	3. Single-item scales	*https://dbr.education.uconn.edu*
		4. Multi-item scales	Five Direct Behavior Rating Multi-Item Scales: Sensitivity to the Effects of Classroom Interventions (Matta et al., 2020)
Brief Behavior Rating Scales (BBRS)	Method for collecting brief ratings of students across settings and periods of time (e.g., 1 week or month).	5. Behavior and Feelings Survey (BFS)	*https://weiszlab.fas.harvard.edu*
		6. Social Skills Improvement System (SSIS) Brief Scales	*https://ssiscolab.com*
Goal attainment scaling (GAS)	Method for assessing performance using a standardized rating format and individualized indicators of progress	See Ruble et al. (2012) for an example	Goal Attainment Scaling: A Progress Monitoring Tool for Behavioral Interventions (Coffee & Ray-Subramanian, 2009)
Intervention data	Data that are collected as natural by-product of intervention implementation and which can be used to monitor student response.	7. Check-In/Check-Out (CICO) Daily Progress Report (DPR) scores	Responding to Problem Behavior in Schools: The Check-In/Check-Out Intervention (Hawken et al., 2020)

Given the variety of student needs, schools will likely need to build a library of progress monitoring tools from which they can select in preparing to monitor a student. As they build this library, educators should consider multiple factors in evaluating the quality of each potential tool (see Christ et al., 2009). First, a progress monitoring tool should be *defensible*, as documented through psychometric evidence. Such evidence should speak to the reliability of the tool's scores and the validity of inferences made in consideration of those scores. Importantly, evidence should also indicate the tool is sensitive to changes in student functioning, thus allowing it to document student response to intervention. Finally, evidence should indicate that a measure is fair and free of bias, such that its scores can be interpreted similarly for students of various backgrounds.

Second, a tool should be *flexible* in that it can be used to evaluate a range of behaviors or skills, thus increasing its relevance across students. Some measures are defensible but minimally flexible, including brief behavior rating scales corresponding to only a few behaviors or skills that are completed in the same way for each student. Other assessment methods are highly flexible. For instance, systematic direct observation (SDO) can be adapted on a student-by-student basis by constructing operational definitions and selecting observation procedures aligned with the behavior (e.g., interval recording or time-sampling methods). DBR is also a flexible method in that (1) single-item DBR scales can be used to evaluate a range of operationally defined behaviors (Briesch et al., 2016) and (2) several multi-item DBR scales have been developed, each corresponding to a different behavior or skill (e.g., academic engagement, organizational skills, and disruptive behavior). Finally, goal attainment scaling (GAS) can be adapted to assess a range of intervention-related goals, each of which can be assessed in several dimensions (e.g., frequency, extent, latency, or intensity; Kiresuk et al., 2014).

Third, progress monitoring tools should be *repeatable*, being capable of administration on a frequent and ongoing basis. Behavior is inherently variable and subject to changes in the environment. A student can be highly engaged one day and off-task the next. They can interact with peers on Monday and avoid all interactions on Tuesday. Such variability means that more progress monitoring data are needed to estimate the behavior accurately (Volpe & Briesch, 2012). Behaviors that are particularly variable should be evaluated every day or multiple times per week. Behaviors that are more stable and build slowly, such as social or adaptive skills, can be monitored less frequently, such as on a weekly basis. Frequent data collection ensures that updated information is available for timely intervention decisions, ensuring students receive the support they require and that resources are not wasted on unnecessary intervention.

Fourth, progress monitoring tools should be *efficient*. The need for efficiency is inherently tied to repeatability. Progress monitoring requires a large amount of data collection. Progress monitoring tool administration should require minimal time and effort to ensure the practice's sustainability and the quality of collected data. Most progress monitoring tools can be completed in only seconds or minutes (e.g., DBR and GAS tools). Others require more time and extensive training for administration (e.g., SDO).

Fifth, it should be possible to apply progress monitoring tools *within a culturally responsive evaluation (CRE) framework*. CRE can guide practitioners toward culturally responsive progress monitoring and complements the goals of CRPBIS, which were described above. CRE posits the imperative need for culturally sensitive assessment tools, inclusive data collection, and active involvement of diverse decision-making teams throughout data collection. The next steps for practitioners engaging in CRE will be discussed below.

CULTURALLY RESPONSIVE EVALUATION

CRE is a framework pioneered by Hood et al. (2015), a concept influenced by education assessment and culturally responsive pedagogy (Ladson-Billings, 1995a, 1995b). CRE is a comprehensive framework for working with other educators, school staff, caregivers, and students to conduct a culturally responsive assessment and evaluation rooted in appreciating cultural differences. Essential takeaways from CRE have been adapted for progress monitoring and are discussed below.

Good practice in supporting students in educational settings involves forming a decision-making team. The decision-making team encompasses a diverse group of key partners to obtain a whole-child view of the student. Key partners may include caregivers, community members, school psychologists, school social workers, and teachers. Key partners hold a meaningful role throughout the progress monitoring and decision-making process. The decision-making team ensures that cultural humility, an ongoing process involving self-reflection and lifelong inquiry about cultural biases and sensitivity toward others (Yeager & Bauer-Wu, 2013), is at the forefront throughout the progress monitoring process and that monitored behaviors are aligned with cultural values. Additionally, decision-making teams can provide additional data on the student, including but not limited to history and background information, identified priorities, and offering information and advice on other sources of progress monitoring and strategies to gather additional data points.

Upon forming a decision-making team, it is essential that the team engage in an educational process to familiarize themselves with the community. Here, the community denotes both the school environment and the unique cultural context of the students. During this process, it is important that the decision-making team is aware of their own culture and how it affects their prior experiences, assumptions, and implicit biases through a cultural humility lens. However, it is essential to distinguish between cultural humility and competency, as these concepts offer distinct perspectives on engaging with culturally and linguistically diverse students and families in educational settings. Earlier in this chapter, the differences between the cultural deterministic and the cultural instrumentalist approach were discussed. As a reminder, cultural determinism posits that culture shapes individual behavior, while cultural instrumentalism views culture as a tool to achieve outcomes. Similarly, whereas cultural competency emphasizes acquiring specific knowledge and skills about different cultures, cultural humility goes beyond this by promoting a commitment to self-reflection and continuous learning in interactions with culturally and linguistically diverse populations (Fisher, 2020). Continuous learning includes educating oneself on the community's location, people, relationships, communication styles, and the system of that community. For example, it is essential to note the power differentials of each culture and how a decision-making team's values and norms would interface with them. The overarching goal is to enter the community respectfully in order to progress monitor effectively.

Effective progress monitoring begins with clearly defined assessment goals and thoughtful planning of progress monitoring tools. A mixed methodology is recommended to ensure a comprehensive understanding of progress. When employing qualitative tools, the focus and the wording of questions are imperative. Decision-making teams can contribute input and reach consensus on the most effective approach. For instance, when evaluating a student proficient in a language other than English, the presence of a translator or interpreter is crucial for obtaining accurate data. Ensuring the cultural and linguistic validity of the assessment tool is important when working with diverse populations. Scrutinizing tools for potential cultural biases or omissions is necessary, and if an assessment is not available in the student's language, a language committee with expertise must facilitate forward and backward translations of the tool.

After completing progress monitoring data collection, a crucial next step involves exploring the cultural context to ensure accurate data analysis. This process is supported by the involvement of key partners, who provide valuable perspectives while examining diverse data sources, ranging from individuals and documents to databases. As the data are reviewed, new questions may emerge, prompting additional questions that would bring the decision-making team together for crucial discussion. Additionally, effective communication of the collected data is necessary, often requiring tailored outcomes to suit the understanding of specific audiences. For example, lay language should be used when sharing progress monitoring information with linguistically diverse individuals. If the progress monitoring data show adverse outcomes, collaboration with decision-making teams becomes imperative to organize appropriate next steps, promoting student well-being.

In sum, CRE is a valuable framework for integrating cultural sensitivity with progress monitoring in educational settings. This approach recognizes the importance of assessing academic progress and considering cultural backgrounds and experiences to obtain a holistic understanding of the student's development in a culturally sensitive and inclusive manner. Concurrently, progress monitoring can be implemented within CRPBIS by considering the culture of each school and ensuring open decision-making processes to families and communities from marginalized backgrounds. Adaptability remains key, allowing assessment tools and procedures to be tailored to meet the needs of students from all marginalized backgrounds. Educators must acknowledge and address their biases throughout the evaluation process, fostering an educational environment rooted in inclusivity, reflexivity, and equity.

PROCEDURES

Solidifying the procedures for progress monitoring is crucial for its implementation. Following student identification and selection of tools for progress monitoring, school personnel must then make logistical decisions regarding the monitoring process. Key considerations of progress monitoring SEB challenges include the informants, frequency, and location of data collection. The following section will discuss these considerations, their variability dependent on the target of interest, and cultural responsiveness.

Regarding school-based SEB assessment, the use of a multi-informant approach is critical given that each informant provides unique information about student functioning (De Los Reyes et al., 2019). This appears especially pertinent as recent research suggests discordance in SEB reports across teachers and students (von der Embse et al., 2023). As such, it is important to choose various informants who are well-suited to rate student outcomes. The methods of progress monitoring can help inform informant selection. For instance, SDOs may be best suited for school psychologists, given that they are often time-intensive and require training to conduct properly. Considering the practicality and brief function of other progress monitoring tools (e.g., DBRs), various school personnel can be appropriate informants to collect data, contingent on their capacity to examine periods in which the behavior or construct of interests occurs. Most often, a primary informant will be a lead classroom teacher (Chafouleas et al., 2010). Yet, there are often challenges when selecting informants. Students move from different classes throughout the day, making it difficult to choose which teachers should be collecting data and when (Bruhn et al., 2018). Moreover, some teachers may have difficulty teaching and collecting data simultaneously (Epstein, 2010). Therefore, before choosing informants, planning and preparation are necessary to ensure teachers or other relevant personnel have the skills to collect accurate data. This can be accomplished through progress monitoring tool training (e.g., *https://dbrtraining.education.uconn.edu*).

Determining the frequency of assessment is also important. The frequency of data collection is often dependent on the behavior of interest and the intervention implemented. Scholars recommend that when progress monitoring teams can make robust assumptions about the nature of the behavior of interest, it is reasonable to collect data less frequently (von der Embse et al., 2022). For instance, with behavioral interventions (e.g., behavior skills training), linearity and consistency of behavior improvement are expected to be seen, reducing the need for frequent data collection. Alternatively, there may be significant variability in internalizing behaviors, as there is often an array of factors that heighten these concerns. In such cases where internalizing challenges are the interest of progress monitoring data collection, it would be prudent to employ more frequent assessments to better understand a student's response to an intervention.

When beginning to monitor SEB difficulties, teams should identify where and when data will be collected. The location of data collection should be chosen based upon the behavior of interest and each student's unique needs. Unless progress monitoring teams desire to have a comparison point to examine, it would be sufficient to solely examine locations or periods in which the target behavior or construct is of heightened concern. Say, for example, a child has particular difficulty with behavioral disruptions or outbursts during math instruction from 10:00 A.M. to 11:30 A.M. Either SDO or DBR use during this time frame and in the classroom would be satisfactory in monitoring how these behaviors change in response to an intervention. Deciding the *when* and *where* of data collection is a necessary first step, and thoughtful consideration should be given to ensure a student's response to an intervention is well-documented.

Notably, there is significant variability in guidance for monitoring progress depending on the target behavior and chosen intervention. For example, internalizing difficulties are especially difficult to monitor as they often exist privately within a student. Consequently, external informants must examine outward depictions of internalizing symptoms (e.g., crying). This necessitates enhancing procedural components of progress monitoring, such as including self-report informant mechanisms, which may not be essential for externalizing challenges (e.g., aggression and disruptions), which are readily observable and more easily documented. For more challenging SEB concerns, teams may opt to enhance the frequency of data collection to better gauge student responsiveness to an intervention. For instance, if a student has several behavioral difficulties across the school day (e.g., reading instruction, gym class, or group math work), it would be advisable to examine behaviors in each setting to see if these behaviors are equally improving in response to an intervention.

Interventions themselves may evoke heterogeneity in data collection processes. CICO is an example of an intervention that naturally produces progress monitoring data. At the foundation of CICO is the daily progress report (DPR), which teachers complete throughout each school day to provide behavioral feedback to students. DPR scores are then aggregated across the day and used to determine whether the student met their daily point goal. These aggregated scores can be evaluated across days to determine the extent to which student behavior has improved. Research on the defensibility of DPR scores is limited, but the available evidence supports their use in progress monitoring (Stage et al., 2012).

In sum, progress monitoring procedures are heavily reliant on both the target behavior and intervention of choice. Progress monitoring teams should be flexible when developing their strategy for data collection, as each student will present with individual concerns that cannot be accurately gauged via a one-size-fits-all approach. The need for cultural responsiveness further underlies the need to avoid a one-size-fits-all approach to progress monitoring.

It is essential to weigh cultural considerations when monitoring SEB challenges. Each student referred for targeted or intensive services arrives with unique needs and cultural background; thus, it will be important to tailor progress monitoring procedures to each student. To enhance the cultural responsiveness of progress monitoring, efforts can be made to enhance procedural considerations. Firstly, while social desirability and the desire to be viewed in a positive light have been somewhat of a concern (Harter, 1986), self-reporting of SEB difficulties still constitutes a crucial method of gauging student functioning. This is especially important in the context of cultural considerations. For instance, Asian American youth are unlikely to be referred for school-based mental health services (Guo et al., 2014), potentially partially explained by the model minority stereotype. Conversely, teachers rate Black students as significantly more likely to have SEB risk compared to their White peers (Izumi & Eklund, 2023; Splett et al., 2018). As such, solely relying on teacher reports of SEB difficulties is not prudent. Indeed, research suggests that students are more accurate reporters of internalizing difficulties compared to teachers (Margherio et al., 2019), which is especially important given that Asian American students often suffer more from internalizing than externalizing concerns (Huang et al., 2012). In addition to self-reports of SEB concerns, it would be wise to seek caregiver perspectives on progress. Because schools often conform to and prioritize middle-class American culture, ethnic–racial minority youth are frequently confronted with a cultural mismatch in their schools, which can disrupt accurate assessment processes (Allen et al., 2013; Jagers et al., 2019). This discordance in cultural matches may lead school staff to label or mark behavior as negative that would be construed as positive or neutral in the home setting. Acquiring caregiver perspectives would help mitigate these concerns and be useful in comparing and contrasting informant views of progress. Therefore, incorporating self-reports or various perspectives (e.g., teacher, parent, or other school staff) into the progress monitoring data collection process can provide a broader and holistic depiction of student functioning.

GOAL SETTING

As mentioned previously, setting goals for SEB performance can be difficult since there is no standard growth rate for improvement (Chafouleas et al., 2010). Furthermore, goals are inextricably linked to the type of data being collected, meaning the decisions school-based personnel face when selecting a progress monitoring tool will directly affect the goals they set for students. Therefore, the purpose of this subsection is not to delineate a unified goal selection procedure design to suit all settings, systems, interventions, and populations. Instead, readers are directed toward several practical considerations that will be helpful in developing meaningful and culturally responsive goals for the students they serve.

First, consider what is achievable during the monitoring period. How often will the progress monitoring data be reviewed? Is the intervention expected to produce immediate effects? What would adequate progress look like? Answering these questions will shed light on whether a goal is timely and achievable. For example, Bruhn and colleagues (2020) encouraged teachers to review progress monitoring data (i.e., percentage of positive behavior) every 3–5 days to make decisions about the effectiveness of multi-component self-monitoring intervention that was implemented over 7 weeks. This schedule suggests that they expected to see some positive change within the first week of implementation but may not have expected pronounced effects until the final week. On the other hand, Commisso and colleagues (2019) suggested that a student would be considered unresponsive to an intervention if they did not show adequate performance (i.e., 80% of daily points earned for at least 5 days) over 2 weeks. These two examples illustrate that the goals we set are tied not only to our assessment selection but also to our monitoring and data review period.

Second, consider setting multiple goals, including both a longer-term mastery goal and a shorter-term goal that can be used to assess more proximal response to intervention. As suggested in the preceding paragraph, decision-making teams may want to determine if a student is responding to an intervention long before deciding about the magnitude of that response. It can be helpful to set short-term goals for that purpose. For example, McDaniel and Bruhn (2016) set an initial goal of 40% of DPR points earned for two students. This goal represented the average of the students' baseline DPR points and was selected so that they could achieve some success early in the implementation period. On the other hand, the students' longer-term mastery goal was 80% of DPR points earned. This is an extremely common mastery goal used to evaluate the effectiveness of CICO (Hawken et al., 2015). To bridge the gap between these goals, McDaniel and Bruhn (2016) increased students' goals to their average DPR performance in the previous phase of the study until they reached 80%. In this way, comparing students' performance to short-term goals can be used to make modifications or adaptations to an intervention while giving students a more realistic performance target. Long-term mastery goals can be used to make final determinations about whether an intervention was effective within the broader context of an MTSS framework.

Finally, consider the level of individualization that will go into goal setting. As mentioned previously, it is very common to use a universal mastery goal (e.g., 80% of DPR points) within CICO. This might make sense for a standardized protocol intervention that is implemented as a Tier 2 strategy schoolwide; however, for more individualized interventions, such as adapted Tier 2 strategies or Tier 3 strategies, it may be necessary to create more individualized goals that are sensitive to the student's unique needs. Ruble and colleagues (2012) describe how GAS can be used to create individualized progress monitoring measures. Although GAS uses a standardized rating system (i.e., a 5-point scale ranging from −2 to +2), each level is personalized around the student's specific SEB goal, where a −2 reflects the baseline level of performance, a 0 reflects the expected level of improvement, and a +2 reflects much more than expected improvement. Assigning meaning to these ratings is up to the intervention and decision-making teams. Ruble and colleagues (2012) provide an example for a fictitious student where a −2 rating signifies that the student "may use aggression as a way to request; relies on adult prompts to make requests" (p. 1979). At the midpoint of the scale, a 0 rating signifies that the student "will make 10 different requests per day independently or as a response to a question" (p. 1979). On the other extreme, a rating of +2 signifies that the student "will make 20 different requests per day independently or as a response to a question" (p. 1979). This kind of flexibility allows school-based personnel to create idiosyncratic progress monitoring goals for students that reflect change in outcomes that are most meaningful to them and those around them.

DATA ANALYSIS

The final step in the progress monitoring process is decision making following an analysis of data. Decision making can occur at the level of the individual student (e.g., intensify to Tier 3, reduce support, or adapt existing supports) or at the school-, district-, or statewide level (e.g., modify standard Tier 2 protocol implemented with all at-risk students). The analysis of student-level progress monitoring data is typically handled through two different approaches, visual analysis and statistical analysis. The analysis of school-, district-, or statewide data is typically accomplished through descriptive or statistical analysis (e.g., McDaniel et al., 2022).

Visual Analysis

Visual analysis of progress monitoring data involves a visual inspection of the data plotted in a linear graph with the outcome on the *y*-axis and the passage of time on the *x*-axis. Although it is viewed as a subjective method compared to statistical analysis, the application of a standardized linear graph construction and visual analytic process can increase consistency in decision making (e.g., Lewis et al., 2022). There are six data characteristics that visual analysts should consider when examining progress monitoring data, including (1) level, (2) trend, (3) variability, (4) consistency, (5) overlap, and (6) immediacy (Horner et al., 2005).

Although a thorough review of each characteristic is outside the scope of this chapter, researchers have written at length about each and have developed standardized processes for examining each (e.g., Lane & Gast, 2014). Visual analysts are tasked with synthesizing their judgments about each characteristic to arrive at a decision regarding the effect of the intervention on the outcome being measured. Because linear graphs provide a depiction of change over time, decision-making teams may use visual analysis to decide whether an intervention is having any effect on the student's performance and, if so, whether the effect is large enough to achieve goal attainment within a reasonable amount of time.

Figure 13.1 depicts a graph of hypothetical DBR single-item scale data specific to student academic engagement and disruptive behavior. Data were collected across two phases, including baseline and intervention. Baseline academic engagement data were stable and low, suggesting room for improvement. Engagement immediately improved upon intervention implementation, with the level increasing and data trending upward. There was no overlap in engagement data between the two phases, suggesting a clear change in performance. During baseline, disruptive behavior data were elevated and rising, again suggesting the need for support. Behavior immediately decreased in level and trended downward following intervention implementation. The lack of overlap in disruptive data between phases again suggests a clear change in functioning.

Statistical Analysis

Statistical analysis offers a quantitative assessment of student performance and, unlike visual analysis, will produce results that are independent of analyst judgments and perceptual differences. There are many different statistical analytic options that school-based personnel can use to interpret progress monitoring data (e.g., Dowdy et al., 2021; Jamshidi et al., 2023), many more than could be reasonably reviewed in this chapter. Instead, we will describe one option that is likely to apply to most progress monitoring data sets.

The percent of goal obtained (PoGO) (Ferron et al., 2020) is an easily interpretable statistic that represents the percent change in an outcome between a student's baseline or pre-intervention performance and their most recent performance, using their mastery goal as the performance target. For example, recall that McDaniel and Bruhn (2016) found that students were earning approximately 40% of their CICO DPR points at baseline and had set a mastery goal of 80% of DPR points. If, after 6 weeks of implementation, a student was earning 60% of DPR points, PoGO would equal 50% because their DPR scores increased halfway

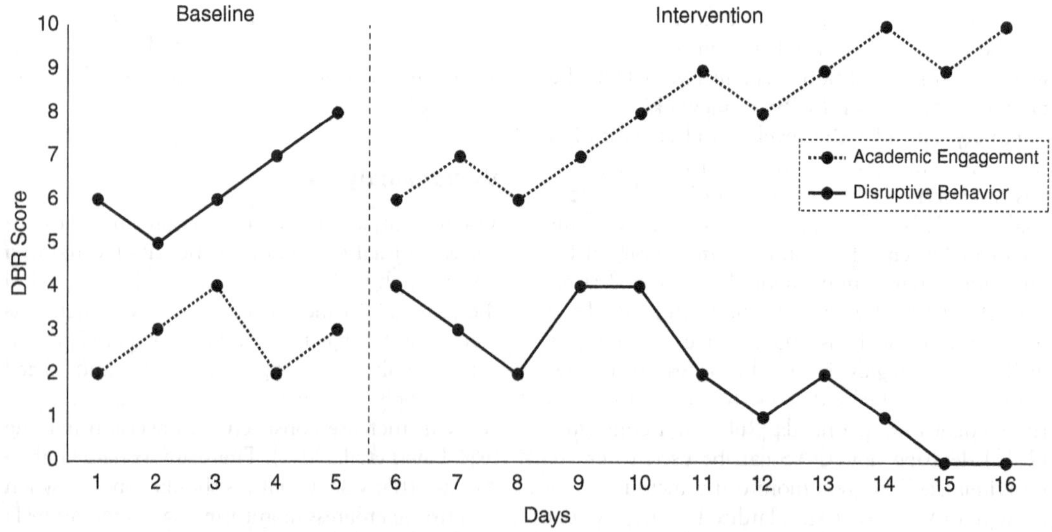

FIGURE 13.1. Example graph of hypothetical Direct Behavior Rating (DBR) scores.

to the mastery goal. On the other hand, if they earned 80% of their DPR points after 6 weeks, PoGO would equal 100%. Ferron and colleagues (2020) provide guidelines for interpreting PoGO with scores of less than 20% indicating little to no effect, scores between 20 and 40% indicating a small effect, scores between 40 and 60% indicating a medium effect, scores between 60 and 80% indicating a large effect, and scores above 80% indicating a very large effect.

Systems Analysis

School-based personnel may wish to make decisions about whether Tier 2 or Tier 3 interventions are effective from a systems-level (i.e., school, district, or state) perspective or whether they are producing equitable outcomes across students from different cultures and identities. To accomplish this, it is necessary to aggregate and synthesize individual student data. For example, Hawken and colleagues (2015) synthesized students' average percentage of DPR points earned within the CICO intervention during an entire school year and found that most (i.e., 83–86%) students receiving the intervention had average DPR scores at or above 80%, suggesting the intervention was functioning well. In another example, McIntosh and colleagues (2021) found that Black students received three times as many office discipline referrals (ODR) as White students in a set of rural public schools. They assessed the effects of an equity-focused PBIS approach by tracking risk differences for receiving an ODR by race, documenting a reduction in risk difference for Black students over a year of implementation. These examples highlight how systems-level data can be used to evaluate the functioning and effectiveness of Tier 2 and Tier 3 systems on a level larger than the individual student.

CONCLUSION

Progress monitoring plays a vital role in MTSS frameworks, serving as the primary means by which we can (1) evaluate the effectiveness of interventions and (2) make timely decisions that promote intervention success. Engaging in progress monitoring requires educators to make a number of decisions, including those related to tool selection, the design of progress monitoring procedures, goal setting, and the analysis of resulting data. Schools can seek to design broad and general progress monitoring solutions, but given the complexity of students and the diversity of their backgrounds and needs, there will likely be a need for individualized progress monitoring designs for many students. This chapter offered several ideas educators can consider and questions they might ask in designing a process that will meet their needs and promote their success within MTSS.

REFERENCES

Allen, A., Scott, L. A., & Lewis, C. W. (2013). Racial microaggressions and African American and Hispanic students in urban schools: A call for culturally affirming education. *Interdisciplinary Journal of Teaching and Learning, 3*(2), 117–129.

Bal, A. (2011). *Culturally responsive school-wide Positive Behavioral Interventions and Supports framework*. Wisconsin Department of Public Instruction.

Bal, A. (2018). Culturally responsive positive behavioral interventions and supports: A process-oriented framework for systemic transformation. *Review of Education, Pedagogy, and Cultural Studies, 40*(2), 144–174.

Briesch, A. M., Chafouleas, S. M., Dineen, J. N., McCoach, D. B., & Donaldson, A. (2022). School building administrator reports of screening practices across academic, behavioral, and health domains. *Journal of Positive Behavior Interventions, 24*(4), 266–277.

Briesch, A. M., Riley-Tillman, T. C., & Chafouleas, S. M. (2016). *Direct Behavior Rating: Linking assessment, communication, and intervention*. Guilford Press.

Bronfenbrenner, U. (1977). Toward an experimental ecology of human development. *American Psychologist, 32*(7), 513–531.

Bruhn, A. L., McDaniel, S. C., Rila, A., & Estrapala, S. (2018). A step-by-step guide to Tier 2 behavioral progress monitoring. *Beyond Behavior, 27*(1), 15–27.

Bruhn, A. L., Rila, A., Mahatmya, D., Estrapala, S., & Hendrix, N. (2020). The effects of data-based, individualized interventions for behavior. *Journal of Emotional and Behavioral Disorders, 28*(1), 3–16.

Chafouleas, S. M., Briesch, A. M., Riley-Tillman, T. C., Christ, T. J., Black, A. C., & Kilgus, S. P. (2010). An investigation of the generalizability and dependability of Direct Behavior Rating Single Item Scales (DBR-SIS) to measure academic engagement and disruptive behavior of middle school students. *Journal of School Psychology, 48*(3), 219–246.

Christ, T. J., Riley-Tillman, T. C., & Chafouleas, S. M. (2009). Foundation for the development and use of Direct Behavior Rating (DBR) to assess and evaluate student behavior. *Assessment for Effective Intervention, 34*(4), 201–213.

Coffee, G., & Ray-Subramanian, C. (2009). Goal Attainment Scaling: A progress-monitoring tool for behavioral interventions. *School Psychology Forum, 3*, 1–12.

Commisso, C. E., Gaier, K., Kern, L., Majeika, C. E., Van Camp, A. M., Wehby, J. H., & Kelly, S. (2019). How to make adaptations to Check In/Check Out to increase its effectiveness. *TEACHING Exceptional Children, 52*(1), 30–37.

Dart, E. H., Arora, P. G., Collins, T. A., & Doll, B. (2019). Progress monitoring measures for internalizing symptoms: A systematic review of the peer-reviewed literature. *School Mental Health, 11*, 265–275.

Dart, E. H., Arora, P., Collins, T., Stark, K., Cook, C. R., Duong, M. T., et al. (2020). Developing a brief behavior rating scale for progress monitoring of depression in school settings. *Assessment for Effective Intervention, 45*(3), 163–172.

De Los Reyes, A., Cook, C. R., Gresham, F. M., Makol, B. A., & Wang, M. (2019). Informant discrepancies in assessments of psychosocial functioning in school-based services and research: Review and directions for future research. *Journal of School Psychology, 74*, 74–89.

Dowdy, A., Peltier, C., Tincani, M., Schneider, W. J., Hantula, D. A., & Travers, J. C. (2021). Meta-analyses and effect sizes in applied behavior analysis: A review and discussion. *Journal of Applied Behavior Analysis, 54*(4), 1317–1340.

Drevon, D. D., Hixson, M. D., Wyse, R. D., & Rigney, A. M. (2019). A meta-analytic review of the evidence for Check-In Check-Out. *Psychology in the Schools, 56*(3), 393–412.

Eklund, K., & Dowdy, E. (2014). Screening for behavioral and emotional risk versus traditional school identification methods. *School Mental Health, 6*, 40–49.

Eklund, K., Kilgus, S. P., Barber, A., Dubose, K., Collins, B. A., & Eikenmeyer, M. (2023). The effect of student race/ethnicity on the diagnostic accuracy of the Social, Academic, and Emotional Behavior Risk Screener (SAEBRS). *Psychology in the Schools, 60*(10), 3878–3895.

Elharake, J. A., Akbar, F., Malik, A. A., Gilliam, W., & Omer, S. B. (2022). Mental health impact of COVID-19 among children and college students: A systematic review. *Child Psychiatry & Human Development, 54*, 913–925.

Epstein M. (2010). *Reducing behavior problems in the elementary school classroom.* What Works Clearinghouse Webinar Transcript.

Ferron, J., Goldstein, H., Olszewski, A., & Rohrer, L. (2020). Indexing effects in single-case experimental designs by estimating the percent of goal obtained. *Evidence-Based Communication Assessment and Intervention, 14*(1–2), 6–27.

Fisher, E. S. (2020). Cultural humility as a form of social justice: Promising practices for global school psychology training. *School Psychology International, 41*(1), 53–66.

Guo, S., Kataoka, S. H., Bear, L., & Lau, A. S. (2014). Differences in school-based referrals for mental health care: Understanding racial/ethnic disparities between Asian American and Latino youth. *School Mental Health, 6*, 27–39.

Harter, S. (1986). Cognitive-developmental processes in the integration of concepts about emotions and the self. *Social Cognition, 4*(2), 119–151.

Hawken, L. S., Bundock, K., Barrett, C. A., Eber, L., Breen, K., & Phillips, D. (2015). Large-scale implementation of Check-In, Check-Out: A descriptive study. *Canadian Journal of School Psychology, 30*(4), 304–319.

Hawken, L. S., Crone, D. A., Bundock, K., & Horner, R. H. (2020). *Responding to problem behavior in schools: The Check-In, Check-Out intervention.* Guilford Press.

Heck, O. C., Komer, J., & Ormiston, H. E. (2022). Incorporating student self-report for progress monitoring: Tapping into their expertise. *Communiqué, 51*(3), 30–33.

Hill, E., Volpe, R. J., & Briesch, A. M. (2023). Psychometric properties of the classroom observation of engagement, disrespectful and disruptive behaviors. *School Psychology Review, 52*(6), 735–746.

Hood, S., Hopson, R. K., & Kirkhart, K. (2015). Culturally responsive evaluation: Theory, practice, and future implications. In K. E. Newcomer, H. Hatry, & J. Wholey (Eds.), *Handbook of practical program evaluation* (4th ed., pp. 281–317). Wiley.

Horner, R. H., Carr, E. G., Halle, J., McGee, G., Odom, S., & Wolery, M. (2005). The use of single-subject research to identify evidence-based practice in special education. *Exceptional Children, 71*(2), 165–179.

Huang, K. Y., Calzada, E., Cheng, S., & Brotman, L. M. (2012). Physical and mental health disparities among young children of Asian immigrants. *The Journal of Pediatrics, 160*(2), 331–336.

Izumi, J. T., & Eklund, K. (2023). Universal screening for social-emotional and behavioral risk: Differential item functioning on the SAEBRS. *School Psychology, 38*(4), 238.

Jagers, R. J., Rivas-Drake, D., & Williams, B. (2019). Transformative social and emotional learning (SEL): Toward SEL in service of educational equity and excellence. *Educational Psychologist, 54*(3), 162–184.

Jamshidi, L., Heyvaert, M., Declercq, L., Fernández-Castilla, B., Ferron, J. M., Moeyaert, M., et al. (2023). A systematic review of single-case experimental design meta-analyses: Characteristics of study designs, data, and analyses. *Evidence-Based Communication Assessment and Intervention, 17*(1), 6–30.

Kauhanen, L., Wan Mohd Yunus, W. M. A., Lempinen, L., Peltonen, K., Gyllenberg, D., Mishina, K., et al. (2023). A systematic review of the mental health changes of children and young people before and during the COVID-19 pandemic. *European Child & Adolescent Psychiatry, 32*(6), 995–1013.

Kilgus, S. P., Collier-Meek, M. A., Johnson, A. H., & Jaffery, R. (2014). Applied empiricism: Ensuring the validity of causal response to intervention decisions. *Contemporary School Psychology, 18*, 1–12.

Kilgus, S. P., Riley-Tillman, T. C., Stichter, J. P., Schoemann, A. M., & Bellesheim, K. (2016). Reliability of direct behavior ratings–social competence (DBR-SC) data: How many ratings are necessary? *School Psychology Quarterly*, *31*(3), 431–442.

Kiresuk, T. J., Smith, A., & Cardillo, J. E. (2014). *Goal Attainment Scaling: Applications, theory, and measurement*. Psychology Press.

Ladson-Billings, G. (1995a). But that's just good teaching! The case for culturally relevant pedagogy. *Theory Into Practice*, *34*(3), 159–165.

Ladson-Billings, G. (1995b). Toward a theory of culturally relevant pedagogy. *American Educational Research Journal*, *32*(3), 465–491.

Lane, K. L., Oakes, W. P., Cantwell, E. D., Common, E. A., Royer, D. J., Leko, M. M., et al. (2019). Predictive validity of Student Risk Screening Scale—Internalizing and Externalizing (SRSS-IE) scores in elementary schools. *Journal of Emotional and Behavioral Disorders*, *27*(4), 221–234.

Lane, J. D., & Gast, D. L. (2014). Visual analysis in single case experimental design studies: Brief review and guidelines. *Neuropsychological Rehabilitation*, *24*(3–4), 445–463.

Lewis, H. H., Radley, K. C., & Dart, E. H. (2022). The effect of graph standardization on intervention evaluation of practitioner-created graphs. *Psychology in the Schools*, *59*(3), 471–479.

Margherio, S. M., Evans, S. W., & Owens, J. S. (2019). Universal screening in middle and high schools: Who falls through the cracks? *School Psychology*, *34*(6), 591–602.

Matta, M., Volpe, R. J., Briesch, A. M., & Owens, J. S. (2020). Five Direct Behavior Rating multi-item scales: Sensitivity to the effects of classroom interventions. *Journal of School Psychology*, *81*, 28–46.

McDaniel, S. C., & Bruhn, A. L. (2016). Using a changing-criterion design to evaluate the effects of Check-In/Check-Out with goal modification. *Journal of Positive Behavior Interventions*, *18*(4), 197–208.

McDaniel, S. C., Cohen, D., & Bruhn, A. L. (2022). Evaluating school-level student outcomes of a systematic Tier 2 framework. *Behavioral Disorders*, *47*(3), 176–186.

McIntosh, K., Girvan, E. J., Fairbanks Falcon, S., McDaniel, S. C., Smolkowski, K., Bastable, E., et al. (2021). Equity-focused PBIS approach reduces racial inequities in school discipline: A randomized controlled trial. *School Psychology*, *36*(6), 433–444.

Moore, S., Long, A. C., Coyle, S., Cooper, J. M., Mayworm, A. M., Amirazizi, S., et al. (2023). A roadmap to equitable school mental health screening. *Journal of School Psychology*, 96, 57–74.

Pentimonti, J. M., Walker, M. A., & Edmonds, R. Z. (2017). The selection and use of screening and progress monitoring tools in data-based decision making within an MTSS framework. *Perspectives on Language and Literacy*, *43*(3), 34–40.

Ruble, L., McGrew, J. H., & Toland, M. D. (2012). Goal Attainment Scaling as an outcome measure in randomized controlled trials of psychosocial interventions in autism. *Journal of Autism and Developmental Disorders*, *42*, 1974–1983.

Shapiro, E. S., & Clemens, N. H. (2023). *Academic skills problems: Direct assessment and intervention* (5th ed.). Guilford Press.

Shinn, M. R. (2008). Best practices in using curriculum-based measurement in a problem-solving model. In A. Thomas & J. Grimes (Eds.), *Best practices in school psychology V* (pp. 671–697). National Association of School Psychologists.

Splett, J. W., Trainor, K. M., Raborn, A., Halliday-Boykins, C. A., Garzona, M. E., Dongo, M. D., & Weist, M. D. (2018). Comparison of universal mental health screening to students already receiving intervention in a multitiered system of support. *Behavioral Disorders*, *43*(3), 344–356.

Stage, S. A., Cheney, D., Lynass, L., Mielenz, C., & Flower, A. (2012). Three validity studies of the Daily Progress Report in relationship to the Check, Connect, and Expect Intervention. *Journal of Positive Behavior Interventions*, *14*(3), 181–191.

Stecker, P. M., Fuchs, L. S., & Fuchs, D. (2005). Using curriculum-based measurement to improve student achievement: Review of research. *Psychology in the Schools*, *42*(8), 795–819.

Sugai, G., & Horner, R. H. (2020). Sustaining and scaling Positive Behavioral Interventions and Supports: Implementation drivers, outcomes, and considerations. *Exceptional Children*, *86*(2), 120–136.

Vannest, K. J. (2012). Implementing interventions and progress monitoring subsequent to universal screening. *School Psychology Forum*, *6*(4), 119–136.

Volpe, R. J., & Briesch, A. M. (2012). Generalizability and dependability of single-item and multiple-item Direct Behavior Rating scales for engagement and disruptive behavior. *School Psychology Review*, *41*(3), 246–261.

von der Embse, N. P., Eklund, K., & Kilgus, S. P. (2022). *Conducting behavioral and mental health assessments in MTSS*. Taylor & Francis.

von der Embse, N., Kim, E., Ross, D., Kilgus, S., & Koza, T. (2023). Multi-informant assessment of internalizing concerns: Rater concordance and implications for decision-making. *Journal of Psychopathology and Behavioral Assessment*, *45*(1), 234–246.

Weist, M. D., Hoover, S. A., Daly, B. P., Short, K. H., & Bruns, E. J. (2023). Propelling the global advancement of school mental health. *Clinical Child and Family Psychology Review*, *26*(4), 851–864.

Yeager, K. A., & Bauer-Wu, S. (2013). Cultural humility: Essential foundation for clinical researchers. *Applied Nursing Research*, *26*(4), 251–256.

PART III

ASSESSMENT OF VARIOUS DISORDERS

CHAPTER 14

Assessment of Autism

Anna Krasno, Julia Juechter, and Kaylin Russell

Autism is a neurodevelopmental diagnosis that is a genetically based difference in brain development (Muhle et al., 2004). It is characterized by differences in social communication skills and specific behaviors such as a preference for sameness, sensory hyper- or hyposensitivities or interests, repetitive speech or motor movements, and intense interests. Autism impacts how an individual experiences the world, what they find salient in the environment (Jones et al., 2023; Wang et al., 2015), their interpersonal interactions, and certain behaviors they may exhibit. Autism is one of the most common neurodevelopmental conditions, with approximately 1 in 31 children in the United States being diagnosed (Centers for Disease Control and Prevention [CDC], 2025). However, worldwide estimates place the prevalence of autism at 1 in 100 children (Zeidan et al., 2022). Though prevalence estimates have increased over time, significant variation exists both within and among different sociodemographic groups (Zeidan et al., 2022). Thus, it is important for clinicians in all settings (e.g., private sector, hospital, clinic, and school) to be well trained in neurodiverse-affirming and culturally responsive identification and assessment of children and youth on the autism spectrum.

Although the medical model of autism conceptualizes autism as a disorder that is a defect within a person, the neurodiversity paradigm posits that autism is a part of human biodiversity and an inherent part of a person's identity (Blume, 1998; Singer, 1998). The neurodiversity paradigm framework has implications for how autism assessment can be conducted in a neurodiversity-affirming manner, which then helps to guide support approaches moving forward. Although the *Diagnostic and Statistical Manual of Mental Disorders, Fifth Edition, Text Revision* (DSM-5-TR) (American Psychiatric Association, 2022) diagnosis is autism spectrum disorder, this chapter will use the word *autism* to refer to those with the diagnosis to better align with a neurodiversity-affirming framework. This chapter also acknowledges that DSM-5-TR language in the autism diagnostic criteria is deficit-based and uses stigmatizing words such as *abnormal, poor,* and *lack.* We understand that this is the language that is used to guide diagnosis; however, we are pushing for a large shift or reframe when it comes to understanding autism and autism assessment by using difference-based objective language (i.e., "differences in social–emotional reciprocity" instead of "deficits in social–emotional reciprocity" and "preference for sameness" instead of "rigid or inflexible"). The next iterations of diagnostic criteria (e.g., DSM and *International Classification of Diseases* [ICD]) will likely not be published for a few more years, so many clinicians in the field are trying to translate deficit-focused criteria into strengths-focused language. It is possible to describe the same actions, responses, and preferences that define what it means to be autistic with a strengths-based lens (Rutherford & Johnston, 2022). Using objective language throughout the assessment process, from consent to report writing and feedback, is a powerful way to shift how a family thinks about their child and how the child thinks about themselves. Specifically, clinicians should use the phrase "area of challenge/difficulty" instead of "deficit," "co-occurring" instead of "comorbid," and, for very young children, consider using "high probability" of autism rather than "at risk" (Bottema-Beutel et al., 2020; Brown et al., 2021). Additionally, when speaking with families, using both identity-first and person-first language is recommended in order to recognize variability in language preferences across the autism community (Lord et al., 2022). When report writing, clinicians should be mindful that the autistic child will likely read the report (if not now, when they are older) and use strength-based and neurodiverse-affirming language throughout the report.

Sociodemographic and cultural factors that may impact the assessment process must be considered to ensure accurate diagnosis across diverse populations. Culturally responsive practice extends beyond merely accommodating clients with limited English proficiency. Factors such as socioeconomic status, cultural norms and expectations, gender differences, cultural relevance of assessment tools, and the cultural competence and training of clinicians need to be addressed during the assessment process to ensure an accurate diagnosis of autism.

Cultural norms and expectations significantly influence the recognition and interpretation of autism symptoms by shaping social behavior, communication styles, and developmental milestones. For example, maintaining eye contact is seen as attentive in many Euro-American cultures but confrontational in some Asian cultures. Similarly, acceptable physical distance during interactions varies across cultures. These differences can lead to misinterpretation of behaviors such as avoiding eye contact or preferring more personal space. Communication norms also play a role; some cultures prioritize verbal communication while others emphasize nonverbal cues, with Euro-American cultures valuing direct communication and many Asian cultures preferring indirect communication. Additionally, developmental milestones differ, with European American cultures encouraging early independence and other cultures emphasizing interdependence. These cultural differences can lead to varying interpretations of a child's abilities, potentially resulting in misdiagnosis of developmental delays or autism symptoms. Clinicians should not interpret different racial and ethnic groups as monoliths; within racial groups, there are cultural subgroups with their own variability in social norms and experiences (Henderson et al., 2024).

Specifically, intersectionality of identities needs to be considered in the assessment process. Autism may be stigmatized in certain cultures, leading to parents blaming themselves for their child's differences and challenges (Stahmer et al., 2019). Families may also have a history of negative interactions with health care providers, mistrust the system, and feel undervalued or unheard by medical professionals (Brown et al., 2021; Moseley et al., 2007). In some cultures, stigma associated with developmental conditions can lead to reluctance in seeking a diagnosis. Additionally, cultural attitudes toward medical interventions and therapies vary; some families may prefer traditional or alternative treatments over conventional medical approaches. These scenarios require clinicians to practice cultural humility and understand intersectionality during the process of thoughtfully determining and delivering diagnoses.

Socioeconomic status (SES), health care access, and availability of diagnostic services all significantly impact timely and accurate autism diagnosis. Families with higher SES often have greater financial resources, education, and awareness, enabling them to access early interventions and specialized care, leading to faster diagnoses. Conversely, families with lower SES may face financial barriers, limited access to specialists, and longer wait times in public health care systems, potentially delaying diagnosis and intervention. Geographic location also plays a role, as urban areas typically have a higher concentration of specialists and resources compared to rural areas (Drahota et al., 2020; Stahmer et al., 2019).

The availability of culturally appropriate diagnostic tools is crucial for accurate assessment, particularly for children from diverse backgrounds. Standardization bias in autism assessment instruments poses significant challenges when evaluating clients with limited English proficiency (LEP). These instruments are often developed and standardized based on English-speaking populations, which can result in inaccurate assessments for LEP individuals due to language barriers and cultural differences in communication and behavior. Research indicates that standardized tools may not fully capture the nuances of autism symptoms in non-English-speaking populations, leading to potential underdiagnosis or misdiagnosis (Smith et al., 2019). Additionally, the reliance on verbal communication in many assessment tools can disadvantage LEP clients, as their language proficiency may not accurately reflect their cognitive or social abilities (Klinger et al., 2015). In addition to language barriers, a lack of culturally humble training further exacerbates these issues, as clinicians may struggle to accurately assess children who do not speak English fluently or for whom English is not their first language (Zuckerman et al., 2013). This bias underscores the need for culturally and linguistically adapted assessment instruments to ensure equitable and accurate diagnosis of autism across diverse populations.

Finally, clinician bias in assessing children from different gender identities, racial identities, ethnic identities, or cultural backgrounds for autism can significantly influence diagnostic outcomes, often leading to disparities in diagnosis and treatment. Factors contributing to this bias include implicit biases, which are unconscious attitudes or stereotypes that affect clinicians' understanding, actions, and decisions (FitzGerald & Hurst, 2017). Racially and ethnically minoritized children are often diagnosed with autism later than their White peers, and their caregivers report experiencing significant barriers in the diagnostic process (Constantino et al., 2020; Fisher et al., 2023; Pearson & Meadan, 2018; Stahmer et al., 2019; Zuckerman et al., 2013). Research indicates that clinicians may have preconceived notions about the prevalence and presentation of autism in different racial or cultural groups, potentially leading to underdiagnosis or misdiagnosis in minoritized populations (Mandell et al., 2007). Specifically, anti-Black racism significantly impacts the assessment and diagnostic process for Black autistic people, and Black autistic children are 2.6 times more likely to be misdiagnosed than White autistic children (Mandell et al., 2007; Straiton & Sridhar, 2022).

Clinician biases also impact underdiagnosis in evaluating children assigned female at birth (Lockwood et al., 2021; Rynkiewicz et al., 2016) and gender-diverse children. Assigned female at birth children are more likely than assigned male at birth children to be misdiagnosed and underdiagnosed for autism (Gillberg, 1993). This is because the current gold standard autism assessments are developed based on the phenotype of autistic boys, which does not include many characteristics of autistic girls (Rynkiewicz et al., 2018). It is also important for clinicians to note that there is a high occurrence of autism in gender-diverse and transgender individuals, highlighting the importance of providers to inquire about gender identity with all assessment clients approximately 11 years and older when assessing for autism (Greene et al., 2024). These biases highlight the need for culturally humble and gender-diverse normed diagnostic tools and training programs to improve the accuracy and equity of autism diagnoses across diverse populations.

The present chapter will examine several important areas of assessment of autism. First, the diagnostic features of autism will be reviewed. Second, essential components of culturally humble assessment of autism will be discussed. Third, considerations for providing an autism diagnosis to children and families within the context of a feedback appointment will be outlined. Fourth, considerations for recommending appropriate interventions when engaging with children and families from historically underserved and marginalized groups will be explored. Finally, future directions for autism assessment are offered.

DIAGNOSTIC CRITERIA FOR AUTISM SPECTRUM DISORDER

The primary diagnostic criteria for autism include persistent differences in social communication and social interaction across multiple contexts, such as difficulties in social–emotional reciprocity, nonverbal communicative behaviors, and developing, maintaining, and understanding relationships. Additionally, individuals must exhibit restricted, repetitive patterns of behavior, interests, or activities, as evidenced by at least two of the following: stereotyped or repetitive motor movements, use of objects, or speech; insistence on sameness, inflexible adherence to routines, or ritualized patterns of verbal or nonverbal behavior; highly restricted, fixated interests that are abnormal in intensity or focus; and sensory reactivity or unusual interest in sensory aspects of the environment (American Psychiatric Association, 2013). Characteristics of autism must be present in the early developmental period (but may not become fully manifest until social demands exceed limited capacities or may be masked by learned strategies in later life). Autism can sometimes be identified in children as young as 18 months old, but a reliable diagnosis can be provided as young as at the age of 24 months (Hyman et al., 2020).

DSM-5-TR and the *International Classification of Diseases, 11th Revision* (ICD-11) (World Health Organization, 2019) are both widely used diagnostic tools in the field of mental health, but their usage varies by country and context (First, 2009). DSM-5-TR is primarily used in the United States. It is published by the American Psychiatric Association and is the standard classification of mental disorders used by mental health professionals in the United States. Many mental health professionals in Canada also use DSM-5-TR, although the ICD-10-CA (Canadian Institute for Health Information, 2019) is also recognized. Some other countries may use DSM-5-TR, particularly in academic and research settings, but it is less commonly used as the primary diagnostic tool outside of North America. ICD-11 is used globally and is endorsed by the World Health Organization. It is the international standard for reporting diseases and health conditions. Most European countries use ICD-11 for diagnostic purposes in both general and mental health care. Many Asian countries also use ICD-11, although some may use it in conjunction with their own national diagnostic systems.

It is important that the diagnostic criteria for autism spectrum disorder found in DSM-5-TR (where they appear on pp. 56–57) and in ICD-11 (which makes the criteria accessible via search at *https://icd.who.int/browse/2025-01/mms/en*) not be interpreted in a literal sense only, as presentations of the diagnostic social communication criteria significantly vary across individuals on the spectrum. The examples listed in the criteria are *only illustrative*, *not exhaustive*, of the ways in which autism can present. Interpreting these criteria at face value may lead to the cultural, racial, and gender biases in the diagnostic process that are discussed in the introductory section of this chapter. For example, camouflaging and masking are complex mechanisms used to compensate for social differences in autistic individuals, particularly females, which often leads to misdiagnosis, late diagnosis, or underdiagnosis (Tubío-Fungueiriño et al., 2021). Masking of autistic traits can be effective for fitting into non-autistic spaces but can take a significant toll mentally, emotionally and physically. This is why it is important to note the statement in the DSM-5-TR and ICD-11 diagnostic criteria: "symptoms may not become fully manifest until social demands exceed limited capacities or may be masked by learned strategies in later life." Additionally, autism is often missed in young children with co-occurring mental health conditions, as clinicians often have trouble teasing apart autism from (or diagnosing before/instead of autism) co-occurring anxiety, depression, obsessive–compulsive disorders, oppositional defiant disorders, and attention-deficit/hyperactivity disorder (ADHD) (Gabrielsen et al., 2023, Chapter 8, pp. 155–172). Although not noted in the DSM-5-TR criteria, emotion-regulation challenges and challenging behaviors are often common in autistic children (England-Mason, 2020; Matson & Nebel-Schwalm, 2007) and should be considered during the assessment process to avoid the potential misdiagnosis of autism as mood disorders, oppositional defiant disorder, etc.

With regard to the levels of autism, we find that they sometimes have utility; however, other times they can be misnomers for a child's actual experience. Additionally, some children may have abilities that meet one level and abilities that meet a different level; thus, assigning one level does not describe their true abilities. It can be more meaningful to identify each child's individual areas of strength and areas of support need. Similarly, using terms such as "high" or "low-functioning" are inaccurate ways of describing an person with autism's functioning. These lead to misunderstanding of who the person is, and they do not account for time, context, values, sensory systems, ways of being independent, and the fact that people change, grow, and fluctuate in the levels of support they need across their lifespan (Hartman et al., 2023).

Additionally, the diagnosis of autism spectrum disorder under DSM-5-TR and the special education eligibility criteria for autism under the Individuals with Disabilities Education Act (IDEA, 2004) serve different purposes and have distinct criteria. DSM-5-TR provides a clinical framework for medically diagnosing autism based on specific criteria, including persistent differences in social communication and social interaction and restricted, repetitive patterns of behavior, interests, or activities. These symptoms must be present in the early developmental period and cause a clinically significant impact in social, occupational, or other important areas of functioning. In contrast, IDEA focuses on determining eligibility for special education services in the educational context. Under IDEA, a child must exhibit characteristics of autism that significantly affect verbal and nonverbal communication and social interaction, generally evident before age 3 years, and these characteristics must adversely affect the child's educational performance. The federal government's educational guidelines define autism as

> a developmental disability significantly affecting verbal and nonverbal communication and social interaction, generally evident before age three that adversely affects a child's educational performance. . . . Other characteristics often associated with autism are engaging in repetitive activities and stereotyped movements, resistance to environmental change or change in daily routines, and unusual responses to sensory experiences. The term autism does not apply if the child's educational performance is adversely affected primarily because the child has an emotional disturbance, as defined in [IDEA]. (IDEA, 20 U.S.C. § 1400, 2004)

CLINICAL AND SCHOOL-BASED ASSESSMENTS

Whereas health care professionals use DSM-5-TR diagnosis to identify and support autism, IDEA eligibility criteria are used by educational professionals (e.g., school psychologists) to ensure that children on the autism spectrum receive appropriate support and services in the school setting. Educational professionals are not providing a medical diagnosis but determining eligibility for special education using IDEA eligibility criteria. To determine a child's eligibility for a school classification of autism spectrum disorder, a comprehensive developmental assessment must be completed in the school setting that includes a multimethod, multisource, and multisetting approach. In comparison, medical diagnoses typically function to provide useful information to the client and their family so they can access resources and interventions outside of the school setting and financial support from insurance companies. Medical diagnoses are not made to determine need for special education services, and academic performance does not have a bearing on the diagnostic decision; however, there is a similar multimethod, multisource, and multisetting evaluation approach that is suggested in clinical practice (American Psychiatric Association, 2013; Mandell & Palmer, 2005). It can be the case that a child with a medical diagnosis of autism is not found eligible for special education services under autism as the primary or even secondary designation. This can be because their educational performance is not impacted or they are found as eligible under a different designation that is more applicable for in-school support.

The aspects of evaluation can differ between school-based special education eligibility evaluations and medical diagnostic testing. Assessment of autism in both settings includes documentation of the child's symptoms that are associated with autism, including social communication and social interactions; restricted, repetitive patterns of behavior, interests, and/or activities; early presence of autism characteristics; and significant clinical impact on functioning. For a medical diagnosis of autism, there must be documentation of restricted, repetitive patterns of behavior, interests, and/or activities in the developmental history, in addition to differences in social communication (American Psychiatric Association, 2013). However, for school-based eligibility, students are not required to demonstrate restricted, repetitive patterns of behavior, interests, and/or activities.

COMPONENTS OF AUTISM ASSESSMENT

A diagnosis of autism requires a comprehensive clinical assessment using both direct observational measures of the child, parent/caregiver questionnaires, parent/caregiver interviews, observations across settings, and self-report measures depending on the child's age and language level (Bigham et al., 2023). All instruments used during an evaluation should represent a range of potential functioning that is in line with the child's developmental level. Additionally, because of the symptom variability noted across age, development, and environment, it is critical for any professional conducting an autism evaluation to choose instruments and interviews that are appropriate for the child's presentation (Goldstein et al., 2008; Kroncke et al., 2016). It is also important to understand that many measures used in autism assessment were developed in the context of research studies, which often have strict inclusion criteria and do not represent the general population (Lebersfeld, 2020). There is a need for the development of evidence-based neurodiversity-affirming assessment tools for all ages (Rutherford & Johnston, 2022).

Conducting culturally competent assessments is essential for achieving fair and accurate diagnoses across diverse populations. According to the American Psychological Association (2017), several key guidelines should be followed to ensure cultural humility in assessments. First, clinicians need to be aware of the cultural context of the individual being evaluated, including an understanding of cultural norms, values, and practices that may affect behavior and symptom expression. Second, it is essential to use assessment tools that have been validated for the specific cultural group of the individual. In cases where such tools are not available, clinicians should recognize and disclose the limitations and potential biases of the tools they are using. Assessments should be conducted in the individual's preferred language whenever possible, and qualified interpreters should be utilized to facilitate accurate communication if language barriers exist. Additionally, although not noted in the American Psychological Association guidelines, when conducting the observation and interviews, the examiner should consider that the family members being interviewed may be neurodivergent (whether formally diagnosed or not), as autism is genetically based (Havdahl et al., 2021). The manner in which some parent interview questions are stated on autism-specific interviews can come across as stigmatizing and are worded using the medical model. Examiners may opt to slightly change the wording of such questions to be more neurodiverse-affirming and less stigmatizing. For example, instead of asking, "How old was your child when you first wondered if there might be something not quite right with their development?" (Rutter et al., 2003), the examiner may shift this to "How old was your child when you first wondered if something was different about their development?" Making accommodations, when necessary, is recommended when conducting clinical interviews and giving surveys to neurodivergent clients and families (Wright, 2019).

Developmental History

A thorough developmental history that includes age at which developmental milestones were obtained (speech and motor skills) and functioning across the social behavior domain (comfortability with eye contact, imitation, and response/initiation of joint attention, behavior, and sensory sensitivities) is essential at the start of the assessment process. Both structured and non-structured clinical interviews are useful in documenting early childhood development and behaviors, as well as current behavioral differences. The Autism Diagnostic Interview—Revised (ADI-R) (Rutter et al., 2003) is a semistructured diagnostic interview given to a parent or caregiver by a clinician who is trained in the ADI-R's administration and scoring. The interview asks the caregiver in-depth, detailed questions about the child's developmental history and behaviors associated with autism. The ADI-R can be quite useful in differentiating autism from other diagnoses, as it asks questions specific to autism that parents/caregivers are likely not asked by other providers or pediatricians. Additionally, if the child had engaged in high levels of masking or effortfully hid their autistic characteristics, it is possible that the parent may not have observed certain behaviors during childhood.

Table 14.1 provides a list of potential questions that may be included when conducting an informal interview with parents/caregivers about their child's early development.

Testing Environment

In structuring the testing environment, standardization techniques of assessments must be followed to obtain valid results. Management of behaviors that will lead to increased cooperation and motivation is also essential in order to obtain accurate estimates of functioning. In some cases, it may be possible for a parent or caregiver to be present during the testing session, which may ease anxiety for the child, and it is required for a parent or caregiver to be present during the administration of Autism Diagnostic Observation Schedule, Second Edition (ADOS-2), Modules Toddler 1 and 2 (Lord et al., 2012). For very young children or children who are non-speaking, it would likely be inappropriate to separate them from their caregiver during the evaluation. When possible, it may be beneficial to schedule the evaluation into separate sessions across more than one evaluation day. This may reduce fatigue for the child so the examiners may see a general estimate of the child's abilities and presentation. This may increase a child's comfort level (i.e., examiners may see fewer masking behaviors from the child on the second day of the evaluation).

To help promote motivation and comfort for the child, the examiner should allow for brief play and warm-up time for the child as they enter the assessment environment. Warm-up time is also typically an appropriate time to discuss with the family and child what the assessment period will include. For older children, it may be appropriate to have a conversation with them about why they are at the appointment and offer space for them to ask questions. This practice follows neurodiverse-affirming guidelines by promoting autonomy for the child

TABLE 14.1. Questions for Developmental History Interviews with Parents/Caregivers

Category	Questions
	Medical history
Prenatal and birth history	Were there any complications during pregnancy or birth? Was the child born prematurely or full-term? Were there any issues noted at birth?
Medical conditions	Does the child have any chronic medical conditions? Has the child had any serious illnesses or hospitalizations?
Family medical and mental health history	Is there a family history of developmental differences, including autism? Are there any other family members with similar symptoms? What is the family's mental health history?
	Developmental milestones
Motor skills	When did the child start to crawl, walk, and run? Have there been any concerns about the child's motor coordination?
Social communication milestones	How does the child communicate? When did the child say their first words? When did the child start forming sentences? What are examples of their first words and phrases?
Self-care skills	Tell me about the child's self-care skills, such as feeding themselves and getting dressed. Tell me about how toilet training went: Were there any issues? How is the child with washing their hands and taking a bath or showering?
	Environmental and cultural circumstances
Recent stressors	Tell me about any recent stressors, legal issues, or crises that may be impacting the child/family.
Impact of COVID-19	How was the child impacted by the COVID-19 pandemic?
Trauma	Describe any history or incidences of traumatic/potentially traumatic incidents that the child has experienced.
Discrimination	Has the child experienced discrimination, prejudice, or racism? If so, how has that impacted them?
	Communication
Verbal communication	Tell me about the child's verbal communication. How would you describe the child's vocabulary and language skills? Does the child engage in echolalia or repetitive language? (Give examples for families who may not understand this jargon.)
Nonspeaking communication	Does the child use gestures, such as pointing or waving? How does the child express their needs and emotions without words?
Understanding	Does the child understand and follow simple instructions? How well does the child understand spoken language?
	Social interactions
Interaction with peers	How does the child interact with other children? Does the child show interest in playing with others? Does the child have friends or a best friend?

(continued)

TABLE 14.1. *(continued)*

Category	Questions
Interaction with adults	How does the child interact with family members and other adults? How does the child respond to social cues? Are they able to read social cues from your observation?
Play behavior	What types of play does the child engage in? Does the child engage in imaginative or pretend play? Does their play vary, or does it follow a similar pattern each time?
	Sensory sensitivity
Sensory preferences	Does the child have any strong preferences or aversions to certain textures, sounds, lights, smells, tastes, clothing, or foods? How does the child react to loud noises or bright lights? How does the child react to physical touch?
Behavioral responses	Does the child show any unusual reactions to sensory stimuli, such as covering ears or avoiding certain textures? Are there any specific situations that seem to overwhelm the child?
	Restricted interests and repetitive behavior
Repetitive actions	Does the child engage in repetitive behaviors, such as hand-flapping, rocking, or spinning objects? How often do these behaviors occur?
Focused interests	Does the child have any intense interests or fixations on specific topics or objects? How does the child react if they are unable to engage in these interests?
Routine and change	How does the child handle changes in routine or unexpected events? Does the child insist on following specific routines or rituals?

(Waddington et al., 2023). The use of a visual schedule that will allow the child to see the order of the test administration and can also be used to provide structure for children who prefer routine or difficulty with transitions. Additionally, the examiner may allow the examinee to earn rewards or offer the choice for breaks to play with preferred items after completing tasks, if that is motivating and meaningful for the child. Some children also require more movement than others, so the examiners may allow children to move around the evaluation room as needed and should avoid forcing children to sit still or strapping young children into high chairs. Examiners may also offer the option for children to sit on their caregiver's lap during developmental testing or cognitive testing if that is most comfortable for the family.

Developmental and Intellectual Functioning

Evaluating a child's developmental or intellectual functioning is an essential component of an autism assessment because it provides valuable insights into their developmental or cognitive abilities and identifies areas where they may excel or require additional support. Tools such as cognitive and developmental assessments enable clinicians to gain a comprehensive understanding of the child's cognitive or developmental profile, which can significantly influence the diagnosis and the intervention strategies employed. These assessments are vital for distinguishing autism from other developmental conditions that may present with similar symptoms but have different cognitive characteristics. The Wechsler Intelligence Scale for Children—Fifth Edition (WISC–V) (Wechsler, 2014) and Differential Ability Scales—Second Edition (DAS-II; Elliott, 2007) are common cognitive evaluations used in the context of autism evaluations. The WISC–V ranges from 6 to 16 years, 11 months (16:11) of age (adolescents 17:0 and older would be given the Wechler Adult Intelligence Scale—Fourth Edition [WAIS–IV; Wechsler, 2008]). The DAS-II is divided into two batteries: the Early Years battery (ages 2:6 to 8:11 years) and the School-Age battery (5:0 to 17:11 years). The DAS-II offers more teaching items than the WISC–V, but the WISC–V core subtests examine processing speed, whereas the DAS-II does not. Given the common systematic differences in overall scores across these two assessments for autistic populations, choice of assessment should be considered carefully.

Different factors involved in cognitive assessment administration may lead to an underestimation of the child's cognitive abilities. Factors to consider when administering a cognitive assessment to an autistic child as opposed to a non-autistic child include that such tests generally require the child to act cooperatively with an unfamiliar examiner in a new environment for a long period of time, have inherent non-autistic social demands/expectations, and require the child to engage in activities that may not be motivating (Kuriakose, 2014). There are also time limits to providing some answers that may impact final scores. For example, a child who takes longer to provide the correct answer for an item may obtain a lower score than their ability because they provided the answer outside the time limit, or the child may prefer to say all of the incorrect answers first and then the correct answer, which extends the amount of time taken to answer. It can also be the case that autistic children prefer to follow their own interests during the tasks rather than answer the questions given by the examiner (i.e., the correct answer is "red balloon," but because the child loves blue, they choose "blue balloon," despite having an understanding of the task at hand). Additionally, the child with autism might interpret the standardized instructions literally and require additional verbal information that is not part of the standardized scripted procedure to understand the task. There has not yet been developed a cognitive assessment measure specifically for autistic populations.

When children are chronologically younger and/or developmentally functioning at an age below the DAS-II and the WISC–V age ranges, developmental functioning should be assessed rather than cognitive functioning. The Bayley Scales of Infant and Toddler Development, Third Edition (Bayley, 2005), ranges from 1 to 42 months of age, and the Mullen Scales of Early Learning (Mullen, 1995) ranges from birth to 68 months of age. These developmental assessments can be helpful in assessing for developmental delays. Developmental delays are important to consider in autism assessment for young children, given that recent studies show that 62.3% of children with global developmental delay (GDD) also have autism, and 30–80% of children with autism have co-occurring GDD or intellectual disability (Shan et al., 2022).

For non-speaking and minimally verbal children above the age ranges for the Mullen and Bayley assessments, cognitive tests such as the Stanford–Binet Intelligence Scales, Fifth Edition (SB-5) (Roid & Pomplun, 2012) and the Leiter International Performance Scale, Third Edition (Leiter-3) (Roid & Koch, 2017) are more appropriate. The Leiter-3 is a nonverbal assessment of cognitive functioning, which can be useful for assessing cognitive abilities in individuals with speech, hearing, and language impairments or who are not native English speakers. The SB-5 Abbreviated Battery IQ (ABIQ) can be used to obtain a general estimate of a child's verbal and nonverbal abilities, given the Leiter only assesses nonverbal cognitive abilities. The ABIQ is based on two routing subtests: one nonverbal (Object Series/Matrices) and one verbal (Vocabulary). The SB-5 ABIQ can provide a brief picture of a child's verbal and nonverbal skills. Examiners may choose to administer the Leiter in addition to the SB-5 to get a better idea of the child's specific strengths within their nonverbal abilities since the SB-5 has high verbal demands and may result in an underestimate of one's nonverbal strengths and abilities.

Understanding a child's intellectual and developmental functioning also aids in the development of educational and therapeutic plans that are specifically tailored to their needs, ensuring that the support provided is both appropriate and effective. By identifying cognitive or developmental strengths, clinicians and educators can leverage these areas to enhance learning and development, while also addressing any cognitive or developmental weaknesses that may need targeted intervention. In essence, assessing intellectual or developmental functioning not only contributes to a more accurate and comprehensive autism diagnosis but also plays a crucial role in designing individualized, effective treatment plans that promote the best possible outcomes for the child.

However, it is important to note that cultural bias in cognitive and developmental assessments can manifest in several ways, potentially affecting the accuracy and fairness of the assessment. Language barriers are a significant source of bias, as testing items may use language, idioms, or expressions unfamiliar to individuals from different cultural or linguistic backgrounds, leading to misunderstandings and incorrect answers. Instructions and questions may not be fully comprehensible to non-native speakers, affecting their ability to perform well (Fagan & Holland, 2002). Content relevance is another issue, as testing items may include culturally specific knowledge or experiences that are not universally shared, disadvantaging individuals from different cultural backgrounds. Educational disparities also play a role, as differences in educational systems, curricula, and access to quality education can affect evaluation performance. Socioeconomic factors further complicate the issue, as socioeconomic status can influence access to learning resources, extracurricular activities, and enrichment opportunities, which can affect cognitive development and evaluation performance.

Language and Communication

Before beginning the assessment process, it is crucial for clinicians to evaluate the language proficiency of both the child and caregiver. Limited proficiency in the assessment language can hinder the child's ability to comprehend and respond to tasks, potentially leading to misdiagnosis (Kremer-Sadlik, 2005). Bilingual or multilingual individuals may show different language development patterns, which could be mistaken for language deficits linked to autism (Hambly & Fombonne, 2012). Variations in dialect and accent can influence the interpretation of verbal responses and language use. Additionally, the language used in parent–child interactions might differ from the assessment language, affecting the accuracy of reported behaviors (Yu, 2013).

In evaluating potential autism, assessing receptive, expressive, and pragmatic language is crucial for understanding an individual's communicative abilities. Receptive language can be measured through standardized tests like the Peabody Picture Vocabulary Test, 5th Edition (PPVT-5) (Dunn, 2019) and the Clinical Evaluation of Language Fundamentals, 5th Edition (CELF-5) (Wiig et al., 2013), which gauge comprehension of vocabulary and spoken language. Expressive language is assessed using tools such as the Expressive Vocabulary Test, 3rd Edition (EVT-3) (Williams, 2019) and the CELF-5, focusing on language production, including vocabulary, grammar, and sentence structure. The Preschool Language Scales, 5th Edition (PLS-5) (Zimmerman et al., 2011) can also be used to assess auditory comprehension and expressive communication for children from birth to age 7:11 years. Pragmatic language, related to the social use of language, can be evaluated with the Test of Pragmatic Language–2 (TOPL-2) (Phelps-Terasaki & Phelps-Gunn, 2007), the Children's Communication Checklist–2 (CCC-2) (Bishop, 2003), and the Comprehensive Assessment for Spoken Language, 2nd Edition (CASL-2) (Carrow-Woolfolk, 2017), which assess skills like conversation initiation, understanding non-literal language, inference, and use of social skills. Additionally, naturalistic observations and reports from parents/caregivers or teachers offer valuable insights into the individual's everyday functional language use. A child may have advanced vocabulary and fluent expressive language but have difficulty using this language in a socially functional and flexible manner (Dennis et al., 2001). Combining these assessments provides a detailed language profile, essential for accurately diagnosing autism and developing effective support strategies (Lord et al., 2012; Bishop, 2003; Phelps-Terasaki & Phelps-Gunn, 2007).

Clinical Observation

Both structured and unstructured observations of the child are an essential component of assessment for autism. Clinicians evaluate many behaviors during clinical observations, including verbal and nonverbal social communication abilities, play skills, engagement in reciprocal interaction, and the presence of restricted and repetitive behaviors and interests. The ADOS-2 (Lord et al., 2012) is a widely used tool in the assessment of autism. The ADOS-2 is a semistructured, standardized assessment of communication, social interaction, play or imaginative use of materials, and restricted and repetitive behaviors. It incorporates the use of planned social occasions, referred to as "presses" in which a behavior of a particular type is likely to appear. Based on the interaction, the behaviors are coded and entered into an algorithm. The ADOS-2 captures observable autistic characteristics and should always be paired with a thorough developmental history caregiver interview and clinical interview with the child if appropriate, as it can be the case that autistic behaviors are present but are masked or hidden.

It is important for clinicians to consider that the ADOS-2 coding system is based on non-autistic social communication expectations and ways of interacting. The assessment does not acknowledge that for autistic individuals, speaking at length on one topic, for example, is a valid form of communication and can be a strength (Hartman et al., 2023). The ADOS-2 is divided into five different modules depending on the age and expressive language skills of the person being evaluated. Modules 1 and 2 are most commonly used with preschool-age children. Module 1 is appropriate for children with only single words or no speech, and Module 2 is intended for use with young children with phrase speech; however, it may also be used with children of any age who are not verbally fluent. Module 3 is for use with verbally fluent children and adolescents, while Module 4 is used with verbally fluent older adolescents and adults. The ADOS-2 also includes a Toddler Module for use with toddlers 12 to 30 months of age who do not consistently use phrase speech (Lord et al., 2012).

During the COVID-19 pandemic, the Brief Observation of Symptoms of Autism (BOSA) (Dow et al., 2022) was developed. The BOSA is a telehealth social observation with standardized materials and activities that can be coded by clinicians trained in the ADOS-2. It consists of a 12- to 14-minute interaction between the individual being assessed and a caregiver or clinician. The BOSA has utility in providing increased accessibility to an autism diagnosis for those who do not live near an autism center, permitting a more specialized evaluation.

In addition, the Childhood Autism Rating Scale, Second Edition (CARS-2) (Schopler et al., 2010) is a rating scale completed by a trained clinician and is based on direct observations. Although background information in the form of clinical records and parent reports may be incorporated into the clinician's CARS-2 ratings of behavior, these scales are not given to caregivers and/or teachers to be completed individually. The CARS-2 includes two rating booklets—the Standard Version (CARS-2-ST) and a High-Functioning Version (CARS-2-HF). There is also a separate CARS-2 questionnaire for parents/caregivers.

The Monteiro Interview Guidelines for Diagnosing the Autism Spectrum, Second Edition (MIGDAS-2) (Monteiro & Stegall, 2018) is a comprehensive tool that includes interviews with the child, their caregivers, and other significant people in their life, such as teachers, to gather a well-rounded view of the child's functioning (Monteiro & Stegall, 2018). Clinicians are guided to observe the child in various settings and situations to identify behaviors indicative of autism. Detailed questions about the individual's developmental milestones, medical history, and early behaviors are included to provide a comprehensive background. The guidelines also cover sensory processing and motor behaviors and assess the individual's social interactions, communication skills, and the presence of any repetitive or restrictive behaviors. The MIGDAS-2 includes a protocol for verbal adolescents that engages them in a safe and affirming manner to learn more about their experiences across many domains, including sensory preferences. While the MIGDAS-2 is not a standardized test with numerical scores, it provides a qualitative framework for clinicians to interpret the gathered information and make a diagnostic decision.

When administering autism assessment tools such as the ADOS-2, the CARS-2, and the MIGDAS-2, it is crucial to consider cultural and linguistic factors that may introduce bias. Different cultures have varying norms for social interactions and communication styles, which may be misinterpreted as indicators of autism (Mandell & Novak, 2005). For all behaviors reported, cultural understanding must be used to interpret whether the behaviors are specific to autism or not. Levels of awareness, understanding, and stigma associated with autism vary across cultures can impact how parents report behaviors (Kinnear et al., 2016). In some communities, stigma may lead to underreporting of symptoms due to fear of social repercussions. The way emotions are expressed and understood can differ significantly between cultures, potentially leading to misinterpretation of affective behaviors (Dyches et al., 2004). For example, some cultures may express emotions more subtly, which could be misread as a lack of emotional response. Cultural differences in play and socialization practices can also affect the interpretation of social and communicative behaviors during assessments (Harrison et al., 2017). Additionally, pragmatic language use, including idioms, humor, and indirect communication, varies across cultures and can impact the assessment of communication skills (Yu, 2013). For example, understanding and using idiomatic expressions may be challenging for individuals from different linguistic backgrounds.

Rating Scales

Rating scales are a useful and efficient method of collecting information from parents, caregivers, and child and adolescent self-reports about current and past behaviors directly related to autism. Additionally, rating scales may be completed by individuals such as teachers, behavior specialists, and interventionists who also see the client across a breadth of situations under differing conditions to help provide the clinician with a holistic view of the client's presentation. Rating scales assessing adaptive functioning, symptoms and characteristics of autism, executive functioning, and other internalizing and externalizing behaviors children may exhibit are available.

Adaptive behavior skills are important and essential to promote the independent functioning of autistic individuals (Pugliese et al., 2015) and have been found to show a better predictive outcome when compared to cognitive ability and language abilities. The Vineland Adaptive Behavior Scales, Third Edition (Vineland–3) (Sparrow et al., 2016); the Adaptive Behavior Assessment System, Third Edition, caregiver and self-report (ABAS-3) (Harrison & Oakland, 2015); and the Developmental Profile, Fourth Edition (DP-4) (Alpern, 2020) each evaluate key domains of adaptive functioning: communication, daily living skills, socialization, and motor skills. For autism assessment, the Communication and Social domains of adaptive skills questionnaires help identify communication and socialization differences, which are primary characteristics of autism. Critical items in the Maladaptive Behaviors domain of adaptive behavior rating scales, such as the Vineland–3, also address stereotyped or repetitive motor movements, repetitive speech, fixated interests, and sensory issues. Additionally, the ABAS-3 self-report starts at age 16 and can be used to augment the ABAS-3 caregiver/parent report or the Vineland caregiver interview/report.

Rating scales focusing primarily on core characteristics of autism are an essential component of all autism evaluations. The Autism Spectrum Rating Scales (ASRS) (Goldstein & Naglieri, 2009) measure behaviors associated with autism in children and youth ages 2 to 18 years, featuring separate forms for ages 2 to 5 and 6 to 18, with both parent and teacher versions available. The ASRS Full-Scale Form accurately classified 89.5% of children ages 2 to 5 and 90.1% of those ages 6 to 18. The Gilliam Autism Rating Scale, Third Edition (GARS-3) (Gilliam, 2014) is a screening tool for identifying autism-specific behaviors in individuals ages 3 to 22 years, completed by parents and/or teachers, and includes six subscales and an overall Autism Index, although it lacks a matched control group in its normative sample. The Social Communication Questionnaire (SCQ) (Rutter et al., 2003) is a 40-item screener based on parent/caregiver reports, designed as a companion to the ADI-R, focusing on autism-specific behaviors and can be completed with minimal clinician support. The SCQ's most meaningful score is the total score from the Lifetime form, with a recommended cutoff of 15, though this may yield false positives in certain populations (Berument et al., 1999; Bishop & Norbury, 2002; Sappok et al., 2015). The Social Responsiveness Scale, Second Edition (SRS-2) (Constantino & Gruber, 2012) is a 65-item rating scale for measuring autism symptoms, including social interactions, communication, and repetitive behaviors, with forms for different age groups and can be completed by various respondents. The SRS-2 provides *T*-scores for five treatment subscales and a total score reflecting social communication deficits. However, it is notable that the SRS-2 has not been normed for children with Level 3 autism (i.e., requiring very substantial support) (Thurm & Klaiman, 2023). The Autism-Spectrum Quotient (AQ) (Baron-Cohen et al., 2001) is a 50-item questionnaire for adolescents and adults age 16 and older that assesses five symptom clusters: social skills, attention switching, attention to detail, communication, and imagination. Furthermore, the Camouflaging Autistic Traits Questionnaire (CAT-Q) (Hull et al., 2019) is a self-report measure of social camouflaging behaviors in adolescents and adults age 16 and up of average to higher intelligence. The CAT-Q may be helpful for clinicians to use with adolescents who do not at that time meet full diagnostic criteria due to their ability to mask their autistic traits.

Broadband behavior rating scales allow for examination of co-occurring symptoms beyond characteristics of autism. The Behavior Assessment System for Children—Third Edition (BASC-3) (Reynolds & Kamphaus, 2004) evaluates clinical and adaptive behavior and emotional functioning in individuals ages 2 to 25 years. It includes parent, teacher, and self-report forms, with clinical and adaptive scales varying by age group. Research has demonstrated that autistic children obtain higher scores on the Atypicality, Withdrawal, Functional Communication, and Developmental Social Disorders (DSD) scales than allistic children, including those with developmental delays (Volker et al.,

2010; Bradstreet et al., 2017). The BASC-3 Self Report of Personality can be administered starting as young as ages 8–11 (Child Version) and ages 12–21 (Adolescent Version).

Several rating scales including the Behavior Rating Inventory of Executive Function, Second Edition (BRIEF-2) (Gioia et al., 2015), Barkley Deficits in Executive Functioning Scale (BDEFS) (Barkley, 2011), Comprehensive Executive Function Inventory (CEFI) (Naglieri et al., 2013), Conners Fourth Edition (Conners 4) (Conners, 2022), and Brown Executive Function/Attention Scales (Brown EF/A) (Brown, 2003) are available to assess executive functioning. Executive functioning refers to a set of cognitive processes that are essential for controlling behavior and achieving goals. These processes include planning, working memory, attention, problem solving, verbal reasoning, inhibition, mental flexibility, task initiation, and monitoring of actions. Autistic individuals often experience executive functioning challenges that can significantly impact their daily functioning (Naglieri & Goldstein, 2013). Challenges with inhibition can result in impulsive actions, difficulty waiting for turns, and struggles in social situations requiring self-control. Cognitive flexibility, the ability to shift thinking and adapt to change, is often difficult for autistic individuals, leading to distress when routines are disrupted. Individuals on the spectrum may also exhibit difficulties with initiation, requiring prompts or external cues to begin tasks. Self-monitoring, or the ability to evaluate and adjust one's behavior, can be challenging, impacting learning and social interactions. Emotional regulation difficulties are common, leading to heightened anxiety, frustration, and meltdowns, which can lead to the misdiagnosis of mood disorders in undiagnosed autistic females (Kentrou et al., 2024). Lastly, attention control challenges can make it difficult to focus on relevant information while ignoring distractions, impacting academic performance and learning.

When interpreting results, it is important to keep in mind that these assessment tools may be subject to cultural bias, which can affect their validity and reliability when used with diverse populations. Many commonly used rating scales are based on normative data that primarily reflect Euro-American populations, thus limiting their relevance to different cultures. Cultural differences in parenting styles, child-rearing practices, and behavioral expectations can significantly influence how behaviors are rated (Rudy & Grusec, 2006). Behaviors deemed problematic in one culture may be perceived as normal or even desirable in another. For instance, high energy levels might be encouraged and valued in some cultures but considered disruptive in others (Conners, 2019). Additionally, cultural differences in the importance of social reciprocity and emotional expression can impact how behaviors are assessed on rating scales for autism symptoms.

There is a need to norm rating scales for gender-diverse individuals. The CAT-Q (non-binary norms) and the Conners 4 (norms included non-binary and transgender individuals) are the only autism-related rating scales known to the authors that acknowledge gender diversity. Finally, although several rating scales are available in multiple languages, it is important to confirm the availability of specific language versions with the publishers, as translations may be updated or expanded over time. (See Table 14.2 for a list of frequently used assessments specifying the languages in which they are widely available.) Although translations exist, it is essential to ensure that the instruments have been culturally adapted and validated for use in the target population to maintain the accuracy and reliability of the assessment. When using translated versions, it is advisable to involve qualified interpreters who are familiar with the clinical context to ensure accurate administration and interpretation of results (Hambleton et al., 2005).

PROVIDING DIAGNOSTIC RESULTS

Delivering the diagnostic results to the child and family is as important of a process as the rest of the evaluation and is an opportunity to speak about the child and their support needs in a strengths-based and neurodiverse-affirming manner (Rutherford & Johnston, 2022). The way the results are delivered, and the words that are used, can have a powerful impact on how the family and child understands autism and how the child experiences the world. From the outset of the evaluation, establishing trust and rapport with the family is paramount, as that established relationship helps with the receiving of the diagnosis. Throughout the entire process, how the examiner talks about autism is modeling for how the family will come to understand it. Reframing autism using neurodiverse-affirming language throughout the process sets up feedback to be potentially less stressful or anxiety-provoking. For example, imagine how the parent will receive the diagnosis if the examiner

TABLE 14.2. Language Availability of Commonly Used Rating Scales

Instrument	Languages available	Publisher
Adaptive Behavior Assessment System, Third Edition (ABAS-3)	English, Spanish	Western Psychological Services (WPS)
Autism Behavior Checklist (ABC)	English, Spanish, French, German, Italian, Dutch, Chinese (Simplified), Japanese, Korean, Portuguese (Brazilian), Russian, Turkish	Pro-Ed
Autism Spectrum Rating Scales (ASRS)	English, Spanish, French, German, Italian, Dutch, Chinese (Simplified), Japanese, Korean, Portuguese (Brazilian), Russian, Turkish	Multi-Health Systems (MHS)
Barkley Deficits in Executive Functioning Scale (BDEFS)	English	Guilford Press
Behavior Assessment System for Children—Third Edition (BASC-3)	English, Spanish	Pearson
Behavior Rating Inventory of Executive Function, Second Edition (BRIEF-2)	English, Spanish	Psychological Assessment Resources (PAR)
Brown Executive Function/Attention Scales (Brown EF/A)	English	Pearson
Comprehensive Executive Function Inventory (CEFI)	English, Spanish	Multi-Health Systems (MHS)
Child Behavior Checklist (CBCL)	English, Spanish, French, German, Italian, Dutch, Chinese (Simplified and Traditional), Japanese, Korean, Portuguese (Brazilian), Russian, Turkish, Arabic, Hebrew, and many more	ASEBA (Achenbach System of Empirically Based Assessment)
Conners Comprehensive Behavior Rating Scales (Conners CBRS)—Conners 4	English, Spanish, French	Multi-Health Systems (MHS)
Developmental Behavior Checklist (DBC)	English, Spanish, French, German, Italian, Dutch, Chinese (Simplified), Japanese, Korean, Portuguese (Brazilian), Russian, Turkish, Arabic, Hebrew, and many more	Monash University
Developmental Profile, Fourth Edition (DP-4)	English, Spanish	Western Psychological Services (WPS)
Gilliam Autism Rating Scale, Third Edition (GARS-3)	English, Spanish	Pro-Ed
Social Responsiveness Scale, Second Edition (SRS-2)	English, Spanish, French, German, Italian, Dutch, Chinese (Simplified), Japanese, Korean, Portuguese (Brazilian), Russian, Turkish	Western Psychological Services (WPS)
Vineland Adaptive Behavior Scales, Third Edition (Vineland–3)	English, Spanish, French, German, Italian, Dutch, Chinese (Simplified), Japanese, Korean, Portuguese (Brazilian), Russian, Turkish	Pearson

has used only deficit-based language in the way they have talked about autism and the way in which the questions are phrased versus using difference-based and objective language. It is the examiner's role to work to destigmatize how autism is perceived. A meta-analysis of parent experiences of autism diagnosis found that tone and a strength-based approach employed when delivering the diagnosis is important to caregivers (Makino et al., 2021). Additionally, partnering with parents during the feedback, asking how they feel receiving a diagnosis for their child, and being open to all and any type of questions from the parents sets up a safe and affirming space for collaborating on next steps for the child (Brown et al., 2021).

When giving an autism diagnosis, it is crucial to be very clear about why the diagnosis is being given. Several studies have reported that parents experience an inadequate explanation of the diagnosis when given (Makino et al., 2021). Naming exact behaviors that were observed during the assessment and providing exact details that the child and family provided within the framework of the autism diagnostic criteria is helpful for the family in understanding the information. Using objective language in a non-judgmental manner to describe autism provides modeling for how the family moves forward in their understanding of autism. Understanding and explaining a diagnosis from a strength-based approach can result in validating and affirming the child and family. For example, when a child is no longer described as having "challenging behavior," but their actions are understood within the context of their sensory and social differences, the family is better placed to meet the child's individual needs (Rutherford & Johnston, 2022).

Families can have varying ideas about what autism is and what it means for their child and can show a myriad of different responses to the diagnostic decision. It is important for the clinician to exude empathy and validation to all ways in which the family receives a diagnosis, as some parents might become emotional or question the diagnosis, while others might be pleased, in celebration of neurodivergence. It is also helpful for families when clinicians explain that there is not one piece of information that makes or breaks the diagnostic decision and that all information gathered is considered in a holistic manner to arrive at a decision (e.g., toe walking on its own does not make an autism diagnosis; it is when toe walking is present along with other diagnostic criteria).

To promote self-understanding, offering to provide the feedback results to the child directly should be considered and adjusted based on the child's age and language level. The child has the right to know the findings. Understanding the findings can be therapeutic for the child in helping them have language and words to express how they experience the world. As they get older and encounter potentially challenging situations or see their peers having more ease with skills than them, understanding how their brain is wired differently can be empowering (Oredipe et al., 2023). It can also help guide support approaches. Providing a social story to the child based on the assessment process can also be informative and helpful for explaining to the child in developmentally appropriate terms the results of testing (Tharinger et al., 2008).

A common question during feedback can be, "Where is my child on the spectrum?" It is common that parents' views of autism include a spectrum that is considered to be a straight line (e.g., more to less autistic). The authors find it can be more helpful to describe the autism spectrum not as a line but as a circle, with multiple pie pieces and facets about that person, that are dynamic and changing with time (see autism_sketches, 2022). Engaging the client in making their own circle and naming the pieces of themselves that are strengths and areas that need support can aid in their understanding of their differences more so than being told a number they are on the spectrum. The authors have found that using the circle image instead of the straight line for the autism spectrum has been incredibly helpful in families' understanding of the spectrum and the unique strengths and areas of support need for their child. Additionally, the family feels validated that the clinicians have taken the time to understand the unique needs of their child and can speak to the child's individual strengths.

If the child is not part of feedback, it is recommended that the family tell the child about their diagnosis at some point in childhood so they can understand themselves and the language to describe their experiences (Oredipe et al., 2023). While it is important for caregivers to use their intuition and knowledge of the child in making this decision, a cue for identifying the right time can be when the child starts asking questions about topics that have to do with their diagnosis or if the child notices they do things differently than their peers and they begin to ask about that. The way that caregivers provide the information impacts how the child feels and views the information (Crane et al., 2019). When provided in an affirming way, the child can associate strengths with the diagnosis. The information can be shared over informal chats, walks, while driving in the car, or on other casual activities; information can initially be minimal and build over time. Depending on the age of the child, inviting them directly into the feedback session can provide the opportunity to hear the results directly from the clinician or assessment team in a strength-based and affirming manner. It is more often the case that child clients are initiating their own evaluations because they want to understand their differences. In those cases, there is no question that the client should be part of feedback.

GUIDELINES FOR RECOMMENDING SUPPORT SERVICES

Though there are many evidence-based interventions for autistic children and their families, intervention supports are not one-size-fits-all. When thinking about recommendations, clinicians should first consider the family's socioeconomic status and access to resources and then provide feasible and accessible recommendations for each family. When considering appropriate support services, it is also important to consider the family's cultural values, norms, and beliefs. For example, clinicians should ask the family about their relationship with the neurodiversity movement, as families who embrace and celebrate their neurodivergent identities may impact how they interpret recommendations and may impact which recommendations are meaningful and helpful for their family. Sharing online resources (blogs, Reddit, books, etc.) about neurodiversity is often helpful for families, as the neurodiversity movement is an evolving community.

Assessment clinicians can help to empower families to advocate for their child's needs within educational and health care systems by providing resources to help them navigate these systems (Mandell & Novak, 2005). Within the recommendations section of the diagnostic report, clinicians can provide specific recommendations for the school setting, as the new medical diagnosis of autism and the formal report may lead to the child receiving special education for the first time. Clinicians should encourage the family to share this report with their child's school to promote service access for the child within the school setting.

When implementing autism-specific intervention and support services with children and families with new diagnoses, there are many family-level factors to consider. It is important for the clinician to acknowledge the family's religious and spiritual beliefs and incorporate these into the intervention plan when appropriate to enhance family engagement (Poston & Turnbull, 2004). Delivering interventions in the child's and family's preferred language and using bilingual therapists or interpreters when necessary (Zuckerman et al., 2013) are crucial considerations when working with families. Additionally, families may value respect for authority, collectivism, and community orientation in their family system (Betancourt et al., 2003) and may include extended family members in decision making and caregiving (Kuhn & Carter, 2006). Clinicians should practice cultural humility by recognizing these family styles and practices and providing guidance that aligns with their approach while promoting positive outcomes for the child and family (Kuhn & Carter, 2006). Furthermore, clinicians should aim to maintain flexibility and adaptability in their intervention approach to accommodate the family's cultural needs and preferences and seek continuous feedback from the family to ensure social validity (Beagan, 2003).

FUTURE DIRECTIONS

The field of autism rapidly evolves, and what is documented in this chapter regarding assessment is likely to shift and change in the near future. Clinicians should continue to seek out ongoing cultural competence training to ensure that they understand the diverse cultural, linguistic, and socioeconomic backgrounds of the families they serve (Beagan, 2003; Betancourt et al., 2003) as well as training on the intersection of autism with gender diversity so they feel equipped to assess trans, nonbinary, and other gender-diverse youth (Mawson, 2024). Transgender children are over six times as likely as binary individuals to report an autism diagnosis (Mawson, 2024). We also call on rating scale measures to be more inclusive with regard to gender identity choices on their forms so that those who self-report are not misgendered nor compared to a sample in which they are not represented.

Autistic voices should be included in developing new assessment measures, employing the concept of ethical listening to include both speaking and nonspeaking voices (Lebenhagen, 2020). The current diagnostic language and most assessment measures were developed from the medical model framework with assumptions that non-autistic ways of communicating are "appropriate," while anything different from that is considered "abnormal" and "unusual" (Henderson et al., 2024). Because of this framework and what we know about masking and differences in presentations across genders, race, and ethnicity, no one assessment (e.g., an ADOS-2 total score) should be taken alone in determining an autism diagnosis. Measures should be developed from an affirming perspective that creates a safe and validating assessment space, similar to the MIGDAS-2 framework. Autistic children have reported that safety and security were core factors impacting their lived experiences (Mullally et al., 2024). Therefore, listening to experiences within the context of the assessment process can help to reveal more hidden presentations of autism and ensure that the lived experiences of the child and family are being accurately captured. Although the diagnostic criteria are written as face value and observable characteristics, clinicians must consider that being able to compensate for challenges does not mean that the challenges are absent (Henderson et al., 2024); thus, although clinicians may not directly observe certain autistic traits, this does not necessarily mean the child is not autistic. A deeper investigation and understanding of how widely autism can present within the diagnostic process is required. The field requires updated standards for understanding presentations of autism in assigned female at birth children, trans/non-binary youth, Black, Indigenous, and children of color and the intersection of these identities. During the assessment process, taking all information gathered into the diagnostic decision and acknowledging the child's identities is crucial.

Another essential step is to engage in community outreach and education to increase understanding of autism, as we know that based on prevalence in the United States, there is a person with autism in any room of 36 people. Such outreach may include practitioners and providers who work in clinical settings, as there are still many misperceptions and knowledge gaps about autism in the general community (Jones et al., 2021) and amongst those with advanced degrees in psychology (Harris et al., 2020). Furthermore, within the diagnostic psychological community, increasing understanding of differential diagnosis between autism, ADHD, obsessive–compulsive disorder (OCD), trauma symptomatology, social anxiety, bipolar disorder, giftedness, and other neurodevelopmental disorders is crucial for diagnostic decision making (de Lima et al., 2023). Lastly, psychologists collaborating with primary care providers to increase their understanding of autism has increased satisfaction rates for both providers and families and has positively impacted referral rates and wait times for evaluations (Hine et al., 2018). We suspect that collaboration and consultation with teachers and school staff, speech–language pathologists, occupational therapists, and physical therapists may also have this positive impact on the experiences of providers and the families that they work with.

Increasing access to an autism assessment is an important equity issue. The field must consider increasing implementation of telehealth evaluations to reach families in remote or underserved areas, reducing travel-related barriers, and providing access to specialists (Juárez et al., 2018). Families also experience disparities in the time it takes them to receive a diagnosis (Shaw et al., 2022). Even when autism traits are present, families of color may face difficulty in accessing a specialty evaluation due to lack of language interpreters, transportation, work leave, and childcare needs (Tregnago & Cheak-Zamora, 2012). Clinicians should aim to embed supports into their assessment processes to help reduce these barriers for families (e.g., provide interpreters, telehealth appointments, evening appointment availability, and childcare).

CONCLUSION

This chapter outlined many components involved in autism assessment. This included reviewing the diagnostic features of autism, components of culturally humble assessment, considerations for feedback appointments, recommending support services, and future directions for autism assessment. Our hope is that this chapter motivates clinicians to practice cultural humility during the diagnostic process, embed a neurodiverse-affirming approach into assessment procedures, and collaborate with providers of other disciplines within their community. We also urge researchers to develop new rating scale measures and adapt existing measures to be more inclusive regarding gender identity. Ultimately, our field has come a long way but is ever-evolving and requires continued improvements in how we support a range of families in access to and quality of autism evaluations. It is the ethical responsibility of clinicians to remain informed about current best practices in autism assessment and the direction in which the field is moving.

REFERENCES

Alpern, G. D. (2020). *DP-4: Developmental Profile 4*. Western Psychological Services.

American Psychiatric Association. (2013). *Diagnostic and statistical manual of mental disorders* (5th ed.). American Psychiatric Publishing.

American Psychiatric Association. (2022). *Diagnostic and statistical manual of mental disorders* (5th ed., text rev.). American Psychiatric Publishing.

American Psychological Association. (2017). *Multicultural guidelines: An ecological approach to context, identity, and intersectionality*. Author. *www.apa.org/about/policy/multicultural-guidelines.pdf*

autism_sketches [@autism_sketches]. (2022, April 2). *The autism spectrum is NOT linear* [Drawing]. Instagram. *www.instagram.com/p/Cb2ykmTMOTN/?utm_source=ig_web_copy_link&igsh=MzRlODBiNWFlZA==*

Barkley, R. A. (2011). *Barkley Deficits in Executive Functioning Scale (BDEFS)*. Guilford Press.

Baron-Cohen, S., Wheelwright, S., Skinner, R., Martin, J., & Clubley, E. (2001). The Autism-Spectrum Quotient (AQ): Evidence from Asperger syndrome/high-functioning autism, males and females, scientists and mathematicians. *Journal of Autism and Developmental Disorders, 31*, 5–17.

Bayley, N. (2005). *Bayley Scales of Infant and Toddler Development, Third Edition (Bayley–III®)* [Database record]. APA PsycTests.

Beagan, B. L. (2003). Cultural competence and health care: Educating medical students in a multicultural society. *Journal of the American Medical Association, 289*(9), 1173–1175.

Berument, S. K., Rutter, M., Lord, C., Pickles, A., & Bailey, A. (1999). Autism screening questionnaire: diagnostic validity. *The British Journal of Psychiatry, 175*(5), 444–451.

Betancourt, J. R., Green, A. R., Carrillo, J. E., & Ananeh-Firempong, O. (2003). Defining cultural competence: A practical framework for addressing racial/ethnic disparities in health and health care. *Public Health Reports, 118*(4), 293–302.

Bigham, M., Keister, D., Johnston, S., & Rieske, R. (2023). Comprehensive assessment of autism spectrum disorders. In J. L. Matson (Ed.), *Handbook of applied behavior analysis for children with autism* (pp. 59–78). Springer International.

Bishop, D. V. M. (2003). *Children's Communication Checklist, Second Edition (CCC-2)*. Psychological Corporation.

Bishop, D. V., & Norbury, C. F. (2002). Exploring the borderlands of autistic disorder and specific language impairment: A study using standardised diagnostic instruments. *Journal of Child Psychology and Psychiatry, 43*(7), 917–929.

Blume H. (1998, September). Neurodiversity: On the neurological underpinnings of geekdom. *The Atlantic. www.theatlantic.com/magazine/archive/1998/09/neurodiversity/305909*

Bottema-Beutel, K., Kapp, S. K., Lester, J. N., Sasson, N. J., & Hand, B. N. (2020). Avoiding ableist language: Suggestions for autism researchers. *Autism in Adulthood*. Advance online publication.

Bradstreet, L. E., Juechter, J. I., Kamphaus, R. W., Kerns, C. M., & Robins, D. L. (2017). Using the BASC-2 parent rating scales to screen for autism spectrum disorder in toddlers and preschool-aged children. *Journal of Abnormal Child Psychology, 45*, 359–370.

Brown, H. M., Stahmer, A. C., Dwyer, P., & Rivera, S. (2021). Changing the story: How diagnosticians can support a neurodiversity perspective from the start. *Autism, 25*(5), 1171–1174.

Brown, T. E. (2003). *Brown Executive Function/Attention Scales: Manual*. Pearson.

Canadian Institute for Health Information. (2019). *ICD-10-CA: International statistical classification of diseases and related health problems, 10th revision, Canadian edition* (2019). Canadian Institute for Health Information. *www.cihi.ca/en/icd-10-ca-and-cmd-10-ca*

Carrow-Woolfolk, E. (2017). *Comprehensive Assessment of Spoken Language, Second Edition (CASL-2)*. Western Psychological Services.

Centers for Disease Control and Prevention. (2025, April 17). *Prevalence and early identification of autism spectrum disorder among children aged 4 and 8 years—Autism and Developmental Disabilities Monitoring Network, 16 sites, United States, 2022* (Morbidity and Mortality Weekly Report, Surveillance Summaries, Vol. 74, No. 2). U.S. Department of Health & Human Services. *https://www.cdc.gov/mmwr/volumes/74/ss/ss7402a1.htm*

Conners, C. K. (2019). *Conners Comprehensive Behavior Rating Scales*. Multi-Health Systems.

Conners, C. K. (2022). *Conners Continuous Performance Test, Fourth Edition Manual*. Multi-Health Systems.

Constantino, J. N., Abbacchi, A. M., Saulnier, C., Klaiman, C., Mandell, D. S., Zhang, Y., et al. (2020). Timing of the diagnosis of autism in African American children. *Pediatrics, 146*(3), 1–9.

Constantino, J. N., & Gruber, C. P. (2012). *Social Responsiveness Scale, Second Edition (SRS-2)*. Western Psychological Services.

Crane, L., Jones, L., Prosser, R., Taghrizi, M., & Pellicano, E. (2019). Parents' views and experiences of talking about autism with their children. *Autism, 23*(8), 1969–1981.

de Lima, T. A., Zuanetti, P. A., Nunes, M. E. N., & Hamad, A. P. A. (2023). Differential diagnosis between autism spectrum disorder and other developmental disorders with emphasis on the preschool period. *World Journal of Pediatrics, 19*(8), 715–726.

Dennis, M., Lazenby, A. L., & Lockyer, L. (2001). Inferential language in high-function children with autism. *Journal of Autism and Developmental Disorders, 31*, 47–54.

Drahota, A., Sadler, R., Hippensteel, C., Ingersoll, B., & Bishop, L. (2020). Service deserts and service oases: Utilizing geographic information systems to evaluate service availability for individuals with autism spectrum disorder. *Autism, 24*(8), 2008–2020.

Dow, D., Holbrook, A., Toolan, C., McDonald, N., Sterrett, K., Rosen, N., et al. (2022). The brief observation of symptoms of autism (BOSA): Development of a new adapted assessment measure for remote telehealth administration through COVID-19 and beyond. *Journal of Autism and Developmental Disorders, 52*(12), 5383–5394.

Dunn, D. M. (2019). *Peabody Picture Vocabulary Test–Fifth Edition: Manual.* Pearson.

Dyches, T. T., Wilder, L. K., Sudweeks, R. R., Obiakor, F. E., & Algozzine, B. (2004). Multicultural issues in autism. *Journal of Autism and Developmental Disorders, 34,* 211–222.

Elliott, C. D. (2007). *Differential Ability Scales* (2nd ed.). Harcourt Assessment.

England-Mason, G. (2020). Emotion regulation as a transdiagnostic feature in children with neurodevelopmental disorders. *Current Developmental Disorders Reports, 7,* 130–138.

Fagan, J. F., & Holland, C. R. (2002). Equal opportunity and racial differences in IQ. *Intelligence, 30*(4), 361–387.

First, M. B. (2009). Harmonisation of ICD–11 and DSM–V: Opportunities and challenges. *The British Journal of Psychiatry, 195*(5), 382–390.

Fisher, A. P., Lynch, J. D., Jacquez, F. M., Mitchell, M. J., Kamimura-Nishimura, K. I., & Wade, S. L. (2023). A systematic review examining caregivers' of color experiences with the diagnostic process of autism spectrum disorder. *Autism, 27*(4), 876–889.

FitzGerald, C., & Hurst, S. (2017). Implicit bias in healthcare professionals: A systematic review. *BMC Medical Ethics, 18*(1), 19.

Gabrielsen, T.P., Begay, K.K., Campbell, K., Hahn, K., & Harrington, L.T. (2023). *Assessment of autism in females and nuanced presentations.* Springer, Cham.

Gillberg, C. (1993). Autism and related behaviours. *Journal of Intellectual Disability Research, 37*(4), 343–372.

Gilliam, J. E. (2014). *GARS-3: Gilliam Autism Rating Scale–Third Edition.* Pearson.Gioia, G. A., Isquith, P. K., Guy, S. C., & Kenworthy, L. (2015). *Behavior Rating Inventory of Executive Function, Second Edition (BRIEF2).* PAR.

Goldstein, S., & Naglieri, J. A. (2009). *Autism spectrum rating scales.* Multi-Health System.

Goldstein, S., Naglieri, J. A., & Ozonoff, S. (Eds.). (2008). *Assessment of autism spectrum disorders.* Guilford Press.

Greene, R. K., Rutter, T. M., Phelps, R. A., Olsen, E. K., Harmon, R., & Moyer, D. N. (2024). Diagnostic assessment of autism spectrum disorder in transgender and gender diverse youth. *The Clinical Neuropsychologist, 39*(3) 599–620.

Hambleton, R. K., Merenda, P. F., & Spielberger, C. D. (2005). *Adapting educational and psychological tests for cross-cultural assessment.* Psychology Press.

Hambly, C., & Fombonne, E. (2012). The impact of bilingual environments on language development in children with autism spectrum disorders. *Journal of Autism and Developmental Disorders, 42,* 1342–1352.

Harris, B., McClain, M. B., Schwartz, S., & Haverkamp, C. R. (2020). Knowledge of autism spectrum disorder among school psychology graduate students. *Contemporary School Psychology, 24*(2), 239–247.

Harrison, A. J., Long, K. A., Tommet, D. C., & Jones, R. N. (2017). Examining the role of race, ethnicity, and gender on social and behavioral ratings within the Autism Diagnostic Observation Schedule. *Journal of Autism and Developmental Disorders, 47,* 2770–2782.

Harrison, P. L., & Oakland, T. (2015). *Adaptive Behavior Assessment System, Third Edition.* Western Psychological Services.

Hartman, D., O'Donnell-Killen, T., Doyle, J. K., Kavanagh, M., Day, A., & Azevedo, J. (2023). *The adult autism assessment handbook: A neurodiversity affirmative approach.* Jessica Kingsley Publishers.

Havdahl, A., Niarchou, M., Starnawska, A., Uddin, M., van der Merwe, C., & Warrier, V. (2021). Genetic contributions to autism spectrum disorder. *Psychological Medicine, 51*(13), 2260–2273.

Hine, J. F., Herrington, C. G., Rothman, A. M., et al. (2018). Embedding autism spectrum disorder diagnosis within the medical home: Decreasing wait times through streamlined assessment. *Journal of Autism and Developmental Disorders, 48,* 2846–2853.

Henderson, D., Wayland, S., & White, J. (2024). *Is this autism?: A companion guide for diagnosing.* Routledge.

Hull, L., Mandy, W., Lai, M. C., Baron-Cohen, S., Allison, C., Smith, P., & Petrides, K. V. (2019). Development and validation of the camouflaging autistic traits questionnaire (CAT-Q). *Journal of Autism and Developmental Disorders, 49,* 819–833.

Hyman, S. L., Levy, S. E., Myers, S. M., Kuo, D. Z., Apkon, S., Davidson, L. F., et al. (2020). Identification, evaluation, and management of children with autism spectrum disorder. *Pediatrics, 145*(1), 1–5.

Individuals With Disabilities Education Act, 20 U.S.C., § 1400, and (2004).

Jones, S. C., Akram, M., Gordon, C. S., Murphy, N., & Sharkie, F. (2021). Autism in Australia: Community knowledge and autistic people's experiences. *Journal of Autism and Developmental Disorders, 51*(10), 3677–3689.

Jones, W., Klaiman, C., Richardson, S., Aoki, C., Smith, C., Minjarez, M., et al. (2023). Eye-tracking–based measurement of social visual engagement compared with expert clinical diagnosis of autism. *JAMA, 330*(9), 854–865.

Juárez, A. P., Weitlauf, A. S., Nicholson, A., Pasternak, A., Broderick, N., Hine, J., et al. (2018). Early identification of ASD through telemedicine: Potential value for underserved populations. *Journal of Autism and Developmental Disorders, 48*, 2601–2610.

Kentrou, V., Livingston, L. A., Grove, R., Hoekstra, R. A., & Begeer, S. (2024). Perceived misdiagnosis of psychiatric conditions in autistic adults. *EClinicalMedicine, 71*, 1–12.

Kinnear, S. H., Link, B. G., Ballan, M. S., & Fischbach, R. L. (2016). Understanding the experience of stigma for parents of children with autism spectrum disorder and the role stigma plays in families' lives. *Journal of Autism and Developmental Disorders, 46*, 942–953.

Klinger, L. G., Ence, W. A., & Meyer, A. (2015). Caregiver perceptions of diagnostic feedback for children with autism spectrum disorder. *Journal of Autism and Developmental Disorders, 45*(10), 3274–3284.

Kremer-Sadlik, T. (2005). To be or not to be bilingual: Autistic children from multilingual families. *Proceedings of the 4th International Symposium on Bilingualism* (pp. 1225–1234).

Kroncke, A. P., Willard, M., & Huckabee, H. (2016). *Assessment of autism spectrum disorder: Critical issues in clinical, forensic, and school Settings*. Springer.

Kuhn, J. C., & Carter, A. S. (2006). Maternal self-efficacy and associated parenting cognitions among mothers of children with autism. *American Journal of Orthopsychiatry, 76*(4), 564–575.

Kuriakose, S. (2014). Concurrent validity of the WISC-IV and DAS-II in children with autism spectrum disorder. *Journal of Psychoeducational Assessment, 32*(4), 283–294.

Lebenhagen, C. (2020). Including speaking and non-speaking autistic voice in research. *Autism in Adulthood, 2*(2), 128–131.

Lebersfeld, J. B. (2020). *Diagnosis and screening of autism spectrum disorder in clinical populations*. Doctoral dissertation, The University of Alabama at Birmingham.

Lockwood Estrin, G., Milner, V., Spain, D., Happé, F., & Colvert, E. (2021). Barriers to autism spectrum disorder diagnosis for young women and girls: A systematic review. *Review Journal of Autism and Developmental Disorders, 8*(4), 454–470.

Lord, C., Charman, T., Havdahl, A., Carbone, P., Anagnostou, E., Boyd, B., et al. (2022). The Lancet Commission on the future of care and clinical research in autism. *The Lancet, 399*(10321), 271–334.

Lord C., Rutter M., DiLavore P. C., Risi S., Gotham K., & Bishop S. (2012). *Autism Diagnostic Observation Schedule, Second Edition*. Western Psychological Services.

Makino, A., Hartman, L., King, G., Wong, P. Y., & Penner, M. (2021). Parent experiences of autism spectrum disorder diagnosis: A scoping review. *Review Journal of Autism and Developmental Disorders*, 8, 267–284.

Mandell, D. S., Ittenbach, R. F., Levy, S. E., & Pinto-Martin, J. A. (2007). Disparities in diagnoses received prior to a diagnosis of autism spectrum disorder. *Journal of Autism and Developmental Disorders, 37*(9), 1795–1802.

Mandell, D. S., & Novak, M. (2005). The role of culture in families' treatment decisions for children with autism spectrum disorders. *Mental Retardation and Developmental Disabilities Research Reviews, 11*(2), 110–115.

Mandell, D. S., & Palmer, R. (2005). Differences among states in the identification of autistic spectrum disorders. *Archives of Pediatrics & Adolescent Medicine, 159*(3), 266–269.

Matson, J. L., & Nebel-Schwalm, M. (2007). Assessing challenging behaviors in children with autism spectrum disorders: A review. *Research in Developmental Disabilities, 28*(6), 567–579.

Mawson, A. R. (2024). The transgender phenomenon: Needs for research. *Journal of Public Health Policy, 45*(1), 179–182.

Monteiro, M. J., & Stegall, S. (2018). *Monteiro Interview Guidelines for Diagnosing the Autism Spectrum, Second Edition (MIGDAS-2)*. PAR.

Moseley, K. L., Freed, G. L., Bullard, C. M., & Goold, S. D. (2007). Measuring African-American parents' cultural mis-trust while in a healthcare setting: A pilot study. *Journal of the National Medical Association, 991*(1), 15–21.

Muhle, R., Trentacoste, S. V, & Rapin, I. (2004). "The genetics of autism." *Pediatrics* 113(5), e472–e486.

Mullally, S. L., Wood, A. E., Edwards, C. C., Connolly, S. E., Constable, H., Watson, S., Rodgers, J., Rose, K., & King, N. (2024). Autistic voice: Sharing autistic children's experiences and insights. *medRxiv*, 2024–07.

Mullen, E. M. (1995). *Mullen Scales of Early Learning* (AGS ed.). American Guidance Service.

Naglieri, J. A., Goldstein, S., & Davis, L. B. (2013). *Comprehensive Executive Function Inventory (CEFI)*. Multi-Health Systems.

Oredipe, T., Kofner, B., Riccio, A., Cage, E., Vincent, J., Kapp, S. K., Dwyer, P., & Gillespie-Lynch, K. (2023). Does learning you are autistic at a younger age lead to better adult outcomes? A participatory exploration of the perspectives of autistic university students. *Autism, 27*(1), 200–212.

Pearson, J. N., & Meadan, H. (2018). African American parents' perceptions of diagnosis and services for children with autism. *Education and Training in Autism and Developmental Disabilities, 53*(1), 17–32.

Phelps-Terasaki, D., & Phelps-Gunn, T. (2007). *Test of Pragmatic Language, Second Edition (TOPL-2)*. Pro-Ed.

Poston, D. J., & Turnbull, A. P. (2004). Role of spirituality and religion in family quality of life for families of children with disabilities. *Education and Training in Developmental Disabilities, 39*(2), 95–108.

Pugliese, C. E., Anthony, L., Strang, J. F., Dudley, K., Wallace, G. L., & Kenworthy, L. (2015). Increasing adaptive behavior skill deficits from childhood to adolescence in autism spectrum disorder: Role of executive function. *Journal of Autism and Developmental Disorders*, *45*, 1579–1587.

Reynolds, C. R., & Kamphaus, R. W. (2015). *Behavior Assessment System for Children, Third Edition (BASC-3)*. Pearson.

Roid, G. H., & Koch, C. (2017). Leiter-3: Nonverbal cognitive and neuropsychological assessment. *Handbook of Nonverbal Assessment*, 127–150.

Roid, G., & Pomplun, M. (2012). The Stanford–Binet Intelligence Scales. In D. P. Flanagan & P. L. Harrison (Eds.), *Contemporary intellectual assessment: Theories, tests, and issues* (3rd ed., pp. 249–268). Guilford Press.

Rudy, D., & Grusec, J. E. (2006). Cultural differences in parenting styles and their effects on teens' self-esteem, perceived parental relationship satisfaction, and self-satisfaction. *Journal of Adolescence, 29*(5), 703–716.

Rutherford, M., & Johnston, L. (2022). Rethinking autism assessment, diagnosis, and intervention within a neurodevelopmental pathway framework. In Marco Carotenuto (Ed.), *Autism spectrum disorders: Recent advances and new perspectives* (pp. 83–100). IntechOpen.

Rutter, M., Bailey, A., & Lord, C. (2003). *The Social Communication Questionnaire*. Western Psychological Services.

Rutter, M., Le Couteur, A., & Lord, C. (2003). *Autism Diagnostic Interview—Revised*. Western Psychological Services.

Rynkiewicz, A., & Łucka, I. (2018). Autism spectrum disorder (ASD) in girls. Co-occurring psychopathology. Sex differences in clinical manifestation. *Psychiatria Polska, 52*(4), 629–639.

Rynkiewicz, A., Schuller, B., Marchi, E., Piana, S., Camurri, A., Lassalle, A., & Baron-Cohen, S. (2016). An investigation of the "female camouflage effect" in autism using a computerized ADOS-2 and a test of sex/gender differences. *Molecular Autism, 7*, 1–8.

Sappok, T., Heinrich, M., & Underwood, L. (2015). Screening tools for autism spectrum disorders. *Advances in Autism, 1*(1), 12–29.

Schopler, E., Van Bourgondien, M. E., Wellman, G. J., & Love, S. R. (2010). *Childhood Autism Rating Scale–Second Edition (CARS-2)*. Western Psychological Services.

Shan, L., Feng, J. Y., Wang, T. T., Xu, Z. D., & Jia, F. Y. (2022). Prevalence and developmental profiles of autism spectrum disorders in children with global developmental delay. *Frontiers in Psychiatry, 12*, 794238.

Shaw, K. A., McArthur, D., Hughes, M. M., Bakian, A. V., Lee, L. C., Pettygrove, S., & Maenner, M. J. (2022). Progress and disparities in early identification of autism spectrum disorder: Autism and developmental disabilities monitoring network, 2002–2016. *Journal of the American Academy of Child & Adolescent Psychiatry, 61*(7), 905–914.

Singer J. (1998). "Why can't you be normal for once in your life? From a 'problem with no name' to a new category of disability." In M. Corker & S. French (Eds.), *Disability discourse* (pp. 59–67). Open University Press.

Smith, T., Polloway, E. A., Patton, J. R., & Dowdy, C. A. (2019). *Autism spectrum disorders across the lifespan: A comprehensive guide for educators, clinicians, and parents*. Springer.

Sparrow S. S., Cicchetti D. V., & Saulnier C. A. (2016) *Vineland Adaptive Behavior Scales, Third edition*. Pearson.

Stahmer, A. C., Vejnoska, S., Iadarola, S., Straiton, D., Segovia, F. R., Luelmo, P., et al. (2019). Caregiver voices: Cross-cultural input on improving access to autism services. *Journal of Racial and Ethnic Health Disparities*, 6, 752–773.

Straiton, D., & Sridhar, A. (2022). Call to action for autism clinicians in response to anti-Black racism. *Autism, 26*(4), 988–994.

Tharinger, D. J., Finn, S. E., Hersh, B., Wilkinson, A., Christopher, G. B., & Tran, A. (2008). Assessment feedback with parents and preadolescent children: A collaborative approach. *Professional Psychology: Research and Practice, 39*(6), 600.

Thurm, A., & Klaiman, C., (2023, August). The importance of cognition in autism diagnostic evaluation. International Collaboration for Diagnostic Evaluation of Autism Webinar.

Tregnago, M. K., & Cheak-Zamora, N. C. (2012). Systematic review of disparities in health care for individuals with autism spectrum disorders in the United States. *Research in Autism Spectrum Disorders*, 6(3), 1023–1031.

Tubío-Fungueiriño, M., Cruz, S., Sampaio, A., Carracedo, A., & Fernández-Prieto, M. (2021). Social camouflaging in females with autism spectrum disorder: A systematic review. *Journal of Autism and Developmental Disorders, 51*, 2190–2199.

Volker, M. A., Lopata, C., Smerbeck, A. M., Knoll, V. A., Thomeer, M. L., Toomey, J. A., & Rodgers, J. D. (2010). BASC-2 PRS profiles for students with high-functioning autism spectrum disorders. *Journal of Autism and Developmental Disorders, 40*, 188–199.

Waddington, H., Jordan, P., Scott, E., Minnell, H., Patrick, L., van der Meer, L., et al. (2023). Community perspectives on support goals for young autistic children: A qualitative investigation. *Neurodiversity, 1*, 27546330231218587.

Wang, S., Jiang, M., Duchesne, X. M., Laugeson, E. A., Kennedy, D. P., Adolphs, R., & Zhao, Q. (2015). Atypical visual saliency in autism spectrum disorder quantified through model-based eye tracking. *Neuron*, 88(3), 604–616.

Wechsler, D. (2008). *Wechsler Adult Intelligence Scale—Fourth Edition*. Pearson.

Wechsler, D. (2014). *Wechsler Intelligence Scale for Children—Fifth Edition*. Pearson.

Wiig, E. H., Semel, E., & Secord, W. A. (2013). *Clinical evaluation of language fundamentals* (5th ed.). Pearson.

Williams, K. T. (2019). *Expressive Vocabulary Test* (3rd ed.). NCS Pearson.

World Health Organization. (2019). *International statistical classification of diseases and related health problems* (11th ed.). Author.

Wright, A. J. (2019). *Essentials of psychological assessment supervision*. Wiley.

Yu, B. (2013). Issues in bilingualism and heritage language maintenance: Perspectives of minority-language mothers of children with autism spectrum disorders. *American Journal of Speech–Language Pathology, 22*(1), 10–24.

Zeidan, J., Fombonne, E., Scorah, J., Ibrahim, A., Durkin, M. S., Saxena, S., et al. (2022). Global prevalence of autism: A systematic review update. *Autism research, 15*(5), 778–790.

Zimmerman, I. L., Steiner, V. G., & Pond, R. E. (2011). *Preschool Language Scales, Fifth Edition (PLS-5)*. Pearson.

Zuckerman, K. E., Mattox, K., Donelan, K., Batbayar, O., Baghaee, A., & Bethell, C. (2013). Pediatrician identification of Latino children at risk for autism spectrum disorder. *Pediatrics, 132*(3), 445–453.

CHAPTER 15

Assessment of Attention-Deficit/ Hyperactivity Disorder

Nadia Bounoua, Hong NT Bui, Nicholas Marsh, Daria Taubin, and Andrea Chronis-Tuscano

According to the Centers for Disease Control and Prevention (CDC), attention-deficit/hyperactivity disorder (ADHD) is one of the most prevalent neurodevelopmental disorders in childhood (Reuben et al., 2024). ADHD is defined by core symptom clusters of inattention and hyperactivity, present before age 12 and exceeding what is expected for children their age (American Psychiatric Association, 2013). ADHD is associated with cross-situational impairments in social and academic and/or occupational domains across the lifespan and can contribute to the later development of comorbid conditions, including anxiety, depression, and substance misuse. Importantly, youth with ADHD are at risk for serious outcomes, including increased risk for suicide and a reduced lifespan of 10–15 years (Barkley & Fischer, 2019; Cherkasova et al., 2022; Franke et al., 2018). Early and accurate diagnosis is critical to intervention and prevention of long-term negative outcomes.

Data from the 2022 CDC National Survey of Children's Health reported that 11.4% of children in the United States received an ADHD diagnosis in 2022 (Danielson et al., 2024). This prevalence rate was an increase from previous years and was the first since the COVID-19 pandemic. Importantly, this report also revealed disparities in ADHD diagnosis across sociodemographic groups.[1] For example, more boys than girls were diagnosed with ADHD, a sex difference that has been well-acknowledged in the field (American Psychiatric Association, 2022). Although it is possible that these differences reflect true sex-related prevalence, research shows that ADHD among girls has been historically underdiagnosed. This difference is driven partially by the fact that females may display greater symptoms of inattention and internalizing problems and adopt compensatory strategies that make recognition of ADHD symptoms more difficult for assessors (Chronis-Tuscano, 2022; Hinshaw et al., 2022). Racial and ethnic differences in prevalence were also noted in this report. Specifically, Asian American and Hispanic youth were less likely to receive an ADHD diagnosis than youth from other racial groups. It is likely that these differences emerged from a myriad of factors, including culturally embedded beliefs

[1] A note on terminology: Throughout this paper, we sought to follow the guidelines on terminology outlined in the American Psychological Association's (2023) Inclusive Language Guide. When citing specific findings from peer-reviewed literature, we chose to adhere to the language used by the authors to describe their study sample.

about ADHD, stigma about mental health more broadly, and barriers to help-seeking behaviors.

Although the guidelines for evidence-based assessment of ADHD have been well established for decades and are widely adopted by the American Academy of Pediatrics (AAP) (Wolraich et al., 2019) and the American Association of Child and Adolescent Psychiatry (AACAP) (Pliszka, 2007), little guidance is provided for incorporating cultural considerations into the diagnostic process. Importantly, Mulraney et al. (2022) show there are significant limitations in how the current assessment tools perform across informants and populations. The objectives of this chapter are to (1) provide an overview of current practices relevant to ADHD assessment and diagnosis, including an overview of widely used instruments and differential diagnosis considerations; (2) discuss culturally relevant factors pertaining to the assessment of ADHD with families and youth across ecological contexts, and (3) introduce future directions in the field of culturally sensitive youth ADHD assessment.

OVERVIEW OF ADHD ASSESSMENT METHODS

In their seminal article, Pelham et al. (2005) lay out the various components of evidence-based assessment of ADHD. Evidence-based ADHD assessment involves diagnostic interviews with parents and older children (>9 years), collection of parent and teacher symptom checklists with strong psychometric properties, additional clinical and psychoeducational assessment to evaluate common comorbidities (e.g., other neurodevelopmental disorders, mood disorders, anxiety disorders, and potential learning disabilities), and classroom observations when possible. Ideally, all of these are taken into consideration with assessing impairment alongside symptoms. Indeed, Pelham et al. (2005) emphasize that the main focus on ADHD assessment should be on monitoring levels of *impairment*, rather than symptom count, given that the degree of impairment is what prompts treatment seeking and is what children and families wish to reduce (Chronis-Tuscano et al., 2013).

Diagnostic Interviews

Experts recommend the use of semistructured clinical interviews conducted with parents in ADHD assessment (Pelham et al., 2005). A widely used semistructured clinical interview used to assess youth with symptoms of ADHD is the ADHD module in the Kiddie Schedule for Affective Disorders and Schizophrenia for School-Age children (K-SADS) (Kaufman et al., 1997), which has shown excellent reliability and predictive validity (Jarbin et al., 2017). In general, the K-SADS interview has demonstrated good reliability and validity across a variety of cultures and populations (Kim et al., 2004; de la Peña et al., 2018; Ünal et al., 2019). In addition to assessing ADHD symptoms, diagnostic interviews can provide additional context and clarity for differential diagnoses, as well as provide insight into the developmental time course and persistence of symptoms and impairments. Importantly, these interviews provide an opportunity for interviewers to solicit examples of symptom presentations, allowing caregivers to "paint a picture" of their child, which can be used to ascertain the severity and impairment of any one symptom in relation to developmental norms.

Symptom Checklists

Even though clinical interviews are the gold-standard assessment, the most widely used assessment tools for ADHD are rating scale measures eliciting the symptom reports by caregivers, teachers, and, to a lesser extent, the youth's self-report of symptoms. The measures may include longer comprehensive surveys of child mental health symptoms or ADHD symptom-based rating scales (e.g., Vanderbilt ADHD Diagnostic Rating Scale, Wolraich et al., 1998; Conners 4th edition, Conners, 2022). These measures are easily disseminated and brief to fill out, making the barrier to assessment low for collecting reports—particularly from parents and teachers. Given that a diagnosis of ADHD requires cross-situational impairment, obtaining information from multiple informants is critical. Teachers typically have a better reference than parents for how other children of the same age and sex behave and therefore can better gauge when a child's behavior may be developmentally inappropriate. It is not uncommon for parents and teachers to disagree on symptoms and level of impairment (De Los Reyes, 2011); however, this is expected because children behave differently across various contexts and with different demands or expectations. Thus, it is unlikely that a single measure, completed by a single informant, is comprehensively accurate (Mulraney et al., 2022). Incorporating both teacher questionnaires and parent questionnaires helps provide symptoms of ratings across contexts and settings and improves assessment of ADHD. However, less time-efficient than using multi-informant self-report measures of symptoms alone, a thorough assessment of ADHD should consist of both questionnaires and clinical interviews.

Pierce and Reid (2004) highlight two main issues regarding the cross-cultural assessment of ADHD: rater "bias" (i.e., differences in use of diagnostic criteria by raters due to their own cultural background; raters attributing severity differences due to culture only) and the development of assessment measures without consideration of cultural differences. Both issues have implications for the assessor. Furthermore, while symptom checklists have been adapted for use across cultures, few robust, validated symptom checklists are available for use cross-culturally (Maldonado et al., 2019). Additional research is needed to explore the effectiveness of these tools in non-Western samples.

Differential Diagnosis

Estimates suggest that more than half of children with ADHD also have a co-occurring mental, behavioral, and/or developmental disorder (Cuffe et al., 2020; Danielson et al., 2024). Given high rates of comorbidity and symptom overlap, ADHD assessment ideally will include the evaluation of symptoms and impairment associated with several different disorders. Additionally, ADHD assessment should obtain a clear developmental time course to determine whether symptoms are chronic (as in ADHD and autism) or episodic (as in depression). Establishing a developmental timeline can be helpful in distinguishing between ADHD and common comorbidities, with ADHD typically emerging earlier and showing a more chronic course, but also often worsening during developmental periods that tax executive functioning (e.g., the transitions to elementary school, middle school, and high school). Below, we briefly discuss common disorders that share overlapping symptoms with ADHD and provide suggestions for differential diagnosis to aid in assessments.

Disruptive Disorders

Perhaps the most common co-occurring disorders that present during a diagnostic assessment of childhood ADHD are disruptive disorders, such as oppositional defiant disorder (ODD) and conduct disorder (CD). Although distinct disorders, ODD, CD, and ADHD share similar symptom presentations, particularly in the domains of impulsive behaviors, emotion dysregulation, and impairments in social and academic functioning. Differentiating symptoms of ODD/CD and ADHD can be difficult, especially given their high rates of comorbidity. Thus, it is helpful to have a multi-informant assessment that includes a diagnostic interview to provide clarity in symptom presentations. For example, a child may have difficulty following instructions, and this could present as either a symptom of ODD or ADHD. Similarly, it may be difficult for parents and teachers alike to disentangle intent to cause harm (reflective of CD) from hyperactivity symptoms with, for example, a child who may squeeze a family pet or harm a younger sibling. A clinician collecting additional information about the developmental context, environmental demands, caregiver expectations, and intentions behind these behaviors can provide diagnostic clarity (e.g., due to distraction versus defiance against authority).

Other Neurodevelopmental and Intellectual Disorders

Given that ADHD is classified as a childhood neurodevelopmental disorder, it is perhaps unsurprising that there is substantial comorbidity between ADHD and other neurodevelopmental disorders, such as autism spectrum disorders (ASD). Although diagnostically distinct, ADHD and ASD may share phenotypes (e.g., impairments in social and executive functioning) that may complicate accurate diagnosis (for review, see Antshel & Russo, 2019). Thus, it is imperative that successful evaluation of ADHD considers the potential co-occurring symptoms of ASD or if symptoms are better otherwise explained by ASD. Similarly, assessments should also consider the high likelihood of other intellectual and/or learning disorders (e.g., DuPaul & Volpe, 2009). For ADHD assessment, this can complicate conceptualization because of long-standing documentation of ADHD symptoms associated with academic underachievement. Often, cognitive and neuropsychological testing can be used to supplement an ADHD assessment to identify co-occurring intellectual or learning difficulties. It is important to note that individuals with ADHD do not have a distinct psychometric cognitive profile, suggesting that results of cognitive and neuropsychological testing alone cannot be used to diagnose ADHD (Barkley, 2019). Thus, while cognitive testing alone is not an appropriate tool for the diagnosis of ADHD, it can be critical in accurately differentiating underachievement from a specific learning disorder in children. Additionally, it is ideal for evidence-based assessment to also include observations of the child in different situations (e.g., school, with peers, or with parents; Pelham et al., 2005) for differential and diagnostic clarity. However, this may be less feasible for providers that are not embedded in the school system, as travel and observation time may not be reimbursed. However, observing the child in their natural environment is an important component as it is more objective and allows comparison to same-age peers.

Mood and Anxiety Disorders

There are a host of other mood and anxiety symptoms that can complicate the assessment process for ADHD symptoms given their common co-occurrence. In a review, Reale et al. (2017) report that rates of co-occurring depression, anxiety disorders, and bipolar disorders occur in 16–26%, 10–40%, and 11–75% of children with ADHD, respectively. These comorbidities may arise secondary to ADHD, given concerns about missing details or poor self-concept as a result of negative feedback from one's environment (Chronis-Tuscano et al., in press). Assessors should thus be aware of the potential overlap of ADHD and internalizing symptoms during youth ADHD assessments.

Trauma- and Stress-Related Disorders

Research shows that youth with ADHD are more likely to endorse some degree of trauma exposure (e.g., Briscoe-Smith & Hinshaw, 2006). Moreover, although ADHD and post-traumatic stress disorder (PTSD) are distinct disorders, these disorders share a number of overlapping symptoms. For example, difficulties in concentration, distraction, disorganization, impulsivity, restlessness, and difficulty sleeping are a few symptoms/associated features that cut across both diagnoses (Boodoo et al., 2022; National Child Traumatic Stress Network, 2016). Indeed, in a systematic review and meta-analysis, Spencer et al. (2016) found that ADHD and PTSD have a bidirectional association. Thus, particularly among trauma-exposed youth, assessors should consider timing of exposure to potentially traumatic events and onset of symptom severity to delineate the influence of trauma exposure on presenting ADHD symptoms.

Demographic Differences in Differential Diagnosis in Relation to ADHD Assessment

The issue of differential diagnosis is critical when conducting ADHD assessments, particularly in diverse samples. For instance, research shows that Black/African American children are more likely to receive a diagnosis of CD and ODD for behaviors that are more likely diagnosed as mood, anxiety, developmental, or adjustment disorders in non-Hispanic White children. This has been implicated in overdiagnosis of ODD/CD and underdiagnosis of ADHD in African American children (Fadus et al., 2020; Fairman et al., 2020). This may be due to implicit biases held by assessors. For example, research shows that African American boys are viewed as older and less innocent than non-Hispanic White peers and that clinicians are more likely to view behaviors of African Americans as more dangerous and disobedient than similar behaviors among non-Hispanic White peers (Fadus et al., 2020). Research also suggests that youth's sex and race influence the likelihood of diagnosis of comorbid ASD and learning disorders in the context of ADHD (Federico et al., 2024; Pastor & Reuben, 2005). Moreover, meta-analytic work has shown that girls with ADHD were more likely to meet criteria for externalizing (e.g., ODD and CD) and internalizing disorders than girls without ADHD, regardless of race or ethnicity (Tung et al., 2016). These findings highlight the importance of considering biases and differential diagnosis when completing ADHD assessments with diverse groups.

ADHD Assessment Across Settings

Schools

Schools represent an important ecological context for the identification and assessment of ADHD in children and adolescents. Starting as early as 4 years old, schools become the primary context in which children spend time. Indeed, research shows that teachers are second to parents in most common referral sources for ADHD (DuPaul & Stoner, 2014). Schools provide an opportunity for early identification, and school-based assessments may be more easily implemented, as teachers and school mental health professionals may be able to more quickly identify ADHD symptoms based on developmental norms. School personnel can provide insight into symptom presentation in the school environment, given that they can easily observe child behavior in the classroom, bolstering evidence of impairment across settings. Moreover, research shows that intervening with youth with ADHD in the school setting promotes generalization of treatment gains through practice opportunities in the natural environment (Evans et al., 2003). Schools represent a promising avenue for reducing barriers to care, particularly for youth with marginalized identities. Indeed, research shows that youth from lower-income backgrounds and racially minoritized groups were more likely to only access mental health care in educational settings (Ali et al., 2019). It is important to note that schools should not be the only context in which ADHD symptoms are assessed, but rather reports from school personnel, in conjunction with caregivers, is ideal for a comprehensive assessment of ADHD.

Despite the promise of school settings for the identification and assessment of ADHD, research shows that at least one in five students with ADHD do not receive school-based services for ADHD. Further, research demonstrates that receipt of school-based services is likely impacted by a myriad of culturally relevant factors, with children from lower socioeconomic status and non-English speaking families less likely to receive school-based services (DuPaul et al., 2019). Recent work from Shippen et al. (2022) focused on understanding barriers and facilitators to ADHD school-based services among Black youth in an urban high school context. Results from qualitative analyses of focus groups involving caregivers and adolescents with ADHD, as well as teachers and school mental health professionals, revealed multiple school-based barriers to ADHD care. These included a lack of training and support for teacher and school staff, low teacher knowledge of ADHD, and larger systematic components of the school structure (e.g., classroom size and limited ability to modify classroom environment) (Shippen et al., 2022). Given the importance of the school context in ADHD assessment for youth, it is crucial that ADHD identification and assessments are culturally informed and sensitive.

Medical Settings

The medical system serves as another important ecological context for the assessment of ADHD. It is well established that sociocultural factors impact how families navigate the medical system, including access to care, interactions with providers, and financial burdens associated with treatment (Garney et al., 2021). Primary care settings are where parents often first voice concerns related to ADHD (Visser et al., 2015), and the AAP recommends routine screening for ADHD symptoms in children ages 4 and older (Wolarich et al., 2019). Primary care may also provide a more accessible environment for providers to initiate conversations about ADHD with families, particularly if families have built a trusting relationship with their child's pediatrician (Lui et al., 2023). Similarly, parents may prefer to undergo assessment via screening questionnaires at pediatrician offices rather than full diagnostic interviews due to time constraints.

Even though having conversations about ADHD-related concerns with trusted providers is preferred by some parents, several systems-level barriers to this exist in primary care, including significant demand on primary care providers to see a high patient load and provide a variety of services over a relatively brief appointment (Lui et al., 2023). Additionally, significant racial and ethnic disparities exist in access to, and experiences in, primary care. For example, a large-scale study of Medicare beneficiaries found differing patterns of specialty referral practices in primary care physicians for Black and White patients (Landon et al., 2021), suggesting disparate levels of access to specialists across racial groups. Integrated behavioral health has been proposed as a potential strategy to increase access to mental health providers within the primary care system and reduce health disparities (see O'Loughlin et al., 2019 for a review), as trusted providers can provide a "warm handoff" and initiate the process of an ADHD assessment.

Taken together, a complete diagnostic battery that includes assessing a range of disorders in semistructured clinical interviews is strongly recommended to consider the developmental/temporal course of symptoms and the settings in which they occur and ascertain which syndromes best describe the symptoms and impairment reported. Clinical judgment, standardized phrasing in interview questions, and symptom anchors can assist in removing some of the uncertainty in overlap between symptoms across these disorders and form a more accurate case conceptualization of the etiology behind the symptoms. Accurate assessment of ADHD symptoms must consider the possibilities of co-occurring symptoms, overlapping but distinct symptoms, and developmental norms to provide successful differential diagnoses. Diagnostic case formulation is strengthened by assessing symptoms from reporters across settings (e.g., home, school, medical, and community). Despite efforts to remain objective and use evidence-based assessment strategies, implicit biases held by clinicians may still influence their attributions about behaviors or diagnoses. Given that clinician observations and judgment play a significant role in both identifying youth in need of further assessment for ADHD, as well as interpreting assessment results, biases may lead to both inaccurately over-pathologizing developmentally and culturally appropriate behavior in youth, as well as prematurely dismissing symptoms in youth by labeling them as deviant, dangerous, or deliberately misbehaving.

CULTURALLY RELEVANT PRACTICE CONSIDERATIONS

As discussed, a diagnosis of ADHD requires an evaluation ideally involving multiple informants and methods, which is impacted by informant and provider beliefs and biases (Bussing et al., 2003; Fadus et al., 2020). Thus, moving toward culturally informed assessment of ADHD requires an understanding of characteristics of not only the child, but also their larger environmental context.

We developed a developmental–transactional model of ADHD, which depicts multiple contextual influences on the developmental course of ADHD (see Figure 15.1; Johnston & Chronis-Tuscano, 2015). For instance, a child with ADHD both influences and is influenced by their environment. Children with ADHD are understood to be more sensitive to stressors, including exposure to parental mental health difficulties, interparental discord, etc. And, oftentimes, their challenging behaviors elicit negative responses from caregivers, teachers, and their peers. Parents' own characteristics may make it easier or more difficult for them to provide the type of consistent, structured environment in which their children are most likely to thrive. In addition to bidirectional influences of child and parent/family factors, broader contextual factors such as school, neighborhood, culture, and socioeconomic status can influence the child and parent directly and indirectly as risk or protec-

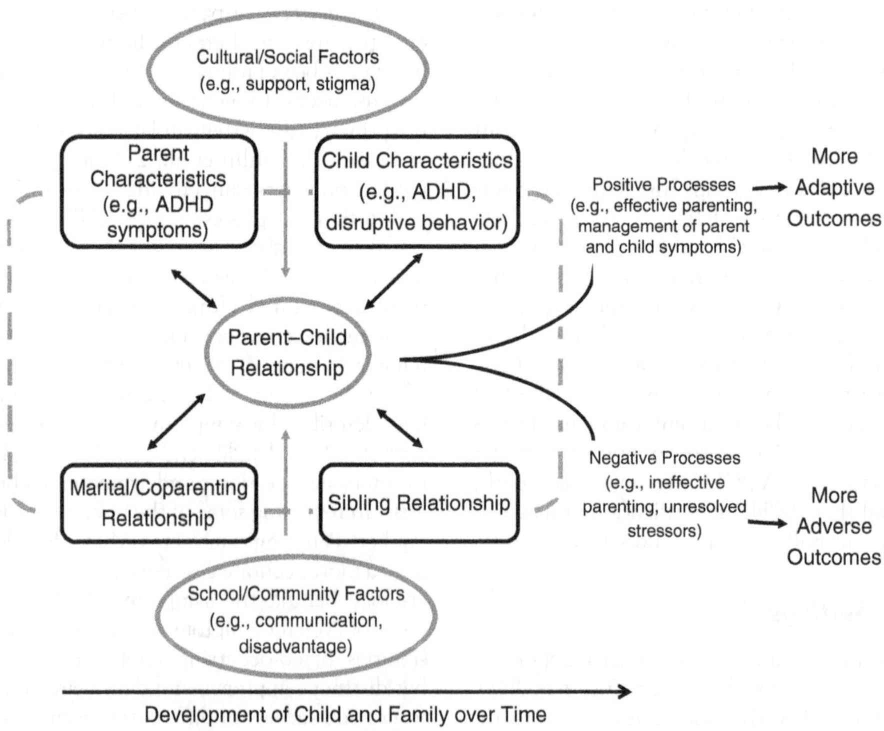

FIGURE 15.1. Transactional model of ADHD in families (Johnston & Chronis-Tuscano, 2015). Reprinted with permission from The Guilford Press.

tive factors. For instance, poverty, racism, neighborhood violence, and other contextual stressors can directly influence the child or adversely affect parenting quality via the stress these factors place on their caregivers. An understanding of all of these dynamic, transactional influences is an important part of assessment and treatment planning (Chronis-Tuscano et al., 2020).

Often, caregivers serve as primary informants given their proximity to youth and the detailed developmental histories required for ADHD diagnoses. Even though the term "caregivers" often encapsulates primary (e.g., parents), extended (e.g., siblings, aunts/uncles, and grandparents), and/or foster/custodial members, most of the research on the caregiver role in assessment focuses on parents. However, we acknowledge the importance of extending this literature to other caregivers within the youth's environment (Malik et al., 2017; Thompson et al., 2017), as approaches to child assessment may vary across different caregivers.

In this section, we discuss the various ways culture can impact ADHD problem recognition and the initiation and experience of the assessment process (e.g., how parents describe symptoms, etc.). We then suggest clinical considerations that should be incorporated to promote inclusion and increase sensitivity during ADHD assessment and a culturally informed case conceptualization. An abundance of literature focuses on parental factors impacting the initiation of *treatment* for youth ADHD (e.g., attitudes and beliefs; Baweja et al., 2021; Berger et al., 2008; Bussing et al., 2012; Spencer et al., 2021), but far less is known about how cultural factors may impact *assessments* for youth ADHD. In the next section, we draw from components of the American Psychiatric Association's Cultural Formulation Interview (CFI), which holds promise as a brief, skills-based method to improve culturally informed assessment of symptoms by collecting the client's perspective and sociocultural context (Lewis-Fernández et al., 2016). Research has shown that the CFI can improve communication through building rapport by prompting assessors to collect new culturally relevant data related to clients' cultural definitions and perceptions of the causes of ADHD, in addition to factors affecting help-seeking behaviors (Jarvis et al., 2020). Similarly, the ADHD-Help Seeking Behavior Model (ADHD-HSB) (Eiraldi et al., 2006) also provides a useful framework for understanding the role of culture in parents' problem recognition, decision to seek help, service selection, and service utilization for ADHD.

Cultural Considerations in ADHD Problem Recognition

First, initiation of an ADHD assessment requires problem recognition, or identifying specific behaviors as impairing or problematic (Cauce et al., 2002). Problem recognition is heavily influenced by cultural factors, including caregivers' conceptualizations about ADHD and attributions about the causes of ADHD (e.g., whether ADHD is neurobiological, alternative explanations for child behavior; Bussing et al., 2007), as well as cultural expectations of appropriate behavior (Pham, 2015). Further, research shows that parental beliefs of the etiology and conceptualization of ADHD may impact service utilization among Latinx families (Haack & Gerdes, 2011; Lawton et al., 2014). Such beliefs and conceptualizations are often shaped by parents' access to knowledge about ADHD (Paidipati et al., 2017). For example, research has shown that Latinx families may have limited exposure to information about ADHD, which may impact their understanding of their child's ADHD symptoms (Eiraldi et al., 2006; Gerdes et al., 2014). Moreover, some research shows that families from ethnic minority or low socioeconomic backgrounds may perceive some ADHD symptoms as developmentally normative and less problematic, which may delay help-seeking via diagnosis and treatment; thus, they may be less likely to perceive these behaviors as problematic (Arcia & Fernández 2003; Gerdes et al., 2014; Slobodin & Masalha, 2020). Other commonly held beliefs of alternative causes of ADHD behaviors include familial/family discord (Haack et al., 2018), personality (Yeh et al., 2004), and stressful life events (Bussing et al., 2003), which may influence help-seeking behaviors.

Cultural Considerations in ADHD-Help Seeking Behaviors

Assessors should also assess cultural factors that impact parents and caregivers' attempts to address problems once they have been identified. These behaviors, also known as help-seeking, can be defined as attempts to obtain external assistance to address mental health concerns and include the pursuit of treatment and assessment for ADHD (Rickwood & Thomas, 2012). Help-seeking is impacted by several factors, including the makeup and size of parents' social networks, as well as experiences with stigma. Notably, the size and composition of one's social networks impact parental help-seeking and may vary across racial groups (Bussing et al., 2003). Furthermore, research shows that Black parents are more likely to seek help from religious leaders regarding their children's internalizing and externalizing problems compared to White parents, whereas White parents are more likely to seek self-help resources for internalizing problems (Thurston et al., 2018).

The likelihood of help-seeking for ADHD is also impacted by experiences with stigma. A systematic review identified that a significant number of parents from underrepresented ethnic backgrounds also express concern about the stigmatization of their children should they receive an ADHD diagnosis (Kappi & Martel, 2022). This is concerning given that families who report low levels of stigma were more likely to have positive attitudes about ADHD treatment (Taylor & Ansthel, 2021). Less is known about whether stigma impacts parental attitudes regarding ADHD assessment in similar ways. For Asian Americans in particular, the model minority myth, or the stereotype that Asians may not require individual, institutional, or societal help due to inherent "resilience," may impact rates of referral for ADHD assessments and experiences of stigma, impacting help-seeking behaviors (Jhawar & Antshel, 2023). Given that the valence and intensity of stigma continue across development (Lebowitz, 2016), it is necessary to consider the effects of stigma preceding, during, and after the completion of ADHD assessments.

STRUCTURAL BARRIERS TO ADHD ASSESSMENTS ACROSS SETTINGS

Providers should be aware that several structural barriers may interfere with the completion of a comprehensive and culturally sensitive ADHD assessment. First, it is important for assessors to keep in mind that time and resources may be a barrier for families to access and complete ADHD assessments. ADHD assessments are typically expensive and time-consuming and may require taking off time from work and school. Further, as described above, ADHD assessments require standardized assessments from multiple informants. Additionally, multiple barriers, such as prohibitive out-of-pocket or copay costs, exist within the medical system that may limit one's ability to access assessment services for ADHD, and research suggests that these barriers disproportionately impact individuals from historically minoritized ethnic and racial groups (Bailey et al., 2014). Rates of ADHD diagnosis have also been shown to vary based on type of insurance, with some research suggesting that children with public insurance are more likely to be diagnosed with ADHD than those with private insurance (Danielson et al., 2018), which is consistent with findings that public insurance (i.e., Medicaid) may have more extensive mental health service coverage than some private insurers (Pastor et al., 2017). Other barriers to accessing care within the medical system include lack of access to non-English speaking providers or interpreter services (Slobodin & Masalha, 2020). Indeed, research shows that language barriers make it more challenging to obtain evidence-based information about ADHD and to advocate for the child across systems of care (e.g., Araujo et al., 2017; Rothe, 2005).

Parent concern about harm due to medical racism (Shi et al., 2021) and mistrust of the medical system more broadly (Paidipati et al., 2017) may be a barrier for caregivers engaging in help-seeking behavior for ADHD assessment. Indeed, results of national polling have shown that 36% of parents from African American backgrounds and 19% of parents from Hispanic/Latinx backgrounds report concerns that racism would negatively impact their child's ability to receive appropriate ADHD care (Bailey et al., 2014). This may be particularly salient for caregivers in the context of considering assessment for ADHD given parental concerns about whether their child receiving an ADHD diagnosis would lead to their child receiving stimulant pharmacotherapy (Berger-Jenkins et al., 2012; Lui et al., 2023).

All of these factors can impact the likelihood of families to seek out, initiate, and complete ADHD assessments for their children. Providers seeking to reduce barriers may consider evaluating options for helping families navigate their insurance options, investigating alternatives for uninsured or underinsured families, as well as maximizing access to language-appropriate services. Previous reviews have identified barriers to ADHD treatment services (e.g., Bailey et al., 2014; Slobodin & Masalha, 2020); yet more research is needed to identify barriers to the *assessment* of childhood ADHD specifically.

Shared Decision Making in ADHD Assessment

As previously discussed, families begin the assessment process with their own set of causal beliefs about ADHD and child behavior more broadly, preferences for service selection, and biases and experiences with stigma impacting their help-seeking behaviors. Family-centered care, or care that is planned in consideration of the entire family and not just the individual, has been proposed as a promising approach for several patient populations (Kokorelias et al., 2019). More specifically, shared decision making, or intentional collaboration between providers and family members regarding care decisions, is particularly promising for populations with ADHD, given the potential to personalize care approaches, (re)establish provider–family trust, and reduce stigma (Fiks et al., 2011). In fact, the shared decision model has been shown to be strongly supported by families across Euro-American, African American/African Caribbean, and Mexican American backgrounds with ADHD (Davis et al., 2012). Clients who engaged in shared decision making reported higher treatment satisfaction, had increased treatment completion rates, and exhibited better clinical outcomes (Baweja et al., 2021; Lindhiem et al., 2014). Moreover, shared decision-making practices have shown promise in bolstering the ability of parents of youth with ADHD to make informed decisions about their child's care (Brinkman et al., 2013). However, other research has found that shared decision making increased the odds of ADHD treatment for White and multiracial children, but not for Black and Hispanic/Latinx families (Hinojosa et al., 2020), highlighting the need to investigate *for whom* and *within which contexts* shared decision making is most effective. Importantly, despite its promise in promoting service uptake, shared decision making within the *assessment* context has not been explored within ADHD populations. Such work needs to be extended to assessment decisions and procedures to investigate the effectiveness of shared decision making on assessment completion rates and follow-up with treatment care.

Culturally informed approaches to shared decision making should focus on understanding the family's beliefs, values, and preferences and collaborating with family members in their decision to pursue an ADHD assessment. For example, by eliciting families' explanatory models of ADHD behaviors, providers can gain insight into potential barriers to assessment seeking (e.g., normalizing of behavior, attributions to personality, or relational stress). Furthermore, culturally informed shared decision-making approaches can allow providers to more thoroughly discuss any potential concerns that family members may have surrounding the decision to seek an ADHD assessment. For example, some family members may be concerned about experiencing judgment from extended family or their community as a consequence of seeking ADHD assessment services for their child (Malik et al., 2017). Given research on the importance of social networks for certain cultural groups, providers may want to discuss the implications of an ADHD diagnosis on social network support, as caregivers may experience strain from their social networks as a result. Other caregivers may fear stigma or misunderstanding from others in their community when their child receives an ADHD diagnosis. Without considering these factors during the assessment process, providers may be at risk of misunderstanding core motivations, and family members may further experience mistrust of their providers or lose interest in completing the ADHD assessment process.

In order to conduct a culturally sensitive assessment, mental health providers should consider cultural and other broad contextual factors when evaluating diverse youth. The American Psychiatric Association's CFI is a useful starting point for assessors to consider how cultural factors may impact the ADHD assessment process. Assessors should also consider structural (e.g., time, money, and transportation) and systemic (e.g., stigma and medical racism) barriers impacting the family's initiation and follow-through with ADHD assessments. Shared decision making is one potential culturally informed approach to ADHD assessment; however, more research is needed to investigate *for whom* and *within which contexts* shared decision making is most effective.

FUTURE DIRECTIONS

In this final section, we discuss emerging trends in the field of ADHD assessments. This includes potential future directions to reduce ADHD-related disparities.

Elucidating ADHD Disparities across Groups

Available data shows that disparities continue to exist in the assessment of ADHD, impacting youth from different racial/ethnic and socioeconomic backgrounds, among other social determinants of health. More work is needed to further understand which youth are being overlooked. For example, while sex differences in ADHD prevalence are well defined, very little research on prevalence and experiences of ADHD in gender diverse individuals exists (Goetz & Adams, 2022). Additionally, it remains unclear whether lower prevalence rates among some racial groups (e.g., Asian American and Latinx youth) reflect true differences in prevalence or lower likelihood of identification based on culturally embedded belief systems and/or biases. Further, although most research to date has focused on identifying disparities based on single identities (e.g., sex and race), it is becoming increasingly clear that intersectional approaches are needed to fully encapsulate the influential factors contributing to these disparities (Danielson et al., 2024; Morgan & Hu, 2023). Moreover, while examining trends across identity groups is useful, assessors should also evaluate the degree to which cultural factors relate to the ADHD assessment process for each individual child and family.

Acknowledgment of Parent Mental Health in Youth ADHD Assessments

As reviewed above, caregivers play a critical role in the assessment of youth ADHD. Additional research is needed to explore assessment of ADHD in children whose parents may also have ADHD and/or other mental health difficulties. It is well established that ADHD has a strong genetic component (Faraone & Larsson, 2019), and it is estimated that 25–50% of children with ADHD have at least one parent with ADHD (Johnston et al., 2012). Research has demonstrated that children whose parents have ADHD have poorer developmental and treatment outcomes (Chronis-Tuscano et al., 2017). However, less is known about how parent ADHD may impact help-seeking behavior or assessment of child ADHD. Given the strong familial component of ADHD, more research is needed to examine the utility of familywide assessments. Specifically, it will be useful to understand the acceptability and feasibility of assessing caregiver ADHD during youth ADHD assessments and the extent to which these symptoms may impact the assessment of youth ADHD. Familywide assessments of ADHD within primary care could be one avenue to address parent ADHD and mental health more broadly, but may require special considerations. Indeed, in a qualitative study assessing perspectives on screening of parent ADHD in pediatric primary care settings, findings demonstrated that parents may feel hesitant about divulging information about their own mental health due to the child-focused nature of the visit, despite provider enthusiasm regarding the holistic family-centered approach (Lui et al., 2023). In line with prior research, parents also shared hesitancy about medication and mental health help-seeking due to experiences with stigma. Thus, more research is needed to further evaluate the acceptability of familial and provider attitudes toward familywide screening of ADHD to inform culturally sensitive practices regarding parental ADHD screening.

Furthermore, additional research is needed to assess whether assessment of child ADHD may prompt caregivers to seek assessment for their own symptoms of ADHD or vice versa. Parents who have prior personal or professional experience with ADHD are 2.17 times more likely to recognize problem behavior (Thurston et al., 2015). However, it is unclear whether parents' own ADHD may impact their problem recognition and help-seeking behaviors. For example, parents with ADHD may underreport their children's ADHD symptoms due to empathizing with similar experiences. On the other hand, parents with ADHD may be more likely to recognize ADHD symptoms in their own children. Given beliefs about ADHD greatly impact likelihood of help-seeking behavior (Johnston & Freeman, 2002; Wright et al., 2015), additional research is needed to elucidate the decision-making processes underlying the pursuit of child ADHD assessments based on familial-level factors such as parental mental health.

Strengths-Based Approach to ADHD Assessments

More research is needed to show how ADHD-related strengths can be incorporated into the assessment framework, which may appeal to caregivers and youth alike. Qualitative research studies have highlighted several potential areas of strength associated with ADHD, including creativity, ability to think in unconventional ways, spontaneity, hyperfocus on topics of interest, drive to try new things, resilience, and emotional intelligence (Nordby et al., 2023; Sedgwick et al., 2019). However, to date, quantitative literature investigating these strengths is limited. Though less is known about incorporating strengths into ADHD assessment, strengths-based assessment practices are increasingly being utilized in assessments for autism (Brown et al., 2021), including introducing parents to strengths associated with autism at the time of diagnosis, moving away from deficit-based language (i.e., using "challenge/difficulty" instead of "deficit"), and reframing the goals of assessment away from "fixing" and toward helping parents gain a better understanding of their child's experiences to support their continued growth (Brown et al., 2021).

Another aspect of strengths-based assessment involves introducing caregivers to the neurodiversity framework (Singer, 1999), which conceptualizes differences in neurological functioning experienced by individuals with autism, ADHD, learning disabilities, and other neurological or developmental conditions as valuable dimensions of diversity to be celebrated and accommodated rather than deficits or dysfunctions to be eliminated. Work in the autism literature has called for introducing the neurodiversity framework to caregivers as part of the assessment and diagnosis process for autism, training providers on the neurodiversity movement, and facilitating greater participation of individuals with lived experience in both clinical and research practices (Schuck et al., 2022). More research is needed to examine how the neurodiversity framework can be integrated into evidence-based assessment for ADHD.

Expanding ADHD Services to Reduce ADHD Disparities

More research is needed to identify broad, systemic changes that may address barriers to ADHD assessments, with the ultimate goal of reducing disparities in ADHD identification, diagnosis, and care. One promising avenue may be to include lay health workers (e.g., community health workers and peer providers) in the ADHD assessment process (Barnett et al., 2021). For example, parent or family navigators, who often come from similar backgrounds as the families they assist, may be useful resources for families seeking ADHD assessments for their children, as they may be able to assist patients with the assessment process (e.g., coordinating across multiple systems and completion of assessments), while also addressing potential barriers (e.g., housing, food, and transportation) that may otherwise interfere with the completion of a comprehensive ADHD assessment. Family navigation has been shown to improve assessment-related outcomes in the context of autism spectrum disorders (e.g., Feinberg et al., 2021); however, more work is needed to understand the role family navigation programs can play in reducing disparities in ADHD diagnosis and treatment receipt.

Considering ADHD Content on the Internet/Social Media

Recently, there has been a spike in online information seeking about ADHD, with Google searches of "ADHD" and related terms increasing significantly since 2020 (Hartnett & Cummings, 2023). Data from the widely used social media app TikTok has revealed that "ADHD" is one of the most popular health-related hashtags on the platform (Zenone et al., 2021). These patterns have prompted concerns from the clinical community, citing potential unmanageable increases in demand for ADHD assessment (Hartnett & Cummings, 2023), as well as significant concerns about the accuracy and quality of information about ADHD being presented on social media platforms (Yeung et al., 2022). Others have raised concerns about potential tensions between provider concerns about misinformation and ensuring that those seeking assessment for ADHD based on information they found on the internet and social media feel validated and heard in their concerns (Eagle & Ringland, 2023). Indeed, while the popularization of social media platforms has been an avenue to increase awareness around ADHD, it may also perpetuate harmful myths and stereotypes (Hinshaw & Scheffler, 2014; Sciutto, 2015). Given social media platforms like TikTok are extremely popular among youth, more research will be needed to explore how social media content about ADHD may impact families' desires or expectations around assessment for ADHD.

CONCLUSION

Although well-established guidelines for evidence-based assessment of ADHD exist, relatively little attention has been paid to cultural factors that may impact diagnosis and help-seeking. It is well documented that disparities exist in which youth receive an ADHD diagnosis and which do not. The ADHD-Help Seeking Behavior Model provides a useful framework for understanding the role of culture in problem recognition, decision to seek help, service selection, and service utilization for ADHD. Ultimately, there is a need for more provider training on cultural considerations in the assessment of ADHD in diverse youth. In particular, training providers in cultural humility (e.g., using the Cultural Formulation Interview) and shared decision making are necessary to gain a deeper understanding of the child within the cultural and broader environmental context. Inclusion of lay health workers, from similar backgrounds as the families and with lived experience, across schools, pediatric primary care, and specialty mental health settings, can assist parents with navigating the often-complicated process of obtaining an ADHD assessment and accessing evidence-based services.

REFERENCES

Ali, M. M., West, K., Teich, J. L., Lynch, S., Mutter, R., & Dubenitz, J. (2019). Utilization of mental health services in educational setting by adolescents in the United States. *Journal of School Health*, 89(5), 393–401.

American Psychiatric Association. (2013). *Diagnostic and statistical manual of mental disorders* (5th ed.). Author.

American Psychiatric Association. (2022). *Diagnostic and statistical manual of mental disorders* (5th ed., text rev.). Author.

American Psychological Association. (2023). *Inclusive language guide* (2nd ed.).Author. *www.apa.org/about/apa/equity-diversity-inclusion/language-guidelines.pdf*

Antshel, K. M., & Russo, N. (2019). Autism spectrum disorders and ADHD: Overlapping phenomenology, diagnostic issues, and treatment considerations. *Current Psychiatry Reports, 21*, 1–11.

Araujo, E. A., Pfiffner, L., & Haack, L. M. (2017). Emotional, social and cultural experiences of Latino children with ADHD symptoms and their families. *Journal of Child and Family Studies, 26*, 3512–3524.

Arcia, E., & Fernández, M. C. (2003). From awareness to acknowledgment: The development of concern among Latina mothers of children with disruptive behaviors. *Journal of Attention Disorders*, 6(4), 163–175.

Bailey, R. K., Jaquez-Gutierrez, M. C., & Madhoo, M. (2014). Sociocultural issues in African American and Hispanic minorities seeking care for attention-deficit/hyperactivity disorder. *The Primary Care Companion for CNS Disorders, 16*(4), 10–4088.

Barkley, R. A. (2019). Neuropsychological testing is not useful in the diagnosis of ADHD: Stop it (or prove it)! *The ADHD Report, 27*(2), 1–8.

Barkley, R. A., & Fischer, M. (2019). Hyperactive child syndrome and estimated life expectancy at young adult follow-up: The role of ADHD persistence and other potential predictors. *Journal of Attention Disorders, 23*(9), 907–923.

Barnett, M. L., Luis Sanchez, B. E., Green Rosas, Y., & Broder-Fingert, S. (2021). Future directions in lay health worker involvement in children's mental health services in the U.S. *Journal of Clinical Child & Adolescent Psychology, 50*(6), 966–978.

Baweja, R., Soutullo, C. A., & Waxmonsky, J. G. (2021). Review of barriers and interventions to promote treatment engagement for pediatric attention deficit hyperactivity disorder care. *World Journal of Psychiatry, 11*(12), 1206.

Berger, I., Dor, T., Nevo, Y., & Goldzweig, G. (2008). Attitudes toward attention-deficit hyperactivity disorder (ADHD) treatment: Parents' and children's perspectives. *Journal of Child Neurology, 23*(9), 1036–1042.

Berger-Jenkins, E., McKay, M., Newcorn, J., Bannon, W., & Laraque, D. (2012). Parent medication concerns predict underutilization of mental health services for minority children with ADHD. *Clinical Pediatrics, 51*(1), 65–76.

Boodoo, R., Lagman, J. G., Jairath, B., & Baweja, R. (2022). A review of ADHD and childhood trauma: Treatment challenges and clinical guidance. *Current Developmental Disorders Reports*, 9(4), 137–145.

Brinkman, W. B., Hartl Majcher, J., Poling, L. M., Shi, G., Zender, M., Sucharew, H., et al. (2013). Shared decision-making to improve attention-deficit hyperactivity disorder care. *Patient Education and Counseling*, 93(1), 95–101.

Briscoe-Smith, A. M., & Hinshaw, S. P. (2006). Linkages between child abuse and attention-deficit/hyperactivity disorder in girls: Behavioral and social correlates. *Child Abuse & Neglect, 30*(11), 1239–1255.

Brown, H. M., Stahmer, A. C., Dwyer, P., & Rivera, S. (2021). Changing the story: How diagnosticians can support a neurodiversity perspective from the start. *Autism: The International Journal of Research and Practice, 25*(5), 1171–1174.

Bussing, R., Gary, F. A., Mills, T. L., & Garvan, C. W. (2007). Cultural variations in parental health beliefs, knowledge, and information sources related to attention-deficit/hyperactivity disorder. *Journal of Family Issues, 28*(3), 291–318.

Bussing, R., Gary, F. A., Mills, T. L., & Wilson Garvan, C. (2003). Parental explanatory models of ADHD: Gender and cultural variations. *Social Psychiatry and Psychiatric Epidemiology, 38*, 563–575.

Bussing, R., Koro-Ljungberg, M., Noguchi, K., Mason, D., Mayerson, G., & Garvan, C. W. (2012). Willingness to use ADHD treatments: A mixed methods study of perceptions by adolescents, parents, health professionals and teachers. *Social Science & Medicine, 74*(1), 92–100.

Cauce, A. M., Domenech-Rodríguez, M., Paradise, M., Cochran, B. N., Shea, J. M., Srebnik, D., & Baydar, N. (2002). Cultural and contextual influences in mental health help seeking: A focus on ethnic minority youth. *Journal of Consulting and Clinical Psychology, 70*(1), 44.

Cherkasova, M. V., Roy, A., Molina, B. S., Scott, G., Weiss, G., Barkley, R. A., et al. (2022). Adult outcome as seen through controlled prospective follow-up studies of children with attention-deficit/hyperactivity disorder followed into adulthood. *Jour-*

nal of the American Academy of Child & Adolescent Psychiatry, *61*(3), 378–391.

Chronis-Tuscano, A. (2022). ADHD in girls and women: A call to action–reflections on Hinshaw et al. (2021). *Journal of Child Psychology and Psychiatry*, *63*(4), 497–499.

Chronis-Tuscano, A., Chacko, A., & Barkley, R. (2013). Key issues relevant to the efficacy of behavioral treatment for ADHD. *American Journal of Psychiatry*, *170*(7), 799–799.

Chronis-Tuscano, A., French, W., Strickland, J., Sasser, T., Gonzalez, E. N. S., Whitlock, K. B., & Stein, M. A. (2020). Acute effects of parent stimulant medication versus behavioral parent training on mothers† ADHD, parenting behavior, and at-risk children. *The Journal of Clinical Psychiatry*, *81*(5), 21254.

Chronis-Tuscano, A., Oddo, L. E., Schwartz, K. T. G., & Meinzer, M. C. (in press). Co-occurring ADHD, disruptive behavior disorders, and depression. In J. W. Pettit & T. M. Olino (Eds.-in-Chief), R. C. Boyd, B. C. Chu, E. P. Hayden, & D. A. Pizzagalli (Assoc. Eds.), *APA handbook of depression: Vol. 1. Classification, co-occurring conditions, and etiological processes*. American Psychological Association, 159–175.

Chronis-Tuscano, A., Wang, C. H., Woods, K. E., Strickland, J., & Stein, M. A. (2017). Parent ADHD and evidence-based treatment for their children: Review and directions for future research. *Journal of Abnormal Child Psychology*, *45*, 501–517.

Conners, C. K. (2022). *Conners, 4*™. Multi-Health Systems.

Cuffe, S. P., Visser, S. N., Holbrook, J. R., Danielson, M. L., Geryk, L. L., Wolraich, M. L., & McKeown, R. E. (2020). ADHD and psychiatric comorbidity: Functional outcomes in a school-based sample of children. *Journal of Attention Disorders*, *24*(9), 1345–1354.

Danielson, M. L., Claussen, A. H., Bitsko, R. H., Katz, S. M., Newsome, K., Blumberg, S. J., et al. (2024). ADHD prevalence among US children and adolescents in 2022: Diagnosis, severity, co-occurring disorders, and treatment. *Journal of Clinical Child & Adolescent Psychology*, *53*(3), 343–360.

Danielson, M. L., Visser, S. N., Chronis-Tuscano, A., & DuPaul, G. J. (2018). A national description of treatment among United States children and adolescents with attention-deficit/hyperactivity disorder. *The Journal of Pediatrics*, *192*, 240–246.

Davis, C. C., Claudius, M., Palinkas, L. A., Wong, J. B., & Leslie, L. K. (2012). Putting families in the center: Family perspectives on decision making and ADHD and implications for ADHD care. *Journal of Attention Disorders*, *16*(8), 675–684.

de la Peña, F. R., Villavicencio, L. R., Palacio, J. D., Félix, F. J., Larraguibel, M., Viola, L., et al. (2018). Validity and reliability of the kiddie schedule for affective disorders and schizophrenia present and lifetime version DSM-5 (K-SADS-PL-5) Spanish version. *BMC Psychiatry*, *18*, 1–7.

De Los Reyes, A. (2011). Introduction to the special section: More than measurement error: Discovering meaning behind informant discrepancies in clinical assessments of children and adolescents. *Journal of Clinical Child & Adolescent Psychology*, *40*(1), 1–9.

DuPaul, G. J., Chronis-Tuscano, A., Danielson, M. L., & Visser, S. N. (2019). Predictors of receipt of school services in a national sample of youth with ADHD. *Journal of Attention Disorders*, *23*(11), 1303–1319.

DuPaul, G. J., & Stoner, G. (2014). *ADHD in the schools: Assessment and intervention strategies*. Guilford Press.

DuPaul, G. J., & Volpe, R. J. (2009). ADHD and learning disabilities: Research findings and clinical implications. *Current Attention Disorders Reports*, *1*(4), 152–155.

Eagle, T., & Ringland, K. E. (2023). "You can't possibly have ADHD": Exploring validation and tensions around diagnosis within unbounded ADHD social media communities. In *Proceedings of the 25th International ACM SIGACCESS Conference on Computers and Accessibility* (pp. 1–17).

Eiraldi, R. B., Mazzuca, L. B., Clarke, A. T., & Power, T. J. (2006). Service utilization among ethnic minority children with ADHD: A model of help-seeking behavior. *Administration and Policy in Mental Health and Mental Health Services Research*, *33*, 607–622.

Evans, S. W., Langberg, J., & Williams, J. (2003). Achieving generalization in school-based mental health. *Handbook of school mental health advancing practice and research*, 335–348.

Fadus, M. C., Ginsburg, K. R., Sobowale, K., Halliday-Boykins, C. A., Bryant, B. E., Gray, K. M., & Squeglia, L. M. (2020). Unconscious bias and the diagnosis of disruptive behavior disorders and ADHD in African American and Hispanic youth. *Academic Psychiatry*, *44*, 95–102.

Fairman, K. A., Peckham, A. M., & Sclar, D. A. (2020). Diagnosis and treatment of ADHD in the United States: Update by gender and race. *Journal of Attention Disorders*, *24*(1), 10–19.

Faraone, S. V., & Larsson, H. (2019). Genetics of attention deficit hyperactivity disorder. *Molecular Psychiatry*, *24*(4), 562–575.

Feinberg, E., Augustyn, M., Broder-Fingert, S., Bennett, A., Weitzman, C., Kuhn, J., et al. (2021). Effect of family navigation on diagnostic ascertainment among children at risk for autism: A randomized clinical trial from DBPNet. *JAMA Pediatrics*, *175*(3), 243–250.

Fiks, A. G., Hughes, C. C., Gafen, A., Guevara, J. P., & Barg, F. K. (2011). Contrasting parents' and pediatricians' perspectives on shared decision-making in ADHD. *Pediatrics*, *127*(1), e188–e196.

Franke, B., Michelini, G., Asherson, P., Banaschewski, T., Bilbow, A., Buitelaar, J. K., et al. (2018). Live fast, die young? A review on the developmental trajectories of ADHD across the lifespan. *European Neuropsychopharmacology*, *28*(10), 1059–1088.

Federico, A., Zgodic, A., Flory, K., Hantman, R. M., Eberth, J. M., Mclain, A. C., & Bradshaw, J. (2024).

Predictors of autism spectrum disorder and ADHD: Results from the National Survey of Children's Health. *Disability and Health Journal, 17*(1), 101512.

Garney, W., Wilson, K., Ajayi, K. V., Panjwani, S., Love, S. M., Flores, S., et al. (2021). Social-ecological barriers to access to healthcare for adolescents: A scoping review. *International Journal of Environmental Research and Public Health, 18*(8), 4138.

Gerdes, A. C., Lawton, K. E., Haack, L. M., & Schneider, B. W. (2014). Latino parental help seeking for childhood ADHD. *Administration and Policy in Mental Health and Mental Health Services Research, 41*, 503–513.

Goetz, T. G., & Adams, N. (2022). The transgender and gender diverse and attention deficit hyperactivity disorder nexus: A systematic review. *Journal of Gay & Lesbian Mental Health, 28*(1), 2–19.

Haack, L. M., & Gerdes, A. C. (2011). Functional impairment in Latino children with ADHD: Implications for culturally appropriate conceptualization and measurement. *Clinical Child and Family Psychology Review, 14*, 318–328.

Haack, L. M., Meza, J., Jiang, Y., Araujo, E. J., & Pfiffner, L. (2018). Influences to ADHD problem recognition: Mixed-method investigation and recommendations to reduce disparities for Latino youth. *Administration and Policy in Mental Health and Mental Health Services Research, 45*(6), 958–977.

Hartnett, Y., & Cummings, E. (2024). Social media and ADHD: Implications for clinical assessment and treatment. *Irish Journal of Psychological Medicine, 41*(1), 132–136.

Hinojosa, M. S., Hinojosa, R., & Nguyen, J. (2020). Shared decision making and treatment for minority children with ADHD. *Journal of Transcultural Nursing, 31*(2), 135–143.

Hinshaw, S. P., Nguyen, P. T., O'Grady, S. M., & Rosenthal, E. A. (2022). Annual research review: Attention-deficit/hyperactivity disorder in girls and women: Underrepresentation, longitudinal processes, and key directions. *Journal of Child Psychology and Psychiatry, 63*(4), 484–496.

Hinshaw, S. P., & Scheffler, R. M. (2014). *The ADHD explosion: Myths, medication, money, and today's push for performance.* Oxford University Press.

Jarbin, H., Andersson, M., Råstam, M., & Ivarsson, T. (2017). Predictive validity of the K-SADS-PL 2009 version in school-aged and adolescent outpatients. *Nordic Journal of Psychiatry, 71*(4), 270–276.

Jarvis, G. E., Kirmayer, L. J., Gómez-Carrillo, A., Aggarwal, N. K., & Lewis-Fernández, R. (2020). Update on the Cultural Formulation Interview. *Focus, 18*(1), 40–46.

Jhawar, N., & Antshel, K. (2023). Asian Indian American parental help-seeking intentions for ADHD. *Research on Child and Adolescent Psychopathology, 51*(11), 1551–1563.

Johnston, C., & Chronis-Tuscano, A. (2015). Families and ADHD. In R. A. Barkley (Ed.), *Attention-deficit hyperactivity disorder: A handbook for diagnosis and treatment* (4th ed., pp. 191–209). Guilford Press.

Johnston, C., & Freeman, W. (2002). Parents' beliefs about ADHD: Implications for assessment and treatment. *The ADHD Report, 10*(1), 6–9.

Johnston, C., Mash, E. J., Miller, N., & Ninowski, J. E. (2012). Parenting in adults with attention-deficit/hyperactivity disorder (ADHD). *Clinical Psychology Review, 32*(4), 215–228.

Kappi, A., & Martel, M. (2022). Parental barriers in seeking mental health services for attention deficit hyperactivity disorder in children: systematic review. *Journal of Attention Disorders, 26*(3), 408–425.

Kaufman, J., Birmaher, B., Brent, D., Rao, U. M. A., Flynn, C., et al. (1997). Schedule for affective disorders and schizophrenia for school-age children-present and lifetime version (K-SADS-PL): Initial reliability and validity data. *Journal of the American Academy of Child & Adolescent Psychiatry, 36*(7), 980–988.

Kim, Y. S., Cheon, K. A., Kim, B. N., Chang, S. A., Yoo, H. J., Kim, J. W., et al. (2004). The reliability and validity of Kiddie-Schedule for affective disorders and schizophrenia-present and lifetime version-Korean version (K-SADS-PL-K). *Yonsei Medical Journal, 45*(1), 81–89.

Kokorelias, K. M., Gignac, M. A., Naglie, G., & Cameron, J. I. (2019). Towards a universal model of family centered care: A scoping review. *BMC Health Services Research, 19*, 1–11.

Landon, B. E., Onnela, J. P., Meneades, L., O'Malley, A. J., & Keating, N. L. (2021). Assessment of racial disparities in primary care physician specialty referrals. *JAMA Network Open, 4*(1), e2029238–e2029238.

Lawton, K. E., Gerdes, A. C., Haack, L. M., & Schneider, B. (2014). Acculturation, cultural values, and Latino parental beliefs about the etiology of ADHD. *Administration and Policy in Mental Health and Mental Health Services Research, 41*, 189–204.

Lebowitz, M. S. (2016). Stigmatization of ADHD: A developmental review. *Journal of Attention Disorders, 20*(3), 199–205.

Lewis-Fernández, R., Aggarwal, N. K., Hinton, L., Hinton, D. E., & Kirmayer, L. J. (Eds.). (2016). *DSM-5® handbook on the Cultural Formulation Interview.* American Psychiatric Publishing, Inc.

Lindhiem, O., Bennett, C. B., Trentacosta, C. J., & McLear, C. (2014). Client preferences affect treatment satisfaction, completion, and clinical outcome: A meta-analysis. *Clinical Psychology Review, 34*(6), 506–517.

Lui, J. H., Danko, C. M., Triece, T., Bennett, I. M., Marschall, D., Lorenzo, N. E., Stein, M. A., & Chronis-Tuscano, A. (2023). Screening for parent and child ADHD in urban pediatric primary care: Pilot implementation and stakeholder perspectives. *BMC Pediatrics, 23*(1), 354.

Maldonado, B. N., Chandna, J., & Gladstone, M. (2019). A systematic review of tools used to screen and assess for externalising behaviour symptoms in low and middle income settings. *Global Mental Health*, 6, e13.

Malik, T. A., Rooney, M., Chronis-Tuscano, A., & Tariq, N. (2017). Preliminary efficacy of a behavioral parent training program for children with ADHD in Pakistan. *Journal of Attention Disorders, 21*(5), 390–404.

Morgan, P. L., & Hu, E. H. (2023). Sociodemographic disparities in ADHD diagnosis and treatment among US elementary schoolchildren. *Psychiatry Research, 327*, 115393.

Mulraney, M., Arrondo, G., Musullulu, H., Iturmendi-Sabater, I., Cortese, S., Westwood, S. J., et al. (2022). Systematic review and meta-analysis: Screening tools for attention-deficit/hyperactivity disorder in children and adolescents. *Journal of the American Academy of Child & Adolescent Psychiatry, 61*(8), 982–996.

National Child Traumatic Stress Network. (2016). *Is it ADHD or child traumatic stress? A guide for clinicians* [Fact sheet]. *www.nctsn.org/resources/it-adhd-or-child-traumatic-stress-guide-clinicians*

Nordby, E. S., Guribye, F., Nordgreen, T., & Lundervold, A. J. (2023). Silver linings of ADHD: A thematic analysis of adults' positive experiences with living with ADHD. *BMJ Open, 13*(10), e072052.

O'Loughlin, K., Donovan, E. K., Radcliff, Z., Ryan, M., & Rybarczyk, B. (2019). Using integrated behavioral healthcare to address behavioral health disparities in underserved populations. *Translational Issues in Psychological Science*, 5(4), 374–389.

Paidipati, C. P., Brawner, B., Eiraldi, R., & Deatrick, J. A. (2017). Parent and family processes related to ADHD management in ethnically diverse youth. *Journal of the American Psychiatric Nurses Association, 23*(2), 90–112.

Pastor, P. N., & Reuben, C. A. (2005). Racial and ethnic differences in ADHD and LD in young school-age children: Parental reports in the National Health Interview Survey. *Public Health Reports, 120*(4), 383–392.

Pastor, P. N., Simon, A. E., & Reuben, C. A. (2017). ADHD: Insurance and mental health service use. *Clinical Pediatrics*, 56(8), 729–736.

Pelham, Jr, W. E., Fabiano, G. A., & Massetti, G. M. (2005). Evidence-based assessment of attention deficit hyperactivity disorder in children and adolescents. *Journal of Clinical Child and Adolescent Psychology, 34*(3), 449–476.

Pham, A. V. (2015). Understanding ADHD from a biopsychosocial-cultural framework: A case study. *Contemporary School Psychology, 19*, 54–62.

Pierce, C. D., & Reid, R. (2004, August). Attention deficit hyperactivity disorder: Assessment and treatment of children from culturally different groups. In *Seminars in speech and language* (Vol. 25, No. 03, pp. 233–240). Thieme.

Pliszka, S. (2007). Practice parameter for the assessment and treatment of children and adolescents with attention-deficit/hyperactivity disorder. *Journal of the American Academy of Child and Adolescent Psychiatry* 46, 894–921.

Reale, L., Bartoli, B., Cartabia, M., Zanetti, M., Costantino, M. A., Canevini, M. P., & Bonati, M. (2017). Comorbidity prevalence and treatment outcome in children and adolescents with ADHD. *European Child & Adolescent Psychiatry*, 26(12), 1443–1457.

Reuben C, & Elgaddal N. Attention-deficit/hyperactivity disorder in children ages 5–17 years: United States, 2020–2022 (2024). NCHS Data Brief, no 499. National Center for Health Statistics.

Rickwood, D., & Thomas, K. (2012). Conceptual measurement framework for help-seeking for mental health problems. *Psychology Research and Behavior Management*, 173–183.

Rothe, E. M. (2005). Considering cultural diversity in the management of ADHD in Hispanic patients. *Journal of the National Medical Association*, 97(10 Suppl), 17S.

Schuck, R. K., Tagavi, D. M., Baiden, K. M. P., Dwyer, P., Williams, Z. J., Osuna, A., et al. (2022). Neurodiversity and autism intervention: Reconciling perspectives through a naturalistic developmental behavioral intervention framework. *Journal of Autism and Developmental Disorders*, 52(10), 4625–4645.

Sciutto, M. J. (2015). ADHD knowledge, misconceptions, and treatment acceptability. *Journal of Attention Disorders*, 19(2), 91–98.

Sedgwick J. A., Merwood A., & Asherson, P. (2019). The positive aspects of attention deficit hyperactivity disorder: A qualitative investigation of successful adults with ADHD. *ADHD Attention Deficit and Hyperactivity Disorders, 11*(3), 241–253.

Shi, Y., Guevara, L. R. H., Dykhoff, H. J., Sangaralingham, L. R., Phelan, S., Zaccariello, M. J., & Warner, D. O. (2021). Racial disparities in diagnosis of attention-deficit/hyperactivity disorder in a US national birth cohort. *JAMA Network Open*, 4(3), e210321–e210321.

Shippen, N., Horn, S. R., Triece, P., Chronis-Tuscano, A., & Meinzer, M. C. (2022). Understanding ADHD in Black adolescents in urban schools: A qualitative examination of factors that influence ADHD presentation, coping strategies, and access to care. *Evidence-Based Practice in Child and Adolescent Mental Health*, 7(2), 213–229.

Singer, J. (1999). Why can't you be normal for once in your life? From a "problem with no name" to a new category of disability. In M. Corker & S. French (Eds.), *Disability discourse* (pp. 59–67). Open University Press.

Slobodin, O., & Masalha, R. (2020). Challenges in ADHD care for ethnic minority children: A review of the current literature. *Transcultural Psychiatry*, 57(3), 468–483.

Spencer, A. E., Faraone, S. V., Bogucki, O. E., Pope, A. L., Uchida, M., Milad, M. R., et al. (2016). Examining the association between posttraumatic stress disorder and attention-deficit/hyperactivity disorder: A systematic review and meta-analysis. *The Journal of Clinical Psychiatry*, *77*(1), 6862.

Spencer, A. E., Sikov, J., Loubeau, J. K., Zolli, N., Baul, T., Rabin, M., et al. (2021). Six stages of engagement in ADHD treatment described by diverse, urban parents. *Pediatrics*, *148*(4), e2021051261.

Taylor, L. E., & Antshel, K. M. (2021). Factors associated with parental treatment attitudes and information-seeking behaviors for childhood ADHD. *Journal of Attention Disorders*, *25*(4), 607–617.

Thompson, M. J., Au, A., Laver-Bradbury, C., Lange, A. M., Tripp, G., & Shimabukuro, S., & Sonuga-Barke, E. J. (2017). Adapting an attention-deficit hyperactivity disorder parent training intervention to different cultural contexts: The experience of implementing the New Forest Parenting Programme in China, Denmark, Hong Kong, Japan, and the United Kingdom. *PsyCh Journal*, 6(1), 83–97.

Thurston, I. B., Hardin, R., Decker, K., Arnold, T., Howell, K. H., & Phares, V. (2018). Black and white parents' willingness to seek help for children's internalizing and externalizing symptoms. *Journal of Clinical Psychology*, *74*(1), 161–177.

Thurston, I. B., Phares, V., Coates, E. E., & Bogart, L. M. (2015). Child problem recognition and help-seeking intentions among black and white parents. *Journal of Clinical Child & Adolescent Psychology*, *44*(4), 604–615.

Tung, I., Li, J. J., Meza, J. I., Jezior, K. L., Kianmahd, J. S., Hentschel, P. G., O'Neil, P. M., & Lee, S. S. (2016). Patterns of comorbidity among girls with ADHD: A meta-analysis. *Pediatrics*, *138*(4), e20160430.

Ünal, F., Öktem, F., Çetin Çuhadaroğlu, F., Çengel Kültür, S. E., Akdemir, D., Foto Özdemir, D., et al. (2019). Reliability and validity of the schedule for affective disorders and schizophrenia for school-age children-present and lifetime version, DSM-5 November 2016-Turkish adaptation (K-SADS-PL-DSM-5-T). *Turkish Journal of Psychiatry*, *30*(1), 1–8.

Visser, S. N., Bitsko, R. H., Danielson, M. L., Ghandour, R. M., Blumberg, S. J., Schieve, L. A., et al. (2015). Treatment of attention deficit/hyperactivity disorder among children with special health care needs. *The Journal of Pediatrics*, *166*(6), 1423–1430.

Wolraich, M. L., Chan, E., Froehlich, T., Lynch, R. L., Bax, A., Redwine, S. T., et al. (2019). ADHD diagnosis and treatment guidelines: A historical perspective. *Pediatrics*, *144*(4), e20191682.

Wolraich, M. L., Feurer, I. D., Hannah, J. N., Baumgaertel, A., & Pinnock, T. Y. (1998). Obtaining systematic teacher reports of disruptive behavior disorders utilizing DSM-IV. *Journal of Abnormal Child Psychology*, *26*, 141–152.

Wright, N., Moldavsky, M., Schneider, J., Chakrabarti, I., Coates, J., Daley, D., et al. (2015). Practitioner review: Pathways to care for ADHD–a systematic review of barriers and facilitators. *Journal of Child Psychology and Psychiatry*, *56*(6), 598–617.

Yeh, M., Hough, R. L., McCabe, K., Lau, A., & Garland, A. (2004). Parental beliefs about the causes of child problems: Exploring racial/ethnic patterns. *Journal of the American Academy of Child & Adolescent Psychiatry*, *43*(5), 605–612.

Yeung, A., Ng, E., & Abi-Jaoude, E. (2022). TikTok and attention-deficit/hyperactivity disorder: A cross-sectional study of social media content quality. *The Canadian Journal of Psychiatry*, *67*(12), 899–906.

Zenone, M., Ow, N., & Barb'ic, S. (2021). TikTok and public health: A proposed research agenda. *BMJ Global Health*, 6(11), e007648.

CHAPTER 16

Assessment of Intellectual Disabilities

Lindsay M. McCary and Kathryn Smith

Understanding and effectively evaluating intellectual disabilities is paramount for providing individuals with tailored, individualized support and services. Intellectual disabilities encompass a spectrum of cognitive and adaptive impairments that significantly impact an individual's participation in community, school, and home activities. The accurate assessment of these conditions is crucial for informed decision making, personalized interventions, and equitable access to resources. Grounded in principles of validity, equity, and cultural humility, this chapter will explore assessment approaches encompassing cognitive, adaptive, and socioemotional domains to provide practitioners with a holistic understanding of a comprehensive, best-practice assessment of intellectual disabilities. This chapter includes a brief overview of the history of intellectual assessment, main theories of intelligence, and definitions of intellectual disability before further describing best-practice considerations.

HISTORY OF INTELLECTUAL ASSESSMENT

The history of intellectual assessment traces back to the late nineteenth and early twentieth centuries when pioneers such as Alfred Binet and Theodore Simon developed the first standardized intelligence tests. Binet and Simon's groundbreaking work resulted in the creation of the Binet–Simon Scale, aimed at identifying children who might require additional educational support (Binet & Simon, 1916). This scale marked the beginning of systematic efforts to measure cognitive abilities, laying the foundation for the field of psychological assessment. Subsequent developments, such as Lewis Terman's adaptation of the Binet–Simon Scale into the Stanford–Binet Intelligence Scales, contributed to the widespread use of intelligence testing in various contexts, including education, clinical practice, and employment (Terman, 1916). The increased popularity of intelligence tests was not without criticism. Klineberg (1927) studied differences in speed and accuracy on performance measures across racial groups and found bias in measurement related to language and educational differences across groups. He concluded that quantitative differences may overshadow other factors important to consider. Horace Mann Bond was also an early critic of intelligence tests and recognized the tendency for tests to be racially biased and therefore perpetuate racial stereotypes (1924). Yet, over the decades, intelligence tests continued to evolve to incorporate more sophisticated measurement techniques and theoretical frameworks, which revolutionized intelligence tests by emphasizing multiple domains and providing standardized scores based on normative data. This process of evolution has led to significant implications in regard to how intelligence testing is used today, both positive in terms of identification and accessing support and negative in terms of the gravity of decisions sometimes made on a single score and the implications for an individual, as well as continued criticism regarding racial biases inherent in these tests.

MAIN THEORIES OF INTELLIGENCE

The assessment of intellectual disability is underpinned by various theoretical perspectives on intelligence, each offering unique insights into the nature and measurement of cognitive abilities. One prominent theory is the psychometric approach, which views intelligence as a unitary construct that can be quantified through standardized tests. Spearman's two-factor theory posits that intelligence comprises a general factor (*g*) representing overall cognitive ability, as well as specific factors (*s*) accounting for domain-specific skills (Spearman, 1904). This model laid the foundation for the development of intelligence tests such as the Stanford–Binet and Wechsler scales, which aim to measure individuals' overall intellectual functioning across different domains. Spearman's two-factor theory evolved over time to a hierarchical model of intelligence, the Cattell–Horn–Carroll (CHC) theory of intelligence. CHC provides a comprehensive framework for understanding the structure of cognitive abilities and guides intellectual assessment practices today. The CHC theory is considered the most comprehensive and empirically supported theory of intelligence and is the foundation on which most new and newly revised intelligence batteries are based. This theory posits a hierarchical model with three strata: the broad abilities at the top, middle-level abilities in the middle, and narrow abilities at the bottom (Schneider & McGrew, 2018). At the broadest level, there are general factors such as Fluid Intelligence (Gf) and Crystallized Intelligence (Gc), representing innate capacity for problem solving and the acquired knowledge and skills, respectively (McGrew, 2009). Middle-level abilities, such as visual processing (Gv), auditory processing (Ga), and processing speed (Gs), further delineate specific cognitive domains, while narrow abilities provide fine-grained assessments of specialized skills within each domain, such as phonological awareness or spatial relations (Schneider & McGrew, 2018). This hierarchical organization enables practitioners to assess a wide range of cognitive abilities systematically, allowing for more precise identification of strengths and weaknesses to facilitate tailored interventions.

In contrast to psychometric theories of intelligence, the cognitive perspective emphasizes the processes underlying intellectual functioning, focusing on *how* individuals acquire, process, and apply information. Spearheaded by Piaget's developmental theory, this approach posits that intelligence emerges through active engagement with the environment and progresses through distinct stages of cognitive development (Piaget, 1952). Moreover, information-processing models such as Sternberg's (1985) triarchic theory and Gardner's (1983) theory of multiple intelligences, offer alternative conceptualizations of intelligence by highlighting diverse cognitive abilities beyond traditional measures of intelligence quotient (IQ). These theories emphasize the role of context, experience, and culture in shaping one's cognitive functioning, thus broadening our understanding of intelligence beyond narrow psychometric assessments.

INTELLECTUAL DISABILITY OVERVIEW

Intellectual disability, or intellectual developmental disorder, as defined by the *Diagnostic and Statistical Manual of Mental Disorders, Fifth Edition, Text Revision* (DSM-5-TR) (American Psychiatric Association, 2022), is part of a group of neurodevelopmental disorders. By definition, neurodevelopmental disorders emerge early in the developmental period and impact language, academic skills, social skills, intellectual ability, and adaptive functioning. Assessing for and identifying these conditions early is therefore paramount in providing appropriate support and services across environments. Intellectual disability is also defined in the *International Classification of Diseases, 11th Revision* (World Health Organization, 2021), as well as by the American Association of Intellectual and Developmental Disabilities (AAIDD, 2020) and Individuals with Disabilities Education Act (IDEA, 2004).

ICD-11 classifies intellectual disability as intellectual functioning approximately two standard deviations below the mean and challenges in adaptive behavior that originate in the developmental period (World Health Organization, 2022). The AAIDD defines intellectual disability as a significant limitation in both intelligence (IQ) and adaptive behavior, specifically in the areas of conceptual, social, and practical domains or adaptive behavior. Further, the AAIDD specifies that intellectual disability originates prior to the age of 22, which is more specific than the ICD-11 or DSM-5-TR criteria, which reference the early developmental period. They further state that the limitations in functioning must be considered within the context of one's environment and be based on valid assessments that consider cultural and linguistic diversity (AAIDD, 2020). Finally, intellectual disability is defined under IDEA as having significantly subaverage intellectual functioning along with deficits in adaptive behavior that are manifested during the developmental period and affect an individual's education performance (IDEA, 2004). What all these definitions highlight is that intelligence testing, or an IQ score, are necessary, but *not sufficient*, components of classifying intellectual disability and the importance of the assessment and understanding of adaptive behavior and the context of the individual.

Intellectual disabilities are heterogeneous, and the cause of intellectual disability is multifactorial, with about 60% of cases having no known etiology (Fletcher & Miciak, 2023). Multifactorial causes may include environmental factors (e.g., toxic exposure, brain trauma, and infection) and psychosocial deprivation (Ellison et al., 2013), in addition to genetic and syndromic causes. Medical and psychiatric comorbidities are also common and an important consideration in the assessment process.

Research indicates that genetic abnormalities, such as chromosomal disorders (e.g., Down syndrome), single gene mutations (e.g., fragile X syndrome), and copy number variations (CNVs), contribute significantly to the etiology of intellectual disability (Vissers et al., 2016). Advances in genomic technologies have facilitated the identification of novel genetic variants implicated in intellectual disability, thus enhancing our understanding of the genetic basis and informing diagnostic and therapeutic intervention (Vissers et al., 2016). Additionally, prenatal factors such as maternal substance abuse, infections, and exposure to toxins or teratogens can disrupt fetal brain development, leading to intellectual impairments (Fletcher & Grigorenko, 2012). Perinatal complications, including premature birth, low birth weight, and birth trauma, are also associated with an increased risk for intellectual disability (Wu et al., 2018). Furthermore, postnatal factors such as traumatic brain injury, severe malnutrition, and inadequate stimulation or nurturing environments can impact cognitive development and contribute to the manifestation of intellectual disability. Understanding the multifaceted nature of intellectual disability etiology is impactful for accurate diagnosis, intervention planning, and support services tailored to individuals' specific needs.

Intellectual disability often co-occurs with various other psychiatric conditions (e.g., anxiety and depression) and neurodevelopmental disabilities (e.g., autism spectrum disorder and attention-deficit/hyperactivity disorder), further complicating the assessment and management. A diagnosis of intellectual disability alone is socially significant and brings additional vulnerability to co-occurring conditions. Prevalence estimates of psychiatric conditions in people with intellectual disability range from 16 to 55% (Fletcher et al., 2016). Evaluating for and understanding the risk of co-occurring psychiatric conditions is essential in the assessment process of intellectual disability. Unfortunately, co-occurring psychiatric conditions often go undiagnosed for several reasons. Some of the reasons include clinician factors such as limited training with intellectually disabled populations and adapted assessment, limitations in assessment methods such as overreliance on self-report of symptoms, and misconceptions held by clinicians and caregivers about the co-occurrence of psychiatric and neurodevelopmental conditions (Buckles, 2016). Often, these misconceptions are based on the concept of "diagnostic overshadowing" in which a clinician may attribute psychiatric symptoms to the diagnosis of intellectual disability rather than a true separate clinical condition (Reiss et al., 1982). The identification of co-occurring psychiatric conditions is supported by the *Diagnostic Manual-Intellectual Disability, Second Edition* (Fletcher et al., 2016). This diagnostic manual includes modifications in assessment practices, including simplified language for clinical interviews, visual supports, and the recommendation to collect information from multiple informants. The manual also includes adapted criteria for psychiatric conditions that reflect the developmental functioning of the individual (Fletcher et al., 2016). The etiology of intellectual disability is also emphasized within this framework as part of the diagnostic and assessment process.

Furthermore, physical health conditions, such as epilepsy, sensory impairments, and motor disabilities, are commonly observed among individuals with intellectual disabilities, necessitating

TABLE 16.1. Key Definitions of Intellectual Disability and Assessment Components

Organization	Definition	Assessment components
American Psychiatric Association, *Diagnostic and Statistical Manual of Mental Disorders, Fifth Edition, Text Revision* (DSM-5-TR), 2022	Problems with general mental abilities that affect functioning in intelligence and adaptive behavior that begin early in the developmental period.	Individually administered and psychometrically valid, comprehensive, culturally appropriate, test of intelligence and consideration of three areas of adaptive functioning: conceptual, social, and practical.
American Association on Intellectual and Developmental Disabilities (AAID), 2020	Condition characterized by significant limitations in both intellectual functioning and adaptive behavior that originates before the age of 22.	Assessment of intellectual functioning, assessment of adaptive behavior, inclusive of conceptual, social, and practical skills and consideration of the community environment, culture, and linguistic diversity.
World Health Association, *International Classification of Diseases, 11th Edition* (ICD-11), 2021	A group of etiologically diverse conditions originating during the developmental period characterized by significantly below average intelligence and adaptive behavior.	Assessment includes appropriately normed, individually administered standardized tests of intelligence as well as measures of adaptive behavior.
Individuals with Disabilities Education Act (IDEA), 2004	Significantly subaverage intellectual functioning along with deficits in adaptive behavior that adversely impact an individual's educational performance and are manifested during the developmental period.	Assessments include all areas of suspected disabilities, including culturally and linguistically appropriate assessment measures.

comprehensive medical evaluations and interdisciplinary interventions (Emerson & Hatton, 2007). Motor and sensory impairments can complicate the assessment and diagnosis process of intellectual disability, as the majority of intellectual assessments are not normed on populations with these conditions or do not allow for sufficient accommodations for sensory and motor impairments. The presence of comorbidities can exacerbate cognitive impairments, impact adaptive functioning, and influence treatment outcomes, highlighting the importance of a holistic approach to assessment and identification. See Table 16.1 for a summary of definitions of intellectual disability.

BEST PRACTICES FOR ASSESSMENT OF INTELLECTUAL DISABILITY

The definition of intellectual disability has evolved over time as more emphasis has been placed on function, or adaptive behavior, and this, in turn, has influenced the assessment process. The population of individuals with intellectual disability is heterogeneous; therefore, assessment methods have evolved to capture the complex strengths and areas for intervention that may be present within the population. Historically, intellectual disability has been diagnosed with an IQ score (mean of 100, standard deviation of 15), with ranges determined to classify the severity of intellectual disability. For example, an IQ of 55–70 was considered mild intellectual disability, 40–55 was considered moderate intellectual disability, and 25–40 was considered severe to profound. However, as the definition of intellectual disability has evolved to become more accepting of individual strengths that co-occur with intellectual deficits and increased emphasis on the importance of adaptive functioning, this classification system has been gradually abandoned by professionals and professional organizations. The 1990s saw the evolution of the diagnostic process of intellectual disability through an increased emphasis on adaptive functioning, which we see carrying over into diagnostic criteria and assessment practices today.

Assessing intellectual disabilities requires a nuanced and multifaceted approach to capture the complexity of cognitive functioning and adaptive skills. Best practice includes utilizing a comprehensive assessment battery inclusive of standardized cognitive assessments as well as standardized

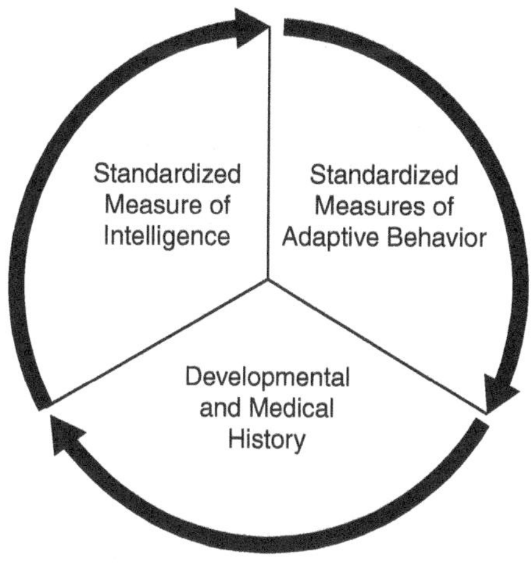

FIGURE 16.1. Key components of a comprehensive assessment for intellectual disability, including use of standardized measures of intelligence, standardized measures of adaptive behavior, and a comprehensive developmental and medical history

assessments of adaptive functioning. Cultural and linguistic factors must be considered as part of a comprehensive assessment, as described further in this section. A key emphasis is a focus on the assessment process rather than relying solely on testing using particular measures. This provides more comprehensive data to fully support individuals as it accounts for context and disability-related fluctuations in performance and outcomes (Hanson et al., 2023). Assessment is the process of integrating information from a variety of sources, including personal data, results from inventories, individual and parent/caregiver/teacher interviews, and observation (American Educational and Research Association et al., 2014). Diagnosis of intellectual disability relies on a comprehensive assessment process, the components of which are illustrated in Figure 16.1.

Assessment of Intellectual Ability

The assessment of intellectual ability is done through administration of standardized, norm-referenced measures of intellectual functioning that produce a standardized IQ. Although the use of standardized IQ tests is fundamental to the assessment and diagnosis of intellectual disability, several limitations exist in the use of these measures with this population. Intelligence assessments are designed and normed based on the general population; therefore, when using these measures with people with intellectual disability, recognition of factors beyond intelligence that may impact performance need to be considered (Coolican et al., 2008). For example, cognitive assessments often rely on verbal or motor responses; therefore, results may be confounded by expressive language or motor delays; likewise, motivation and joint attention may impact performance on these measures, therefore limiting validity (Duckworth et al., 2011). The impact on both reliability and validity of measurement must be considered. Additionally, individuals with intellectual disability are not well-represented in the normative data of common IQ tests, given the low incidence of the condition, therefore limiting interpretation of IQ scores at the lower ends and potentially introducing floor effects (Hanson et al., 2023).

As noted, the assessment of intelligence in the diagnosis of intellectual disability is necessary, but not sufficient (AAIDD, 2020). Other factors that influence intelligence and therefore the IQ score include other co-occurring conditions (e.g., sensory or motor impairments and psychiatric conditions), sociocultural factors, language, and minority status. Therefore, best practice of assessment of intelligence includes that practitioners use an individualized, multifactorial standardized measure of intelligence (AAIDD, 2020; APA, 2022) and avoid using screening measures, short or abbreviated forms, group assessments, or other alternatives. Based on the AAIDD's recommendations (2020), a multifactorial standardized intelligence assessment should include at least three dimensions of intellectual ability and, at minimum, six subtests that represent the composite IQ score. The consideration of the standard error of measurement should be incorporated into the interpretation of the data, along with other measures, when assessing intellectual impairment. Culturally relevant practice examples are shared later in the chapter. See Table 16.2 for common measures of intelligence.

Assessment of Adaptive Functioning

Although intelligence is a useful and necessary construct, it does not accurately reflect how well an individual is able to navigate their environment to meet societal demands and expectations. All definitions of intellectual disability (DSM-5-TR, AAIDD, ICD-11, and IDEA) emphasize the importance of assessment of adaptive behavior as part of the diagnostic assessment process. Generally, adaptive behavior is a person's capacity to perform activities of daily living on a routine

TABLE 16.2. Common Standardized Intellectual Assessment Batteries

Measure	Author(s)	Year	Age range	Assessment method	Domains assessed	Time to administer	Scores/ interpretation	Notes
Bayley Scales of Infant and Toddler Development, Fourth Edition (Bayley–4)	Nancy Bayley, PhD, and Glen P. Aylward, PhD, ABPP	2019	16 days –42 months	Observation, caregiver interview, and direct assessment	General cognitive	30 to 70 minutes (depending upon age of child)	Subtest-level scaled scores, domain-level composite scores, percentile ranks, confidence intervals, developmental age equivalents, and growth scale values	Available in English (Bayley–3 is available in Spanish). Normative sample included 1700 children across 17 age groups, including clinical populations of autism spectrum disorder, developmental delay, Down syndrome, language delay, prematurity, motor impairment, and prenatal drug/alcohol exposure.
Developmental Assessment of Young Children, Second Edition (DAYC-2)	Judith K. Voress, PhD, Taddy Maddox, and Donald D. Hammill, PhD	2012	Birth–5 years	Observation, interview of caregivers, and direct assessment	Five domains: Cognition, Communication, Social–Emotional Development, Physical Development, and Adaptive Behavior	10 to 20 minutes per each domain	Standard scores, percentile ranks, and age equivalents	Normed on national sample of 1,832 children between 2009 and 2011
Differential Ability Scales, Second Edition (DAS-II)	Colin D. Elliott, PhD	2007	2:6–17:11 years	Direct assessment	Core battery: Verbal Reasoning, Nonverbal Reasoning, and Spatial Reasoning Additional subtests: Working Memory, Speed of Information Processing, Visual and Auditory Memory, *and others	Core battery: 45 to 60 minutes; diagnostic subtests: 30 minutes	Standard scores and percentiles by age General Conceptual Ability	Updated normative data for school-age version. Includes data on those with intellectual disability (mild), autism. spectrum disorder, ADHD, deaf or hard of hearing, expressive language disorder, English learners, and specific learning disability in math and reading.

Kaufman Assessment Battery for Children, Second Edition (KABC-II)	Alan S. Kaufman, PhD, and Nadeen L. Kaufman, EdD	2004	3–18 years	Direct assessment		25 to 70 minutes	Age-based standard scores, age equivalents, and percentile ranks	Considered a "culturally fair ability test for all children." Normative sample of 700 children and adolescents ages 3 years to 18 years, 11 months. Matched U.S. population on variables of gender, race/ethnicity, parent education, and region.
Kaufman Brief Intelligence Test, Second Edition, Revised (KBIT-2 Revised)	Alan S. Kaufman, PhD, and Nadeen L. Kaufman, EdD	2022	4–90 years	Direct assessment	Brief measure of verbal and nonverbal intelligence	Approximately 20 minutes	Crystallized (Verbal), Fluid (Nonverbal), IQ Composite: Standard scores and percentile ranks by age	Available in English and Spanish. Revised norms from 2021. Updated to include telehealth administration.
Mullen Scales of Early Learning	Eileen M. Mullen	1995	Birth–68 months	Direct assessment	Five scales: Gross Motor, Visual Reception, Fine Motor, Expressive Language, and Receptive Language	15 to 60 minutes, depending on age	Scales: T-scores, percentile ranks, age equivalents; composite: standard scores, percentile ranks	Normed between 1981 and 1989 on sample of 1,849 children between the ages of 2 days and 69 months. Only native English speakers and individuals with no cognitive and physical impairments were included.
Reynolds Intellectual Assessment Scales–2 (RIAS-2)	Cecil Reynolds, PhD, and Randy Kamphaus, PhD	2015	3–94 years	Direct assessment	Composites for Composite IQ, Verbal IQ, Nonverbal IQ, Memory, and Processing Speed	20 to 25 minutes for intelligence assessment, 10 to 15 minutes for memory assessment, 5 to 10 minutes for processing speed assessment	Standard scores, percentile ranks, T-scores, confidence interval	Normative data based on sample of 2,154 individuals ages 3–94, representative of 2012 U.S. Census. Includes clinical groups of stroke, dementia, hearing impairment, intellectual disability, traumatic brain injury, learning disability, ADHD, and gifted.

(continued)

TABLE 16.2. *(continued)*

Measure	Author(s)	Year	Age range	Assessment method	Domains assessed	Time to administer	Scores/ interpretation	Notes
Stanford–Binet Intelligence Scales, Fifth Edition (SB-V)	Gale H. Roid, PhD	2003	2–85 years	Direct assessment	Composites for Verbal IQ, Nonverbal IQ, Brief IQ, Full Scale IQ; and five factors: Fluid, Knowledge, Quantitative, Visual–Spatial, and Working Memory	Approximately 5 minutes per subtest (up to 10 subtests)		Representative sample of 4,800 individuals across the lifespan.
Wechsler Preschool and Primary Scale of Intelligence, Fourth Edition (WPPSI-IV)	David Wechsler, PhD	2012	2:6–7:7 years	Direct assessment	Full Scale IQ and five core indexes: Verbal Comprehension, Visual–Spatial, Fluid Reasoning, Working Memory, and Processing Speed	Core subtests: Ages 2:6 to 3:11: 30 to 45 minutes, Ages 4:0 to 7:7: 45 to 60 minutes	FSIQ, Primary Index Scores, and Ancillary Index Scores	1,700 children ages 2 years, 6 months to 7 years, 7 months included in normative sample. Stratified to match U.S. census data based on sex, race/ethnicity, parent education level, and geographical region. Includes small representation from clinical groups.
Wechsler Intelligence Scale for Children, Fifth Edition (WISC-V)	David Wechsler, PhD	2014	6:0–16:11 years	Direct assessment	Full Scale IQ and Five core indexes: Verbal Comprehension, Visual–Spatial, Fluid Reasoning, Working Memory, and Processing Speed	Core subtests: ~60 minutes	FSIQ, Primary Index Scores, and Ancillary Index Scores	Normative sample of 2,200 children ages 6 years to 16 years, 11 months. Includes representation from clinical samples including intellectual disability, specific learning disorder, ADHD, disruptive behavior disorder, traumatic brain injury, and autism spectrum disorder.

Wechsler Adult Intelligence Scale, Fourth Edition (WAIS-IV)	David Wechsler, PhD	2008	16:0–99:11 years	Direct assessment	Full Scale IQ and four core domains: Verbal Comprehension, Perceptual Reasoning, Working Memory, and Processing Speed	Core subtests: 60 to 90 minutes	FSIQ, Index Scores, subtest-level scaled scores	Fifth edition to be released in fall 2024. Normative data include 2,200 individuals ages 16 years to 90 years, 11 months. Stratified to match U.S. population based on age, sex, education level, race/ethnicity, and geographic region. Includes data from clinical groups including intellectual disability, autism spectrum disorder, specific learning disability, ADHD, traumatic brain injury, probable dementia, and depression.
Woodcock–Johnson Tests of Cognitive Abilities, Fourth Edition (WJ-IV-Cog)	Frederick Shrank, PhD, Kevin McGrew, PhD, and Nancy Mather, PhD	2014	2–90 years	Direct assessment		5 to 10 minutes per subtest	Standard scores, percentile ranks, age-equivalent (AE) and grade-equivalent scores (GE), Relative Proficiency Index (RPI), W scale, and Cognitive Academic Language Proficiency levels (CALP)	Normative samples included individuals ages 2 years to 90+ years based on 2010 census data. Total of 7,416 participants across 4 blocks.

basis. These skills are learned and performed to meet society's expectations and demands (Shalock et al., 2021) and continue to be learned over time throughout an individual's life. Adaptive behavior has been positively predicted with positive life outcomes (Farley et al., 2009) in individuals with neurodevelopmental disabilities. The American Psychiatric Association (2022) has emphasized the use of adaptive behavior in the diagnosis of intellectual disability, as the construct of adaptive behavior better represents a person's overall level of support needed compared to an individualized assessment of intelligence. Further, assessments of adaptive behavior are intended to measure a person's actual observed behavior rather than their capacity for performing daily activities across areas of conceptual, social, and practical skills. Conceptual deficits of adaptive behavior include domains such as language, reading and writing, math, number and time concepts, money management, and learning from experience. Social deficits represent interpersonal skills, relationships, and self-esteem. Practical skills involve activities of daily living, including personal care, work, use of money, healthcare, and safety (AAIDD, 2020).

Adaptive behavior allows for practitioners to assess how an individual is routinely able to navigate their environment and inform support and intervention that may be most beneficial. Adaptive behavior is needed as an additional component of a high-quality, evidence-based assessment for intellectual disability, as research supports that, although adaptive behavior and intelligence are correlated constructs, they are separate and distinct (Keith et al., 1987). The relationship between adaptive behavior and intelligence further varies based on ability level, with the strongest correlation being at the lower end of the ability scale (Alexander & Reynolds, 2020). The inclusion of adaptive behavior is a best-practice recommendation from both the American Psychiatric Association and AAIDD. The AAIDD specifically recommends evidence of deficits in adaptive behavior across three areas of adaptive functioning—conceptual, social, and practical—rather than a focus on the overall adaptive behavior composite score, although one area is sufficient (AAIDD, 2020). In this definition of adaptive behavior, maladaptive behaviors are considered separately. This is accomplished through formal assessments through the administration of standardized rating scales and semistructured interviews with reliable caregivers (Fletcher et al., 2016). Retrospective administrations are often used to collect information about key components of an individual's developmental history from caregivers who knew the individual during that period. See Table 16.3 for a list of common measures of adaptive behavior.

Taken together, having measures of adaptive functioning along with intellectual assessment provides useful information about an individual's abilities and support needs. Including adaptive behavior measures along with measures of IQ offers several advantages. First, measures of adaptive functioning are less likely to show floor effects than measures of intelligence (Hamburg et al., 2019). Second, measures of adaptive functioning provide information about an individual in everyday contexts, which is not provided by measures of intelligence (Tassé & Mehling, 2017). And finally, the use of informant reports (caregiver/teacher) of adaptive functioning reduces the demands on the individual with intellectual disability, thus providing a more holistic and sensitive assessment of the strengths and growth areas for that individual.

INTERVIEWS, RECORD REVIEW, AND MEDICAL AND DEVELOPMENTAL HISTORY

In the assessment and diagnosis of intellectual disability, interviews, review of medical and educational records, and a thorough developmental history are critical in informing the diagnostic process. Comprehensive clinical interviews with the parents/caregivers and the individual, as appropriate, allow clinicians to gather valuable information regarding the individual's developmental milestones, academic and social functioning, as well as any behavioral or emotional challenges they may face. These interviews provide qualitative data that help in understanding the individual's strengths, limitations, and support needs. Additionally, review of medical and educational documents offers valuable objective data, which can corroborate information obtained through interviews and provide a more holistic understanding of the individual's history and current functioning. Given the high comorbidity of genetic and medical conditions with intellectual disabilities, having a deep understanding of the individual and family medical history is imperative.

Moreover, a thorough developmental history provides contextual information regarding the individual's early milestones, familial and environmental influences, and any significant life

TABLE 16.3. Common Standardized Measures of Adaptive Behavior

Measure	Author(s)	Year	Age range	Assessment method	Domains assessed	Time to administer	Scores/ interpretation	Notes
Adaptive Behavior Assessment System, Third Edition (ABAS-3)	Patti Harrison, PhD, and Thomas Oakland, PhD	2015	0–89 years	Caregiver report Includes: Parent/ Caregiver, Teacher/ Daycare Provider, and Adult Self-Report	Three broad domains: Conceptual, Practical, and Social Eleven total subdomains: Communication, Community Use, Functional Academics, Health and Safety, Home or School Living, Leisure, Self-care, Self-direction, Social, Work, and Motor	15 to 20 minutes	General Adaptive Composite, standard scores, and percentile ranks	Available in English and Spanish
Vineland Adaptive Behavior Scales, Third Edition (Vineland–3)	Sara S. Sparrow, PhD, Domenic V. Cicchetti, PhD, and Celine A. Saulnier, PhD	2016	Birth–90 years	Birth–90 years old: Interview and Parent/ Caregiver Form. 3–21 years old: Teacher Form	Three Broad Domains: Communication, Daily Living Skills, and Socialization			Available in English and Spanish
Adaptive Behavior Evaluation Scale (ABES)	Stephen B. McCarney, EdD, and Samm N. House	2017	4–12 Years		Three broad domains: Conceptual, Social, and Practical	Approximately 20 minutes		
Diagnostic Adaptive Behavior Scale (DABS)	Marc J. Tassé, PhD, Robert L. Schalock, PhD, David Thissen, PhD, Giulia Balboni, PhD, Henry (Hank) Bersani, Jr., PhD, Sharon A. Borthwick-Duffy, PhD, Scott Spreat, EdD, Keith F. Widaman, PhD, and Dalun Zhang, PhD		4–21 years	Caregiver report	Three domains: Conceptual Skills, Social Skills, and Practical Skills			
Adaptive Behavior Diagnostic Scale (ABDS)	Nils A. Pearson, James R. Patton, PhD, and Daniel W. Mruzek, PhD	2016	2–21 years	Interview Rating Scale	Three domains: Conceptual Skills, Social Skills, and Practical Skills	Approximately 30 minutes		

events or traumas that may have impacted their development. This comprehensive understanding of the individual's background helps differentiate between intellectual disability and other potential underlying factors contributing to cognitive or adaptive deficits. By integrating information from interviews, record reviews, and developmental histories, clinicians can formulate accurate diagnoses and have a context from which to interpret standardized assessments.

Given the high co-occurrence of psychiatric conditions and emotional/behavioral disorders with intellectual disability (Fletcher et al., 2016), a comprehensive assessment of intellectual disability also includes the integration of behavioral and social–emotional measures for a holistic understanding of an individual's functioning and to drive treatment and intervention recommendations. While adaptive behavior assessments provide valuable insights into functioning across conceptual, social, and practical domains, they do not provide insight into maladaptive behaviors, which are equally essential for assessing the impact on an individual's daily life. Behavioral and social–emotional measures offer complementary information that enriches the diagnostic process.

DEVELOPMENTAL DELAY AND UNSPECIFIED NEURODEVELOPMENTAL DISORDERS

Related to the assessment of intellectual disability, understanding the nuances of global developmental delay and unspecified neurodevelopmental disorder is important. These are interrelated, yet distinct diagnostic categories present in DSM-5-TR (American Psychiatric Association, 2022). Developmental delay typically refers to significant lags in development, or deviations from expected developmental milestones, in one or more domains, such as motor skills, language, cognition, or social–emotional functioning, during early childhood (American Psychiatric Association, 2022). These delays may be transient or persistent and often warrant thorough assessment to determine the underlying causes and appropriate interventions to support optimal development. Often, measures of intellectual functioning, or cognitive developmental assessments, as well as measures of adaptive behavior, are appropriate to inform intervention practices. In children who do not "catch up" to age-matched peer expectations by school entry, they are often referred for assessment due to concerns of intellectual disability.

Unspecified neurodevelopmental disability encompasses a broader spectrum of conditions characterized by impairments in neurological development, without meeting diagnostic criteria for a specific condition such as intellectual disability, autism spectrum disorder, or attention-deficit/hyperactivity disorder (American Psychiatric Association, 2022).

Assessment practices are similar, with an emphasis on a comprehensive evaluation of cognitive, adaptive, social, and behavioral functioning to determine the individual's strengths, challenges, and support needs. Whereas assessments for developmental delays prioritize identifying specific areas of delay and providing early intervention services tailored to the individual's needs, assessments for unspecified neurodevelopmental disabilities aim to characterize the overall pattern of strengths and functional limitations to guide intervention planning and support.

CULTURALLY RELEVANT PRACTICE CONSIDERATIONS

Ecological Context and Considerations for Diversity, Equity, and Inclusion

Culture provides a context in which people develop and learn. It is difficult to define intelligence, and therefore intellectual disability, without first understanding the individual's cultural context. According to the American Psychological Association (APA) multicultural guidelines, culture includes context, identity, and intersectionality from an ecological approach (APA, 2017). Thus, cultural responsiveness considers the fluid and complex nature of identity and self-definition, including language and communication, social and physical environments, experiences with power, privilege, and oppression, and the intersection of developmental stages and transitions with biosociocultural context. Fundamental to these guidelines is a strengths-based approach in assessment and intervention. This has an important impact on our understanding and interpretation of intellectual assessments for the purpose of identifying intellectual disability. For example, Fagan and Holland (2007) theorized that an IQ score was a measure of an individual's knowledge based on their information-processing ability *and* the information available to them within the cultural context. Therefore, they question whether racial differences in intelligence were due to variations in individuals' cognitive abilities or to disparities in their exposure to information. The authors thus conclude that given differences in opportunities to be exposed to information presented in standardized intelligence assessments, racial differences in intelligence scores can be accounted for by differential access to information rather than true differences.

AAIDD (2020) definition and preamble include that the purpose of defining/diagnosing intellectual disability should be to provide necessary support for an individual rather than to marginalize the individual. Thus, the definition includes several assumptions, including the importance of understanding intellectual limitations within the context of culture and development, which includes accounting for linguistic diversity when conducting assessments. Inherent in the definition is that the normative cultural environment of an individual, inclusive of linguistic diversity, be accounted for in the assessment and consideration of diagnosis. This stems from important concerns that have been raised regarding overrepresentation of individuals from marginalized backgrounds receiving a diagnosis of intellectual disability and overclassification within educational settings (Morgan et al., 2015).

There is also research highlighting the impact of socioeconomic status (SES) on intellectual assessment and interpretation of results. Research supports that SES positively correlates with IQ scores (von Strumm & Plomin, 2015) and that SES is associated with several IQ correlates, including achievement test scores (Brooks-Gunn et al., 1993), grade retentions, and functional literacy (Baydar et al., 1993). The question remains what the main contributor is, as other factors that vary with SES may also impact intelligence assessment, including physical health, home environment, neighborhood characteristics, and early education (Bornstein & Bradley, 2003). Therefore, considering the context of the individual is paramount in deciding whether someone exhibits a true intellectual disability or if their performance on assessments is instead a reflection of their economic background and limits in opportunity.

The American Educational Research Association (AERA), American Psychological Association, and the National Council on Measurement in Education (NCME) endorsed a set of standards for psychological testing (2014) to reduce cultural and contextual biases, citing three foundations of testing psychometric properties of reliability and validity, and a third pillar that impacts the use of intelligence tests with culturally diverse groups, fairness in testing. This pillar emphasizes the importance of context in relation to testing, noting threats to validity that include a variety of contextual factors such as limited English proficiency and other differences related to educational and cultural background.

The nature of our tests—including test content, test context, test response, and opportunities to learn—unfairly impact valid interpretations of test scores from minority groups (AERA et al., 2014). All tests are culturally loaded, meaning there is some degree of cultural specificity within the test content, as their content and format reflect what is important in the cultural context of the community for which it was developed. Cultural loading has important implications for understanding cultural bias. The cultural loading of a particular test can favor certain groups over others. The cultural loading impacts all tests, including measures of adaptive behavior and intelligence. If there is a match of the tasks required on an intelligence test and the cultural background of the individual taking the test, then the individual may have an advantage. If there is not, then the person taking the test may be at a disadvantage (Valencia et al., 2001). Given that all forms of measurement are developed within a cultural context, it is difficult to develop a fundamental cognitive task or adaptive behavior assessment that would not be impacted by cultural loading.

Regarding adaptive behavior, given that this is a construct assessed relative to the demands of one's community and societal expectations, it is crucial that measures of adaptive behavior are revised and updated to reflect the evolving demands and increased complexities of our societies, advances in technology, and cultural variations (von Buttlar et al., 2021). Beyond adapting and updating our measures, research must continue to evaluate the relationships between measures of adaptive functioning and intelligence, given the strong assumed link between the two in our diagnostic criteria.

Cultural and Linguistic Factors Impacting Assessment

Cultural and linguistic factors are nuanced and important to understand and appreciate in the assessment of intellectual abilities. Cultural considerations encompass a broad range of influences, including beliefs, values, norms, and communication styles inherent to different ethnic, racial, and socioeconomic groups. These factors significantly shape one's cognitive development and expression, impacting performance on standardized assessments. For example, some cultures prioritize communal learning over individual achievement, leading to variations in problem-solving approaches and responses to testing stimuli (Rogers-Sirin, 2019). Moreover, language proficiency plays a critical role in intellectual assessment, as linguistic diversity can affect comprehension, expression, and performance on standardized tests (Gottfredson, 2017). Thus, practitioners must consider cultural and linguistic diversity when selecting assessment tools, interpreting results, and making diagnostic decisions to avoid misidentification or overrepresentation of certain cultural or linguistic groups with intellectual disability.

Cultural bias is inherent in many assessment tools used in the assessment of intellectual disability, including intelligence tests. Therefore, practitioners must use culturally fair and linguistically appropriate measures in the evaluation of intellectual functioning. Traditional cognitive tests may reflect the values, experiences, and linguistic conventions of the dominant culture, leading to systematic underestimation of intellectual abilities among individuals from diverse backgrounds (Sattler & Hoge, 2016). To address this issue, practitioners can employ culturally sensitive assessment practices, such as incorporating alternative methods of communication, adapting test materials to reflect diverse experiences, and considering the sociocultural context of those being assessed (García, 2017). Additionally, collaboration with culturally competent interpreters and community members can enhance the validity and reliability of assessments by ensuring accurate interpretation of responses and culturally relevant test administration (López, 2020). The need to incorporate culturally and linguistically valid assessment approaches and the inherent bias present in common intelligence tests underscores the importance of having a multimethod, multisource approach to the assessment of intellectual disability. By integrating cultural and linguistic considerations into the assessment process, practitioners can foster more equitable and culturally responsive practices, ultimately improving the accuracy, validity, and utility of intellectual disability evaluations across populations.

Complementary Options for Assessment

Although standardized assessment and comprehensive clinical and developmental interviews are fundamental to the assessment and diagnosis of intellectual disability, alternative assessment approaches may be used in tandem to support the information gathered through traditional means. Using complementary approaches informs the comprehensive nature of the evaluation and can add valuable information to inform intervention and support.

Dynamic Assessment

Dynamic assessment is an approach that takes into account educational planning and views the individual's strengths and challenges from a learning perspective. This approach is a good way to capture the inherent change over time in learning expected given that intervention is targeted at enhancing cognitive and adaptive abilities in the individual (Lidz & Peña, 1996). The dynamic assessment approach involves an initial assessment, establishment of learning objectives, and evaluation of response to intervention. It is an active form of informal assessment that involves the test–teach–test procedure (Meller & Ohr, 2008). The focus of the assessment is on the process rather than the outcome. Focusing on the process has positive implications for culturally diverse individuals, as there is opportunity for feedback and demonstration of learning that may be missing with traditional assessment practices.

Performance-Based Assessment

Performance-based assessments were designed to address the concerns of standardized assessments, such as intelligence tests (Hintze, 2009). This approach is inclusive of common measures such as curriculum-based measurement used in schools as a progress monitoring tool. Performance-based measures or curriculum-based measures require individuals to solve "real-world tasks" based on what they have learned. These tasks are often based on a curriculum that examines behavior in the natural context and focuses on what is being taught as well as a student's understanding of what is being taught. Performance-based assessments are useful for screening to inform whether further evaluation is necessary for determination of eligibility within a school setting, for goal setting, and for program and/or intervention evaluation (Hintze, 2009).

CONCLUSION

The landscape of assessing intellectual disabilities is evolving, embracing innovative trends that enhance accuracy, sensitivity, and inclusivity in evaluations. Notable trends include the integration of technology into assessment tools, enhanced ecological assessment approaches, and increased recognition of the importance of cultural and linguistic diversity and its impacts on the administration and interpretation of assessments.

The recognition of the importance of cultural diversity has spurred a trend toward the development and validation of culturally fair and linguistically appropriate assessment tools. Researchers and practitioners are actively engaged in developing assessments that are sensitive to the cultural backgrounds and linguistic diversity of the individuals being evaluated (López, 2019; Suzuki et al., 2020). This trend aims to address longstanding concerns about the cultural bias in traditional assessment instruments, ensuring evaluations are equitable across diverse populations.

Emerging trends in the diagnosis and assessment of intellectual disability reflect advancements in understanding the complex interplay between genetic, neurobiological, and environmental factors contributing to cognitive functioning. One notable trend is the integration of neuroimaging techniques, such as functional magnetic resonance imaging (fMRI) and diffusion tensor imaging (DTI), into the assessment process. These neuroimaging methods provide insights into the structural and functional integrity of the brain, aiding in the identification of specific neuroanatomical markers associated with intellectual disability and facilitating early detection and intervention (Fletcher & Grigorenko, 2012). Additionally, the incorporation of genomic sequencing technologies has revolutionized the diagnostic approach by enabling the identification of genetic variants and mutations associated with syndromic and non-syndromic forms of intellectual disability, thereby facilitating personalized treatment strategies and genetic counseling for those impacted (Vissers et al., 2016).

Furthermore, there is a growing recognition of the importance of adopting a strengths-based approach in intellectual disability assessment, emphasizing individuals' abilities and potential rather than solely focusing on deficits. This paradigm shift underscores the need for comprehensive assessment tools that capture the full spectrum of intellectual functioning, including adaptive skills, social competence, and personal strengths (Shalock et al., 2021). Moreover, the increasing emphasis on cultural and linguistic diversity in assessment practices acknowledges the impact of sociocultural factors on the manifestation and interpretation of intellectual disability, necessitating culturally sensitive assessment tools and practices to ensure accurate diagnosis and intervention planning for individuals from a variety of backgrounds (García-Villamisar et al., 2020).

REFERENCES

Alexander, R. M., & Reynolds, M. R. (2020). Intelligence and adaptive behavior: A meta-analysis. *School Psychology Review, 47*, 85–110.

American Association on Intellectual and Developmental Disabilities. (2020). *Intellectual disabilities: Definition, classification, and systems of support* (12th ed.). Author.

American Educational Research Association, American Psychological Association, & National Council on Measurement in Education (Eds.). (2014). *Standards for educational and psychological testing.* American Educational Research Association.

American Psychiatric Association (2022). *Diagnostic and statistical manual of mental disorders* (5th ed., text rev.). Author.

American Psychological Association. (2017). *Multicultural guidelines: An ecological approach to context, identity, and intersectionality.* Author. *www.apa.org/about/policy/multicultural-guidelines*

Baydar, N., Brooks-Gunn, J., & Furstenberg, F. F. (1993). Early warning signs of functional illiteracy: Predictors in childhood and adolescence. *Child Development, 64*(3), 815–829.

Binet, A., & Simon, T. (1916). *The development of intelligence in children.* (E. S. Kite, Trans.). Williams & Wilkins.

Bond, H. M. (1924). Intelligence tests and propaganda. *The Crisis, 28*(2), 61–64.

Bornstein, M. H., & Bradley, R. H. (2003). *Socioeconomic status, parenting, and child development.* Erlbaum.

Brooks-Gunn, J., Guo, G., & Furstenberg, F. F. (1993). Who drops out and who continues beyond high school? A 20-year follow-up of Black urban youth. *Journal of Research on Adolescence, 3*(3), 271–294.

Buckles, J. (2016). The epidemiology of psychiatric disorders in adults with intellectual disabilities. In C. Hemmings & N. Bouras (Eds.), *Psychiatric and behavioral disorders in intellectual and developmental disabilities* (pp. 34–44). Cambridge University Press.

Coolican, J., Bryson, S.E., & Zwaigenbaum, L. (2008). Brief report: Data on the Stanford–Binet Intelligence Scales in children with autism spectrum disorder. *Journal of Autism and Developmental Disorders, 38*(1), 190–197.

Duckworth, A. L., Quinn, P. D., Lynam, D. R., Loeber, R., & Stouthamer-Loeber, M. (2011). Role of test motivation in intelligence testing. *Proceedings of the National Academy of Sciences of the United States of America, 108*(19), 7716–7720.

Ellison, J. W., Rosenfeld, J. A., & Shaffer, L. G. (2013). Genetic basis of intellectual disabilities. *Annual Review of Medicine, 64*, 441–450.

Emerson, E., & Hatton, C. (2007). Mental health of children and adolescents with intellectual disabilities in Britain. *British Journal of Psychiatry, 191*(6), 493–499.

Fagan, J. F., & Holland, C. R. (2007). Racial equality in intelligence: Predictions from a theory of intelligence as processing. *Intelligence, 35*, 319–334.

Farley M.A., McMahon W.M., Fombonne E., Jenson W. R., Miller J., Gardner M., et al. (2009). Twenty-year outcome for individuals with autism and average or near-average cognitive abilities. *Autism Res, 2*, 109–118.

Fletcher, J. M., & Grigorenko, E. L. (2012). Neuropsychology of intellectual disability. In J. L. Matson (Ed.), *Handbook of intellectual disabilities: Integrating theory, research, and practice* (pp. 27–46). Springer.

Fletcher, J. M., & Miciak, J. (2023). Assessment of specific learning disabilities and intellectual disabilities. *Assessment, 31*(1), 53–74.

Fletcher, R. J., Barnhill, J., & Cooper, S. A. (2016). An introduction to the DM-ID-2. In J. Barnwell, S. A. Cooper, and R. Fletcher (Eds.) *Diagnostic manual-intellectual disability 2: A textbook of diagnosis of mental disorders in persons with intellectual disability* (pp. 1–12). NADD Press.

García, J. N. (2017). Culturally responsive assessment in clinical psychology. In J. N. García (Ed.), *Cultural foundations and interventions in Latino/a Mental Health: History, theory, and within-group differences* (pp. 173–197). Routledge.

García-Villamisar, D., Ordóñez-Camblor, N., & Moreno, F. (2020). Cultural aspects in the assessment of intellectual disabilities: A review. In R. Balanzá-Martínez (Ed.), *Cultural neuroscience and psychopathology: Foundations, applications, and future directions* (pp. 267–282). Elsevier.

Gardner, H. (1983). *Frames of mind: The theory of multiple intelligences*. Basic Books.

Gottfredson, L. S. (2017). Mainstream science on intelligence: An editorial with 52 signatories, history, and bibliography. *Intelligence, 63*, 67–81.

Hamburg S., Lowe B., Startin C. M., Padilla C., Coppus A., Silverman W., et al. (2019). Assessing general cognitive and adaptive abilities in adults with Down syndrome: A systematic review. *Journal of Neurodevelopmental Disorders, 11*, 1–16.

Hanson, S. L., Bruyere, S., Forber-Pratt, A., Reesman, J., & Sung, C. (2023). Guidelines for assessment and intervention with persons with disabilities: An executive summary. *American Psychologist, 78*(8), 995–1009.

Hintze, J. M. (2009). Conceptual and empirical issues related to developing a response-to-intervention framework. *Journal of Evidence-Based Practices for Schools, 9*, 128–147.

Individuals with Disabilities Education Act, Sec. 300.8 (c) (6) (2004).

Keith, T. Z., Fehrmann, P. G., Harrison, P. L., & Pottebaum, S. M. (1987). The relation between adaptive behavior and intelligence: Testing alternative explanations. *Journal of School Psychology, 25*(1), 31–43.

Klineberg, O. (1927). Racial differences in speech and accuracy. *The Journal of Abnormal and Social Psychology, 22*(3), 273–277.

Lidz, C. S., & Peña, E. D. (1996). Dynamic assessment: The model, its relevance as a nonbiased approach, and its application to Latino American preschool children. *Language, Speech, and Hearing Services in Schools, 27*(4), 367–372.

Lopez, B. (2019). *Assessing culturally and linguistically diverse students: A practical guide*. Guilford Press.

López, S. R. (2020). Cultural competence in psychological assessment. In J. N. Butcher (Ed.), *Oxford handbook of psychological assessment* (pp. 427–442). Oxford University Press.

McGrew, K. S. (2009). CHC theory and the human cognitive abilities project: Standing on the shoulders of the giants of psychometric intelligence research. *Intelligence, 37*(1), 1–10.

Meller, P. J., & Ohr, P. S. (2008). Family-Oriented, Culturally Sensitive (FOCUS) assessment of young children. In L. A. Suzuki & J. G. Ponterotto (Eds.), *Handbook for multicultural assessment: Clinical, psychological, and educational applications* (pp. 565–593). Jossey-Bass/Wiley.

Morgan, P. L., Farkas, G., Hillemeier, M. M., Mattison, R., Maczuga, S., Li, H., & Cook, M. (2015). Minorities are disproportionately underrepresented in special education. *Education Research, 44*, 278–292.

Piaget, J. (1952). *The origins of intelligence in children*. International Universities Press.

Reiss, S., Levitan, G. W., & Szyszko, J. (1982). Emotional disturbance and mental retardation: Diagnostic overshadowing. *American Journal of Mental Deficiency, 86*(6), 567–574.

Rogers-Sirin, L. (2019). Cultural perspectives on intellectual disability: A review of the literature. *Journal of Intellectual Disability Research, 63*(3), 173–187.

Sattler, J. M., & Hoge, R. D. (2016). *Assessment of children: Cognitive foundations* (6th ed.). Sattler.

Schalock, R. L., Luckasson, R., & Tassé, M. J. (2021). *Intellectual disability: Definition. diagnosis, classification, and systems of supports* (12th ed.). American Association on Intellectual and Developmental Disabilities.

Schneider, W. J., & McGrew, K. S. (2018). The Cattell–Horn–Carroll theory of cognitive abilities. In D. P. Flanagan & P. L. Harrison (Eds.), *Contemporary intellectual assessment: Theories, tests, and issues* (4th ed., pp. 73–163). Guilford Press.

Spearman, C. (1904). "General intelligence," objectively determined and measured. *American Journal of Psychology, 15*(2), 201–292.

Sternberg, R. J. (1985). *Beyond IQ: A triarchic theory of human intelligence*. Cambridge University Press.

Suzuki, L. A., Valencia, R. R., & Ponterotto, J. (Eds.). (2020). *Handbook of multicultural assessment: Clinical, psychological, and educational applications*. Wiley.

Tassé, M. J., & Mehling, M. H. (2017). Measuring intellectual functioning and adaptive behavior in determining intellectual disability. In K. Shogren, L. Scott, E. Dean, and B. Linnenkamp (Eds.) *Handbook of research-based practices for educating students with intellectual disability* (pp. 63–78). Routledge.

Terman, L. M. (1916). *The measurement of intelligence: An explanation of and a complete guide for the use of the Stanford revision and extension of the Binet–Simon Intelligence Scale*. Houghton Mifflin.

Valencia, R. R., Suzuki, L. A., & Salinas, M. F. (2001). Test bias. In R. R. Valencia & L. A. Suzuki (Eds.), *Intelligence testing and minority students: Foundations, performance factors, and assessment issues* (pp. 111–150). Sage.

Vissers, L. E. L. M., Gilissen, C., & Veltman, J. A. (2016). Genetic studies in intellectual disability and related disorders. *Nature Reviews Genetics, 17*(1), 9–18.

von Buttlar, A. M., Zabel, T. A., Pritchard, A. E., & Cannon, A. D. (2021). Concordance of the adaptive behavior assessment system, second and third editions. *Journal of Intellectual Disabilities Research, 65(3)*, 283–295.

von Stumm, S., & Plomin, R. (2015). Socioeconomic status and the growth of intelligence from infancy through adolescence. *Intelligence*, 48, 30–36.

World Health Organization. (2022). *ICD-11: International classification of diseases* (11th revision). Author. *https://icd.who.int*

Wu, C. S., Nohr, E. A., Bech, B. H., Vestergaard, M., Catov, J. M., & Olsen, J. (2018). Health of children born to mothers who had preeclampsia: A population-based cohort study. *American Journal of Obstetrics and Gynecology, 201*(3), 269.e1–269.e10.

CHAPTER 17

Assessment of Depression

Katie Eklund, Madeline Wadington, and Temma Levis

Major depression is an episodic, recurring disorder characterized by persistent and pervasive sadness or unhappiness, loss of enjoyment of everyday activities, irritability, and associated symptoms of lack of energy, difficulty concentrating, negative thinking, and sleep and appetite difficulties. Depression can present in multiple ways according to age, gender, and cultural background. The term *depression* is what the *Diagnostic and Statistical Manual of Mental Disorders, Fifth Edition, Text Revision* (DSM-5-TR), defines as "major depressive episode" or "major depressive disorder" (American Psychiatric Association, 2022). Depression is a leading cause of disability among adolescents ages 10 to 19 years, with an estimated 12.5% of 12- to 17-year-olds experiencing symptoms of major depressive episode in a 12-month period (National Institute of Mental Health [NIH], 2017) and with twice as many females experiencing depression as their male counterparts (NIH, 2023). In addition to causing personal distress, depression also plays a large role in suicide attempts, with one-half of all suicide attempts linked to depression and suicide being the second leading cause of death for adolescents ages 10 to 18 (Centers for Disease Control and Prevention, 2023). Given the high prevalence rates and significant impact it can have on children and adolescents, it is important for clinicians to engage in culturally responsive assessment practices when assessing depressive symptoms.

CHARACTERISTICS OF DEPRESSION

Children who are facing sadness and depressive thoughts and emotions often appear as withdrawn, irritable, cranky, or lethargic. Youth experiencing depression may complain of bodily aches and pains and loss of interest in previously enjoyable activities, experience a sense of worthlessness and blaming oneself, and demonstrate functional impairments in completing their work due to concentration and memory problems. Children can display symptoms of depression at any age; however, symptoms present themselves in various ways depending on the developmental stage of the child. Table 17.1 provides differences in the presentation of depression across children, adolescents, and adults.

Major depressive disorder (MDD) in DSM-5-TR (American Psychiatric Association, 2022) is characterized by discrete episodes of at least 2 weeks' duration (although episodes can last considerably longer) and involving at least five of the following symptoms: depressed mood, loss of interest or pleasure in activities, thoughts of death or suicide, significant weight loss or gain, insomnia or hypersomnia, fatigue or loss of energy, feelings of worthlessness or excessive guilt, and diminished ability to think or concentrate. Although this chapter focuses on MDD, the recommendations around identification and assessment can be applied to

TABLE 17.1. Differences in the Presentation of Depression by Age

Prepubertal children	Adolescents	Adults
• Somatic complaints	• Somatic complaints	• Psychomotor agitation or retardation
• Irritability (non-compliance, temper tantrums)	• Irritability (grumpy, hostile, easily frustrated, angry outbursts)	• Lack of affective reactivity
• Affect is reactive	• Affect is reactive	• Variation in mood throughout the day; mood is worse in the morning
• Frequently comorbid with anxiety, behavior problems, and ADHD	• Extreme sensitivity to rejection, leading to difficulties maintaining relationships	• Early morning waking
	• Hypersomnia	• Frequently comorbid with anxiety
	• Increased appetite and weight gain	

Note. Adapted from Huberty (2012); Maughan et al. (2013); and Rey et al. (2015).

other forms of depression as well. The DSM-5-TR depression criteria have been shown to cluster together, run in families, and have a genetic basis; a large body of evidence accumulated over time now supports the internal consistency of depressive symptoms and the validity of the major depression construct (Costello et al., 2003; Lewinsohn & Essau, 2002; Robins & Guze, 1970). The severity of depressive symptoms can be based on symptom count, intensity of symptoms, and/or level of impairment (Cuijpers et al., 2004). There is often a range of symptoms across mild, moderate, and severe symptoms of depression. Diagnostic guidelines have been developed for primary care clinicians and other mental health professionals who can identify and assist children and youth (Zuckerbrot et al., 2018).

Mild depression can be characterized when observing milder symptoms, a shorter duration of symptoms, and when a patient meets minimal criteria for depression (Selph & McDonagh, 2019). According to DSM-5-TR, mild depression could include five to six symptoms that are mild in severity and when a patient only experiences mild impairment in functioning. Alternatively, severe depression could be observed when a patient experiences all symptoms listed in the DSM-5-TR and with severe impairment in functioning. An adolescent with at least five criteria of major depression should be considered in the severe category if they present with a specific suicide plan, clear intent, or recent attempt; family history of first-degree relatives with bipolar or depression; psychotic symptoms; and severe impairment in functioning (Zuckerbrot et al., 2018). Moderate depression would then fall between these two categories.

Depression can often be manifested in cognitive, behavioral, and physical symptoms (Huberty, 2012). Symptoms of depression can often be more severe manifestations of typical behaviors, such as feeling down or blue, which all individuals may experience at some point. Sadness and unhappiness are components of normal human experience, especially following losses and disappointment. One of the most common concerns voiced by clinicians when diagnosing depression is how to distinguish between normal adolescent behavior and youth with depression. This is because adolescents are often perceived as being irritable, experiencing mood swings, or being bored. Table 17.2 presents some of the differences between typical adolescent behavior and those with clinical depression. Concerns emerge when typical behaviors become more significant or severe to the point when they start to impair an individual's functioning. Additional characteristics of depression and the development of depressive symptoms are described below.

Negative Cognitive Triad

Aaron Beck is credited with creating one of the earliest cognitive models of depression for adults, which has since been extended to children and adolescents. His model suggests that individuals with depression have a "negative cognitive triad" that includes a negative perception of themselves, the future, and this world (Beck, 1987). As part of this model, individuals who are depressive have cognitive biases and errors in thinking that are often incorrect interpretations of situations and events. This includes the development of thinking patterns that process automatic, repetitive, and nega-

TABLE 17.2. Typical Adolescent Behavior versus Clinical Depression

Typical adolescent behavior	Adolescent with clinical depression
• Demonstrates some moodiness, angst, and difficulties, but otherwise no significant and enduring changes in behavior	• A persistent negative mood or persistent irritability; change in previous behavior (e.g., lost interest in everyday activities, repeated complaints of boredom, or dramatic response to perceived rejections)
• Sadness or crying is in response to life events and may be short-lived	• Primary symptoms of depression (lack of pleasure or sadness) present every day, most of the day, for at least two weeks
• Changes in preferred activities, foods, and friends	• Decreased interest in previously enjoyable activities; decreased activity; withdraw into internet, room, and/or self instead of engaging in previously enjoyed relationships or social activities; change in eating patterns
• Risky behaviors can happen but usually contained within reasonable limits of the individual's character	• Engaging in uncharacteristic high-risk, or dangerous, behaviors (e.g., substance abuse, unsafe sex, and reckless driving)
• Infrequent thoughts of death and suicide	• Common or frequent thoughts of suicide and/or attempts

Note. Adapted from Rey et al. (2015) and Selph and McDonagh (2019).

tive thoughts, increasing an individual's susceptibility to depression. In this model, Beck suggested that people develop negative cognitive schemas and structures that incorrectly filter and process incoming information (Beck et al., 1974). Additional research since that time has found that it's not clear if negative thoughts cause depression but rather that depression can cause negative thoughts (Pennington, 2002). And the negative outcomes of dysfunctional thinking can exacerbate depressed mood and adjustment problems (Huberty, 2012).

Learned Helplessness

Depression is also theorized to be due to learned helplessness. A theory of learned helplessness came out of research on animal responses to stress but was applied to humans and characterized by the development of the belief that individuals are not able to deal with adverse contexts (Seligman, 1972). Learned helplessness is developed through the repeated experience of aversive events that are perceived to be unavoidable or unescapable, therefore leading to a sense of not being in control of their outcomes. Learned helplessness is hypothesized to result in three main deficit-based outcomes: reduced motivation, difficulty identifying the association between actions and outcomes, and depression (Abramson et al., 1978; Seligman, 1972). Learned helplessness is then connected to the development of depression, arguing that helplessness leads to the attribution of negative events to internal, permanent, and global causes (e.g., my abilities or personal circumstances will never improve) and continued disengagement with activities that may have at one time been valued (Abramson et al., 1978).

Emotion Regulation in Depression

Scholars have defined depression as a disorder of emotion regulation, emphasizing the connection between challenges with emotion regulation and depressive symptoms (Joorman & Gotlib, 2010). The literature further highlights the complex processes associated with emotion regulation, as evidenced by the development of its definition over the past several years. Broadly, emotion regulation describes the processes by which individuals modify emotional experiences and expression to adapt and respond to contextual demands (Aldao et al., 2010; Gonçalves et al., 2019). Scholars further describe the ways in which emotions are modified, including adaptive strategies, such as reappraisal and problem solving, and maladaptive strategies, such as suppression, rumination, and avoidance, to alter the intensity, duration, and frequency of a particular emotion (Aldao et al., 2010). Emotion regulation skills grow and develop over time, with many of these skills emerging during the school-age years and continuing to develop into late adolescence and early adulthood (Crowell, 2021).

Given the developmental nature of emotion regulation, it plays a key role in social, emotional, and behavioral development. Given the association between emotion regulation and depression symptomatology in youth and, more specifically, the predictive nature between the two, it is important to examine both the present and future impacts on functioning. Adolescents who demonstrate challenges with emotional regulation are also more likely to present with both current and future depressive symptoms (Gonçalves et al., 2019). Siener and Kerns (2012) also explored the relationship between depressive symptoms and ways in which children monitor, evaluate, and modify emotional experiences, finding that children who experienced greater depression symptoms experienced more intense emotions, engaged in more cognitive errors when evaluating their emotions, and were less likely to engage in adaptive coping strategies. As such, an assessment of emotion regulation is an important component of the assessment and treatment of depression among youth.

CULTURALLY RESPONSIVE ASSESSMENT OF DEPRESSION

In a culturally responsive assessment of depression, clinicians are encouraged to start with an initial appraisal of how they integrate conceptualizations of culture within the assessment of a child's needs. *Culture* refers to values, beliefs, language, traditions, and behaviors that are passed from one generation to another within any social group (American Psychological Association, 2023). Psychologically relevant elements may include values of authority or personal control, individualism, collectivism, and spirituality, among others (Betancourt & Lopez, 1993). These culturally relevant elements may influence how individuals report and conceptualize their experience of distress, determine if they seek and/or stay in treatment, as well as their treatment outcome (U.S. Department of Health and Human Services [DHHS], 2021). Culturally responsive approaches to assessment include recognizing, respecting, and responding to the diverse cultural backgrounds of children and youth.

Depression impacts many people across the globe. Sociodemographic correlates of major depression often appear consistent across countries (Kessler & Bromet, 2013). Despite depression being present across countries, cultures, races, and ethnicities, research conducted by the World Health Organization (WHO) examined cross-national differences in depression prevalence in 14 countries around the world (Simon et al., 2002). Results suggest that in countries with higher prevalence rates of depression, individuals report lower levels of impairment, compared to countries with lower rates of prevalence where individuals report higher levels of impairment. Overall, the authors concluded that cross-nationally, there are similarities in the nature and validity of depressive episodes; however, when using the DSM criteria for depressive disorders, individuals from different countries may indicate varying levels of depression severity.

Sociodemographic factors can also impact rates of depression, including prevalence rates and perceptions by gender, age, race, ethnicity, and other cultural identities. A systematic review of qualitative literature conducted by Haroz et al. (2017) examined the diagnostic features of DSM-5 (American Psychiatric Association, 2013) and the relevancy and prevalence of those features worldwide in both Western and non-Western populations. Standard assessment techniques purely based on the DSM were found to not fully capture the experience of depression in all regions of the world. Across the globe, individuals with depression report the DSM features of depressed mood/sadness, fatigue/loss of energy, problems with sleep, appetite/weight problems, suicidal thoughts, loss of interest, and worthless/guilt. However, individuals from around the world also reported features not included in the DSM. Specifically, four of the most reported features of depression include social isolation/loneliness, crying, anger, and general pain, all symptoms that are not included in DSM-5 diagnostic criteria. Additionally, the diagnostic features of difficulty with concentration and psychometric agitation or slowing are often not reported in non-Western populations. Results point to the need for a greater understanding of the unique characteristics and features present within each culture and broadening assessment features of depression to include global indicators inclusive of symptoms, such as pain, anger, and/or crying.

In populations that have experienced trauma, individuals often report guilt, rumination, and feeling suspicious at greater frequencies than individuals who have not experienced trauma (Haroz et al., 2017). The unique symptoms of depression reported by those who have experienced trauma suggest the need for combining assessment measures rooted in the DSM criteria with other forms of assessment. For example, childhood trauma in the form of psychological or physical abuse, emotional or physical neglect, and abuse may have immediate and long-term negative impacts on youth mental health and increase the risk of youth developing depression at some point in their lifetime (Danese, 2020; Fava et al., 2023). It is important to note that there is often overlap in reports of guilt and rumination between individuals who have experienced trauma and individuals with post-traumatic stress disorder (Haroz et al., 2007), and populations who have experienced collective trauma often experience increased overlap in depression and post-traumatic stress symptoms (Momartin et al., 2004). Experiences with trauma are unique to each individual, impacting reported depressive symptoms and necessitating practitioners' use of culturally responsive and trauma-informed assessments of depression.

Risk and Protective Factors

A thorough assessment of depression includes a consideration of risk and protective factors for depression. Across the developmental lifespan, studies of adults, adolescents, and children all indicate a family history of depression and exposure to stressful life events as the most robust risk factors for depression (Maughan et al., 2013). Children who have a family history of depression are up to 3.5 times more likely to be diagnosed with depression (van Dijk et al., 2021). Psychosocial risk factors include family bereavement, separations and conflict, child abuse and neglect, and peer conflict and bullying (e.g., Jaffee et al., 2002; Kendler et al., 2000). Other risk factors include substance use, trauma, psychosocial adversities, and frequent somatic complaints (Clayborne et al., 2019; Fergusson et al., 2000). Caregivers, peers, and primary care clinicians should routinely monitor the psychosocial functioning of all youth because problems in peer and family relationships may be an early indicator of a variety of concerns, including depression (Zuckerbrot et al., 2018).

Conversely, active coping skills, use of problem-solving strategies, and a favorable self-concept have been found to be protective factors against the onset of depression (Van Voorhees et al., 2008). Similarly, having positive connections to family members and perceptions of feeling loved and wanted has been shown to result in a reduction in the onset of depressive episodes. Better school performance and greater peer acceptance are additional protective factors against future risk of a depressive episode (Askeland et al., 2020; Cattelino et al., 2021; Hjemdal et al., 2007).

Sex and Gender Differences

Differences are present in prevalence rates of depression between males, females, and nonbinary youth. There is a steady climb in the rate of depression throughout adolescence for both boys and girls and by ages 13–15; symptoms of depression are seen twice as of often in girls compared to boys (Douglas & Scott, 2014). Across the lifetime, women are also two times more likely to be diagnosed with depression than men (Van de Velde et al., 2010). Symptoms are also variable between males and females, as males report symptoms of irritability, restlessness, troubles with concentration and sleep disturbance, and impulse control (Khesht-Masjedi et al., 2017). However, the same study revealed that females report sadness, depressed mood, hopelessness, self-blame, feelings of fatigue, challenges with concentration, and somatic health symptoms. Put broadly, males often display more externalizing behaviors, and females demonstrate more internalizing behaviors, encouraging a broader assessment of depressive features in diagnosis. Additionally, gender identity can impact youth rates of depression. Youth who identify as transgender and gender-diverse have higher risk of experiencing depression and suicidality (Connolly et al., 2016). The difference in the presentation of depression symptoms between male and female youth and the increased risk for youth who identify as transgender must be taken into consideration throughout the assessment process.

Cultural, Racial, and Ethnic Differences

The expression of depressive symptoms may vary by culture, race, and ethnicity, and additional work is needed to better understand the presentation of these indicators among youth. Parents from different cultural backgrounds report differing thresholds for observed symptoms of depression in their children (Liang et al., 2016). Specifically, patterns in research suggest that parents who identify as Black, Asian American, and Native Hawaiian tend to report fewer internalizing symptoms for their children when compared to White parents reporting their child's concerns (Nguyen et al., 2007). Initial studies have begun to assess validity across diverse samples; however, most studies are based on limited samples of individuals from diverse cultural, racial, and ethnic identities. Additionally, limited information is available regarding cultural adaptations of assessment measures (Newell et al., 2010). A more holistic understanding of how depression begins and is maintained during childhood, adolescence, and adulthood is warranted.

Finally, there are several social justice concerns that impact anxiety among youth, such as disparities in mental health care, increased exposure to social and environmental stressors, and implicit bias in educational practices. The degree to which these systems-level disparities impact experiences of anxiety through heightened physiological responses, reduced social support, and limited access to effective services to offset symptoms of anxiety warrants immediate attention and advocacy efforts.

Minority Stress Theory

Research on rates of depression has pointed to higher levels of depression among minoritized youth from certain identities. The prevailing explanation on health disparities for racially, ethnically, and gender-minoritized youth comes from the minority stress theory (e.g., Brooks, 1981; Jardas et al., 2023; Toomey, 2021), which asserts that on top of all the stressors that all individuals experience, members of many minoritized groups experience a host of unique stressors, which can harm their mental health. As such, clinicians are encouraged to consider both distal or external stressors, such as if youth have experienced victimization, rejection, or discrimination. Clinicians are also encouraged to consider more proximal or internal stressors, such as internalizing stigma associated with their identity or group membership, or expecting discrimination. Clinicians are encouraged to ask youth about their perceptions of both proximal and distal stressors that could heighten symptoms of depression. These factors can help guide a more effective treatment plan, including how to promote interpersonal protective factors (e.g., family connectedness, social support, and affinity spaces) and address how adults and peers can work to address or alleviate contextual factors that may further exacerbate depressive symptoms.

ASSESSMENT OF DEPRESSION ACROSS CONTEXTS

The assessment of depression is relevant for a wide variety of child and adolescent populations and contexts—including, but not limited to, schools, specialty medical care settings, and inpatient and outpatient mental health care. However, the severity of depression can differ across contexts as it may be seen as more severe in mental health settings and milder in school and community settings (Klein, 2024). Tools assessing depression can also vary in their sensitivity to the severity level of depression, so it can be important to consider measures that are sensitive to varying levels of depressive symptoms.

An important consideration in the assessment of depression is whether the underlying latent construct assessed by a measure is comparable across groups, such as individuals of different races, ethnicities, genders, sexual orientation, and cultures. Confirmatory factor analysis can be used to test for measurement invariance (MI). If an instrument is used with two groups and found to lack invariance, it cannot be assumed to measure the same construct in each group (Klein, 2024). Prior research has demonstrated that depression measures are often invariant across a variety of populations in self-report measures (e.g., Mellick et al., 2019; Olino, 2020; Patel et al., 2019). MI is limited as it cannot determine whether existing measures leave out symptoms that are important in identifying depression in some groups but not others. For example, the generalizability of Western conceptualizations and measures of depression can be limiting and not appropriate for children and adolescents from historically minoritized communities (Kirmayer et al., 2022). For example, in some cultures, depression can be experienced as headaches, pain, anger, and/or loneliness (Haroz et al., 2017), which may not be analogous to the Western construct of depression. As previously referenced, for many individuals who identify as male, symptoms of depression present as more externalizing behaviors, including anger, aggression, and substance abuse (Martin et al., 2013). As such, it is important to consider a broad range of behavior in a culturally informed assessment of depression to consider how depression-related symptoms are conceptualized in communities across diverse contexts.

METHODS OF ASSESSMENT

Diagnostic and Semistructured Interviews

Assessing youth for depression should employ a multifaceted approach that includes individual rating scales, observations, and clinical interviews. Often, the assessment includes reports from multiple informants, including the youth, parent, and/

or teacher, among others (Orchard et al., 2019). Diagnostic interviews provide detailed information about symptoms of depression. In a fully structured diagnostic interview, the interviewer follows a detailed script that does not include follow-up questions. In contrast, a semistructured diagnostic interview follows a specific, predetermined format where the interviewer can ask follow-up questions and can ask for specific examples (Klein et al., 2024). Several semistructured interview protocols have been developed to assist clinicians in gaining a comprehensive understanding of youth functioning and depressive symptoms. Examples of these measures are provided below.

Kiddie Schedule for Affective Disorders and Schizophrenia

The Kiddie Schedule for Affective Disorders and Schizophrenia (K-SADS) (Kaufman et al., 1997) is a widely used diagnostic interview for depression that is designed to be used with youth ages 6–18 years old. The K-SADS has been updated as the DSM has been revised, and a recent version of the K-SADS (Townsend et al., 2020) uses DSM-5 criteria to assess for current and lifetime symptoms of depression (Birmaher et al., 2009; Klein et al., 2005). The K-SADS allows for flexibility in its administration and includes screening questions that address criteria for a range of diagnoses and supplemental sections of questions to access more specific criteria for diagnoses that may be flagged as part of the screening. A youth and adult interview protocol is included and is each estimated to last between 30 minutes and 2.5 hours. Reliability on the K-SADS indicates strong interrater reliability and test–retest reliability (Ambrosini, 2000). This semistructured interview has also been translated into multiple languages, such as Spanish (de la Peña, 2018), Farsi (Ghanizadeh et al., 2006), Japanese (Nishiyama et al., 2020), Korean (Kim et al., 2004), and Icelandic (Lauth et al., 2010).

Mini International Neuropsychiatric Interview for Children and Adolescents

The Mini International Neuropsychiatric Interview for Children and Adolescents (MINI-KID) (Sheehan et al., 2010) is an interview assessing current depressive symptoms. The MINI-KID includes modules for various disorders, and each module consists of screening questions. Endorsement of screening questions leads to additional symptom interview questions, with administration lasting approximately 10 to 30 minutes. Research on the MINI-KID indicates strong interrater reliability for mood disorders and moderate test–retest reliability for depressive disorders (Duncan et al., 2018; Sheehan et al., 2010). This semistructured interview has also been translated into Spanish, French, Russian, German, Turkish, Hungarian, and Norwegian Sign Language (Øhre et al., 2014; Sheehan et al., 2010).

Child and Adolescent Psychiatric Assessment

The Child and Adolescent Psychiatric Assessment (CAPA) (Angold & Costello, 1995, 2000) is a broad semistructured interview that can be utilized with children ages 9–17 years to assess for a variety of psychiatric disorders. The CAPA includes self-report and caregiver interviews that provide mandatory and optional questions regarding symptoms during the previous 3 months, taking between 1 and 2 hours to administer (Angold & Costello, 2000). In addition to questions specific to the diagnostic criteria of varying disorders, this interview also includes questions about school performance and family structure, which may provide useful information to clinicians. Asking questions beyond depressive symptomology such as ones related to school and family may help provide the clinician with a more comprehensive picture and understanding of the individual's experience, which may be beneficial when working with youth and families from diverse culturally backgrounds.

Preschool Age Psychiatric Assessment

The Preschool Age Psychiatric Assessment (PAPA) (Egger & Angold, 2004) can be administered to parents of children ages 2–5 years for the purpose of diagnosing a variety of behavioral or emotional problems and can be used to assess depression in preschool age children. The PAPA follows a similar structure to the CAPA and has been modified to include questions that are more developmentally appropriate for younger children. Both the PAPA and CAPA have been translated into Spanish (Angold & Costello, 2000; Egger & Angold, 2004).

The Importance of Multiple Informants

In addition to diagnostic interviews, rating scales are also often used to diagnose depression. Best practice suggests the need to use multiple informants in the assessment process (Kraemer et al., 2003). Observable, externalizing behaviors often have better correspondence between informants, whereas less observable and more internalizing behaviors (e.g., worries and negative thoughts) have less correspondence between informants (De Los Reyes et al., 2015). Parents and teachers often underestimate depressive feelings in children, while adolescents may overestimate symptoms (Orchard et al., 2019). Additionally, reports and questionnaire data from different informants often disagree, as it can be difficult to accurately interpret children's emotions and behavior. It is important to interview the child and adolescent, often across several occasions, to best ascertain an accurate picture of how the young person is feeling. Clinicians should pay careful attention to the young person's report when diagnosing depression, while also integrating feedback from teachers and caregivers. Additionally, multiple informants provide a more comprehensive picture of the settings in which depressive symptoms are showing up, offering detailed information to inform intervention.

Questionnaires and Rating Scales

Patient Health Questionnaire for Adolescents

The Patient Health Questionnaire for Adolescents (PHQ-A) (Johnson et al., 2002) is designed for individuals ages 12 years and older, assessing nine DSM-IV-TR criteria for depressive disorders and examining the presence and severity of depressive symptoms. This screening tool was created from the full version of the Patient Health Questionnaire (Spitzer et al., 1999) and is composed of nine items that are answered on a scale from 0 (*Not at all*) to 3 (*Nearly every day*). The questionnaire includes an assessment of functional impairment, asking how much the symptoms endorsed interfere with daily functioning. Calculated scores range from 0 to 27 and are accompanied by various cutoff scores to indicate severity of symptoms, ranging from minimal to severe depression (Spitzer et al., 1999). This measure demonstrates adequate levels of reliability and validity, as well as adequate levels of sensitivity, specificity, and diagnostic accuracy when compared to other diagnostic measures for depression (Johnson et al., 2002). The PHQ-9 has been validated across many languages and cultures, demonstrating adequate reliability and validity (Anum et al., 2019; Fonseca-Pedrero et al., 2023; Lamela et al., 2020).

Children's Depression Inventory–2

The Children's Depression Inventory–2 (CDI-2) (Kovacs, 2011) is designed for children ages 7–17 years and is a widely used measure to assess depressive symptoms in children and adolescents. The measure includes parent/caregiver, teacher, and self-report forms that utilize two scales: emotional problems and functional problems. The emotional problems subscale is comprised of the negative mood/physical symptoms and negative self-esteem subscales and provides information about feelings of distress and challenges with sleep, appetite, and energy. The functional problems scale is comprised of the ineffectiveness and interpersonal problems subscales and provides information about social relationships and functioning across settings. Each of the 28 items is rated on a scale from 0 to 2, assessing depressive symptoms in the previous two weeks.

A review of the psychometric properties of the CDI-2 and the CDI-2 short form (CDI-2: SR[S]) revealed adequate measures of reliability and validity (Bae, 2012). The CDI and CDI-2 have been translated and validated across many cultures and languages, including Korean (Cho et al., 2022), Spanish (Cumba-Avilés et al., 2020), Japanese (Ozono et al., 2019), and Danish (Sørensen et al., 2005).

Reynolds Child and Adolescent Depression Scales–2

The Reynolds Child Depression Scale–2 (RCDS-2) (Reynolds, 2010), designed for children ages 7–13, and the Reynolds Adolescent Depression Scale–2 (RADS-2) (Reynolds, 2008), designed for adolescents and young adults ages 11–20, are self-report measures to assess the frequency of depressive symptoms. The RCDS-2 is comprised of 30 items and is responded to using a four-point Likert scale ranging from *Almost never* to *All the time* (Reynolds, 2010). Scores obtained are accompanied by descriptions regarding severity of symptoms, ranging from normal to severe clinical depression. This measure demonstrates adequate measures of reliability of reported symptoms, including measures of test–retest reliability (Reynolds & Graves, 1989), as well as strong correlations with other self-report and interview measures that assess depression in children (Reynolds, 2010).

The RADS-2 is designed for use with adolescents ages 11–20 based on the diagnostic criteria for depressive disorders. This 30-item scale provides a depression total score and four subscale scores, including dysphoric mood, anhedonia/negative affect, negative self-evaluation, and somatic complaints. Similar to the RCDS-2, scores obtained on the RADS-2 are accompanied by descriptions regarding severity of symptoms, ranging from normal to severe clinical depression. Regarding its psychometric properties, the RADS-2 demonstrates evidence of reliability, with test–retest reliability coefficients ranging from .77 to .84 (Reynolds, 2008). These measures also demonstrate moderate to strong evidence across dimensions of validity constructs, including criterion-related validity, convergent validity, and clinical validity (Reynolds, 2008). The RADS-2 has also been validated and translated into several languages, including Swedish, and demonstrates sound measures of reliability and validity in the diagnosis of depression (Blomqvist et al., 2021).

Children's Depression Rating Scale—Revised

The Children's Depressions Rating Scale—Revised (CDRS-R) (Poznanski et al., 1984) is a semistructured interview designed to evaluate the severity of depressive symptoms in children ages 6–12 years. This 17-item scale is administered by a clinician based on interviews with the child and/or their caregiver. Each item is scored to indicate level of symptom severity across a range of areas that align with DSM-IV depression criteria. Fourteen of the items are scored based on verbal observations, and three items are scored based on nonverbal observations, including tempo of language, hypoactivity, and nonverbal expression of depressed affect. Early evaluations of the CDRS-R demonstrated adequate measures of reliability (Poznanski et al., 1984). Findings of a meta-analysis examining the psychometric properties of the CDRS-R with adolescents revealed sufficient evidence for various aspects of reliability and validity (Stallwood et al., 2021).

Beck Hopelessness Scale

The Beck Hopelessness Scale (BHS) (Beck et al., 1974) is a 20-item self-report questionnaire that measures aspects of hopelessness in adolescents and adults ages 17 and older. Founded upon the research identifying hopelessness as an important factor in the etiology of depression and long-term risk factor of suicidal behavior, the BHS examines the motivational, affective, and cognitive dimensions of hopelessness about the future to inform diagnostic assessment of depression and associated symptoms (Beck et al., 1974). Items that are answered as true or false and result in a total hopelessness score ranging from 0–20 across three factors: feelings about the future, loss of motivation, and future expectations. Higher scores are indicative of higher levels of feelings of hopelessness. Analyses of the psychometric properties resulted in adequate measures of internal consistency and validity (Steed, 2001). Subsequent analyses indicate sound psychometric properties for the measure in German (Kliem et al., 2018), Italian (Iliceto & Fino, 2015), Finnish (Granö et al., 2017), and Spanish (Hermosilla-De la Torre et al., 2020).

Progress Monitoring Measures

Progress monitoring is an important component of any intervention. Utilizing progress monitoring allows mental health professionals to understand how youth are responding to the intervention and what, if any, adjustments need to be made. Despite broad evidence on the benefits of using progress monitoring to track how an individual is responding to an intervention, little research exists on tools to monitor child and adolescent changes in depression over time (von der Embse et al., 2015). Examples of these progress monitoring tools can be found below.

Brief Behavior Rating Scale for Depression

The Brief Behavior Rating Scale for Depression (BBRS-D) (Dart et al., 2020) is a four-item progress monitoring measure that is designed to assess symptoms of depression in children. It was created from items on the Beck Depression Inventory for Youth and the Children's Depression Inventory. The four items assess stomach pain, sadness, sleep problems, and tiredness. Initial research suggests there is evidence for the validity of the BBRS-D (Dart et al., 2020); however, future research is needed to establish reliability and internal consistency metrics, as well as the utility of the measure across diverse samples.

Behavior and Feelings Survey

The Behavior and Feelings Survey (BFS) (Weisz et al., 2020) is a 12-item progress monitoring measure designed to assess internalizing and externalizing behaviors in youth. The BFS uses a four-point Likert scale ranging from 0 (*not a problem*) to 4 (*a very big problem*), with higher total scores indicating greater challenges. Both self-report and caregiver measures are freely available at *https://weiszlab.fas.harvard.edu/measures*. The brevity and affordability of the measure make it an ideal progress monitoring measure for social, emotional, behavioral, and mental health interventions. Research on the BFS suggests it has strong internal reliability (Rognstad, 2022), test–retest reliability, and good convergent and discriminant validity compared to other well-established measures (Weisz et al., 2020).

Positive and Negative Affect Schedule for Children—Short Form

The Positive and Negative Affect Schedule for Children—Short Form (PANAS-C) (Ebesutani et al., 2012) is designed as a progress monitoring measure for youth experiencing symptoms of depression. The PANAS-C is a 10-item self-report questionnaire that uses a five-point Likert scale to assess symptoms of anxiety and depression. It demonstrates strong reliability and validity estimates in its ability to assess the frequency of positive and negative emotions in children (Ebesutani et al., 2012).

DEPRESSION AND SUICIDAL BEHAVIOR

About 60% of young people with depression report having thought about suicide, and 30% attempt suicide. The risk increases if the young person has a previous suicide attempt; access to firearms; suicides in the family; other comorbid psychiatric disorders (e.g., substance abuse), aggression and impulsivity; and experience of negative events (e.g., disciplinary crises). As such, it is important that any assessment of depressive symptoms includes asking questions about suicidal thoughts and behaviors. Measures such as the Columbia–Suicide Severity Rating Scale (C-SSRS) (Posner et al., 2011) or the screening version of this measure address critical domains of suicidality, allowing clinicians to accurately assess level of risk. Please see the chapter in this book on suicide assessment for a full description of assessment considerations when working with youth who may be experiencing suicidal ideation and/or behaviors.

CONCLUSION

Developing a multimethod and multi-informant assessment plan is needed in the effective identification, diagnosis, and treatment of depression in children and youth. Culturally responsive approaches to assessment include recognizing, respecting, and responding to the diverse cultural backgrounds of all children and youth. This includes semistructured interviews and rating scales that promote effective identification, diagnosis, and treatment planning, as well as progress monitoring tools that lead to valuable data to guide intervention modifications when needed. Given the high prevalence rates of depression among youth, it is critical that clinicians use evidence-based tools that are guided by a culturally informed approach to assessment.

REFERENCES

Abramson, L. Y., Seligman, M. E., & Teasdale, J. D. (1978). Learned helplessness in humans: Critique and reformulation. *Journal of Abnormal Psychology*, *87*(1), 49.

Aldao, A., Nolen-Hoeksema, S., & Schweizer, S. (2010). Emotion-regulation strategies across psychopathology: A meta-analytic review. *Clinical Psychology Review*, *30*, 217–237.

Ambrosini, P. J. (2000). Historical development and present status of the schedule for Affective Disorders and Schizophrenia for School-Age Children (K-SADS). *Journal of the American Academy of Child & Adolescent Psychiatry*, *39*(1), 49–58.

American Psychiatric Association. (2013). *Diagnostic and statistical manual of mental disorders* (5th ed.) Author.

American Psychiatric Association. (2022). *Diagnostic and Statistical Manual of Mental Disorders* (5th ed., text rev.). Author.

American Psychological Association. (2023). *APA dictionary of psychology*. Author. *https://dictionary.apa.org/culture*

Angold, A., & Costello, E. J. (1995). A test–retest reliability study of child-reported psychiatric symptoms and diagnoses using the Child and Adolescent Psychiatric Assessment (CAPA-C). *Psychological Medicine*, *25*(4), 755–762.

Angold, A., & Costello, E. J. (2000). The Child and Adolescent Psychiatric Assessment (CAPA). *Journal of the American Academy of Child & Adolescent Psychiatry*, *39*(1), 39–48.

Anum, A., Adjorlolo, S., & Kugbey, N. (2019). Depressive symptomology in adolescents in Ghana: Examination of psychometric properties of the Patient

Health Questionnaire–9. *Journal of Affective Disorders, 256*, 213–218.

Askeland, K. G., Bøe, T., Breivik, K., La Greca, A. M., Sivertsen, B., & Hysing, M. (2020). Life events and adolescent depressive symptoms: Protective factors associated with resilience. *PLOS One, 15*(6), e0234109.

Bae, Y. (2012). Test review: Children's Depression Inventory 2 (CDI 2). *Journal of Psychoeducational Assessment, 30*(3), 304–308.

Beck, A. T. (1987). Cognitive models of depression. *Journal of Cognitive Psychotherapy, 1*(1), 5–37.

Beck, A. T., Weissman, A., Lester, D., & Trexler, L. (1974). The measurement of pessimism: The Hopelessness Scale. *Journal of Consulting and Clinical Psychology, 42*, 861–865.

Betancourt, H., & Lopez, S. (1993). The study of culture, ethnicity and race in American psychology. *American Psychologist, 48*, 629–637.

Birmaher, B., Ehmann, M., Axelson, D. A., Goldstein, B. I., Monk, K., Kalas, C., et al. (2009). Schedule for Affective Disorders and Schizophrenia for School-Age Children (K-SADS-PL) for the assessment of preschool children: A preliminary psychometric study. *Journal of Psychiatric Research, 43*(7), 680–686.

Blomqvist, I., Ekbäck, E., Dennhag, I., & Henje, E. (2021). Validation of the Swedish version of the Reynolds Adolescent Depression Scale second edition (RADS-2) in a normative sample. *Nordic Journal of Psychiatry, 75*(4), 292–300.

Brooks, V. R. (1981). *Minority stress and lesbian women*. Lexington Books.

Cattelino, E., Chirumbolo, A., Baiocco, R., Calandri, E., & Morelli, M. (2021). School achievement and depressive symptoms in adolescence: The role of self-efficacy and peer relationships at school. *Child Psychiatry & Human Development, 52*(4), 571–578.

Centers for Disease Control and Prevention. (2023). *WISQARS Leading Causes of Death Reports*. Author.

Cho, Y., Lee, E., Hong, S., Joung, Y., & Kim, J. (2022). Reliability and validity of the Korean version of the Children's Depression Inventory 2 short version as a screening tool: A comparison with the standard 28-item version. *Psychiatry Investigation, 19*(1), 54–60.

Clayborne, Z. M., Varin, M., & Colman, I. (2019). Systematic review and meta-analysis: Adolescent depression and long-term psychosocial outcomes. *Journal of the American Academy of Child & Adolescent Psychiatry, 58*(1), 72–79.

Connolly, M. D., Zervos, M. J., Barone, C. J., Johnson, C. C., & Joseph, C. L. M. (2016). The mental health of transgender youth: Advances in understanding. *Journal of Adolescent Health, 59*(5), 489–495.

Costello, E. J., Mustillo, S., Erkanli, A., Keeler, G., & Angold, A. (2003). Prevalence and development of psychiatric disorders in childhood and adolescence. *Archives of General Psychiatry, 60*(8), 837–844.

Crowell, J. (2021). Development of emotion regulation in typically developing children. *Child and Adolescent Psychiatric Clinics of North America, 30*(3), 467–474.

Cuijpers, P., de Graaf, R., & van Dorsselaer, S. (2004). Minor depression: risk profiles, functional disability, health care use and risk of developing major depression. *Journal of Affective Disorders, 79*(1–3), 71–79.

Cumba-Avilés, E., López-Robledo, Y. M., Caro-González. W., & Rosario-Nieves, I. (2020). Pilot validation study for the Spanish-language CDI-2 among adolescents from Puerto Rico. *Revista Puertorriqueña de Psicología, 31*(1), 110–126.

Danese, A. (2020). Annual research review: Rethinking childhood trauma-new research directions for measurement, study design and analytical strategies. *Journal of Child Psychology and Psychiatry, 61*(3), 236–250.

Dart, E. H., Arora, P., Collins, T., Stark, K., Cook, C. R., Duong, M. T., McCarty, C. A., & Doll, B. (2020). Developing a brief behavior rating scale for progress monitoring of depression in school settings. *Assessment for Effective Intervention, 45*(3), 163–172.

de la Peña, F. R., Villavicencio, L. R., Palacio, J. D., Félix, F. J., Larraguibel, M., Viola, L., & Ulloa, R. E. (2018). Validity and reliability of the Kiddie Schedule for Affective Disorders and Schizophrenia present and lifetime version DSM-5 (K-SADS-PL-5) Spanish version. *BMC Psychiatry, 18*, 1–7.

De Los Reyes, A., Augenstein, T. M., Wang, M., Thomas, S. A., Drabick, D. A. G., Burgers, D. E., & Rabinowitz, J. (2015). The validity of the multi-informant approach to assessment child and adolescent mental health. *Psychological Bulletin, 141*(4), 858–900.

Douglas, J., & Scott, J. (2014). A systematic review of gender-specific rates of uni-polar and bipolar disorders in community studies of pre-pubertal children. *Bipolar Disorder, 16*(1), 5–15.

Duncan, L., Georgiades, K., Wang, L., Van Lieshout, R. J., MacMillan, H. L., Ferro, M. A., et al. (2018). Psychometric evaluation of the Mini International Neuropsychiatric Interview for Children and Adolescents (MINI-KID). *Psychological Assessment, 30*(7), 916–928.

Ebesutani, C., Regan, J., Smith, A., Reise, S., Higa-McMillan, C., & Chorpita, B. F. (2012). *Positive and Negative Affect Schedule for Children—Short Form (PANAS-C)* [Database record]. APA PsycTests.

Egger, H. L., & Angold, A. (2004). The Preschool Age Psychiatric Assessment (PAPA): A structured parent interview for diagnosing psychiatric disorders in preschool children. *Handbook of Infant, Toddler, and Preschool Mental Health Assessment, 42*(5), 223–243.

Fava, N. M., Meldrum, R. C., Villar, M. G., Zucker, R. A., & Trucco, E. M. (2023). Adverse childhood experiences, sleep problems, low self-control, and adolescent delinquency: A longitudinal serial mediation analysis. *Development and Psychopathology, 35*(4), 1868–1877.

Fergusson, D. M., Woodward, L. J., & Horwood, L. J. (2000). Risk factors and life processes associated with the onset of suicidal behaviour during adolescence and early adulthood. *Psychological Medicine, 30*(1), 23–39.

Fonseca-Pedrero, E., Díez-Gómez, A., Pérez-Albéniz, A., Al-Halabí, S., Lucas-Molina, B., & Debbané, M. (2023). Youth screening depression: Validation of the Patient Health Questionnaire (PHQ-9) in a representative sample of adolescents. *Psychiatry Research, 328*, 115486.

Ghanizadeh, A., Mohammadi, M. R., & Yazdanshenas, A. (2006). Psychometric properties of the Farsi translation of the Kiddie Schedule for Affective Disorders and Schizophrenia-present and lifetime version. *BMC Psychiatry*, 6(1), 10.

Gonçalves, S. F., Chaplin, T. M., Turpyn, C. C., Niehaus, C. E., Curby, T. W., Sinha, R., Ansell, E. B. (2019). Difficulties in emotion regulation predict depressive symptom trajectory from early to middle adolescence. *Child Psychiatry and Human Development, 50*, 618–630.

Granö, N., Oksanen, J., Kallionpää, S., & Roine, M. (2017). Specificity and sensitivity of the Beck Hopelessness Scale for suicidal ideation among adolescents entering early intervention service. *Nordic Journal of Psychiatry, 71*(1), 72–76.

Haroz, E. E., Ritchey, M., Bass, J. K., Kohrt, B. A., Augustinavicius, J., Michalopoulos, L., et al. (2017). How is depression experienced around the world? A systematic review of qualitative literature. *Social Science & Medicine, 183*, 151–162.

Hermosillo-De la Torre, A. E., Méndez-Sánchez, C., & González-Betanzos, F. (2020). Evidence for the factorial validity of the Beck Hopelessness Scale in Spanish with clinical and non-clinical samples. *Acta Colombiana de Psicología, 23*(2), 159–169.

Hjemdal, O., Aune, T., Reinfjell, T., Stiles, T. C., & Friborg, O. (2007). Resilience as a predictor of depressive symptoms: A correlational study with young adolescents. *Clinical Child Psychology and Psychiatry, 12*(1), 91–104.

Huberty, T. J. (2012). *Anxiety and depression in children and adolescents: Assessment, intervention, and prevention*. Springer Science & Business Media.

Iliceto, P., & Fino, E. (2015). Beck Hopelessness Scale (BHS): A second-order confirmatory factor analysis. *European Journal of Psychological Assessment, 31*(1), 31–37.

Jaffee, S. R., Moffitt, T. E., Caspi, A., Fombonne, E., Poulton, R., & Martin, J. (2002). Differences in early childhood risk factors for juvenile-onset and adult-onset depression. *Archives of General Psychiatry, 59*, 215–222.

Jardas, E. J., Ladd, B. A., Maheux, A. J., Choukas-Bradley, S., Salk, R. H., & Thoma, B. C. (2023). Testing the minority stress model across gender identity, race, and ethnicity among U.S. gender minority adolescents. *Journal of Psychopathology and Clinical Science, 132*(5), 542.

Johnson, J. G., Harris, E. S., Spitzer, R. L., & Williams, J. B. W. (2002). The Patient Health Questionnaire for adolescents: Validation of an instrument for the assessment of mental disorders among adolescent primary care patients. *Journal of Adolescent Health, 30*, 196–204.

Joorman, J., & Gotlib, I. H. (2010). Emotion regulation in depression: Relation to cognitive inhibition. *Cognition and Emotion, 24*(2), 281–298.

Kaufman, J., Birmaher, B., Brent, D., Rao, U., Flynn, C., Moreci, P., et al. (1997). Schedule for Affective Disorders and Schizophrenia for School-Age Children–present and lifetime version (K-SADS-PL): Initial reliability and validity data. *Journal of the American Academy of Child and Adolescent Psychiatry, 36*(7), 980–988.

Kendler, K. S., Thornton, L. M., & Gardner, C. O. (2000). Stressful life events and previous episodes in the etiology of major depression in women: An evaluation of the "kindling" hypothesis. *American Journal of Psychiatry, 157*(8), 1243–1251.

Kessler, R. C., & Bromet, E. J. (2013). The epidemiology of depression across cultures. *Annual Review of Public Health, 34*(1), 119–138.

Khesht-Masjedi, M. F., Shokrgozar, S., Abdollahi, E., Golshahi, M., & Sharif-Ghaziani, Z. (2017). Comparing depressive symptoms in teenage boys and girls. *Journal of Family Medicine and Primary Care*, 6(4), 775–779.

Kim, Y. S., Cheon, K. A., Kim, B. N., Chang, S. A., Yoo, H. J., Kim, J. W., et al. (2004). The reliability and validity of Kiddie-Schedule for Affective Disorders and Schizophrenia–present and lifetime version–Korean version (K-SADS-PL-K). *Yonsei Medical Journal, 45*(1), 81–89.

Kirmayer, L. J., Jarvis, G. E., & Gomez-Carillo, A. (2022). Depression across cultures. In C. B. Nemeroff, A. F. Schatzberg, N. Rasgon, & S. M. Strakowski (Eds.), *The American Psychiatric Association Publishing textbook of mood disorders* (pp. 837–867). American Psychiatric Association Publishing.

Kliem, S., Lohmann, A., Mößle, T., & Brähler, E. (2018). Psychometric properties and measurement invariance of the Beck Hopelessness Scale (BHS): Results from a German representative population sample. *BMH Psychiatry, 18*(1), 110.

Klein, D. N. (2024). Assessment of depression in adults and youth. *Assessment, 31*(1), 110–125.

Klein, D. N., Dougherty, L. R., & Olino, T. M. (2005). Toward guidelines for evidence-based assessment of depression in children and adolescents. *Journal of Clinical Child and Adolescent Psychology, 34*(3), 412–432.

Kraemer, H. C., Measelle, J. R., Ablow, J. C., Essex, M. J., Boyce, W. T., & Kupfer, D. J. (2003). A new approach to integrating data from multiple informants in psychiatric assessment and research: Mixing and matching contexts and perspectives. *American Journal of Psychiatry, 160*(9), 1566–1577.

Kovacs, M. (2011). *Children's Depression Inventory 2nd edition (CDI 2)*. Multi-Health Systems.

Lamela, D., Soreira, C., Matos, P., & Morais, A. (2020). Systematic review of the factor structure and measurement invariance of the patient health questionnaire (PHQ-9) and validation of the Portuguese version in community settings. *Journal of Affective Disorders, 276*, 220–233.

Lauth, B., Arnkelsson, G. B., Magnússon, P., Skarphéðinsson, G. Á., Ferrari, P., & Pétursson, H. (2010). Parent–youth agreement on symptoms and diagnosis: Assessment with a diagnostic interview in an adolescent inpatient clinical population. *Journal of Physiology-Paris, 104*(6), 315–322.

Lewinsohn, P. M., & Essau, C.A. (2002). Depression in adolescents. In I. H. Gotlib & C. L. Hammen (Eds.), *Handbook of depression* (pp. 541–559). Guilford Press.

Liang, J., Matheson, B. E., & Douglas, J. M. (2016). Mental health diagnostic considerations in racial/ethnic minority youth. *Journal of Child and Family Studies, 25*, 1926–1940.

Martin, L. A., Neighbors, H. W., & Griffith, D. M. (2013). The experience of symptoms of depression in men vs women: Analysis of the National Comorbidity Survey Replication. *JAMA Psychiatry, 70*(10), 1100–1106.

Maughan, B., Collishaw, S., & Stringaris, A. (2013). Depression in childhood and adolescence. *Journal of the Canadian Academy of Child and Adolescent Psychiatry, 22*(1), 35–40.

Mellick, W., Hatkevich, C., Venta, A., Hill, R. M., Kazimi, I., Elhai, J. D., & Sharp, C. (2019). Measurement invariance of depression symptom ratings across African American, Hispanic/Latino, and Caucasian adolescent psychiatric inpatients. *Psychological Assessment, 31*(6), 833–838.

Momartin, S., Silove, D., Manicavasagar, V., & Steel, Z. (2004). Comorbidity of PTSD and depression: Associations with trauma exposure, symptom severity and functional impairment in Bosnian refugees resettled in Australia. *Journal of Affective Disorders, 80*(2–3), 231–238.

National Institute of Mental Health. (2017). Major depression among adolescents. *www.nimh.nih.gov/health/statistics/prevalence/major-depression-among-adolescents.shtml*

Newell, M. L., Nastasi, B. K., Hatzichristou, C., Jones, J. M., Schanding Jr, G. T., & Yetter, G. (2010). Evidence on multicultural training in school psychology: Recommendations for future directions. *School Psychology Quarterly, 25*(4), 249.

Nguyen, L., Huang, L. N., Arganza, G. F., & Liao, Q. (2007). The influence of race and ethnicity on psychiatric diagnoses and clinical characteristics of children and adolescents in children's services. *Cultural Diversity and Ethnic Minority Psychology, 13*(1), 18–25.

Nishiyama, T., Sumi, S., Watanabe, H., Suzuki, F., Kuru, Y., Shiino, T., et al. (2020). The kiddie schedule for affective disorders and schizophrenia present and lifetime version (K-SADS-PL) for DSM-5: A validation for neurodevelopmental disorders in Japanese outpatients. *Comprehensive Psychiatry, 96*, 152148.

Øhre, B., Saltnes, H., von Tetzchner, S., & Falkum, E. (2014). Psychometric properties of a sign language version of the Mini International Neuropsychiatric Interview (MINI). *BMC Psychiatry, 14*(1), 148.

Olino, T. M. (2020). Clinical applications of measurement invariance. *Journal of Personality Assessment, 102*(5), 727–729.

Orchard, F., Pass, L., Chessell, C., & Reynolds, S. (2019). Examining parent and child agreement in the diagnosis of adolescent depression. *Child and Adolescent Mental Health, 24*(4), 338–344.

Ozono, S., Nagamitsu, S., Matsuishi, T., Yamashita, Y., Ogata, A., Suzuki, S., et al. (2019). Reliability and validity of the Children's Depression Inventory—Japanese version. *Pediatrics International, 61*(11), 1159–1167.

Patel, J. S., Oh, Y., Rand, K. L., Wu, W., Cyders, M. A., Kroenke, K., & Stewart, J. C. (2019). Measurement invariance of the Patient Health Questionnaire–9 (PHQ-9) depression screener in U.S. adults across sex, race/ethnicity, and education level: Nhanes 2005–2016. *Depression and Anxiety, 36*(9), 813–823.

Pennington, B. F. (2002). *The development of psychopathology: Nature and nurture*. Guilford Press.

Posner, K., Brown, G. K., Stanley, B., Brent, D. A., Yershova, K. V., Oquendo, M. A., et al. (2011). The Columbia-Suicide Severity Rating Scale: Initial validity and internal consistency findings from three multisite studies with adolescents and adults. *The American Journal of Psychiatry, 168*(12), 1266–1277.

Poznanski, E. O., Grossman, J. A., Buchsbaum, Y., Banegas, M., Freeman, L., & Gibbons, R. (1984). Preliminary studies of the reliability and validity of the Children's Depression Rating Scale. *Journal of the American Academy of Child Psychiatry, 23*, 191–19.

Robins, E., & Guze, S. B. (1970). Establishment of diagnostic validity in psychiatric illness: its application to schizophrenia. *American Journal of Psychiatry, 126*(7), 983–987.

Rey, J. M., Bella-Awusah, T. T., Jing, L. (2015). Depression in children and adolescents. In J. M. Rey (Ed), *IACAPAP e-textbook of child and adolescent mental health* (pp. 1–36). International Association for Child and Adolescent Psychiatry and Allied Professions.

Reynolds, W. M. (2008). *Reynolds Adolescent Depression Scale (2nd ed., Short Form—RADS-2: SF)*. Psychological Assessment Resources.

Reynolds, W. M. (2010). *Reynolds Children Depression Scale* (2nd ed.). Psychological Assessment Resources.

Reynolds, W. M., & Graves, A. (1989). Reliability of children's reports of depressive symptomatology. *Journal of Abnormal Child Psychology, 17*(6), 647–655.

Rognstad, K., Helland, S. S., Neumer, S.-P., Baardstu, S., & Kjøbli, J. (2022). Short measures of youth psychopathology: Psychometric properties of the brief problem monitor (BPM) and the behavior and feelings survey (BFS) in a Norwegian clinical sample. *BMC Psychology, 10*(1), 182.

Seligman, M. E. (1972). Learned helplessness. *Annual Review of Medicine, 23*(1), 407–412.

Selph, S. S., & McDonagh, M. S. (2019). Depression in children and adolescents: Evaluation and treatment. *American Family Physician, 100*(10) 609–617.

Siener, S., & Kerns, K. A. (2012). Emotion regulation and depressive symptoms in preadolescence. *Child Psychiatry and Human Development, 43*, 414–430.

Sheehan, D. V., Sheehan, K. H., Shytle, R. D., Janavs, J., Bannon, Y., Rogers, J. E., et al. (2010). Reliability and validity of the Mini International Neuropsychiatric Interview for Children and Adolescents (MINI-KID). *The Journal of Clinical Psychiatry, 71*(3), 17393.

Simon, G. E., Goldberg, D. P., Von Korff, M., & Ustün, T. B. (2002). Understanding cross-national differences in depression prevalence. *Psychological Medicine, 32*(4), 585–594.

Sørensen, M. J., Frydenberg, M., Thastum, M., & Thomsen, P. H. (2005). The Children's Depression Inventory and classification of major depressive disorder: Validation and reliability of the Danish version. *European Child and Adolescent Psychiatry, 14*(6), 328–334.

Spitzer, R. L., Kroenke, K., Williams, J. B., & the Patient Health Questionnaire Primary Care Study Group (1999). Validation and utility of a self-report version of the PRIME-MD: The PHQ primary care study. *JAMA, 282*(18), 1737–1744.

Stallwood, E., Monsour, A., Rodrigues, C., Monga, S., Terwee, C., Offringa, M., & Butcher, N. J. (2021). Systematic review: The measurement properties of the Children's Depression Rating Scale—Revised in adolescents with major depressive disorder. *Journal of the American Academy of Child and Adolescent Psychiatry, 60*(1), 119–133.

Steed, L. (2001). Further validity and reliability evidence for Beck Hopelessness Scale scored in a nonclinical sample. *Educational and Psychological Measurement, 61*(2), 303–316.

Toomey, R. B. (2021). Advancing research on minority stress and resilience in trans children and adolescents in the 21st century. *Child Development Perspectives, 15*(2), 96–102.

Townsend L., Kobak K., Kearney C., Milham M., Andreotti C., Escalera J., et al. (2020). Development of three web-based computerized versions of the Kiddie Schedule for Affective Disorders and Schizophrenia child psychiatric diagnostic interview: Preliminary validity data. *Journal of the American Academy of Child & Adolescent Psychiatry*, 59(2), 309–325.

U.S. Department of Health and Human Services. (2021). *Mental health: Culture, race, and ethnicity—A supplement to mental health* (a report of the Surgeon General). Author.

Van de Velde, S., Bracke, P., & Levecque, K. (2010). Gender differences in depression in 23 European countries. Cross-national variation in the gender gap in depression. *Social Science & Medicine (1982), 71*(2), 305–313.

van Dijk, M. T., Murphy, E., Posner, J. E., Talati, A., & Weissman, M. M. (2021). Association of multigenerational family history of depression with lifetime depressive and other psychiatric disorders in children: Results from the adolescent brain cognitive development (ABCD) study. *JAMA Psychiatry, 78*(7), 778–787.

Van Voorhees, B. W., Paunesku, D., Kuwabara, S. A., Basu, A., Gollan, J., Hankin, B. L., & Reinecke, M. (2008). Protective and vulnerability factors predicting new-onset depressive episode in a representative of U.S. adolescents. *Journal of Adolescent Health, 42*(6), 605–616.

von der Embse, N. P., Scott, E.-C., & Kilgus, S. P. (2015). Sensitivity to change and concurrent validity of direct behavior ratings for academic anxiety. *School Psychology Quarterly: The Official Journal of the Division of School Psychology, American Psychological Association, 30*(2), 244–259.

Weisz, J. R., Vaughn-Coaxum, R. A., Evans, S. C., Thomassin, K., Hersh, J., Ng, M. Y., et al. (2020). Efficient monitoring of treatment response during youth psychotherapy: The behavior and feelings survey. *Journal of Clinical Child and Adolescent Psychology*, 49(6), 737–751.

Zuckerbrot, R. A., Cheung, A., Jensen, P. S., Stein, R. E., Laraque, D., Levitt, A., & GLAD-PC Steering Group. (2018). Guidelines for adolescent depression in primary care (GLAD-PC): Part I. Practice preparation, identification, assessment, and initial management. *Pediatrics, 141*(3), e20174018.

CHAPTER 18

Assessment of Anxiety and Related Disorders

Leandra Parris and Celeste Malone

Despite early descriptions as a disorder of adulthood, anxiety has been found to impact a large proportion of children and adolescents. Prior to 2019, rates of anxiety among children and adolescents ranged from 5% to 17% across the country, with an 8% national average (Bitsko et al., 2022). Prevalence rates doubled during the years of COVID-19, with an estimated 26.5% of youth experiencing symptoms of anxiety during the pandemic. Of note, rates of anxiety for children and adolescents were highest in North America, particularly for children whose schools had closed. Further, while not surprising, rates were significantly higher for high school girls, students who previously struggled academically, youth frequently exposed to pandemic-related media, and those who had conflictual relationships with caregivers (Panchal et al., 2023). Compounding the impact of the global pandemic on anxiety among youth are the inequities in health care and outcomes due to discriminatory systems and structures. For example, racially and ethnically marginalized populations, as well as women and those experiencing economic marginalization, experienced disproportionately higher rates of negative outcomes, such as loss of a loved one, economic hardship, mental health struggles, and hospitalization (Duong et al., 2023). Due to these systemic disparities, one can expect symptoms of anxiety to be greater for children experiencing marginalization.

Although many consider the pandemic over, the process of healing and the long-term impacts of this global tragedy on children's mental health are infinite. Further, other national and local level stressors, such as increased sociopolitical violence, police brutality, and school shootings, continue to add to the worries that children and adolescents experience, worries that can manifest into anxiety-related disorders that, without proper prevention, assessment, and intervention, will undoubtedly impact children's academic performance and well-being. Indeed, children and adolescents experiencing anxiety are more likely to miss school, struggle with academic tasks, engage in disruptive behaviors, and withdraw from their peers (American Psychiatric Association, 2022). Long-term associated outcomes for youth with anxiety disorders include substance abuse, mood disorders, interpersonal dysfunction, and reduced life satisfaction (Essau et al., 2014; Pollard et al., 2023). That said, the manifestation and impact of anxiety can vary based on culture, history, and personal experiences. Other factors, such as genetics and biological determinants, may also contribute. Further complicating the assessment process is that some degree of anxiety is considered normal—even healthy—and the point at which anxiety becomes atypical, or pathological, is not always clear. Possible paths toward pathology are diverse, as are the types of anxiety that may subsequently develop.

Therefore, the assessment of anxiety and related disorders requires a multimethod, multi-informant approach with careful consideration of individual and contextual factors.

Based on the increased understanding of anxiety over the past several years, diagnostic criteria for anxiety disorders were changed in the most recent (fifth edition, text revision) update of the *Diagnostic and Statistical Manual of Mental Disorders* (DSM-5-TR) (American Psychiatric Association, 2022). Most changes in criteria for certain disorders were relatively minor and reflected an increased focus on developmental considerations for symptomology. The most notable change was the distinction of obsessive–compulsive disorders. Previously, obsessive–compulsive disorders were categorized as anxiety-based disorders. Due to the unique presentation of obsessions and compulsive behaviors, these disorders were given a separate classification in DSM-5-TR (American Psychiatric Association, 2022). Despite this distinction, anxiety and obsessive–compulsive disorders are highly related; as such, obsessive–compulsive disorders are also reviewed. Other disorders, particularly those related to stress and trauma responses, are highly comorbid with anxiety disorders and are discussed in other chapters.

In this chapter, we provide a foundation for adopting a socially just, culturally informed approach to assessing anxiety and related disorders in children and youth. We first provide a brief overview of theories of anxiety development in children and adolescents, followed by descriptions of the different anxiety and anxiety-related disorders most salient to youth. The bulk of the chapter will discuss case conceptualization and various assessment techniques for understanding children's experiences with anxiety, with a particular focus on cultural and ecological considerations for both process and interpretation. We end with an eye to the future by outlining areas that warrant further exploration and advocacy.

THEORIES OF ANXIETY

Biological theories of anxiety posit that anxiety is the result of genetic disposition. Twin and family history studies have found that genetics influenced children's vulnerability to anxiety, development of general and separation anxiety, and increased severity of symptoms over time (Beesdo et al., 2009; Waszczuk et al., 2013). That said, no single genetic composition has been identified as resulting in anxious traits or increased risk of anxiety disorders. Similarly, biological factors that were once thought to be clear contributors to anxiety (e.g., sex-based differences due to hormones) are now viewed as less clearly connected. For example, gender differences were found to be limited in early childhood with increased variability between different genders over the lifespan (Beesdo et al., 2009). This suggests that although there may be some biological component related to sex assigned at birth, environmental and social factors related to gender identities may be just as responsible for differences in anxiety disorder experiences. In fact, in most studies, there were environmental variables that were found to be just as, if not more, predictive of anxiety in children than biology (Chen et al., 2015; Smoller, 2016; Waszczuk et al., 2013).

The importance of environment and exposure in the development of anxiety is highlighted in behavioral theories, which include conditioning (classical and operant) and observational learning. The development of anxiety is described as a negative, fear-inducing interaction between the child and the environment that results in a classically conditioned fear response (Beesdo et al., 2009). For example, a child may develop a phobic response to birds after being attacked by a crow. The pain of the attack elicits an unconditioned fearful response that, through association, becomes a conditioned response to crows. This fear response could also generalize to all types of birds. Once the child starts to avoid exposure to birds, they are rewarded by the decrease in anxiety and fear. Through the process of operant conditioning, they continue to avoid not only birds, but places where birds may be present, such as zoos, atriums, and parks.

The process of observational learning has also been demonstrated as a component of anxiety. Research has shown that parent reactions (e.g., facial expressions) to distress play an important role in the development of anxiety in youth (Borelli et al., 2015; Pereira et al., 2014). Using the example of the crow, a child could develop anxiety around birds based on how others respond in the presence of the animal rather than their own interaction and experiences. This is particularly important considering we often downplay the potential impact of events we did not personally witness, despite evidence that fear responses can still develop.

In addition to biological and behavioral theories, the literature has also drawn from cognitive theories to conceptualize anxiety disorders. Cognitive processes shown to impact symptoms of anxiety include involuntary and voluntary attention bias to threats, sensitivity in threat appraisal, cognitive distortions, and increased cognitive vigilance for signs (both internal and external) of fear-inducing stimuli (Beesdo et al., 2009; Pereira et al., 2014). As children interact with the world, they cognitively organize this information to build schemas and expectations. If, in integrating information, a child places too much emphasis on fear-inducing or threatening information, cognitive processes are impacted, and distortions may develop. As children begin to cognitively evaluate and process their environment with greater sensitivity to threat and anxious thought processes, they increase their risk of developing an anxiety disorder (Pereira et al., 2014).

Integrating across multiple theories, Waters and Craske (2016) proposed a cognitive-learning model for conceptualizing anxiety in children. This model includes components of behavioral and cognitive theories, outlining the relations between conditioned or learned fear responses and cognitive processes (e.g., cue appraisal and coping, attention bias). Moderating this relationship are individual characteristics, such as genetic predisposition, temperament, anxious traits, and neurological functioning. The cognitive-learning framework for understanding anxiety in children and adolescents is helpful in guiding assessment. This model illustrates the importance of considering individual (i.e., personality, biology, and cognition) and environmental (e.g., external cues, exposure, and others' behaviors) characteristics, and the interaction of these factors, when assessing anxiety in children.

ANXIETY AND RELATED DISORDERS

Despite being one of the most common psychological ailments experienced by youth (Beesdo et al., 2009), anxiety disorders can be easily overlooked due to their internalized nature. Teachers do not typically identify or refer children with anxiety until their symptoms impact learning, there are substantial behavior changes, or the presence of externalizing behaviors is unresponsive to intervention (Henchliffe & Campbell, 2016). Because cognitive processes and some psychosomatic responses (e.g., increased heart rate and difficulty breathing) may not be readily apparent, these hallmark indicators of anxiety can be easily missed by others. Covert symptoms, such as avoidant or noncompliant behaviors, are more likely to be the source of initial identification and referral for evaluation. Finally, all anxiety disorders share some common characteristics, such as avoidant behavior, extreme and persistent fear, and disproportionate worry (American Psychiatric Association, 2022). Differential diagnoses require the clinician to examine the focus and context of the child's fears and worries. The following sections provide a brief overview of different anxiety-related diagnoses, along with cultural and ecological considerations when available in the literature.

Separation Anxiety Disorder

Separation anxiety disorder (SAD) is characterized by an excessive fear of separation from attachment figures such as parents, caregivers, and siblings. Individuals often limit independent activities away from home or attachment figures (e.g., school, overnight camp, and sleeping alone). The general symptoms associated with anxiety (e.g., persistent worry and somatic complaints) are present with SAD; however, SAD is distinguished from other anxiety disorders in that these symptoms emerge due to separation, or the possibility of separation, from attachment figures. SAD may develop following loss, such as the death of a pet, parental divorce or separation, transition to a new neighborhood, or natural disaster that involved separation from loved ones. Youth with SAD are often described as overly dependent and in need of constant attention because of their reluctance to be separated from attachment figures. They also display persistent worry that something bad will happen to either themselves or their loved one(s) should they be separated or that some danger will force their separation. They may withdraw from others, become inattentive, cry when separated from their caregiver, refuse to go to school or leave certain spaces, and/or have repeated nightmares focused on being separated. This fear of separation must be present for at least 4 weeks and cause significant distress or lead to functional impairment. Onset of SAD typically occurs in early childhood, and its prevalence, roughly 2–4% (American Psychiatric Association, 2022), decreases across the lifespan.

There is limited information regarding potential prevalence differences in separation anxiety among youth. Although it has been more frequently diagnosed in girls (Shear et al., 2006), it is unclear if that is a true difference or a difference in how behaviors are interpreted and subsequently labeled (e.g., upset vs. oppositional). Differences in how we interpret behaviors based on the identities of the child are concerns that must be addressed as early as pre-referral. Understanding implicit biases that exist, such as interpreting the behaviors of boys and children of color to be aggressive or defiant when those same behaviors are interpreted as less severe or unintentional for other children, is crucial to the accurate assessment of separation anxiety. We must also consider whether the school is truly a safe space. Is the child afraid to separate from their caregiver, or are they afraid to be in this space? It is also important to rule out trauma- and stress-related disorders, as symptoms are similar, but the etiology and potential for intervention are different. As part of the assessment process, we must critically examine the degree to which implicit bias, lack of environmental safety, and stress exposure may be impacting the child's symptomology.

Finally, it is important to note that cultural differences exist in terms of what, when, and to what degree familial separations occur and whether such separations are considered common or something to be actively avoided (American Psychiatric Association, 2022). There can be differences in the impact of separation on the child based on familial and cultural expectations, as well as differences in what are acceptable ways to address the child's anxiety. For example, Asian parents perceived their child's separation anxiety to be similar to that of White parents; however, Asian parents were far less likely to ask for help in addressing the symptoms (Nguyen & McAloon, 2018). If involvement from others is not an expectation or wanted when addressing separation concerns, it may require adjustments to how assessment and intervention occur to ensure alignment and collaboration. Far more important than determining if the child's behaviors meet a checklist of criteria is the need to critically examine the purpose of the behaviors, reasons for wanting to avoid separation, the potential influence of bias in assessing behaviors, and impact of cultural values and expectations regarding separation from caregivers.

Selective Mutism

Selective mutism is a rare disorder, with reported prevalence rates below 2% in school-age children (American Psychiatric Association, 2022). Selective mutism primarily occurs in children, with an onset prior to the age of 5 years. Children with selective mutism refrain from speaking in certain social situations despite demonstrating adequate skill in, and comfort with, speaking in other environments. Additional criteria include a detrimental impact on social or achievement performance and symptoms that last for more than 1 month. When assessing a child for selective mutism, it is important to rule out other possible diagnoses, such as social anxiety, communication, autism spectrum, and psychotic disorders (American Psychiatric Association, 2022). Functions of associated behaviors may include anxiety over public speaking, an oppositional attitude toward a particular social situation, and lack of confidence in social or language skills. When assessing, it's important to note that, unlike social anxiety, selective mutism is often context-specific or limited in its scope. Selective mutism can result in decreased performance at school and increased social stress, particularly if a child is not asking for help meeting their needs (e.g., requesting to see the nurse when in pain) or engaging in required academic tasks (e.g., presenting projects). Whereas younger children are more likely to receive this diagnosis, there have been no differences found based on gender or ethnicity (American Psychiatric Association, 2022). However, consideration of multilingual students must be made in terms of confidence and ease of speech and language that may influence when children are comfortable talking. Further, because selective mutism can be interpreted as oppositional, assessment practices should consider selective mutism rather than assuming behaviors are intentionally aggressive or noncompliant.

Specific Phobia

The diagnosis of specific phobia is predicated on a child having an intense fear response to one or more specific objects or situations and is experienced by roughly 3–16% of children and adolescents (American Psychiatric Association, 2022). Potential targets of the phobia are categorized as animal, natural environment (e.g., storms), blood–injection–injury, situational (e.g., enclosed spaces), and other (e.g., costumed characters). In children, this fear response can include clinging to others, crying, refusing to move, and having a tantrum. A diagnosis of specific phobia requires that the child almost always has an anxious response to the stimulus that is disproportionate to the actual threat posed by the object or situation (American Psychiatric Association, 2022). That is, a child who is afraid of a live snake in the wild is considered typical. Yet if a child has the same level of fear response to a snake toy in the safety of their home, they may have a specific phobia (i.e., ophidiophobia). Further, avoidant behaviors and extreme distress or impairment in functioning must be present, such as refusing to enter the classroom because of a picture of a snake on the wall. These fears and behaviors must be persistent, and DSM-5-TR gives a typical timeframe of 6 months. Rule out diagnoses for this disorder include agoraphobia, obsessive–compulsive, stress-related, separation anxiety, and social anxiety disorders. Specific phobias are more common among younger children and, except for blood–injection–injury phobias, girls (American Psychiatric Association, 2022). Further, identifying as Asian or Latinx is associated with decreased frequency of being diagnosed with this disorder (American Psychiatric Association, 2022). Whether these lower rates are due to actual prevalence within these cultures, or due to children in these populations receiving a different diagnosis for the same behaviors, is unclear.

Social Anxiety Disorder

Also called social phobia, social anxiety disorders manifest as a disproportionate fear of social situations that involve the child being the focus of others. The child's fear of rejection and/or humiliation resulting from being evaluated by others causes anxious symptoms (American Psychiatric Association, 2022). In children, these symptoms can be exhibited through tantrums, crying, clinging to others, refusing to speak, and avoidance. Further, to meet diagnostic criteria, children must display these symptoms in the presence of their peers, not just adults. The occurrence of these symptoms should be persistent (DSM-5-TR suggests 6 months) and not attributable to other disorders or medical conditions. If the child is only anxious when speaking or performing in public, the specifier "performance only" can be added to the diagnosis.

Given that this disorder is focused on perceived social pressures or evaluation, it is important to consider the various ways in which culture can inform expectations of social interactions. For instance, individualistic cultures may find withdrawn behavior and more quiet demeanors to be atypical or contrary to social norms, while collectivist cultures may feel those behaviors are to be expected and are quite normal. Brockveld and colleagues (2014) offer helpful guidance on this topic. For example, by withdrawing or holding back, some children may be seeking to maintain balance or group harmony rather than being anxious or stressed about social interactions. Another important consideration is how the child views themselves in terms of their association with others or their self-construal. Children who view themselves as an independent self would put more focus on expressing their inner thoughts and working toward their own wants and needs. In contrast, children with a more interdependent view of self would focus more on regulating themselves and shift to meet the needs of the context they are in and who they are around. Children with an interdependent self are more likely to look for cues from others and be more sensitive to how others see them, which can increase their risk of developing social anxiety. As such, it is important that we consider the cultural values as well as the child's unique view of who they are to understand how and why they may experience social anxiety. Understanding these contexts will help not only provide a more accurate diagnosis, but also better inform next steps.

Panic Disorder

Panic disorder is rare in children but becomes more frequent in adolescence. Youth who have a panic disorder experience sudden, unpredictable increases in fear to the point that they exhibit symptoms such as increased heart rate, shaking, sweating, dizziness, chills, numbness, and chest or stomach pain. In addition to these physical sensations, the child may also feel out of touch with reality or fear losing control and/or dying. It should be noted that these symptoms should not be included in the diagnosis if they are culturally normative. For example, a teacher once referred a student to one of us for hallucinations and seeming out of touch with reality. Observations indicated the child was talking to someone who was not there but otherwise was not disruptive. When talking to the caregivers to get more information, it was revealed that the child's grandmother had recently died and that, in their culture, it was quite common to have conversations with a recently deceased. In this situation, seeming out of touch with reality would be a matter of perception and interpretation, not a diagnostic event. Moreover, the symptoms that were concerning to the teacher were not causing distress or impairment to the child or their family, further validating the culturally informed hypothesis of normative behavior instead of pathology.

Following a panic attack, youth with a panic disorder will consistently fret over having another attack and will engage in avoidance behavior to decrease the risk of a repeat incident. As with other disorders, these attacks and fears meet the criteria for panic disorder only if not better explained by another disorder or medical condition and if they cause significant impairment in the child's functioning. Girls and Native Americans have been found to be at increased risk for panic disorders when compared to boys and other ethnic groups (American Psychiatric Association, 2022). Should a child not meet the diagnostic criteria for a panic disorder but experience a panic attack in conjunction with another disorder or medical condition, a panic attack specifier can be added to the diagnosis.

Generalized Anxiety Disorder

Generalized anxiety disorder (GAD) includes the core criteria of all anxiety disorders (e.g., persistent, causes distress, not due to other conditions, and includes excessive fear or worry). However, youth with GAD find it hard to control their anxiety regarding numerous aspects of their life as opposed to specific situations or stimuli. Children receiving this diagnosis must exhibit one of six symptoms: restlessness, easily tired, difficulty concentrating, irritability, muscle tension, or disturbances in sleep. This disorder is more common in adults but does occur among youth. Research has reported that girls experience GAD more frequently (American Psychiatric Association, 2022). Further, individuals from European cultures or developed countries are at greater risk for GAD (American Psychiatric Association, 2022). Many of the considerations previously noted regarding cultural and ecological differences would be beneficial in addressing GAD as well.

Additional Anxiety Disorders

There are several more anxiety disorders that are less common, but still occur, among children and adolescents. Some have similar criteria as other anxiety disorders, but with specific contributing variables such as substance/medication-induced anxiety disorders (e.g., anxiety following drug use) or anxiety disorder due to another medical condition (e.g., experiencing panic after a medical diagnosis). Agoraphobia is another anxiety-related disorder that may occur in children and is marked by a fear of using public transportation, being in open spaces, being in closed spaces, standing in line/being in a crowd, and/or being outside of the home alone. These fears may focus on perceived threat in that situation (e.g., plane crashing), the inability to escape (e.g., being trapped in an elevator), or the risk of symptoms causing them embarrassment.

A diagnosis of other specified anxiety disorder can be used in situations where a child does not fully meet the criteria for other anxiety disorders, but their symptoms have a significant negative impact on their functioning. This diagnosis can also be used when a child describes culturally specific symptoms (e.g., wind attacks or attack of the nerves; Hofmann & Hinton, 2014) that indicate distress but may not be captured by the current DSM-5-TR descriptions of symptoms. Finally, a diagnosis of unspecified anxiety disorder may be used if an individual has symptoms characteristic of an anxiety disorder but does not meet full criteria for any of the disorders and the clinician chooses not to specify why criteria are not met for a specific disorder or there is insufficient information to make a diagnosis (American Psychiatric Association, 2022). Outside of DSM-5-TR diagnoses, in schools, we often see other forms of anxiety-related struggles, such as test anxiety, that should be considered.

Obsessive–Compulsive Disorders

Obsessive–compulsive disorders are not categorized as anxiety disorders; however, because they include an aspect of worry and the avoidance of anxious symptoms, they are considered closely related disorders (American Psychiatric Association, 2022). Obsessive–compulsive disorder (OCD) requires the presence of obsessions (e.g., persistent, intrusive thoughts) and/or compulsions (e.g., repetitive physical or cognitive behaviors). Children with OCD actively try to disengage from their obsessions to negate the subsequent distress. When those efforts lead to ritualistic compulsions that must be adhered with extreme fidelity, it can cause disruptions in their ability to function. In children, the rationale behind compulsive behaviors can be hard to articulate. Because obsessive thoughts and any compulsive behaviors to avoid them can be very time-consuming, children with OCD may find it hard to complete tasks at school and home in a timely manner. The degree to which a person understands the obsessions and compulsions to be irrational can vary; therefore, the appropriate specifier (i.e., with good/fair, poor, or absent insight) should be included with the diagnosis. In children, OCD is more common among boys than girls; however, this trend reverses over time. Although OCD has been found to be stable across cultures, the specific compulsive behaviors may be influenced by cultural dimensions, such as religion, perceptions of stress, and disparities in health care access and treatment (Nicolini et al., 2017). Additional diagnoses in this category include body dysmorphic disorder, hoarding disorder, trichotillomania (hair pulling), and excoriation disorder (skin picking). Trichotillomania has been observed in children, while body dysmorphic and excoriation disorder most commonly begin in adolescence. Hoarding behaviors have not been consistently observed among youth.

CULTURALLY INFORMED, SOCIALLY JUST ASSESSMENT OF ANXIETY

Ecological Approach

The beginning of the assessment process is case conceptualization, which is vulnerable to not only being underdeveloped but can also be biased and create disparities throughout the assessment process. Therefore, several considerations should be made in our approach to assessing anxiety. First, we must take an ecological approach to understanding the child's presenting concerns. We must consider questions such as:

- How are decisions being made about the child, and in what context? How do those decisions impact their behavior and perceptions of their worries? (i.e., procedural justice; Malone & Proctor, 2019).
- What access does the child have within their environment to address their worries? What resources are (or are not) provided to address challenges they are facing? (i.e., distributive justice; Malone & Proctor, 2019).
- How do others treat the child? Do they validate their worries or dismiss them, which could subsequently make them worse? How do others perceive their behaviors compared to those same behaviors in other students? (i.e., relational justice, Malone & Proctor, 2019).
- What systems are in place to support the child? What systemic barriers exist that may contribute to the child's presenting concerns?
- What biases about the child might I hold? What assumptions am I making about them, their families, and their experiences? What assumptions do I hold about anxiety (i.e., critical reflection)?

Considering the various ecological levels and their interactions, as well as an evaluation of a clinician's own perceptions prior to assessment, will help ensure that the presenting concerns are assessed with an open and curious approach that is client-driven. Throughout case conceptualization, dimensions of the child's culture and ecological context should be included to provide context and understanding of what their anxious or compulsive behaviors may be communicating to us. It is important that we explore the various cultural manifestations of anxiety and how they may be described by the child and their family, as outlined by Hofmann and Hinton (2014). Further, we must always take a strengths-based approach when conceptualizing a case. For example, what is going well with the child? What does the adolescent have available to them? Anxiety can make individuals forget that they are capable and competent individuals, and a strengths-based approach is not only best practice but can also be a form of intervention itself.

Interviews

Best practice for assessing the functioning of a child suggests that an interview with key collaborators (e.g., parents, teachers, and child) take place first. However, interviewing can also be seen as a recursive process that may be repeated throughout the assessment process as new information is gathered and requires clarification or follow-up. The initial interview can be used to identify behaviors of concern, including the possible function, duration, latency, and frequency of anxiety-related symptoms. A functional behavior assessment interview (Frick et al., 2009) with parents, teachers, and even the child can provide a wealth of information for informing next steps and initial data regarding the child's anxious behaviors.

Other interviewing methods include structured or semistructured formats that may use a particular protocol or series of questions to assess anxious behaviors, contributing factors (e.g., environment and demands), related history (e.g., traumatic event), and previous treatments or interventions that have been used and their effectiveness (Frick et al., 2009). There are some well-established diagnostic interviews (see Table 18.1); however, overreliance on these diagnostic interviews may lead the clinician to primarily focus on diagnostic criteria without greater consideration of subclinical symp-

TABLE 18.1. Example Instrumentation for the Assessment of Anxiety in Children and Youth

Instrument	Age range	Relevant subscales/areas	Reporters	Estimated time to complete	Available languages	Additional considerations
Diagnostic Interview for Anxiety, Mood, and OCD and Related Neuropsychiatric Disorders—Child and Adolescent Version (DIAMOND-KID) (Tolin et al., 2023)	6–17 years	Anxiety OCD Trauma- and stress-related	Child Adolescent	Varies	English	Test–retest range from very good to excellent Adequate construct validity Limited available data with diverse populations Adaptations for development, language, and culture recommended
Behavior Assessment System for Children—Third Edition (BASC-3) (Reynolds & Kamphaus, 2015)	2–21 years	Anxiety Test Anxiety	Teacher Parent Child Adolescent	10–20 minutes (Teacher and Parent) 30 minutes (Self-Report)	English Spanish	Broad measure Strong validity and reliability in national sample Mixed evidence of validity with certain student populations
Revised Children's Manifest Anxiety Scales, 2nd Edition (RCMAS-2) (Reynolds & Richmond, 2008)	6–19	Total Anxiety Physiological Worry Social Anxiety Defensiveness Inconsistency	Child Adolescent	10–15 minutes	English Italian Spanish	Short Form available Adequate to excellent validity and reliability Nationally normed with ethnically diverse population
State–Trait Anxiety Inventory for Children (STAI-CH) (Spielberger et al., 1983)	Not given, reading level is fourth grade but can be read to younger children	State Trait	Child Adolescent	20 minutes	Multiple	Quality of language translations not guaranteed by publisher Good to excellent reliability and validity

(continued)

TABLE 18.1. *(continued)*

Instrument	Age range	Relevant subscales/areas	Reporters	Estimated time to complete	Available languages	Additional considerations
Screen for Children's Anxiety Related Disorders (SCARED) (Birmaher et al., 1997)	8–18 years	Generalized Anxiety Separation Anxiety Social Anxiety Panic/Somatic School Avoidance	Parent Child Adolescent	10 minutes	Arabic Chinese English French German Italian Portuguese Spanish Thai	Good to excellent reliability and validity Normed with national sample that is ethnically diverse
Multidimensional Anxiety Scale for Children, 2nd Edition (MASC-2) (March, 2013)	8–19 years	Separation Anxiety/Phobias Social Anxiety Obsessions and Compulsions Physical Symptoms Harm Avoidance Generalized Anxiety Disorder Inconsistency	Parent Child Adolescent	15 minutes	English Italian Spanish	Nationally normed with ethnically diverse sample Good to excellent reliability and validity
Test Anxiety Inventory for Children and Adolescents (TAICA) (Lowe et al., 2008)	Elementary and secondary school ages	Total Anxiety Cognitive Obstruction/Inattention Physiological Hyperarousal Social Humiliation Worry Facilitation Anxiety Lie scale	Child Adolescent	Unknown	English	Norming sample demographics unavailable Per authors, reliability and validity are good to strong
Social Phobia and Anxiety Inventory (SPAI, SPAI-C) (Beidel et al., 1996)	8–14 years (SPAI-C) 14 years and older (SPAI)	SPAI-C: Frequency Range of situations SPAI: Social Phobia Agoraphobia	Child Adolescent	Unknown	English German Portuguese	SPAI-C has good to excellent reliability and validity Limited information available for diverse populations

Social Anxiety Scale for Children, Revised and Adolescents (SASC-R, SAS-A) (La Greca & Stone, 1993; 1998)	SASC-R: 6–11 years SAS-A: 9–18 years	SASC-R: Fear of Negative Evaluation Social Avoidance and Distress—Specific to New Situations Social Avoidance and Distress—General	Child Adolescent	Unknown	English	Adequate to excellent reliability and validity Limited information available for diverse populations, with some evidence of reliability among children with autism spectrum disorder (Schiltz et al., 2021)
Children's Yale–Brown Obsessive Compulsive Scale, 2nd Edition (CY-BOCS-II) (Storch et al., 2019)	6–17 years	Obsession Severity Compulsion Severity Total Severity	Child Adolescent	15–25 minutes	English Italian Thai Chinese Portuguese	Per authors, excellent reliability and strong validity Limited information available for diverse populations
Fear Survey Schedule for Children—Revised (FSSC-R) (Ollendick, 1983)	7–17 years	Failure and Criticism The Unknown Minor Injury and Small Animals Danger and Death Medical Fears	Child Adolescent	Unknown	English Italian Spanish	Adequate to excellent reliability and validity Normed samples from multiple countries

Note. Ratings of reliability and validity from Etkin et al. (2021) unless otherwise noted.

toms, the way these symptoms impact the child's functioning, and any pattern of symptoms (Meyer et al., 2001). For example, a clinician may overfocus on the presence of phobic reactions without considering the child's history of exposure, cultural interpretations of worries, and whether such worries impact all settings or only certain contexts (e.g., school vs. home). Professionals will want to tailor their anxiety-related interview questions based on information gleaned during the initial referral and hypotheses, such as focusing on difficulties separating from whom and when versus examining broader anxieties about infrequent situations, as well as their families' conceptualization of anxiety and its impact on well-being. Further, multiple interviews may be required throughout the assessment process should new information become available (e.g., critical items endorsed).

In addition to obtaining descriptive information regarding a child's anxious systems, interviews provide an opportunity to gather qualitative information about the child's functioning related to their symptoms. Information such as how severe the child perceives their fears and worries, their worldview, family functioning and core values, and interpersonal dynamics can be hard to assess using other measures. Such information can be used to put quantitative results in context and facilitate the development of culturally appropriate recommendations that are not redundant with previous efforts. Further, we recommend using interview protocols that are specifically designed to integrate the identity of the child and other cultural considerations. For example, the use of the Cultural Formulation Interview is effective in increasing engagement with therapy, particularly when provided in the families' native language (Sanchez et al., 2022). This highlights the importance of integrating cultural and ecological considerations across each phase of the assessment of anxiety.

Observations

Typically, behavioral observations take place following interviews so that target behaviors are defined and clarified from the referral. However, there are times when interviews are not possible or available within the time constraints of the assessment process. In situations where the referral question is unclear or vague in terms of anxious behaviors, the use of a general observation system, such as the Behavior Assessment System for Children Student Observation System (BASC SOS) (Reynolds & Kamphaus, 2016), may be useful in identifying the most disruptive behaviors, such as excessive movement and inattention. The BASC SOS also includes a section for qualitative information to help differentiate anxiety symptoms from other disorders that may present in similar ways, such as ADHD. Targeted forms that focus on specific, operationally defined anxious symptoms (e.g., crying, shaking, and chewing nails) can also be used. The clinician should consider the frequency and duration of behaviors when choosing to use partial- or whole-interval sample or momentary time sample. Further, peer comparisons can help differentiate the degree to which anxious symptoms are a manifestation of the classroom or less/more frequent than peers. In addition to general observation systems, clinicians may also use behavioral avoidance tests to assess specific phobias and other anxiety disorders with high levels of avoidance and other observable behaviors (e.g., obsessive–compulsive disorder) to collect objective information about how the child responds to an anxiety-provoking stimulus (Vasey & Lonigan, 2000).

Internalizing behaviors that are often associated with anxiety are often not easily observed or measurable (Frick et al., 2009). Rumination, cognitive distortion, increased heart rate, and other internal signs of anxiety-based distress are not easily detectable by others. This makes the use of behavioral observations difficult when assessing anxiety in children. Fortunately, behavior recording systems are available to help overcome this barrier. Self-monitoring worksheets can be provided to the child if they are mature enough to complete them independently. These worksheets require the child to record antecedent, behavior, and consequence information for incidents that caused them anxiety. Duration, latency, and other details can be included if the child is within the appropriate developmental stage, typically older adolescents. Worksheets completed by the child or adults in their life between assessment sessions can provide information regarding internal functioning or less frequent behaviors that do not typically occur within the time frame of a behavioral observation.

Rating Scales

The most common form of assessment for anxiety is the use of rating scales. Rating scales ask parents, teachers, or the child to indicate the degree to which behaviors, thoughts, and feelings related to anxiety occur. Summative ratings are then compared to the general population to demonstrate whether the child's behaviors exceed what would be expected given their age and sometimes gender (Frick et al., 2009). It is important to note that while rating scales are, for the most part, psychometrically sound, scores are still based on subjective ratings of a person. Excessive negativity, social desirability, anxious tendencies in the rater, and difficulty identifying anxious symptoms can influence scores and subsequent interpretations (Frick et al., 2009). Clinicians must use additional information obtained through the assessment process (e.g., validity checks) to provide context to the ratings, integrate divergent reports, and make clinical judgements regarding the nature of the child's anxiety. It is also important to consider how experiences of anxiety themselves may influence the child's completion of self-report scales, causing them to over- or underidentify symptoms, particularly given they are being evaluated, which can heighten feelings of anxiety.

Further, the degree to which rating scales were normed using diverse populations is a concern that cannot be understated. Whereas larger, omnibus scales have more diverse norming samples (e.g., BASC-3; Kamphaus & Reynolds, 2015), some of the narrowband measures are not as widely used and may not be valid for all cultures. Some have shown promise, such as the Multidimensional Anxiety Scale for Children, 2nd edition (March, 2013) and the Revised Children's Manifest Anxiety Scale (Varela et al., 2008). Another consideration is the way in which ratings scales are scored. Several rating scales for anxiety allow the clinician to indicate the gender of the client. While this is useful in addressing issues of over- and underdiagnosis of anxiety among boys and girls, to date, very few, if any, rating scales allow for the comparison of nonbinary or transgender students. Although scales, such as the BASC-3, can provide a general combined score that does not consider gender, this still does not completely address the disparity. Norms developed on gender in terms of sex assigned at birth do not take into consideration the variations and population differences that exist for nonbinary and transgender students. Similarly, rating scales do not typically provide normed data based on other identities, such as trauma history, economic marginalization, and disability, which can influence the expression and frequency of anxiety. It is important that when using rating scale data, clinicians take into consideration the various factors—cultural, ecological, and subjective perceptions of raters—that the scale cannot do on its own. A score report cannot tell you how a child's experiences and identities influence their feelings of anxiety, only if their ratings are above or below what would be considered statistically average.

Performance-Based and Sociometric Tools

Another set of tools for assessing anxiety in children includes performance-based and sociometric assessment measures. Performance-based and sociometric measures cannot be used as standalone indicators of anxiety and are typically considered supplemental, qualitative information to help illustrate or further support other findings (Whitcomb & Merrell, 2013). At the same time, information obtained from these techniques can be used to provide insight into general adjustment and help build rapport; these techniques have not been found to be effective tools in identifying or differentiating symptoms of anxiety in children (Lack & Thomason, 2013).

Sociometric techniques, such as peer or teacher nomination, can provide information regarding the child's social status and behaviors as observed by their peers. However, like behavioral observations, internal processes associated with anxiety are not observable, and external behaviors may be unnoticed or attributed to other causes. Given the amount of time, resources, personnel, and general difficulties related to asking students to discuss their peers, sociometrics are not likely to be used to assess anxiety of an individual child.

In contrast, research has demonstrated that performance-based techniques may be beneficial in eliciting information about a child's internal functioning, perceptions of their environment, and their relationships with others (Whitcomb & Merrell, 2013). Performance-based techniques used with children include storytelling, sentence completion, and drawings, which may provide evidence of anxiety in terms of how the child describes social situations, themes in how they finish stories or sentences, or characteristics of drawings such as excessive shading (Whitcomb & Merrell, 2013). Most performance-based techniques include a set of prompts that are necessary for contextualizing children's performance and clarifying the child's experiences with symptoms of anxiety. However, as previously noted, the use of performance-based and sociometric assessments is controversial, as evidence shows that rarely do they fit within the scope of school-based evaluation and are often not used in standardized ways (Hojnoski et al., 2006).

Linking Data to Intervention

The primary purpose of assessing anxiety is to determine the most appropriate path toward intervention. Linking comprehensive assessment data to holistic intervention approaches requires an understanding of the physiological, cognitive, social, and cultural variables that shape the way in which anxiety has manifested for the child. Failure to obtain a thorough assessment of these factors may lead to ineffective intervention, which is incomplete at best and harmful at worst. For instance, failing to recognize the cultural significance of quiet and withdrawn behavior may lead to interventions that require a child to do things that not only violate their comfort but their cultural expectations as well. When linking assessment data to next steps, we must carry forward our emphasis on culturally responsive and socially just services by considering questions such as:

- What decisions will these data be used to make, and how might that influence available intervention resources?
- What strengths does the child and/or their family have that interventions can expand on or draw from?
- What are the types of access the child and their family need to support or implement recommendations for intervention? What barriers need to be addressed, and if they cannot be addressed, how does this change potential recommendations?
- What are appropriate targets for success based on the data? How confident are the child and key partners that these targets can be met within a reasonable time frame?

By intentionally reflecting on how the data informs our next steps, rather than simply indicating whether a child has a disorder or not, clinicians are better equipped to provide appropriate services that are culturally responsive and strengths-based as well as sustainable within systems of service.

CASE EXAMPLE

AJ is an 8-year-old, cisgender Mexican American Hispanic boy who is in third grade at Sunnydale Elementary, home of the Wildcats. He was referred for concerns regarding school refusal and decreased performance in school. AJ cries, throws tantrums, and refuses to enter the school. When AJ can be convinced to stay at school, he is inattentive, described as noncompliant by teachers, and does not complete tasks. He was referred for evaluation to determine how best to support his family in increasing his school attendance as well as his school performance. At this point, clinicians are encouraged to reflect and ask questions such as:

1. What assumptions are being made about the noncompliant and school refusal behaviors?
2. What assumptions or perceptions might others have within this situation?
3. What do we know about school refusal and noncompliance among Latino boys within this developmental period? What do we not know and must assess?

To begin the assessment, a record review and classroom observation are conducted. The record review indicated that attendance was historically consistent and then suddenly drops off 2 months prior, coinciding with a tornado that impacted the community. The same pattern was noted for academics, with high levels of performance up until 2 months ago. Disciplinary action for noncompliance and aggression (i.e., tantrums) increased during that same 2-month period. Observational data indicated AJ was off-task 87% of the time during classroom lessons, compared to a peer composite average of 46%. Off-task behaviors included staring at the window, getting up to get closer to a clock to check the time, and asking peers about the weather forecast that day. Teacher reactions to AJ's behaviors were redirections, followed by a raised voice and finally asking AJ to complete his work in the hallway. Guiding questions at this point may include:

1. What impact did the tornado have on AJ's families and local community?
2. Given AJ's strength in academic performance, what is currently causing the lower performance indicators (e.g., missed assignments or low test grades)?
3. Given AJ's behaviors during the observation, is the environment contributing to or alleviating symptoms?

Interviews with AJ's parents indicate that Spanish is the primary language of the family, though everyone speaks fluent English. AJ is an only child, and his parents divorced when he was 4 years old, though they remain amicable. AJ's father lives alone with the family cat, while AJ's mother lives with her mother and grandmother. During the tornado, AJ was with his father, who put him in a safe enclosed space with the cat. The cat attacked AJ during the tornado, and AJ has refused to be around the cat since, which means he no longer stays with his father. AJ will scream and cry when around cats or when seeing cats (including the Wildcat mascot of the school) and will run away if he thinks a cat is nearby. The tornado damaged AJ's mother's house. Although no one was injured, AJ's grandmother and great-grandmother are currently staying with relatives, and AJ and his mom are renting an apartment while waiting on their house to be fixed.

Interviews with the primary teacher indicated she is growing increasingly frustrated with AJ. While understanding at first, she notes that other children have moved on from the tornado. She has started to refer AJ for disciplinary action with the principal for his noncompliant behaviors and tantrums because she "does not know what else to do." AJ's work is exemplary when it is complete, but he often does not finish or misses assignments all together. Previous interventions to try to support AJ included allowing his mom to bring him directly to the classroom and for him to spend the first 20 minutes of the day playing games and talking with the school counselor. These were unsuccessful and, at times, made his behaviors worse. Following interviews with the adults in AJ's life, some guiding questions might include:

1. To what degree does the presence of the Wildcat mascot of the school impact AJ's willingness to attend school?
2. How does AJ perceive the interventions and supports given by others in his life?
3. How does the impact of the tornado influence AJ's behaviors?

At this point, the clinician is likely considering traumatic stress reactions, specific phobia of cats, and separation anxiety as potential classifications for AJ. Given that inattentive behaviors are new, we can likely rule out ADHD, yet a rating scale can help verify this hypothesis. Yet much of what needs to be differentiated between the potential diagnoses can be completed by conducting an interview with AJ. During a child interview, AJ indicates that while the Wildcat mascot is frightening, he can avoid paintings of it by taking certain hallways and staying in certain rooms at school. He remains adamant that he avoids cats and anything like them. He reports feeling bad avoiding his dad and refusing to see him but that he does not feel he can help himself.

AJ indicates that his primary reason for not wanting to go to school is that he is afraid to leave his mom alone because of the tornado. He believes that if he is not with his mom, something bad will happen to her, like "last time when the tornado hit." He also indicates he misses his grandmother and great-grandmother and worries that his mom is alone when he is not there. During the school day, he finds it hard to concentrate and is constantly monitoring the weather. He reports enjoying school, but it seems less important after the tornado. As for his noncompliant behaviors, he indicates he knows his teachers are upset with him, but he's too afraid and too distracted to really do schoolwork, and sometimes, he doesn't hear them when they ask him to do things. There are moments he feels too scared and must "let it out," which leads to tantrums and crying. When asked about the tornado directly, he says he does not think about it constantly but does worry about whether his mom will be hurt in another one. Some guiding questions as we continue:

1. Are AJ's symptoms and behaviors occurring more frequently when compared to a normative sample?
2. How can we differentiate between separation anxiety and traumatic stress-related disorders given AJ's experiences?

Rating scales were completed by AJ's teacher, both of his caregivers (in Spanish, per their preference), and by AJ (in Spanish, per his preference). The BASC-3 was given as it was standard procedures within the school district and would provide adaptive information along with information about ADHD and anxiety-related information. Given AJ's identity as Hispanic, as well as his younger age, he was also given the Fear Survey Schedule for Children—Revised (FSSC-R) (Ollendick, 1983) to assess his potential specific phobia, as well as the Multidimensional Anxiety Scale for Children, 2nd edition (MASC-2) (March, 2013) to assess separation and general anxiety. Both scales have been shown to be valid and reliable for younger, Hispanic populations and available in Spanish, as well as accurate in identifying specific anxiety-related disorders (Etkin et al., 2021; Varela et al., 2008).

Teacher ratings had a flagged validity index, suggesting that her ratings of AJ were perhaps excessively negative of AJ. As such, the clinically significant scores regarding conduct, externalizing, and school problems must be approached with caution. These findings suggest that AJ's fear-based responses were disruptive to the classroom and teacher and were being interpreted as a problem behavior rather than a stress response. Parent ratings were quite similar to one another, with levels of anxiety being high, with some adaptive scores related to independence being lower than average.

AJ's BASC-3 ratings were clinically significant for anxiety, relationships with parents, and attitude to teachers (but not school). AJ's ratings on the FSSC-R were clinically significant for fears regarding Minor Injury and Small Animals but were average in all other areas. It might be surprising that AJ did not score higher on Danger and Death, but it should be noted the FSSC-R focuses on danger and death to self while AJ's fears around danger and injury focus on his mom. AJ's ratings on the MASC-2 were average for all subscales except Separation Anxiety/Phobia, which was significantly elevated.

Taken together, a full case conceptualization of AJ's current functioning can be created (see Table 18.2). Clearly, AJ misses the presence of his extended family and feels their absence increases the risk of harm for his mother. His separation anxiety and focus on his mom's safety are impacting his ability to attend and perform at school. Further, while his phobic response to cats is not impacting him at school—despite the mascot being a Wildcat—it is having a negative impact on his relationship with his father and should be addressed. Traumatic stress-related disorders can be ruled out, as he is not having intrusive thoughts or other traumatic stress-related symptoms (e.g., startle reflexes and avoidant behaviors related to the traumatic event). ADHD and conduct problems can also be ruled out, as only one informant noted those concerns, and rating scale information indicated those ratings were skewed.

In summary, AJ is experiencing separation anxiety following exposure to a tornado, as well as a phobia of cats triggered by his experience with his family cat during the tornado. Developmental considerations suggest that separation anxiety is not a common experience for his age and thus more representative of an atypical response. Cultural considerations were made throughout the assessment process and should be used to develop a plan for intervention and supports (e.g., arranging ways for the extended family to spend more time with AJ and his mom and connecting AJ's family with a Spanish-speaking counselor or therapist to address specific phobias). Ecologically, it will be important to work with AJ's teacher to address the overdiscipline of AJ and her negatively skewed view of his behaviors, which are not intentionally noncompliant or aggression, but rather a symptom of anxiety.

FUTURE DIRECTIONS

Moving forward, there remains much we do not know about the manifestation of anxiety based on cultural factors. For example, there are several constructs across other cultures (see Hofmann & Hinton, 2014) that are related to anxiety. As we are starting to integrate these conceptualizations of anxiety with best practices, we must move toward a more global and holistic understanding of how anxiety begins and is maintained throughout childhood and adolescence.

Further, limited information regarding cultural adaptations of assessment processes (e.g., interviews and rating scales) is available. Although some instruments have started to assess validity across cultures, these are largely based on limited samples from racially/ethnically and economically diverse populations. Other aspects of culture, such as disability, religion, indigeneity, sexual orientation, and gender diversity beyond male/female, have not sufficiently been examined to inform best practices in the assessment of anxiety. Similarly, many scales may be available in English and Spanish, but there is much left to learn about anxiety among linguistically diverse student populations. Finally, there are several social justice concerns that impact anxiety among youth, such as disparities in mental health care, increased exposure to social and environmental stressors, and implicit bias in educational practices. The degree to which these systems-level disparities impact experiences of anxiety through heightened physiological responses, reduced social support, and limited access to effective services to offset symptoms of anxiety warrants immediate attention and advocacy efforts.

CONCLUSION

Anxiety-based disorders in children can be difficult to assess as symptoms can present differently across developmental stages, genders, and cultural groups. Therefore, it is important to use a developmental, ecological approach to the assessment of anxiety that is multimodal and multi-informant. Further, culturally responsive assessment of anxiety requires a social justice lens, which considers systems that impact the child, provides information for advocacy with and on behalf of the child, the impact of cultural variables that influence anxiety experiences and supports, and careful considerations of appropriate instrumentation. Assessing all aspects of the child's experiences that might contribute to anxiety is crucial to an accurate diagnosis and, more importantly, effective intervention design and implementation.

TABLE 18.2. Case Conceptualization for the Assessment of Anxiety for AJ

Referral	AJ was referred by both his teacher and caregivers for school refusal and noncompliant, inattentive behaviors, as well as extreme fear of the family cat.
Cultural considerations	AJ is a cisgender, 8-year-old boy who is Hispanic and in the third grade. His, and his family's, primary language is Spanish with fluent English skills. AJ is typically developing with no history of medical or educational concerns. His family is concerned in the middle socioeconomic range, and his mom's extended family is very present in his daily life.
Ecological considerations	AJ's parents divorced 2 years ago but are amicable. AJ's teacher has an excessively negative view of his behavior. A tornado impacted the community, destroying AJ's primary home, though no one was injured.

Potential hypotheses	Risk factors	Protective factors	Data: Relevant areas of growth	Data: Relevant areas of strength	Data reconciliation	Final hypothesis
• Conduct problems • ADHD—inattention • Traumatic-stress disorder • School phobia • Specific phobia • Separation anxiety	• Exposure to natural disaster • Attacked by family cat • Negative relationship with teacher	• Supportive caregivers • Strong academic skills • Evidence of problem solving (e.g., avoiding school mascot)	Significantly high self-ratings of: • Separation anxiety • Fear of small animals • Poor attitude toward teacher	Average self-ratings of: • Social anxiety • Generalized anxiety • Interpersonal concerns • Attitude to school	Likes school but refuses to go => school refusal is more about leaving mom	Exposure to tornado has led to separation anxiety specific to separation from his mom and potential phobia of cats that impacts his home life.
			Significantly high adult ratings of: • Anxiety • Inattention • Leadership skills (low ratings)	Average adult ratings of: • Hyperactivity • Depression • Functional communication	Inattentive but average score for ADHD => Inattention is anxiety-based	Ruled out: • *Conduct problems*: other explanations more plausible • *ADHD*: Inattention is anxiety-based • *Traumatic stress disorder*: other diagnoses are better fit given focus of worries and symptoms • *School phobia*: AJ is not afraid of school - behaviors are based on fear of being away from mom

REFERENCES

American Psychiatric Association. (2022). *Diagnostic and statistical manual of mental disorders* (5th ed., text rev.). Author.

Beesdo, K., Dipl-Psych, S., & Pine, D. (2009). Anxiety and anxiety disorders in children and adolescents: Developmental issues and implications for DSM-V. *Psychiatric Clinics of North America, 32*, 483–524.

Beidel, D. C., Turner, S. M., & Fink, C. M. (1996). Assessment of childhood social phobia: Construct, convergent, and discriminative validity of the Social Phobia and Anxiety Inventory for Children (SPAI-C). *Psychological Assessment, 8*(3), 235–240.

Birmaher, B., Khetarpal, S., Brent, D., Cully, M., Balach, L., Kaufman, J., & McKenzie Neer, S. (1997). The Screen for Child Anxiety Related Emotional Disorder: Scale construction and psychometric characteristics. *Journal of the American Academy of Child and Adolescent Psychiatry, 36*(4), 545–553.

Bitsko, R. H., Claussen, A. H., Lichstein, J., Black, L. I., Everett Jones, S., Danielson, M. L., et al. (2022). Mental Health Surveillance Among Children—United States, 2013–2019. *MMWR Suppl. 2022*, 71(Suppl. 2), 1–42.

Borelli, J., Rasmussen, H., St. John, H., West, J., & Piacentini, J. (2015). Parental reactivity and the link between parent and child anxiety symptoms. *Journal of Child and Family Studies. 24*, 3130–3144.

Brockveld, K. C., Perini, S. J., & Rapee, R. M. (2014). Social anxiety and social anxiety disorder across cultures. In S. Hofmann and P. DiBartolo (Eds.), *Social anxiety: Clinical, developmental., and social perspectives* (3rd ed.). Academic Press.

Chen, J., Yu, J., Li, X., & Zhang, J. (2015). Genetic and environmental contributions to anxiety among Chinese children and adolescents: A multi-informant twin study. *Journal of Child Psychology and Psychiatry*, 56, 586–594.

Duong, K. N., Le, L. M., Veettil, S. K., Saidoung, P., Wannaadisai, W., Nelson, R. E., et al. (2023). Disparities in COVID-19 related outcomes in the United States by race and ethnicity pre-vaccination era: An umbrella review of meta-analyses. *Frontiers in Public Health, 11*.

Essau, C. A., Lewinsohn, P. M., Olaya, B., & Seeley, J. R. (2014). Anxiety disorders in adolescents and psychosocial outcomes at age 30. *Journal of Affective Disorders, 163*, 125–132.

Etkin, R. G., Shimshoni, Y., Lebowitz, E. R., & Silverman, W. K. (2021). Using evaluative criteria to review youth anxiety measures, part I: Self-report. *Journal of Clinical Child & Adolescent Psychology*, 50(1), 58–76.

Frick, P., Barry, C., & Kamphaus, R. (2009). *Clinical assessment of child and adolescent personability and behavior*. Springer.

Henchliffe, K., & Campbell, M. (2016). Tipping points: Teachers' reported reasons for referring primary school children for excessive anxiety. *Journal of Psychologists and Counsellors in Schools, 26*, 84–99.

Hofmann, S. G., & Hinton, D. E. (2014). Cross-cultural aspects of anxiety disorders. *Current psychiatry reports, 16*, 1–5.

Hojnoski, R. L., Morrison, R., Brown, M., & Matthews, W. J. (2006). Projective test use among school psychologists: A survey and critique. *Journal of Psychoeducational Assessment, 24*(2), 145–159.

Kamphaus, R. W., & Reynolds, C. R. (2015). BASC-3 *Behavioral and Emotional Screening System*. Pearson.

Lack, C. & Thomason, S. (2013). Projective personality assessment of anxiety: A critical appraisal. In D. McKay & E. A. Storch (Eds.), *Handbook of assessing variants and complications in anxiety disorders* (pp. 203–216). Springer.

La Greca, A. M., & Lopez, N. (1998). Social anxiety among adolescents: Linkages with peer relations and friendships. *Journal of Abnormal Child Psychology, 26*, 83–94.

La Greca, A. M., & Stone, W. L. (1993). Social Anxiety Scale for Children-Revised: Factor structure and concurrent validity. *Journal of Clinical Child Psychology, 22*(1), 17–27.

Lowe, P. A., Lee, S. W., Witteborg, K. M., Prichard, K. W., Luhr, M. E., Cullinan, C. M., et al. (2008). The Test Anxiety Inventory for Children and Adolescents: Examination of the psychometric properties of a new multidimensional measure of test anxiety among elementary and secondary school students. *Journal of Psychoeducational Assessment, 26*(3), 215–230.

Malone, C. M., & Proctor, S. L. (2019). Demystifying social justice for school psychology practice. *Communique, 48*(1), 1–21.

March, J. S. (2013). *Multidimensional Anxiety Scale for Children* (2nd ed.). Multi-Health Systems.

Meyer, G. J., Finn, S. E., Eyde, L. D., Kay, G. G., Moreland, K. L., Dies, R. R., et al. (2001). Psychological testing and psychological assessment: A review of evidence and issues. *American Psychologist, 56*(2), 128.

Nguyen, S. A., & McAloon, J. (2018). A cross-cultural comparison of parental perceptions of childhood separation anxiety disorder symptoms and likelihood to seek help. *Journal of Cross-Cultural Psychology*, 49(3), 453–469.

Nicolini, H., Salin-Pascual, R., Cabrera, B., & Lanzagorta, N. (2017). Influence of culture in obsessive–compulsive disorder and its treatment. *Current Psychiatry Reviews, 13*(4), 285–292.

Ollendick, T. H. (1983). Reliability and validity of the revised Fear Survey Schedule for Children (FSSC-R). *Behaviour Research and Therapy, 21*(6), 685–692.

Panchal, U., Vaquerizo-Serrano, J. D., Conde-Ghigliazza, I., Genc, H. A., Marchini, S., Pociute, K., et al. (2023). Anxiety symptoms and disorders during the COVID-19 pandemic in children and adolescents: Systematic review and meta-analysis. *The European Journal of Psychiatry, 37*(4), 1–14.

Pereira, A., Barros, L., Mendonca, D., & Muris, P. (2014). The relationship among parental anxiety, parenting, and children' anxiety: The mediating effect of children's cognitive vulnerabilities. *Journal of Child and Family Studies, 23*, 399–409.

Pollard, J., Reardon, T., Williams, C., Creswell, C., Ford, T., Gray, A., et al. (2023). The multifaceted consequences and economic costs of child anxiety problems: A systematic review and meta-analysis. *JCPP advances, 3*(3), e12149.

Reynolds, C. R., & Kamphaus, R. W. (2015). *Behavior assessment for children: Third edition*. (BASC-3). Pearson.

Reynolds, C. R., & Richmond, B. O. (2008). *Revised Children's Manifest Anxiety Scale—Second Edition (RCMAS-2): Manual.* Western Psychological Services.

Sanchez, A. L., Comer, J. S., & LaRoche, M. (2022). Enhancing the responsiveness of family-based CBT through culturally informed case conceptualization and treatment planning. *Cognitive and Behavioral Practice, 29*(4), 750–770.

Schiltz, H. K., Magnus, B. E., McVey, A. J., Haendel, A. D., Dolan, B. K., & Stanley, R. E., et al., (2021). A psychometric analysis of the Social Anxiety Scale for adolescents among youth with autism spectrum disorder: Caregiver–adolescent agreement, factor structure, and validity. *Assessment, 28*(1), 100–115.

Shear, K., Belnap, B. H., Mazumdar, S., Houck, P., & Rollman, B. L. (2006). Generalized Anxiety Disorder Severity Scale (GADSS): A preliminary validation study. *Depression and Anxiety, 23*(2), 77–82.

Smoller, J. (2016). The genetics of stress-related disorders: PTSD, depression, and anxiety disorders. *Neuropsychopharmacology, 41*, 297–319.

Spielberger, C. D., Gorsuch, R. L., Lushene, R., Vagg, P. R., & Jacobs, G. A. (1983). *Manual for the State–Trait Anxiety Inventory*. Consulting Psychologists Press.

Storch, E. A., McGuire, J. F., Wu, M. S., Hamblin, R., McIngvale, E., Cepeda, S. L., et al. (2019). Development and psychometric evaluation of the children's Yale–Brown Obsessive–Compulsive Scale Second Edition. *Journal of the American Academy of Child & Adolescent Psychiatry*, 58(1), 92–98.

Tolin, D. F., Sain, K. S., Davis, E., Gilliam, C., Hannan, S. E., Springer, K. S., et al. (2023). The DIAMOND-KID: Psychometric properties of a structured diagnostic interview for DSM-5 anxiety, mood, and obsessive-compulsive and related disorders in children and adolescents. *Assessment, 30*(8), 2351–2363.

Varela, R. E., Sanchez-Sosa, J. J., Biggs, B. K., & Luis, T. M. (2008). Anxiety symptoms and fears in Hispanic and European American children: Cross-cultural measurement equivalence. *Journal of Psychopathology and Behavioral Assessment, 30*(2), 132–145.

Vasey, M. W., & Lonigan, C. J. (2000). Considering the clinical utility of performance-based measures of childhood anxiety. *Journal of Clinical Child Psychology, 29*(4), 493–508.

Waszczuk, M., Zavos, H., & Eley, T. (2013). Genetic and environmental influences on relationship between anxiety sensitivity and anxiety subscales in children. *Journal of Anxiety Disorders, 27*, 475–484.

Waters, A., & Craske, M. (2016). Towards a cognitive-learning formulation of youth anxiety: A narrative review of theory and evidence and implications treatment. *Clinical Psychology Review, 50*, 50–66.

Whitcomb, S., & Merrell, K. (2013). *Behavioral, Social, and Emotional Assessment of Children and Adolescents*. Routledge.

CHAPTER 19

Assessment of Disruptive Behavior Disorders

Cody Gion

Human behavior is fundamentally a societal construct, influenced by cultural norms. When actions or behaviors deviate from these norms, they are often labeled as disruptive. It's important to recognize that cultural context, norms, and values significantly shape behavior. These constructs also influence how we perceive and classify behavior as disruptive or otherwise. It's crucial to understand that behavioral expectations vary across and within cultures, leading to diverse values and beliefs about behavioral norms.

Disruptive behavior disorders (DBDs) represent a group of mental health disorders characterized by persistent patterns of noncompliant and defiant behavior that cause distress to others. The *Diagnostic and Statistical Manual of Mental Disorders, Fifth Edition, Text Revision* (DSM-5-TR) defines DBDs as disorders characterized by difficulties in managing aggressive behaviors, self-control, and impulses (American Psychiatric Association, 2022, p. 461). A unique feature of DBDs is that their identification depends on others' interpretation of the behavior, which can introduce bias in diagnosis depending on the interpreter. This reality highlights the need for a culturally responsive approach to data assessment within a dual-factor model framework.

This chapter offers an overview of the symptoms and disparities in the evaluation of the most common DBDs, namely, oppositional defiant disorder (ODD) and conduct disorder (CD). Furthermore, this chapter outlines the components of a comprehensive and culturally sensitive method for assessing and diagnosing DBDs. The chapter concludes with a discussion of the implications and future directions of culturally responsive assessments for DBDs.

SYMPTOMOLOGY OF COMMON DBDs

ODD and CD are defined by distinct characteristics requiring detailed examination. Each of these disorders exhibits a unique set of symptoms that are crucial to their identification (American Psychiatric Association, 2022). The identification of these salient symptoms is not merely an academic exercise, but a practical necessity. It enables us to understand how the symptom profiles of these disorders may interact within diverse environments and among different individuals. This understanding is critical because the manifestation of these disorders can vary significantly based on environmental factors and individual differences (Burke et al., 2010).

A thorough comprehension of the distinctive features of ODD and CD, coupled with their prominent symptoms, is crucial for precise identification and diagnosis. This knowledge provides us with the essential tools to apply a comprehensive evaluation and diagnostic framework. Such a framework enables a deeper understanding of these disorders, ultimately facilitating accurate diagnosis and effective intervention.

Oppositional Defiant Disorder

ODD involves regular displays of rage, disagreeableness, and difficult moods. Individuals with ODD tend to have temper tantrums and are quick to express annoyance. Argumentative and defiant behavior, such as clashing with authority figures, refusing to follow rules, and displaying a vindictive attitude that can lead to holding grudges and blaming others for their mistakes, are common features of this disorder (American Psychiatric Association, 2022).

The criteria for diagnosing ODD are found on pages 522–523 of DSM-5-TR (American Psychiatric Association, 2022). The behaviors listed there cause significant distress to the individual exhibiting them or those close to them. DSM5-TR classifies the severity of this disorder into three categories: mild, moderate, and severe. A mild classification implies that these behaviors cause significant disturbances in one particular setting (e.g., at home, school, or work), whereas a severe classification indicates that these behaviors cause significant disturbances in at least three distinct settings (and sometimes more) (American Psychiatric Association, 2022).

Certain symptoms of ODD can suggest the presence of comorbid conditions or predict specific negative outcomes. Chronic irritability and oppositional behavior are two symptoms that are consistent across genders and are key factors in diagnosing youth with ODD (Herzhoff & Tackett, 2016). Chronic irritability can predispose young people to experience peer rejection, victimization, anxiety, depression, and even suicidality (Burke et al., 2021; Evans et al., 2016; Mikolajewski et al., 2017; Stringaris & Goodman, 2009; Stringaris et al., 2012). On the other hand, oppositional behaviors are associated with externalizing behavior, delinquency, substance abuse, symptoms of attention-deficit/hyperactivity disorder (ADHD), and an increased likelihood of being diagnosed with CD in the future (Burke et al., 2021; Mikolajewski et al., 2017; Stringaris et al., 2012; Waldman et al., 2021). There is also evidence suggesting that grandiosity should be considered when evaluating ODD, as these symptoms may predict later conduct and behavioral issues (Burke et al., 2022). For example, clinicians will want to consider factors of inflated self-importance, unrealistic abilities, or a sense of superiority, in addition to other characteristics of ODD. This information may provide insights into other comorbid conditions and drive the scope of evaluation.

Understanding the relationships between irritability, oppositionality, and specific outcomes and other symptoms can help clinicians conduct a more comprehensive evaluation than focusing solely on the symptoms of ODD. For instance, knowing that irritability is closely linked to depressive and anxious symptoms, clinicians may choose to gather additional information about internalizing behaviors that may not be immediately obvious. Similarly, understanding the close links between oppositional behaviors and harmful externalizing behaviors can support the collection of information about externalizing behavior across contexts that extend beyond mere oppositionality.

Conduct Disorder

CD, according to the American Psychiatric Association (2022), is a mental health condition marked by ongoing aggressive actions toward people and animals, as well as delinquent behaviors like property damage, dishonesty, or theft. It also exhibits oppositional traits like those seen in ODD. The criteria for diagnosing CD are found on pages 530–532 of DSM-5-TR.

The symptoms of CD are predictive of several negative outcomes. These include lower academic achievement, increased rates of exclusion from school, rejection by peers, tension within the family, personal injury, engagement in criminal activities, substance abuse, further antisocial and delinquent behavior, and even suicidality (Biederman et al., 2008; Erskine et al., 2016; Wei et al., 2016).

CD is a highly heterogeneous disorder, meaning it can have a unique presentation in different individuals (Fanti, 2018). This heterogeneity is evident in youth who display callous-unemotional traits and those who exhibit aggressive and nonaggressive antisocial behavior (Klahr & Burt, 2014). Youth with callous-unemotional traits tend to have more severe and persistent symptoms over time. Those who display aggressive antisocial behavior often have an onset of CD that emerges in early childhood, while non-aggressive antisocial behavior seems to most frequently occur in adolescence (Maughan et al., 2004). Interestingly, there appears to be little evidence to suggest that the qualifier of Limited Positive Emotions (e.g., lack of empathy, remorse, and overall callousness) adds anything meaningful to the diagnosis of CD (Colins et al., 2020; Déry et al., 2019).

Understanding how CD may manifest differently across individuals or within the same individual at different points in time provides valuable information that can guide the assessment of CD. Clinicians should consider obtaining data that not only depicts antisocial behavior but also the type of antisocial behavior (i.e., aggressive vs. non-aggressive). They may tailor their assessments toward specific symptoms based on the age of the youth. Additionally, they should consider whether callous-unemotional traits are present, as this could inform the type of treatment that might be needed.

Prevalence and Disproportionality of ODD and CD

The prevalence of CD and ODD in children ages 18 years or younger is relatively uniform across various geographical regions and cultures, with rates of 3.2% and 3.3%, respectively. This consistency implies that the diagnostic criteria for these disorders hold validity across diverse cultures (Canino et al., 2010).

Whereas the overall prevalence of CD and ODD remains stable, significant differences emerge concerning gender and race. Males are more likely to be diagnosed with both ODD and CD compared to females, a trend observed irrespective of cultural or geographical differences (Demmer et al., 2017; Erskine et al., 2013; Lavigne et al., 2009; Polanczyk et al., 2015). Interestingly, the gender disparity for CD decreases as children transition into adolescence and adulthood (from a ratio of 3:1 to 2:1), and for ODD, it becomes nearly equal (from 1.5:1 to approximately 1:1) (Lavigne et al., 2009; Moffitt & Caspi, 2001; Polanczyk et al., 2015).

Studies indicate that Black children are more likely to be diagnosed with DBDs (including ODD and CD) compared to White children (DelBello et al., 2001; Lau et al., 2004; Nguyen et al., 2007). This observation is concerning, especially considering these studies have found no significant differences in disruptive behavior symptoms between White and Black children. However, the perception of these symptoms may vary among teachers and caregivers (Downey & Pribesh, 2004; Mattuck, 2022).

Moreover, Black children are less likely to be diagnosed with affective disorders such as anxiety and depression compared to White children (DelBello et al., 2001; Lau et al., 2004; Nguyen et al., 2007). Additionally, Black and Hispanic youth are more likely to be diagnosed with CD and ODD, but less likely to receive a diagnosis of ADHD compared to White children (Fadus, 2020; Morgan et al., 2013; Schneider & Eisenberg, 2006). These disparities exist despite evidence suggesting that Black children experience ADHD at similar rates as White children (Miller et al., 2009). The underdiagnosis of ADHD can have significant implications for treatment, as it can limit access to medications, therapeutic services, and other interventions (Mehta et al., 2009).

These disparities in diagnosis across gender and race highlight the importance of culturally responsive assessment of DBDs. In this chapter, we will adopt a step-by-step approach to culturally responsive assessment, outlining considerations for inclusivity to ensure that all children, regardless of their race, gender, or other intersectional identities, receive accurate diagnoses and appropriate treatment.

COMPREHENSIVE AND CULTURALLY SENSITIVE APPROACH TO ASSESSING DBDs

In the evaluation of DBDs, a comprehensive and culturally sensitive approach is essential (Burke et al., 2024). This involves a guiding framework that effectively navigates the assessment process. The assessment extends beyond the specific DBDs, implying that the focus is not confined to the symptoms and behaviors typically linked to these disorders. Instead, a broader array of factors that could impact the individual's behavior is considered.

An ecological approach is adopted to assess environmental factors, entailing investigation of the individual's environment and circumstances. This pinpoints elements that may either alleviate or intensify the symptoms of DBDs, allowing for a more detailed understanding of the individual's behavior within their environmental context. Data are compiled from diverse sources and settings using a dual-factor framework. This strategy enables a more comprehensive and precise depiction of the individual's behavior, involving the gathering of information from various environments and different sources of data.

Data are also collected across multiple informants and contexts, soliciting input from a variety of individuals who interact regularly with the person being assessed. These informants could encompass parents, teachers, peers, and other pertinent individuals. Active checks for bias in diagnostic decision making are conducted, requiring awareness of preconceptions and biases, and taking measures to ensure they do not unfairly influence the assessment. See Frick et al. (2020, Chapter 15) for a detailed process for integrating and interpreting assessment information across multiple sources.

A comprehensive and thorough evaluation can result in a close connection between the assessment information and treatment planning, ensuring that the insights derived from the assessment directly guide the formulation of an effective treatment plan. These concepts are integrated into every phase of the assessment process, rather than applied in isolation. This holistic approach ensures the assessment of DBDs is thorough, precise, and culturally sensitive.

PLANNING THE EVALUATION

When assessing youth, it's vital to consider the referral source. Clinicians should be aware of the referring party, which could be a parent, school, government organization, and/or physician, and collect any initial information related to the referral reason. It's important to know if any screenings were conducted and to have access to any historical information. It's also crucial to understand who perceives the presenting problem. It's necessary to determine if the youth, caregivers, or others agree that there is a problem or if their views differ.

Children diagnosed with DBDs often have additional diagnoses or conditions. For instance, a diagnosis of ODD, CD, or both increases the chance of also being diagnosed with ADHD or other affective disorders like depression or anxiety (Boylan et al., 2007; Lahey et al., 2002). Furthermore, various DBDs share many characteristics, including deficits in impulse control, self-control, and aggressive behaviors. This overlap can make diagnosis and treatment more complex (Maughan et al., 2004).

Considering this evidence, it's clear that a comprehensive, holistic approach is necessary when assessing DBDs. This approach should consider all potential comorbid conditions and their interrelationships. By adopting this approach, clinicians can gain a more profound understanding of the child's current behaviors and create more effective treatment strategies.

CULTURALLY RESPONSIVE PROCEDURES FOR DATA COLLECTION

For effective diagnostic decision making in youth suspected of having DBDs, it's crucial to employ a diverse and comprehensive range of data collection methods. These data should be gathered from various contexts and sources, utilizing both standardized and naturalistic measures. It's important to focus not only on the individual behaviors of the youth but also on the broader environmental context. In the following sections, we will outline beneficial procedures for data collection.

Culturally Sensitive Interviewing Strategies for DBDs

Understanding the mental constructs, beliefs, and environments where disruptive behaviors may surface is crucial when employing a culturally sensitive interviewing approach. Gathering insights from caregivers and young individuals alike can illuminate how these behaviors are perceived and establish if they are deemed normal within a specific cultural context. Paying attention to how young people and their families articulate their thoughts, feelings, and actions is of utmost importance.

Cultural Formation Interview

The American Psychiatric Association developed the Cultural Formulation Interview (CFI), a set of 16 questions aimed at understanding an individual's cultural perspective on their presenting problems. This tool aids clinicians in understanding how cultural factors may influence symptom expression, help-seeking behaviors, and service expectations (American Psychiatric Association, 2022). The CFI serves as a valuable instrument to use during an initial interview with young people and their caregivers. It assists in framing the problem from the perspective of the youth and family rather than from the perception of a clinician or other provider(s). The use of open-ended questions empowers the individuals being interviewed and gives them a voice in the process.

This approach can make families from diverse backgrounds feel recognized and listened to, which can guide subsequent steps in the evaluation process. When families feel acknowledged and safe, they may be more willing to share sensitive information. This could include parenting styles, a history of disruptive behavior or related mental health conditions, and any potentially traumatic events. Such information can often provide context to the evaluation process and contribute to the development of effective, targeted treatment.

Parenting Styles

Conducting interviews with caregivers about their parenting styles and philosophies can shed light on potential risk factors and protective measures related to DBDs. Parenting styles that are excessively punitive, devoid of warmth, or exhibit physical aggression can instigate oppositional or aggressive behavior in children (Stormshak et al., 2000). On the other hand, positive and proactive parenting strategies such as setting limits, providing reinforcement, and active parental involvement can foster more socially acceptable behaviors (Leijten et al., 2019). Interestingly, a reciprocal relationship seems to exist between children with DBDs and maladaptive parenting practices (Burke et al., 2008). This suggests that harsh parenting practices may heighten the probability of DBDs and vice versa. This emphasizes the importance of an open and nonjudgmental interview process that acts as a supportive resource for families.

Family History of DBDs

Research has shown that the presence of a familial history of DBDs or related mental health issues can influence the development and manifestation of DBDs in children (Hudziak et al., 2005; Stringaris et al., 2012). In addition to formal diagnosis, it is crucial for clinicians to investigate symptoms indicative of DBDs or similar disorders. This could involve asking about symptoms such as chronic irritability, oppositional behavior, conduct problems, depression, or anxiety. Clinicians should also provide diverse examples of how these symptoms could manifest in different individuals. For instance, chronic irritability could manifest as yelling at another person or complete withdrawal. Expanding the scope of mental health history to encompass a broad range of symptoms could help reveal underlying familial history and enhance understanding of symptomology and expression of DBDs that would otherwise be overlooked.

History of Traumatic Events

Understanding the potentially traumatic experiences of youth can provide valuable insights that aid the diagnostic and treatment process. The presence of DBDs has been tightly linked to a history of abuse (Maniglio, 2014). Moreover, exposure to interpersonal violence, whether at home or in the community, could potentially predispose youth to develop DBDs (Boden et al., 2010; Kersten et al., 2017). However, discussing these experiences can be challenging for families. Therefore, clinicians should ensure they establish a strong rapport with interviewees before broaching these sensitive topics. It's crucial to maintain an open and responsive demeanor throughout the interview process, allowing families the option to revisit these topics if necessary. By maintaining open lines of communication throughout the evaluation process, clinicians can create a safe environment for gathering additional sensitive information when the time is right.

Gathering Existing Data

There may be a wealth of available data that can aid in determining the intensity of DBD symptoms across various environments. School and community environments often have multiple sources of data available, and they are where youth spend most of their time.

School Performance Data

The school environment can either alleviate or intensify symptoms of disruptive behavior. For example, schools that implement positive and proactive approaches to behavioral support may serve as a protective factor, whereas schools that rely heavily on exclusionary discipline may put students, especially youth of color, at risk for DBDs (Rosenbaum, 2020; Waddell et al., 2018). Details about grades, attendance records, disciplinary referrals, report cards, suspension and expulsion incidents, changes in special education placements, academic evaluation results, and the number of schools the youth has attended can provide meaningful insights into the youth's performance at school and the extent to which the problem varies across contexts.

Community-Based Data

Understanding the community and gathering pertinent information is also essential to bolster resilience and pinpoint potential risks. Data pertaining to youth may encompass records of juvenile arrests or detentions, visits to hospitals or emergency rooms, and comprehensive medical histories. The association with deviant peer groups can escalate the risk of DBDs (Boden et al., 2010). It is crucial to be aware of supportive peer groups and trustworthy adults for effective assessment and treatment planning. Furthermore, identifying additional community resources that are accessible and cater to their racial, gender, ethnic, ability, and other intersecting identities can serve as beneficial channels that foster overall well-being.

Direct Observation

Systematic direct observation of behavior in natural environments can yield valuable insights into the nature of the behavior, as well as potential antecedents and consequences that may reinforce the behavior across various settings (Hintz et al., 2002). Furthermore, such observation can shed light on practices and mechanisms that encourage socially acceptable behavior and promote skill development. By observing across diverse contexts, at different times of the day, across various days, and by multiple observers, we can better assess the frequency, intensity, and duration of the behavior.

Behavior Reporting

In behavioral assessment, direct observation of behaviors of interest isn't always feasible or practical. Young individuals may exhibit certain behaviors only in specific environments, such as their home or school, or around certain individuals with whom they are comfortable. In these cases, behavior reporting becomes a vital tool that can be used alongside other assessment measures (Chafouleas et al., 2009).

Numerous methods are available for behavior reporting. When choosing a method, it's essential to consider its practicality and acceptability to the information provider, who could be a parent or teacher. Additionally, clinicians should evaluate the reliability and validity of the selected methods to ensure they yield accurate and consistent results.

One well-established method of behavior reporting is the Parent Daily Report (PDR). The PDR, which includes a list of 35 common behavioral issues, has been used for many years across various settings and has proven its reliability and accuracy in capturing youth behavior (Chamberlain & Reid, 1987). When using the PDR, clinicians contact the parent daily to identify which behaviors were displayed in the past 24 hours and whether these behaviors caused any stress. This tool can provide insights into the frequency of behaviors and the extent to which they are perceived as problematic by the parent or caregiver.

Another effective tool for behavior reporting is the Daily Behavior Report Card (DBRC), typically completed by a teacher. DBRCs are highly adaptable and can be tailored to various target behaviors and settings. They involve diverse data collection methods where teachers provide information on behaviors of interest within the school setting. DBRCs have been widely accepted among teachers and are often used for data collection (Riley-Tillman et al., 2008). School systems may likely already be able to provide this information without further need for additional assessment. Chafouleas et al. (2002) provide an overview of the implementation of these measures in a school setting. Although the psychometric properties of DBRCs as a stand-alone measure can vary, they are generally considered effective when used in conjunction with other established behavioral assessment measures (see Chafouleas et al., 2009).

The application of behavior reporting within a multi-measure approach can significantly improve the reliability and validity of the assessment process and can be a practical and acceptable method to gather additional information. It also aligns with the best practice of collecting data from multiple sources, which can help reduce bias in decision making. This comprehensive approach ensures a more accurate and holistic understanding of the individual's behavior, thereby enabling more effective interventions and support.

Standardized Assessments

The use of standardized assessments, primarily in the form of rating scales and structured interviews, is a crucial part of evaluating DBDs. These tools can offer valuable normative data about disruptive behaviors. Burke et al. (2024) provide a comprehensive list of these assessment tools and discuss their relevance to various DBD categories. However, when applying these assessments within a culturally sensitive context, clinicians need to exercise caution.

First, clinicians need to be careful in selecting the appropriate measure by taking into consideration the specific population and purpose they were designed to serve. Clinicians should align this information with the demographic data of the student and caregivers to ensure accuracy and relevance. Language barriers can impact the validity of the obtained data; hence, offering interpretation services and adapting assessment approaches can mitigate biases across diverse cultural and linguistic groups.

Second, clinicians should review the reliability and validity of each tool. They should opt for measures with robust psychometric properties while being aware of potential variations when applied by different raters or within distinct assessment sections. Given that perceptions of behavior can vary among parents, teachers, and youth (Mitchison et al., 2022), employing multiple measures from varied sources over time enhances reliability and validity. Additionally, considering that DBDs often coexist with other disorders like impulsivity, depression, and anxiety disorders, a comprehensive approach involving multiple assessment tools and methods focusing on a range of symptoms is recommended.

Finally, a detailed review of each item within the selected measures is vital to understand the nature of the questions asked and information gathered. There's evidence indicating racial disparities in reporting internalizing symptoms (Nguyen et al., 2007); thus, clinicians might need to employ informal questioning techniques to gather comprehensive data.

Clinicians should avoid overreliance on standardized assessments and instead adopt a holistic approach that incorporates various perspectives. Reports generated should encompass scores, interpretations, and identified patterns while validating behavioral perspectives from youth against those from caregivers or teachers, ensuring a balanced view that respects diverse insights into DBD manifestations across different settings.

APPROACHES TO ENHANCE DIAGNOSTIC ACCURACY FOR DBDs

After collecting and analyzing data, clinicians may arrive at a working differential diagnosis for DBDs. To mitigate biases during the diagnostic verification process, clinicians can take several steps.

Present Data Holistically

When presenting with data related to DBDs, clinicians must avoid the pitfall of selectively including information that only supports their pre-existing beliefs. This phenomenon, known as confirmation bias, can unintentionally distort the process (Mendel et al., 2011). Instead, clinicians have a critical role in presenting data in a transparent manner. Rather than disregarding outliers or data points that deviate from the norm, these should be actively discussed within the team. This approach not only enhances diagnostic accuracy but also helps stakeholders feel more validated in the process (Perkins et al., 2018). These divergent data points often provide valuable insights and contribute to a more accurate understanding of the situation. By adopting a holistic approach to data presentation, clinicians can ensure that all relevant information is considered, leading to a full understanding of the issue at hand.

Reference Diagnostic Criteria

Clinicians should consistently refer to the diagnostic criteria specific to DBDs of interest. Despite its seemingly straightforward nature, a study by First et al. (2018) revealed that nearly half of clinicians (49.8%) did not reference criteria at all, and 32.0% only did so occasionally when making diagnostic decisions. Establishing a practice of referencing diagnostic criteria serves as a critical check to determine if the collected data support a diagnosis. By adhering to these criteria, clinicians ensure that their assessments are grounded in evidence-based guidelines, minimizing the influence of personal biases. Additionally, knowledge and discussion of presenting symptoms and criteria have been shown to influence how individuals experience the diagnosis of a mental health disorder. Active discussion about symptomology can empower and normalize the presence of mental conditions for individuals diagnosed (Perkins et al., 2018).

Examine Cultural and Contextual Considerations

Recognizing the cultural and contextual factors surrounding DBDs is essential. These factors significantly influence how symptoms manifest and how individuals respond to interventions. Clinicians should remain attuned to cultural nuances, family dynamics, socioeconomic context, and community influences. A culturally sensitive approach ensures that diagnostic decisions account for the unique experiences and backgrounds of the individuals being evaluated.

Use a Team-Based Approach

Analyzing consolidated data should involve a collaborative team approach, facilitated by the clinician. Although clinicians possess expert diagnostic knowledge of DBDs, they should avoid an exclusive expert-only stance. Instead, they must rely on a diverse team that includes various participants. These participants may encompass the child, caregivers, educators, mental health workers, cultural liaisons, and other relevant agencies (e.g., the Department of Human Services or community support personnel). By incorporating multiple perspectives, the clinician is able to gain additional insight into interpreting collected data. Moreover, this approach fosters a holistic understanding of the individual's behavior, considering various contexts and viewpoints (Perkins et al., 2018).

Check for Understanding and Bias

Clinicians play a vital role in distilling complex data into a format that is both understandable and easily digestible by others. This task involves not only meticulous analysis and interpretation of the data but also effective communication of the findings in a clear and concise manner. It is crucial to allow sufficient time for clarification of any information or instructions being provided (Perkins et al., 2018). This means not rushing through explanations, but rather presenting data and information in a comprehensive and easy-to-understand manner. It's important to break down complex concepts into simpler terms and use visual aids or examples, where possible, to help illustrate points.

To ensure effective communication and understanding, language interpretation services should be readily available for both caregivers and the child. This is particularly important in situations where the primary language of the caregivers and/or the child is not the same as that of the service provider. The availability of such services can greatly enhance the quality of care and the overall experience. However, the responsibilities of clinicians extend beyond mere understanding of presented information. They should actively foster an environment that promotes open dialogue and the exchange of ideas.

Active listening techniques are another key component of effective communication. These techniques involve summarizing the information provided by the caregivers or the child to ensure that it has been correctly understood. This could involve paraphrasing their words or concisely repeating the information. In addition, asking clarifying questions can help to fill in any gaps in understanding or to confirm certain details. These questions should be open-ended to encourage more detailed responses and provide a clearer picture of the situation or issue at hand. Lastly, it's important to affirm the perspectives of the caregivers and the child. This means acknowledging their feelings, opinions, and experiences, and validating them. This can help to build trust, promote open communication, and ensure that they feel heard and understood. This approach fosters a more collaborative relationship and can lead to better outcomes in assessment and care.

Furthermore, clinicians should recognize and respect the diverse knowledge and experiences that everyone brings to the table. This includes acknowledging different ways of knowing and understanding, which may be influenced by cultural backgrounds, personal experiences, or areas of expertise. By valuing these varied perspectives, clinicians enrich their own understanding and make more informed decisions.

In summary, clinicians have a dual role when establishing diagnoses of DBDs: effectively summarizing and communicating data and cultivating a collaborative and inclusive environment that appreciates diverse viewpoints and ways of knowing. This approach not only enhances the decision-making process but also fosters a culture of respect and mutual understanding.

TREATMENT RECOMMENDATIONS

Treatment recommendations should be closely linked to information gathered throughout the evaluation, be evidence-based, and seek to amplify strengths. Below are important guidelines when presenting potential treatment recommendations.

Formative Data

We have presented methods for collecting low-inference data to support the decision making of both diagnosis and treatment throughout this chapter (i.e., interviews, direct observations, behavior reporting, and behavior rating scales). Treatment recommendations should avoid high-inference decision making. Extending recommendations that are loosely related to the presenting issues may result in ineffective treatment. There should be a clear line from the information gathered to the conditions that are serving to maintain the current symptomology. The team should be clear on the most pressing and problematic symptoms that need to be addressed and the conditions in which those symptoms are most likely to be present. For example, data from direct observations or behavioral reporting might serve to identify the specific target behaviors of focus across specific contexts, or a team may choose to focus on lessening the symptom of irritability during the times it is most severe based on information from standardized assessments and interviews. There are infinite scenarios that can serve to guide decision making. The guiding premise is to closely connect data to intervention selection and implementation.

Evidence-Based Treatments

There are many effective treatment options for youth with DBDs (see Comer et al., 2013; McCart & Sheidow, 2016). Identifying appropriate interventions, however, must extend beyond simply picking from a list of attractive candidates. Teams should discuss the potential impact, feasibility, and cultural and contextual appropriateness of various intervention options (Horner et al., 2014). One way of assessing cultural and contextual fit may be to use a motivational interviewing process where the team discusses the acceptability of the interventions, identifies any potential barriers, and adjusts the non-essential elements of the intervention to support better implementation (Gion et al., 2022). The information gathered from this process can increase the likelihood of involvement and adherence.

Strengths-Based Focus

Treatment should not just focus on lessening problematic symptoms but should instead promote strengths within the youth and their environment. Teams should utilize the data on strengths collected throughout the assessment process to leverage favorable conditions. For example, connecting youth to positive peer groups and adults may serve to lessen symptoms of deviant behavior by providing opportunities for healthier replacement activities (e.g., Sinclair et al., 2019). Tapping into the youth's interests or aspirations can motivate them toward more positive outcomes (Gallagher et al., 2010). This focus also promotes the understanding of a dual-factor framework to mental health, whereby severe symptoms of a disorder may be experienced alongside high levels of well-being (see Chapter 5 for additional information on the dual-factor framework).

FUTURE DIRECTIONS IN ASSESSMENT FOR DBDs

This chapter proposed a comprehensive and culturally responsive method for assessing DBDs. This method is based on a framework that includes (1) a broad assessment scope, (2) an ecological approach to data collection and treatment recommendations, (3) a dual-factor approach that evaluates both strengths and problematic symptoms from the perspectives of various informants and stakeholders, and (4) active checks for bias. Future research and practice could aim to validate this model across youth with diverse backgrounds, identities, and abilities. Although we drew from multiple established sources to guide our decision making, our process remains research-informed. Developing a strong evidence base of comprehensive approaches to the assessment of DBDs may reduce disparities in the identification of DBDs among diverse populations and subgroups.

While there is abundant information on how to assess risk factors and problematic symptoms in youth with DBDs, there is less information on protective factors or strengths-based assessment approaches (Rashid, 2015). A dual-factor approach in future research could help identify coexisting characteristics of well-being in youth with DBDs and guide the development of more effective, strengths-focused treatment options.

Future research and practice should also focus on early identification methods for youth at risk of developing DBDs. Keenan and Wakschlag (2002) suggested that typical and atypical problems can be differentiated using a modified DSM model among individuals as young as 2 years old. However, there is no consensus on how to conceptualize and measure problems in young children, and there are concerns about including a DBD category for young children in the DSM. Regardless of the debate on including DBDs in early childhood, it is clear that accurate early screening is vital for interventions aimed at preventing the development of externalizing disorders and delinquent behaviors (Hill et al., 2004). The lack of widespread implementation of practices for universal screening and promotion and prevention treatment options is problematic and should be examined as a potential way to reduce the risk of DBDs and their negative impacts on youth mental and behavioral health.

Finally, due to the academic and social demands placed on students, schools are often where youth exhibit symptoms of DBDs. Schools are community fixtures and can serve as connection points across agencies. There is limited information and guidance on how DBDs intersect with educational eligibility for services provided by the Individuals with Disabilities Education Act (IDEA). School providers are tasked with interpreting information and analyzing it within school disability categories. The category of emotional disturbance can be problematic due to the exclusion of students considered "socially maladjusted," a term that remains undefined by the IDEA, leading to potential ambiguity in its interpretation (Sec. 300.8 (c) (4)). Efforts to align DBDs within the framework of school-based services should be considered and articulated to promote clarity and collaboration across mental health and education agencies.

In conclusion, the implementation of culturally responsive assessments for DBDs is not just a matter of best practice; it's a crucial step toward creating more inclusive and equitable support for youth with DBDs. Culturally responsive assessment practices aim to provide a more accurate and comprehensive understanding of a youth's psychological symptoms and behavior by considering their cultural context and cultural formulation. The approach outlined in this chapter can help avoid misdiagnosis and ensure youth receive appropriate and effective support. By ensuring that assessment practices are culturally responsive, we can help to ensure that all youth, regardless of their cultural background, receive the support and understanding they need to thrive.

REFERENCES

American Psychiatric Association. (2022). *Diagnostic and statistical manual of mental disorders* (5th ed., text rev.). Author.

Biederman, J., Petty, C. R., Dolan, C., Hughes, S., Mick, E., Monuteaux, M. C., & Faraone, S. V. (2008). The long-term longitudinal course of oppositional defiant disorder and conduct disorder in ADHD boys: Findings from a controlled 10-year prospective longitudinal follow-up study. *Psychological Medicine, 38*(7), 1027–1036.

Boden, J. M., Fergusson, D. M., & Horwood, L. J. (2010). Risk factors for conduct disorder and oppositional/defiant disorder: Evidence from a New Zealand birth cohort. *Journal of the American Academy of Child & Adolescent Psychiatry, 49*(11), 1125–1133.

Boylan, K., Vaillancourt, T., Boyle, M., & Szatmari, P. (2007). Comorbidity of internalizing disorders in children with oppositional defiant disorder. *European Child & Adolescent Psychiatry, 16*, 484–494.

Burke, J. D., Butler, E. J., Shaughnessy, S., Karlovich, A. R., & Evans, S. C. (2024). Evidence-based assessment of DSM-5 disruptive, impulse control, and conduct disorders. *Assessment, 31*(1), 75–93.

Burke, J. D., Hipwell, A. E., & Loeber, R. (2010). Dimensions of oppositional defiant disorder as predictors of depression and conduct disorder in preadolescent girls. *Journal of the American Academy of Child & Adolescent Psychiatry, 49*(5), 484–492.

Burke, J. D., Johnston, O. G., & Butler, E. J. (2021). The irritable and oppositional dimensions of oppositional defiant disorder: Integral factors in the explanation of affective and behavioral psychopathology. *Child and Adolescent Psychiatric Clinics of North America, 30*(3), 637–647.

Burke, J. D., Johnston, O. G., & Perkins, A. G. (2022). Where should psychopathic traits be placed in a diagnostic framework? Evidence for a grandiose–manipulative specifier for ODD. *Research on Child and Adolescent Psychopathology, 50*(10), 1289–1298.

Burke, J. D., Pardini, D. A., & Loeber, R. (2008). Reciprocal relationships between parenting behavior and disruptive psychopathology from childhood through adolescence. *Journal of Abnormal Child Psychology, 36*, 679–692.

Canino, G., Polanczyk, G., Bauermeister, J. J., Rohde, L. A., & Frick, P. J. (2010). Does the prevalence of CD and ODD vary across cultures? *Social Psychiatry and Psychiatric Epidemiology, 45*, 695–704.

Chafouleas, S. M., Riley-Tillman, T. C., & Christ, T. J. (2009). Direct Behavior Rating (DBR): An emerging method for assessing social behavior within a tiered intervention system. *Assessment for Effective Intervention, 34*(4), 195–200.

Chafouleas, S. M., Riley-Tillman, T. C., & McDougal, J. L. (2002). Good, bad, or in-between: How does the Daily Behavior Report Card rate? *Psychology in the Schools, 39*(2), 157–169.

Chamberlain, P., & Reid, J. B. (1987). Parent observation and report of child symptoms. *Behavioral Assessment*. 9(1), 97–109.

Colins, O. F., Van Damme, L., Hendriks, A. M., & Georgiou, G. (2020). The DSM-5 with limited prosocial emotions specifier for conduct disorder: A systematic literature review. *Journal of Psychopathology and Behavioral Assessment, 42*, 248–258.

Comer, J. S., Chow, C., Chan, P. T., Cooper-Vince, C., & Wilson, L. A. (2013). Psychosocial treatment efficacy for disruptive behavior problems in very young children: A meta-analytic examination. *Journal of the American Academy of Child & Adolescent Psychiatry, 52*(1), 26–36.

DelBello, M. P., Lopez-Larson, M. P., Soutullo, C. A., & Strakowski, S. M. (2001). Effects of race on psychiatric diagnosis of hospitalized adolescents: A retrospective chart review. *Journal of Child and Adolescent Psychopharmacology, 11*(1), 95–103.

Demmer, D. H., Hooley, M., Sheen, J., McGillivray, J. A., & Lum, J. A. (2017). Sex differences in the prevalence of oppositional defiant disorder during middle childhood: A meta-analysis. *Journal of Abnormal Child Psychology, 45*, 313–325.

Déry, M., Begin, V., Toupin, J., & Temcheff, C. (2019). Clinical utility of the limited prosocial emotions specifier in the childhood-onset subtype of conduct disorder. *The Canadian Journal of Psychiatry, 64*(12), 838–845.

Downey, D. B., & Pribesh, S. (2004). When race matters: Teachers' evaluations of students' classroom behavior. *Sociology of Education, 77*(4), 267–282.

Erskine, H. E., Ferrari, A. J., Nelson, P., Polanczyk, G. V., Flaxman, A. D., Vos, T., et al. (2013). Research review: Epidemiological modeling of attention-deficit/hyperactivity disorder and conduct disorder for the Global Burden of Disease Study 2010. *Journal of Child Psychology and Psychiatry, 54*(12), 1263–1274.

Erskine, H. E., Norman, R. E., Ferrari, A. J., Chan, G. C., Copeland, W. E., Whiteford, H. A., & Scott, J. G. (2016). Long-term outcomes of attention-deficit/hyperactivity disorder and conduct disorder: A systematic review and meta-analysis. *Journal of the American Academy of Child & Adolescent Psychiatry, 55*(10), 841–850.

Evans, S. C., Pederson, C. A., Fite, P. J., Blossom, J. B., & Cooley, J. L. (2016). Teacher-reported irritable and defiant dimensions of oppositional defiant disorder: Social, behavioral, and academic correlates. *School Mental Health, 8*, 292–304.

Fadus, M. C., Ginsburg, K. R., Sobowale, K., Halliday-Boykins, C. A., Bryant, B. E., et al. (2020). Unconscious bias and the diagnosis of disruptive behavior disorders and ADHD in African American and Hispanic youth. *Academic Psychiatry, 44*, 95–102.

Fanti, K. A. (2018). Understanding heterogeneity in conduct disorder: A review of psychophysiological studies. *Neuroscience & Biobehavioral Reviews, 91*, 4–20.

First, M. B., Rebello, T. J., Keeley, J. W., Bhargava, R., Dai, Y., Kulygina, M., et al. (2018). Do mental health professionals use diagnostic classifications the way we think they do? A global survey. *World Psychiatry, 17*(2), 187–195.

Frick, P. J., Barry, C. T., & Kamphaus, R. W. (2020). *Clinical assessment of child and adolescent personality and behavior*. Springer International.

Gallagher, R., Kurtz, S., & Blackwell, S. C. (2010). Engaging adolescents with disruptive behavior disorders in therapeutic change. In D. Castro-Blanco & M. S. Karver (Eds.), *Elusive alliance: Treatment engagement strategies with high-risk adolescents* (pp. 139–158). American Psychological Association.

Gion C., McIntosh K., & Falcon S. (2022). Effects of a multifaceted classroom intervention on racial disproportionality. *School Psychology Review, 51*(1), 67–83.

Herzhoff, K., & Tackett, J. L. (2016). Subfactors of oppositional defiant disorder: Converging evidence from structural and latent class analyses. *Journal of Child Psychology and Psychiatry, 57*(1), 18–29.

Hill, L. G., Coie, J. D., Lochman, J. E., & Greenberg, M. T. (2004). Effectiveness of early screening for externalizing problems: Issues of screening accuracy and utility. *Journal of Consulting and Clinical Psychology, 72*(5), 809.

Hintze, J. M., Volpe, R. J., & Shapiro, E. S. (2002). Best practices in the systematic direct observation of student behavior. *Best Practices in School Psychology, 4*, 993–1006.

Horner, R., Blitz, C., & Ross, S. W. (2014). *The importance of contextual fit when implementing evidence-based programs*. Office of the Assistant Secretary for Planning and Evaluation (ASPE). *https://aspe.hhs.gov/sites/default/files/migrated_legacy_files//44416/ib_Contextual.pdf*

Hudziak, J. J., Derks, E. M., Althoff, R. R., Copeland, W., & Boomsma, D. I. (2005). The genetic and environmental contributions to oppositional defiant behavior: A multi-informant twin study. *Journal of the American Academy of Child & Adolescent Psychiatry, 44*(9), 907–914.

Individuals with Disabilities Education Act. (2004). Sec. 300.8 (c)(4). *https://sites.ed.gov/idea/regs/b/a/300.8*

Keenan, K., & Wakschlag, L. S. (2002). Can a valid diagnosis of disruptive behavior disorder be made in preschool children? *American Journal of Psychiatry, 159*(3), 351–358.

Kersten, L., Vriends, N., Steppan, M., Raschle, N. M., Praetzlich, M., Oldenhof, H., et al. (2017). Community violence exposure and conduct problems in children and adolescents with conduct disorder and healthy controls. *Frontiers in Behavioral Neuroscience, 11*. *www.frontiersin.org/journals/behavioral-neuroscience/articles/10.3389/fnbeh.2017.00219*

Klahr, A. M., & Burt, S. A. (2014). Practitioner review: Evaluation of the known behavioral heterogeneity in conduct disorder to improve its assessment and treatment. *Journal of Child Psychology and Psychiatry, 55*(12), 1300–1310.

Lahey, B. B., Loeber, R., Burke, J., & Rathouz, P. J. (2002). Adolescent outcomes of childhood conduct disorder among clinic-referred boys: Predictors of improvement. *Journal of Abnormal Child Psychology, 30*, 333–348.

Lau, A. S., Garland, A. F., Yeh, M., Mccabe, K. M., Wood, P. A., & Hough, R. L. (2004). Race/ethnicity and inter-informant agreement in assessing adolescent psychopathology. *Journal of Emotional and Behavioral Disorders, 12*(3), 145–156.

Lavigne, J. V., LeBailly, S. A., Hopkins, J., Gouze, K. R., & Binns, H. J. (2009). The prevalence of ADHD, ODD, depression, and anxiety in a community sample of 4-year-olds. *Journal of Clinical Child & Adolescent Psychology, 38*(3), 315–328.

Leijten, P., Gardner, F., Melendez-Torres, G. J., van Aar, J., Hutchings, J., Schulz, S., Knerr, W., & Overbeek, G. (2019). Meta-analyses: Key parenting program components for disruptive child behavior. *Journal of the American Academy of Child and Adolescent Psychiatry, 58*(2), 180–190.

Maniglio, R. (2014). Prevalence of sexual abuse among children with conduct disorder: A systematic review. *Clinical Child and Family Psychology Review, 17,* 268–282.

Mattuck, S. (2022). Effects of child and parent race on reported externalizing and internalizing symptoms: Findings from the PACCT study. *Graduate Student Journal of Psychology, 18.*

Maughan, B., Rowe, R., Messer, J., Goodman, R., & Meltzer, H. (2004). Conduct disorder and oppositional defiant disorder in a national sample: developmental epidemiology. *Journal of Child Psychology and Psychiatry, 45*(3), 609–621.

McCart, M. R., & Sheidow, A. J. (2016). Evidence-based psychosocial treatments for adolescents with disruptive behavior. *Journal of Clinical Child & Adolescent Psychology, 45*(5), 529–563.

Mehta, S., Nagar, S., & Aparasu, R. (2009). Unmet prescription medication needs in US children. *Journal of the American Pharmacists Association, 49*(6), 769–776.

Mendel, R., Traut-Mattausch, E., Jonas, E., Leucht, S., Kane, J. M., Maino, K., et al. (2011). Confirmation bias: Why psychiatrists stick to wrong preliminary diagnoses. *Psychological Medicine, 41*(12), 2651–2659.

Mikolajewski, A. J., Taylor, J., & Iacono, W. G. (2017). Oppositional defiant disorder dimensions: Genetic influences and risk for later psychopathology. *Journal of Child Psychology and Psychiatry, and Allied Disciplines, 58*(6), 702–710.

Miller, T. W., Nigg, J. T., & Miller, R. L. (2009). Attention deficit hyperactivity disorder in African American children: What can be concluded from the past ten years? *Clinical Psychology Review, 29*(1), 77–86.

Mitchison, G. M., Liber, J. M., & Njardvik, U. (2022). Parent and teacher ratings of ODD dimensions and emotion regulation: Informant discrepancies in a two-phase study. *Journal of Child and Family Studies, 31*(2), 1–11.

Moffitt, T. E., & Caspi, A. (2001). Childhood predictors differentiate life-course persistent and adolescence-limited antisocial pathways among males and females. *Development and Psychopathology, 13*(2), 355–375.

Morgan, P. L., Staff, J., Hillemeier, M. M., Farkas, G., & Maczuga, S. (2013). Racial and ethnic disparities in ADHD diagnosis from kindergarten to eighth grade. *Pediatrics, 132*(1), 85–93.

Nguyen, L., Huang, L. N., Arganza, G. F., & Liao, Q. (2007). The influence of race and ethnicity on psychiatric diagnoses and clinical characteristics of children and adolescents in children's services. *Cultural Diversity and Ethnic Minority Psychology, 13*(1), 18–25.

Perkins, A., Ridler, J., Browes, D., Peryer, G., Notley, C., & Hackmann, C. (2018). Experiencing mental health diagnosis: a systematic review of service user, clinician, and carer perspectives across clinical settings. *The Lancet. Psychiatry, 5*(9), 747–764.

Polanczyk, G. V., Salum, G. A., Sugaya, L. S., Caye, A., & Rohde, L. A. (2015). Annual research review: A meta-analysis of the worldwide prevalence of mental disorders in children and adolescents. *Journal of Child Psychology and Psychiatry, 56*(3), 345–365.

Rashid, T. (2015). Strength-based assessment. In S. Joseph (Ed.), *Positive psychology in practice: Promoting human flourishing in work, health, education, and everyday life* (pp. 519–542). Wiley.

Riley-Tillman, T. C., Chafouleas, S. M., Briesch, A. M., & Eckert, T. L. (2008). Daily behavior report cards and systematic direct observation: An investigation of the acceptability, reported training and use, and decision reliability among school psychologists. *Journal of Behavioral Education, 17,* 313–327.

Rosenbaum, J. (2020). Educational and criminal justice outcomes 12 Years after school suspension. *Youth & Society, 52*(4), 515–547.

Schneider, H., & Eisenberg, D. (2006). Who receives a diagnosis of attention-deficit/ hyperactivity disorder in the United States elementary school population? *Pediatrics, 117*(4), e601–e609.

Sinclair, A. C., Gesel, S. A., & Lemons, C. J. (2019). The effects of peer-assisted learning on disruptive behavior and academic engagement. *Journal of Positive Behavior Interventions, 21*(4), 238–248.

Stringaris, A., & Goodman, R. (2009). Three dimensions of oppositionality in youth. *Journal of Child Psychology and Psychiatry, 50*(3), 216–223.

Stringaris, A., Mikolajewski, A. J., Taylor, J., & Iacono, W. G. (2012). Oppositional defiant disorder dimensions: Genetic influences and risk for later psychopathology. *Journal of Child Psychology and Psychiatry, 58*(6), 702–710.

Stormshak, E. A., Bierman, K. L., McMahon, R. J., & Lengua, L. J. (2000). Parenting practices and child disruptive behavior problems in early elementary school. *Journal of Clinical Child Psychology, 29*(1), 17–29.

Waddell, C., Schwartz, C., Andres, C., Barican, J. L., & Yung, D. (2018). Fifty years of preventing and treating childhood behaviour disorders: A systematic review to inform policy and practice. *BMJ Mental Health, 21*(2), 45–52.

Waldman, I. D., Rowe, R., Boylan, K., & Burke, J. D. (2021). External validation of a bifactor model of oppositional defiant disorder. *Molecular Psychiatry, 26*(2), 682–693.

Wei, H. T., Lan, W. H., Hsu, J. W., Bai, Y. M., Huang, K. L., Su, T. P., et al. (2016). Risk of suicide attempt among adolescents with conduct disorder: A longitudinal follow-up study. *The Journal of Pediatrics, 177*, 292–296.

CHAPTER 20

Assessment of Bipolar and Related Disorders

Shelley R. Hart

Bipolar disorder (BD) is a complex diagnosis characterized by distinct periods, that is, episodes of depression and mania or hypomania (American Psychiatric Association, 2022). Specifically related to diagnosis in youth, bipolar and related disorders share symptoms with multiple other disorders—both specific symptoms, such as criteria of a depressive episode, and nonspecific symptoms, such as irritability or hyperactivity. In combination with high levels of comorbidity, it is often difficult to separate BD from other diagnoses, in particular, major depressive disorder (MDD) or unipolar depression, disruptive mood dysregulation disorder (DMDD), and attention-deficit/hyperactivity disorder (ADHD) (Singh et al., 2014).

Diagnosing BD in youth is not without controversies in the literature (e.g., Elhosary & Birmaher, 2022). Further, research terminology may be confusing for practicing clinicians (e.g., "pediatric" or "early onset" are typically defined as onset prior to 18 years, incorporating both pre- and pubertal-age youth). It is generally accepted that BD can occur in prepubertal youth (referred to as "children" throughout this chapter); however, the presentation of BD in children can look quite different from adolescents and adults, who tend to share similar patterns and prognosis (Baldessarini et al., 2012; Janiri et al., 2021; Singh et al., 2014).

Recent estimates of the international prevalence rates for bipolar spectrum disorder in youth are 3.9% (Van Meter et al., 2019), making it more common than autism or schizophrenia (Goldstein et al., 2017). The spectrum includes bipolar I, which requires the presence of a manic episode, and bipolar II, which tends to be the more depressive presentation of BD disorders, the not otherwise specified (NOS) and other specified bipolar and related (OS-BRD) disorders, and cyclothymia (Goldstein et al., 2017). The spectrum of disorders is a challenging one. For example, youth with BD report a lower quality of life than those with chronic medical conditions, behavioral disorders, and other non-behavior/non-mood disorders (McGinty et al., 2023). This may be, in part, due to the chronic experience of depressive symptoms (including subthreshold symptoms), particularly for those with BD II (Karanti et al., 2020).

Importantly, the risk for suicide for those with BD is high. Notably, in a review of suicidal thoughts and behaviors for youth diagnosed with BD (outpatient 42.9%, inpatient 21.4%, and community 35.7%), the majority reported either past (57.4%) or current (50.4%) suicidal ideation. A quarter of the sample reported a current suicide attempt (25.5%; 21.3% reported a past suicide attempt; Hauser et al., 2013). In comparison to adults, those with a pediatric onset experienced 33% more suicide attempts (Baldessarini et al., 2012).

Although treatment options are less than optimal, missing a diagnosis of BD puts an individual at substantial risk for depressive, manic, or hypomanic episodes, increasing the allostatic load for the individual (Muneer, 2016). Allostatic load implies a cumulative burden on the body and brain of individuals as they attempt to maintain homeostasis during episodes or subthreshold states that are common, particularly for individuals with an early onset of BD. In adults, more affective episodes are associated with more functional and cognitive impairments (Colomer et al., 2023). Missed diagnoses also increase the opportunity for an incorrect treatment protocol—for example, stimulant medication for ADHD before a mood-stabilizing medication—although unequivocal evidence to support risks related to this has not yet been provided (Singh et al., 2014).

This chapter will provide an overview of BD in children and adolescents focusing on identification and assessment. As characteristics associated with BD may adversely impact a child in the educational context, a discussion of special education will follow. The chapter will conclude with culturally relevant practices and future directions for assessment of BD in youth. A substantial literature base exists examining neurological and biological aspects of this disorder; however, that will not be covered in this chapter (interested readers are referred to Scaini et al., 2020, for a review).

IDENTIFICATION AND DIAGNOSTIC CRITERIA

The most common diagnostic tools in the world are the *Diagnostic and Statistical Manual of Mental Disorders* (currently in its fifth text revision edition [DSM-5-TR]; American Psychiatric Association, 2022) and the *International Statistical Classification of Diseases and Related Health Problems* (currently in its 11th edition [ICD-11]; World Health Organization, 2019). The DSM is the official classification system in the United States, although its influence extends beyond, while the ICD, which covers medical disorders as well as psychiatric ones, extends globally.

Both systems include various diagnoses within the bipolar and related disorders that include combinations of manic, hypomanic, or depressive symptoms. Table 20.1 highlights the three main diagnoses of bipolar and related disorders: bipolar I, bipolar II, and cyclothymia. Cyclothymic disorder is much less commonly diagnosed or researched, and so the primary focus of this chapter will be on bipolar I and II. DSM-5-TR also includes bipolar related to substances or medical conditions, as well as other and unspecified bipolar and related disorders. ICD-11 includes coding for other and unspecified bipolar or related disorders. These di-

TABLE 20.1. The Three Main Bipolar and Related Diagnoses

	Manic episode	Hypomanic episode	Major depressive episode	Distinguishing features
Bipolar I	• Required ○ Current or past	• Not required but may be present ○ Current or historical ○ Only if a manic episode exists	• Not required, but may be present ○ Current or historical ○ Only if a manic episode exists	• Characterized by manic symptoms
Bipolar II	• Cannot be present ○ Current or past	• Required ○ Current or past	• Required ○ Current or past	• Requires criteria are met for both hypomanic and major depressive episodes • Hypomanic symptoms are the same as manic symptoms ○ With a shorter duration (at least 4 days vs. 7 days), and ○ Less impairment (unequivocal change in functioning but not marked impairment)

(continued)

TABLE 20.1. *(continued)*

	Manic episode	Hypomanic episode	Major depressive episode	Distinguishing features

Cyclothymia	• Cannot be present
	  ○ Current or past
		• Cannot be present
		  ○ Current or past
			• Cannot be present
			  ○ Current or past
				• Within a 2-year span (1 year for youth), numerous periods of both hypomanic and depressive symptoms
				• Hypomanic symptoms
				  ○ Present for at least half the time
				  ○ Cannot be absent for more than 2 months

Note. Based on *Diagnostic and Statistical Manual of Mental Disorders, 5th Edition, Text Revision* (American Psychiatric Association, 2022) and *International Statistical Classification of Diseases and Related Health Problems, 11th Edition* (World Health Organization, 2019). Specific criteria for episodes can be found on pages 140–142; criteria for bipolar I can be found on pages 142–143, criteria for bipolar II can be found on pages 152–153, and criteria for cyclothymia can be found on pages 159–160 (American Psychiatric Association, 2022).

agnoses are the result of combinations of episodes and symptoms related to mania and depression.

Episodes of Bipolar and Related Disorders

Distinct changes in mood and behavior that are substantially developmentally atypical are necessary for a diagnosis of bipolar I, bipolar II, or cyclothymic disorder. Symptoms must meet duration and impairment criteria and generally cannot be the result of substances or another medical condition. Two of the three episodes are unique to BD: mania and hypomania. Additionally, major depressive episodes are required for a bipolar II diagnosis but, while commonly present, are not required for a diagnosis of bipolar I.

Manic Episode

Episodes of mania are defined by distinct changes in mood—that is, elevated, expansive, or irritable mood—and abnormal and persistent increases in energy or activity (Criterion A; American Psychiatric Association, 2022). Updates from DSM-IV-TR to DSM-5 included adding increases in energy or activity as a core symptom, with the goal to improve diagnostic precision as individuals may be more likely to remember changes in energy more than changes in mood, and changes in energy align with Kraepelin's original description of BD (Calabrese et al., 2017). That is, nonspecific, or overall, increases in energy or activity may represent the hallmark shifts of a manic or hypomanic episode. Meta-analyses of pediatric cases identified increases in energy were present in over three-quarters of the cases of manic symptom presentation (i.e., 76–96%; Kowatch et al., 2005; Van Meter & Youngstrom, 2018).

Elated or euphoric mood is experienced as feeling excessively good, cheerful, or "high." Closely related, an expansive mood may encompass indiscriminate enthusiasm in interpersonal, sexual, or occupational interactions. In an early, but still relevant and noteworthy meta-analysis, Kowatch and colleagues (2005) found that 45–87% of cases reported elated or euphoric mood. Importantly, for youth, irritability may more likely be the overarching valence of mood. This same meta-analysis highlighted that approximately 80% of cases reported irritability as the predominant mood, and most cases reported both irritability and euphoria or elated mood (Kowatch et al., 2005). Van Meter and Youngstrom's (2018) more recent meta-analysis identified similar results (77% of cases with predominant mood as irritability).

Irritability is a challenging symptom present in many psychiatric disorders. For several decades, the presence and primacy of irritability was a particularly polarizing issue within the field regarding pediatric BD (Goldstein et al., 2017; Hart et al., 2014). Further research has essentially quelled the debate by demonstrating that irritability is episodic and shifts with the manic episode, and a call for a developmental subtype dominated by severe irritability has faded (Goldstein et al., 2017). Additionally, creation of the DMDD (American Psychiatric Association, 2022) was thought to capture the severely irritable symptom presentation (Hart et al., 2014). More discussion of DMDD can be found later in this chapter.

In addition to the changes in mood and energy level, a manic episode requires the presence of three of seven symptoms (four if the mood is irritable). These symptoms focus on (1) elevated sense of self (i.e., grandiosity or inflated self-esteem); (2) increases in energy (i.e., a decreased need for sleep, being more talkative than usual or feeling pressured to keep talking, increased goal-directed activity, or psychomotor agitation); (3) risk taking (e.g., unrestricted spending sprees, impulsive investments, and sexual indiscretions); or (4) challenges in thought (i.e., distractibility, flight of ideas, or subjective experience of racing thoughts; American Psychiatric Association, 2022).

The changes in mood and energy included in a manic episode must be present most of the day almost every day for a period of at least 1 week, or any length of time if hospitalization is needed (Criterion A of DSM-5-TR; American Psychiatric Association, 2022). Significant impairment in social or occupational functioning, hospitalization, or presence of psychotic features is required (Criterion C). Three of the seven symptoms must be evident (or four if the predominant mood is irritable; Criterion B). Kowatch and colleagues' (2005) meta-analysis demonstrated that most of the symptoms were reported by a vast majority of youth. Table 20.2 provides an overview of these symptoms as they might present in school-age youth, along with the weighted rate—percentage—reported by Kowatch and colleagues (2005; Hart et al., 2014). It is important to note that mood will influence how these symptoms present. For example, a youth whose predominant mood is irritable will likely respond to racing thoughts in a

TABLE 20.2. Examples of Presentation of Mania in School-Age Children

Symptom	% of cases	Note	Younger child	Adolescent
Inflated self-esteem/ grandiosity	78%	Estimation of abilities not reality-based and, when confronted, are unable to acknowledge reality (don't "give up" on them, despite contradicting evidence); estimation of abilities is inappropriate to context and may cause impairing consequences	Child claims he can run faster than a car, and when his friends question him, he runs out to the street to prove them wrong	Youth posts videos on Instagram, posing as an "influencer" while having 10 followers
Decreased need for sleep	72%	Circadian rhythms off—not simply a lack of sleep, but not being tired despite a lack of sleep	Child who normally needs a nap refuses it and has an increased level of energy past normal bedtime	Parents find youth in the living room early in the morning, alert and active, claiming to have not slept all night
Talkativeness	82%	Pressured, loud, rapid speech; others may have difficulty interjecting into the monologue; youth may be unable to monitor speech despite consequences	Parents are asked to keep a child home during a basketball game as the child had talked throughout the previous game, interrupting the coach and distracting players on the bench and on the court (and repeated these behaviors during the week's practices)	Youth's friends tell parents that they needed to leave the movie halfway through the night before because the youth was talking throughout and other moviegoers were visibly annoyed and verbally threatening

(continued)

TABLE 20.2. *(continued)*

Symptom	% of cases	Note	Younger child	Adolescent
Flight of ideas	56%	Challenges following thoughts through; youth may have difficulty articulating thoughts as they move so quickly that they cannot hold on to them	Child stops in the middle of a story, flowing directly into an entirely new train of thought without a breath; when caregiver points it out, trying to bring her back to the first story, the child looks blankly and cannot remember what the story was about	Youth becomes agitated when trying to describe thinking around math homework, stating he has an "Energizer bunny" in his head
Distractibility	84%	Extreme challenges focusing as a result of internal or external stimuli	Child is observed in their room moving quickly from one play toy to another, seemingly based on what happens to be in their eyesight at the moment	Youth gets up from the dinner table before finishing meal to get something from his room he was talking to his brother about and is gone for an extended period of time; when caregiver goes to find him, he is sitting on his bed looking at a book
Goal-directed activity	(not reported)	Described as "mission mode;" youth may have difficulty transitioning from one activity to another	Child throws self on ground, screaming and pounding fists and feet, after multiple attempts to move him away from the Tonka trucks and inside for lunch	Youth is found in the basement in the morning, having stayed up all night to work on coding their program
Pleasurable activities	69%: poor judgment 38%: hypersexuality	Might be excessive risk-taking behavior; hypersexuality is important to note (once ruling out sexual abuse), as it seems to be specific to bipolar disorders	Child climbs on the roof yelling excitedly to caregiver to show how high up they are	Youth accesses medical support after unprotected sex with multiple partners at several parties over the weekend

Note. Adapted with permission from Hart et al. (2014). Percentages adapted with permission from Kowatch et al. (2005).

different way than one whose predominant mood is expansive or elated.

Hypomanic Episode

Hypomania literally means "beneath" or "mild" mania. An episode of hypomania includes the same symptoms as in a manic episode; however, the duration and impairment criteria are different. That is, unequivocal and distinct changes in mood must be present nearly every day for 4 days and must be apparent to, or observable by, others, but cannot be severe enough to cause significant impairment. Hypomania can be a challenge to diagnose, as characteristics may overlap with highly valued and attractive traits (e.g., highly energetic, gregarious, and friendly with an accelerated work productivity; Doran, 2008). Even when the predominant mood is irritable, it may be seen as part of their personality, and it is unlikely these individuals (or caregivers) would seek treatment or remember these periods or that clinicians would recognize these as hypomanic symptoms (Hart et al., 2014).

The duration requirement of 4 days in DSM-5-TR has continued to spark discussion in the literature. Many researchers have called the 4-day designation "arbitrary" (Miller et al., 2016). In a large longitudinal study, Angst and colleagues (2003) demonstrated that those who met the 4-day criterion were not different from those who did not in terms of important clinical features (e.g., family history, age of onset for symptoms, number of days spent experiencing hypomanic or depressive symptoms, treatment of depression, suicide attempts, comorbidities, or criminal history). Although much of DSM-5-TR and ICD-11 concur in BD, the ICD-11 hypomanic criteria are more vague, requiring "several days" of symptoms (World Health Organization, 2019). ICD-11 also does not require additional symptoms if the mood is only irritable (i.e., DSM-5-TR requires four vs. three of the seven symptoms if the mood is only irritable). These differences result in significantly more hypomanic episodes being recognized using this diagnostic system (Angst et al., 2020). As missed hypomanic episodes are an important factor in undiagnosed BD, it would seem that the ICD-11 criteria are superior.

Major Depressive Episode

Major depressive episodes are characterized by at least 2 weeks of either depressed mood or anhedonia (i.e., loss of interest in previously pleasurable activities). These symptoms are perhaps more familiar than those of mania or hypomania. They include (1) disruptions in weight (i.e., gain or loss when not dieting); (2) sleep (i.e., inability to sleep or sleeping too much); (3) activity (i.e., psychomotor retardation or agitation); (4) energy (i.e., fatigue or loss of energy); (5) concentration (i.e., diminished ability to think or indecisiveness); (6) feelings of guilt or worthlessness; and (7) suicidal thoughts and behaviors (American Psychiatric Association, 2022). Five symptoms (with at least one being depressed mood or anhedonia) must be present nearly every day for the 2-week period (Criterion A), cause significant distress or impairment in functioning (Criterion B), and not be attributable to substances or another medical condition (Criterion C).

It is important to note that it is common for the initial episode to be a major depressive episode, for individuals with BD to spend a substantial amount of time experiencing depressive symptoms, and for individuals with MDD to transition to BD in their lifetime (Angst et al., 2005; Judd et al., 2003). Depressive symptoms have been shown to be at least as debilitating and sometimes more so than manic or hypomanic symptoms (Judd et al., 2003). Differentiation between MDD and BD will be discussed later.

Diagnoses

Bipolar I

Bipolar I is the more classic presentation of BD. For a diagnosis of bipolar I, an individual must experience a manic episode. They may have a history of major depressive episodes, but interestingly, that is not necessary for a diagnosis of bipolar I. They may also experience multiple hypomanic episodes (American Psychiatric Association, 2022). This presentation is traditionally thought to be the more impaired in comparison to bipolar II. For example, in a large national registry study in Sweden, Karanti and colleagues (2020) found that these individuals had higher rates of treatment—that is, more medications prescribed, including mood stabilizers, antipsychotic drugs, and more psychoeducation or electroconvulsive therapy. They also had higher rates of hospitalizations, more elated episodes, and more physical challenges, such as higher body mass index, and more endocrine, nutritional, and metabolic diseases. Other research has shown lower levels of functioning, more cerebrovascular problems, more psychosis, and more mixed features and rapid cycling. However, past research has also indicated that individuals with this diagnosis tend to recover to premorbid levels of psychosocial functioning more than those with a bipolar II diagnosis (Judd et al., 2003).

Bipolar II

A bipolar II diagnosis is believed to be the more depressive and chronic presentation of BD. This diagnosis requires both current or past hypomanic and major depressive episodes (American Psychiatric Association, 2022). A manic episode cannot be part of the individual's history, as that would indicate a bipolar I diagnosis. Bipolar I is traditionally thought to be the more impaired presentation; however, more recent evidence has demonstrated that bipolar II is a complex condition with its own challenging course. Individuals with bipolar II have been shown to have an earlier onset; higher rates of psychiatric comorbidity with earlier onset of these disorders, particularly anxiety, attention-deficit/hyperactivity, and eating disorders; more frequent major depressive episodes; generally more depressive or hypomanic episodes each year with shorter asymptomatic periods, more antidepressant prescriptions and psychotherapy; and more frequent suicide attempts than those with a bipolar I diagnosis (Judd et al., 2003; Karanti et al., 2020). Individuals with a bipolar II diagnosis frequently convert to a bipolar I diagnosis within their lifetime (Angst et al., 2005). However, individuals with bipolar II have also been shown to be more likely to have completed higher education degrees (Karanti et al., 2020).

Cyclothymia

Cyclothymic disorder is less commonly understood, diagnosed, or researched than bipolar I or II (e.g., Faedda et al., 2004) and represents a milder expression of the symptoms. For children, 1 year of hypomanic and depressive symptoms without meeting full criteria for a manic, hypomanic, or major depressive episode is required (for adults, 2 years is required; American Psychiatric Association, 2022). An individual cannot be diagnosed with cyclothymia if they experience a manic, hypomanic, or major depressive episode. Prospective studies have indicated that cyclothymia may be an early presentation (i.e., prodrome) of bipolar I and II (Howes et al., 2011). It has been shown to be reliably distinguishable from nonbipolar disorders and tends to have an earlier onset than bipolar II or unipolar depression in pediatric cases (Van Meter et al., 2013). Interestingly, characterized by a milder expression of symptoms, longitudinal studies have demonstrated that youth with cyclothymia have similar levels of impairment in functioning as those with a BD I or II diagnosis (Birmaher et al., 2009; Van Meter et al., 2013).

Course, Prognosis, and Developmental Challenges to Diagnosis

BD is a complex diagnosis, made even more complicated when diagnosing youth. Once believed not to exist in children, recent systematic reviews and meta-analyses highlight its presence in youth. Bolton et al.'s (2021) review found that approximately 45% of cases had an onset prior to age 18 years, with a peak age of onset between 15 and 25 years old. In their review, Liu et al. (2022) found that over one-quarter (27.7%) of cases had an onset prior to 13 years old, with 37.6% having their first episode between 13 and 18 years old. Importantly, de Girolamo et al.'s (2016) review and meta-analysis identified that, on average, individuals experienced an almost 7-year delay in diagnosis.

The persistence of BD has also been highlighted in recent studies. In their longitudinal study, Hafeman et al. (2021) found that 63% of youth had a childhood onset, and over half of those who had mania or hypomania in childhood also had a hypomanic or manic episode in adolescence (57%). Additionally, a large portion of those who had a hypomanic or manic episode in adolescence also had a manic or hypomanic episode in young adulthood. Another longitudinal study found that only a very small minority of youth diagnosed with BD were asymptomatic with normal functioning in the year prior to follow-up (6%). In contrast, almost half (48%) continued to meet full diagnostic criteria (i.e., have a current episode; Wozniak et al., 2022). In their longitudinal study, Faedda et al. (2004) found that almost three-quarters of their sample (74%) displayed psychopathology prior to age 3 years, primarily in mood and sleep disturbances, hyperactivity, aggression, and anxiety.

The presentation and course for those with a childhood onset may look different than for those with an adolescent onset, who historically have been thought to resemble an adult presentation more closely. For example, in a large adult retrospective study, Baldessarini and colleagues (2012) demonstrated that individuals with adolescent and adult onset did not differ in terms of clinical indicators (i.e., family history of BD, number of episodes per year, percent of time ill, comorbidities, number of hospitalizations, or suicide attempts). In comparison, those with a childhood onset experienced more episodes per year, more comorbidities, and an increased likelihood of family history of BD. There were differences noted between all the groups in terms of functioning in adulthood, with the childhood onset group demonstrating the most impairment; however, those with an onset prior to age 18 years were more likely to have impaired functioning, including lower employment and more frequent suicide attempts, than those with an adult onset. Birmaher and colleagues (2009) also found that those with an early onset, in addition to a long illness duration, low socioeconomic status, and a family history of mood disorders, experienced poorer outcomes.

Additionally, those with an earlier onset have been shown to experience mixed states or rapid cycling more than those with a later onset. Mixed features and rapid cycling are specifiers in DSM-5-TR, meaning that they are coded along with a manic, hypomanic, or major depressive episode to help understand the course and aid in treatment. To add the mixed features specifier, an individual must meet the full criteria for the dominant episode plus three additional symptoms of the other pole that are experienced most days. That is, mania or hypomania is one pole, and depression is the other, so, for example, to add the mixed features specifier, an individual who met the criteria for a manic or hypomanic episode would also need to experience at least three symptoms of depression on most days. A designation of rapid cycling requires at least four mood episodes within a 12-month period, separated by at least 2 months of remission or a switch to the opposite pole (American Psychiatric Association, 2022).

In their systematic review, Janiri et al. (2021) found that over half (55.2%) of individuals with an early onset had mixed states or features. Those with mixed states also tended to have higher rates of comorbidities, particularly ADHD, oppositional defiant disorder (ODD), and anxiety (Janiri et al., 2021). In a longitudinal study of adults conducted over almost 15 years, approximately 25% of the sample experienced a rapid cycling course (Coryell et al., 2003). Half of those individuals had no periods of remission (i.e., 2 months symptom-free) within a 1-year period. This group was more likely to be female, have an early onset of the disorder, and demonstrate a poorer course, including more depressive symptoms, suicide attempts, suicide attempts with higher lethality and intent to die, and multiple suicide attempts.

In addition to women having more rapid cycling and mixed features, DSM-5-TR (American Psychiatric Association, 2022) identifies gender differences in diagnosis and patterns of comorbidity. For example, women may be more likely to be diagnosed with bipolar II disorder, have comorbid eating and alcohol use disorders, and experience more depressive symptoms than do men.

Comorbidities and Differential Diagnoses

It is generally accepted that the presence of comorbidities tends to worsen the course and outcome of BD in youth, yet they are unfortunately common. However, Goldstein and colleagues (2017) warn against "double counting" overlapping symptoms so as not to overinflate rates of comorbidity (p. 527). Instead, they encourage clinicians to identify discrete mood episodes with overlapping symptoms that are (1) more significant than what is typical (baseline) for an individual and (2) concurrent with mood episodes, which would then count the symptom for BD. On the other hand, symptoms that persist outside of a mood episode (e.g., during remission of a bipolar episode) would result in a true symptom of another disorder.

For example, hyperactivity is a possible overlapping symptom for a BD/ADHD comorbidity. Hyperactive symptoms that mark a change from what is normal for an individual and occur only while the individual is experiencing a manic episode would not represent symptoms of a comorbidity but align with a BD-only diagnosis. However, if these symptoms persisted as the manic episode abated, they would also aid in the diagnosis of ADHD.

There are common comorbidities associated with BD in youth. Additionally, there are several disorders that are important to differentiate from BD. Determining what is a true comorbidity and differentiating between these disorders is an important task for a clinician aiming to identify and diagnose BD in youth.

Common Comorbidities

Table 20.3 provides comorbidities identified by two reviews spanning four decades of research (Fahrendorff et al., 2023; Kowatch et al., 2005). These reviews do not overlap in the studies they included, yet it is clear that the rates are very similar. It is important to note that there is wide variation (i.e., range) in the reported rates. Additionally, not all studies included in the reviews reported on all comorbidities. For example, in the Fahrendorff et al. (2023) review, 16 of the 20 studies reported on ADHD diagnoses in their BD youth samples. In those studies, the range of comorbidities ranged from 0–87%, with a weighted mean prevalence, or average, of approximately 60%.

Externalizing types of disorders are the most common comorbidities, with ADHD and ODD having the highest frequencies. On average, almost two-thirds of youth with BD also experience ADHD, and around one-half also experience ODD, with about one in five demonstrating conduct disorder (CD). For internalizing disorders, anxiety is the most common, with, on average, one-quarter of youth with BD experiencing this comorbidity. Apart from substance use disorders (Goldstein & Bukstein, 2010), most comorbidities tend to precede BD. However, while youth with BD have high rates of comorbidities with these disorders, the reverse is not necessarily true (e.g., in the population of all youth with ADHD, BD is not common; Biederman et al., 1996). While not a comprehensive review, also identified in Table 20.3

TABLE 20.3. Common Comorbidities in Youth with BD

Disorder	Weighted mean prevalence[a]	Weighted mean prevalence[b]	Additional comorbidity and differentiation information
ADHD	62% (29–87%)	60% (0–87%)	Symptoms significantly more likely to be present in youth with bipolar disorder[c], elevation of these symptoms is most common in those with comorbidity (vs. bipolar alone)[d]: • Elated mood • Grandiosity • Hypersexuality • Decreased need for sleep (important to distinguish between youth who have insomnia, which may be the case for those with ADHD; however, their need for sleep does not change[e]) • Racing thoughts • Psychiatric hospitalizations[e]
ODD	53% (25–79%)	47.0% (6–89%)	Family history of bipolar disorder much more likely[f], aggression (when present) is more disorganized and impulsive[g], and defiant behaviors may be more typically mood-related[e] in youth with bipolar disorder
Anxiety	27% (15–43%)	24% (0–77%)	• Differences exist between types of anxiety disorders: separation (29%), agoraphobia (27%), generalized (GAD; 24%), social (24%), obsessive–compulsive (OCD; 21%), panic (19%), simple phobia (19%), post-traumatic stress (6%)[b] • Likely developmental differences in type of anxiety with younger individuals more likely to have GAD and separation anxiety disorders and adolescent-onset youth demonstrating more panic, OCD, and social phobias[h] • In many cases, youth with comorbid anxiety have multiple anxiety disorders (44%)[b]
CD	19% (11–30%)	21% (0–55%)	Family history of bipolar disorder much more likely[f], aggression (when present) is more disorganized and impulsive[g], and defiant behaviors may be more typically mood-related[e] in youth with bipolar disorder
SUD	12% (5–29%)	13% (0-41%)	The one comorbidity that bipolar disorder seems to precede, so screening and prevention should be a priority[i]
Tourette's (tics)	Not reported	21% (3–32%)	No known scholarship available
ID	Not reported	10.3% (n/a)	No known scholarship available
ASD	Not reported	10% (2–30%)	Those with ASD typically have a much earlier onset and are more likely to experience[e]: • Developmental delays • Impairments in social functioning • Impairments in verbal and nonverbal communication • Stereotyped or repetitive body movements, speech, or use of objects • Hyper- or hyporeactivity to sensory stimuli • Highly restricted or fixated interests • Inflexible adherence to routines, sameness, or ritualized patterns
ED	Not reported	5% (0–13%)	No known scholarship available

Note. Adapted from [a]Kowatch et al. (2005), [b]Fahrendorff et al. (2023), [c]Geller et al. (1998), [d]Diler et al. (2007), [e]Singh et al. (2014), [f]Wozniak et al. (2001), [g]Joshi and Wilens (2009), [h]Eser et al. (2020), and [i]Goldstein and Bukstein (2010). ADHD = attention-deficit/hyperactivity disorder; ODD = oppositional defiant disorder; CD = conduct disorder; SUD = substance use disorder (includes alcohol use disorder); ID = intellectual disability; ASD = autism spectrum disorder; ED = eating disorder. Only one study reported an ID comorbidity; therefore, a range was not included.

are some additional tips for understanding these comorbidities and possibly distinguishing between them when assessing BD. Far less scholarship is available for comorbidity with Tourette's (tic disorders), intellectual disability, autism, and eating disorders.

The frequency of these comorbidities means that when assessing youth for BD, it will be important to, at the least, also screen for these disorders through clinical interview and with specific measures. Although it is outside the scope of this chapter, the clinician should plan on having screening and assessment tools for these comorbidities available and including them in the assessment plan as needed. Additionally, interpretation of comorbidities should require the presence of overlapping symptoms outside of the mood episode (Goldstein et al., 2017). Recognition that these disorders commonly precede presentation (or diagnosis) of BD also means that clinicians working with youth with these disorders should be familiar with BD to potentially identify symptoms early in the course.

Differential Diagnoses

Equally important to an accurate identification of BD is differentiating it from typical behaviors and other diagnoses. Formally, DSM-5-TR identifies disorders or precursors to onset that must be ruled out prior to a diagnosis (e.g., a manic episode that occurs during antidepressant therapy; American Psychiatric Association, 2022). Additionally, with the reorganization that occurred in DSM-5, bipolar and related disorders are now positioned between schizophrenia spectrum and other psychotic disorders and depressive disorders to acknowledge the relationship BD has with these disorders.

Table 20.4 provides guidance for clinicians in differentiation activities. In general, differential diagnosis benefits from identification of the course of the symptoms: episodic symptoms lend themselves to a BD diagnosis, while chronic features that do not shift with mood lend themselves to a depressive or psychotic disorder diagnosis.

TABLE 20.4. Differentiation of BD with Typical Development, Depressive Disorders, and Psychotic Disorders

Differentiate BD from . . .	Guidance for identification of BD
Typical development	Symptoms[a]: • Must persist • Cause social, academic, or family impairment • Represent a significant change from baseline • Like grandiosity and elation, must be inappropriate to context • Like pathological elation, decreased need for sleep and hypersexuality are relatively specific to bipolar disorder
Major depressive disorder	Presence of multiple risk factors increases the likelihood of bipolar disorder, and characteristics may include: • Early onset of MDD (prior to age 25)[a,b] • Atypical depressive features (excessive hunger, excessive sleep or need for sleep, excessive tiredness)[a] • Unique experiences with antidepressants (inefficacy)[a,b] • Family history of schizophrenia or mood disorder[a,b] • Psychotic features[a] • Highly recurrent depression[a] • Psychiatric comorbidities (e.g., ADHD, SUD)[b] • Obesity[b]
Disruptive mood dysregulation disorder	Episodic irritability is the defining feature (chronic irritability of DMDD is more likely to be associated with major depressive than bipolar disorder)[a]
Psychotic disorders	• Psychotic features that are mood congruent and present only during a mood episode[c] • Hyperactivity, increased speech, and aggression may be more likely in those with mood disorders with psychotic features than in those with psychotic disorders[d]

Note. Adapted from [a]Singh et al. (2014), [b]Kung et al. (2024), [c]Pavuluri et al. (2004), and [d]Fis and Gumustas (2018).

Depressive Disorders

Depressive disorders discussed here include MDD and DMDD. Diagnostic criteria explicitly exclude BD from coexisting with these disorders. However, the issues related to differentiation are very different. Depressive episodes are often the index (first) episode for individuals, and irritability may be a common experience for youth with BD; therefore, distinguishing between these disorders is often a complex task for clinicians.

In a recent national longitudinal study of 130,793 individuals (10–29 years old) diagnosed with MDD, 13.8% of individuals converted from MDD to BD during the 11-year follow-up (Kung et al., 2024). The conversion rate was highest in the first year following an MDD diagnosis (significant predictors are highlighted in Table 20.4). These findings support prior research that identified family history of psychiatric disorders (primarily mood disorders; Singh et al., 2014), earlier age of MDD onset, and antidepressant resistance as important predictors of a transition. Additionally, these researchers found that psychiatric comorbidities, lower income, more visits to a mental health clinic, and obesity also predicted conversion.

DMDD was added to DSM-5 and not without controversy. The intention of the DMDD diagnosis was to capture the phenotype of BD characterized by predominantly chronic irritability. DMDD criteria require severe, recurrent temper outbursts (on average three or more times per week) that are grossly out of proportion to the situation and inconsistent with developmental level, with a persistent irritable or angry mood most of the day (American Psychiatric Association, 2022). It exists within a hierarchy in that if criteria for BD are met, DMDD is not diagnosed; however, if criteria for both DMDD and ODD are met, a DMDD diagnosis is conferred.

As irritability exists in over a dozen diagnoses, Evans and colleagues (2021) recently tested the accuracy of clinicians to correctly diagnose using DSM-5-TR and ICD-11. Generally, ICD-11 outperformed DSM-5-TR, but of specific interest to this issue, the researchers examined the accuracy of clinicians to identify DMDD using DSM-5-TR (ICD-11 does not recognize DMDD). When presented with various cases, clinicians failed to assign a DMDD diagnosis, even when it was appropriate, using DSM-5-TR, and were more likely to assign a diagnosis to cases with irritability that was developmentally appropriate. Additionally, although clinicians were able to identify BD, they were less likely to be able to differentiate between BD and DMDD or ODD when irritability was present. Again, most advice for differentiation seems to center on irritability that comes and goes with mood—that is, irritability that either begins or significantly increases during a mood episode—versus irritability that is chronic and seems to be simply part of temperament (Goldstein et al., 2017).

Psychotic Disorders

DSM-5-TR includes specific criteria ruling out schizophrenia, schizoaffective, schizophreniform, and delusional disorders. However, psychotic features, delusions, or hallucinations, aspects that most typically define those disorders, are also included as a specifier in BD.

As with other guidance on differentiation, psychotic features that seem to wax and wane with mood episodes appear to be more connected to BD, while those that remain stable throughout the course of the disorder are more connected to a psychotic disorder (Pavuluri et al., 2004). Additionally, Fis and Gumustas (2018) found that there was a significant difference in symptom presentation for adolescents with a psychotic diagnosis in comparison to those with a mood diagnosis. Those with a mood diagnosis, such as BD, were more likely to demonstrate hyperactivity, increased speech, and aggression. Those with a psychotic disorder were more likely to experience hallucinations, disorganized speech, and withdrawal or isolation. The group with psychotic disorders was also more likely to have higher psychotic symptoms and general psychopathology scores. These researchers emphasize the importance of not underestimating the presence of a mood disorder with psychotic features.

ASSESSMENT STRATEGIES AND TOOLS

Youngstrom and colleagues (2005) offer 12 recommendations for an evidence-based approach to assessing BD in youth. While an older resource, the tenets still hold true. These recommendations offer concrete advice (e.g., use of multi-informants) and philosophical stances (e.g., believe BD can exist in youth) that will aid in identification. Generally, they center around knowledge (e.g., being an up-to-date, yet critical, consumer of the literature and recognizing the base rate of BD in your area) and data gathering (e.g., using screenings; gathering detailed family history; looking for abrupt changes in mood and the "handle" symptoms more specific to BD, including elevated mood, grandiosity, pressured speech, racing thoughts, and hypersexuality; and continuing to gather data on key symptoms during treatment). Importantly, these authors recommend an actuarial approach, which requires clinical sophistication and combines (1) base rate, (2) change in likelihood based on family history, and (3) change in likelihood based on screening results. While this process provides a posterior probability estimate (i.e., after symptoms are developed), Van Meter and colleagues (2021) have developed and begun testing a risk calculator that aims to evaluate future probability of BD.

The gold standard for assessment of BD is the clinical interview (Hours, 2025). Rating scales are also an essential assessment tool for BD; psychometric support for measures specific for use with BD in youth continues to advance—including supporting translation into multiple languages (e.g., Chi et al., 2023; de Pablo et al., 2022; Youngstrom et al., 2020, 2021). Useful measures may be omnibus (or broad)—covering an array of internalizing and externalizing behaviors or experiences—and narrow (or specific)—focusing on one aspect of behavior or experience. Table 20.5 provides an overview of these measures. Although depressive symptoms are an important part of the assessment for BD, measures that focus exclusively on depression are not included in this discussion as they will be covered elsewhere (see Chapter 17, this volume, on depressive disorders).

Clinical (Semistructured/Structured) Interview

The clinical interview relies on knowledge of the diagnostic criteria, including how symptoms present most commonly in youth, comorbid conditions, and disorders that require differentiation. Hours (2025) encourages clinicians to obtain the following information from family members during

TABLE 20.5. Assessment Tools for BD

Tool	General information
Semistructured/structured interviews	
K-SADS-PL	• Ages 6 to 18 years • Addresses multiple diagnoses • If primary symptom is endorsed, further probing occurs (so variable numbers of items will be administered based on each case) • Lengthy process • Extensions of this tool are available with more specific (and briefer) interviews for mania and depression • Multiple versions of the K-SADS-PL are available at: *www.pediatricbipolar.pitt.edu/clinical-services/clinical-tools*
YMRS	• Ages 5 to 17 years • 11 items • Four items are double-weighted (irritability, speech, thought content, and disruptive/aggressive behavior) • Industry standard interview to quantify symptom severity (five levels of severity available) • Parent version of the YMRS is available at: *www.tn.gov/content/dam/tn/mentalhealth/documents/Pages_from_CY_BPGs_483-488.pdf*
Omnibus/broad rating scales	
ASEBA/CBCL	• Ages 6 to 18 years (also a version for 1.5 to 5 years) • Conflicting evidence exists to support a pediatric BD profile (CBCL-PBD) consisting of elevated Attention Problems, Aggressive Behavior, and Anxious/Depressed subscales • CBCL Externalizing Scale may be useful in identification and has outperformed the CBCL-PBD • Cost associated: *www.aseba-web.org*

(continued)

TABLE 20.5. *(continued)*

Tool	General information
BASC-3	• Ages 2 to 21 years • Has not been researched in diagnosis of BD • Caregiver, teacher, and self-report forms • Has a Structured Development History (SDH) report • Has screening forms available (Behavior and Emotional Screening System; BESS) • Has multiple scales that may aid in identification (e.g., Emotional Behavior Disorder Probability Index) as well as special education eligibility (e.g., Emotional Disturbance Qualification Scales) • Cost associated: *www.pearsonassessments.com/store/usassessments/en/Store/Professional-Assessments/Behavior/BASC-3-Family-of-Assessments/p/P100010000.html*
SDQ	• Ages 2 to 17 years • Has not been researched in diagnosis of BD • Caregiver, teacher, and self-report forms available • Available in many different languages • May aid in identification of youth with behavioral and emotional dysregulation • Forms available at: *www.sdqinfo.org/a0.html*
Narrow/specific rating scales	
P-GBI	• Ages 5 to 17 years • Mania and depression screener • Caregiver completed • Short forms (of the original 73 items) exist with one 10-item form for mania and 10 items for depression (two parallel 10-item forms) • Caregiver version of the forms is available: *https://trello.com/b/dYUKINRP/translated-measures-dashboard*
CMRS-P	• Ages 5 to 17 years • Mania screener • Caregiver completed • 21 items • Brief version consisting of 10 items also available (Brief CMRS-P) • Rated on scale from "Never/Rarely" (0) to "Very Often" (3) • Cut score of 20 (full version) or 10 (brief version) should prompt further assessment
CBQ	• Ages 5 to 17 years • Caregiver completed • 65 items • Available for caregiver to complete at: *www.jbrf.org/the-child-bipolar-questionnaire*
GBI	• Ages 11 to 18 years • Mania and depression screener • Self-report • Short forms exist with one 10-item form for mania and 10 items for depression (two parallel 10-item forms); also one 7-item mania and one 7-item depression scales also exist with less content coverage • Self-report version of the forms is available: *https://trello.com/b/dYUKINRP/translated-measures-dashboard*
MDQ-A	• Ages 12 years to adulthood • Based on MDQ for adults available: *www.dbsalliance.org/pdfs/MDQ.pdf* • Version for caregivers also available (MDQ-P): *https://osf.io/h9vbs*

Note. K-SADS-PL = Kiddie Schedule for Affective Disorders and Schizophrenia—Present and Lifetime (Kaufman et al., 1997); YMRS = Young Mania Rating Scale (Young et al., 1978); CDRS-R = Child Depression Rating Scale—Revised (Poznanski et al., 1984); ASEBA = Achenbach System of Empirically Based Assessment (Achenbach & Rescorla, 2001); BASC-3 = Behavior Assessment System for Children—3rd Edition (Reynolds et al., 2015); SDQ = Strengths and Difficulties Questionnaire (Goodman, 1997); P-GBI = Parent General Behavior Inventory (Youngstrom et al., 2020); GBI = General Behavior Inventory (Youngstrom et al., 2021); CMRS = Child Mania Rating Scale (Pavuluri et al., 2006); MDQ-A = Mood Disorders Questionnaire—Adolescent (Wagner et al., 2006).

the clinical interview: (1) perinatal, developmental, and medical–surgical history; (2) psychosocial events and history of abuse; (3) psychiatric history, including any comorbidities; (4) frequency, intensity, number, and duration of mood episodes; and (5) severity and psychosocial impact of symptoms.

Specialized training may be required to conduct formal clinical interviews, particularly when structured or semistructured interview measures are used. The most common semistructured interview used in assessment of BD is the *Kiddie Schedule for Affective Disorders and Schizophrenia—Present and Lifetime* version (K-SADS-PL; Kaufman et al., 1997). This is a lengthy interview that incorporates child and parent reports with clinician judgment to measure current and past symptoms of mood, anxiety, and psychotic and disruptive behavior disorders in children 6–18 years old. If a primary symptom for a diagnosis is endorsed, further probes elicit more information about the symptoms for that disorder. The K-SADS-PL has been updated to reflect DSM-5 and has been translated into 16 languages.

Additionally, extensions of the K-SADS-PL have been developed to explicitly examine mania and depression. These are newer additions to the older semistructured interviews that focus on mania—the Young Mania Rating Scale (YMRS; Young et al., 1978)—and depression—the Child Depression Rating Scale—Revised (CDRS-R; Poznanski et al., 1984). Goldstein and colleagues (2017) highlighted that these semistructured interviews remain the best available methods to identify BD and concluded that psychometrically, there is very little distinction between these interview tools. However, in their meta-analysis comparing different strategies and measures, Youngstrom and colleagues (2015) stated that due to the varied performance of the YMRS, its use is not recommended in lieu of the other, narrow-focused rating scales, which have stronger evidence supporting their use.

Identification of the "handle" symptoms of BD (i.e., symptoms that tend to provide the most helpful differentiation between BD and other disorders, such as elevated mood, grandiosity, pressured speech, racing thoughts, and hypersexuality) and inquiry about the episodic nature of symptoms and the presence of symptoms at "subthreshold" (i.e., milder than diagnoseable) level, are important tasks of the clinical interview. Additionally, inquiry into a potential "prodrome" (i.e., early presentation)—high level of energy, less need for sleep, difficulty thinking and concentrating, and loud speech—can aid in diagnosis (Hours, 2025).

Omnibus or Broad Rating Scales

Omnibus or broad measures do not necessarily include items specific to symptoms of BD; however, several have clinical utility in the diagnostic process. The Achenbach System of Empirically Based Assessment (ASEBA)—particularly the Child Behavior Checklist (CBCL; Achenbach & Rescorla, 2001)—has been discussed in terms of a pediatric BD profile. This profile includes elevated scores on the attention problems, aggressive behavior, and anxious/depressed subscales. However, as outlined in Goldstein et al. (2017), this profile was outperformed by the CBCL externalizing scale in identifying BD, suggesting that the profile is not empirically supported.

Youngstrom et al.'s (2015) meta-analysis demonstrated that narrow rating scales (described below) were better at identifying BD than omnibus scales. These authors noted that omnibus scales appeared to be better at ruling out, rather than ruling in, BD. However, it has also been suggested that if a clinician was already using the ASEBA in their assessment, adding narrow scales was redundant and likely unnecessary in diagnosis, but might provide useful ongoing information for treatment purposes (Youngstrom et al., 2021). Other omnibus scales have not had direct research related to BD. However, they may provide useful supplemental information.

Narrow or Specific Rating Scales

Several rating scales have demonstrated the ability to identify BD and differentiate it from other disorders (e.g., ADHD). Again, included in this discussion are only scales that focus on both mania/hypomania and depression or exclusively on mania/hypomania. Most of these scales focus on caregiver report, which has been shown to be superior to teacher- and self-report in identification of BD (Youngstrom et al., 2015), and many are freely available. In Youngstrom et al.'s (2015) meta-analysis, these caregiver reports all performed equally well and included the Parent General Behavior Inventory (P-GBI; Youngstrom et al., 2009), the Child Mania Rating Scale (CMRS; Pavuluri et al., 2006), and the Child Bipolar Questionnaire (CBQ; Papolos et al., 2006). The P-GBI has since been updated to include a short form for mania and two parallel forms for depression (Youngstrom et al., 2020).

Self-report scales are also valuable in the assessment of BD in adolescents, particularly as self-report may better differentiate some of the "handle" symptoms (e.g., racing thoughts, flight of ideas, elation, grandiosity, and decreased need for sleep; Tillman et al., 2004). Additionally, self-report is typically the easiest form of data to collect and may be the only option in certain circumstances (e.g., foster care and forensic situations). Two self-report scales are included in Table 20.5, the General Behavior Inventory (GBI; Depue et al., 1981) and Mood Disorders Questionnaire (MDQ; Hirschfeld, 2002). The GBI has also been recently updated to include a short form for mania and two parallel forms for depression (Youngstrom et al., 2021; *note*: two additional brief forms following a 7 Up [manic symptoms] and 7 Down [depressive symptoms; Youngstrom et al., 2013, 2021] were also evaluated and performed well but had less content coverage).

ADDITIONAL CONSIDERATIONS IN ASSESSMENT

There are several additional issues to consider when assessing youth for BD. First, suicide risk is unfortunately high in this population, and any assessment for BD would be remiss without addressing it. In a systematic review, Hauser and colleagues (2013) found that more than half of youth with BD disclosed current suicidal ideation (50.4%), while over one-quarter reported a suicide attempt (25.5%). Huber et al. (2023) found that in comparison to youth with an MDD diagnosis, those with BD experienced more frequent and more severe suicidal ideation and felt less in control of their suicidal thoughts, and deterrents were less likely to stop them from acting on their suicidal ideation. Goldstein and colleagues (2022) found that the risk for suicide in youth with BD was 60 times greater than for the general population, and 13.7% had more than two suicide attempts during their 13-year follow-up. These researchers proposed a clinical risk calculator that relies on information commonly gathered during assessment, which, when scores are elevated, may indicate the need for more detailed suicide risk assessment (see Table 20.6 for predictors).

Second, it can be anticipated that youth experiencing BD symptoms (and other factors, such as neurological differences; e.g., Scaini et al., 2020) may have challenges in an educational context. Additionally, challenges in the educational context have been shown to put youth at risk for a BD onset (Rabelo-da-Ponte et al., 2024). Even though a diagnosis of BD is not expected to fall within the school-based mental health professional's duties typically, knowledge of this disorder is valuable. Conversely, while assessing special education eligibility is not typically part of a community-based clinician's duties, knowledge of special education is valuable. Both professionals benefit from information that the other might gather during an assessment. For example, a school psychologist may benefit from information a clinical psychologist obtained during a clinical assessment that highlighted racing thoughts, pressured speech, psychomotor agitation, and increased goal-directed activities as being dominant symptoms, which informed eligibility as a student with an "other health impairment" rather than mood-dominant symptomatology, which would suggest emotional disturbance (ED) as the more appropriate desig-

TABLE 20.6. Suicide Risk Predictors for Bipolar Youth (Factors Included in the Suicide Risk Calculator)

1. *Age of mood onset*: younger conferring more risk
2. *Nonsuicidal self-injurious behavior*: presence of this in an individual's history
3. *Current age*: older conferring more risk
4. *Psychosis*: presence of this in an individual's history
5. *Socioeconomic status (SES)*: lower SES conferring more risk
6. *Most severe depressive symptoms in past 6 months*: highest depression scores in last 6 months
7. *History of suicide attempt*: presence of this in an individual's history
8. *Family history of suicidal behavior*: presence of this in an individual's history
9. *Substance use disorder*: presence of this in an individual's history
10. *Lifetime history of physical/sexual abuse*: presence of this in an individual's history

Note. Adapted from Goldstein et al. (2022). These 10 predictors accounted for over 90% of the cross-validated relative influence (in order of relative influence).

nation. For a comprehensive overview of identifying, assessing, and treating youth with BD in the educational context, readers are referred to Hart et al. (2014).

Third, issues related to physical development will be important to attend to during assessment. For example, individuals with thyroid dysfunction may experience changes in mood, and physicians recommend treating the physical issue first, which may resolve the mood issue (Chakrabarti, 2011). Hours (2025) recommends that an assessment of BD include laboratory tests to rule out physical illnesses, including complete blood count; electrolyte panel; liver functioning test; lipid panel; fasting blood sugar test; examination of thyroid-stimulating hormone, vitamin B12, and folic acid levels; iron tests; and measurement of hormone levels. A urine drug screen will also be helpful.

CULTURALLY RELEVANT PRACTICE CONSIDERATIONS

Alarcón (2009) defines culture as norms, meanings, and values used to construct a view of the world. It includes factors such as language, values, traditions, religion, gender and sexual orientation, socioeconomic status, and moral practices. This author highlights the ethnocentrism of the DSM and its "benign neglect" of issues related to culture over time, stressing that culture in clinical assessments is typically limited to issues of race, ethnicity, language, or migrant status. In response to criticisms such as this, workgroups were convened to more adequately address issues of race, ethnicity, culture, and gender in the updates to DSM-5 and DSM-5-TR (American Psychiatric Association, 2022).

Rates of pediatric BD have not highlighted international differences (Van Meter et al., 2019). However, this does not preclude cultural differences in symptom expression, identification of symptomatology as problematic, or practices that implicitly or explicitly are biased against or for certain groups. For example, African American males in the United States were at higher risk of being diagnosed with schizophrenia when presenting with psychosis rather than BD when appropriate (American Psychiatric Association, 2022). Youngstrom and colleagues (2015) commented that, although they did not find cultural bias in the measures they examined (i.e., differential item functioning and structural invariance), reading level of the measures was important to examine, as lower caregiver reading level may inhibit gathering of accurate information.

DSM-5-TR features a "Cultural Formulation" section that includes an Outline for Cultural Formulation and a Cultural Formulation Interview (CFI; American Psychiatric Association, 2022). The Outline provides a framework for exploring the intersection of an individual's identities with their mental health challenges. It encourages the systematic assessment of demographic and socially and culturally defined characteristics (e.g., age, ethnoracial background, and religious affiliation), experiences and perceptions of their symptoms (e.g., cultural idioms of distress), social determinants of health (e.g., access to resources), and cultural features of the relationship between the clinician and individual (e.g., differences in language, cultural background, and education level). This framework stresses the importance of engaging in this work with every individual, not simply those with unfamiliar (or different) cultural backgrounds.

The CFI offers protocols for systematically obtaining this information and includes three tools: the core CFI, an Informant version for collateral information, and Supplementary modules (American Psychiatric Association, 2022). Four domains are included in the CFI that include exploring how an individual assigns meaning and factors that influence coping and help-seeking.

First, the clinician is encouraged to explore an individual's cultural definition of the problem, that is, presenting concerns, narrative of their understanding of the illness, how they would describe their issues to others close to them, and what they would describe as being most distressing about the illness. Questions such as "People often understand their problems in their own way, which may be similar to or different from how doctors describe the problem. How would *you* describe the problem?" (American Psychiatric Association, 2022, p. 864) attempt to clarify the presenting issue from the point of view of the individual and important others in their lives.

Second, the clinician is asked to explore cultural perceptions of cause, context, and support, that is, what social supports exist that help with the issue, are there social stressors that contribute to the problems, are there culturally relevant idioms of distress, how do close others understand the cause of the illness, and how does the individual's cultural identity impact the illness, or how does it influence other challenges. Questions such as "Sometimes, aspects of people's background or identity can make their [problem] better or worse.

By background I mean, for example, the languages you speak, where you or your family are from, your race or ethnic background, your gender or sexual orientation, or your faith or religion . . . are there any aspects of your background or identity that make a difference to your [problem]?" (American Psychiatric Association, 2022, p. 865) aim to uncover meaning around causes, stressors, and supports that may be relevant for understanding the challenges and helpful for treatment.

Third, the clinician is encouraged to help the individual identify cultural factors affecting self-coping and past help-seeking, that is, past forms of self-coping and help-seeking. Questions such as "Often, people look for help from many different sources, including different kinds of doctors, helpers, or healers. In the past, what kinds of treatment, help, advice, or healing have you sought for your [problem]?" (American Psychiatric Association, 2022, p. 866) are posed to elicit experiences of self-coping and help-seeking.

Fourth, the clinician is asked to inquire about cultural factors that may affect current help-seeking, that is, treatment preferences of the individual and others close to them. Questions such as, "Sometimes doctors and patients misunderstand each other because they come from different backgrounds or have different expectations. Have you been concerned about this and is there anything that we can do to provide you with the care you need?" attempt to clarify differences in backgrounds, as well as the individual's understanding of their needs and expectations of help and what kinds of help others might have recommended.

Utilization of these tools in combination with a clinician's examination of their biases and understanding of how their own background influences their assessment processes will improve the diagnostic validity of BD in youth. Interested readers are encouraged to access the *DSM-5® Handbook on the Cultural Formulation Interview* for more practical guidance on effective use of the CFI (Lewis-Fernández et al., 2016).

CONCLUSION

Assessment of BD in youth has advanced substantially over the last two decades. These advances have resulted in acknowledgement that this disorder can and does exist in youth. In theory, better identification leads to more timely intervention and appropriate treatment. This could be lifesaving, particularly in recognition of the high risk for suicidal thoughts and behaviors. However, misdiagnosis and underdiagnosis remain an issue. Improvements in knowledge of BD for school- and community-based mental health professionals continue to be required. Next steps for clinicians may include exploring the role of assessment in treatment, and for those interested, a more comprehensive review of working with BD youth in the schools is referred to Hart et al. (2014).

REFERENCES

Achenbach, T. M., & Rescorla, L. A. (2001). *Manual for the ASEBA school-age forms & profiles*. University of Vermont.

Alarcón, R. D. (2009). Culture, cultural factors and psychiatric diagnosis: Review and projections. *World Psychiatry, 8*, 131–139.

American Psychiatric Association. (2022). *Diagnostic and statistical manual of mental disorders* (5th ed., text rev.).

Angst, J., Adjacic-Gross, V., & Rössler, W. (2020). Bipolar in ICD-11: Current status and strengths. *International Journal of Bipolar Disorders, 8*, Article 3.

Angst, J., Benazzi, F., Adjacic, V., Eich, D., & Rössler, W. (2003). Toward a re-definition of subthreshold bipolarity: Epidemiology and proposed criteria for bipolar-II, minor bipolar disorders and hypomania. *Journal of Affective Disorders, 73*, 133–146.

Angst, J., Sellaro, R., Stassen, H. H., & Gamma, A. (2005). Diagnostic conversion from depression to bipolar disorder: Results of a long-term prospective study of hospital admissions. *Journal of Affective Disorders, 84*, 149–157.

Baldessarini, R. J., Tondo, L., Vazquez, G. H., Undurraga, J., Bolzani, L., Yildiz, A., et al. (2012). Age at onset versus family history and clinical outcomes in 1665 international bipolar-I disorder patients. *World Psychiatry, 11*, 40–46.

Biederman, J., Faraone, S., Mick, E., Wozniak, J., Chen, L., Ouellette, C., et al. (1996). Attention-deficit hyperactivity disorder and juvenile mania: An overlooked comorbidity? *Journal of the American Academy of Child and Adolescent Psychiatry, 35*, 997–1008.

Birmaher, B., Axelson, D., Goldstein, B., Strober, M., Gill, M. K., Hunt, J., et al. (2009). Four-year longitudinal course of children and adolescents with bipolar spectrum disorders: The Course and Outcome of Bipolar Youth (COBY) study. *American Journal of Psychiatry, 166*(7), 795–804.

Bolton, S., Warner, J., Hariss, E., Geddes, J., & Saunders, K. E. A. (2021). Bipolar disorder: Trimodal age-at-onset distribution. *Bipolar Disorders, 23*(4), 341–356.

Calabrese, J. R., Gao, K., & Sachs, G. (2017). Diagnosing mania in the age of DSM-5. *American Journal of Psychiatry, 174*(1), 8–10.

Colomer, L., Fico, G., Gutierrez, F., Pujal, E., Baldaqui, N., Murru, A., & Vieta, E. (2023). Lifetime number of affective episodes and functioning in a cohort of patients with bipolar disorder: A cross-sectional study. *European Psychiatry, 66*(S1), S384.

Coryell, W., Solomon, D., Turvey, C., Keller, M., Leon, A. C., Endicott, J., et al. (2003). The long-term course of rapid-cycling bipolar disorder. *Archives of General Psychiatry, 60*, 914–920.

Chakrabarti, S. (2011). Thyroid functions and bipolar affective disorder. *Journal of Thyroid Research, 2011*, Article 306367.

Chi, S., M., Y. E., Ko, J. K., Han, C., Pavuluri, M., & Lee, M.-S. (2023). Development of a Korean version of the Child Mania Rating Scale: Korean validity and reliability study. *Psychiatry Investigation, 20*(10), 946–950.

de Girolamo, G., Bani, M., Dagani, J., Ferrari, C., Pastore, A., & Signorini, G. (2016). Age of onset of bipolar disorders: A systematic review and meta-analysis. *European Psychiatry, 335*, S56–S71.

de Pablo, G. S., Moreno, D., Gonzalez-Pinto, A., Paya, B., Castro-Fonieles, J., Baeza, I., et al. (2022). Affective symptom dimensions in early-onset psychosis over time: A principal component factor analysis of the Young Mania Rating Scale and the Hamilton Depression Rating Scale. *European Child & Adolescent Psychiatry, 31*, 1715–1728.

Depue, R. A., Slater, J. F., Wolfstetter-Kausch, H., Klein, D., Goplerud, E., & Farr, D. (1981). A behavioral paradigm for identifying persons at risk for bipolar depressive disorder: A conceptual framework and five validation studies. *Journal of Abnormal Psychology, 90*, 381–437.

Doran, C. M. (2008). *The hypomania handbook: The challenge of elevated mood.* Lippincott Williams & Wilkins.

Elhosary, M., & Birmaher, B. (2022). Pediatric bipolar disorder: Misinformation with unintended negative consequences for children and adolescents. *European Neuropsychopharmacology, 59*, 4–6.

Eser, H. Y., Taskiran, A. S., Ertinmaz, B., Mutluer, T., Kiliç, Ö., Morey, A. Ö., et al. (2020). Anxiety disorders comorbidity in pediatric bipolar disorder: A meta-analysis and meta-regression study. *Acta Psychiatrica Scandinavica, 141*, 327–339.

Evans, S. C., Roberts, M. C., Keeley, J. W., Rebello, T. J., de la Peña, F., Lochman, J. E., et al. (2021). Diagnostic classification of irritability and oppositionality in youth: A global field study comparing ICD-11 with ICD-10 and DSM-5. *The Journal of Child Psychology and Psychiatry, 62*(3), 303–312.

Faedda, G., Baldessarini, R., Glovinsky, I., & Austin, N. (2004). Pediatric bipolar disorder: phenomenology and course of illness. *Bipolar Disorders, 6*(4), 305–313.

Fahrendorff, A. M., Pagsberg, A. K., Kessing, L. V., & Maigaard, K. (2023). Psychiatric comorbidity in patients with pediatric bipolar disorder: A systematic review. *Acta Psychiatrica Scandinavica, 148*, 110–132.

Fis, N. P., & Gumustas, F. (2018). Early-onset psychosis: What is the diagnostic outcome? *European Journal of Psychiatry, 32*(4), 159–165.

Geller, B., Williams, M., Zimerman, B., Frazier, J., Beringer, L., & Warner, K. L. (1998). Prepubertal and early adolescent bipolarity differentiate from ADHD by manic symptoms, grandiose delusions, ultra-rapid or ultradian cycling. *Journal of Affective Disorders, 51*, 81–91.

Goldstein, B. I., Birmaher, B., Carlson, G. A., DelBello, M. P., Findling, R. L., Fristad, M., et al. (2017). The International Society for Bipolar Disorders Task Force report on pediatric bipolar disorder: Knowledge to date and directions for future research. *Bipolar Disorders, 19*, 524–543.

Goldstein, B. I., & Bukstein, O. G. (2010). Comorbid substance use disorders among youth with bipolar disorder: Opportunities for early identification and prevention. *Journal of Clinical Psychiatry, 71*, 348–358.

Goldstein, T. R., Merranko, J., Hafeman, D., Gill, M. K., Liao, F., Sewall, C., et al. (2022). A risk calculator to predict suicide attempts among individuals with early-onset bipolar disorder. *Bipolar Disorders, 24*, 749–757.

Goodman, R. (1997). *Strengths and Difficulties Questionnaire (SDQ)* [Database record]. APA PsycTests.

Hafeman, D. M., Goldstein, T. R., Strober, M., Merranko, J., Gill, M. K., Liao, F., et al. (2021). Prospectively ascertained mania and hypomania among young adults with child- and adolescent-onset bipolar disorder. *Bipolar Disorders, 23*(5), 463–473.

Hart, S. R., Brock, S. E., & Jeltova, I. (2014). *Identifying, assessing, and treating bipolar disorder at school.* Springer.

Hauser, M., Galling, B., & Correll, C. U. (2013). Suicidal ideation and suicide attempts in children and adolescents with bipolar disorder: A systematic review of prevalence and incidence rates, correlates, and targeted interventions. *Bipolar Disorders, 15*, 507–523.

Hirschfeld, R. M. A. (2002). The Mood Disorder Questionnaire: A simple, patient-rated screening instrument for bipolar disorder. *Primary Care Companion to the Journal of Clinical Psychiatry, 4*(1), 9–11.

Hours, C. (2025). Pediatric bipolar disorder: A practical guide for clinicians. *Child Psychiatry & Child Psychology and Human Development, 56*(1), 63–72.

Howes, O. D., Lim, S., Theologos, G., Yung, A. R., Goodwin, G. M., & McGuire, P. (2011). A comprehensive review and model of putative prodromal features of bipolar affective disorder. *Psychological Medicine, 41*(8), 156–177.

Huber, R. S., Boxer, D. Smith, C. J., Renshaw, P. F., Yurgelun-Todd, D. A., & Kondo, D. G. (2023). Detailed assessment of suicidal ideation in youth with bipolar disorder versus major depressive disorder. *Bipolar Disorders, 25*, 200–208.

Janiri, D., Conte, E., De Luca, I., Simone, M. V., Moccia, L., Simonetti, A., et al. (2021). Not only mania or depression: Mixed states/missed features in pediatric bipolar disorders. *Brain Sciences, 11*, Article 434.

Joshi, G. G., & Wilens, T. (2009). Comorbidity in pediatric bipolar disorder. *Child and Adolescent Psychiatric Clinics of North America, 18*, 291–319.

Judd, L. L., Akiskal, H. S., Schettler, P. J., Coryell, W., Maser, J., Rice, J. A., et al. (2003). The comparative clinical phenotype and long term longitudinal episode course of bipolar I and II: A clinical spectrum or distinct disorders? *Journal of Affective Disorders, 73*, 19–32.

Karanti, A., Kardell, M., Joas, E., Runeson, B., Pålsson, E., & Landén, M. (2020). Characteristics of bipolar I and II disorder: A study of 8766 individuals. *Bipolar Disorders, 22*, 392–400.

Kaufman, J., Birmaher, B., Brent, D., Rao, U., Flynn, C., Moreci, P., et al. (1997). Schedule for Affective Disorders and Schizophrenia for School-Age Children-Present and Lifetime version (K-SADS-PL): Initial reliability and validity data. *Journal of the American Academy of Child & Adolescent Psychiatry, 36*, 980–988.

Kowatch, R. A., Youngstrom, E. A., Danielyan, A., & Findling, R. L. (2005). Review and meta-analysis of the phenomenology and clinical characteristics of mania in children and adolescents. *Bipolar Disorders, 7*, 483–496.

Kung, F.-H., Tsai, C.-K., Cheng, C.-M., Tsa, S.-J., Su, T.-P., Chen, T.-J., et al. (2024). Diagnostic conversion to bipolar disorder among adolescents and young adults with major depressive disorder: A nationwide longitudinal study. *European Child & Adolescent Psychiatry, 33*(10), 3625–3635.

Lewis-Fernández, R., Aggarwal, N. K., Hinton, L., Hinton, D. E., & Kirmayer, L. J. (2016). *DSM-5® handbook on the Cultural Formulation Interview*. American Psychiatric Publishing.

Liu, L., Meng, M., Zhu, X., & Zhu, G. (2022). Research status in clinical practice regarding pediatric and adolescent bipolar disorders. *Frontiers in Psychiatry, 13*, Article 882616.

McGinty, K. R., Janos, J., Seay, J., Youngstrom, J. K., Findling, R. L., Youngstrom, E. A., & Freeman, A. J. (2023). Comparing self-reported quality of life in youth with bipolar versus other disorders. *Bipolar Disorders, 25*, 648–660.

Miller, S., Dennehy, E. B., & Suppes, T. (2016). The prevalence and diagnostic validity of short-duration hypomanic episodes and major depressive episodes. *Current Psychiatry Reports, 18*, Article 27.

Muneer, A. (2016). Staging models in bipolar disorder: A systematic review of the literature. *Clinical Psychopharmacology and Neuroscience, 14*(2), 117–130.

Papolos, D., Hennen, J., Cockerham, M. S., Thode, H. C. J., & Youngstrom, E. A. (2006). The Child Bipolar Questionnaire: A dimensional approach to screening for pediatric bipolar disorder. *Journal of Affective Disorders, 95*, 149–158.

Pavuluri, M. N., Henry, D. B., Devineni, B., Carbray, J., & Birmaher, B. (2006). Child mania rating scale: Development, reliability and validity. *Journal of the American Academy of Child and Adolescent Psychiatry, 45*, 550–560.

Pavuluri, M. N., Herbener, E. S., & Sweeney, J. A. (2004). Psychotic symptoms in pediatric bipolar disorder. *Journal of Affective Disorders, 80*, 19–28.

Poznanski, E. O., Grossman, J. A., Buchsbaum, Y., Banegas, M., Freeman, L., & Gibbons, R., (1984). Preliminary studies of the reliability and validity of the Children's Depression Rating Scale. *Journal of the American Academy of Child Psychiatry, 23*(2), 191–197.

Rabelo-da-Ponte, F., Marchionatti, L. E., Watts, D., Roza, T. H., Amoretti, S., Barros, F. C., et al. (2024). Premorbid intelligence quotient and school failure as risk markers for bipolar disorder and major depressive disorder. *Journal of Psychiatric Research, 169*, 160–165.

Reynolds, C. R., Kamphaus, R. W., & Vannest, K. J. (2015). *BASC-3: Behavior Assessment System for Children* (3rd ed.). Pearson.

Scaini, G., Valvassori, S. S., Diaz, A. P., Lima, C. N., Benevenuto, D., Fries, G. R., & Quevedo, J. (2020). Neurobiology of bipolar disorders: A review of genetic components, signaling pathways, biochemical changes, and neuroimaging findings. *Brazilian Journal of Psychiatry, 42*(5), 536–551.

Singh, M. K., Ketter, T., & Chang, K. D. (2014). Distinguishing bipolar disorder from other psychiatric disorders in children. *Current Psychiatry Reports, 16*, Article 516.

Tillman, R., Geller, B., Craney, J. L., Bolhofner, K., Williams, M., & Zimerman, B. (2004). Relationship of parent and child informants to prevalence of mania symptoms in children with a prepubertal and early adolescent bipolar disorder phenotype. *American Journal of Psychiatry, 161*(7), 1278–1284.

Van Meter, A., Moreira, A. L., & Youngstrom, E. (2019). Updated meta-analysis of epidemiologic studies of pediatric bipolar disorder. *The Journal of Clinical Psychiatry, 80*(3), Article 18r12180.

Van Meter, A., & Youngstrom, E. A. (2018). Early identification of bipolar disorder: A meta-analytic approach. *Journal of the American Academy of Child & Adolescent Psychiatry, 57*(10S), S302.

Van Meter, A., Youngstrom, E. A., Demeter, C., & Findling, R. L. (2013). Examining the validity of cyclothymic disorder in a youth sample: Replication and extension. *Journal of Abnormal Child Psychology, 41*(3), 367–378.

Van Meter, A. R., Hafeman, D. M., Merranko, J., Youngstrom, E. A., Birmaher, B. B., Fristad, M. A., et al. (2021). Generalizing the prediction of bipolar disorder onset across high-risk populations. *Journal of the American Academy of Child & Adolescent Psychiatry, 60*(8), 1010–1019.

Wagner, K. D., Hirschfeld, R. M. A., Emslie, G. J., Findling, R. L., Gracious, B. L., & Reed, M. L. (2006). Validation of the Mood Disorder Questionnaire for bipolar disorders in adolescents. *Journal of Clinical Psychiatry, 67*, 827–830.

World Health Organization. (2019). *International statistical classification of diseases and related health problems* (11th ed.).

Wozniak, J., DiSalvo, M., Farrell, A., Joshi, G., Uchida, M., Faraone, S. V., et al. (2022). Long term outcomes of pediatric bipolar-I disorder: A prospective follow-up analysis attending to full syndromatic subsyndromal and functional types of remission. *Journal of Psychiatric Research, 151*, 667–675.

Young, R. C., Biggs, J. T., Ziegler, V. E., & Meyer, D. A. (1978). A rating scale for mania: Reliability, validity and sensitivity. *British Journal of Psychiatry, 133*(5), 429–435.

Youngstrom, E. A., Algorta, G. P., Youngstrom, J. K., Frazier, T. W., & Findling, R. L. (2021). Evaluating and validating GBI mania and depression short forms for self-report of mood symptoms. *Journal of Clinical Child & Adolescent Psychology, 50*(5), 579–595.

Youngstrom, E. A., Findling, R. L., Youngstrom, J. K., & Calabrese, J. R. (2005). Toward an evidence-based assessment of pediatric bipolar disorder. *Journal of Clinical Child and Adolescent Psychology, 34*, 433–448.

Youngstrom, E. A., Frazier, T. W., Demeter, C., Calabrese, J. R., & Findling, R. L. (2009). Developing a ten item mania scale from the Parent General Behavior Inventory for children and adolescents. *Journal of Clinical Psychiatry, 69*(5), 831–839.

Youngstrom, E. A., Genzlinger, J. E., Egerton, G. A., & Van Meter, A. R. (2015). Multivariate meta-analysis of the discriminative validity of caregiver, youth, and teacher rating scales for pediatric bipolar disorder: Mother knows best about mania. *Archives of Scientific Psychology, 3*, 112–137.

Youngstrom, E. A., Murray, G., Johnson, S. L., & Findling, R. L. (2013). The 7 Up 7 Down Inventory: A 14-item measure of manic and depressive tendencies carved from the General Behavior Inventory. *Psychological Assessment, 25*(4), 1377–1383.

Youngstrom, E. A., Van Meter, A., Frazier, T. W., Youngstrom, J. K., & Findling, R. L. (2020). Developing and validating short forms of the Parent General Behavior Inventory mania and depression scales for rating youth mood symptoms. *Journal of Clinical Child & Adolescent Psychology, 49*(2), 162–177.

CHAPTER 21
Assessment of Trauma

Kirby L. Wycoff and Kelly N. Moore

Across the world, more and more young people are experiencing the damaging impacts of trauma and chronic adversity. For many young people, particularly racially and ethnically minoritized (REM) youth, this will also include various forms of racism, systematic oppression, and structural supremacy. Approximately two-thirds of children in the United States report that they have experienced at least one traumatic event by the time they reach age 16 (Substance Abuse and Mental Health Services Administration, 2016). These could include anything from psychological, physical, or sexual abuse to community and school violence, the sudden loss of a loved one, or sexual exploitation. The Centers for Disease Control and Prevention (CDC), drawing on the work of Finkelhor et al. (2015), indicates that in the United States at least one in seven children experiences child abuse or neglect every year. The hallmark public health study by Felitti et al. (1998) found that adverse childhood experiences (ACEs) are both common and harmful. ACEs include abuse, neglect, parental mental illness, and domestic violence, and can have profoundly negative impacts on young people, leading to long-term impacts on physical and mental health. These experiences can disrupt brain development, impair learning and behavior, increase the risk of substance abuse, and contribute to chronic health problems like heart disease and diabetes later in life (Felitti et al., 1998).

Further, countless youth in the United States are subjected to the ongoing trauma of racism and discrimination, which only adds an additional layer of chronic traumatic stress on the lived experiences of many young people (Brondolo et al., 2016). Racism and discrimination are broadly defined as "the processes, norms, ideologies, and behaviors that perpetuate racial inequality" (Gee et al., 2012, p. 130). Both racism and discrimination have a well-documented negative impact on the mental health of REM youth and can play a significant role on youth wellness both in and out of the school setting (Brondolo et al., 2016; Malone et al., 2022; Turner, 2019). A robust systematic review of over 120 studies identified a clear and substantial connection between racial discrimination and multiple poor outcomes, including mental health challenges (anxiety and depression), low self-esteem, and general psychological maladjustment (Priest et al., 2013).

The American Academy of Pediatrics (Trent et al., 2019) notes that racism is a core determinant of child health and a well-established driver of health inequities (Gee et al., 2012), or the unfair and avoidable differences in health status across different groups of people. These avoidable health disparities (also referred to as health inequities) are not the result of individual choices or genetics but are instead linked to economic, political, and social conditions, including racism. The World Health Organization notes that social determinants of health (SDOH), which influence health equity, are the "non-medical factors that influence health outcomes. They are the conditions in which people are born, grow, work, live, and age, and the wider set of forces and systems shaping the conditions of daily life. These forces and systems include economic policies and systems, development agendas, social norms, social policies, and political systems" (World Health Organization, 2024, para. 3). Things like food insecurity, housing insecurity, access to health care, social inclusion, unemployment, income, education, and racism are all examples of SDOH. The SDOH framework suggests a continuum where, at one end, higher social status leads to greater access to resources, contributing to improved health outcomes and even longer life expectancy (Alegría et al., 2018; Marmot & Bell, 2016).

All of this suggests that mental health professionals who provide assessment and intervention for youth have a critically important role to play. First and foremost, for mental health providers conducting assessments of youth or providing treatment to youth, we advocate for an integrated model or approach that includes both a trauma-informed and culturally responsive perspective. In fact, being truly trauma informed also requires deeply considering the influence of race, identity, and culture, and SDOH. At their core, both perspectives are intended to authentically meet people where they are at and give agency and choice in the assessment process. The remainder of this chapter will focus on an integrated and holistic approach to the behavioral and emotional assessment of youth that prioritizes trauma-informed and culturally responsive perspectives.

UNDERSTANDING THE HISTORY

Defining trauma-informed practices (including assessment practices) starts with defining trauma. Trauma itself has existed since the beginning of time. Human suffering is a part of the human condition: "The concept and consciousness of trauma in the Western world have appeared, disappeared, and reappeared as social, political, and historical conditions have changed" (Sugiman et al., 2008, p. 98).

In 1866, John Erich Erichsen was one of the first to offer a written description of a type of trauma syndrome that appeared to involve psychological functioning (not just physical impact) while examining railway accidents (Report of the Commission, 1862). Erichsen wrote about "railway spine," which was later conceptualized by German neurologist Hermann Oppenheim (1889) as a type of "traumatic neurosis" that appeared to capture the psychological aspects of physical trauma or nerve damage caused by a shocking event or experience (Keller & Chappell, 1996). This unfolding of events led to an awareness that physical trauma could be associated with psychological challenges and impairment.

The collective awareness and consciousness of trauma became more amplified in the United States throughout a series of wars, starting with World War I, when returning soldiers were diagnosed with shell shock. This was further amplified in the 1970s, when an entire generation of military service members returned from the Vietnam War, having seen and done traumatizing things. At this time, many returning war veterans had significant challenges with adjustment in the postwar period. This impacted the later conceptualization of posttraumatic stress disorder (PTSD) in the diagnostic manuals that sought to identify psychiatric conditions. PTSD was first included in the *Diagnostic and Statistical Manual of Mental Disorders* (DSM) in its third iteration (DSM-III), released in 1980. The timing of this, relative to the Vietnam War, is noteworthy and over the years the definition of PTSD has included controversy (Pai et al., 2017). Despite this deep history of trauma, it is only in more recent decades that there has been increased intentionality around how we treat, support, and understand those who have experienced trauma (Roessner & Becker, 2015).

DEFINING TRAUMA

A concise definition of trauma is a task that is both simple and complex, as a shared and common operational definition of trauma remains elusive (Rossen & Wycoff, 2022). The most compact definition of trauma is one that refers to experiences or circumstances that cause significant physical and psychological stress responses. The more complex reality is that understanding and defining trauma might be more nuanced. Three of the most commonly cited definitions of trauma emerge from the DSM's fifth edition (DSM-5), the Substance Abuse and Mental Health Services Administration (SAMHSA), and the original ACEs study that the CDC and Kaiser Permanente conducted. Although not all three are intended for assessment purposes, all three are used to conceptualize trauma and will be briefly discussed in the following.

Diagnostic and Statistical Manual of Mental Health Disorders, Fifth Edition

DSM-5 (American Psychiatric Association, 2013) is the diagnostic manual used in the United States and globally for determining the presence of mental illness, and this conceptualization of trauma may be the one most familiar to most mental health providers. The most recent iteration of the DSM was released in 2013, and with it came considerable updates to its conceptualization and definition. In the current version (DSM-5), PTSD was moved out of the section on anxiety disorders and into a new diagnostic category titled "trauma- and stressor-related disorders."

There are seven disorders listed in the DSM-5 trauma- and stressor-related disorders section: (1) PTSD, (2) acute stress disorder, (3) adjustment disorder, (4) reactive attachment disorder, (5) disinhibited social engagement disorder, (6) other specified trauma- and stressor-related disorder, and (7) unspecified trauma- and stressor-related disorder (American Psychiatric Association, 2013).

DSM-5 underwent a text revision (DSM-5-TR) update in 2022 (American Psychiatric Association, 2022). While the core diagnostic criteria for PTSD remained unchanged, one key addition was a more inclusive range of examples for what constitutes a traumatic event under Criterion A. The aim of this change was to better reflect the diversity of experiences that can lead to trauma, including cultural and racial trauma. This update also acknowledged how cultural factors can shape trauma responses, providing more guidance for clinicians assessing trauma across different cultural contexts—for example, hearing about a school shooting in your community or learning about a young Black man being shot by a police officer. Previous versions of the DSM did not account for the fact that indirect exposure to trauma can still be just as relevant to the eventual unfolding of a traumatic stress response.

As much as the changes noted previously are largely viewed as positive improvements, there remain many critiques about how DSM-5 conceptualizes trauma. For example, Bremness and Polzin (2014) wrote a commentary response to van der Kolk et al.'s (2009) earlier proposal to include a diagnosis of developmental trauma disorder in DSM-5. The proposal by van der Kolk et al. (2009) to include a developmental trauma disorder in DSM-5 was ultimately denied. Their proposal (and the one that we suggest clinicians use) advocated for a perspective that acknowledged the particularly damaging effects that trauma can have when experienced during key developmental periods. They wrote:

> The goal of introducing the diagnosis of Developmental Trauma Disorder is to capture the reality of the clinical presentations of children and adolescents exposed to chronic interpersonal trauma and thereby guide clinicians to develop and utilize effective interventions and for researchers to study the neurobiology and transmission of chronic interpersonal violence. Whether or not they exhibit symptoms of PTSD, children who have developed in the context of ongoing danger, maltreatment, and inadequate caregiving systems are ill-served by the current diagnostic system, as it frequently leads to no diagnosis, multiple unrelated diagnoses, an emphasis on behavioral control without recognition of interpersonal trauma and lack of safety in the etiology of symptoms, and a lack of attention to ameliorating the developmental disruptions that underlie the symptoms. (van der Kolk et al., 2009, para. 1)

Bremness and Polzin (and others) were critical of the fact that developmental trauma disorder was not included in DSM-5 and noted that DSM-5's definition of trauma fundamentally failed to address the significant role of ongoing stress and adversity during key developmental periods. Bremness and Polzin (2014) advocate for the approach championed by Carrey (2008), which highlights the idea that when we assess and diagnose youth, we *must* consider developmental psychopathology, attachment theory, and neuropsychology, as well as resiliency factors (Bremness & Polzin, 2014; Carrey, 2008). This is also an approach that we advocate for mental health professionals involved in assessing youth.

Substance Abuse and Mental Health Services Administration

For many, SAMHSA provides an improved definition of what is found in DSM-5, with a particular focus on expanding beyond a single-incident traumatic event. According to SAMHSA, "Individual trauma results from an event, series of events, or set of circumstances that is experienced by an individual as physically or emotionally harmful or life-threatening and that has lasting adverse effects on the individual's functioning and mental, physical, social, emotional, or spiritual well-being" (2014, p. 7). If we unpack this definition further, we see three core components of the SAMHSA definition, often referred to as the "three E's." First, the trauma emerges from an *event*, a series of events, or a set of circumstances. Second, the *experienced* part of the definition focuses on the subjective experience or how the individuals involved subjectively interpret the event. Finally, the third E focuses on the *effects* or functional impact of the actual trauma on the person(s) involved.

The National Child Traumatic Stress Network (NCTSN) is a program that was established through SAMHSA. Specifically, NCTSN was created in 2000 as a part of SAMHSA's efforts to improve the standard of care for children and families who have experienced trauma.

NCTSN has a similar approach to SAMHSA's approach, defining complex trauma as follows:

> Complex trauma describes both children's exposure to multiple traumatic events—often of an invasive, interpersonal nature—and the wide-ranging, long-term effects of this exposure. These events are severe and pervasive, such as abuse or profound neglect. They usually occur early in life and can disrupt many aspects of the child's development and the formation of a sense of self. Since these events often occur with a caregiver, they interfere with the child's ability to form a secure attachment. Many aspects of a child's healthy physical and mental development rely on this primary source of safety and stability. (NCTSN, n.d., para. 1)

Adverse Childhood Experiences Study

The Adverse Childhood Experiences (ACEs) study is a seminal research project that investigated the long-term effects of trauma experienced during childhood on later-life health and well-being. The ACEs study predates both SAMHSA and DSM-5 definition of trauma and forms the foundation for all that came after it. In the 1990s, Felitti et al. (1998) conducted a landmark public health study to examine adversity in childhood. Despite the fact that their initial connection emerged from a discussion on the treatment of severe obesity, their work soon shifted to become a much broader examination of the ACEs study. In their retrospective study in which participants reflected and reported on adversity they experienced in childhood, approximately 17,000 participants reported a range of stressors that they experienced during childhood (physical abuse, neglect, sexual abuse, parental incarceration, food security, parental mental illness, domestic violence, and more). The findings revealed a strong, graded relationship between the number of ACEs and a wide range of negative health and social outcomes, including increased risks of chronic diseases, mental illness, substance abuse, and decreased lifespan. There was a dose–response relationship; essentially, the more childhood adversity experienced by an individual, the higher likelihood an individual had of experiencing poor outcomes later in life. This study highlighted the critical impact that early exposure to trauma can have on an individual's future, underscoring the importance of prevention and early intervention. The original ACEs study helped to launch a global awareness of the importance of a trauma-informed approach in education, health care, and social service settings (Felitti et al., 1998). The instrumentation developed by the study team included 10 items, and although it was not intended as a diagnostic or assessment tool, it is often used to help conceptualize early exposure to trauma and adversity. The Philadelphia ACEs project expanded on the original ACEs study and added items that address important issues like witnessing violence, experiencing discrimination, living in foster care, being exposed to adverse neighborhood experiences, and more (Health Federation of Philadelphia, 2013). Of note, the utility of such a tool (either the original or expanded inventory) as an early screener is an issue that carries diverse perspectives and has both potential benefits and drawbacks. We encourage clinicians to strongly consider the potential cost-risk analysis of using something like the ACEs inventory as a large-scale screening instrument. For example, McLennan, McTavish, et al. (2020) offer a number of questions to consider when making the decision about whether to use the ACEs inventory as a screening tool. Asking questions like these may provide useful guidance: "Is the screening approach accurate?"; "What are the potential harms associated with screening?"; "Does an evidence-based intervention exist that will improve outcomes for high-risk groups identified through screening?"; "Is this evidence-based intervention available for those screening positive?"; "Have other critical domains been considered?" (McLennan, Macmillan, et al., 2020). Essentially, while there are in fact benefits to be gained from gathering this information, there are drawbacks as well. The decision to use this instrument should not be taken lightly. For additional dialogue on this issue, see Choi et al. (2019), McLennan, Macmillan, et al. (2020); McLennan, McTavish, et al. (2020); SmithBattle et al. (2022), and Whiteside-Mansell et al. (2022).

UNDERSTANDING TRAUMA THROUGH THE LENS OF POWER

Irrespective of an individual's conceptualization of trauma, we would recommend a holistic view of trauma that integrates all three of the aforementioned conceptualizations in some capacity. Further, we advocate for a core understanding of the fact that *power* is at the center of all traumas. This is one of the reasons why issues of identity and positionality are so critically important when considering trauma-informed, culturally responsive approaches to assessment. American psychiatrist and researcher Judith Herman (1992) notes:

> Psychological trauma is an affiliation of the powerless. At the moment of trauma, the victim is rendered helpless by overwhelming force. When the force is that of nature, we speak of disasters. When the force is that of other human beings, we speak of atrocities. Traumatic events overwhelm the ordinary systems of care that give people a sense of control, connection, and meaning. (p. 33)

When we consider the impact of trauma on youth, the issue of power is particularly salient. In a world where young people have so much of their daily lives managed by adults who (often necessarily) need to provide guidance, structure, boundaries, and more, youth at times can feel like nothing is in their control. This is no more apparent than in situations or environments when adults (or other youth with more power) abuse that power, capitalize on their vulnerability, and cause harm. Power and trauma are inextricably connected, and even more so for young people.

DEFINING TRAUMA-INFORMED PRACTICES

Defining trauma informed starts by asking, "What does being trauma informed really mean?" Being *trauma informed* means shifting and changing your own understanding to include a new pair of eyes that help you understand and make sense of the world around you. Being trauma informed is not a checklist or a list of things to do; rather, it is a way to be. Being trauma informed is a process, not a destination. It is not a checklist by which one can say, "If I do these things, then I am trauma informed." Yes, guidelines and principles can support the journey toward becoming trauma informed, but at its core we must recognize that embracing a trauma-informed ethos is about who we are and how we see the world.

Healing Empowering Advocacy Leading Pennsylvania (HEAL PA) is a statewide collaborative initiative in Pennsylvania. It brings together volunteers from various sectors, including trauma experts, government agencies, and community stakeholders, to work toward making Pennsylvania a trauma-informed and healing-centered state. The initiative's core mission is to promote trauma-informed care across all levels of the state. This includes setting goals and implementing strategies to prevent trauma, support healing, and ensure that trauma survivors receive compassionate care throughout the state. The HEAL PA action teams are expected to innovate and push the boundaries to keep Pennsylvania at the forefront of trauma-informed care practices. The first author has been a member of HEAL PA since its inception in 2018, when she was one of 25 trauma experts in the Commonwealth selected by the governor to lead the initiative. HEAL PA notes that being trauma informed means "Providing an atmosphere that allows every individual to feel validated and affirmed with each and every contact at the entity" (HEAL PA, 2020). The University of Buffalo School of Social Work (n.d.) notes that being trauma informed means that we understand, acknowledge, and consider the deep and pervasive nature of trauma stress and promote environments of healing and recovery rather than practices and services that may inadvertently re-traumatize. Being authentically trauma informed means continuously challenging ourselves to seek to understand those around us. As clinicians, it is important to not to make assumptions about others and why they do what they do but rather carry with us a deep understanding that every single person has their own unique lived experiences. In this chapter, we are focusing on trauma-informed assessment approaches, which require an integration of culturally responsive approaches.

THE INTERSECTION OF TRAUMA AND CULTURE

It may seem obvious to consider the cultural background of a child when assessing for trauma and trauma symptoms. However, many clinicians may benefit from additional training. Because training programs in behavioral health are so varied in their emphasis on cultural competence and culturally responsive care, additional professional development and supervision may be needed to ensure clinicians are considering culture as a top-of-mind concept to integrate into assessment. To understand why a child's cultural background is so important for assessing for trauma, the following section describes how cultural factors may impact the risk for trauma exposure and recovery.

How Culture Influences the Perception of Trauma and Mental Health

The experience of trauma is not uncommon. National surveys have indicated that approximately 37% of youth survey respondents reported experiencing physical abuse (Finkelhor, et al., 2015). SAMHSA also reported that two-thirds of youth have experienced some form of trauma, such as neglect, national disasters, loss of a loved one, abuse, and others. A report issued by the National Child Traumatic Stress Initiative under SAMHSA indicated that two-thirds of its study population will have experienced some form of trauma by the age of 16. Experiencing trauma does not always guarantee being *impacted* by trauma. Not every child who experiences trauma will go on to have posttraumatic symptoms or meet the criteria for PTSD. Those who engage in what Foa et al. (2006) have called natural recovery are usually those who have protective factors that aid them during and after a trauma. Assari (2020) found that non-Hispanic Black youth between the ages of 8 and 11 years who experience trauma did not benefit from recovery from the same protective factors as their non-Hispanic White counterparts. These protective factors include parental education level and family income, but the degree of protection varies when considering race. Findings suggested that non-Hispanic Black youth reported higher numbers of trauma exposure, even when parental education and family income were equivalent to their White counterparts (Assari, 2020). Findings like this indicate that protective factors cannot be generalized to all groups and professionals engaging in assessment should consider cultural differences that may impact outcomes. Sometimes the decision to assess and to what extent are often made based on risk and protective factors. Professionals should be aware that all protective factors do not have the equivalent levels of protection based on Assari's findings.

Studies have found a correlation between perceived discrimination and endorsement of ACEs (Campbell et al., 2020; Gangamma et al., 2020; Helminen et al., 2022). There is also evidence that the experience of discrimination as a result of systemic racism, sexism, xenophobia, homophobia, and transphobia not only increases the risk of exposure to trauma but can also contribute to the exacerbation of symptoms. Also, the impact of culture and trauma is illustrated by the fact that individuals who experience interpersonal violence or trauma have a greater likelihood of developing PTSD (Forbes et al., 2011; Mauritz et al., 2013). To experience trauma by virtue of one's cultural identity is akin to this concept because the targeted nature of being abused or violated simply because of who one is can feel interpersonal in nature, thus making it harder to overcome (Forbes et al., 2011; Mauritz et al., 2013). Power and proximity to power as it relates to racial identity or other aspects of identity are relevant when considering the impact of trauma. When considering the intersection of identity and trauma, it is also important to consider the role of power. Also, certain cultural identities such as race, socioeconomic status, or geographic location can result in disproportionate exposure to trauma in the community and among members of that community. The correlation between poverty and adverse community environments can lead to vulnerability for individuals to experience trauma (Chappelle et al., 2021).

There is some evidence that people from different cultural backgrounds have different presentations of trauma symptoms. Hinton and Lewis-Fernández (2011) found that the prevalence of PTSD numbing-avoidance symptom clusters varied across cultures, with some cultural groups expressing more of these cluster symptoms consistent with PTSD than others. They surmised that part of these differences may be attributed to cultural norms in different countries as they relate to coping strategies and managing physiological arousal when overwhelmed with emotion or distress. Nevertheless, these variations suggest that traditional assessment approaches may not yield accurate findings when trying to assess and treat trauma and possible PTSD, especially when clients represent diverse backgrounds. This is not to say that traditional assessments are not helpful. Rather, in the absence of integrating a culturally responsive approach to trauma assessment, symptoms may be overlooked, which can lead to misdiagnoses and/or increased risk for re-traumatization.

Evidence also indicates that, when it comes to race, clinicians often misdiagnose Black clients in behavioral health settings. For example, Gara et al. (2019) found that Black clients were more likely to be diagnosed with serious mental health conditions such as schizophrenia or bipolar disorder when, after archival record review, many clients fit the criteria for major depressive disorder or other less severe conditions. With these more severe diagnoses come more significant treatment interventions, such as antipsychotic medications, intensive therapies, and more. Gara suggests that this is consistent with trends in behavioral health, where Black youth and adults receive more severe diagnoses that are *also* often more stigmatizing and treatment-resistant (e.g., oppositional defiant disorder, conduct disorder, schizophrenia, psychotic disorders) (Gara et al., 2019). Furthermore, the diagnosis of PTSD as a primary diagnosis is noticeably absent despite the evidence that trauma exposure can lead to symptoms that often overlap with many of those listed here. By not assessing for trauma, clinicians may miss critical details about trauma exposure that might help them better map out effective treatment interventions (Gara et al., 2019).

TRAUMA-INFORMED, CULTURALLY RESPONSIVE ASSESSMENT APPROACHES

"The necessity of an assessment framework that considers the potential impact (not definite but *potential* impact) of trauma as a driving factor in a child's current challenges and impairments cannot be overstated. Even when the referral question has nothing (seemingly) to do with the trauma, the trauma-competent professional will build this possibility into their hypothesis-testing approach" (Wycoff & Franzese, 2019, p. 183). Culturally responsive care refers to adjusting our practice in a manner that considers the unique cultural identity of those receiving care without compromising the quality of care provided.

Methods of Inquiry and Psychological Assessment

The scientific method is a systematic process by which we can investigate a problem, seek to answer a question, and generate new information or new knowledge (Carey, 1994). This method is essential to use in the assessment process. One of the key aspects of the scientific method of generating hypotheses is to try and explain or make sense of whatever question we are trying to answer (Carey, 1994; Millar, 2005). In the world of psychological assessment, hypothesis testing means that we might have an idea (or a hypothesis) about why the young person we are working with might be struggling. Our idea (or hypothesis) should emerge from the initial referral question that the youth (or their caregiver has) about the current situation. A hypothesis is a possible explanation (for the challenges that the young person has); it is not yet a known thing, a guarantee, or a truth, but rather a hypothesis that we have to test out and explore further. The scientific method, in general, and hypothesis testing, in particular, are tools of science that allow us to use research to answer a question (Carey, 1994; Millar, 2005). The scientific method is a cyclical and iterative process that allows us to answer the referral question for a youth and their caregiver or whoever made the referral. As we work toward building a trauma-informed approach to assessment, having a solid understanding of the assessment process in general is essential. Wycoff and Franzese (2019) discuss the cyclical, iterative approach to psychological assessment and scientific method, providing a summary in Table 21.1 of how to use these steps.

Holistic Assessment Approaches

As with any assessment, building and using a framework to guide how we approach the work is critical. Constructing a trauma-informed assessment framework calls for considering the ecological context within which the young person exists. Adopting a social-ecological approach to assessing youth mental health allows us to consider the complex interplay between individual, familial, community, and societal factors that influence their overall wellness and mental and behavioral health. This holistic perspective ensures that interventions address not only the child's immediate symptoms but also the broader environmental contexts that contribute to their mental health. By understanding these dynamic influences, we can create more effective, tailored strategies that support sustainable, positive outcomes for young people.

Multiple researchers and authors advocate for a model of assessment (and treatment) of trauma that fully considers the child's ecological context and positionality (Rossen & Wycoff, 2022; Saxe et al., 2007; Tishelman et al., 2010; Wycoff

Table 21.1. Steps to Using the Scientific Method in Assessment

Step in the Process	Considerations for Assessment
Step #1: *Make an observation*	What do I notice about a particular child in this specific setting? What referral question brought this young person to me for further assessment?
Step #2: *Formulate a question*	Why do I think that problem is occurring for this young person in this setting?
Step #3: *Formulate a hypothesis*	What do I know to be true for children who typically struggle with this? What do my observations tell me about this child thus far? Based on my expertise and preliminary observations, what may be a reasonable hypothesis about this child's difficulties? If my hypothesis is correct, data will support this and demonstrate these same trends.
Step #4: *Gather data to test hypothesis*	Build the assessment battery. What information do I need to test this prediction/hypothesis? Where and how will I collect these data? Be sure to include multiple informants and multiple domains of functioning. Be thorough and intentional in building the assessment battery. Ask yourself, "What do I need to know, and what tools do I have to help me test my hypothesis?"
Step #5: *Refine, alter, expand, or reject your hypothesis*	Remember, the scientific method is an iterative process. Do the data confirm or disconfirm your original hypothesis? If it is not confirmed, you reject the hypothesis. Or you expand it, alter it, and go back to developing a testable prediction and gathering data to test those predictions.
Step #6: *Synthesize and communicate results*	Using the data gathered, synthesize the results and build a clear picture or story about what is going on for this young person. Work with relevant stakeholders, including the young person themselves, to discuss the results and, most importantly, what steps can now be taken to ensure that the client can get the support and services they need to be successful.

& Franzese, 2019). Use of a social-ecological approach aligns with a more holistic and trauma-informed approach in that it seeks more deeply and fully to understand the big picture of what might be going on for a young person. This approach allows us to consider multiple layers of influence on a child's mental health, including family dynamics, peer interactions, community resources, and broader societal factors, rather than focusing solely on the individual and what might be "wrong with them." When we focus exclusively on "what is wrong with this individual" (or are only focusing on what diagnostic criteria or eligibility criteria we need to meet), we are (perhaps unintentionally) operating from a deficit-based lens. This deficit-based approach unnecessarily limits our thinking and diminishes our ability to think expansively and creatively about what might be troubling a young person and how best to support them. Sandy Bloom (psychiatrist) and the late Joseph Foderaro (social worker), along with their colleague Ruth Ann Ruan (nurse), founded the Sanctuary Model of Trauma-Informed Care while working together on an inpatient psychiatric unit in Philadelphia in the middle to late 1980s. The Sanctuary Model is an organizational change model intended to shift organizations from being trauma-inducing to trauma-informed and healing spaces. It was Foderaro who famously noted in a personal conversation with Bloom (1995) that a trauma-informed approach shifted the conversation from "What is wrong with you?" to "What has happened to you?" (Foderaro, 2001; see Wycoff & Franzese, 2019, pp. 44–57, for a more robust discussion of the Sanctuary Model). We are advocating for the very same approach here—one that asks, "What is going on here? What has this person endured, experienced, and been exposed to?" and "How does this fit into the puzzle of what they are experiencing now?" In a personal conversation with Foderaro shortly before he died in early 2022, he reminded me (Kirby Wycoff) of the significance of the work we were all doing and the absolute imperative to train future mental health clinicians to understand and embrace an authentic trauma-informed ethos. He candidly shared that doing so "makes all the difference in the world." We maintain that a more holistic, trauma-informed approach allows us to recognize how traumatic experiences at any of the social-ecological levels can impact a child's development and well-being and emphasizes creating supportive environments that foster resilience and healing. Addressing the full ecological context within which a young person exists ensures that assessments and interventions are comprehensive and sensitive to the diverse factors that affect mental health.

Evaluating children within their ecological context involves assessing the various environmental systems that influence their development and behavior. This holistic approach considers the multiple layers of influence that might impact a young person. One of the most well-known social-ecological theorists is Urie Bronfenbrenner (1979), who highlights five nested and interconnected environmental systems. This systems-thinking and social-ecological theory approach can help conceptualize the trauma-informed assessment process and help build the framework for approaching the work. Consider the various levels in the social-ecological theory, such as the microsystem, mesosystem, exosystem, macrosystem, and chronosystem. As you read further, visualize a Russian matryoshka (nesting) doll. The smallest doll in the middle is the child you are working with (i.e., the young person with the "identified problem" or for whom the referral question is focused). The larger dolls around the smaller dolls are each of the layers of the system. At every level, we must consider the role that adversity and chronic traumatic stress may have on the individual and their functioning. What follows are examples of how we can evaluate children across the interconnected environment systems.

Microsystem

The microsystem is the immediate environment that the young person exists within. This includes family, school, peers, and even the local neighborhood, and it would involve either day or regular interactions. The relationships and interactions here can have a direct impact on a young person.

ASSESSMENT CONSIDERATIONS

- Family: Assess the child's relationships with parents, siblings, and other family members or kinship networks. Consider assessing emotional support, communication patterns, parenting styles, and home environment, among others.
- School: Evaluate the child's interactions with teachers, peers, and the learning environment. Consider academic performance, social skills, and classroom behavior.
- Peers: Observe the child's friendships and social networks. Assess social competence, peer acceptance, and the quality of peer relationships.
- Neighborhood: Consider the safety, resources, and community support available in the child's immediate living environment.

Mesosystem

The mesosystem focuses on the interactions or interconnections between the various microsystems. For example, this could include an examination of how the school system and family interact. Here, we are concerned with the relationships and connections between the child and their environment.

ASSESSMENT CONSIDERATIONS

- Family–school link: Examine the communication and relationships between the child's family and school. Consider how family involvement in education influences the child's academic and social development. Also, consider how school, in turn, may influence the child and family's experiences. Be sure to consider how past (even intergenerational) encounters with educational systems might affect the family's perceptions of the school.
- Peer–family link: Assess how peer relationships might be influenced by family dynamics and vice versa. How are peer groups intersecting with the family system? Are they a protective factor? Why or why not?
- Peer–school link: How might peer interactions impact academic performance? Are there elements of the peer relationships that are particularly salient to the young person's school experience?
- Community involvement: Assess the child's participation in community activities and how these interactions may support or hinder their development.

Exosystem

The exosystem refers to the larger social system that does not directly involve the individual but indirectly impacts them. This could include extended family, parents' workplaces, community services, and social media. Changes or events in this system can significantly affect the individual's microsystems.

ASSESSMENT CONSIDERATIONS

- Parental work environment: Evaluate how parents' work conditions and stress levels affect the child's home environment and development.
- Community services: Assess the availability and quality of community resources such as health care, recreational facilities, and social services that indirectly impact the child.
- Media exposure: Consider the effects of media, including television, the internet, and social media, on children's behavior and attitudes.

Macrosystem

The macrosystem refers to the broader cultural and societal context in which the other systems are embedded (think back to the Russian nesting dolls). This includes cultural values, laws, customs, and resources. The macrosystem shapes the overall environment and influences the systems within it.

ASSESSMENT CONSIDERATIONS

- Cultural norms and values: Assess the cultural background and societal values that shape the child's beliefs, behaviors, and expectations.
- Socioeconomic status: Consider the family's economic situation and its impact on the child's access to resources and opportunities.
- Policies and legislation: Evaluate the impact of local, state, and national policies on the child's life, such as education policies, child protection laws, and health care access.

Chronosystem

The chronosystem refers to environmental changes over time, which encompasses the changes over an individual's life course. This can include both life transitions, such as starting school or changing jobs, and broader societal changes, such as economic shifts, technological advancements, or global pandemics.

ASSESSMENT CONSIDERATIONS

- Life transitions: Assess how significant life changes, such as moving to a new school, parental divorce, or the birth of a sibling, might impact the child's development.
- Historical events: Consider how broader societal changes and historical events, such as economic recessions, natural disasters, or pandemics, influence the child's environment and development over time.

Building a Trauma-Informed Assessment Battery

Operating within the social-ecological framework and using the scientific method to guide the inquiry and assessment process are essential when conducting assessments. Notably, even when the referral question does not include trauma or adversity among the driving questions or factors in the child's current functioning, the trauma-competent professional will build this lens (and be open to the possibility) that these are present (Wycoff & Franzese, 2019). If the presence of complex trauma is known, it is crucial to be thorough in exploring this further. Although a full curation of all available assessment tools is beyond the scope of this chapter, we encourage readers to reference *The Essentials of Trauma-Informed Assessment and Intervention in School and Community Settings* (Wycoff & Franzese, 2019) for more information.

The NCTSN (n.d., para. 6) further suggests that assessing complex trauma is as it sounds—complex. We must consider that a child could be exposed to a wide range of potentially traumatic events, as well as the impact of that adversity across various domains of functioning. Further, it is critical that the person who is conducting the assessment has the necessary training and credentials to conduct the assessment, employing an interdisciplinary team-based approach. When assessing for complex trauma, NCTSN suggests the following:

- "Assess for a wide range of traumatic events. Determine when they occurred so that they can be linked to developmental stages."
- "Assess for a wide range of symptoms (beyond PTSD), risk behaviors, functional impairments, and developmental derailments."
- "Gather information using various techniques (clinical interviews, standardized measures, and behavioral observations)."
- "Gather information from a variety of perspectives (child, caregivers, teachers, other providers, etc.)."
- "Try to make sense of how each traumatic event might have impacted developmental tasks and derailed future development. Note: this may be challenging given the number of pervasive and chronic traumatic events a child may have experienced throughout his or her young life."

- "Try to link traumatic events to trauma reminders that may trigger symptoms or avoidant behavior. Remember that trauma reminders can be remembered both in explicit memory and out of awareness in the child's body and emotions." (NCTSN, n.d., para. 7)

Safe and Supportive Assessment Environments

The therapeutic alliance is the cornerstone of all psychological interventions and mental health assessment processes. The therapeutic alliance refers to the trust that is built between a client and a helping professional. It often refers to the emotional bond or connection between the client and helper and involves agreement on goals and tasks, truthfulness, and openness (Krause et al., 2011; Manso & Rauktis, 2011). Therapeutic alliance, or the trusting relationship between the client and the helper, is consistently noted as predicting more positive outcomes across multiple populations and interventions (Barber et al., 2009; Martin et al., 2000).

The therapeutic alliance is critical for all clients, especially those who may have experienced trauma. For some clients, it may be more challenging to build than for others. Research suggests that adults who have a history of childhood abuse may struggle with creating this trusting relationship due to their own history of violations of trust and failure to be protected from harm (Lawson et al., 2020). Intentional focus on building a trusting relationship with the client (the young person being assessed) *and* the caregiving, familial, or kinship system is critically important. Weak therapeutic alliances are often associated with poor treatment outcomes, particularly for survivors of childhood abuse (Eltz et al., 1995).

Establishing both psychological and physical safety is an important aspect of any assessment and even more so for the trauma-informed professional. This includes authentic dialogue around informed consent and discussing with the client and support system how the assessment process will unfold, what it will entail, and how the information will be used. The specific circumstances under which the assessor must break confidentiality must also be addressed. This is particularly relevant when considering the potential influence of intergenerational exploitation and harm done by school systems and health care systems of minoritized communities. The young person and their support system should be included in data collection efforts for the assessment. However, the discussion about the actual trauma that may have happened should be discussed in private. This means the child should not be asked about their trauma history in the presence of parents or any others who may have an investment in nondisclosure (NCTSN, n.d.).

Assessment as Advocacy

The trauma-informed clinician must be aware of their own identity and positionality as it relates to the assessment process and the youth. Candid and authentic self-reflection and work-around issues of race, gender, sexuality, power, access to resources, and history are critically important for the clinician who seeks to be genuinely trauma informed in their assessment processes. This includes a candid reflection on privilege and power and how it intersects with our clients lived experiences. "When we identify where our privilege intersects with somebody else's oppression, we'll find our opportunities to make real change" (Oluo, 2019, p. 64). This is true for the assessment process as well. Approaching the assessment process with a trauma-informed lens gives us the opportunity to be a part of change and to fight against a system that continues to give advantage to some while disadvantaging others. "If you live in this system of white supremacy, you are either fighting the system or you are complicit. There is no neutrality to be had toward systems of injustice; it is not something you can just opt out of" (Oluo, 2019, p. 49). We suggest that trauma-informed professionals view their work as an opportunity for advocacy and fighting pervasive injustice. It means having hard conversations with ourselves and those around us about our own identities, lived experiences, and positionality. It may be hard, uncomfortable work, but it is necessary work. "You have to get over the fear of facing the worst in yourself. You should instead fear unexamined racism. Fear the thought that right now, you could be contributing to the oppression of others, and you don't know it. But do not fear those who bring that oppression to light. Do not fear the opportunity to do better" (Oluo, 2019, p. 224). Understanding ourselves, who we are, how we are positioned and our complicity in White supremacy culture is an instrumental component of being a trauma-informed clinician. We strongly encourage all readers to lean into this opportunity for growth and self-reflection. This is hard but necessary work.

Strategies for Conducting Culturally Sensitive Assessments

Clinicians interested in culturally sensitive assessments must first have flexibility about what they may have been taught in traditional psychology training programs. Although most trauma assessments have been normed with diverse populations, the challenge is that many standardized measures for assessing trauma are focused on the distinct criteria that are described in DSM. There are other types of traumas described earlier that are not adequately captured by these standardized measures alone. A culturally informed approach to trauma assessment helps to yield more rich information that can be layered into the results from traditional measures.

Modifications to Traditional Assessment Tools for a Culturally Responsive Approach

A culturally responsive approach to assessing trauma history and related issues was explored by de Arellano and Danielson (2008) when they proposed a model called a culturally INFORMED approach. In their evaluation of standard practices of assessing for trauma in youth, they suggested that language matters when asking youth and their family questions about topics related to trauma, many of which are stigmatizing in nature. These authors elaborate their approach with an acronym based on the letters in INFORMED, which, in short, encourages clinicians to analyze multiple perspectives (via demographic research, family/community member surveys, and so on) and assessment strategies (such as means of delivery, types of assessment, and varieties of trauma) prior to designing and administering assessments that are both uniquely tailored and maximally effective for particular clients. (See de Arellano & Danielson, 2008, for full description of the INFORMED approach.)

This approach can be impactful as it amplifies the fact that trauma assessment must also be trauma *informed*. And trauma-informed work and culturally responsive work are inextricably linked because trauma-informed assessment and treatment are intended to meet people where they are and to offer them a voice and choice to share. They also respect the boundaries of clients and encourage providers to think broadly about how to obtain information about trauma.

Traditional trauma assessment could include tools such as the *Trauma Symptom Checklist for Children* (Briere, 1996), the *PTSD Symptom Scale* (Foa et al., 2016), and the *Stressful Life Events Screening Questionnaire* (Goodman et al., 1998). Many of these tools are well established and can serve as a part of a larger assessment that factors in some of the references listed in the aforementioned INFORMED approach. This is necessary as many traditional trauma assessments use language that is stigmatizing and could potentially result in respondents' reticence to answer authentically. For example, asking clients, "Have you ever been physically abused . . . ?" may be unclear, since some cultures have different definitions of what abuse is or looks like. Rather, asking the more specific question, "Have you ever been hit by someone so hard that it left you with a bruise, broken bone, or serious injury requiring medical care . . . ?" bypasses the need for the client to interpret what abuse means. Engaging in culturally responsive, trauma-informed assessment should mean that the provider recognizes that language matters when trying to get an accurate idea of the client's experience.

Interpreting Assessment Results through a Culturally Responsive Lens

Assessment reports and subsequent treatment guidelines can often follow a client as they move on in life. Even though many clinicians may not consider this, they are in a position of power in their role of interpreting data, analyzing, and writing final reports that may impact a person's school or work accommodations, access to mental or physical healthcare, establish their fitness to parent, or be released from prison. The power of assessment interpretation cannot be denied, and considering trauma and culture should be an integral part of this process when it comes to determining final disposition and future recommendations.

If trauma and culturally informed assessments are guided by best practice, they include both standardized measures for trauma and related symptoms such as depression and anxiety. Additionally, these assessments should include qualitative data with information about cultural background and general beliefs about aspects that may contribute to the referral. For example, if evaluating a parent who has been accused of child abuse, the clinician should consider including the parent's answers to questions about their own history and how they were raised. This may help a reader to understand what biases or assumptions the parent may have about how best to raise a child. To what extent does their cultural background (e.g., religious beliefs, family of origin values) connect to their decisions as a parent? The intent behind these considerations being captured in a report is not meant to excuse dangerous behaviors but instead could inform interventions that target the specific underlying reasons for why the behavior happened in the first place and may provide insights into the presence of intergenerational trauma.

Consider an example of writing a report for a parenting evaluation for this fictional parent in the example just mentioned. If a person is abusive because they enjoy inflicting pain on defenseless people, the intervention is far different than for a person who strikes a child because they were raised to believe that if they are not tough on their child, the child may grow up to be reckless and engage in behaviors that may result in them receiving more severe punishment when they are older. In the first instance, the intention of the behavior is dangerous. In the latter instance, the person seems to be seeking to protect someone. For the latter, the suggested intervention may intend to help the parent explore safer methods of protection and unlearning values that lead to abusive behaviors.

Essentially, the question here is whether a trauma assessment is truly one if it is *not* culturally informed. Based on much of the evidence and the ever-changing social climate, it seems that for those who are engaging in trauma assessment, it is ethically imperative to consider culture as a part of the assessment process. This is not intended to be an additional element in the assessment process but rather to operate with the assumption that a person's cultural background—remembering to think broadly about culture as having nested layers—is inextricably tied to their perception of trauma, their behavioral and emotional expression of trauma, and their recovery from trauma. Clinicians can also consider how the recommendations they derive from trauma assessments may or may not be feasible to address based on environmental contexts and systems. Unfortunately, assessment recommendations may be limited in their implementation if those assessments are embedded in systems that are not trauma and culturally informed. In these instances, clinicians may consider including these caveats in their reports to ensure that any barriers or facilitators for recommendations are fully documented and understood by the client(s). Recommendations should be written precisely and include best strategies for implementation, taking into account the salient cultural identities of the client, while taking care not to over/under prescribe recommendations based on any generalizations of cultural factors too. Emphasizing the importance of cultural considerations when implementing recommendations helps those who have to implement them to be more intentional about how they will proceed with the client/student.

CASE EXAMPLE

Creating a Parallel Process—An Organizational Trauma-Informed Assessment and Pilot Program Implementation

The following case study provides an example of how engaging in a trauma-informed, culturally responsive assessment at multiple levels of a system can improve interventions for youth impacted by trauma.

In a school district located in a densely populated and diverse city, a school in one of the more impoverished areas of the city invited a school-based mental health team to help them improve student behaviors in the classroom. To accomplish this task, the mental health team developed an adaptation of the organizational trauma assessment (NCTSN, n.d.) in partnership with the school, and once completed, developed a pilot program development to be implemented by the school. The process consisted of roughly four phases: *needs assessment, program development, pilot implementation*, and *feedback*. The goal was to develop a pilot program aimed at creating an integrated trauma-informed school-based support system. As a result of this needs assessment, the mental health team created a pilot program focused on training for school staff on trauma-informed care, culturally responsive practices in schools, and self-care for teachers. Specific educator and staff training helped them recognize and label potential trauma symptoms in students. The training for staff not only resulted in enhanced knowledge of how trauma symptoms appear in the classroom, but it also helped the educators to have better targeted interventions for helping students who struggled behaviorally in class. For example, understanding that for many children impacted by trauma externalizing and disruptive classroom behaviors may be related to underlying fears of potential danger or feelings of inadequacy led to fewer children being removed from class as a primary consequence. Rather, teachers were able to better anticipate these behaviors and support students in the moment before behaviors were out of control.

This is an example of how a trauma-informed and culturally responsive assessment can be implemented at both the individual and program/organizational level.

On the latter level, this process can help to improve the overall culture of an organization, potentially mitigating issues at the programmatic and individual levels of a system.

CONCLUSION

Trauma-informed and culturally responsive assessment approaches are critically important when assessing the social, emotional, and behavioral needs of youth because they can help ensure that evaluations are sensitive to the unique experiences and backgrounds of each individual. These approaches help identify and address the underlying factors contributing to a child's difficulties, such as past trauma or cultural stressors, which standard assessments might overlook. By incorporating these methods, practitioners can develop more effective, personalized interventions that promote healing and resilience, ultimately leading to better long-term outcomes for youth.

REFERENCES

Alegría, M., NeMoyer, A., Bagué, I. F., Wang, Y., & Alvarez, K. (2018). Social determinants of mental health: Where we are and where we need to go. *Current Psychiatry Reports, 20*(11), 95.

American Psychiatric Association. (2013). Trauma- and stressor-related disorders. In *Diagnostic and statistical manual of mental disorders* (5th ed.). American Psychiatric Publishing.

American Psychiatric Association (2022). *Diagnostic and statistical manual of mental disorders* (5th ed., text rev). American Psychiatric Publishing.

Assari, S. (2020). Family socioeconomic status and exposure to childhood trauma: Racial differences. *Children, 7*(6), 57.

Barber, J. P., Connolly, M. B., Crits-Christoph, P., Gladis, L., & Siqueland, L. (2009). Alliance predicts patients' outcome beyond in-treatment change in symptoms. *Journal of Consulting and Clinical Psychology, 77*(5), 880–888.

Bloom, S. (1995). Creating sanctuary in the school. *Journal for a Just and Caring Education, 1*(4), 403–433.

Bremness, A., & Polzin, W. (2014). Commentary: Developmental trauma disorder: A missed opportunity in DSM V. *Journal of the Canadian Academy of Child and Adolescent Psychiatry, 23*(2), 142–145.

Briere, J. (1996). *Trauma symptom checklist for children (TSCC)*. Psychological Assessment Resources.

Brondolo, E., Ng, W., Pierre, K.-L. J., & Lane, R. (2016). Racism and mental health: Examining the link between racism and depression from a social cognitive perspective. In A. N. Alvarez, C. T. H. Liang, & H. A. Neville (Eds.), *The cost of racism for people of color: Contextualizing experiences of discrimination* (pp. 109–132). American Psychological Association.

Bronfenbrenner, U. (1979). *The ecology of human development: Experiments by nature and design*. Harvard University Press.

Campbell, J. A., Walker, R. J., Garacci, E., Dawson, A. Z., Williams, J. S., & Egede, L. E. (2020). Relationship between adverse childhood experiences and perceived discrimination in adulthood. *Journal of Affective Disorders, 277*, 999–1004.

Carey, S. S. (1994). *A beginner's guide to scientific method*. Wadsworth.

Carrey, N. (2008). Guest editorial: Classification in child psychiatry. *Journal of the Canadian Academy of Child and Adolescent Psychiatry, 17*(2), 49.

Chappelle, N., & Tadros, E. (2021). Using structural family therapy to understand the impact of poverty and trauma on African American adolescents. *The Family Journal, 29*(2), 237–244.

Choi, K. R., McCreary, M., Ford, J. D., Rahmanian Koushkaki, S., Kenan, K. N., & Zima, B. T. (2019). Validation of the traumatic events screening inventory for ACEs. *Pediatrics, 143*(4), e20182546.

Centers for Disease Control and Prevention. (n.d.). About child abuse and neglect. Author. *www.cdc.gov/violenceprevention/childabuseandneglect/fastfact.html*

de Arellano, M. A., & Danielson, C. K. (2008). Assessment of trauma history and trauma-related problems in ethnic minority child populations: An INFORMED approach. *Cognitive and Behavioral Practice, 15*(1), 53–66.

Eltz, M. J., Shirk, S. R., & Sarlin, N. (1995). Alliance formation and treatment outcome among maltreated adolescents. *Child Abuse & Neglect, 19*(4), 419–431.

Felitti, V. J., Anda, R. F., Nordenberg, D., Williamson, D. F., Spitz, A. M., Edwards, V., et al. (1998). Relationship of childhood abuse and household dysfunction to many of the leading causes of death in adults: The Adverse Childhood Experiences (ACE) Study. *American Journal of Preventive Medicine, 14*(4), 245–258.

Finkelhor, D., Turner, H. A., Shattuck, A., & Hamby, S. L. (2015). Prevalence of childhood exposure to violence, crime, and abuse: Results from the National Survey of Children's Exposure to Violence. *JAMA Pediatrics, 169*(8), 746–754.

Foa, E. B., Huppert, J. D., & Cahill, S. P. (2006). Emotional Processing Theory: An update. In B. O. Rothbaum (Ed.), *Pathological anxiety: Emotional processing in etiology and treatment* (pp. 3–24). Guilford Press.

Foa, E. B., McLean, C. P., Zang, Y., Zhong, J., Rauch, S., Porter, K., et al. (2016). Psychometric properties of the Posttraumatic Stress Disorder Symptom Scale Interview for DSM-5 (PSSI-5). *Psychological Assessment, 28*(10), 1159–1165.

Foderaro, J. (2001). Creating a nonviolent environment: Keeping sanctuary safe. In L. A. Levesque (Ed.), *Violence: A public health menace and a public health approach* (pp. 57–82). American Public Health Association.

Forbes, D., Fletcher, S., Parslow, R., Phelps, A., Meaghan, O., Bryant, R. A., et al. (2011). Trauma at the hands of another: Longitudinal study of differences in the posttraumatic stress disorder symptom profile following interpersonal compared with noninterpersonal trauma. *The Journal of Clinical Psychiatry, 72*(3), 21208.

Gangamma, R., Tor, S., Whitt, V., Hollie, B., Gao, Q., Stephens, A., et al. (2020). Perceived discrimination as a mediator of ACEs and psychological distress. *The American Journal of Family Therapy, 49*(3), 282–298.

Gara, M. A., Minsky, S., Silverstein, S. M., Miskimen, T., & Strakowski, S. M. (2019). A naturalistic study of racial disparities in diagnoses at an outpatient behavioral health clinic. *Psychiatric Services, 70*(2), 130–134.

Gee, G. C., Walsemann, K. M., & Brondolo, E. (2012). A life course perspective on how racism may be related to health inequities. *American Journal of Public Health, 102*(5), 967–974.

Goodman, L. A., Corcoran, C., Turner, K., Yuan, N., & Green, B. L. (1998). Assessing traumatic event exposure: General issues and preliminary findings for the Stressful Life Events Screening Questionnaire. *Journal of Traumatic Stress, 11*(3), 521–542.

HEAL PA. (2020). *Trauma-Informed PA: A plan to make Pennsylvania a trauma-informed, healing-centered state*. HEAL PA.org. *https://uploads.strikinglycdn.com/files/106bcfa4-d9e6-4c74-85ca-560d78fe1e3e/HEAL%20Trauma-Informed%20PA.pdf?t=1669742562?id=3962583*

Health Federation of Philadelphia. (2013). *Philadelphia ACE survey*. *www.philadelphiaaces.org/philadelphia-ace-survey*

Helminen, E. C., Scheer, J. R., Edwards, K. M., & Felver, J. C. (2022). Adverse childhood experiences exacerbate the association between day-to-day discrimination and mental health symptomatology in undergraduate students. *Journal of Affective Disorders, 297*, 338–347.

Herman, J. L. (1992). *Trauma and recovery: The aftermath of violence—from domestic abuse to political terror*. Basic Books.

Hinton, D. E., & Lewis-Fernández, R. (2011). The cross-cultural validity of posttraumatic stress disorder: Implications for DSM-5. *Depression and Anxiety, 28*(9), 783–801.

Keller, T., & Chappell, T. (1996). The rise and fall of Erichsen's disease (railroad spine). *Spine, 21*(14), 1597–1601.

Krause, M., Altimir, C., & Horvath, A. O. (2011). Deconstructing the therapeutic alliance: Reflections on the underlying dimensions of the concept. *Clinical and Health, 22*(3), 267–283.

Lawson, D. M., Skidmore, S. T., & Akay-Sullivan, S. (2020). The influence of trauma symptoms on the therapeutic alliance across treatment. *Journal of Counseling & Development, 98*(1), 29–40.

Malone, C. M., Wycoff, K., & Turner, E. A. (2022). Applying a MTSS framework to address racism and promote mental health for racial/ethnic minoritized youth. *Psychology in the Schools, 59*(12), 2438–2452.

Manso, A., & Rauktis, M. E. (2011). What is the therapeutic alliance and why does it matter? *Reclaiming Children and Youth, 19*(4), 45.

Marmot, M., & Bell, R. (2016). Social inequalities in health: A proper concern of epidemiology. *Annals of Epidemiology, 26*(4), 238–240.

Martin, D. J., Garske, J. P., & Davis, M. K. (2000). Relation of the therapeutic alliance with outcome and other variables: A meta-analytic review. *Journal of Consulting and Clinical Psychology, 68*(3), 438–450.

Mauritz, M. W., Goossens, P. J., Draijer, N., & Van Achterberg, T. (2013). Prevalence of interpersonal trauma exposure and trauma-related disorders in severe mental illness. *European Journal of Psychotraumatology, 4*(1), 19985.

McLennan, J. D., MacMillan, H. L., & Afifi, T. O. (2020). Questioning the use of adverse childhood experiences (ACEs) questionnaires. *Child Abuse & Neglect, 101*, 104331.

McLennan, J. D., McTavish, J. R., & MacMillan, H. L. (2020). Routine screening of ACEs: Should we or shouldn't we? In G. J. G. Asmundson & T. O. Afifi (Eds.), *Adverse childhood experiences: Using evidence to advance research, practice, policy, and prevention* (pp. 145–159). Academic Press.

Millar, R. (2005). What is "scientific method" and can it be taught? In R. Levinson (Ed.), *Teaching science* (pp. 172–185). Routledge.

National Child Traumatic Stress Network (NCTSN). (n.d.). *Assessment and screening*. Author. *www.nctsn.org/what-is-child-trauma/trauma-types/complex-trauma/screening-and-assessment*

Oluo, I. (2019). *So you want to talk about race*. Hachette UK.

Pai, A., Suris, A. M., & North, C. S. (2017). Posttraumatic stress disorder in the DSM-5: Controversy, change, and conceptual considerations. *Behavioral Sciences, 7*(1), 7.

Priest, N., Paradies, Y., Trenerry, B., Truong, M., Karlsen, S., & Kelly, Y. (2013). A systematic review of studies examining the relationship between reported racism and health and wellbeing for children and young people. *Social Science & Medicine, 95*, 115–127.

Report of the Commission. (1862). Influence of railway traveling on public health. *The Lancet, 1*, 79–84.

Roessner, V., & Becker, A. (2015). Chapter 5: Epidemiology, course, and outcomes of Tourette syndrome. In J. T. Walkup, J. A. Mink, & P. J. Hollenbeck (Eds.), *Tourette syndrome* (pp. 79–92). Oxford University Press. *www.ncbi.nlm.nih.gov/books/NBK207202*

Rossen, E., & Wycoff, K. L. (2022). Best practices in trauma-informed schools. In P. L. Harrison, S. L. Proctor, & A. Thomas (Eds.), *Best practices in school psychology* (7th ed.). National Association of School Psychologists.

Saxe, G. N., Ellis, B. H., & Kaplow, J. B. (2007). *Collaborative treatment of traumatized children and teens: The trauma systems therapy approach*. Guilford Press.

SmithBattle, L., Loman, D. G., Yoo, J. H., Cibulka, N., & Rariden, C. (2022). Evidence for revising the adverse childhood experiences screening tool: A scoping review. *Journal of Child & Adolescent Trauma, 15*(1), 89–103.

Substance Abuse and Mental Health Services Administration (SAMHSA), National Child Traumatic Stress Initiative. (2016). *National Child Traumatic Stress Initiative*. Author. *https://store.samhsa.gov/sites/default/files/sma16-4923_0.pdf*

Sugiman, P., Chana, T., Oikawa, M., & Takagaki, T. (2008). *Remapping memory: The politics of timespace*. University of British Columbia Press.

Tishelman, A. C., Haney, P., Greenwald O'Brien, J., & Blaustein, M. E. (2010). A framework for school-based psychological evaluations: Utilizing a "trauma lens." *Journal of Child & Adolescent Trauma, 3*(4), 279–302.

Trent, M., Dooley, D. G., & Dougé, J. (2019). The impact of racism on child and adolescent health. *Pediatrics, 144*(2), e20191765.

Turner, E. A. (2019). *Mental health among African Americans: Innovations in research and practice*. Rowman & Littlefield.

University at Buffalo School of Social Work. (n.d.). *What is trauma-informed care?* Institute on Trauma and Trauma-Informed Care. *https://socialwork.buffalo.edu/social-research/institutes-centers/institute-on-trauma-and-trauma-informed-care/what-is-trauma-informed-care.html*

van der Kolk, B., Pynoos, R., Cicchetti, D., Cloitre, M., D'Andrea, W., Ford, J., & Teicher, M. (2009). *Proposal to include a Developmental Trauma Disorder diagnosis for children and adolescents in DSM-V. https://complextrauma.org/wp-content/uploads/2019/03/Complex-Trauma-Resource-3-Joseph-Spinazzola.pdf*

Whiteside-Mansell, L., McKelvey, L., Lewis, K., & Peters, R. (2022). Screening for adverse childhood experiences (ACEs) before age 3: Evidence for the family map inventory. *HS Dialog: The Research to Practice Journal for the Early Childhood Field, 25*(2).

World Health Organization. (2024). *Social determinants of health*. Author. *www.who.int/social_determinants/thecommission/finalreport/key_concepts/en*

Wycoff, K. L., & Franzese, B. (2019). *Essentials of trauma-informed assessment and intervention in school and community settings*. Wiley.

PART IV

SPECIAL CONSIDERATIONS

CHAPTER 22

Twice-Exceptionality

Jon W. Goodwin and Katherine Schabilion

When the U.S. Congress passed the landmark civil rights legislation of Public Law 94-142 (Education for All Handicapped Children Act of 1975), it enshrined the right for all children, including those with disabilities, to have access to a "free appropriate public education," or what is routinely referred to by educators as a FAPE (Yell, 2018; Ysseldyke et al., 2023). As it pertains to school psychologists tasked with evaluating students who may be suspected of having disabilities, determination of the "appropriate" component of FAPE rests, at least in part, on there being an appropriate, comprehensive individualized assessment of each referred student. At the time that Public Law 94-142 was initially enacted, recognition and understanding of how high-ability (or "gifted") students may also have an educationally relevant disability were limited, and as such, the training of school psychologists on how to assess such students traditionally has not been a priority of graduate training programs. However, the most recent reauthorization of special education law, the Individuals with Disabilities Education Improvement Act of 2004 (IDEA, 2004), acknowledges that students with high intellectual ability and co-occurring disabilities may receive special education services and are afforded the protection of IDEA 2004 and its implementing regulations (Baldwin et al., 2015). Therefore, it is vital that school psychologists understand the complex and multifaceted needs of high-ability students who are also impacted by disability (Assouline & Whiteman, 2011; Foley-Nicpon & Assouline, 2020).

Twice-exceptionality is a term used to describe students who may simultaneously demonstrate advanced intellectual or scholastic ability while also being impacted by one or more areas of educationally relevant disability (Assouline & Whiteman, 2011). The paradox of possessing both scholastic strengths and areas in need of support is often perplexing to affected students, their parents, and their educators, and may confound school teams tasked with providing appropriate support services. This chapter aims to provide an overview of how the intersection of giftedness and disability confers unique challenges to school psychologists and warrants special consideration when conducting psychoeducational evaluations.

DEFINITIONS

In order to understand how to support twice-exceptional students, it is necessary to understand the characteristics that define the population. Recent work undertaken to establish a definition for twice-exceptionality yielded the following output:

> Twice-exceptional learners are students who demonstrate the potential for high achievement or creative

> productivity in one or more domains such as math, science, technology, the social arts, the visual, spatial, or performing arts or other areas of human productivity AND who manifest one or more disabilities as defined by federal or state eligibility criteria. These disabilities include specific learning disabilities; speech and language disorders; emotional/behavioral disorders; physical disabilities; Autism Spectrum Disorders (ASD); or other health impairments, such as Attention Deficit/Hyperactivity Disorder (ADHD). These disabilities and high abilities combine to produce a unique population of students who may fail to demonstrate either high academic performance or specific disabilities. Their gifts may mask their disabilities and their disabilities may mask their gifts. (Reis et al., 2014)

This definition contains two elements: high ability and disability. Therefore, complete understanding of twice-exceptional students requires a deeper exploration of both elements.

Giftedness

The study of twice-exceptionality has been largely centered within the field of gifted education. In 1972, the first definition of *gifted students* was introduced at the federal level through the *Marland Report*:

> Gifted and talented children are those identified by professionally qualified persons who by virtue of outstanding abilities are capable of high performance. These are children who require differentiated educational programs and/or services beyond those normally provided by the regular school program in order to realize their contribution to self and society. (Marland, 1972)

More recently, the National Association for Gifted Children (NAGC) established an agreed-upon definition of *giftedness*:

> Students with gifts and talents perform—or have the capability to perform—at higher levels compared to others of the same age, experience, and environment in one or more domains. They require modification(s) to their educational experience(s) to learn and realize their potential. (NAGC, 2019)

It is important to note that the field is reckoning with the use of the term gifted due to the heavy baggage that term carries (National Working Group on Advanced Education, 2023). Alternatives, including "advanced," "talented," "high ability," and others, have been proposed by various scholars, but there is not, at the time of writing, a consensus in the field. For the sake of clarity, throughout this chapter the authors will use the term "high ability" to describe this element of twice-exceptionality.

Disability

This element of twice-exceptionality has a more established research base and definition. In educational contexts, a *child with a disability* means a child (1) with intellectual disabilities, hearing impairments (including deafness), speech or language impairments, visual impairments (including blindness), serious emotional disturbance, orthopedic impairments, autism, traumatic brain injury, other health impairments, or specific learning disabilities; and (2) who, by reason thereof, needs special education and related services (IDEA, 2004). Specific to twice-exceptionality, some types of disabilities have received more exploration than others. Specifically, most research on twice-exceptional populations has studied individuals with specific learning disabilities, attention-deficit/hyperactivity disorder (ADHD), and autism spectrum disorder (ASD). More recently, exploration of students with disabilities included in IDEA's emotional disturbance category (e.g., anxiety, depression, and other emotional and behavioral disorders) has increased. Educational determinations of disability are made based on criteria from special education law (IDEA, 2004), whereas clinical diagnoses apply criteria from medical classification systems, typically the *Diagnostic and Statistical Manual of Mental Disorders, Fifth Edition, Text Revision* (DSM-5-TR; American Psychiatric Association, 2022), and/or the *International Classification of Diseases, 11th Revision* (ICD-11; World Health Organization, 2019).

MASKING

The identification of twice-exceptional students is a complex endeavor that warrants a careful, thorough psychoeducational assessment to better understand areas of both talent and disability. One of the most significant challenges in identifying twice-exceptional students is the phenomenon of masking, which refers to how an affected student's talent domains can obfuscate detection of their disability, or vice versa (Baldwin et al., 2015). Just as a mask obscures an individual's face from recognition by others, twice-exceptional individuals may present with disability-related challenges that preclude others from recognizing their areas of advanced academic ability, artistic creativity, or scholastic talent (Lewis, 2021). Likewise, twice-exceptional students, often through well-honed compensatory strategies or extraordinary effort, may experience disability-related challenges that are not readily apparent to parents, educators, and school teams, which consequently may go unrecognized throughout their K–12 educational career. For some twice-exceptional students, the confluence of both talent and disability interferes with the expression of both exceptionalities. For these students, their scholastic abilities may appear to be average, and they may be unidentified or unserved for either exceptionality (Baldwin et al., 2015). Because twice-exceptional students may neither attain high scholastic achievement nor fully manifest their disabilities, frustration may abound across parents, teachers, and affected students themselves without appropriate identification and support services to address strengths and weaknesses (Lewis, 2021). As a twice-exceptional student's strengths and challenges evolve with each academic year, they are at risk for being mislabeled as an underachiever or "lazy" (Lewis, 2021).

MISDIAGNOSIS AND MISSED DIAGNOSIS

A misdiagnosis occurs when a high-ability student is incorrectly identified as having a disability (Amend & Beljan, 2009), whereas a missed diagnosis occurs when a disability is indeed present but disability-related behaviors are minimized or dismissed because of advanced intellect or creativity (Amend & Peters, 2012). Because the severity of seemingly disability-related symptoms can obfuscate areas of talent, behavioral or attentional issues displayed by a student tend to be urgently addressed by professionals, without giving consideration to potential underlying causes related to contextual factors such as insufficient instructional rigor or a lack of appropriate academic accommodations. This may happen because a comprehensive evaluation approach is eschewed for briefer, less comprehensive, symptom-focused evaluation methods. This is understandable given that (1) clinical and educational diagnostic nosology's are based on the extent to which a person suspected of having a disability presents with specific polythetic criteria (Mash & Barkley, 2014), and (2) student support personnel and mental health professionals often have limited knowledge of high-ability students and may not have a framework from which to discern whether or not displayed behaviors are "typical" of giftedness (Amend & Peters, 2012). However, as with differential diagnosis in medicine, psychologists should be careful not to come to conclusions that lead to inadvertent misdiagnosis of high-ability and twice-exceptional students (Amend & Peters, 2012). For example, a student's "inattentiveness" and "minimal engagement" within a classroom may be misinterpreted as indicative of a potential attention disorder, yet a thorough evaluation may reveal it actually to be boredom or frustration due to a student's mastery of grade-level curricular content. However, it is also plausible that another student presenting with similar issues of "inattentiveness" or "minimal engagement" may simply be dismissed as an underachiever or lazy. In this scenario, referral for further evaluation may be delayed or denied, precluding identification of an actual disability that may truly be present.

There are also concerns among some professionals that high-ability students are unnecessarily pathologized for displaying idiosyncratic or anomalous behaviors and characteristics that may be attributable to their advanced intellect. That is, for high-ability students, peculiarity does not always indicate pathology, and difference does not equate disorder. For example, what may appear to be distractibility and inattention may simply be a manifestation of a high-ability student's creativity, spontaneity, and imagination (Probst & Piechowski, 2012). In another example, a high-ability student who has deep interest in a seemingly esoteric subject may have their intellectual curiosity mistaken as an indicator of autism symptomatology. The perspective that children with advanced intellectual ability run the risk of being deemed pathological despite or perhaps because of their intelligence has led many within the field of gifted education to espouse Polish psychiatrist Kazimierz Dabrowski's (1964) theory of positive disintegration as a framework for understanding the social–emotional development of gifted children. A key concept within Dabrowski's theory is the notion that intellectually and artistically gifted youth are predisposed to experience their external and internal environments with greater sensitivity, intensity, and nuance than their average peers (Daniels & Piechowski, 2009; Probst & Piechowski, 2012). These intensely experienced sensitivities, or overexcitabilities, are purported to manifest in several forms, including in psychomotor, sensual, intellectual, imaginational, and emotional expressions (Probst & Piechowski,

2012). According to Dabrowski, overexcitabilities and their expressions, which may include existential crises, depression, or anxiety, are essential for emotional growth in gifted individuals. Although a comprehensive overview of Dabrowski's theory is beyond the scope of this chapter, for an outline of the theory, see Ackerman (2009).

While we have encountered students and clients whose peculiarities (or "quirks") were primarily attributable to their intellectual precocity instead of a psychological disorder, it is also our experience that confidently ruling out the presence of a disorder or disability can only be determined through a comprehensive psychoeducational assessment. More importantly, if a high-ability student is experiencing distress that is interfering with their subjective well-being, it requires intervention and monitoring regardless of whether their distress is believed to be due to overexcitabilities or a true psychological disorder.

ASYNCHRONOUS DEVELOPMENT

The concept of "asynchronous development" has long been discussed in the field of gifted education (see Silverman, 1997). This term can be used to describe many different populations of students, but within the context of high ability, *asynchronous development* refers to the fact that different domains of ability do not necessarily develop at the same pace, and therefore children with exceptional abilities in one or more areas may have average or even weak abilities in other areas (Silverman, 1997). The construct of twice-exceptionality is practically defined by this concept (Reis et al., 2014).

As it applies to assessment, practitioners can expect to see a higher degree of variability across test scores for twice-exceptional students than is typically seen in other populations, because their profiles are characterized by both significant strengths and significant weaknesses. Beyond quantitative test scores, assessors may receive qualitative comments indicating that one area/skill is very natural for the child, whereas another, seemingly related skill is inexplicably difficult.

This asynchronous or uneven development can be both a result and a cause of difficulties associated with twice-exceptionality. That is, uneven development can be the result of neurodevelopmental differences like ASD, ADHD, and specific learning disability (SLD), wherein certain abilities (e.g., executive functioning, social communication, specific academic skills) develop at a slower pace or in a different manner than typical. However, asynchronous development can also contribute to difficulties, especially social–emotional ones, when twice-exceptional students feel out of sync with peers and frustrated by their differences (Pfeiffer & Stocking, 2000) and when they recognize the implications of their relative or normative weaknesses and struggle with self-confidence or perceived failure to meet expectations, whether real or imagined. In addition, the ways that twice-exceptional students cope with their uneven development and compensate for relatively weaker skills may not align with environmental expectations, which can have social and emotional implications (Cornoldi et al., 2023). A common example in practice is the twice-exceptional student who is talented in math but has significant difficulty complying with demands to show their work on math assignments due to a significant weakness in fine motor coordination.

PRACTICAL CONSIDERATIONS FOR TWICE-EXCEPTIONAL ASSESSMENT

Although the intersections of talent and disability have been considered since the 1920s, much of the scholarship in this area has relied on clinical experiences and anecdotes in lieu of empirical research, and even the empirical work has relied largely on qualitative rather than quantitative methodology (Foley-Nicpon et al., 2011). Research in this area is growing, however, and sufficient research exists to make some conclusions regarding assessment of high-ability students with ADHD, ASD, SLD, and emotional disabilities (e.g., mood, anxiety, and related disorders). Across disability domains, research has consistently indicated that comprehensive evaluations employing intraindividual comparisons of strengths and weaknesses are the best way to identify twice-exceptional students (Foley-Nicpon et al., 2011; Gilman et al., 2013).

ADHD/Other Health Impairment

Assessment of ADHD in high-ability students can be complicated due to the overlaps between the two categories (Lee & Olenchak, 2015). Characteristics like fidgetiness, inattentiveness, off-task behaviors, and disobedience/questioning of authority can occur in both groups (Antshel, 2008; Webb & Latimer, 1993), though they may manifest in different settings and for different reasons

(Lee & Olenchak, 2015). Specifically, high-ability students may be easily bored during class when the work is not aligned with their instructional level, but not in other contexts (Lee & Olenchak, 2015), whereas people with ADHD display frequent inattentive and/or hyperactive/impulsive symptoms across multiple contexts (American Psychiatric Association, 2022). Given the overlap of behavioral characteristics between high-ability students and those with ADHD, concerns regarding possible misdiagnosis are prevalent (Hartnett et al., 2004; Webb et al., 2005). Other research, however, has shown a pattern of similar cognitive and behavioral characteristics between high-ability students with ADHD and average-ability students with ADHD, which indicates that "dual diagnosis" of ADHD and high abilities is also possible (Gomez et al., 2020; Mullet & Rinn, 2015). In addition, comparison of high-ability and average-ability students without ADHD showed that high-ability students without ADHD did not display significantly more inattentive or hyperactive/impulsive symptoms than average-ability students without ADHD (Gomez et al., 2020).

Based on this information, approaches to diagnosing ADHD in average-ability students can be largely employed with high-ability students as well. However, some differences have been noted between high-ability and average-ability students with ADHD, particularly on performance measures, which may have implications for accurate diagnosis. Specifically, high-ability students with ADHD have been shown to perform better than average-ability students with ADHD overall on tests of attention (e.g., continuous performance tests), especially regarding omission errors, commission errors, and response sensitivity (Chae et al., 2003). Therefore, an absence of elevations on these elements of assessment should not necessarily preclude diagnosis of ADHD in students known to have high abilities. Rather, diagnosis of ADHD in high-ability students must be based on a confluence of information about the individual's functioning across multiple settings, even if performance concerns are not observed in the clinic setting. Professionals assessing for ADHD in high-ability students are encouraged to rely more heavily on parent, teacher, and self-report information obtained via rating scales, such as the ADHD Rating Scale (in its fifth edition at the time of writing; DuPaul et al., 2016) and the Behavior Rating Inventory of Executive Functioning (in its second edition; Gioia et al., 2015), and interviews.

ASD

Extensive research has been conducted regarding ASD, although much of the literature has focused on those with average to below-average cognitive abilities. Limited empirical research is available regarding high-ability people with ASD (Assouline et al., 2009). What research does exist suggests that high-ability students may be at greater risk of missed diagnosis because social difficulties may be attributed to their high abilities or they may be more able to compensate for difficulties given their advanced cognitive skills (Neihart, 1999). Diagnostically, assessments of adaptive behavior and executive functioning (Assouline et al., 2009), as well as consideration of how students interact with intellectual peers and recognize how others perceive them (Webb et al., 2005), may be keys to accurately identifying ASD in high-ability students.

Best practices for assessing ASD in general have been well established and include collection of a detailed developmental history and direct observation and interaction with the child (Lord et al., 2020). Common tools used in the assessment process include the Autism Developmental Interview—Revised (ADI-R; Rutter et al., 2003) and the Autism Diagnostic Observation Schedule—Second Edition (ADOS-2; Lord et al., 2012). Among high-ability students, the combination of developmental history and current functioning can be especially important due to the high potential that presentation of current symptoms may be reduced by masking and/or compensatory strategies.

Assouline et al. (2009) proposed a theoretical schema of gifted students with social difficulties wherein "Type B" students are characterized by high cognitive ability and moderate social impairment due to a mismatch between their skills and their environment, while "Type C" students are characterized by high cognitive abilities and severe social impairment that cannot be explained by environmental mismatch. Both profiles are at risk for misdiagnosis, with Type B students having the potential of being assigned an inaccurate ASD diagnosis, and Type C students having the potential of their true disability being missed due to inaccurate assumptions that their social difficulties are an aspect of their high abilities. Case study analysis of two profoundly gifted students, one Type B and one Type C, revealed differences in only a few areas, including cognitive processing speed, autism diagnostics, adaptive behavior, and psychosocial functioning (Assouline et al., 2009).

Similar results were found in a correlational study by Doobay et al. (2014), in which high-ability youth with ASD were found to have significantly lower adaptive functioning and psychosocial functioning compared to high-ability youth without ASD. However, high-ability youth with ASD displayed limited insight into their own psychosocial functioning, as evidenced by minimal reports of social–emotional concerns on self-report rating scales despite significant concerns on parallel parent- and/or teacher-report scales (Doobay et al., 2014; Foley-Nicpon et al., 2010).

Assessment of ASD in high-ability students requires a comprehensive evaluation, including collection of extensive developmental history, observation of social behaviors, and consideration of adaptive and psychosocial functioning through reports from parents and teachers (Assouline et al., 2009; Doobay et al., 2014; Lord et al., 2020). Self-reports of psychosocial functioning, though not always aligned with parent and teacher reports (Doobay et al., 2014; Foley-Nicpon et al., 2010), can also be helpful to identify areas of perceived strength and/or weakness to increase individual buy-in for intervention. In addition, although they have not yet been specifically studied in high-ability youth, executive functioning (EF) deficits are commonly observed in people with ASD (see McCrimmon et al., 2016, for discussion), and measurement of EF skills through direct testing and/or behavior ratings from parents and teachers can support both diagnosis and intervention planning for high-ability students with ASD.

It is worth noting that ASD and ADHD are both neurodevelopmental disorders that often feature executive dysfunction as a shared, transdiagnostic impairment. Furthermore, findings from a recent meta-analytic review indicate that the prevalence of ADHD in individuals with ASD ranges from 50 to 70% (Rong et al., 2021). Although there are no reliable epidemiological estimates for comorbidity of ASD and ADHD in high-ability youth, school psychologists and other clinicians may nonetheless be tasked with determining whether either or both conditions are present in a twice-exceptional student. Because high-ability individuals with either ASD or ADHD may present with EF deficits, the assessment of EF is necessary, but not sufficient, for accurate determination of differential versus dual diagnosis. As mentioned earlier, when evaluating for ASD, a comprehensive assessment should include thorough assessment of a child's past development and current social communication, as well as an evaluation of adaptive behavior (Assouline et al., 2009). Adaptive behavior may be particularly useful in providing diagnostic clarity when attempting to differentiate the functional impairments of ASD in high-ability students from those associated with ADHD in high-ability students, with the former exhibiting marked impairments within the social domain of adaptive functioning (Assouline et al., 2008).

Emotional Disturbance/Mood, Anxiety, and Related Disorders

Social–emotional functioning of high-ability students has long been a source of debate within the field of gifted education (Duplenne et al., 2024). There have been assertions that high-ability individuals are more vulnerable to social–emotional difficulties (see Baudson, 2016, for discussion). However, much of the research has indicated that "giftedness" provides social and emotional advantages (e.g., higher self-concept, life satisfaction; Ogurlu, 2021) or at least does not negatively impact personality, motivation, and well-being (see Bergold et al., 2021). That said, just as there are high-ability people with ADHD, ASD, and SLD, there are high-ability people with emotional and behavioral disorders as well.

Given that the rates of social–emotional–behavioral problems occur at generally similar rates for high-ability students and average-ability students, similar methods for identifying these problems can be employed regardless of an individual's ability level. However, the causes and sources of emotional distress can be different for high-ability students when compared to average-ability students. Pfeiffer and Stocking (2000) identified several characteristics of high-ability students that may contribute to emotional difficulties, including perfectionism, overexcitabilities or emotional intensity, and high levels of moral sensitivity and concern (e.g., concerns for justice, fairness, and equality). Underserved populations of high-ability students, including twice-exceptional students as well as students of minoritized racial/ethnic groups or low socioeconomic status, are also suspected to be at greater risk of psychosocial challenges (Pfeiffer & Stocking, 2000), due at least in part to the difficulty accessing appropriate talent development services.

Unique manifestations and impacts of emotional and behavioral disorders beyond diagnostic criteria may also present in high-ability students. A recent study examining characteristics of obsessive–compulsive disorder (OCD) among high-ability students indicated that the combination of high ability and OCD resulted in lower self-concept and greater parent-reported externalizing and internalizing problems when compared to OCD alone (LeBeau et al., 2024). Another study found that higher verbal intelligence scores were associated with rumination and worry, two cognitive processes underlying anxiety (Penney et al., 2015); the authors speculated that those with higher verbal skills can consider "past and future events in greater detail, leading to more intense rumination and worry" (p. 92). From clinical experience, high-ability individuals seem to contend with more existential and societal worries (e.g., worries about death, social justice, environmental concerns) at younger ages than typical, which seems to align with the perspective that advanced verbal reasoning permits greater awareness and exploration of topics that, unfortunately, can develop into maladaptive social–emotional manifestations.

Specific Learning Disability

The identification of students with SLD has been fraught with controversy (Dombrowski et al., 2004; Mather & Gregg, 2006), and the introduction of the additional variable of high ability further complicates matters (see Lovett & Lewandowski, 2006). In addition to considerations regarding SLD identification methods (e.g., ability-achievement discrepancy, response to intervention, pattern of strengths and weaknesses), considerations for determining whether high-ability students have SLD include whether to use intraindividual discrepancies or normative impairment criteria (Lovett & Sparks, 2011; Maddocks, 2018).

Regardless of the method by which high-ability students with SLD are identified, there are emotional and behavioral implications that are important for school psychologists to recognize. For example, the asynchrony experienced by these students may contribute to reduced self-concept, especially in academic domains, similar to average-ability students with SLD (Shany et al., 2013). Additionally, high-ability students with SLD may display anxiety and/or avoidance in relation to their domain(s) of academic weakness. For example, in the authors' clinical experience, "behavior" concerns related to refusal of certain academic tasks can often be explained by the presence of a significant intraindividual weakness in that academic domain. It is essential to consider the asynchrony of cognitive and academic profiles among high-ability students with SLD in order to provide appropriate social–emotional support.

Cultural Considerations for Identification and Assessment of Twice-Exceptional Students

High-ability and twice-exceptional students, like any other group of students in schools, "come from all racial, ethnic, and cultural populations, as well as all economic strata" (NAGC, 2019, para. 1). However, students from minoritized racial, ethnic, and socioeconomic groups are significantly and persistently underserved by talent development programming (Rinn et al., 2020), while simultaneously being overrepresented within special education (Gindal et al., 2019). This is particularly notable in the context that students with disabilities are significantly less likely to be referred for gifted education programming (Barnard-Brak et al., 2015; Cain et al., 2019; McCallum et al., 2013). Therefore, because students of color are more likely to be referred for disability-related programming, and students identified as having disabilities are less likely to be referred for gifted programming, this further limits the opportunity for twice-exceptional students from minoritized groups to receive talent development opportunities.

To address the underrepresentation of culturally, linguistically, and economically diverse high-ability and twice-exceptional students, simply changing identification procedures will likely be insufficient. It is necessary to shift from a deficit-focused approach to a strengths-based approach that emphasizes early and repeated access to rigorous educational environments (Davis & Robinson, 2018). Culturally responsive practices that help twice-exceptional students develop positive identities will further contribute to their success in school (Mayes & Moore, 2016). Finally, implementing practices that increase equity in identification for gifted programs, such as those described in the following, will benefit all high-ability and twice-exceptional students from racially, culturally, and linguistically diverse backgrounds by increasing access to advanced learning opportunities.

Redefining schoolwide identification practices for high-ability students is necessary to increase access to accelerated learning programs for students from historically underrepresented backgrounds. Traditionally, consideration for inclusion within gifted education programs has heavily relied on teacher nomination, which has likely contributed to the persistent problem of underrepresentation of Black and Latinx students in gifted programs. One potential means of redressing referral biases and expanding access to gifted programming for diverse students is to implement universal screening to detect students who may benefit from accelerated learning opportunities (Card & Giuliano, 2016). Just as many schools have moved toward a multi-tiered system of support (MTSS) service delivery model, universal screening for giftedness can be conducted if districts are willing to marshal the resources to integrate appropriate screening tools within their MTSS frameworks. Measures of cognitive reasoning that can be group administered, such as the Cognitive Abilities Test (CogAT; Lohman, 2011) or the Naglieri Nonverbal Ability Test (NNAT; Naglieri, 2008), have the potential to help educators cast a wider net and find high-ability students who otherwise would not be considered for gifted programs based on teacher nomination, such as twice-exceptional students or students of color.

Notably, some research has shown that both traditional and nonverbal tests of cognitive ability, such as the CogAT and NNAT, may do little to redress the gap in identification of historically underrepresented students for gifted and talented programs (Giessman et al., 2013). However, this problem can be mitigated by employing these existing instruments within a "use test differently" paradigm to better identify underrepresented high-ability students (Peters & Engerrand, 2016). The "use tests differently" paradigm is a potential solution to underrepresentation that emphasizes using instruments commonly used within K–12 education (e.g., achievement tests, ability tests) in different and novel ways; it is an alternative to the "use different tests" paradigm that tends to focus on the development, selection, and/or administration of measures that are purportedly bias-free and culture neutral (Peters & Engerrand, 2016). Perhaps the most widely accepted "use tests differently" method is the utilization of local norming groups instead of national norming groups to support more proportional representation within gifted programs.

Many districts rely on identification criteria that require students to perform at or above the 95th percentile on nationally normed tests of both cognitive ability and academic achievement (Lohman, 2013). Such restrictive criteria for identification for advanced educational programming present several challenges to diversifying gifted education programs, especially in large, urban, decentralized school districts. The most glaring problem is twofold: (1) Some minority-majority schools within large districts may nominally have access to the gifted and talented program, yet no students actually are served because they are unable to qualify based on nationally normed measures; and (2) some predominantly White schools may have an outsized segment of their students identified as gifted. Instead of such restrictive eligibility criteria being uniformly imposed districtwide, Lohman (2013) recommends that districts consider operationalizing giftedness (i.e., the top 5% of students) at the building level to increase access to gifted and talented programs. For more information on how group-administered tests of cognitive ability can be locally normed at the building or district level, see Lohman (2013).

Additionally, there is some reluctance to administer measures of intellectual ability to students of color due to a history of their inappropriate use and interpretation. For example, there has been a well-documented history of Black students being disproportionately and inappropriately identified as having "educable mental retardation" in the 1970s (Grant, 1992). However, there is general consensus that major contemporary intelligence tests, whose primary purpose is to predict academic performance, are not biased predictors of scholastic achievement for racial/ethnic minority groups (Erwin & Worrell, 2012; Nisbett et al., 2012). For Black and Latinx students who are being evaluated for special education services, an assessment of cognitive ability may reveal intellectual strengths that can help guide intervention planning beyond remediation of externalizing behaviors or academic deficits.

CONCLUSION

Although research has shown that a comprehensive assessment is the best way to accurately identify twice-exceptional students (Assouline et al., 2009; Foley-Nicpon et al., 2011), limited time and financial resources make such an approach difficult for school psychologists to implement. These students, and all who serve them, will benefit from additional research into facets of twice-exceptionality that can inform accurate identification of needs for both talent development and disability accommodation/remediation. Additionally, limited intervention research has been conducted with twice-exceptional populations, which leaves even those students who are identified as twice-exceptional without empirically validated interventions to support them. Increased investigation of interventions that benefit specific populations of twice-exceptional students (e.g., social skills curricula for high-ability students with ASD, EF instruction for high-ability students with ADHD) will facilitate improved support for their areas of need while also accounting for their talent areas. Finally, continued research into talent development approaches, including academic acceleration, with twice-exceptional students can help to inform decision making when such approaches are considered.

Reconsideration of the common understanding of giftedness and the traditional frameworks of gifted education will also be beneficial and necessary to facilitate appropriate provision of advanced learning opportunities to students who need them, including culturally and linguistically diverse and twice-exceptional students. That is, the conception of giftedness as innate ability (National Working Group on Advanced Education, 2023) should be replaced with an understanding of gifted education as "a path to challenge students who are not being challenged through existing services" (Peters, 2022; p. 89). Shifting the focus from innate characteristics to individual needs will allow for more accurate and equitable identification for talent development programming, and therefore more opportunities to find and develop talents existing systems tend to miss.

Although bilingual/multilingual learners are one of the fastest growing segments of the United States' K–12 student population (Irwin et al., 2023), most American school psychologists are monolingual English speakers (Goforth et al., 2021). For twice-exceptional students who speak English as a second language, the psychoeducational assessment process is even more complex and requires specialized knowledge of not only the intersection of disability and giftedness but also bilingual/multilingual learning and development. The field of gifted education is increasingly recognizing the need to accurately identify high-ability students who may be multilingual learners (Haller-Gryc, 2022). Furthermore, the field is also recognizing the critical role that school psychologists can and should have in redressing racial/ethnic disparities in access to gifted programming (Ford et al., 2016). Therefore, social–emotional and behavioral assessment of twice-exceptional students who are bilingual or English language learners is likely an area for much-needed future research. Overall, twice-exceptional students pose a unique challenge for school psychologists to assess and serve, and this population will benefit from continued research into best practices for identifying and supporting both their strengths and areas of challenge.

REFERENCES

Ackerman, C. M. (2009). The essential elements of Dabrowski's theory of positive disintegration and how they are connected. *Roeper Review, 31*, 81–95.

Amend, E. R., & Beljan, P. (2009). The antecedents of misdiagnosis: When normal behaviors of gifted children are misinterpreted as pathological. *Gifted Education International, 25*, 121–143.

Amend, E. R., & Peters, D. B. (2012). Misdiagnosis and missed diagnosis of gifted children: The importance of accurate assessment. In T. L. Cross & J. R. Cross (Eds.), *Handbook for counselors serving students with gifts and talents: Development, relationships, school issues, and counseling needs/interventions* (pp. 585–596). Prufrock Press.

American Psychiatric Association. (2022). *Diagnostic and statistical manual of mental disorders* (5th ed., text rev.).

Antshel, K. M. (2008). Attention-deficit/hyperactivity disorder in the context of a high intellectual quotient/giftedness. *Developmental Disabilities Research Reviews, 14*(4), 293–299.

Assouline, S. G., Foley-Nicpon, M., & Doobay, A. (2009). Profoundly gifted girls and autism spectrum disorder: A psychometric case study comparison. *Gifted Child Quarterly, 53*(2), 89–105.

Assouline, S. G., Nicpon, M. F., Colangelo, N., & O'Brien, M. (2008). *The paradox of giftedness and autism: Packet of information for professionals (PIP)—Revised.* Connie Belin & Jacqueline N. Blank International Center for Gifted Education and Talent Development (NJ1).

Assouline, S. G., & Whiteman, C. S. (2011). Twice-exceptionality: Implications for school psychologists in the post-IDEA 2004 era. *Journal of Applied School Psychology, 27*(4), 380–402.

Baldwin, L., Baum, S., Pereles, D., & Hughes, C. (2015). Twice-exceptional learners: The journey toward a shared vision. *Gifted Child Quarterly, 38*, 206–214.

Barnard-Brak, L., Johnsen, S. K., Hannig, A. P., & Wei, T. (2015). The incidence of potentially gifted students within a special education program. *Roeper Review, 37*(2), 74–83.

Baudson, T. G. (2016). The mad genius stereotype: Still alive and well. *Frontiers in Psychology, 7*, Article 368.

Bergold, S., Hostel, M. R., & Steinmayr, R. (2021). Do mass media shape stereotypes about intellectually gifted individuals? Two experiments on stigmatization effects from biased newspaper reports. *Gifted Child Quarterly, 65*(1), 75–94.

Cain, M. K., Kaboski, J. R., & Gilger, J. W. (2019). Profiles and academic trajectories of cognitively gifted children with autism spectrum disorder. *Autism, 23*(7), 1663–1674.

Card, D., & Giuliano, L. (2016). Universal screening increases the representation of low-income and minority students in gifted education. *Proceedings of the National Academy of Sciences, 113*(48), 13678–13683.

Chae, P. K., Kim, J. H., & Noh, K. S. (2003). Diagnosis of ADHD among gifted children in relation to KEDI-WISC and TOVA performance. *Gifted Child Quarterly, 47*(3), 192–201.

Cornoldi, C., Giofrè, D., & Toffalini, E. (2023). Cognitive characteristics of intellectually gifted children with a diagnosis of ADHD. *Intelligence, 97*, 1–8.

Dabrowski, K. (1964). *Positive disintegration*. Little, Brown.

Daniels, S., & Piechowski, M. M. (Eds.). (2009). *Living with intensity: Understanding the sensitivity, excitability, and emotional development of gifted children, adolescents, and adults*. Great Potential Press.

Davis, J. L., & Robinson, S. A. (2018). Being 3e, a new look at culturally diverse gifted learners with exceptional conditions: An examination of the issues and solutions for educators and families. In S. B. Kaufman (Ed.), *Twice exceptional: Supporting and educating bright and creative students with learning difficulties* (pp. 278–289). Oxford University Press.

Dombrowski, S. C., Kamphaus, R. W., & Reynolds, C. R. (2004). After the demise of the discrepancy: Proposed learning disabilities diagnostic criteria. *Professional Psychology: Research and Practice, 35*, 364–372.

Doobay, A. F., Foley-Nicpon, M., Ali, S. R., & Assouline, S. G. (2014). Cognitive, adaptive, and psychosocial differences between high ability youth with and without autism spectrum disorder. *Journal of Autism and Developmental Disorders, 44*(8), 2026–2040.

DuPaul, G. J., Power, T. J., Anastopoulos, A. D., & Reid, R. (2016). *ADHD Rating Scale-5 for children and adolescents: Checklists, norms, and clinical interpretation*. Guilford Press.

Duplenne, L., Bourdin, B., Fernandez, D. N., Blondelle, G., & Aubry, A. (2024). Anxiety and depression in gifted individuals: A systematic and meta-analytic review. *Gifted Child Quarterly, 68*(1), 3–85.

Education for All Handicapped Children Act of 1975, Pub. L. No. 94-142, 89 Stat. 773. (1975). *www.govinfo.gov/content/pkg/STATUTE-89/pdf/STATUTE-89-Pg773.pdf*

Erwin, J. O., & Worrell, F. C. (2012). Assessment practices and the underrepresentation of minority students in gifted and talented education. *Journal of Psychoeducational Assessment, 30*, 74–87.

Foley-Nicpon, M., Allmon, A., & Stinson, R. D. (2011). Empirical investigation of twice-exceptionality: Where have we been and where are we going? *Gifted Child Quarterly, 55*(1), 3–79.

Foley-Nicpon, M., & Assouline, S. A. (2020). High ability students with coexisting disabilities: Implications for school psychological practice. *Psychology in the Schools, 57*, 1615–1626.

Foley-Nicpon, M., Doobay, A. F., & Assouline, S. G. (2010). Parent, teacher, and self perceptions of psychosocial functioning in intellectually gifted children and adolescents with autism spectrum disorder. *Journal of Autism and Developmental Disorders, 40*, 1028–1038.

Ford, D. Y., Wright, B. L., Washington, A., & Henfield, M. S. (2016). Access and equity denied: Key theories for school psychologists to consider when assessing Black and Hispanic students for gifted education. *School Psychology Forum, 10*(1), 265–277.

Giessman, J. A., Gambrell, J. L., & Stebbins, M. S. (2013). Minority performance on the Naglieri Nonverbal Ability Test, versus the Cognitive Abilities Test, form 6: One gifted program's experience. *Gifted Child Quarterly, 57*(2), 101–109.

Gilman, B. J., Lovecky, D. V., Kearney, K., Peters, D. B., Wasserman, J. D., Silverman, L. K., et al. (2013). Critical issues in the identification of gifted students with co-existing disabilities: The twice-exceptional. *SAGE Open, 3*(3).

Gindal, T., Schifter, L. A., Schwartz, G., & Hehir, T. (2019). Racial differences in special education identification and placement: Evidence across three states. *Harvard Educational Review, 89*(4), 525–553.

Gioia, G. A., Isquith, P. K., Guy, S. C., & Kenworthy, L. (2015). *Behavior Rating Inventory of Executive Function®, Second Edition (BRIEF®2)*. Western Psychological Services.

Goforth, A. N., Farmer, R. L., Kim, S. Y., Naser, S. C., Lockwood, A. B., & Affrunti, N. W. (2021). Status of school psychology in 2020: Part 1, Demographics of the NASP membership survey. *NASP Research Reports, 5*(2). *www.nasponline.org/research-and-policy/research-center/member-surveys*

Gomez, R., Stavropoulos, V., Vance, A., & Griffiths, M. D. (2020). Gifted children with ADHD: How are they different from non-gifted children with ADHD? *International Journal of Mental Health and Addiction, 18*, 1467–1481.

Grant, P. (1992). Using special education to destroy Black boys. *Negro Educational Review, 63*, 17–21.

Haller-Gryc, I. (2022). When teachers are the gatekeepers of gifted and talented programs: Potential factors for English learners' underrepresentation and possible solutions. *Journal of English Learner Education, 14*(1), 4.

Hartnett, D. N., Nelson, J. M., & Rinn, A. N. (2004). Gifted or ADHD? The possibilities of misdiagnosis. *Roeper Review, 26*, 73–76.

Individuals with Disabilities Education Act, 20 U.S.C. § 1400 et seq. (2004). *www.govinfo.gov/content/pkg/PLAW-108publ446/pdf/PLAW-108publ446.pdf*

Irwin, V., Wang, K., Tezil, T., Zhang, J., Filbey, A., Jung, J., et al. (2023). *Report on the Condition of Education 2023*. NCES 2023-144. National Center for Education Statistics. *https://nces.ed.gov/programs/coe*

LeBeau, B., Foley Nicpon, M., Doobay, A. F., Schabilion, K., Smith, C., Berns, A. J., & Assouline, S. G. (2024). Academic, clinical, and psychosocial profiles for high ability individuals with obsessive–compulsive disorder. *Roeper Review, 46*(2), 103–119.

Lee, K. M., & Olenchak, F. R. (2015). Individuals with a gifted/attention deficit/hyperactivity disorder diagnosis: Identification, performance, outcomes, and interventions. *Gifted Education International, 31*(3), 185–199.

Lewis, L. R. (2021). Twice-exceptionality: Maximizing academic and psychosocial success in youth. *Journal of Health Service Psychology, 47,* 191–196.

Lohman, D. F. (2011). *Cognitive Abilities Test, Form 7.* Riverside Publishing.

Lohman, D. F. (2013). Identifying gifted students: Nontraditional uses of traditional measures. In C. M. Callahan & H. L. Hertberg-Davis (Eds.), *Fundamentals of gifted education: Considering multiple perspectives* (pp. 112–127). Routledge.

Lord, C., Brugha, T. S., Charman, T., Cusack, J., Dumas, G., Frazier, T., et al. (2020). Autism spectrum disorder. *Nature Reviews Disease Primers,* 6(1), 5.

Lord, C., Rutter, M., DiLavore, P. C., Risi, S., Gotham, K., & Bishop, S. (2012). *Autism diagnostic observation schedule: ADOS-2.* Western Psychological Services.

Lovett, B. J., & Lewandowski, L. J. (2006). Gifted students with learning disabilities: Who are they? *Journal of Learning Disabilities,* 39(3), 482–571.

Lovett, B. J., & Sparks, R. L. (2011). The identification and performance of gifted students with learning disability diagnoses: A *quantitative synthesis. Journal of Learning Disabilities,* 46(4), 304–316.

Maddocks, D. L. (2018). The identification of students who are gifted and have a learning disability: A comparison of different diagnostic criteria. *Gifted Child Quarterly,* 62(2), 175–192.

Marland, S. P., Jr. (1972). *Education of the gifted and talented: Report to the Congress of the United States by the U.S. Commissioner of Education and background papers submitted to the U.S. Office of Education* (Vols. 1 and 2) (Government Documents, Y4.L 11/2: G36). U.S. Government Printing Office.

Mash, E. J., & Barkley, R. A. (Eds.). (2014). *Child psychopathology* (3rd ed.). Guilford Press.

Mather, N., & Gregg, N. (2006). Specific learning disabilities: Clarifying, not eliminating, a construct. *Professional Psychology: Research and Practice, 37*(1), 99–106.

Mayes, R. D., & Moore, J. L. (2016). The intersection of race, disability, and giftedness: Understanding the education needs of twice-exceptional, African American students. *Gifted Child Today,* 39(2), 73–127.

McCallum, R. S., Bell, S. M., Coles, J. T., Miller, K. C., Hopkins, M. B., & Hilton-Prillhart, A. (2013). A model for screening twice-exceptional students (gifted with learning disabilities) within a response to intervention paradigm. *Gifted Child Quarterly, 57*(4), 209–222.

McCrimmon, A. W., Matchullis, R. L., Altomare, A. A., & Smith-Demers, A. D. (2016). Executive functions in autism spectrum disorder. In J. L. Matson (Ed.), *Handbook of assessment and diagnosis of autism spectrum disorder* (pp. 403–425). Springer.

Mullet, D. R., & Rinn, A. N. (2015). Giftedness and ADHD: Identification, misdiagnosis, and dual diagnosis. *Roeper Review, 37*(4), 195–207.

Naglieri, J. A. (2008). *Naglieri Nonverbal Ability Test* (2nd ed.). NCS Pearson.

National Association for Gifted Children. (2019). *A definition of giftedness that guides best practice. https://nagc.org/page/what-is-giftedness*

National Working Group on Advanced Education. (2023). *Building a wider, more diverse pipeline of advanced learners.* Thomas B. Fordham Institute. *https://fordhaminstitute.org/national/research/building-wider-more-diverse-pipeline-advanced-learners*

Neihart, M. (1999). The impact of giftedness on psychological well-being: What does the empirical literature say? *Roeper Review, 22*(1), 10–17.

Nisbett, R. E., Aronson, J., Blair, C., Dickens, W., Flynn, J., Halpern, D. F., & Turkheimer, E. (2012). Intelligence: New findings and theoretical developments. *American Psychologist, 67,* 130–159.

Ogurlu, U. (2021). A meta-analytic review of emotional intelligence in gifted individuals: A multilevel analysis. *Personality and Individual Differences, 171,* 1–11.

Penney, A. M., Miedema, V. C., & Mazmanian, D. (2015). Intelligence and emotional disorders: Is the worrying and ruminating mind a more intelligent mind? *Personality and Individual Differences, 74,* 90–93.

Peters, S. J. (2022). The challenges of achieving equity within public school gifted and talented programs. *Gifted Child Quarterly,* 66(2), 82–94.

Peters, S. J., & Engerrand, K. G. (2016). Equity and excellence: Proactive efforts in the identification of underrepresented students for gifted and talented services. *Gifted Child Quarterly,* 60(3), 159–171.

Pfeiffer, S. I., & Stocking, V. B. (2000). Vulnerabilities of academically gifted students. *Special Services in the Schools, 16*(1/2), 83–93.

Probst, B., & Piechowski, M. (2012). Overexcitabilities and temperament. In T. L. Cross & J. R. Cross (Eds.), *Handbook for counselors serving students with gifts and talents: Development, relationships, school issues, and counseling needs/interventions* (pp. 53–73). Prufrock Press.

Reis, S. M., Baum, S. M., & Burke, E. (2014). An operational definition of twice-exceptional learners: Implications and applications. *Gifted Child Quarterly,* 58(3), 217–230.

Rinn, A. N., Mun, R. U., & Hodges, J. (2020). *2018–2019 State of the states in gifted education.* National Association of Gifted Children and the Council of State Directors of Programs for the Gifted. *www.nagc.org/2018-2019-state-states-gifted-education*

Rong, Y., Yang, C. J., Jin, Y., & Wang, Y. (2021). Prevalence of attention-deficit/hyperactivity disorder in individuals with autism spectrum disorder: A meta-analysis. *Research in Autism Spectrum Disorders, 83,* 101759.

Rutter, M., Le Couteur, A., & Lord, C. (2003) *Autism Diagnostic Interview—Revised.* Western Psychological Services.

Shany, M., Wiener, J., & Assido, M. (2013). Friendship predictors of global self-worth and domain-specific self-concepts in university students with and without learning disability. *Journal of Learning Disabilities, 46,* 444–452.

Silverman, L. K. (1997). The construct of asynchronous development. *Peabody Journal of Education, 72*(3–4), 36–58.

Webb, J. T., Amend, E. R., Webb, N. E., Goerss, J., Beljan, P., & Olenchak, F. R. (2005). *Misdiagnosis and dual diagnoses of gifted children and adults: ADHD, bipolar, CD, Asperger's, depression, and other disorders.* Great Potential Press.

Webb, J. T., & Latimer, D. (1993). ADHD and children who are gifted. *Exceptional Children, 60*(2), 183.

World Health Organization. (2019). *International classification of diseases and related health problems* (11th ed.). *https://icd.who.int*

Yell, M. L. (2018). *Law and special education* (5th ed.). Pearson.

Ysseldyke, J. E., Chaparro, E. A., & VanDerHeyden, A. M. (2023). *Assessment in special and inclusive education* (14th ed.). Pro-Ed.

CHAPTER 23

Functional Behavior Assessment

Tai A. Collins, Jakayla Fulwood, Nneka Bonner, and Joseph Lampton

Behaviors of concern take considerable time and energy to address within educational settings. Challenging behaviors can have harmful effects on the students who engage in them, as they can lead to loss of instructional time, changes in placement, disciplinary action, and physical harm, resulting in poor academic, behavioral, social–emotional, and mental health outcomes. These behaviors can also disrupt the learning of other students. Teachers regularly indicate feeling underprepared to address inappropriate behaviors, as behavior management has been reported as a primary stressor and contributing factor to leaving the education field (Flower et al., 2017). This challenge is particularly salient for teachers who support students with intellectual, developmental, emotional, and behavioral disabilities, as the rates of inappropriate behaviors can be particularly stressful and harmful to everyone in the educational community, including the students themselves (Esteves et al., 2021; Flower et al., 2017).

When youth engage in challenging behaviors, the viewpoint should not be that the students are "broken." This deficit-based interpretation of behaviors can be harmful and incomplete, as it does not acknowledge the environmental variables that contribute to the behavior (Collins & Hawkins, 2023). Students' inappropriate behaviors often confer some benefit for them, such as increased attention from staff and/or peers, escape from educational or social demands, access to preferred items or activities, and/or automatic reinforcement (Cooper et al., 2019). Antecedent variables can also influence behaviors, such as lack of sleep, food insecurity, boredom, lack of attention, and staff behaviors that escalate situations, among many others (Cooper et al., 2019). As such, functional behavior assessment (FBA) strategies are used to analyze the various factors related to a behavior to identify a hypothesized function of the behavior (e.g., attention, access, escape, and/or automatic reinforcement). FBA also informs the development of function-based interventions aimed at manipulating environmental variables to occasion more appropriate behaviors and reduce the likelihood of inappropriate behaviors (Collins & Hawkins, 2023).

When experiencing challenging behaviors, it is crucial to recognize that these are emotionally charged situations for all involved and that biases factor into the conceptualization of the situation and the resulting response. Racially and ethnically minoritized students and students with disabilities continuously receive disproportionate rates of exclusionary discipline in the United States (e.g., Enders et al., 2022). Research has shown that Latinx students, for example, are more likely to receive disciplinary action rather than behavioral intervention, resulting in poor outcomes such as loss of valuable instructional time (Moreno &

Bullock, 2015). These inequitable responses to behaviors are a result of a variety of factors, including educator bias, racism, and ableism, that affect how staff view and respond to perceived problem behaviors (Collins & Hawkins, 2023). Given that FBA provides a framework to analyze challenging behaviors and inform intervention, FBA approaches must be culturally informed so that they promote positive outcomes and avoid exacerbating harm to marginalized and minoritized youth (Collins & Hawkins, 2023).

Culturally informed approaches to FBA are needed to alleviate bias in assessment, case conceptualization, and prioritization of behaviors and promote equitable and socially just outcomes for youth. Ethical codes of the National Association of School Psychologists and Behavior Analyst Certification Board indicate the responsibility of educational professionals to protect the rights and educational opportunities of all students, which means that we are required to engage in anti-racist and anti-ableist practices that challenge bias across all areas of responsibility (Fong et al., 2016; Harrison et al., 2023). For example, Blake et al. (2016) discussed the cultural synchrony hypothesis, which posits that teachers who do not share a racial/ethnic identity with minoritized students may misperceive culturally appropriate behaviors and make decisions that result in disciplinary actions for students. If an FBA were to be conducted without an understanding of the body of literature around teachers' racialized biases and their effects on students' behaviors, we run the risk of failing to understand a critical variable occasioning and potentially exacerbating the problem behavior, thereby compounding the harm that minoritized and marginalized students experience in schools. Toward a culturally informed approach to FBA, this chapter will (1) define FBA, (2) describe culturally informed FBA, (3) discuss cultural considerations within FBA, and (4) identify gaps in the literature and future directions for culturally informed FBA.

DEFINING FBA

FBA procedures are used to analyze a functional relationship between environmental maintaining variables and challenging behaviors to inform effective intervention design (Cooper et al., 2019). The usefulness of FBAs in education can be illustrated by the Individuals with Disabilities Education Act of 1990 (IDEA), which ensured the right to free public education in the least restrictive environment for individuals with disabilities (Asmus et al., 2002). IDEA mandated the use of the FBA to address target behaviors when a child's behavior difficulties result in changing their educational placement or result in a student with a disability being repeatedly suspended (Asmus et al., 2002). However, IDEA does not identify specific strategies and techniques for assessment, so despite the recognized utility of FBA procedures, FBA policies, criteria, and procedures vary by state (Asmus et al., 2002).

There are three approaches to FBAs: indirect, descriptive analysis, and functional analysis (Iwata & Worsdell, 2005). Indirect methods include rating scales, questionnaires, checklists, and interviews (e.g., Motivation Assessment Scale; Durand & Crimmins, 1988; Functional Assessment Checklist: Teachers and Staff; March et al., 2000), which are used to gather information pertaining to the target behavior and the conditions under which it occurs. Indirect assessment provides an efficient approach to obtaining information about the target behavior and is frequently used in schools to address a variety of concerns. Indirect FBAs are also frequently used as a preliminary step to more resource-intensive FBAs, as the results can inform descriptive FBAs and functional analyses. When conducting indirect FBAs, it is important to consider the subjective and unreliable nature of verbal reports, which are open to interpretation and can vary across interviewees (Iwata & Worsdell, 2005).

Descriptive FBAs

Descriptive FBAs can be described as direct observation of the target behavior and the circumstances surrounding it. The most commonly used approach to descriptive analysis is ABC (i.e., **A**ntecedent, **B**ehavior, **C**onsequence) recording, which records each instance of the behavior, in addition to what occurs immediately before and after the target behavior (Cooper et al., 2019). The results are summarized to identify correlations between the antecedents, consequences, and the challenging behavior (Iwata & Worsdell, 2005). These results may inform intervention, as well as the conditions of a functional analysis. When comparing the results of descriptive FBAs and functional analyses, Contreras et al. (2023) found exact correspondence between 50% of comparisons in 48 studies. Additionally, structured descriptive assessments were more likely than unstructured assessments to accurately predict functions (defined as finding the same hypothesized function as a functional analysis; Contreras et al., 2023). Descriptive

FBAs were also found to be more likely to predict the absence of a function, as opposed to the presence of a function (Contreras et al., 2023). While descriptive analysis is the most frequently used method of assessment, it is limited in that it has no control over environmental factors and cannot directly test which factors are contributing to the target behavior (Iwata & Worsdell, 2005).

Functional Analyses

Functional analyses (FAs) consist of manipulating the antecedents and consequences of the target behavior to determine the functional variables (Iwata & Worsdell, 2005). The client is exposed to a variety of conditions (e.g., attention, escape, alone, play), and the rates of the target behavior in each condition are compared. In an attention condition, attention is withheld, and access to attention is contingent on the occurrence of the target behavior (Iwata & Worsdell, 2005). In a typical escape condition, a demand is presented, and if the target behavior occurs, the demand is removed for a brief period and then presented again (Iwata & Worsdell, 2005). In the alone condition, which is used to test for behaviors maintained by automatic reinforcement, the client is left in a relatively empty room with no socially mediated consequences for the target behavior (Cooper et al., 2019). In a play condition, which acts as a control to which results of other conditions are compared, the client is given free access to preferred items and social interaction (Iwata & Worsdell, 2005). In some instances, FAs can also include an access condition, which consists of providing the client with access to a preferred object or edible a few minutes prior to the start of the condition, removing it at the start of the condition, and returning the object or edible briefly contingent on the target behavior. The rates of the target behavior in each condition are carefully compared to identify a hypothesized function (Iwata & Worsdell, 2005).

The FA is the only FBA method that can identify a causal relationship between the target behavior and its function (Iwata & Worsdell, 2005). It provides important information to inform intervention decisions and helps to determine which interventions are likely to be effective in altering the environmental factors to promote appropriate behaviors and reduce inappropriate behaviors. Functional analysis has some disadvantages, as it is complex, time-consuming, and requires high levels of training and a high degree of consistency when implementing the conditions (Cooper et al., 2019; Iwata & Worsdell, 2005).

Brief and Trial-Based Functional Analyses

Brief functional analysis (BFA) was developed to capitalize on the ability of the FA to manipulate contingencies while being more practical for use in a variety of settings (Cooper et al., 2019). In a BFA, the sequence of test and control conditions is based on hypotheses from descriptive FBAs, sessions are shorter, and there are fewer exposures to the conditions (Muething et al., 2017). The research is mixed about the correspondence between BFAs and FAs, indicating that more research is needed to determine the conditions under which a BFA is likely to result in a similar hypothesized function to a traditional FA (e.g., Muething et al., 2017). More research is needed to assess the correspondence between FAs and BFAs; however, BFAs hold promise as a feasible approach to determining the function of challenging behaviors.

Another alternative to a full FA is a trial-based functional analysis (TBFA), in which each condition involves the manipulation of the motivation related to a target behavior. For example, in an attention condition, a trial consists of a phase when the motivating operation (MO) is present (i.e., ignoring or attention deprivation) for a minute. At the end of the minute, or if the target behavior occurs during the MO present phase, the MO absent phase (i.e., presentation of attention) begins for one minute. The MO present and absent phases related to each hypothesized function are repeatedly presented until a pattern of behavior emerges (e.g., increased rates of the target behavior in the attention MO present phase relative to MO absent phase). LaRue et al. (2010) compared the results of traditional FAs and TBFAs for five clients. Researchers found exact correspondence with four clients and partial correspondence with the other, while the TBFAs took an average of approximately 32 minutes compared to an average of 208 minutes for full FAs (LaRue et al., 2010). These results illustrate fairly high correspondence between FAs and TBFAs, which instills confidence that TBFAs and FAs are likely to yield similar results.

CULTURALLY RELEVANT PRACTICE CONSIDERATIONS

Culture-evasive assessments of target behaviors are likely to miss valuable information regarding the variables maintaining the behavior and can result in harmful interventions that can advance oppressive systems and fail to incorporate the client's strengths (Collins & Hawkins, 2023). As such, FBAs must be informed by the culture of the client and the environments they navigate. Diversity among school-based populations is increasing in the United States, while the teaching population remains homogenous, with most teachers and school staff being White women (La Salle et al., 2019). Issues such as racism and implicit bias can increase disproportionality in discipline referrals and skew educators' objectivity regarding their behavioral expectations of culturally minoritized students (Enders et al., 2022; Moreno, 2021). Given what we know about teachers' racialized biases and the potential for clashes between cultures (e.g., Blake et al., 2016; Moreno & Gaytán, 2013), as well as the rampant racial ethnic disproportionality in discipline (e.g., Kunesh & Noltemeyer, 2019), it is imperative that the FBA assessments that we use to analyze target behaviors are culturally informed and socially just.

Collins and Hawkins (2023) outlined best practices in conducting culturally relevant FBAs, including work prior to, during, and after assessment (described in more detail later). Prior to assessment, school psychologists and other professionals should advocate for equitable and culturally affirming school systems. It is essential that children experience positive and culturally relevant learning environments that affirm their identities and strengths. Many inappropriate behaviors can be avoided or de-escalated when youth experience care and support in schools, and they can be exacerbated when they experience apathy and discrimination. School professionals should be intentional about improving our knowledge and skills related to social justice, such as understanding one's own identities and how they intersect with the various identities of students and staff in schools. Practicing cultural humility, which involves self-reflection and constructive criticism, openness, self-awareness, positive interactions, and avoiding complacency (Steefel et al., 2016), allows us to ask the right questions and advocate for equity. Best practice is to include FBA processes in all consultation (Collins & Hawkins, 2023). The processes of indirect and direct descriptive FBAs (e.g., interviews, observations) are often used when consulting around various concerns in schools. An FBA lens should be used during our work in schools, as we should be looking for patterns in antecedents and consequences related to a variety of behaviors. This would allow us to notice and alleviate any alarming trends occurring with specific populations of students or staff, or in specific settings, thereby informing preventative strategies that promote students' wellness and educational outcomes. Each of these pre-FBA strategies is essential in setting the stage for culturally informed FBAs, as engaging in FBA in schools without social justice-oriented systems and staff can result in blaming students for problems caused by the systems they navigate.

With the prior considerations as a foundation, Collins and Hawkins (2023) identified five best practices during the FBA process: (1) centering student voice, (2) engaging families, (3) developing a shared definition of the challenging behavior, (4) conducting direct observations, and (5) developing a functional hypothesis informed by culture. First, students' voices should be solicited and centered throughout the FBA process, because too often we avoid discussing the concerns with youth and gaining their perspective on what they are experiencing and why they are engaging in behaviors. Students are the experts of their own experiences and can provide valuable insight to inform our functional hypothesis and intervention. Second, families should be engaged as partners in the FBA process, as they can provide valuable information about the child's culture, values, and functioning in various contexts. Families have rich cultural knowledge and expertise that often go unacknowledged in the FBA process and educational practices in general (Moll et al., 1992). Fewer than half of special educators and support staff who responded to a survey about culturally informed FBAs indicated that their schools always provide written and oral communication to families in the families' first language (Moreno et al., 2017). This raises ethical questions about consent and family engagement in the FBA process and emphasizes the need for the ethical use of interpretation and translation services. Third, a shared definition of the target behavior must be developed, as various partners (e.g., teachers, staff, families, students) must be clear on the goals of assessment and intervention. Individuals' attributions of behaviors can be affected by their cultural norms and expectations, identities (e.g., gender, age, ability), and various other factors, so it is important that everyone on the team supporting a student reaches consensus on the behaviors of concern. Conducting direct observations is a fourth best practice, as we should not solely rely on individuals' reports of problem behaviors. Direct observations can reveal environmental factors that individuals may be unaware of or do not report through formal interviews or rating scales (e.g., teachers' lack of positive attention focused on the student, distracting behaviors of other students), with observations yielding a more complete and valid FBA. Intervention ideas can also be sparked when the setting of interest is observed and evaluated. Finally, developing a culturally relevant functional hypothesis includes using all of the data collected to summarize the environmental variables contributing to a target behavior. A culturally informed functional hypothesis considers the student's strengths, the staff behaviors that may exacerbate the target behavior, and includes a consideration of more distal issues such as school climate, school policies, and the sociopolitical environment in which all partners are operating (Collins & Hawkins, 2023). This hypothesis contrasts with a typical deficit-oriented functional hypothesis that blames the student for their behaviors and fails to consider the various factors that affect individuals' functioning in school contexts.

Collins and Hawkins (2023) identified two best practices following a culturally relevant FBA. First, a culturally informed intervention should be developed using FBA data. A more complete and student-centered case conceptualization forms when a culturally relevant FBA is conducted, thereby allowing us to develop a culturally relevant intervention with a high likelihood of success. For example, we may hypothesize that a student's refusal to complete academic work is maintained by escape from the academic task and exacerbated by harmful interactions with the teacher. Intervention may involve reinforcement for work completion and building academic skills, but a culturally informed approach would also involve improving the teacher-student relationship and professional development for the teacher. Interventions should be codeveloped with youth and families, as their strengths, values, and voices should be centered. The final best practice is to continuously evaluate students' progress in response to intervention, as culturally relevant FBA is an ongoing process informed by changes in students' behaviors and environmental variables. Case conceptualization and functional hypotheses are not static. Rather, they evolve as environmental variables change and should always be informed by the best available evidence. Intentionally incorporating these practice considerations prior to, during, and after an FBA can result in a culturally informed assessment of a situation and culturally relevant intervention that promotes students' wellness and actively challenges any systemic barrier to their success.

FUTURE DIRECTIONS

Recent advancements in the FBA literature have revealed three future directions for the use of culturally relevant FBA practices. First, researchers must continue to examine the practicality of FBA in a variety of contexts and determine how to conduct culturally relevant FBAs with validity and reliability in settings with limited resources. Second, the thoughtful and ethical incorporation of technology, including telehealth and artificial intelligence (AI), must continue to be explored. Finally, the ongoing racial reckoning occurring in the United States and across the world highlights the importance of incorporating critical theories into FBA to inform socially just, anti-racist, and anti-ableist conceptualizations of behaviors.

Practical Approaches to FBA

Advancements in FBA methodology such as BFA and TBFA have allowed for the use of functional analysis methodologies in schools with limited resources; however, concerns about the practicality of these assessments remain (e.g., time, complexity, risk; Hanley, 2012). Future research should continue to explore the feasibility and social validity of these assessments and develop additional ways to manipulate environmental contingencies to inform functional hypotheses while promoting practicality for teachers, school staff, and students. In addition, research should continue to examine the validity and cultural relevance of indirect and direct FBA methodologies. Open-ended functional interviews and observations (Hanley, 2012) allow for a more robust exploration of the variety of environmental variables acting on a behavior and give respondents more flexibility in sharing their perspectives (Saini et al., 2019). More research is needed to validate the use of open-ended interviews, determine the likelihood that they predict a similar functional hypothesis to a full functional analysis, and improve the cultural relevance of the questions. Moreno and Gaytán (2013) provided an example of an open-ended functional interview form developed for Latinx families, with questions in both English and Spanish. Additional research is needed to inform how FBA questions should be translated, the training and qualifications necessary for educators to conduct FBAs in various languages, and the social validity of the questions among different populations.

Given concerns about the acceptability and practicality of FAs in schools, Kilgus et al. (2017,

2019) developed the Intervention Selection Profile—Function (ISP-F). This assessment uses direct behavior rating methodology (Chafouleas, 2011), in which teachers briefly rate the frequency with which operationally defined target behaviors result in function-based consequences (e.g., adult attention, peer attention, escape/avoidance, and access to activities/tangibles). Results from the literature support the use of the ISP-F, particularly for behaviors maintained by peer and adult attention (Eklund et al., 2023; Kilgus et al., 2017, 2019). Additional research is needed to further validate the ISP-F for other hypothesized functions and determine the acceptability and feasibility of this assessment. Additionally, future research could allow students to conduct their own ratings related to their behaviors, which could improve their self-determination and offer opportunities for them to be more active in case conceptualization and intervention development. Issues of teacher bias in the rating of behaviors should also be addressed within the ISP-F literature. Additional practical approaches to indirect FBAs, direct FBAs, and FAs should continue to be developed and validated for use in educational settings.

Incorporating Technology into FBA

Innovations in technology are regularly incorporated into educational practices. Researchers have examined the use of telehealth strategies in schools, such as the use of smartphones, telepresence robots, computers, and tablets in teleconsultation (e.g., King et al., 2023). The use of technology during problem-solving consultation, which may include indirect and direct FBA methodologies, has been applied in a variety of settings, such as schools, homes, and clinics. Aerial drones and mounted cameras have been used to record students' behaviors, potentially increasing the types of settings where behaviors can be reliably observed (e.g., playground) and the feasibility of recording in schools (King et al., 2021). Future research should examine the reliability, validity, and feasibility of FBAs conducted remotely. Ethical concerns such as the growing digital divide (i.e., inequitable access to technology); students' and families' consent to recording, storage, and use of recorded observation data; and best practices in developing relationships and centering students' and families' values in teleconsultation should also be explored.

Researchers have also used technology to train various partners in FBA methodology. For example, Romani et al. (2023) trained occupational therapists and special education teachers to conduct preference assessment (i.e., identifying preferred items) and FAs via remote behavioral skills training. Tereshko et al. (2023) trained graduate students via video conferencing on conducting accurate descriptive FBAs (i.e., ABC recording). Although promising, the research on telehealth-delivered behavioral skills training to teach practitioners to conduct FBAs is in its early stages, as few studies incorporate student outcomes or skill usage (Nylen & King, 2023). Future studies should expand training to professionals in school and clinical settings, as much of the research focuses on graduate students in applied behavior analysis programs (Nylen & King, 2023), evaluate the accessibility of remote delivery of FBA skills, and meaningfully integrate culture and cultural humility into training. In addition to these areas, the recent proliferation of AI poses exciting opportunities and ethical and equity concerns in schools. Future research should examine how to meaningfully and ethically incorporate AI into FBAs, as well as factors related to educators' acceptability and use of AI in behavioral assessment and intervention.

Incorporating Critical Theories into FBA

The murders of unarmed Black people by police prompted a racial reckoning in the United States. All institutions, including educational ones, have been forced to examine their inherent inequities. Behavioral assessment in schools is not without its inequities, as racial bias is evident in how we perceive and respond to behaviors, and behavioral assessment often fails to examine the effects of racial trauma on behaviors. As such, FBAs should be informed by theories that explain and examine racism. Ladson-Billings and Tate (1995) applied Critical Race Theory (CRT) to the field of education, positing that gender and socioeconomic status are insufficient to account for the rampant inequities in education. Rather, racism is endemic to the policies, laws, curricula, funding, and practices of educational systems, and the academic, behavioral, social, and emotional functioning of racially/ethnically minoritized children cannot be separated from the racism they experience in education and the broader world. Tenets of CRT include an acknowledgement that racism is endemic to American systems; the centering of minoritized and marginalized voices through storytelling and counter-storytelling; and challenges of color-evasiveness, race neutrality, and meritocracy. When applied to behavioral assessment, and FBA in particular, CRT can be used to explain how racism and unconscious bias can affect teachers' attributions of perceived problem behaviors in minoritized youth, how deficit-oriented conceptualizations of students' functioning are constructed, and how color-blind interventions are developed. A CRT-informed FBA approach would be anti-racist, intentionally centering students' strengths and involving them and their families in promoting their wellness (e.g., Enders et al., 2022). CRT-informed FBAs could also incorporate sociopolitical events as factors in the conceptualizations of cases. For example, Heidelburg et al. (2022) noted that physical and psychological safety in schools (i.e., freedom from bias and racism from educators and peers) is a prerequisite for Black students' wellness and educational outcomes. As such, future research should intentionally incorporate a critical approach to assessing minoritized students' educational environment within FBAs, necessitating an assessment of racism and racial trauma and a case conceptualization that accurately reflects minoritized students lived experience.

In addition to furthering racist policies and practices, traditional FBAs can also perpetuate an ableist conceptualization of disability as disordered functioning (Annamma et al., 2013). Like comparisons of racially and ethnically minoritized youth's behaviors to white standards, Dis/ability Critical Race Studies (DisCrit; Annamma et al., 2013) scholars note that the behaviors of disabled individuals are compared to societal expectations of "normal" functioning, also based on heteronormative, white, middle-class standards. This leads to bias-prone judgments of the federal definition of emotional and behavioral disorders that fail to consider the environments in which students function and the cultural hierarchies that establish expectations of normal, appropriate behavior (Liang et al., 2024). The pervasive issue of ableism cannot be separated from racism but must be viewed from an intersectional lens that acknowledges the individual and interconnected effects of racism, ableism, and sexism on various communities. Fields such as Disability Studies and Disability Studies in Education (DSE) (e.g., Baglieri et al., 2011) have challenged (1) definitions of ability and disability, (2) neutrality and objectivity in school-based assessment and research, and (3) notions of equity in the conceptualization of difference in schools. Given that FBAs are often conducted with students classified as having emotional and behavioral disorders (often a result of intersectional bias and deficit thinking), future FBA research should center anti-ableist critical theories such as DisCrit and DSE, among others.

CONCLUSION

FBA provides a framework to assess the environment a client interacts with to determine the antecedents and consequences of target behaviors. Although there is a vast evidence base supporting the use of FBA, more research is needed to adequately position FBA as an anti-oppressive methodology that can be used to promote equity in educational systems. Minoritized and marginalized individuals' functioning cannot be separated from the oppression they face or the historical and present trauma they carry, and a failure to incorporate these critical issues into a conceptualization of their functioning can cause further harm. Future research is needed to develop practical, technologically sound, anti-racist, and anti-ableist FBA methodologies that will allow us to advance social justice in an increasingly diverse and technologically connected world.

REFERENCES

Annamma, S. A., Connor, D., & Ferri, B. (2013). Dis/ability Critical Race Studies (DisCrit): Theorizing at the intersections of race and dis/ability. *Race Ethnicity and Education*, *16*(1), 1–31.

Asmus, J. M., Vollmer, T. R., & Borrero, J. C. (2002). Functional behavioral assessment: A school-based model. *Education and Treatment of Children*, *25*, 67–90.

Baglieri, S., Valle, J. W., Connor, D. J., & Gallagher, D. J. (2011). Disability Studies in Education: The need for a plurality of perspectives on disability. *Remedial and Special Education*, *32*(4), 267–278.

Blake, J. J., Smith, D. M., Marchbanks, M. P., Seibert, A. L., Wood, S. M., & Kim, E. S. (2016). Does student-teacher racial/ethnic match impact Black students' discipline risk? A test of the cultural synchrony hypothesis. In R. J. Skiba, K. Mediratta, M. Karega Rausch (Eds.), *Inequality in school discipline: Research and practice to reduce disparities* (pp. 79–98). Springer.

Chafouleas, S. M. (2011). Direct behavior rating: A review of the issues and research in its development. *Education & Treatment of Children*, *34*, 575–591.

Collins, T. C., & Hawkins, R. H. (2023). Best practices for linking functional behavioral assessment data to culturally relevant interventions. In P. Harrison, S. Proctor, & A. Thomas (Eds.), *Best practices in school psychology* (7th ed., pp. 137–148). National Association of School Psychologists.

Contreras, B. P., Tate, S. A., Morris, S. L., & Kahng, S. (2023). A systematic review of the correspondence between descriptive assessment and functional analysis. *Journal of Applied Behavior Analysis, 56*(1), 146–165.

Cooper, J., Heron, T., & Heward, W. (2019). *Applied behavior analysis* (3rd ed.). Pearson.

Durand, V. M., & Crimmins, D. B. (1988). Identifying the variables maintaining self-injurious behavior. *Journal of Autism and Developmental Disorders, 18*(1), 99–117.

Eklund, K., Kilgus, S. P., Zahn, M., von der Embse, N. P., Willenbrink, J., Davis, E., & Twombly, T. (2023). Intervention Selection Profile-Function: An examination of decisional accuracy relative to traditional FBA data. *School Psychology, 38*(2), 110–118.

Enders, O. G., Buonomo, K., & Robertson, R. (2022). Addressing race and implicit bias in the functional behavior assessment process: A pilot study of preservice teacher training modules. *Multiple Voices for Ethnically Diverse Exceptional Learners, 22*(1), 6–23.

Esteves, J., Perry, A., Spiegel, R., & Weiss, J. A. (2021). Occurrence and predictors of challenging behavior in youth with intellectual disability with or without autism. *Journal of Mental Health Research in Intellectual Disabilities, 14*(2), 189–201.

Flower, A., McKenna, J. W., & Haring, C. D. (2017). Behavior and classroom management: Are teacher preparation programs really preparing our teachers? *Preventing School Failure: Alternative Education for Children and Youth, 61*(2), 163–169.

Fong, E. H., Catagnus, R. M., Brodhead, M. T., Quigley, S., & Field, S. (2016). Developing the cultural awareness skills of behavior analysts. *Behavior Analysis in Practice*, 9, 84–94.

Hanley, G. P. (2012). Functional assessment of problem behavior: Dispelling mythos, overcoming implementation obstacles, and developing new lore. *Behavior Analysis in Practice*, 5(1), 54–72.

Harrison, P., Proctor, S., & Thomas, A. (Eds.). (2023). *Best practices in school psychology* (7th ed.). National Association of School Psychologists.

Heidelburg, K., Phelps, C., & Collins, T. A. (2022). Reconceptualizing school safety for Black students. *School Psychology International, 43*(6), 591–612.

Iwata, B. A., & Worsdell, A. S. (2005). Implications of functional analysis methodology for the design of intervention programs. *Exceptionality, 13*(1), 25–34.

Kilgus, S. P., Kazmerski, J. S., Taylor, C. N., & von der Embse, N. P. (2017). Use of direct behavior ratings to collect functional assessment data. *School Psychology Quarterly, 32*(2), 240–253.

Kilgus, S. P., von der Embse, N. P., Eklund, K., Izumi, J., Peet, C., & Meyer, L. (2019). Reliability, validity, and accuracy of the Intervention Selection Profile-Function: A brief functional assessment tool. *School Psychology, 34*(5), 531–540.

King, H. C., Bloomfield, B., Fischer, A. J., Dart, E., & Radley, K. (2021). A comparison of digital observations of students from video cameras and aerial drones. *Journal of Educational and Psychological Consultation, 31*(3), 360–381.

King, H. C., Wu, S., Bloomfield, B. S., Fischer, A. J., & Martone, L. E. (2023). A practical guide on problem-solving teleconsultation in schools. *Journal of Educational and Psychological Consultation, 33*(2), 181–200.

Kunesh, C. E., & Noltemeyer, A. (2019). Understanding disciplinary disproportionality: Stereotypes shape pre-service teachers' beliefs about Black boys' behavior. *Urban Education, 54*(4), 471–498.

Ladson-Billings, G., & Tate IV, W. F. (1995). Toward a Critical Race Theory of education. *Teachers College Record, 97*(1), 47–68.

La Salle, T. P., Wang, C., Wu, C., & Rocha Neves, J. (2019). Racial mismatch among minoritized students and White teachers: Implications and recommendations for moving forward. *Journal of Educational and Psychological Consultation, 30*(3), 314–343.

LaRue, R. H., Lenard, K., Weiss, M. J., Bamond, M., Palmieri, M., & Kelley, M. E. (2010). Comparison of traditional and trial-based methodologies for conducting functional analyses. *Research in Developmental Disabilities, 31*(2), 480–487.

Liang, C. T., Rosati, S. A., Fluharty, M., Gabrilowitz, R., Carter, D., Mui, V., & Freeman, J. (2024). A DisCrit critique of practices for youth with or at risk of emotional and behavioral disorders. *Journal of Emotional and Behavioral Disorders, 32*(1), 36–46.

March, R. E., Horner, R. H., Lewis-Palmer, T., Brown, D., Crone, D. A., Todd, A. W., & Carr, E. G. (2000). *Functional Assessment Checklist for Teachers and Staff (FACTS)*. University of Oregon.

Moll, L., C., Amanti, C., Neff, D., & Gonzalez, N. (1992). Funds of knowledge for teaching: Using a qualitative approach to connect homes and classrooms. *Theory Into Practice, 31*(2), 132–141.

Moreno, G. (2021). Stemming exclusionary school discipline: Implementing culturally attuned positive behavior practices. *Emotional and Behavioural Difficulties, 26*(2), 176–186.

Moreno, G., & Bullock, L. M. (2015). Offering behavioral assistance to Latino students demonstrating challenging behaviors. *The International Journal of Emotional Education, 7*(2), 36–48.

Moreno, G., & Gaytán, F. X. (2013). Reducing subjectivity in special education referrals by educators working with Latino students: Using functional behavioral assessment as a pre-referral practice in student support teams. *Emotional and Behavioural Difficulties, 18*(1), 88–101.

Moreno, G., Wong-Lo, M., & Bullock, L. M. (2017). Investigation of the practice of the functional behavioral assessment: Survey of educators and their experiences in the field. *The International Journal of Emotional Education*, 9(1), 54–70.

Muething, C. S., Call, N. A, Mevers, J. L., Zangrillo, A. N., Clark, S. B., & Reavis, A. R. (2017). Correspondence between the results of functional analyses and brief functional analyses. *Developmental Neurorehabilitation*, *20*(8), 549–559.

Nylen, B., & King, S. (2023). Training practitioners to conduct a functional behavior assessment via telehealth-delivered behavioral skills training: A systematic literature review. *Journal of Behavioral Education*, *33*, 746–768.

Romani, P. W., Young, K., Boorse, A. L., & Carson, B. (2023). Evaluation of a telehealth training program to teach educators to implement behavioral assessment and treatment. *Education and Treatment of Children*, 46, 5–22.

Saini, V., Ubdegrove, K., Biran, S., & Duncan. R. (2019). A preliminary evaluation of interrater reliability and concurrent validity of open-ended indirect assessment. *Behavior Analysis in Practice*, *13*, 114–125.

Steefel, L., Foronda, C., Baptiste, D. L., Reinholdt, M. M., & Ousman, K. (2016). Cultural humility: A concept analysis. *Creative Nursing*, *22*(3), 210–212.

Tereshko, L., Weiss, M. J., Harper, J., & Ross, R. K. (2023). Impact of a training package to improve the effectiveness of descriptive assessment data. *Behavior Analysis in Practice*, *16*, 232–250.

CHAPTER 24

Assessing Mindfulness with Youth

Tyler L. Renshaw, Mei-ki Chan, Mary L. Phan, and Caleb D. Farley

Mindfulness is a contemporary psychological construct that is theorized to play a pivotal role in supporting broad behavioral and mental health across the lifespan (Lee et al., 2021). The last decade has occasioned a surge in mindfulness research and practice with children and adolescents, mostly conducted in educational settings and for prevention-oriented purposes (Roeser et al., 2023). This chapter describes the current context of assessing mindfulness with youth, particularly as it relates to informing service delivery in educational settings. We begin by providing brief background on how mindfulness is defined and used in applied service settings more generally. We then turn to a more thorough description of how mindfulness practices are used as prevention with youth in educational settings, which draws out the importance of assessing mindfulness to inform service delivery. Next, the chapter transitions into a review of mindfulness assessments that are available for youth, followed by a discussion of considerations regarding culturally responsive implementation and interpretation of these assessments. We close by offering recommendations for research that may help advance culturally responsive mindfulness assessment into the future.

DEFINING AND USING MINDFULNESS

Mindfulness is a modern mental health construct that has evolved from ancient roots in Eastern Buddhist philosophy (Baer, 2003). Public interest in mindfulness has become increasingly widespread in contemporary culture due to several influential meditation teachers, including Thich Nhat Hanh and Jon Kabat-Zinn, who have published best-selling books that adapt Eastern approaches to mindfulness for Western audiences (e.g., Hahn, 1999; Kabat-Zinn, 2003). Hanh (1976) has described mindfulness poetically as "the miracle which can call back in a flash our dispersed mind and restore it to wholeness so that we can live each minute of life" (p. 14). Kabat-Zinn (2003) has defined mindfulness in commonsense language as "paying attention in a particular way: on purpose, in the present moment, and nonjudgmentally" (p. 145).

Over the past 50 years, mindfulness has not only become a mainstay in modern society, it has also been increasingly incorporated into clinical and educational service settings as a behavioral and mental health intervention (see Kabat-Zinn, 2003, for a brief history). This transition has motivated clinical scientists and educational researchers to operationalize the construct for the purposes of better studying and understanding it. Baer (2003), for example, has defined mindfulness within clinical psychology as "the nonjudgmental observation of the ongoing stream of internal and external stimuli as they arise" (p. 125). Some researchers have focused more narrowly on the attentional component of mindfulness (e.g., Brown & Ryan, 2003), whereas others have emphasized the self-relational component regarding how one responds to their own internal experiences (e.g., Bishop et al., 2004). As another example, within the field of school psychology, Renshaw (2020) has defined mindfulness as an applied skillset with two core component skills: *present-moment awareness* (i.e., attentional component) and *responding with acceptance* (i.e., self-relational component). We adopt this skills-based conceptualization of mindfulness throughout the remainder of this chapter.

Although mindfulness has been used in health care settings with adults for over 50 years (Kabat-Zinn, 2003), it has been used in applied service settings with youth only for about half that time (Roeser et al., 2023). Over the past two and half decades, mindfulness-based interventions (MBIs) have emerged as an evidence-based approach for supporting youths' behavioral and mental health in both clinical and educational service settings (Renshaw et al., 2022; Renshaw & Cook, 2017). MBIs include a variety of treatment packages, manuals and curricula, and other flexible intervention procedures that aim to train youth in mindfulness skills and then support them in using these skills for the purposes of improving valued outcomes (Renshaw, 2020). MBIs are designed to be thoroughly secular in nature, grounded in the assumption that mindfulness "can be learned or practiced . . . without appealing to [Eastern] culture or Buddhist authority to enrich or authenticate it" (Kabat-Zinn, 1994, p. 12). There are two big ideas driving the use of MBIs with youth in applied settings: (1) mindfulness skills can be learned like any other skills—through effective training within supportive environments—and (2) mindfulness skills can play a pivotal role in positively affecting multiple valued outcomes across the lifespan, similar to other pivotal competencies like social and academic skills (Renshaw et al., 2022).

The benefits of using MBIs with youth have now been demonstrated through systematic reviews and meta-analyses reporting on dozens of studies conducted in clinical and educational settings, with most of these studies being carried out in schools for prevention-oriented purposes (Roeser et al., 2023). MBIs have been shown to have desirable effects on a variety of valued youth outcomes, including (but not limited to) resilience to stress, executive functioning, internalizing problems, externalizing problems, prosocial skills, physical health, subjective well-being, coping ability, quality of peer relationships, mood, academic achievement, and academic behaviors (e.g., Black, 2015; Carsley et al., 2018; Dunning et al., 2019; Felver et al., 2016; Kallapiran et al., 2015; Klingbeil, Fischer, et al., 2017; Klingbeil, Renshaw, et al., 2017; Maynard et al., 2017; Semple et al., 2017; Zenner et al., 2014; Zoogman et al., 2015). The upshot of the research base, to date, seems to be that using MBIs as prevention may offer youth a range of social, emotional, behavioral, and academic benefits that are wider in scope than other common prevention approaches used in schools (Klingbeil, Renshaw, et al., 2017; Phan et al., 2022).

MINDFULNESS FOR PREVENTION IN SCHOOLS

Within schools, the multi-tiered system of support (MTSS) framework is typically used to structure efficient and effective prevention because it integrates a continuum of system-wide resources, strategies, structures, and practices that address barriers to student learning (Merrell et al., 2022). Traditional MTSS models use a three-tiered service delivery system addressing different levels of prevention: the *universal level* (Tier 1) is characterized by low-intensity supports provided to all students to buffer the onset and exacerbation of risk, as well as to promote well-being; the *targeted level* (Tier 2) is differentiated by moderate-intensity supports delivered to some students who show elevated levels of risk; and the *intensive level* (Tier 3) is indicated by high-intensity supports for a few students who are demonstrating the most severe and chronic risk (Merrell et al., 2022). MBIs are currently used with youth in schools at each of these three levels of prevention (Felver et al., 2013).

The application of MBIs at Tier 1 for universal prevention usually relies on treatment packages and curricula that support the implementation of mindfulness skills training at the classwide or schoolwide level. Mindfulness may also be incorporated into new or updated social–emotional learning (SEL) programming that targets skills related to self-awareness, self-management, social awareness, relationship skills, and responsible decision making (see the CASEL Program Guide for an overview of available SEL curricula: *https://pg.casel.org*). Given the bulk of research on MBIs with youth has been conducted within schools at the classroom level, MBIs are most likely to be effective with youth when used for prevention-oriented purposes at the universal level of service delivery (Klingbeil, Renshaw, et al., 2017; Roeser et al., 2023). Examples of empirically supported mindfulness curricula at Tier 1 include (but are not limited to) *MindUP* (The Hawn Foundation, 2011), *A Still Quiet Place* (Saltzman, 2014), *Mindful Schools* (Brensilver et al., 2020), and *Learning to Breathe* (Broderick, 2021). The *Strong Kids* curricula are examples of long-standing evidence-based SEL programs that have been updated to infuse mindfulness skills in the service of supporting other SEL skills (see *https://strongkidsresources.com*). A descriptive review of several mindfulness curricula available for use at the universal level can be found in Semple et al.'s (2017) article on the topic.

At Tier 2, training in mindfulness skills is often incorporated into small-group interventions provided outside of the classroom, but it may also be built into brief but targeted supports provided to individual students within the classroom. Less research has been conducted to support the use of MBIs with youth for targeted prevention compared with universal prevention. Yet the research base at this level is promising and growing. A few studies have found that small-group MBIs have positive effects on youths' emotional outcomes (Cotton et al., 2016; Esmaeilian et al., 2018; Semple et al., 2010; Syeda & Andrews, 2021). Moreover, a couple of studies have found that MBIs integrated into brief but targeted supports for individual students in classrooms have yielded some modest academic and behavioral benefits (Axelrod & Santagata, 2022; Franzmann et al., 2025). An example of the former approach is using a mindfulness-based cognitive therapy (MBCT) manual to support a small group of students presenting with anxiety risk (Syeda & Andrews, 2021), whereas an example of the latter approach is integrating mindful breathing exercises into the Check-In/Check-Out procedure to support students with classroom behavior problems (Franzmann et al., 2025). Given the more limited research with targeted interventions, it is recommended that MBIs at Tier 2 be used mostly as an adjunct or complement to other evidence-based interventions for targeted problems (Renshaw et al., 2017).

Using MBIs at Tier 3 for intensive prevention typically takes the form of school-based psychotherapy provided outside of the classroom but during the school day, wherein the therapeutic approach used by the clinician relies—primarily or supplementally—on training mindfulness skills. Although there is not nearly as much evidence to support using MBIs at this level when compared with the universal level, there is substantially more evidence to support Tier 3 MBIs compared with Tier 2 MBIs. For example, a meta-analysis of single-case design studies demonstrated that individualized MBIs were effective for reducing disruptive behavior among youth with developmental disabilities and psychiatric diagnoses in both school and home settings (Klingbeil, Fischer, et al., 2017). Furthermore, systematic reviews of research conducted on evidence-based mindfulness-infused psychotherapies with youth—including dialectical behavior therapy (DBT; Day et al., 2022) and acceptance and commitment therapy (ACT; Fang & Ding, 2020)—suggest these MBIs can be used successfully in clinical and educational service settings to improve both psychosocial and academic outcomes. Considering the more limited evidence available at Tier 3, MBIs used for intensive prevention in schools typically draw heavily from evidence-based interventions originally designed and validated in outpatient treatment settings (Renshaw et al., 2023).

Although the evidence base for using MBIs for prevention-oriented purposes in schools has grown substantially over the past decade (Roeser et al., 2023), the use of *mindfulness assessments* for informing MBIs with youth has received far less attention during this same period (Renshaw et al., 2022). This discrepancy in research and practice is concerning, given that selecting, using, and interpreting results from evidence-based assessments is critical for guiding all evidence-based interventions with youth, including MBIs. Yet it is also not surprising, given that evidence-based assessment has historically been overlooked and undervalued within the evidence-based practice movement for supporting youths' behavioral and mental health (Mash & Hunsley, 2005). We propose that mindfulness assessments should serve at least two important functions toward informing the use of MBIs for prevention in schools:

1. Identifying youth who could benefit from MBIs: differentiating those with higher and lower levels of baseline mindfulness skills.
2. Evaluating youths' responsiveness to MBIs: monitoring changes (or the lack thereof) in mindfulness skills as a function of intervention.

We believe using mindfulness assessments for these purposes may help educators and mental health professionals to make better data-based decisions regarding the appropriateness and effectiveness of using MBIs with youth at universal, targeted, and intensive levels of prevention.

MINDFULNESS ASSESSMENTS FOR YOUTH

While mindfulness assessments have been well-validated for adults, far less validation work has been done on mindfulness assessments for youth, and especially with youth who are culturally diverse (Bender et al., 2023; Eklund et al., 2017; Goodman et al., 2017; Guerra et al., 2019; McKeering & Hwang, 2019; Schutt & Felver, 2020). That said, the number and quality of available mindfulness assessments for youth have grown steadily over the past half-decade. For example, in the first review on this topic conducted by Eklund et al. (2017), only a few self-report mindfulness assessments for youth were identified as having validation evidence: the Child and Adolescent Mindfulness Measure (CAMM; Greco et al., 2011), the Mindful Attention Awareness Scale for Adolescents (MAAS-A; Brown et al., 2011), and the Mindful Thinking and Action Scale for Adolescents (MTASA; West et al., 2007). Yet in a recent systematic review, Bender et al. (2023) identified 11 mindfulness assessments for youth that each had at least some supporting validity evidence: (1) the CAMM; (2) a revised CAMM for children (CAMM-R; Mezo et al., 2020); (3) the MAAS-A; (4) a revised MAAS-A for children (MAAS-C; Lawlor et al., 2014); (5) the MTASA; (6) the Comprehensive Inventory of Mindfulness Experiences for Adolescents (CHIME-A; Johnson et al., 2017); (7) the Five Facet Mindfulness Questionnaire, Adolescent Short Form (FFMQ-A-SF; Cortazar et al., 2020); (8) the Mindful Student Questionnaire (MSQ; Renshaw, 2017); (9) the Mindfulness Inventory for Children and Adolescents (MICA; Briere, 2011); (10) the Mindfulness Scale for Pre-Teens, Teens, and Adults (MSPTA; Droutman, 2015); and (11) the Self-Compassion Scale for Youth (SCS-Y; Neff et al., 2021).

Our review of mindfulness assessments in this section draws from Bender et al.'s (2023) systematic review on the topic because we believe that it is the most comprehensive synthesis available to date. Instead of focusing on all 11 mindfulness assessments reported in their review, we narrow in on a selection of five assessments that are representative of the larger group: the CAMM, the MAAS-A, the FFMQ-A-SF, the MSQ, and the SCSF-Y. We intentionally selected this handful of mindfulness assessments for inclusion in this chapter based on two key criteria: uniqueness (i.e., how they differentiated in structure and content from other assessments) and accessibility (i.e., if they were freely available in the public domain for use in research and practice). Readers interested in learning more about the other six mindfulness assessments that are not covered in this chapter (i.e., the CAMM-R, the MAAS-C, the MTASA, the CHIME-A, the MICA, and the MSPTA) are encouraged to read the excellent coverage provided in Bender et al. (2023).

Much of the review of the five selected mindfulness assessments that follows is similar to content presented in Bender and colleagues (2023). However, our review of each assessment adds two additional aspects to their analysis. First, we evaluate and report on the valence for each of the scale scores derived from these assessments. Positive valence (+) indicates that the scale score is derived from items (considering phrasing and scoring) that directly represent the presence of mindfulness. Negative valence (–), on the other hand, indicates that the scale score is derived from items that indirectly represent mindfulness by operationalizing its opposite or incompatible experiences—what we refer to as *mindlessness*. Finally, ambiguous valence (/) indicates the scale score is derived from items with a mix of both positive and negative valences, typically by using reverse scoring for some (but not all) items within the scale.

Second, we build on Bender et al.'s (2023) analysis by adding information regarding the constructs that are measured by each scale score for each assessment by evaluating and reporting on the mindfulness skills that are tapped by these scale scores. This evaluation is guided by the skills-based conceptualization of mindfulness discussed earlier in this chapter and is based on our perceptions of the face validity of scales' item content in representing the two core mindfulness skills: present-moment awareness and responding with acceptance. We also evaluate and report on the valence of the identified mindfulness skills for each assessment, using the same coding system previously described (i.e., + or – or /). A narrative review of each of the five selected mindfulness assessments is provided next, followed by a discussion of considerations related to using and interpreting these measures to inform service delivery with youth in applied settings. A summary of the key characteristics of the five selected mindfulness assessments reviewed in the following is provided in Table 24.1.

Review of Five Representative Mindfulness Assessments

Child and Adolescent Mindfulness Measure

The CAMM (Greco et al., 2011) is a self-report rating scale that has been validated for assessing mindfulness with youth ages 10–17. This assessment is composed of 10 Likert-type items measuring one overarching mindfulness construct that is purported to tap into core mindfulness processes: acting with awareness (e.g., "It's hard for me to pay attention to only one thing at a time") and accepting without judgment (e.g., "I get upset with myself for having feelings that don't make sense"). Youth respond to items using 5-point scaling options that ask them to rate their level of agreement with each statement: 0 = never true, 1 = rarely true, 2 = sometimes true, 3 = often true, and 4 = always true.

The CAMM is scored by summing all item scores to create a composite score. No reverse scoring is necessary. Lower scores are interpreted as representing higher levels of mindfulness, and vice versa. Our evaluation of CAMM items indicated that the overall composite scale was characterized by a negative score valence, and that this overall scale represents both present-moment awareness and responding with acceptance skills. Thus, both mindfulness skills indicated by the measure are characterized by negative valences.

TABLE 24.1. Key Characteristics of the Five Selected Mindfulness Assessments

	Assessment characteristic				
Mindfulness assessment	Age	Scales [# items] (valence)	Response scaling	M. Skills (valence)	Language versions
CAMM	10–17 years	Mindfulness [10] (–)	5-point agreement: 0 = never true 4 = always true	PMA (–) RWA (–)	English, Spanish, Chinese, Greek, French, Turkish, Dutch
MAAS-A	14–18 years	Mindfulness [14] (–)	6-point frequency: 1 = almost always 6 = almost never	PMA (–)	English, Spanish, Chinese, French, Turkish, Dutch
FFMQ-A-SF	14–18 years	Observing [5] (+) Describing [5] (/) Acting with Awareness [5] (–) Nonjudging [5] (–) Nonreactivity [5] (+) *Mindfulness [25] (/)	5-point agreement: 1 = never or very rarely true 5 = very often or always true	PMA (/) RWA (/)	English, Spanish
MSQ	10–14 years	Mindful Attention [5] (+) Mindful Acceptance [5] (+) Approach & Persistence [5] (n/a) *Mindfulness [10] (+)	4-point frequency: 1 = almost never 4 = almost always	PMA (+) RWA (+)	English, Chinese
SCS-Y	11–15 years	Self-Kindness [3] (+) Self-Judgment [3] (–) Common Humanity [3] (n/a) Isolation [3] (n/a) Mindfulness [3] (+) *Self-Compassion [17] (n/a)	5-point frequency: 1 = almost always 5 = almost never	RWA (/)	English, Spanish, Chinese, Greek, Persian, Turkish, Swedish

Note. CAMM = Child and Adolescent Mindfulness Measure; MAAS-A = Mindful Attention Awareness Scale–Adolescents; FFMQ-A-SF = Five Facet Mindfulness Questionnaire, Adolescent Short Form; MSQ = Mindful Student Questionnaire, SCS-Y = Self-Compassion Scale for Youth. + = positive valence; – = negative valence; / = mixed valence; n/a = valence not applicable because scale is not tapping a mindfulness construct/skill. * = composite scale comprised of two or more subscales. M. Skills = mindfulness skills; PMA = present-moment awareness; RWA = responding with acceptance.

Mindful Attention Awareness Scale for Adolescents

The MAAS-A (Brown et al., 2011) is a self-report rating scale that has been validated for assessing mindfulness with youth ages 14–18. This assessment is composed of 14 Likert-type items measuring one overarching mindfulness construct that focuses narrowly on mindful attention (e.g., "It seems I am 'running on automatic,' without much awareness of what I'm doing" and "I find myself doing things without paying attention"). Youth respond to items using 6-point scaling options that ask them to rate how frequently they experience each statement: 1 = almost always, 2 = very frequently, 3 = somewhat frequently, 4 = somewhat infrequently, 5 = very infrequently, and 6 = almost never.

The MAAS-A is scored by summing all item scores to create a total score and then dividing this total score by the number of items (14) to create a mean scale score. No reverse scoring is necessary. Lower mean scores are interpreted as greater levels of mindfulness, and vice versa. Our evaluation of MAAS-A items indicated that the overall composite scale score had a negative valence and that this overall scale represents only the present-moment awareness skill, which, therefore, also presented a negative valence.

Five Facet Mindfulness Questionnaire, Adolescent Short Form

The FFMQ-A-SF (Cortazar et al., 2020) is a self-report rating scale that has been validated for assessing mindfulness with youth ages 14–18. This assessment is composed of 25 Likert-type items that are allocated to five different subscales: Observing (5 items; e.g., "I pay attention to sensations, such as the wind in my hair or sun on my face"); Describing (5 items; e.g., "I'm good at finding words to describe my feelings"); Acting with Awareness (5 items; e.g., "When I do things, my mind wanders off and I'm easily distracted"); Nonjudging (5 items; e.g., "I disapprove of myself when I have irrational ideas"); and Nonreactivity (5 items; e.g., "I perceive my feelings and emotions without having to react to them"). These items and scales are adapted from the full version of the FFMQ, originally designed for use with adults, which includes 39 items representing the same five subscales (Baer et al., 2006). Youth respond to items using 5-point scaling options that ask them to rate their agreement with each statement: 1 = never or very rarely true, 2 = rarely true, 3 = sometimes true, 4 = often true, and 5 = very often or always true.

The FFMQ-A-SF is scored by summing items to produce subscales scores and then summing subscale scores to create a total Mindfulness scale score. Reverse scoring is required for all items in the Acting with Awareness and Nonjudging subscales and some items in the Describing subscale. Higher scores at both the subscale and total scale levels are interpreted as greater levels of mindfulness, and vice versa. Our evaluation of FFMQ-A-SF items indicated mixed levels of score valence across subscales: The Observing and Nonreactivity subscales showed positive valence, whereas the Acting with Awareness and Nonjudging subscales had negative valence, and the Describing subscale presented ambiguous valence. As a result of mixed valence across the subscales, the total Mindfulness scale presented ambiguous valence. Moreover, we concluded that, taken together, items from the Observing, Describing, and Acting with Awareness subscales indicated the present-moment awareness skill with ambiguous valence, and that items from the Nonjudging and Nonreactivity subscales also indicated the responding with acceptance skill with ambiguous valence.

Mindful Student Questionnaire

The MSQ (Renshaw, 2017) is a self-report rating scale that has been validated for assessing mindfulness with youth ages 10–14. This assessment is composed of 15 Likert-type items that are allocated to three subscales: Mindful Attention (5 items; e.g., "When I am at school, I notice when my feelings change from good to bad"), Mindful Acceptance (5 items; e.g., "When I am feeling bad at school, I still am kind to myself"), and Approach and Persistence (5 items; e.g., "When I am doing something hard at school, I try to keep going until I finish"). Notably, the Approach and Persistence subscale is not conceptualized as a measure of mindfulness but rather as a school-based behavioral outcome that mindfulness should, in theory, facilitate (i.e., greater levels of student mindfulness should yield greater levels of approach and persistence behavior with difficult situations at school). Youth respond to items using 4-point scaling options that ask them to rate their relative frequency of experience with each statement: 1 = almost never, 2 = sometimes, 3 = often, and 4 = almost always.

The MSQ is scored by summing items to produce subscale scores and then summing subscale scores to create a total Mindful Student scale score. No reverse scoring of items is required, and the Approach and Persistence subscale score is excluded from the overall mindfulness score. Higher scores at both the subscale and total scale levels are interpreted as greater levels of mindfulness, and vice versa. Our evaluation of MSQ items for the purposes of this chapter indicated positive score valence at the subscale level and, thus, at the total scale level. Furthermore, we concluded that items from the Mindful Attention subscale indicated the present-moment awareness skill with positive valence, and that items from the Mindful Acceptance subscale indicated the responding with acceptance skill with positive valence.

Self-Compassion Scale for Youth

The SCS-Y (Neff et al., 2021) is a self-report rating scale that has been validated for assessing mindfulness with youth ages 11–15. This assessment is composed of 17 Likert-type items that are allocated to five subscales: Self-Kindness (3 items; e.g., "I'm kind to myself when things go wrong and I'm feeling bad"); Self-Judgment (3 items; e.g., "I'm really hard on myself when I do something wrong"); Common Humanity (3 items; e.g., "When I'm sad or unhappy, I remember that other people also feel this way at times"); Isolation (3 items; e.g., "When I'm sad or down, it seems like I'm the only one who feels this way"); and Mindfulness (3 items; e.g., "When something upsets me, I try to notice my feelings and not get carried away by them"). Notably, the Common Humanity and Isolation items measure constructs that are outside of mindfulness skills; however, the Self-Kindness and Self-Judgment subscales tap constructs that could also be considered mindfulness skills. Youth respond to items using 5-point scaling options that ask them to rate their relative frequency of experience with each statement: 1 = almost never, 2 = not very often, 3 = sometimes, 4 = very often, and 5 = almost always.

The SCS-Y is scored by summing items to produce subscales scores and then summing subscale scores plus scores from two additional items (i.e., "When I feel frustrated or disappointed, I think about it over and over again" and "When I'm feeling bad or upset, I can't think of anything else at the time") to create a total Self-Compassion scale score. Reverse scoring is required for all items in the Self-Judgment and Isolation subscales, as well as for the two additional items included in the total scale. For the total scale, a grand mean is calculated by dividing the total score by the number of items (17). Higher scores at both the subscale and total scale levels are interpreted as greater levels of dispositions contributing to self-compassion, and vice versa. Our evaluation of the SCS-Y items indicated mixed levels of score valence across subscales: the Self-Kindness and Mindfulness subscales showed positive valence, whereas the Self-Judgment subscales had negative valence. The valence of the other two subscales and the total scale were not evaluated because they did not tap constructs that represented mindfulness per se. Moreover, we concluded that, taken together, items from the Self-Kindness, Self-Judgment, and Mindfulness subscales indicated the present-moment awareness skill with ambiguous valence.

Considerations for Use and Interpretation

Earlier in this chapter, we proposed that mindfulness assessments should serve at least two important functions toward informing the use of MBIs for prevention in schools. First, mindfulness assessments should help identify youth who could benefit from MBIs by providing data that could be used to differentiate youth with higher and lower levels of baseline mindfulness skills. Second, mindfulness assessments should be used to evaluate youths' responsiveness to MBIs by generating data that could be used to monitor changes (or lack thereof) in mindfulness skills as a function of intervention. In this subsection, we consider how the shared and variable characteristics of the five representative mindfulness assessments we have reviewed inform considerations regarding use and interpretation of scores for these two important functions. A summary of these considerations is provided in Table 24.2. Broader consideration of use and interpretation of mindfulness assessments in the context of culturally responsive practice with youth in schools follows in the next section.

Shared Characteristics

The representative set of mindfulness assessments we reviewed share a few basic characteristics in common. To begin with, they all rely on the same assessment method (i.e., rating scale) and informant (i.e., self-report). They are also all relatively brief (i.e., ranging from 10–25 items) and each makes use of Likert-type response options (i.e., ranging from 4-point to 6-point scales). Whether

TABLE 24.2. Considerations for Use and Interpretation Based on the Shared and Variable Characteristics of Mindfulness Assessments

Shared Characteristics

1. Nature of data derived from mindfulness assessments is limited and highly similar: brief, narrowband, self-report rating scales.
2. Mindfulness assessments are only available and accessible for older children and adolescents who have the requisite reading ability and self-awareness.
3. Scores from mindfulness assessments are interpreted based on internally referenced logic: higher scores indicate great levels of mindfulness, and vice versa.
4. Data from mindfulness assessments are best used for idiographic or intra-individual evaluation, unless local norms or criterions are established at the schoolwide level.

Variable Characteristics

1. Some mindfulness assessments are only validated with adolescents, whereas others are also validated with older children.
2. Some mindfulness assessments are only available in English and one other language, whereas others are available in several languages.
3. The number and nature of scales varies across mindfulness assessments, suggesting some assessments provide more information than others.
4. Representation of core mindfulness skills—present-moment awareness and responding with acceptance—varies across assessments.
5. Most mindfulness assessments tap skills across life domains, but at least one assessment specifically focuses on youths' mindfulness skills at school.
6. Some mindfulness assessments employ frequency-based response scaling, whereas others employ agreement-based response scaling.
7. Score valences differ substantially across mindfulness assessments, presenting with a range of positive, negative, and ambiguous valences.

mindfulness assessments are used for the first (i.e., identification) or second (i.e., outcome monitoring) functions related to informing MBIs, the implication for users is that the nature of data derived across these assessments will be limited and highly similar: narrowband self-report ratings. Mindfulness assessments are therefore not available for youth who do not have the requisite reading ability or the self-awareness necessary to complete self-report rating scales. Other assessment methods beyond rating scales (e.g., direct observation and interview) have yet to be validated for gauging mindfulness with youth; multi-informant rating scale systems (e.g., teacher and parent report forms) have also not been validated for assessing mindfulness. Unfortunately, this means mindfulness assessments are not yet possible with very young children, and that they are unlikely to be accessible for many youth living with significant intellectual and developmental disabilities.

Another shared characteristic of these mindfulness measures is that the scores derived from each are interpreted similarly, based on internally referenced logic, wherein scores are considered to indicate relatively higher or lower levels of mindfulness. It is noteworthy that none of these mindfulness assessments have evidence for norm-referenced interpretation of scores, meaning that scores cannot be used to make normative inferences regarding how one youth's level of mindfulness relates to their peers' levels of mindfulness (e.g., average, below average, above average). Similarly, none of these assessments have evidence for criterion-based interpretation of scores, indicating that scores cannot be used to estimate the probability with which one youth's level of mindfulness may predict responsiveness to MBIs or other valued outcomes (e.g., development of psychosocial risk or academic attainment). The major implication for users is that scores from mindfulness assessments do not provide compelling information about youth's need for or potential benefit from MBIs at any level of school-based prevention. We therefore recommend users consider complementary assessment data from norm-referenced or criterion-based measures of psychosocial or academic risk to adequately justify decisions regarding identifying youth for MBIs, especially at the targeted and intensive levels of service delivery.

Regarding the second function (i.e., outcome monitoring of MBIs), the implication for users is that mindfulness assessments only offer data that could be used for idiographic or intra-individual evaluation of responsiveness to intervention, at least at the intensive (Tier 3) and targeted (Tier 2) levels of service delivery. We therefore recommend again that users should consider complementary monitoring data from norm-referenced or criterion-based measures of whatever valued outcomes are germane to the youth (e.g., internalizing symptoms, coping ability, academic behaviors) to adequately justify decisions regarding determining youths' responsiveness to MBIs. That said, if a mindfulness assessment were used at the universal level (Tier 1), then users could establish local norm-referenced or criterion-based scoring and interpretation procedures at the schoolwide level. These local scoring procedures could then be used to inform evaluations of youths' responsiveness to MBIs across any tier of prevention—universal, targeted, or intensive—within the local school context. If users are interested in establishing local norms or criteria, we further recommend updating these data and accompanying decision rules on a regular basis (e.g., every 3–5 years).

Variable Characteristics

The representative set of mindfulness assessments we reviewed also have variable characteristics, which suggest differentiated considerations for use and interpretation. One key characteristic that varies across assessments is the age range of youth for which the scores have been validated (see Table 24.1). Both the MAAS-A and the FFMQ-A-SF have been validated only with older adolescents (14 to 18 years old), whereas the CAMM, MSQ, and SCS-Y have been validated with adolescents and older children (lower bound of 10 to 11 years old). So, users may have more or fewer options for which mindfulness assessment to use to inform MBIs, depending on the age range of youth they are serving. The available language versions also differ across assessments. Each assessment is available in English, and most are also available in Spanish and Chinese; however, only three of the five reviewed assessments have several language versions available (see Table 24.1). Users who are serving youth who speak native languages other than English, Spanish, and Chinese are therefore likely to have more limited options among these assessments, if they have an option at all.

Another key characteristic that varies across mindfulness assessments is the number and nature of scales for each measure. Both the CAMM and the MAAS-A produce a single-scale score representing mindfulness. The MSQ has two subscales that contribute to a total mindfulness scale, whereas the FFMQ-A-SF has five subscales that contribute to a total mindfulness scale. The SCS-Y has three subscales that tap aspects of mindfulness, yet these subscales contribute to a self-compassion total score, not a mindfulness total score. Given these differences, we recommend that users select assessments with scales that best match the level and scope of their intended service delivery. For example, mindfulness assessments with single-scale scores might be better suited for informing universal MBIs because the data will be simpler for users to collect and analyze at the level of an entire school population. In contrast, assessments with multiple scale scores may be more useful for informing intensive MBIs because subscale scores may provide users with insight into idiographic differences in mindfulness skills that could guide identification of intervention targets or clarify how an intervention affects different aspects of mindfulness over time.

Users should be aware that the number of scales alone does not provide information about how well the assessment indicates the two core mindfulness skills of present-moment awareness and responding with acceptance (see Table 24.1). The CAMM and MAAS-A both have only one scale that purports to measure mindfulness, yet our evaluation of item content indicated that the CAMM represents both skills, whereas the MAAS-A only taps present-moment awareness. As another example, both the FFMQ-A-SF and SCS-F are composed of five subscales, with the items of the former representing both mindfulness skills and the items of the latter indicating only responding with acceptance. The MSQ, on the other hand, has two subscales with items that represent both mindfulness skills. But unlike all the other assessments, which phrase items in a general way that solicits responding across life domains, the MSQ items are contextualized specifically within youths' experiences at school. Thus, when selecting appropriate mindfulness assessments to inform MBIs in schools, we recommend that users consider which mindfulness skills (i.e., one or the other, or both) and which context of skill application (i.e., school only, or all life contexts) best match the inferences they would like to make about the data obtained from the assessment. For instance, MBIs at the targeted level that are focused on improving students' social behavior at school may be better informed by data from the MSQ, whereas MBIs at the intensive level that are supporting students at risk for clinical-level mood disorders may be better served by data from the FFMQ-A-SF.

The five mindfulness assessments we reviewed also differed across two additional characteristics: the nature of response scaling for scores and the valence of scores (+ or – or /). Regarding response scaling, the MAAS-A, MSQ, and SCS-Y employ frequency-based response options, whereas the CAMM and FFMQ-A-SF rely on agreement-based responding (see Table 24.1). Although such scaling is unlikely to influence users' selection of mindfulness assessments for informing MBIs for prevention-oriented purposes in schools, it should influence how users interpret the scores obtained from these mindfulness assessments. Interpretation of scores is especially important when evaluating youths' responsiveness (or lack thereof) to MBIs. For example, an increased level of agreement with an experience stated in an item (e.g., "I push away thoughts that I don't like") may or may not be correlated with an increased level of frequency with which youth report experiencing that item, and vice versa. Users may therefore observe different baseline levels and treatment trends in data, depending on how response scaling differs across selected measures. To control for this potential bias in scale construction, users monitoring outcomes in response to intensive MBIs may wish to use multiple measures of mindfulness with different response scaling (e.g., the CAMM and the MAAS-A). But implementing multiple mindfulness measures to inform universal and targeted MBIs may be impractical or unwise because it complicates data analysis and interpretation at these levels.

Similarly, we suggest that understanding differences in score valences across mindfulness assessments should have implications for how users interpret scores related to youths' responsiveness to MBIs. Our evaluation of item content indicated that the CAMM and MAAS-A have negative score valences, that the FFMQ-A-SF and SCS-Y have ambiguous (mixed) score valences, and that the MSQ has positive score valences (see Table 24.1). Interpretation of positive valence scores is relatively straightforward: users can infer changes in self-reported mindfulness. Yet interpretation of negative valence scores is more complicated: users must infer changes in mindfulness from self-reported changes in mindlessness (i.e., experiences that are opposite or incompatible with mindfulness). Interpretation of ambiguous valence scores is likewise nuanced: users infer an increase in mindfulness that is based on a mixture of self-reported changes in both mindfulness and mindlessness. Given that it is possible for youth to report changes in mindlessness without necessarily experiencing changes in mindfulness, users should be aware that they are required to make higher-level inferences when using mindfulness assessments that have negative or ambiguous score valences.

CULTURALLY RESPONSIVE CONSIDERATIONS

When incorporating mindfulness assessments to inform MBIs in educational settings, it is critical to consider more than just the shared and variable characteristics among the measures themselves. It is also imperative to consider the features of the local community and other cultural aspects related to using mindfulness assessments to ensure both the well-being of youth who are served and the effectiveness of the services being provided in schools. Recent guidelines have been published regarding how researchers, educators, and mental health professionals can work toward designing and implementing culturally responsive MBIs in schools (Phan & Renshaw, 2023, 2024; Phan et al., 2025; Renshaw & Phan, 2023). But similar guidelines have yet to be published regarding how to use and interpret mindfulness assessments in culturally responsive ways for the purpose of informing MBIs in schools. What follows in this section is an initial effort to provide guidelines toward this end. We begin with general considerations regarding culturally sensitive practices related to mindfulness assessment and then transition to more specific considerations related to using mindfulness assessments in culturally responsive ways at the schoolwide, classroom, and individual student levels.

General Cultural Sensitivity Considerations

Related to cultural sensitivity, the foremost consideration for users is to be aware that different cultures may have diverse perspectives on mindfulness more generally, and that these perspectives may influence their valuing of mindfulness assessments more specifically. The primary variable at play here is likely to be spiritual and religious beliefs or worldviews. Although MBIs are currently understood and implemented as secular practices in schools, they have evolved and been adapted from ancient Eastern philosophy and associated religious traditions, as discussed earlier in this chapter (see Kabat-Zinn, 2003). Information about the origins of mindfulness is widely available in modern society via the internet and books on this topic. Yet the history regarding how mindfulness has been translated from Eastern to Western audiences—and from a seemingly religious practice into an evidence-based clinical and educational intervention—is more nuanced and not as widely available online or in print, especially for lay audiences. It is therefore understandable that MBIs and, by extension, mindfulness assessments may be misunderstood by consumers as being religious practices or something "other" that does not align with their spiritual or religious worldview.

We therefore recommend that educators and mental health professionals explicitly consider the beliefs and values of local community members—including educators, parents, and students themselves—who will be participating in MBIs and mindfulness assessments. To address any misconceptions or concerns that may arise within the community, it may be necessary to offer educational resources to help caregivers and students understand the secular purpose and benefits of MBIs so that there is shared understanding of why mindfulness assessments are being used. Furthermore, we suggest presenting mindfulness assessment in a way that is inclusive and sensitive to various secular and spiritual perspectives by emphasizing the common ground that mindfulness skills share with the values of the local community, including the school, the family, and other levels of community. For example, when working within a school community that values SEL, mindfulness skills can be framed as sub-skills that contribute to the development of core social–emotional competencies, such as self-awareness and self-management (Lawlor, 2016). As another example, when serving students within communities of families that adhere to Judeo-Christian values, mindfulness skills can be framed as supporting the family's desires for their children to develop into benevolent and compassionate adults (see Monteiro et al., 2017, for an exploration of other examples on this topic).

Schoolwide Considerations

Prior to implementing a schoolwide mindfulness assessment, the school team should first assess the culture within the school context in order to develop a mindfulness assessment protocol that responds to the social, political, cultural, and educational needs of students and other community members. We recommend users consider and adapt the guidance provided by other scholars regarding conducting culturally responsive mental health screening and programming in schools (Khalifa et al., 2016; Kiperman et al., 2024; Moore et al., 2023; Nastasi et al., 2004; Romer et al., 2020). In addition to accounting for cultural variables (e.g., race/ethnicity, socioeconomic status, religious identities) related to the student population the school serves and acknowledging cultural differences among students, educators and mental health professionals should also consider involving students, caregivers, and school staff in the development process, data collection, interpretation, and use of results of mindfulness assessments following the Participatory Culture-Specific Intervention Modeling approach (see Kiperman et al., 2024, for detailed guidance on applying this model). As part of this process, users of mindfulness assessments can gather information from the school community regarding their attitudes and perspectives about the following topics:

1. Goals of implementing mindfulness assessment at the schoolwide level
2. Understandings of mindfulness and how it relates to the contents of assessments
3. Prior experiences with mindfulness and similar universal assessment procedures (e.g., social–emotional or mental health screenings)
4. Potential barriers to participation in mindfulness assessments
5. Preferred ways to share and use results from assessments with the school community
6. Other cultural values that should be considered throughout the process

Soliciting such information prior to implementing mindfulness assessments will help facilitate the school community's engagement with the assessment procedure and provide users of the assessment an opportunity to proactively address any identified barriers prior to implementation of the universal protocol (Bakhuys Roozeboom et al., 2020; Romer et al., 2020).

After gauging the local school culture, we recommend that implementers collaborate with community members to develop the school's cultural-specific model for mindfulness assessment. This entails embedding community members' values, suggestions, and perceived challenges to guide the implementation of mindfulness assessments at the schoolwide level. Depending on the school's ecological needs (e.g., languages preferred for assessment and age ranges of youth participating in assessment) and other logistical considerations (e.g., available resources and time), the school might identify two to three potentially viable mindfulness measures based on evidenced reliability and validity and the cultural context in the school community. These potential measures could then be shared with the broader community for the purposes of soliciting feedback that contributes to selecting a final or preferred mindfulness assessment. Ideally, the final selected mindfulness measure should match the users' goals related to identification or outcome monitoring (as discussed in the previous section) as well as be acceptable to consumers.

Given mindfulness assessment is still a nascent field of research and practice, few assessment tools have been validated across cultural groups (Bender et al., 2023). Depending on the goals of the MBI at the universal level, users should also consider selecting complementary outcome assessments to administer alongside the mindfulness assessment, such as measures of emotion regulation, mental health symptoms, subjective well-being, or behavior problems (see other chapters in this book for discussion of considerations related to using and interpreting such assessments). Regardless of the mindfulness assessment that is ultimately selected, we recommend that the school pilot the assessment protocol with students, educators, and caregivers to solicit their feedback regarding potential modifications prior to full-scale implementation, such as revising item wording or removing culturally inappropriate items (Dowdy et al., 2014). Relatedly, if a school already has other Tier 1 self-report assessment protocols in place, such as universal mental health screeners, we suggest incorporating the mindfulness assessment into the existing universal assessment system for piloting and feedback prior to implementation.

Once the mindfulness assessment protocol has been selected and appropriately adapted, we recommend that implementers take care to ensure the administration allows for students and families to have equal opportunities to access the assessment and results. Key strategies toward this end may include providing different language versions of the measure and resulting reports, offering the self-report measure in accessible response formats (e.g., online or paper-and-pencil), and implementing at an agreed-on time for preferred administration (e.g., homeroom period or other non-core instructional time). Finally, we recommend that the culture-specific model of mindfulness assessment developed at the local level should itself be continuously monitored and revised based on regular input from the served community. Users interested in more detailed information regarding culturally responsive approaches to universal assessment are encouraged to consider the guidelines provided by Kiperman et al. (2024) and Moore et al. (2023).

Classroom Considerations

Most of the schoolwide considerations we discussed are also applicable at the classroom level, but on a smaller scale. Similarly, culturally responsive assessment in the classroom should be student-centered (Nortvedt et al., 2020). When classroom cultures are considerably different from the school-level culture, then there may be a need to develop a culture-specific assessment model tailored to select classrooms. A potential discrepancy in schoolwide versus classroom cultures is likely to be identified while engaging the processes described earlier toward a culture-specific mindfulness assessment protocol. No new or different procedures are necessarily needed beyond what was covered earlier. Rather, the guidance provided by Kiperman et al. (2024) and Moore et al. (2023) is just as applicable toward this end. Classroom considerations are also relevant beyond universal prevention, especially for targeted MBIs that involve supporting individual students in classrooms or, alternatively, pulling students from the same classroom to receive small-group mindfulness training together.

Moreover, when classroom-level cultural patterns are identified, we recommend that educators and mental health professionals implementing mindfulness assessments should respect students' perceptions of both mindfulness and assessment more broadly. This includes cultivating awareness regarding how the assessment protocol may conflict with students' culturally based ways of participating (see Cumming & van der Kleij, 2016, for further discussion of this topic) and providing alternative ways of engagement to accommodate cultural variations throughout the assessment process. The general cultural sensitivity considerations discussed earlier can be applied to inform this situation by gathering information about attitudes and perspectives that can be used to guide classroom-level adaptations. Moreover, classroom-level adaptations can be used to inform individual student adaptations, which are discussed next.

Individual Student Considerations

When using mindfulness assessments with individual students, at either targeted or intensive levels of prevention, users should interpret scores within the context of students' psychosocial history and cultural backgrounds. This guideline is equally important when making data-based decisions regarding both identification for MBIs and outcome monitoring responsiveness to MBIs. As discussed earlier in this chapter, all mindfulness assessments rely on self-reporting because they focus on an individual's appraisal of their mindfulness skills, which are indicated by experiences of covert or private events (i.e., thoughts and feelings that are only available via subjective perceptions). Research has shown that youths' ages, abilities, cultural backgrounds, prior experiences, and other characteristics can influence their self-reported mindfulness scores in ways that may inaccurately reflect the target traits (Goodman et al., 2017).

For instance, most mindfulness assessments tap into present-moment awareness of physical sensation, which has been found to correlate with internalizing psychopathology and risky behaviors, such as binge drinking (e.g., Leigh et al., 2005). It is therefore possible that youth experiencing anxiety, trauma, and mood concerns may score higher on scales indicating present-moment awareness not because of the strength of their mindfulness skills, but rather because of the salience of their somatic symptoms (Goodman et al., 2017). Ultimately, users must be critical consumers of mindfulness assessment scores, being careful to make only inferences that are warranted by the data. Users would also do well to employ complementary well-validated outcome measures and idiographic monitoring methods to strengthen their inferences, especially at the intensive level of service delivery.

CONCLUSION

This chapter has overviewed the current context of assessing mindfulness with youth, particularly as it relates to informing culturally responsive service delivery in educational settings. In this final section, we close by offering two directions for research that may help advance culturally responsive mindfulness assessment into the future.

First, we recommend that future research focus on ensuring that the evidence base of validation studies for any given mindfulness assessment is representative of the diverse youth the measure is intended to serve. To date, the evidence base for any given mindfulness assessment has been far from representative, due to most validation studies having been conducted with samples characterized by little racial/ethnic, linguistic, and socioeconomic diversity. It is true that some assessments (e.g., the MAAS-A) have a much more diversified research base than other assessments (e.g., the MSQ), at least in terms of language adaptations and cross-national studies (see Table 24.1). Yet little research has directly evaluated the differential psychometrics of responses to mindfulness assessments from diverse youth within the same study. We suggest measurement invariance and generalizability theory studies may be especially useful for helping researchers to parse group and rater effects on mindfulness measures (cf. Briesch et al., 2014; Pendergast et al., 2017). And we are optimistic that insight gained from such studies may eventually help inform users' expectations regarding culturally based patterns of responding to these assessments, which may, in turn, inform adaptations and interpretation.

Second, we recommend that future research focus on reflexively evaluating the guidelines we provided here (see the previous section) regarding how to go about developing and implementing culturally responsive mindfulness assessment protocols in schools. We acknowledge that our guidelines leaned heavily on available guidelines provided for similar but different assessment purposes (e.g., Kiperman et al., 2024; Moore et al., 2023; Nastasi et al., 2004). Thus, the effectiveness of these guidelines for serving their intended purpose is an open research question that begs for an empirical answer. We suggest that studies evaluating the social validity and social consequences of mindfulness assessments may be especially useful toward this end because they may provide complementary evidence—beyond psychometrics—that allows researchers to determine if assessment protocols are valued by the school community (social validity) and if they add value to the services provided to youth at school (social consequences; cf. Miller, 2023). We expect that a focused line of research on this front will eventually produce more refined and parsimonious guidelines than what we offered here.

In closing, we would like to reiterate the promise of mindfulness and MBIs for supporting the broad behavioral and mental health of youth via multi-tiered prevention in schools. We would also like to reemphasize our advocacy for mindfulness assessments to serve at least two important functions within this context: identifying youth who might benefit from MBIs and evaluating youths' responsiveness to MBIs. We hope the information provided in this chapter provides researchers and implementers of mindfulness assessments with foundational knowledge and perspective that enhances their ability to use and interpret these measures in both critical and culturally responsive ways. We recognize that much work remains to be done to establish an evidence base for guiding culturally responsive mindfulness assessments into the future. And we encourage interested readers to pick up where we leave off by carrying this work forward.

REFERENCES

Axelrod, M. I., & Santagata, M. L. (2022). Evaluating a mindfulness-based intervention to improve academic engagement. *Journal of Applied School Psychology, 38*(3), 262–282.

Baer, R. A. (2003). Mindfulness training as clinical intervention: A conceptual and empirical review. *Clinical Psychology: Science and Practice, 10*, 125–143.

Baer, R. A., Smith, G. T., Hopkins, J., Krietemeyer, J., & Toney, L. (2006). *Five Facet Mindfulness Questionnaire (FFMQ)*. APA PsycTests.

Bakhuys Roozeboom, M. C., Schelvis, R. M., Houtman, I. L., Wiezer, N. M., & Bongers, P. M. (2020). Decreasing employees' work stress by a participatory, organizational level work stress prevention approach: A multiple-case study in primary education. *BMC Public Health, 20*(1), 676.

Bender, S. L., Lawson, T., & Palacios, A. M. (2023). Mindfulness measures for children and adolescents: A systematic review. *Contemporary School Psychology, 27*(1), 104–117.

Bishop, S. R., Lau, M., Shapiro, S., Carlson, L., Anderson, N. D., Carmody, J., et al. (2004). Mindfulness: A proposed operational definition. *Clinical Psychology: Science and Practice, 11*(3), 230–241.

Black, D. S. (2015). Mindfulness training for children and adolescents: A state-of-the-science review. In K. W. Brown, J. D. Creswell, & R. M. Ryan (Eds.), *Handbook of mindfulness: Theory, research, and practice* (pp. 283–310). Guilford Press.

Brensilver, M., Hardy, J., & Sofer, O. J. (2020). *The Mindful Schools curriculum and teacher's guide*. Norton.

Briere, J. (2011). *Mindfulness Inventory for Children and Adolescents* [Unpublished manuscript]. University of Southern California.

Briesch, A. M., Swaminathan, H., Welsh, M., & Chafouleas, S. M. (2014). Generalizability theory: A practical guide to study design, implementation, and interpretation. *Journal of School Psychology, 52*(1), 13–35.

Broderick, P. C. (2021). *Learning to Breathe: A mindfulness curriculum for adolescents to cultivate emotion regulation, attention, and performance*. New Harbinger.

Brown, K. W., & Ryan, R. M. (2003). The benefits of being present: Mindfulness and its role in psychological well-being. *Journal of Personality and Social Psychology, 84*(4), 822–848.

Brown, K. W., West, A. M., Loverich, T. M., & Biegel, G. M. (2011). Assessing adolescent mindfulness: Validation of an adapted Mindful Attention Awareness Scale in adolescent normative and psychiatric populations. *Psychological Assessment, 23*(4), 1023–1033.

Carsley, D., Khoury, B., & Heath, N. L. (2018). Effectiveness of mindfulness interventions for mental health in schools: A comprehensive meta-analysis. *Mindfulness, 9*(3), 693–707.

Cortazar, N., Calvete, E., Fernández-González, L., & Orue, I. (2020). Development of a short form of the Five Facet Mindfulness Questionnaire—Adolescents for children and adolescents. *Journal of Personality Assessment, 102*(5), 641–652.

Cotton, S., Luberto, C. M., Sears, R. W., Strawn, J. R., Stahl, L., Wasson, R. S., et al. (2016). Mindfulness-based cognitive therapy for youth with anxiety disorders at risk for bipolar disorder: A pilot trial. *Early Intervention in Psychiatry, 10*, 426–434.

Cumming, J. J., & van der Kleij, F. M. (2016). Effective enactment of assessment for learning and student diversity in Australia. In D. Laveault & L. Allal (Eds.), *Assessment for learning: Meeting the challenge of implementation* (pp. 55–73). Springer.

Day, C. M., Smith, A., Short, E. J., & Bater, L. (2022). Dialectical behavior therapy skills groups for youth in schools: A systematic review. *Adolescent Research Review, 7*(2), 267–284.

Dowdy, E., Kamphaus, R. W., Twyford, J. M., & Dever, B. V. (2014). Culturally competent behavioral and emotional screening. In M. D. Weist, N. A. Lever, C. P. Bradshaw, & J. Sarno Owens (Eds.), *Handbook of school mental health: Research, training, practice, and policy* (pp. 311–321). Springer.

Droutman, V. (2015). Mindfulness scale for pre-teens, teens, and adults. In R. J. Semple (Chair), *Clinical applications of mindfulness* [Symposium]. Bridging the Hearts and Minds of Youth: Mindfulness and Compassion in Clinical Practice, Education, and Research Conference, San Diego, CA, United States.

Dunning, D., Griffiths, K., Kuyken, W., Crane, C., Foulkes, L., Parker, J., & Dalgleish, T. (2019). The effects of mindfulness-based interventions on cognition and mental health in children and adolescents—A meta-analysis of randomized controlled trials. *Journal of Child Psychology and Psychiatry, and Allied Disciplines, 60*(3), 244–258.

Eklund, K., O'Malley, M., & Meyer, L. (2017). Gauging mindfulness in children and youth: School-based applications. *Psychology in the Schools, 54*(1), 101–114.

Esmaeilian, N., Dehghani, M., Dehghani, Z., & Lee, J. (2018). Mindfulness-based cognitive therapy enhances emotional resiliency in children with divorced parents. *Mindfulness, 9*(4), 1052–1062.

Fang, S., & Ding, D. (2020). A meta-analysis of the efficacy of acceptance and commitment therapy for children. *Journal of Contextual Behavioral Science, 15*, 225–234.

Felver, J. C., Celis-de Hoyos, C. E., Tezanos, K., & Singh, N. N. (2016). A systematic review of mindfulness-based interventions for youth in school settings. *Mindfulness, 7*, 34–45.

Felver, J. C., Doerner, E., Jones, J., Kaye, N. C., & Merrell, K. W. (2013). Mindfulness in school psychology: Applications for intervention and professional practice. *Psychology in the Schools, 50*(6), 531–547.

Franzmann, T. K., Renshaw, T. L., Bundock, K., Pinkelman, S. E., & Joslyn, P. R. (2025). Integrated behavioral supports: Combing PBIS and SEL at Tier 2. *School Mental Health, 17*(1), 173–188.

Goodman, M. S., Madni, L. A., & Semple, R. J. (2017). Measuring mindfulness in youth: Review of current assessments, challenges, and future directions. *Mindfulness, 8*, 1409–1420.

Greco, L. A., Baer, R. A., & Smith, G. T. (2011). Assessing mindfulness in children and adolescents: Development and validation of the Child and Adolescent Mindfulness Measure (CAMM). *Psychological Assessment, 23*(3), 606–614.

Guerra, J., García-Gómez, M., Turanzas, J., Cordón, J. R., Suárez-Jurado, C., & Mestre, J. M. (2019). A brief Spanish version of the Child and Adolescent Mindfulness Measure (CAMM). A dispositional mindfulness measure. *International Journal of Environmental Research and Public Health, 16*(8), 1355.

Hanh, T. N. (1976). *The miracle of mindfulness! A manual on meditation*. Beacon Press.

Hanh, T. N. (1999). *The miracle of mindfulness: An introduction to the practice of meditation*. Beacon Press.

The Hawn Foundation. (2011). *The MindUP curriculum: Brain-focused strategies for learning and living. Grades Pre-K–2*. Scholastic.

Johnson, C., Burke, C., Brinkman, S., & Wade, T. (2017). Development and validation of a multifactor mindfulness scale in youth: The Comprehensive Inventory of Mindfulness Experiences—Adolescents (CHIME-A). *Psychological Assessment, 29*(3), 264–281

Kabat-Zinn, J. (1994). *Wherever you go, there you are: Mindfulness meditation in everyday life*. Hyperion.

Kabat-Zinn, J. (2003). Mindfulness-based interventions in context: Past, present, and future. *Clinical Psychology: Science and Practice, 10*(2), 144–156.

Kallapiran, K., Koo, S., Kirubakaran, R., & Hancock, K. (2015). Effectiveness of mindfulness in improving mental health symptoms of children and adolescents: A meta-analysis. *Child and Adolescent Mental Health, 20*(4), 182–194.

Khalifa, M. A., Gooden, M. A., & Davis, J. E. (2016). Culturally responsive school leadership: A synthesis of the literature. *Review of Educational Research, 86*(4), 1272–1311.

Kiperman, S., Clark, K., Renshaw, T. L., Anderson, J. R., Bernstein, E., & Willenbrink, J. B. (2024). Guidelines toward more socially just mental health screening in schools. *School Psychology, 39*(2), 151–166.

Klingbeil, D. A., Fischer, A. J., Renshaw, T. L., Bloomfield, B. S., Polakoff, B., Willenbrink, J. B., et al. (2017). Mindfulness-based interventions with youth: A comprehensive meta-analysis of single-subject design studies. *Psychology in the Schools, 54*(1), 70–87.

Klingbeil, D. A., Renshaw, T. L., Willenbrink, J. B., Copek, R. A., Chan, K. T., Haddock, A., & Clifton, J. D. (2017). Mindfulness-based interventions with youth: A comprehensive meta-analysis of group-design studies. *Journal of School Psychology, 63*, 77–103.

Lawlor, M. S. (2016). Mindfulness and social emotional learning (SEL): A conceptual framework. In K. A. Schonert-Reichl & R. W. Roeser (Eds.), *Handbook of mindfulness in education: Integrating theory and research into practice* (pp. 65–80). Springer.

Lawlor, M. S., Schonert-Reichl, K. A., Gadermann, A. M., & Zumbo, B. D. (2014). A validation study of the Mindful Attention Awareness Scale adapted for children. *Mindfulness, 5*(6), 730–741.

Lee, J., Kim, K. H., Webster, C. S., & Henning, M. A. (2021). The evolution of mindfulness from 1916 to 2019. *Mindfulness, 12*, 1849–1859.

Leigh, J., Bowen, S., & Marlatt, G. A. (2005). Spirituality, mindfulness and substance abuse. *Addictive Behaviors, 30*(7), 1335–1341.

Mash, E. J., & Hunsley, J. (2005). Evidence-based assessment of child and adolescent disorders: Issues and challenges. *Journal of Clinical Child and Adolescent Psychology, 34*(3), 362–379.

Maynard, B. R., Solis, M. R., Miller, V. L., & Brendel, K. E. (2017). Mindfulness-based interventions for improving cognition, academic achievement, behavior, and socioemotional functioning of primary and secondary school students. *Campbell Systematic Reviews, 13*(1), 1–144.

McKeering, P., & Hwang, Y.-S. (2019). A systematic review of mindfulness-based school interventions with early adolescents. *Mindfulness, 10*(4), 593–610.

Merrell, K. W., Ervin, R. A., Gimpel Peacock, G., & Renshaw, T. L. (2022). *School psychology for the 21st century: Foundations and practices* (3rd ed). Guilford Press.

Mezo, P. G., Herc, H. C., Pritchard, K. J., & Bullock, W. A. (2020). Evaluation and a proposed revision of the CAMM among underrepresented elementary school children. *Assessment for Effective Intervention, 45*(3), 235–239.

Miller, F. G. (2023). Assessment in action: Toward a more complete and justice-oriented understanding of the social consequences of educational measures. *School Psychology, 38*(3), 192–198.

Monteiro, L. M., Compson, J. F., & Musten, F. (Eds.). (2017). *Practitioner's guide to ethics and mindfulness-based interventions*. Springer.

Moore, S., Long, A. C. J., Coyle, S., Cooper, J. M., Mayworm, A. M., Amirazizi, S., et al. (2023). A roadmap to equitable school mental health screening. *Journal of School Psychology*, 96, 57–74.

Nastasi, B. K., Moore, R. B., & Varjas, K. M. (2004). *School-based mental health services: Creating comprehensive and culturally specific programs*. American Psychological Association.

Neff, K. D., Bluth, K., Tóth-Király, I., Davidson, O., Knox, M. C., Williamson, Z., & Costigan, A. (2021). Development and validation of the Self-Compassion Scale for Youth. *Journal of Personality Assessment*, *103*(1), 92–105.

Nortvedt, G. A., Wiese, E., Brown, M., Burns, D., McNamara, G., O'Hara, J., et al. (2020). Aiding culturally responsive assessment in schools in a globalising world. *Educational Assessment, Evaluation and Accountability*, *32*(1), 5–27.

Pendergast, L. L., von der Embse, N., Kilgus, S. P., & Eklund, K. R. (2017). Measurement equivalence: A non-technical primer on categorical multi-group confirmatory factor analysis in school psychology. *Journal of School Psychology*, *60*, 65–82.

Phan, M. L., & Renshaw, T. L. (2023). Guidelines for implementing and adapting evidence-based interventions with marginalized youth in schools. *American Journal of Orthopsychiatry*, 93(3), 256–268.

Phan, M. L., & Renshaw, T. L. (2024). Guidelines for adapting mindfulness-based school interventions with youth who are racially and ethnically marginalized. *Journal of Educational and Psychological Consultation*, *35*(3), 285–316.

Phan, M. L., Renshaw, T. L., Caramanico, J., Greeson, J. M., MacKenzie, E., Atkinson-Diaz, Z., et al. (2022). Mindfulness-based school interventions: A systematic review of outcome evidence quality by study design. *Mindfulness*, *13*(7), 1591–1613.

Phan, M. L., Renshaw, T. L., & Farley, C. D. (2025). Guidelines for increasing access to mindfulness-based interventions in under-resourced schools. *Contemporary School Psychology*, *29*(1), 188–199.

Renshaw, T. L. (2017). Preliminary development and validation of the Mindful Student Questionnaire. *Assessment for Effective Intervention*, *42*(3), 168–175.

Renshaw, T. L. (2020). Mindfulness-based intervention in schools. In C. Maykel & M. A. Bray (Eds.), *Promoting mind–body health in schools: Interventions for mental health professionals* (pp. 145–160). American Psychological Association.

Renshaw, T. L., & Cook, C. R. (2017). Mindfulness in the schools—Historical roots, current trends, and future directions. *Psychology in the Schools*, *54*(1), 5–12.

Renshaw, T. L., Fischer, A. J., & Klingbeil, D. A. (2017). Mindfulness-based intervention in school psychology. *Contemporary School Psychology*, *21*(4), 299–303.

Renshaw, T. L., & Phan, M. L. (2023). Using implementation reporting to advance culturally sensitive and equity focused mindfulness programs in schools. *Mindfulness*, *14*(2), 307–313.

Renshaw, T. L., Weeks, S. N., Roberson, A. J., Upton, S. R., Barr, J. D., Phan, M. L., & Farley, C. D. (2022). Cultivating mindfulness in schools to promote well-being. In K. Allen, M. J. Furlong, D. Vella-Brodrick, & S. Suldo (Eds.), *Handbook of positive psychology in schools: Supporting process and practice* (3rd ed; pp. 135–148). Routledge.

Renshaw, T. L., Weeks, S. N., Roberson, A. J., & Vinal, S. (2023). ACT in schools: A public health approach. In M. P. Twohig, M. E. Levin, & J. M. Peterson (Eds.), *Oxford handbook of acceptance and commitment therapy* (pp. 564–583). Oxford University Press.

Roeser, R. W., Greenberg, M. T., Frazier, T., Galla, B. M., Semenov, A. D., & Warren, M. T. (2023). Beyond all splits: Envisioning the next generation of science on mindfulness and compassion in schools for students. *Mindfulness*, *14*(2), 239–254.

Romer, N., von der Embse, N., Eklund, K., Kilgus, S., Perales, K., Splett, J. W., et al. (2020). *Best practices in university social emotional, and behavioral screening: An implementation guide* (Version 2.0). School Mental Health Collaborative, University of Wisconsin–Madison.

Saltzman, A. (2014). *A Still Quiet Place: A mindfulness program for teaching children and adolescents to ease stress and difficult emotions*. New Harbinger.

Schutt, M. K. A., & Felver, J. (2020). Mindfulness in education. In N. Singh & S. Joy (Eds.), *Mindfulness-based interventions with children and adolescents* (pp. 57–73). Routledge.

Semple, R. J., Droutman, V., & Reid, B. A. (2017). Mindfulness goes to school: Things learned (so far) from research and real-world experiences. *Psychology in the Schools*, *54*(1), 29–52.

Semple, R. J., Lee, J., Rosa, D., & Miller, L. F. (2010). A randomized trial of mindfulness-based cognitive therapy for children: Promoting mindful attention to enhance social-emotional resiliency in children. *Journal of Child and Family Studies*, *19*(2), 218–229.

Syeda, M. M., & Andrews, J. J. W. (2021). Mindfulness-based cognitive therapy as a targeted group intervention: Examining children's changes in anxiety symptoms and mindfulness. *Journal of Child and Family Studies*, *30*(4), 1002–1015.

West, A. M., Penix-Sbraga, T., & Poole, D. A. (2007). *Measuring mindfulness in youth: Development of the Mindful Thinking and Action Scale for Adolescents* [Unpublished manuscript]. Central Michigan University.

Zenner, C., Herrnleben-Kurz, S., & Walach, H. (2014). Mindfulness-based interventions in schools—A systematic review and meta-analysis. *Frontiers in Psychology*, *5*, 603–623.

Zoogman, S., Goldberg, S. B., Hoyt, W. T., & Miller, L. (2015). Mindfulness interventions with youth: A meta-analysis. *Mindfulness*, *6*, 290–302.

CHAPTER 25

Considering Fairness and Culture in Social and Emotional Learning Assessment

Christopher J. Anthony, Katherine E. Frye, Timothy C. Horn, Pui-Wa Lei, and James Clyde DiPerna

Attention to social and emotional aspects of learning (i.e., social and emotional learning [SEL]) has grown in prominence since the turn of the century but has taken on new urgency in light of the substantial negative effects of the global COVID-19 pandemic. Although the full impact of the pandemic on students' social and emotional development has yet to be fully understood (Gross & Hamilton, 2023), it is clear that youth today face substantial mental health challenges. For example, it is estimated that 30 to 40% of students have experienced negative mental health effects (Hamilton & Gross, 2021) as a result of the pandemic, with rates of depression, anxiety, and suicide among children and adolescents at decades-long highs (American Academy of Pediatrics et al., 2021). Furthermore, there is extensive evidence that the effects of the pandemic have been unevenly distributed, with students from marginalized backgrounds experiencing much worse effects (e.g., Goldhaber et al., 2022; Tai et al., 2022). As a result of these trends, educators, policymakers, parents, and students themselves have strengthened calls for more comprehensive attention to SEL in schools throughout the United States and around the world.

To support growth in SEL service delivery, schools need well-developed, efficient, and psychometrically strong assessments. Regardless of the particular conceptualization of SEL (i.e., which theoretical or organizational framework is adopted), social and emotional development is broadly conceptualized as bioecological—children learn and grow within contexts in which various environmental systems (e.g., school, family, community, culture) interact and impact development (Bronfenbrenner & Morris, 2006; Osher et al., 2020). Thus, SEL assessments must consider how these environmental contexts affect children's ability both to develop and to demonstrate SEL skills. Guidance on developing and conducting equitable[1] and high-quality school-based assessments (e.g., DiPerna et al., 2022; Holman et al., 2023; McKown, 2017) calls for not only clearly defining both the SEL skills to be measured and the purpose of assessments but also selecting assessments with strong psychometric properties and evidence of fairness across relevant student subgroups.

Amidst calls for greater attention to fairness and psychometric quality, the K–12 student population has become substantially more diverse

[1] As noted by Cipriano and Strambler (2025), the term *equity* has many different definitions and connotations. We use their definition when we use the term in this chapter: "The assurance that everyone has access to the opportunities and resources to address their needs" (p. 58). They also note that equity is akin to "applied fairness" (p. 58), which also coheres with our use of the term.

over the past few decades. For example, in 2000, 61.2% of children in the United States identified as White non-Hispanic compared to an estimated 48.6% of children by 2024 (Federal Interagency Forum on Child and Family Statistics, 2023). In addition, the percentage of Hispanic children increased from 17.2% in 2000 to 25.9% in 2024, and the percentage of children identified as "two or more races" more than doubled (2.2% to 5.0%) across this timeframe. These demographic shifts pose challenges—and opportunities—for an educational system that historically has emphasized more culturally homogenous curricular and instructional approaches. An understanding of the diverse makeup of today's students is crucial in SEL intervention and assessment, given the evidence of disparities in social–emotional competence related to race, ethnicity, socioeconomic status, and other sociocultural characteristics (e.g., T. M. Jones et al., 2020; Rowe & Trickett, 2018; West et al., 2020).

CULTURALLY INFORMED SEL PRACTICES

In response to these trends, the SEL field has increasingly emphasized cultural responsiveness and equity in which all students receive access to high-quality education and support, regardless of their backgrounds or characteristics (e.g., Barnes et al., 2023; Collaborative for Academic, Social, and Emotional Learning [CASEL], n.d.; Jagers et al., 2018; McCall et al., 2023). Broadly, the terms *culturally responsive* and *culturally relevant* have been used in educational research and pedagogy to describe how teachers and schools integrate cultural knowledge, values, frames of reference, and experiences in all aspects of learning (Gay, 2010; Ladson-Billings, 1995, as cited in Aronson & Laughter, 2016). These terms have also been used in the school psychology field broadly (e.g., Goforth & Pham, 2023) as well as the SEL space specifically to refer to how SEL skills are taught and practiced (e.g., Kendziora et al., 2021; McCallops et al., 2019). The term *transformative SEL* (TSEL) refers to an approach to SEL that encompasses considerations for social justice, equity, and empowerment with the goal of fostering educational equity (Jagers et al., 2019). TSEL considers how individuals, interactions, and institutions can be transformed to promote positive development and outcomes for *all* people. Jagers et al. (2019) align the five SEL domains (i.e., self-awareness, self-management, social awareness, relationship skills, responsible decision making) described by CASEL with justice-oriented concepts to outline the competencies needed for students to grow into global citizens (i.e., equity elaborations). These competencies include (1) consideration of how biases, collective histories, intersecting identities, and differing social and cultural norms influence behaviors, (2) the importance of agency and belonging in managing behaviors and relationships, as well as (3) how making caring and ethical choices as a group (e.g., collective efficacy) can promote collective well-being. TSEL also incorporates addressing systemic inequities and supporting both adults and youth in embracing culture and enacting change. In these ways, TSEL expands the conceptualization of SEL and definitions of various SEL competencies to create a socially just, culturally responsive, and equitable framework.

Efforts to promote equitable and culturally informed practices in SEL intervention and programming have increased over the past two decades (e.g., Gagnier et al. 2022; Garner et al., 2014; Kendziora et al., 2021; Kurtz et al., 2022; McCallops et al., 2019). Coulehan (n.d.) describes culturally responsive embedded SEL as mastering SEL skills "in ways that are defined by and consistent with their community and cultural context," such as through what language is used, how behavior is modeled, and how cultural values and members of the community are embedded within the SEL framework guiding programming. Importantly, more work is needed to increase cultural responsiveness in SEL service delivery. For example, some researchers caution that universal SEL programs may not generalize for diverse or marginalized populations, given the lack of empirical attention to diversity characteristics and analyses of subgroup effects in evaluating program outcomes (Lee et al., 2023; Rowe & Trickett, 2018). In addition, some work (e.g., Lee et al., 2023) suggests that universal SEL may benefit diverse subgroups of students but not reduce existing social–emotional disparities. Jagers et al. (2019) recommend the use of student-centered approaches such as project-based learning and youth participatory action research (e.g., Ozer et al., 2021) for creating transformative SEL programs, and the use of culturally relevant education for creating and sustaining culturally responsive learning communities.

A Need for Culturally Informed SEL Assessment

Despite global and national efforts to understand and appreciate how cultural diversity and issues of equity impact education and development (e.g., American Psychological Association, 2021; National Association of School Psychologists, 2021; Organization for Economic Co-operation and Development, n.d.), and clear efforts to develop culturally informed SEL prevention and intervention resources, these efforts have not yet been translated into best practices for assessment. Although it may not be feasible (or possible) to consider every cultural variable when creating and/or using an assessment, school-based practitioners need guidance on how to make culturally informed assessment decisions. The goals for the remainder of this chapter are to briefly summarize relevant literature and share a broad model that considers fairness in the promotion of culturally informed assessment practices for both test developers and practitioners. The chapter concludes with a brief summary of how fairness-related data may be considered in SEL assessment manuals and recommendations for better addressing culturally fair assessment practices in the future.

Culturally Informed Assessment

Although the term is increasing in popularity, there currently is no universal definition or standard for what qualifies as a "culturally informed" assessment. Relatedly, there is no universal definition for culturally informed SEL assessment. Authors have tended to use the term "culturally informed" in the context of ensuring that (a) individuals from different cultural, ethnic, and linguistic backgrounds are fairly treated during assessment processes; (b) assessments measure skills that are relevant considering a person's cultural background; and (c) scores produced by these assessments provide fair estimates of skills across various demographic characteristics (e.g., Fujii, 2016; López, 2002; Mercado & Venta, 2022; Tanaka-Matsumi et al., 1996). Other organizations have provided guidance more broadly on "multicultural" competence with some specific considerations for conducting assessments with culturally and linguistically diverse populations (e.g., American Psychological Association, 2017). Recent publications (e.g., Pickens, 2022) have put forth some guidance on how a culturally responsive lens can be utilized in SEL assessment, such as identifying potential implicit biases through rater effects, utilizing strengths-based assessments to identify protective and promotive factors, applying cultural contextual considerations to the assessment process, and supporting usability of SEL assessments to promote equitable access to services. However, this guidance mostly applies to the *use* of SEL assessments; the underlying assumption is that currently published SEL assessments adequately included considerations of culture and equity in their development. In addition, this literature does not offer explicit guidance regarding how future SEL assessments can be developed to be more culturally appropriate. We describe some of the guidance identified in the literature regarding how SEL assessments should be developed, used, and interpreted in practice.

S. Jones et al. (2019) emphasized the need for SEL constructs to be precisely defined and noted that it is imperative to consider how socioeconomic and cultural context impact SEL competencies, which have been conceptualized based on the dominant or majority culture. McKown (2019) described the tension between cultural variation in the student population and standardization efforts to have consistent procedures and items that measure the construct in the same way for each test taker, in addition to potential concerns with highlighting group differences in SEL that may reinforce inequality. Standardization efforts generally intend to create assessments that measure skills consistently with minimal error; however, assuming that standardized items, formats, and content can be used equally to measure skills across student groups introduces important challenges for both test developers and test users. Some of these challenges include test bias, test score inequalities, and erroneous frames of reference that assume SEL is understood and demonstrated the same way for all students. Indeed, McKown (2019) cautioned, "To the extent that important SEL skills are *not* represented in a student SEL skill assessment . . . the omission of culturally salient skills may undermine its universal relevance" (p. 218). Furthermore, Anthony et al. (2023) described how some purported SEL skills may be culturally loaded and thus not ideal for assessing the SEL competencies of culturally and linguistically diverse students. For example, an SEL skill item targeting eye contact during conversation may disadvantage members from cultures that discourage eye contact, and thus, if assessed, scores on this item may represent variation in cultural values rather than true differences in students' SEL skills. Moreover, Jagers et al. (2018) highlighted the importance of considering issues of measurement bias and equivalence in SEL assessment, such as including cultural indices as moderators or mediators, considering the importance of community and peer networks, and augmenting surveys with interviews, observations, and/or youth participatory action approaches. These additional procedures may increase the time, resources, and cost of assessment development and evaluation, but they represent actionable steps to identify evidence of culturally informed SEL assessment.

In addition, calls for equity-oriented SEL assessment include recommendations for expanding the operational definitions of SEL competencies through prototype analysis, a procedure in which the most salient features of a target construct that are relevant to the intended population are used to define the measured construct (El Mallah, 2022). This systematic approach includes participatory action research with stakeholders from the target population to understand how SEL competencies are conceived in that community rather than simply using expert-created or "universal" definitions of SEL competencies. Notably, El Mallah stated, "SEL competencies are multidimensional constructs, the definitions of which are negotiated between individuals and their cultural worlds" (2019, p. 292). El Mallah argued that using a racial equity lens, performing content validation, and examining conceptual equivalence of SEL constructs across groups are key to equity-oriented SEL assessment.

Culturally Informed Assessment within the Context of Assessment Fairness

In contrast to the term *culturally informed*, other relevant terms have received much more discussion and definition. As noted earlier, the term *equity* has several definitions but can be conceptualized as "applied fairness" (Cipriano & Strambler, 2025, p. 58). This is helpful as there is ample guidance on what the term *fairness* means in the context of psychological and educational assessment (e.g., American Educational Research Association [AERA] et al., 2014; Dorans & Cook, 2016; Johnson & Geisinger, 2022), and this discussion can help clarify how an SEL assessment might be culturally informed. Indeed, the *Standards for Educational and Psychological Testing* (i.e., *Standards*; AERA et al., 2014) provides an entire chapter to guide consideration of fairness that addresses (1) ensuring that procedures needed to complete the assessment are equally accessible to all relevant groups (e.g., items are translated into other languages and do not include idioms or expressions that are particular to one group); (2) eliminating, to the greatest extent possible, measurement bias via statistical methods of evaluating differential item and test functioning; (3) considering whether test items require knowledge that is not relevant to the construct of interest (e.g., reading skills necessary to enable performance on a math test with word problems); and (4) considering the unique configuration of characteristics that each child brings to the assessment scenario (e.g., their intersecting identities and experiences).

The *Standards* also lay out threats to fairness, including differences in the test content across groups, differences in the testing context across groups, and differences in opportunities to learn across contexts. It is important to note that the *Standards* explicitly exclude simple mean differences across groups as a definition of unfairness. In the presence of overall distributional differences, the *Standards* urge increased caution and consideration of fairness, but simple conclusions of unfairness should not follow from mere group differences in assessment scores. Despite its explicit consideration of fairness, there is no single fairness definition in the *Standards* to guide consideration of culturally informed assessment.

The Comprehensive Assessment of Fairness Evidence Framework

Although the broad and somewhat disparate stipulations and considerations about fairness in the *Standards* provide much richness about the concept, the content provides little specific guidance regarding the development and implementation of assessments to promote fairness. To address this limitation, Anthony et al. (2023) developed the comprehensive assessment of fairness evidence (CAFE) model as a guide for both test developers and practitioners regarding how to consider and promote fairness. This model can also provide tangible guidance regarding how to develop and implement SEL assessments in a culturally informed manner.[2]

The CAFE model (Figure 25.1) includes two broad components: an *evidence framework*, which lays out the broad domains in which empirical evidence can be used to inform questions of fairness; and an *evaluation process*, which guides the application of collected empirical evidence to address particular questions of score uses or interpretations. The evidence framework consists of two broad domains of fairness-related evidence: procedural fairness and substantive fairness. *Procedural fairness* evidence involves consideration of testing/assessment procedures and whether they

[2] We briefly describe the CAFE model in this chapter, but interested readers can refer to Anthony et al. (2023) for full discussion, explication, and illustration.

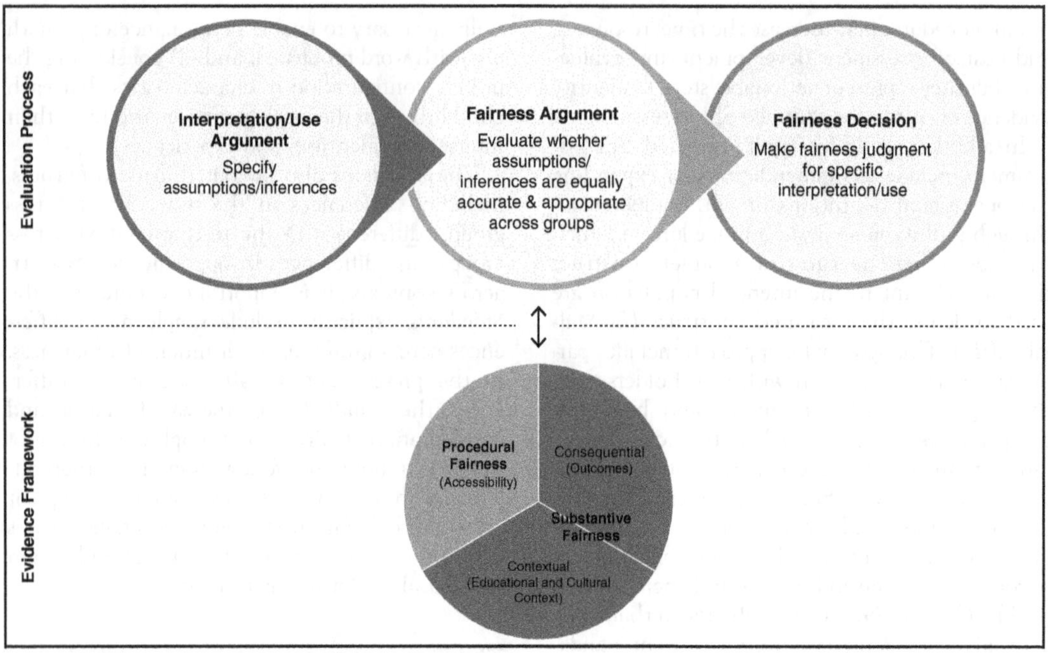

FIGURE 25.1. Comprehensive appraisal of fairness evidence (CAFE) model. Reprinted with permission from Anthony et al. (2023). Copyright © 2023 Elsevier.

are equally accessible for all relevant test-taking groups. *Substantive fairness* evidence involves broader considerations of what is reasonable and appropriate regarding interpretation and use of test/assessment scores. Although "reasonable and appropriate" is at least somewhat subjective, the CAFE model is intended to help clarify questions and identify relevant evidence to help answer them.

Substantive fairness is divided into two parts: evidence of contextual fairness and consequential fairness. *Contextual fairness* involves evaluation of evidence regarding the different social and cultural environments that characterize the lived experiences of relevant subgroups. This domain is central to ensuring culturally fair SEL assessment. It encompasses both traditional psychometric approaches (e.g., differential item functioning [DIF] testing; measurement invariance testing) and broader descriptive approaches, such as utilizing surveys to gauge the appropriateness of SEL item content across groups and focus groups to consider item content in depth with various stakeholder groups representing different cultural backgrounds. Contextual fairness includes both cultural contexts and educational contexts, which specifically focus on whether different groups have had differential opportunities to learn SEL behaviors represented within SEL assessments.

Finally, *consequential fairness* involves consideration of the outcomes of various test score interpretations and uses, and whether these outcomes are reasonable and appropriate. From a broad perspective, this involves evaluating score distributions across relevant groups. Beyond overall distributional differences, however, it is important to consider what the application of recommended decision rules might imply for likely outcomes. For example, if the application of recommended scoring rules resulted in 25% of one cultural group being identified for further services but only 5% of another cultural group, the implications of such a disparity would be important to consider when evaluating whether a particular proposed score use is fair (or would lead to outcomes considered fair). Such information should be readily available for measures developed or normed on nationally representative samples. Beyond these broad samples, however, it is important to consider local contexts and specific cultural groups represented within those contexts, even if they represent a small portion of a broader national population.

The second overarching component of the CAFE model is the *evaluation process*. The evaluation process draws heavily from Kane's (e.g., 2010) approach to test score validation with a special emphasis on fairness, and it involves three steps. First, a particular score interpretation (e.g., this score reflects students' skills in self-awareness) or use (e.g., this score should be used to identify children for Tier 2 SEL services) is specified. When doing so, specific assumptions or inferences are also stated. Second, a fairness argument is engaged in which each assumption or inference is considered in light of the empirical evidence provided via the evidence framework. Different aspects of the evidence framework may be relevant for different types of decisions. For example, for broad construct interpretations (e.g., this score reflects students' self-awareness skills), procedural and contextual fairness evidence may be most relevant to ensure that no construct-irrelevant variance is introduced either from differences in access to the procedures of the assessment or cultural/educational differences across groups. In contrast, usage-type questions (e.g., this score should be used to identify students for further Tier 2 SEL supports) might weigh consequential data more heavily as disparities in referral to or receipt of school-based services may ultimately be deemed unfair, regardless of whether the scores accurately reflect a construct of interest.

Critically, the CAFE model is not meant to provide simple answers to complex problems (e.g., a score interpretation or use is simply "fair" or "unfair"), but rather as a framework that guides the generation and evaluation of empirical data relative to specific questions to promote fairness throughout the assessment process. For example, procedural and contextual fairness evidence may be present in which all students can access test items and there is no empirical indication of cultural influence on the functioning of items, but distributional differences across groups are also present. This may happen if one cultural subgroup scores much higher than another on average. Thus, the decision about fairness may come down to whether the proposed action, such as implementing an intervention program, has empirical evidence for providing a benefit for all groups regardless of average SEL score.

Taking Stock: Fairness Evidence Presented in SEL Assessment Manuals

As an additional benefit, the CAFE model also provides a helpful lens for considering broadly what fairness evidence exists for currently available SEL measures and narrowly what evidence exists for culturally informed development and practice. Such a broad survey of currently available measures can also serve as a basis for recommendations for future development. As such, we have completed such a review using a list of practitioner-accessible SEL measures (Horn et al., 2025; Winkelman et al., 2023)[3] and evaluated each measure's manual according to the CAFE model. Practitioner accessibility is a major consideration because few professionals in schools have access to empirical articles reviewing psychometric evidence, often due to paywalls, time, or other related barriers. Thus, any evidence of fairness or culturally informed development limited to articles published in peer-reviewed journals would be unavailable for consideration for most practitioners. However, users could review psychometric information if presented in a measure's manual.

Additionally, we sought to limit our review to those assessments that practitioners would come across if they were searching for SEL measures. Thus, we reviewed a variety of compendia produced by states and educational organizations listing potential assessments for practitioner use. These compendia were developed with the explicit purpose of guiding practitioners in their selection of SEL assessments for use in schools. The search included 22 compendia from 16 states and eight educational organizations (e.g., RAND Education and Labor, American Institutes for Research [AIR], CASEL, Institute of Education Sciences [IES]) that had lists of recommended SEL measures for practitioners. The search produced a list of 514 SEL assessments, but many measures were eliminated from further consideration due to lack of (1) current norming samples (i.e., post the year 2000); (2) student level assessment (e.g., a scale of teacher SEL competence rather than student SEL competence would not be considered); (3) any empirical support (i.e., at least one publication utilizing the measure); and/or (4) a technical manual. This substantially reduced the number to 26 assessments that were reviewed.

To conduct our review, several independent coders evaluated manuals based on whether there was any evidence related to various facets of pro-

[3] Our research team has been utilizing this list of measures for broad analysis of the state of SEL measures available to practitioners, including reliability and validity in addition to fairness. We present only initial fairness findings in this chapter, but more in-depth findings are available in Horn et al. (2025).

cedural, contextual, and/or consequential fairness. Due to the fact that these measures were not explicitly developed to align with the CAFE framework, we approached this coding task generously and considered a criterion to be met if there was any evidence that could be interpreted in light of the CAFE model, even if that evidence was not construed in the manual as related to fairness considerations. For example, if a manual presented score distributions for students from different racial/ethnic backgrounds, such evidence could be used to consider consequential fairness even if the authors simply presented the information as part of reporting the standardization sample and did not explicitly discuss fairness. If there was evidence found for any of the three broad categories, further coding was conducted within each fairness category. Table 25.1 provides a brief overview of some commonly used behavioral and SEL measures that were evaluated by this coding process.

As stated previously, the cornerstone of evaluating procedural fairness evidence is to consider the accessibility of the assessment. Thus, we coded whether test developers explicitly noted procedures for considerations of readability, test translations, accommodations, or modifications to better meet the needs of examinees. Most of the reviewed SEL assessments contained some type of procedural fairness (87.5%). Readability levels refer to the level of education the test taker needs to effectively read a test item (e.g., DuBay, 2004). Half of the manuals coded explicitly stated that they used a form of readability level standards to inform item development. Test translations were available in half of the manuals, with most translations done for Spanish only. However, not all of these translations were subjected to validation procedures to ensure equivalency. Although it is important to make these translations for fairness consideration, it is equally important to ensure the translated versions go through the same rigorous validation process as those of the original test.

Evaluating contextual fairness evidence involves asking questions about potential environmental differences in culture or instruction between relevant subgroups that may affect an individual's scores on a measure. Although some contextual fairness analyses (e.g., DIF analysis) can be done post hoc with data collected for multiple subgroups, most analyses that would qualify as informing contextual fairness would require a priori planning (e.g., conducting focus groups on item content). As a result, far fewer manuals had any evidence of contextual fairness evaluations (41.7%) than procedural fairness (87.5%). The lower presence of contextual fairness evidence is likely attributed to the greater number of resources (and foresight/planning) needed for test developers to adequately demonstrate that their test minimized group differences stemming from content and structure. For example, just 20.8% of manuals included expert review panels to evaluate the cultural appropriateness of each test item.

There are also statistical methodologies to explore if the items are functioning in the same way for different groups, such as the previously mentioned DIF analyses and measurement invariance. However, just 16.6% of manuals reviewed included DIF analyses, and 8.3% included measurement invariance to statistically examine group differences due to test content and internal structure. When group differences were examined, the most common groups utilized in analyses were gender, age, and disability status. Unfortunately, currently published SEL assessment manuals generally do not include analyses to determine if students with different racial, ethnic, or language backgrounds perform differently, making contextual fairness related to cultural identities a critical area to be addressed in SEL assessment so that test users can access this evidence. To increase evidence of contextual fairness in SEL assessment manuals, resources need to be intentionally allocated to these efforts during test development.

Evaluating consequential fairness evidence considers questions related to score use, such as whether there are score differences for subgroups and whether there are downstream implications (e.g., school placement decisions) due to these score differences. Our analyses indicate that 37.5% of the coded SEL manuals had evidence of subgroup outcome differences produced by means and standard deviations, t-tests, and/or analysis of variance. As with contextual fairness evidence, the most common subgroup outcome differences examined were for gender (54.1%), disability status (50.0%), and age (41.6%). No SEL manuals in the sample examined the downstream consequences of differential score usage based on groups (e.g., the percentages of children considered "at risk" based on application of suggested cut scores to the standardization sample). Notwithstanding the fact that it is absent, examples of these consequences might include outcome data from changes in school placement or intervention progress at the subgroup level. Examining downstream effects of the differences in outcomes requires a higher level of planning and

TABLE 25.1. Overview of Fairness Evidence in Select SEL Measures

		Broadband			SEL Specific				
		BASC-3	CBCL	Conners-3	DESSA	DESSA Mini	SEARS	SSIS-RS	SSIS SEL
	Publication date	2015	2001	2008	2014	2011/2014	2008	2008	2017
	Ages	2–25	1.5–18	6–18	Grades K–8	Grades K–8	5–18	3–18	3–18
	Raters	T, P, S	T, P, S	T, P, S	T, P	T, P	T, P, S	T, P, S	T, P, S
Procedural	Test readability	✓	-	✓	✓	✓	✓	✓	✓
	Translations	✓	✓	✓	-	-	✓	✓	✓
	Reading accommodations	-	✓	✓	✓	-	✓	✓	-
Contextual	Cultural appropriateness ratings	-	✓	-	-	-	-	✓	-
	Biased language consideration	-	-	-	-	✓	-	✓	-
	Differential item functioning	✓	-	-	-	-	-	✓	✓
	Measurement invariance	-	-	-	-	-	-	-	-
Consequential	Subgroup outcome differences	✓	✓	✓	-	-	-	-	-
	Subgroup decision differences	-	-	-	-	-	-	-	-

Note. This table represents a small sample of commonly used tests reviewed by Horn et al. (2024). T = Teacher; P = Parent; S = Student. BASC-3 = Behavior Assessment System for Children—Third Edition; CBCL = Child Behavior Checklist; DESSA = Devereux Student Strengths Assessment; SEARS = Social Emotional Assets and Resilience Scales; SSIS-RS = Social Skills Improvement System—Rating Scales.

resources to collect this information during development and/or validation efforts.

Overall, fairness evidence was less prominent than reliability or validity evidence in the coded SEL measures, and most available evidence did not focus on groups that are centrally relevant for culturally informed assessment. This should perhaps not come as a surprise, given that fairness has only garnered significant attention in recent SEL assessment literature, whereas guidance on validity evidence has been widely available for decades. Moving forward, we hope that guidance from the CAFE model will be accessible and useful to both test developers and test consumers. Lastly, it should be noted that the study did not comprehensively capture all questions to ask when considering fairness evidence of SEL measures. However, it can serve as a useful starting point.

FURTHER HORIZONS: EXPANDING CULTURALLY FAIR SEL ASSESSMENT

This review clearly indicates that there is much work to be done to ensure SEL assessments are culturally informed and fair. Importantly, fairness is a relatively new principle used in the assessment process. In the remaining pages of this chapter, we highlight several recommendations for advancing consideration of cultural fairness in SEL assessment development and use in practice.

Recommendations for SEL Assessment Developers

We provide three broad considerations for the development of culturally informed SEL assessments: (1) committing to clarity and transparency, (2) intentionally planning data collection efforts to facilitate considerations of fairness, and (3) collecting more culturally relevant data to inform a broader consideration of culture and fairness.

Clarity and Transparency Matter

One thing we noted in the process of reviewing SEL manuals was that in many cases, assessment authors' intentions regarding data were unclear. Manuals rarely specified the particular inferences, uses, decisions, or evidence that presented data were supposed to inform. We believe this lack of clarity is problematic enough when considering reliability and validity but will become worse still as assessment developers begin to include fairness-related information more routinely in test manuals. Thus, it is important to consider transparency and clarity when describing how data are supposed to be used within test manuals.

With regard to specific content to clarify, assessment developers should be specific about which steps were taken not only to examine validity and reliability evidence but also evidence of fairness (potentially based on guiding frameworks such as the CAFE model). Information about sampling efforts and the sociocultural characteristics of all samples should be included in these manuals. If certain groups are omitted from field-testing and/or standardization data collection, test developers should address how these omissions may limit generalizability, use, and interpretation of scores. Analyses regarding how items, the test, and the underlying construct function across different groups of students (e.g., by grade range, by sex, by race or ethnicity) should be reported. Such analyses may include item response theory, DIF, Differential Test Functioning, and measurement invariance testing. If subscales or scales demonstrate significant differences across groups of test-takers, guidance on interpreting scores should be provided. As most manuals can be created using digital formats, traditional constraints (e.g., paper) should be less relevant than in previous decades because test authors could append technical updates to their digital manuals. Online appendices could also provide a meaningful repository for accumulated fairness-related evidence.

Beyond clarity, transparency is also important for ensuring the trustworthiness of data presented in manuals. Thus, when possible, SEL test developers should incorporate open science practices such as making data collection efforts explicitly clear in test manuals and sharing data to promote transparency and trustworthiness in the data used to create assessments. Transparency also pertains to disclosing pertinent information about the test developers and sources of funding. Affiliations, conflicts of interest, and whether additional data or materials are available elsewhere should be clearly documented.

Be Intentional about Developing Tests with Fairness Evidence

As noted previously, currently used SEL measures have much less evidence that informs contextual fairness considerations than either procedural or consequential fairness. This is likely because contextual fairness evidence generally requires some amount of forethought and planning (e.g., focus groups including members of different cultural subgroups) and/or specialized analyses (e.g., measurement invariance testing or DIF analysis), whereas the other types of analyses are either already routine (e.g., procedural fairness focused on considerations of item reading level) or able to be interpreted from data collected for nonexplicitly fairness-related considerations (e.g., consequential fairness information generated by comparing SEL scores across boys and girls, despite the likelihood that the authors intended this as a known-group comparison validity analysis).

Designing assessments with fairness in mind will need to become one of the primary goals of the assessment development process, alongside the current emphasis on reliability and validity evidence. For example, although most normative samples are specifically designed to be nationally representative, such samples may not provide sufficient cases to conduct intensive DIF analyses, including relevant subgroups. Test development with an eye toward contextual fairness evidence may require intentional oversampling of smaller cultural subgroups where possible to allow for sufficient sample size to analyze potential bias concerns, followed by weighting procedures for national norms. Such sampling would allow fine-grained analysis of item functioning for different subgroups as well as a broad and nationally representative comparison sample. Likewise, test developers should plan to collect broad evidence to evaluate whether there are cultural differences between subgroups relevant for SEL behaviors included on particular items from the outset of test development (e.g., plan for subgroup analyses with students from different racial and ethnic subpopulations), just as they would routinely plan to collect data to inform reliability (e.g., test-retest samples) and validity (e.g., collecting various concurrent validity measures). Developing tests to inform contextual fairness evidence will necessarily be more intensive than current industry standards regarding test development, and as such, testing companies and researchers should budget and plan accordingly.

Beyond contextual fairness evidence, assessment developers should be more thoughtful about how they ensure procedural fairness, such as validating linguistic translations rather than just providing them. Consequential fairness should also be considered, such as comparing outcomes of applying recommended cut scores to score distributions across subgroups. In sum, fairness must become as central a part of test development as reliability and validity if SEL practices are to become truly culturally informed and fair.

Collect (More) Information

As evidenced by the dearth of empirical evidence bearing on fairness in currently used and recommended SEL measures, it is clear that the first step toward empirically grounded fairness in SEL assessment will be to begin routinely collecting data to inform fairness considerations. Establishing fairness evidence is an ongoing activity that begins prior to test standardization and extends beyond test publication and dissemination. From an ecological standpoint, every child represents a unique constellation of variables, such as their families, classrooms, schools, communities, and broader culture. Although it is unrealistic to expect test developers to collect and report on each of these variables during data collection, much broader data collection will be necessary to truly move toward culturally informed SEL assessment. Test developers may consider reporting on sociocultural factors, including: (1) community-level factors such as geographic region, locale, and racial/ethnic makeup; (2) school-level factors such as school type (e.g., public, charter, private religious), school size, average socioeconomic status, percentage of students receiving free or reduced lunch; (3) classroom-level factors such as class size, teacher characteristics (e.g., gender, race, ethnicity, age, years teaching, level of education); and (4) student characteristics (e.g., gender, race, ethnicity, socioeconomic status, disability status, primary language). Information about both the raters and rated students is important in considering variables that may have influenced ratings. As noted in our review of currently available measures, most fairness-related evidence is for variables that are less relevant to culture (e.g., age or gender), and future efforts for culturally fair or informed SEL assessment will have to substantially increase the amount of background data collected to inform broader considerations of cultural fairness.

Recommendations for SEL Assessment Users

We provide three broad considerations for the use of culturally informed SEL assessments in practice: (1) using the CAFE model locally, (2) involving stakeholders, and (3) linking assessments to intervention.

Use the CAFE Model Locally

The CAFE Model was not just designed for test developers. Rather, it is simply a framework intended to facilitate collecting data relevant to fairness-related questions and systematically considering those data in light of a particular proposed test score interpretation or use. The principles of procedural, contextual, and consequential fairness can and should be applied by school psychology practitioners when evaluating and selecting SEL assessments. Those in charge of selecting SEL assessments should consider the specific culture of students in their school(s), review test manuals to ensure that their school's student community is represented, and review test materials to determine (1) whether the test seems to be accessible, (2) whether the test seems relevant based on the opportunities students have had to learn the skill(s) assessed, and (3) whether the consequences of test decisions make sense for the children they serve.

Furthermore, the evaluation process portion of the framework is specifically relevant for applied practice, as practitioners are the ones who actually have to decide on particular test score interpretations or uses in schools. We encourage practitioners not to shy away from fairness-related questions, but instead to grapple with them using empirical data wherever possible. Indeed, facilitating this goal was the genesis of the CAFE model. The CAFE framework is designed to help practitioners be systematic and empirical in their consideration of fairness-relevant data and hopefully lead to better decisions that promote better outcomes for all children.

Beyond the evaluation process, there are also instances in which empirical data relevant for the evidence framework is not (and likely cannot be) provided by test publishers and local assessment users can provide it. For cultural subgroups that were not considered by test developers, assessment users can attempt to fill in the gaps of knowledge via local data. For example, with regard to contextual fairness evidence, if a practitioner works in an area in which a particular cultural subgroup that was not considered in the development of an assessment is highly represented, that practitioner might consider hosting focus groups or even distributing a survey evaluating the cultural aspects of items included in the assessment. With regard to consequential fairness, practitioners can and should examine score distributions across groups as well as implied decisions using standard cut points. The CAFE model will not dictate appropriate answers but will enable a broader consideration of potential cultural issues at play in particular SEL assessments and put reasonable constraints on appropriate use of those assessments.

Involve Stakeholders

Understanding the values and priorities of important stakeholders such as school administrators, parents/guardians, community members, and district leaders is vital to ensuring that SEL assessments are developed and used to meet the needs of different communities. This will need to occur not just during data collection to ensure contextual or procedural fairness, but throughout the assessment and intervention process. Hosting focus groups or feedback sessions with school and community members can be especially beneficial in areas with large cultural communities (e.g., ethnic enclaves) to ensure that SEL practices are aligned with the skills, behaviors, and values of community members rather than a singular dominant cultural group. These practices could include gathering input and feedback about both SEL assessments and programming. Coulehan (n.d.) outlined an excellent example of cocreating materials through authentic partnerships by including school board members from an Alaskan school district and Alaska Native community members in dialogue about *culturally responsive embedded SEL* (CRESEL). In addition, Lea et al. (2021) described how conducting focus groups about racial and ethnic equity with school and community personnel of color as well as students of color informed school-based SEL-related strategies to promote SEL development and school climate. These practices highlight ways in which stakeholders can be included in efforts to improve culturally informed SEL service delivery.

Link Assessments to Intervention

As previously noted, Cipriano and Strambler's (2025) definition of equity is used to highlight the importance of access to opportunities and resources to meet students' needs. Assessment is undoubtedly part of thorough systems of supporting the development of SEL competencies, but assessment alone cannot provide the opportunities and resources needed for equitable school-based practices. As such, it is critical that SEL assessments be linked with empirically supported intervention and prevention programs.

The importance of this feature of promoting culturally fair outcomes should be brought into clear focus by the CAFE framework's evaluation process phase. In this process, a proposed test interpretation or use is evaluated, using evidence collected in accordance with the evidence framework, regarding whether it is appropriate in general and equally appropriate across relevant subgroups. In a large number of cases, we contend that the appropriate course of action in the face of low SEL scores will be to provide support to foster SEL growth. Beyond overall evidence, the CAFE model would also point toward the use of interventions with empirical evidence that intervention effects are similar across considered subgroups (or evidence of increased efficacy with groups scoring lower on average on the SEL measures in question).

For example, if an SEL assessment team is determining how to use SEL screening data in the context of substantial procedural and contextual fairness evidence (i.e., students from all relevant subgroups can access test items and culture does not lead to major differences in the meaning of item content), but problematic consequential fairness evidence (e.g., one subgroup has substantially lower scores than another on average), the assessment team should strongly consider implementation of intervention programs to help close observed gaps. Even better than an intervention with basic empirical evidence would be one that explicitly considered cultural background as a moderator or was developed via culturally informed principles. Perhaps best of all would be an intervention with *better* evidence to help the cultural group with lower SEL scores such that implementation of the intervention would not only help develop overall skills but also close existing gaps in SEL skills across groups. This example illustrates that in a quest for appropriate and fair decision making, assessment should be linked with empirically validated intervention and prevention programs.

CONCLUSION

In general, the onus of developing and using culturally informed and fair SEL assessments is on all of us—test developers, researchers, and practitioners. Test developers should strive to (1) intentionally include contextual and cultural factors in test development and validation and (2) explicitly address how fairness and minimization of bias were incorporated into test procedures and items as well as in determining test consequences and uses. Researchers should consider what gaps exist in published assessments regarding accessibility, context, and consequences for different groups of students, and seek to establish empirical evidence in new and existing measures when using various SEL assessments with diverse groups of students. Finally, school-based practitioners should consider fairness, equity, and culture in all areas related to assessment: selection, administration, interpretation, and decision making. It is the responsibility of test consumers to carefully examine evidence of fairness to determine if a test is an appropriate fit for the populations they serve. Our collective endeavors toward creating and using culturally informed SEL assessments are in progress, but there is yet much more work to be done.

REFERENCES

American Academy of Pediatrics, American Academy of Child and Adolescent Psychiatry, & Children's Hospital Association. (2021, October 21). *AAP-AACAP-CHA declaration of a national emergency in child and adolescent mental health*. Author. *www.aap.org/en/advocacy/child-and-adolescent-healthy-mental-development/aap-aacap-cha-declaration-of-a-national-emergency-in-child-and-adolescent-mental-health*

American Educational Research Association, American Psychological Association, & National Council on Measurement in Education. (2014). *Standards for educational and psychological testing*. American Educational Research Association.

American Psychological Association. (2017). *Multicultural guidelines: An ecological approach to context, identity, and intersectionality*. Author. *www.apa.org/about/policy/multicultural-guidelines.pdf*

American Psychological Association. (2021, April 8). *Equity, diversity, and inclusion framework*. Author. *www.apa.org/about/apa/equity-diversity-inclusion/framework*

Anthony, C. J., Elliott, S. N., DiPerna, J. C., & Lei, P.-W. (2023). To be fair: Development and illustration of the comprehensive appraisal of fairness evidence (CAFE) model to advance SEL assessment practices. *Social and Emotional Learning: Research, Practice, and Policy, 1*, 100006.

Aronson, B., & Laughter, J. (2016). The theory and practice of culturally relevant education: A synthesis of research across content areas. *Review of Educational Research*, 86(1), 163–206.

Barnes, T. N., Brown, J. E., Stoffers, M., Jackson, J., Xia, Y., Wells, A. G., & Bryant, A. (2023). Increasing equity in SEL for students from marginalized populations. In K. Schonert-Reichel, M. Strambler, & S. Rimm-Kaufman (Eds.), *Social and emotional learning in action: Creating systemic change in schools* (pp. 35–52). Guilford Press.

Bronfenbrenner, U., & Morris, P. (2006). The bioecological model of human development. In W. Damon & R. M. Lerner (Eds.), *Handbook of child psychology* (Vol. 1, pp. 793–828). Wiley.

Cipriano, C., & Strambler, M. (2025). On SEL and equity. In J. Durlak, C. Domitrovich, & J. Mahoney

(Eds.), *Handbook of social and emotional learning* (2nd ed., pp. 57–70). Guilford Press.

Collaborative for Academic, Social, and Emotional Learning. (n.d.). *How does SEL support educational equity and excellence?* Author. *https://casel.org/fundamentals-of-sel/how-does-sel-support-educational-equity-and-excellence*

Coulehan, H. (n.d.). *Culturally responsive embedded social and emotional learning: A comprehensive approach to building skills for life*. Association of Alaska School Boards. *https://aasb.org/culturally-responsive-embedded-social-and-emotional-learning-a-comprehensive-approach-to-building-skills-for-life*

DiPerna, J. C., Lei, P-W., Anthony, C. J., & Elliott, S. N. (2022). Principled and practical approaches to developing SEL assessments. In J. Burros, S. H. Rikoon, & M. W. Brenneman (Eds.), *Assessing competencies for social and emotional learning: Conceptualization, development, and applications* (pp. 79–98). Routledge.

Dorans, N. J., & Cook, L. L. (Eds.). (2016). *Fairness in educational assessment and measurement*. Routledge.

DuBay, W. H. (2004, August). *The principles of readability*. *https://files.eric.ed.gov/fulltext/ED490073.pdf*

El Mallah, S. (2022). Toward equity-oriented assessment of social and emotional learning: Examining equivalence of concepts and measures. *Urban Education, 57*(2), 289–317.

Federal Interagency Forum on Child and Family Statistics. (2023). *America's children: Key national indicators of well-being, 2023. Demographic background*. *www.childstats.gov/americaschildren/demo.asp*

Fujii, D. (2016). *Conducting a culturally-informed neuropsychological evaluation*. American Psychological Association Press.

Gagnier, K. M., Okawa, A., & Jones-Manson, S. (2022, February 4). *Designing and implementing social emotional learning programs to promote equity* [White paper produced by AnLar and the Office of Elementary and Secondary Education; Education, Innovation, and Research Program (EIR)]. *https://oese.ed.gov/files/2022/03/FINAL-EIR_SEL-Programs-White-Paper.pdf*

Garner, P. W., Mahatmya, D., Brown, E. L., & Vesely, C. K. (2014). Promoting desirable outcomes among culturally and ethnically diverse children in social emotional learning programs: A multilevel heuristic model. *Educational Psychology Review, 26*(1), 165–189.

Gay, G. (2010). *Culturally responsive teaching: Theory, research, and practice* (2nd ed.). Teachers College Press.

Goforth, A. N., & Pham, A. V. (2023). *Culturally responsive school-based practices: Supporting mental health and learning of diverse students*. Oxford University Press.

Goldhaber, D., Kane, T. J., McEachin, A., & Morton, E. (2022). *A comprehensive picture of achievement across the COVID-19 pandemic years: Examining variation in test levels and growth across districts, schools, grades, and students* (Working Paper No. 265-0522). American Institutes for Research, National Center for Analysis of Longitudinal Data in Education Research. *https://eric.ed.gov/?id=ED620384*

Gross, B., & Hamilton, L. (2023, February). *Student mental health and well-being: A review of evidence and emerging solutions*. Center on Reinventing Public Education. *https://eric.ed.gov/?id=ED620384*

Hamilton, L., & Gross, B. (2021, August). *How has the pandemic affected students' social-emotional well-being? A review of the evidence to date*. Center on Reinventing Public Education. *https://files.eric.ed.gov/fulltext/ED614131.pdf*

Holman, A. R., D'Costa, S., & Janowitch, L. (2023). Toward equity in school-based assessment: Incorporating collaborative/therapeutic techniques to redistribute power. *School Psychology Review, 52*(5), 534–547.

Horn, T. C., Winkelman, E., Murthy, H., Anthony, C. J., Kozlowski, K., & Yost, M. (2025). That's valid, but let's be fair: Synthesizing fairness and validity evidence in practitioner-accessible SEL assessments. *School Psychology Review*. Advance online publication. *www.tandfonline.com/doi/full/10.1080/2372966X.2025.2532367*

Jagers, R. J., Rivas-Drake, D., & Borowski, T. (2018). *Equity and social and emotional learning: A cultural analysis*. Collaborative for Academic, Social, and Emotional Learning Assessment Work Group. *https://measuringsel.casel.org/wp-content/uploads/2018/11/Frameworks-Equity.pdf*

Jagers, R. J., Rivas-Drake, D., & Williams, B. (2019). Transformative social and emotional learning (SEL): Toward SEL in service of educational equity and excellence. *Educational Psychologist, 54*(3), 162–184.

Johnson, J. L., & Geisinger, K. F. (Eds.). (2022). *Fairness in educational and psychological testing: Examining theoretical, research, practice, and policy implications of the 2014 standards*. American Educational Research Association.

Jones, S., Farrington, C. A., Jagers, R., Brackett, M., & Kahn, J. (2019, January 15). *National commission on social, emotional, and academic development: A research agenda for the next generation*. Aspen Institute. *www.aspeninstitute.org/publications/a-research-agenda-for-the-next-generation*

Jones, T. M., Fleming, C., & Williford, A. (2020). Racial equity in academic success: The role of school climate and social emotional learning. *Children and Youth Services Review, 119*.

Kane, M. T. (2010). Validity and fairness. *Language Testing, 27*(2), 177–182.

Kendziora, K., Li, Y., & Spier, E. (2021, September). *Culturally responsive, embedded, social and emotional learning (CRESEL) in Alaska project: Final evaluation report*. American Institutes for Research. *https://files.eric.ed.gov/fulltext/ED620281.pdf*

Kurtz, K. D., Pearrow, M., Battal, J. S., Collier-Meek, M. A., Cohen, J. A., & Walker, W. (2022). Adapting social emotional learning curricula for an urban context via focus groups: Process and outcomes. *School Psychology Review, 52*(5), 548–562.

Ladson-Billings, G. (1995). Toward a theory of culturally relevant pedagogy. *American Educational Research Journal, 32*(3), 465–491.

Lea, C. H., McCowan, K. J., Jones, T. M., & Malorni, A. (2021). Adult and student perspectives on racial and ethnic equity-informed school-based strategies. *Psychology in the Schools*, 59(10), 1–20.

Lee, J., Shapiro, V. B., & Kim, B.-K. E. (2023). Universal school-based social and emotional learning (SEL) for diverse student subgroups: Implications for enhancing equity through SEL. *Prevention Science, 24*, 1011–1022.

López, S. R. (2002). Teaching culturally informed psychological assessment: Conceptual issues and demonstrations. *Journal of Personality Assessment, 79*(2), 226–234.

McCall, C. S., Romero, M. E., Yang, W., & Weigand, T. (2023). A call for equity-focused social-emotional learning. *School Psychology Review*, 52(5), 586–607.

McCallops, K., Barnes, T. N., Berte, I., Fenniman, J., Jones, I., Navon, R., & Nelson, M. (2019). Incorporating culturally responsive pedagogy within social-emotional learning interventions in urban schools: An international systematic review. *International Journal of Educational Research*, 94, 11–28.

McKown, C. (2017). Social-emotional assessment, performance, and standards. *Future of Children, 27*(1), 157–178.

McKown, C. (2019). Challenges and opportunities in the applied assessment of student social and emotional learning. *Educational Psychologist, 54*(3), 205–221.

Mercado, A., & Venta, A. (2022). *Cultural competency in psychological assessment: Working effectively with Latinx populations*. Oxford University Press.

National Association of School Psychologists. (2021). *The importance of addressing equity, diversity, and inclusion in schools: Dispelling myths about critical race theory*. Author. *www.nasponline.org/resources-and-publications/resources-and-podcasts/diversity-and-social-justice/social-justice/the-importance-of-addressing-equity-diversity-and-inclusion-in-schools-dispelling-myths-about-critical-race-theory*

Organization for Economic Co-operation and Development. (n.d.). *OECD and the sustainable development goals: Delivering on universal goals and targets*. Author. *www.oecd.org/dac/sustainable-development-goals.htm*

Osher, D., Cantor, P., Berg, J., Steyer, L., & Rose, T. (2020). Drivers of human development: How relationships and context shape learning and development. *Applied Developmental Science, 24*(1), 6–36.

Ozer, E. J., Shapiro, V. B., & Duarte, C. (2021, August). *Opportunities to strengthen SEL impact through Youth-led Participatory Action Research (YPAR)*. The Pennsylvania State University. *https://prevention.psu.edu/wp-content/uploads/2022/09/PSU-Youth-Empowerment-Brief-REV.pdf*

Pickens, I. B. (2022). Integrating a culturally responsive lens into social, emotional, and behavioral assessment within tiered decision-making frameworks. *School Psychology Review, 51*(1), 55–58.

Rowe, H. L., & Trickett, E. J. (2018). Student diversity representation and reporting in universal school-based social and emotional learning programs: Implications for generalizability. *Educational Psychology Review, 30*, 559–583.

Tai, D. B. G., Sia, I. G., Doubeni, C. A., & Wieland, M. L. (2022). Disproportionate impact of COVID-19 on racial and ethnic minority groups in the United States: A 2021 update. *Journal of Racial and Ethnic Health Disparities*, 9(6), 2334–2339.

Tanaka-Matsumi, J., Seiden, D. Y., & Lam, K. N. (1996). The culturally informed functional assessment (CIFA) interview: A strategy for cross-cultural behavioral practice. *Cognitive and Behavioral Practice*, 3(2), 215–233.

West, M. R., Pier, L., Fricke, H., Hough, H., Loeb, S., Meyer, R. H., & Rice, A. B. (2020). Trends in student social-emotional learning: Evidence from the first large-scale panel student survey. *Educational Evaluation and Policy Analysis, 42*(2), 279–303.

Winkelman, E., Yost, M., Alfonso, Z., Kozlowski, K., Horn, T. C., & Anthony, C. J. (2023, February). *A systematic review of commonly recommended SEL assessments* [Paper presentation]. National Association of School Psychologists Annual Convention, Denver, CO, United States.

CHAPTER 26

Early Childhood Assessment

Rachel Stein and Kizzy Albritton

According to the Federal Interagency Forum on Child and Family Statistics (2023), there were approximately 22 million children 0 to 5 years old in the United States in 2022. Among this population, approximately 10–15% of preschool-age children may present with one or more developmental delays or disabilities (Choo et al., 2019), and 20% of children under 7 years old may experience social–emotional challenges (Vasileva et al., 2021). Given the potentially large numbers of young children with delays and disabilities, early detection is an important step toward mitigation and early intervention. Specifically, when identification and diagnosis are timely, young children more quickly access support and intervention that is associated with long-term benefits, including more positive long-term education, health, and mental health indicators (Lovett et al., 2017; Sandler, 2019; Sansavini et al., 2021).

Assessment in early childhood poses several challenges that are essential to consider in order to accurately identify young children's needs. First, it is important to note that there is a large degree of variability in which young children may reach developmental milestones, and some level of difficulty with social–emotional regulation is developmentally appropriate for this age group. Second, assessment tools that are isolated from a young child's day-to-day experience (e.g., adaptive skills that they have not practiced, tasks that are culturally irrelevant in the family environment where they spend time) often do not yield helpful information. Third, young children are still developing communication skills that professionals often rely on (e.g., self-reports of affective experiences) as part of a comprehensive assessment. Given the complexities in development among young children and mounting evidence indicating the benefits associated with assessing for and identifying neurodevelopmental conditions and mental health needs during the early developmental period, it is necessary to utilize an assessment approach that provides contextualized information about a young child's functional skills through a family-centered and culturally relevant frame.

Despite both the known prevalence rates of early childhood neurodevelopmental and mental health needs and the benefits of early service provision, the rates of children receiving services are not commensurate (e.g., Finkelhor et al., 2021; Macy et al., 2014). Furthermore, there are known disparities in whose needs are identified early, with some groups of minoritized and/or marginalized children less likely to be referred for services and subsequently receive early identification (Angell et al., 2018; Durkin et al., 2017). For example, although there has been a significant increase in prevalence rates of autism spectrum disorder (ASD) over the last decade, African American and Latinx children are often less likely to be diagnosed when compared to White peers (Angell et al., 2018). Although there are a variety of reasons why needs and services are not aligned, including limited access to quality services and lack of Spanish-speaking service providers, assessment processes are a crucial consideration. How and where young children are assessed, and whether the assessment considers both individual identity factors and context, are all crucial. In this chapter, the term *young children* will be used to refer to children between the ages of 0 and 8 years old, and the term *early childhood* will be used to refer to the developmental time frame for this population of children.

This chapter will explore several key areas of early childhood assessment. First, theoretical frameworks specific to the early childhood period will be discussed. Second, we will orient the reader to the various settings in which early childhood assessments occur. Third, we will discuss approaches to early childhood assessment, including unique features, special considerations, and best practices, particularly when working with young children and families from historically marginalized and minoritized backgrounds. Last, future directions for early childhood assessment are explored. Throughout each section we will integrate information about culturally responsive approaches to assessing young children, as this is an overarching theme, meriting discussion as part of each topic raised.

THEORETICAL FRAMEWORKS TO CONSIDER DURING EARLY CHILDHOOD ASSESSMENT

Understanding a young child's development may be the most critical first step and component when conducting an early childhood assessment. As such, it is necessary to apply a developmental theoretical framework that is applicable to young children and the multiple and varying systems in which they interact. Although a comprehensive discussion of all frameworks examining early childhood development is beyond the scope of this chapter, there are two particular frameworks that are most applicable: Bronfenbrenner's (1994) ecological framework and García Coll et al.'s (1996) integrative model of child development for minority youth. What follows is a brief discussion of each framework.

Within Bronfenbrenner's (1994) ecological approach, the focus is not merely on the child but instead on the environment and the incongruity between the child and the environment. Bronfenbrenner (1994) characterized these environments as "nested structures," often referred to as the microsystem, mesosystem, exosystem, and macrosystem. *Microsystems* are often defined as the most immediate settings, activities, and interpersonal relationships that an individual engages with. For young children, the microsystem is often family members and other daily caretakers, such as child care providers or early childhood teachers if the child is participating in an early childhood education program. The *mesosystem* is the interrelationship between two or more settings that have a direct impact on the individual's development. In the case of young children, this interrelationship is between the child's home setting and school setting (i.e., early childhood classroom or day care center). The *exosystem* is also the interrelationship between two or more settings; however, there is an indirect influence on the individual. Examples include the interrelationship between the child's home setting and the parent's work setting. Last, the *macrosystem* "consists of the overarching pattern of micro-, meso-, and exosystems characteristic of a given culture or subculture" (Bronfenbrenner, 1994, p. 40). Development in the early years is often complex and rarely follows a linear path; therefore, it is necessary to have a clear understanding of each level of the child's environment since doing so will increase our knowledge and ability to successfully assess the child's needs and address those needs. Ultimately, children are bound to their environments, and assessment of the child cannot be separated from the environment (Morse, 1993).

While Bronfenbrenner's (1994) ecological framework is an important first step, it is also necessary to utilize a theoretical framework that attends to the systemic and structural barriers impacting the development of young children from racially and ethnically minoritized backgrounds, particularly given the increasing racial and ethnic diversity of early childhood populations. García Coll et al.'s (1996) integrative model for the study of developmental competencies in minority children was one of the first models to examine constructs that were specific to children of color. In this model, García Coll et al. (1996) address the need to (1) closely examine constructs and experiences that uniquely influence the development of children of color and (2) closely examine the constructs and experiences that influence the development of *all* children but may differentially impact children from racially and/or ethnically minoritized backgrounds. Furthermore, García Coll et al. (1996) argue the importance of social position and how "the effect of social position is mediated through the pervasive social mechanisms of racism, prejudice, discrimination, and oppression" (p. 1895). As a result, young children of color may have extremely limited access to certain resources or opportunities that directly impact their developmental competencies. For example, Ewen and Herzfeldt-Kamprath (2016) found that access to high-quality early childhood programs was a twofold challenge for Black children in that they are the least likely to have access to high-quality early childhood programs and the most likely to be enrolled in low-quality early childhood programs. This social position of limited access to high-quality early childhood settings further increases the opportunity gap between young Black children and their same-age peers. In summary, a young child's development does not occur in a vacuum but instead is highly influenced by the systems they interact with each day. Theoretical frameworks such as the ecological model (Bronfenbrenner, 1994) and the integrative model (García Coll et al., 1996) provide the necessary foundation to accurately understand the myriad of influences on early childhood development and are a prerequisite to understanding when and if a child is not meeting developmental expectations.

EARLY CHILDHOOD ASSESSMENT SETTINGS

Early childhood assessment takes place in a variety of settings that may vary depending on the purpose of the assessment, the source of the referral, the type of concern, or access to assessment. Although there is variability in the types of settings, these settings can be broadly categorized as educational settings and noneducational settings. For example, early childhood assessments that take place in pediatric primary care, private evaluation settings, or specialized clinical settings (e.g., autism evaluations through a clinic at a children's hospital) would be categorized as noneducational settings. Instead, evaluations that take place in school settings (e.g., through preschool special education) would be categorized as educational settings. Each setting may have different objectives, resources, and systemic constraints that change the nature of the assessment. In the following sections, we offer a discussion of the two broad categorizations. Throughout this chapter the terms *assessment* and *evaluation* are both used to describe the process of determining a young child's needs, although evaluation is frequently the term used in educational statutes.

Noneducational Settings

Pediatric Primary Care

It is recommended that pediatric primary care providers regularly screen young children for developmental concerns and provide follow-up recommendations (e.g., a referral to Child Find) when indicated by the screening process (Hagan et al., 2017), although data suggest that only about a third of providers do so (Hirai et al., 2018). Although physicians are a frequent source of referrals, particularly to educationally based Child Find services (Barger et al., 2018), referrals themselves are not equitable, and some families are referred for concerns more readily than others. Research has explored a variety of factors that appear to contribute to whether and when a family is referred for follow-up related to development or mental health concerns for a young child. Families who are economically marginalized, from minoritized backgrounds, have less education, and/or speak a primary language other than English are less likely to be referred for assessment than families without these characteristics (Morgan et al., 2012). Numerous studies have documented that a range of systemic and interpersonal challenges result in disparities in referrals, assessments, and service provision for children from culturally and linguistically diverse backgrounds. As this pertains to assessment it is particularly important that providers are attuned to their own biases; recognize how differences in culture, context, and experience influence development and disability; and understand how few assessment tools are appropriate for accurately evaluating culturally and linguistically diverse children (Huerta et al., 2021; Sapiets et al., 2021).

Private Practice: Licensed Mental Health Provider

Early childhood assessments may occur in the office or practice of an appropriately licensed individual, most often a psychologist or psychiatrist. Of the types of assessments that a young child might participate in, assessments that take place in a private practice setting typically have the fewest constraints. In a private practice setting, evaluators usually work with families to understand the presenting concerns and administer any assessment tools they believe are most appropriate. Following the administration of assessment measures, the assessor will typically write an extensive report and may provide a *Diagnostic and Statistical Manual of Mental Disorders, Fifth Edition, Text Revision* (DSM-5-TR; American Psychiatric Association, 2022) diagnosis and recommendations when appropriate. Outside of any state regulations around their professional practice, the limitations around assessments in the private practice setting tend to be pragmatic. For instance, not all private practice evaluators are willing or able to observe a child with their peers, and frequently assessments only take place within an office setting. Additionally, while private practice assessments may be paid for by insurance, they are often paid for by the family seeking services and can be costly. In addition to the cost, private practices are more likely to be clustered in urban and suburban areas, which also limits access for some families and communities.

Clinic-Based Practices

In some instances, early childhood assessments may take place in clinic-based practices, such as those housed within children's hospitals or other specialized pediatric settings. Clinic-based assessments often have a focus or specialty, such as feeding and eating assessments, developmental assessments, or autism spectrum assessments. When a child presents with a concern that aligns with a specific type of clinic, they may be referred to that clinic for assessment. For example, the most common scenario involving a clinic-based assessment is when a child with autism-like behaviors is referred to a clinic that focuses on ASD assessment. Oftentimes, assessments in clinic settings are multidisciplinary, including evaluations and feedback from several types of providers. For instance, a psychologist, physician, speech and language pathologist, and developmental specialist might all be involved in the information gathering process and synthesis. Although clinic-based assessments frequently include multimodal information gathering, they typically take place in an office setting. As a result, they rarely include observations or gather information from other places or providers (e.g., child care setting, early childhood teacher), beyond what is self-reported by a parent or caregiver. Once the assessment is complete, providers will typically write a report summarizing their assessment and may include a DSM-5-TR diagnosis when appropriate. Oftentimes, insurance or other medical coverage will pay for clinic-based assessments, although these can be very difficult to access due to scarcity and long wait-lists.

Educational Settings

Under the Individuals with Disabilities Education Act (IDEA, 2004), states are mandated to ensure that very young children with delays and disabilities are "identified, located, and evaluated" (Sec 300.111 & Sec 303.302). For children 0 to 3 years old this falls under IDEA Part C, and for children 3 years old and older, this falls under the statutes of IDEA Part B (IDEA, 2004). Although legally anyone may make a referral to Child Find, physicians are the most common referral source in early childhood (Barger, 2018).

IDEA Part C statutes dictate that assessments for children 0 to 3 years old must be conducted by qualified personnel using multidisciplinary approaches to assess a child's strengths and needs. Additionally, the family's "resources, priorities, and concerns" (Sec. 1436) must be included in the assessments. The law further stipulates that assessments must be nondiscriminatory and, whenever feasible, conducted in the child's native language. There are several ways that a child 0 to 3 years old might be found eligible for services. First, states can set their own list of auto-eligibility categories, such as medically diagnosed congenital conditions that qualify a child without an assessment (Sec. 303.321 [3][i]). Second, a delay can be established, with states setting their own criteria for the degree of delay required, in one or more of the five federally outlined domains: cognitive, adaptive, social–emotional, physical, and communication (Sec. 303.321 [a]). Last, informed clinical opinion may also be used to determine eligibility in some states, as long as it does not negate the results from other assessment methods.

IDEA Part B governs children over 3 years old, with IDEA Part B 619 focused specifically on preschool special education. Assessments under IDEA Part B must use a variety of tools and information sources to establish whether the child has a disability, as well as its educational impact. For preschool-age children, the educational impact may include having an effect on the child's ability to participate in age-appropriate activities (IDEA Sec. 1414 [b] [2]), a broader definition than just examining educational outcomes (e.g., grades, standardized scores). The eligibility categories outlined under IDEA Part B include 12 different categories (specific learning disability, intellectual disability, hearing impairment, speech or language impairment, visual impairment, serious emotional disturbance, orthopedic impairment, autism, traumatic brain injury, other health impairment, deaf-blindness, or multiple disabilities) that states may elect to use or combine into categories that capture the same needs (IDEA Sec. 300.8 [a]). IDEA (Sec. 300.111 [b]) also specifies that a developmental delay is an optional designation that states may use as Part B criteria for determining eligibility for children ages 3 through 9 or a more restrictive age range within that, which varies due to state-level educational statutes.

Given the evaluation and eligibility criteria outlined under IDEA, assessments that take place as part of educational evaluations for either IDEA Part C or Part B follow certain stipulations that may vary from assessments in other settings. First, educationally based assessments typically have a more narrowly defined goal than the other types of assessments previously described. Second, educationally based assessments are multidisciplinary and involve multiple professionals who investigate across potential areas of concern. However, the most frequently involved professionals are early childhood special educators and speech and language pathologists; medical professionals or psychologists are rarely involved (Stein & Steed, 2023). Last, state guidelines around eligibility criteria may dictate, at least in part, what types of assessment tools are used. For example, if a state requires a standard deviation from the mean to determine the delay criteria under IDEA Part C, then teams may be confined to certain standardized assessment options.

CONCEPTUALIZING AND CONDUCTING EARLY CHILDHOOD ASSESSMENTS

Best practices suggest that the purpose of assessing a young child, or the referral concern, should guide the assessment. For example, if a child is referred due to concerns around social interactions with other children, the assessment should include observing the child with peers as well as gathering reports about the child's competency with peers. There may also be variations in the approach to assessment, depending on the setting where the assessment will take place (e.g., educational environment, private practice) and related systemic regulations. For most of the aforementioned providers, assessments are conducted to determine the extent to which a child may be experiencing neurodevelopmental and/or mental health challenges. Relatedly, assessments frequently aim to ascertain the type of support or intervention that may help the young child mitigate challenges or remediate missing skills. Early childhood assessment shares some similarities with assessment more broadly in that most states require the administration of a standardized (e.g., norm-referenced) measure when seeking to determine if a young child needs additional support, either through state-level early intervention programs or early childhood special education programs. And while there has been an increase in the type and number of standardized assessment measures available, the assessment of young children—particularly young children from racially and ethnically minoritized backgrounds and economically marginalized backgrounds—is more complex than just administering an assessment measure. Indeed, there are several elements of early childhood assessment that are unique or warrant special consideration.

The first consideration is the recommended practices for early childhood assessment outlined by the Division for Early Childhood (DEC, 2014), an organization devoted to providing support for families and young children with or at risk for developmental delays and disabilities. Although these broadly align with what is stipulated under IDEA's statutes for early childhood assessment, they are more specific and apply across practice settings. It is important to highlight that the DEC recommendations are very family-focused, including emphasizing the role of the family and articulating assessment preferences as well as providing information as part of the assessment. The DEC recommendations are also comprehensive, indicating the importance of multimodal assessment, including thinking about the materials, approaches, and sources of information that are included. Last, the DEC recommendations acknowledge the importance of thinking about culture and language when conducting an appropriate assessment, including using a child's primary language and assessing in other languages when relevant.

de Sam Lazaro (2017) expanded on the DEC recommendations, emphasizing the importance of authentic assessment and the triangulation of multiple types of information to draw meaningful and culturally appropriate conclusions from early childhood assessments. Furthermore, Garro (2016) outlined four tenets that individuals should consider when conducting early childhood assessment, and these tenets are consistent with the recommended practices outlined by the DEC. The first tenet highlights the need to evaluate children, specifically young children, in relation to the circumstances, settings, and other environmental factors that may impact their development. This is crucial given the many ways in which circumstances, settings, and environmental factors can impact development. The second tenet discusses the need to collaborate with and gather input from family members, educators, and other health professionals (e.g., pediatricians) who may hold valuable information regarding the child's functioning. The third tenet focuses on the need for flexibility, as adjustments may be needed during the assessment process, depending on the child's needs. The fourth and final tenet suggests that the assessment process should be dynamic and include multiple data points. In the following sections, we provide an expanded and integrated discussion of the most pertinent practices and tenets when conceptualizing and conducting early childhood assessments.

Developmental Considerations

An overarching element or theme in early childhood assessment is the need to understand the developmental process and the extent to which the pace of early development may influence assessment results. Early childhood is a time of rapid growth and development (National Research Council, 2000). Indeed, young children show incredible growth in acquiring skills across domains, including language, cognitive, emotional, and social development. Skill acquisition across developmental domains helps to prepare the foundation for later functioning and the acquisition of more advanced abilities. For instance, young children move from not understanding or speaking language at birth to often speaking one or more languages with basic competency by around 3 years old (Saletta & Windsor, 2019), usually without intentional instruction. At other points in life, we do see developmental progress, but at a much slower rate.

Human brains change and grow over a long period of time, with early childhood being a time of particularly profound change (Berens & Nelson, 2019). During early childhood, the brain is thought to be particularly "plastic" or able to change, often called *neuroplasticity* (Berens & Nelson, 2019). Additionally, early childhood includes *sensitive periods*, points in development where the brain is primed to learn certain skills or competencies. For instance, the absence of learning any type of language during the early years of development is known to impact language fluency across the lifespan (Berens & Nelson, 2019) because the brain is sensitive or primed for language learning during early development.

Although development is often thought of as a continuous process over time, the reality is that development is discontinuous, with times of more rapid and slower growth (Karasik & Robinson, 2022). Thus, a child assessed before, during, after, or in between periods of rapid development may result in dramatically different findings and conclusions. Recognizing that early childhood assessment is often a snapshot of developmental progress at a specific moment in time is essential to effectively characterize assessment findings and their meaning.

Even though there are natural variations in the pace of development during early childhood, individual progress and growth may be influenced by a variety of factors, including environment, physical and health conditions, and delays and disabilities. For young children from racially and/or ethnically minoritized backgrounds and young children from economically marginalized backgrounds, development may also be impacted by systemic and structural barriers such as limited access to health care, limited access to high-quality child care or early childhood education settings, and food or housing insecurity. Thus, although we can establish broad patterns of developmental progression, individual variation should be expected (Karasik & Robinson, 2022). Additionally, although development is often thought of as a commonly shared human experience, it is heavily influenced by context, including cultural views around young children and what they can do at various points in development. For example, in cultures where young children are more physically confined as infants, motor milestones are typically met later than the "normative" standardized measures, yet these children generally show no long-term delays or consequences from this slower developmental timeline (Karasik & Robinson, 2022).

Understanding early childhood development is essential to accurately assessing a young child. Yet there are clear challenges when trying to effectively understand all of the factors that influence development and to identify instances when a delay may require further evaluation or lead to intervention. As noted previously, adopting a theoretical framework for early childhood development is a critical first step. Both an ecological framework (Bronfenbrenner, 1994) and an integrative model (García Coll et al., 1996) allow individuals to consider all aspects of the environment that the child is embedded within, including familial relationships, community expectations, and cultural values and beliefs. In addition, assessments must consider both normative ranges for developmental progression, as well as exploring why a child might progress at a differential rate to understand when something might be considered outside of the realm of what is expected or when intervention might be beneficial (Karasik & Robinson, 2022).

Screening

Developmental screening is understood to be an important way to identify concerns early and is a practice that has become more common (Radecki et al., 2011). In particular, early education and pediatric settings have increased their use of surveillance and screening to detect young children's concerns (Pizur-Barnekow et al., 2010; Radecki et al., 2011). Ultimately, the goal of screening is to have predictive validity to identify children who will benefit from subsequent assessment and intervention. Cairney et al. (2021) studied the question of whether universal preschool assessment was helpful in identifying later academic challenges. They found that measures that examined a child's developmental progress, particularly the Ages and Stages Questionnaire (ASQ; Squires & Bricker, 2009), alongside teachers' ratings and a developmental history, were the most predictive of later academic challenges (Cairney et al., 2021).

Screening and surveillance may be particularly important for the early identification of children from economically vulnerable families and those from culturally and linguistically diverse backgrounds who are less likely to get connected to early childhood assessment services (Durkin et al., 2010). Developmental screening provides data to identify young children in need of follow-up in a timely manner (Rispoli et al., 2021) and is most likely to happen in pediatric medical settings (Lipkin et al., 2020). However, early education settings and clinical settings may also be appropriate locations for screening (Shahidullah et al., 2020). When young children are screened, the goal is to determine who may benefit from a comprehensive assessment; it is not meant to replace additional information gathering (Radecki et al., 2011).

Various screening tools are available to examine young children's concerns, but the tools need to be both specific enough to identify concerns and sensitive enough to detect them (Radecki et al., 2011). Screening tools are typically designed to either broadly evaluate development or look more narrowly for signs of a specific disability, most often ASD (e.g., Modified checklist for autism in toddlers, revised with follow-up [M-CHAT-R/F]; Robins et al., 2009). Although screening tools vary in their administration, they are often short and may be completed by various individuals who know the child well. Many commonly used screening measures are also available in multiple languages. Table 26.1 provides additional information regarding screening and assessment measures that are frequently used when working in noneducational and educational settings.

Multimodal and Authentic Assessment

There are several widely endorsed best practices in early childhood assessment, including relying on multiple types of information (e.g., observation and standardized tools), emphasizing authentic assessment, incorporating all key caregivers, and including multiple settings where a young child spends time. Historically, most assessments relied on conventional assessment tools, or those types of assessment tools that examined whether a child was able to perform a specific task in a specific situation (e.g., point to which object corresponded to a verbally presented word; Pretti-Frontczak et al., 2023). However, not surprisingly, conventional assessment is not always effective in identifying a child's functional needs in day-to-day lived situations and is particularly problematic for children from some linguistically and racially minoritized backgrounds (de Sam Lazaro, 2017). This has led to an emphasis on authentic assessment as a best practice in effective early childhood evaluation.

Authentic assessment refers to information that is gathered about "naturally occurring behaviors and functional competencies of young children in daily routines by familiar and knowledgeable caregivers in the child's life" (Bagnato & Ho, 2006, p. 7). Under the umbrella of authentic assessments are tools that rely on observations and reports about a child's skills and abilities for routine activities in the environments where they spend time (Neisworth & Bagnato, 2004). Given that many forms of conventional assessment have limited evidence bases to support their use with young children, particularly those with disabilities (Bagnato et al., 2014; Neisworth & Bagnato, 2004), authentic assessment is meant to better align the determination of a child's contextualized

TABLE 26.1. Sample of Commonly Used Early Childhood Assessment Measures

Tool Name	Purpose	Age Range	Languages Available[a]
	Screening Tools		
Ages and Stages Questionnaire (ASQ; Squires & Bricker, 2009).	Screen for delays in gross motor, fine motor, communication, problem solving, and personal-social skills	1–66 months	English, Arabic, Chinese, French, Spanish, Vietnamese
Ages and Stages Questionnaire Social Emotional (ASQ-SE; Squires et al., 2002)	Screen for delays in social–emotional development, specifically self-regulation, compliance, social communication, adaptive functioning, autonomy, affect, and interactions	1–72 months	English, Arabic, French, Spanish
Modified Checklist for Autism in Toddlers, Revised with Follow Up (M-Chat-R/F; Robins et al., 2009)	Autism spectrum disorder screening	16–30 months	Approx. 70 languages
Brief Infant-Toddler Social and Emotional Assessment (BITSEA; Briggs-Gowan & Carter, 2006)	Screen for social–emotional delays and concerns	12–36 months	English, Dutch, Japanese, Spanish
	Standardized Assessment Tools		
Bayley Scales of Infant and Toddler Development (Bayley & Aylward, 2019)	Measures development in cognitive, language, motor, social–emotional and adaptive skills	1–42 months	English
Batelle Developmental Inventory-3 (BDI; Newborg, 2020)	Measures development in adaptive, personal-social, communication, motor, and cognitive development	12 months to 13 years	English, Spanish
Developmental Assessment of Young Children (2nd ed.) (DAYC-2; Voress et al., 2012)	Identifies possible delays in cognitive, communication, social–emotional, physical, and adaptive behavior	Birth to 5 years	
Wechsler Preschool and Primary Scale of Intelligence (4th ed.) (WPPSI-IV; Wechsler, 2012)	Depending on the age of the child assessed, provides full scale and index scales related to a child's cognitive functioning	2:6–7:7 years	Spanish, French, German, Italian, Swedish, Korean, Taiwanese, Japanese, Canadian, Australian, Dutch, Hebrew
Differential Ability Scale–II Early Years (DAS-II; Elliott, 2012)	Measures cognitive abilities and specific learning processes in verbal and nonverbal reasoning, and spatial abilities	2:6–6 years	English, Spanish
Behavior Assessment System for Children (3rd ed.) (BASC-3; Reynolds & Kamphaus, 2015)	Measures behavior and emotional functioning	2–21 years	English, Spanish
Autism Diagnostic Observation Schedule (2nd ed.) (ADOS-2; Lord et al., 2012)	Examines social, imagination, and communication skills to diagnose autism spectrum disorder	12 months and up	
Transdisciplinary Play-Based Assessment (2nd ed.) (TPBA-2; Linder, 2008)	Through observations of play measures sensorimotor, social–emotional, communication, and cognitive development	Birth to 6 years	

[a] Language data are shared based on available information from the assessment tool's publisher.

needs with intervention. Bagnato et al. (2014) examined perceptions related to three authentic assessment tools and found that when compared to conventional assessments, authentic assessment tools were ranked more highly for their authenticity, collaboration, multifactored approach (i.e., information across multiple settings, people, and timepoints using multiple methods), universality, and overall utility. Bagnato et al. (2014) produced several recommendations that are relevant to discussing early childhood assessment in the present context, including focusing on the use of assessment tools that are organized around developmental sequence and functional skills.

Even when using authentic assessment tools, it is essential to contextualize the information that is gathered. It is easy to conflate variations in familial culture and child-rearing practices with delays and disabilities. For example, caregivers may emphasize practicing some skills over others, which can make it hard to differentiate delays that are problematic from those that a child might independently make progress on (Karasik & Robinson, 2022). Standardized conventional assessments in particular are not well suited to differentiating identity related to developmental trends from delays and disabilities. Observations and caregiver information are the best ways to gather information about a child's current functioning and areas of challenge within a context that considers the multitude of factors that can influence development.

Eight principles have been proposed to ensure that authentic assessments are feasible, developmentally appropriate, and center parent-professional partnerships (Neisworth & Bagnato, 2004). Specifically, these eight principles are (1) utility, ensuring that assessments lead to intervention; (2) acceptability, relying on tools that have an agreed-on social worth; (3) using authentic methods and contexts; (4) relying on methods that are equitable and adaptable for individual children; (5) relying on tools with sufficient sensitivity to detect concerns; (6) triangulating data from multiple sources; (7) centering collaboration and parent participation; and (8) using assessment measures that have been tested and normed with a sample that is appropriate for the child being evaluated.

Culturally and Linguistically Responsive Assessment Teams

Best practices in assessment emphasize the use of culturally and linguistically responsive evaluators, including bilingual and culturally representative professionals whenever possible. Although there are benefits to having evaluators who are linguistically and culturally aligned with a family, given that the early childhood assessment workforce largely identifies as White and English speaking (Bureau of Labor Statistics, U.S. Department of Labor, 2018), it is necessary to rely on other practices to ensure valid and fair assessment for racially and linguistically minoritized children. Indeed, IDEA Section 1414 b[3] states that evaluations must be "provided and administered in the language and form most likely to yield accurate information" and be "administered by trained and knowledgeable personnel."

Despite known challenges around implementing best practices (e.g., access to appropriate language supports) when evaluating culturally and linguistically minoritized young children, suggested practices are clear. First, whenever possible, teams should include bilingual and culturally representative personnel. Second, selected assessment tools should be validated for their intended purpose, including being normed to account for cultural and linguistic differences. Third, assessment teams must remain family-centered when evaluating culturally and linguistically minoritized children and learn about a family's language, child rearing, and cultural practices as they pertain to the evaluation. Relatedly, assessment teams must consider the family's concerns and priorities for their child. Finally, when appropriate or necessary, assessment teams should adapt assessment materials or engage in practices such as "testing the limits" to accurately understand a child's strengths and weaknesses, even when it means deviating from standardized evaluation procedures.

Prior research has found that while many early childhood assessment teams use some foundational-level culturally and linguistically responsive practices, such as providing an interpreter or learning about a family's home language practices, fewer evaluators use more sophisticated best practices (Steed et al., 2023). For instance, Steed et al. (2023) found that most evaluators did not use assessment tools that were validated for bilingual children or adapt assessment instruments when evaluating a child who speaks a language other than English. Therefore, evaluators must be more intentional about implementing best practices when evaluating culturally and linguistically minoritized young children and should be careful not to assume that all prior assessments were conducted in a way that accurately represents a child's skills.

FUTURE DIRECTIONS

Over the last decade we have observed significant improvements in the assessment of young children, but there is still a need for additional growth. We argue that emerging research and future directions for best practices in evaluating young children can be divided into (1) the need for professionals with specialized training and knowledge in early childhood assessment; (2) the development of additional assessment measures for racially, culturally, and linguistically diverse populations; and (3) the need for alignment and coordination of integrated early childhood systems.

First, although the last two decades have seen an increase in the number of programs supporting and providing services to young children and their families (Friedman-Kraus et al., 2023), there is still a dearth of professionals with specific training and expertise in working with young children (Early Childhood Personnel Center, 2022b). Relatedly, early childhood professionals frequently do not demographically mirror the populations of children they serve (Early Childhood Personnel Center, 2022a). Second, standardized assessment measures and procedures for young children are not often culturally and linguistically responsive. Third, early childhood systems are poorly integrated and confusing to navigate. This is especially problematic for families who are culturally and linguistically marginalized, limiting their access to assessment and support. The lack of integrated systems has been further impacted by the COVID-19 pandemic (Centers for Disease Control and Prevention, 2023) and other sociocultural influences that have added access barriers to early childhood assessments. Each of these challenges, as well as future directions, is explored in more detail in the following.

Specialized Training and Knowledge

Effective early childhood assessment requires specialized knowledge and training, including recognizing the role of development and context, as described previously. Yet there is some evidence that professionals do not always have the requisite training that would allow them to implement best practices in early childhood assessment (Albritton et al., 2018). In a survey examining the graduate preparation of school psychologists to work in early childhood settings, approximately 44% of respondents indicated receiving only "a little" training with many reporting that they ultimately learned about the role once they were working with young children rather than it being a part of their graduate school training (e.g., building the plane while also flying the plane; Albritton et al. 2018). This lack of requisite training is evidenced by the limited focus of early childhood populations in school psychology coursework. For example, Stein and Albritton (2022) found that of the 48 syllabi submitted by school psychology programs, only 20 syllabi included a focus on assessment of early childhood populations. Furthermore, there was a significant level of variability in the number of class sessions in which early childhood assessment was discussed, with an average of just five sessions.

The lack of specialized training and knowledge regarding early childhood populations broadly, and early childhood assessment specifically, may prevent young children from receiving assessments from professionals such as school psychologists who have expertise regarding their unique development. School psychologists are credentialed to provide early childhood services in over half of the states across the United States (Stein & Albritton, 2022), and as our understanding of the importance of early recognition and intervention increases, it is essential that early childhood assessment personnel have the knowledge and skills to be effective in identifying young children's needs. This includes ensuring that school psychology training programs provide requisite knowledge (Albritton et al., 2018; Stein & Albritton, 2022) as well as a comprehensive understanding of culturally responsive assessment practices for young children (NASP, 2023). Additionally, school psychologists must be actively employed and have full participation in early childhood assessment settings and teams (NASP, 2023).

The Need for Culturally and Linguistically Valid Early Childhood Assessment Tools

It is essential that early childhood assessment measures continue to evolve so that they are valid for diverse individuals, including racially, culturally, and linguistically minoritized young children and their families. Historically, early childhood assessment tools have not focused sufficient attention on considering how results may be influenced by linguistic and identity characteristics of young children. Nonetheless, research has documented disproportionality in early childhood special education for children from historically minoritized backgrounds (Ayala, 2023). Although there are a multitude of reasons for disproportionality in early childhood special education, assessment measures and processes are one important consideration.

Historically, many of the assessment measures available to assess young children were outdated and did not include representative norming samples. More recently some assessments have been updated (e.g., the Bayley Scales of Infant and Toddler Development [Bayley & Aylward, 2019] were updated in 2019), whereas others still in use have not been updated for many years (e.g., the Mullen Scales of Early Learning are from 1995), leaving room for further updates and consideration of whether the norms being used are still relevant. Additionally, many of the existing assessment measures are available in a limited number of languages or may lack consideration of how culture can influence a child's performance. For example, Karasik and Robinson (2022) explored motor development and standardized assessment and concluded that although normed tools have a clinical utility, too often they focus on when motor skills should emerge rather than how they emerge. For children from families where cultural practices accelerate or delay motor development, this may skew results based on caregiving practices rather than providing information about whether a child may benefit from intervention. Indeed, research has found that assessments are more reliable and valid in indicating a young child's needs when both parents and professionals work collaboratively (Neisworth & Bagnato, 2004).

Early Childhood Systems

As described previously, there are a variety of potential settings (e.g., educational settings, private practices, clinics) where a young child might seek and receive an assessment, each with different goals, professionals, and resources. A result of not having an integrated system is that early childhood assessments are frequently confusing to access, and families often do not understand the differences in the types of assessments they might seek. The challenges regarding the lack of a federally coordinated early childhood system have been highlighted by several researchers (Barger et al., 2018; Barger et al., 2019; Macy et al., 2014). In a systematic review examining studies seeking to link young children and families to IDEA Part C services, Barger et al. (2018) found that although there are federal regulations regarding the need to actively identify children who may require early intervention or early childhood special education (i.e., Child Find), state-level interpretation of the federal regulations varies tremendously. Whereas some states have chosen to systematically monitor the development of *all* children, other states have chosen to only focus on those children who are deemed as high risk. Barger et al. (2018) posit that these variations may result in two states potentially having the same number and types of conditions in which early intervention services are needed but differ drastically in the proportion of children who actually receive services, given the targeted population of the state (i.e., all children versus children deemed as high risk).

Research has also documented that racially minoritized families, families with lower levels of education, and those in rural areas are less able to access evaluation services (Thomas et al., 2007). Quebles et al. (2022) specifically explored how systems of care impacted Latinx mothers' experiences seeking assessment and intervention services for their young children and found that most families did have a positive experience, but there were also many instances where they experienced long delays and struggled to get convenient appointments. The research conducted by Quebles et al. (2022) took place in California, where early childhood assessments are conducted through regional centers, which serve as a hub. It is possible that this hub approach mitigated some of the challenges that families may have otherwise faced due to the centralization of services. Until there is a federally coordinated early childhood system, it is urgent that states continue to think about ways to integrate systems in an effort to ease access challenges for families to seek evaluation and support.

CONCLUSION

Early childhood assessment shares several features with best practices in assessments more generally (e.g., using multiple data sources), but it is also distinct from assessing older individuals. Specifically, the rapid pace of development, the importance of context and caregivers, the variety of settings where early childhood assessment takes place, and the potential to misunderstand the role of identity and caregiving on young children are all essential features of accurate assessment in early childhood. When assessing a young child, it is important to let the referral concern guide assessment choices; to collaborate with families and caregivers to understand their child-rearing practices, priorities, and concerns; and to emphasize information gathering and the use of multimodal and authentic assessment tools. Even though there are equity-related concerns around who has access to early childhood assessment, when young children are able to access a thoughtful, well-designed assessment, it has the potential to promote early intervention, thereby improving short- and long-term outcomes for the children and their families.

REFERENCES

Albritton, K., Matthews, R., & Boyle, S. (2018). Is the role of the school psychologist in early childhood truly expanding? A survey examining school psychologists' practices and training experiences. *Journal of Applied School Psychology, 35*(1), 1–19.

American Psychiatric Association. (2022). *Diagnostic and statistical manual of mental disorders* (5th ed., text rev.).

Angell, A. M., Empey, A., & Zuckerman, K. (2018). A review of diagnosis and service disparities among children with autism from racial and ethnic minority groups in the United States. *International Review of Research in Developmental Disabilities, 55*, 145–180.

Ayala, K. (2023). Factors associated with proportionality of representation of children of color in early childhood special education in Illinois. *Journal of Early Childhood Research, 22*(2).

Bagnato, S. J., Goins, D. D., Pretti-Frontczak, K., & Neisworth, J. T. (2014). Authentic assessment as "best practice" for early childhood intervention: National consumer social validity research. *Topics in Early Childhood Special Education, 34*(2), 116–127.

Bagnato, S. J., & Ho, H. Y. (2006). High-stakes testing with preschool children: Violation of professional standards for evidence-based practice in early childhood intervention. *KEDI International Journal of Educational Policy*, 3(1), 22–43.

Barger, B., Rice, C., Simmons, C. A., & Wolf, R. (2018). A systematic review of Part C early identification studies. *Topics in Early Childhood Special Education, 38*(1), 4–16.

Barger, B., Squires, J., Greer, M., Noyes-Grosser, D., Eile, J. M., Rice, C., et al. (2019). State variability in diagnosed conditions for IDEA Part C eligibility. *Infants & Young Children, 32*(4), 231–244.

Bayley, N., & Aylward, G. (2019). *Bayley Scales of Infant and Toddler Development* (4th ed.). Pearson.

Berens, A. E., & Nelson, C. A. (2019). Neurobiology of fetal and infant development. In C. H. Zeanah (Ed.), *Handbook of infant mental health* (4th ed., pp. 41–62). Guilford Press.

Briggs-Gowan, M. J., & Carter, A. S. (2006). *Brief Infant-Toddler Social Emotional Assessment (BITSEA)* [Database record]. APA PsycTests.

Bronfenbrenner, U. (1994). Ecological models of human development. In T. Husen & T. N. Postlethwaite (Eds.), *International encyclopedia of education* (2nd ed., Vol. 3, pp. 1643–1647). Pergamon Press.

Bureau of Labor Statistics, U.S. Department of Labor. (2018). *Occupational outlook handbook, special education teachers. www.bls.gov/ooh/education-training-and-library/special-education-teachers.htm*

Cairney, D.G., Kazmi, A., Delahunty, L., Marryat, L., & Wood, R. (2021). The predictive value of universal preschool developmental assessment in identifying children with later educational difficulties: A systematic review. *PLOS One, 16*(3).

Centers for Disease Control and Prevention. (2023, April 25). Assessing needs related to early identification during COVID-19: A national needs assessment. *www.cdc.gov/ncbddd/actearly/a-national-needs-assessment.html*

Choo, Y. Y., Agarwal, P., How, C. H. & Yeleswarapu, S.P. (2019). Developmental delay: Identification and management and primary care level. *Singapore Medical Journal*, 60(3), 119–123.

de Sam Lazaro, S. L. (2017). The importance of authentic assessments in eligibility determination for infants and toddlers. *Journal of Early Intervention*, 39(2), 88–105.

Division for Early Childhood. (2014). *DEC recommended practices in early intervention/early childhood special education 2014*. Author. *www.dec-sped.org/dec-recommended-practices*

Durkin, M. S., Maenner, M. J., Baio, J., Christensen, D., Daniels, J., Fitzgerald, R.,et al. (2017). Autism spectrum disorder among US children (2002–2010): Socioeconomic, racial and ethnic disparities. *Journal of Public Health, 107*, 1818–1826.

Durkin, M. S., Maenner, M. J., Meaney, F. J., Levy, S. E., DiGuiseppi, C., Nicholas, J. S., et al. (2010). Socioeconomic inequality in the prevalence of autism spectrum disorder: Evidence from a U.S. cross-sectional study. *PLOS One, 5*, e11551.

Early Childhood Personnel Center. (2022a). *Diversifying the early childhood workforce in early childhood special education. https://ecpcta-org.media.uconn.edu/wp-content/uploads/sites/2810/2022/06/Diversifying-EC-Workforce-in-ECSE.pdf*

Early Childhood Personnel Center. (2022b). *ECPC Part C and Part B/619 personnel recruitment and retention survey. https://ecpcta-org.media.uconn.edu/wp-content/uploads/sites/2810/2023/11/Recruitment-and-Retention-Survey-Report-2022.pdf*

Elliott, C. D. (2012). *Differential Ability Scales–II, Early Years (DAS-II)*. Pearson.

Ewen, D., & Herzfeldt-Kamprath, R. (2016). Examining quality across the preschool-to-third-grade continuum. Center for American Progress. *https://cdn.americanprogress.org/wp-content/uploads/2016/01/07110047/Pre-3_AccessToQuality.pdf*

Federal Interagency Forum on Child and Family Statistics. (2023). *America's children: Key national indica-*

tors of well-being, 2023. U.S. Government Printing Office.

Finkelhor, D., Turner, H., & LaSelva, D. (2021). Receipt of behavioral health services among US children and youth with adverse childhood experiences or mental health symptoms. *JAMA Network Open*, *4*(3), e211435–e211435.

Friedman-Krauss, A. H., Barnett, W. S., Hodges, K. S., Garver, K. A., Weisenfeld, G. G., Gardiner, B. A., & Jost, T. M. (2023). *The state of preschool 2023*. National Institute for Early Education Research. *https://nieer.org/yearbook/2022*

García Coll, C., Crnic, K., Lamberty, G., Wasik, B. H., Jenkins, R., Garcia, H. V., & McAdoo, H. P. (1996). An integrative model for the study of developmental competencies in minority children. *Child Development*, *67*(5), 1891–1914.

Garro, A. (2016). Early childhood assessment: An integrative framework. In A. Garro (Ed.), *Early childhood assessment in school and clinical child psychology* (pp. 1–24). Springer.

Hagan, J. F., Shaw, J. S., & Duncan, P. M. (2017). *Bright F = futures: Guidelines for health supervision of infants, children, and adolescents* (4th ed.). American Academy of Pediatrics.

Hirai, A. H., Kogan, M. D., Kandasamy, V., Reuland, C., & Bethell, C. (2018). Prevalence and variation of developmental screening and surveillance in early childhood. *JAMA: Journal of the American Medical Association Pediatrics*, *172*(9), 857–866.

Huerta, L., Cycyk, L. M., Sanford-Keller, H., Busch, A., Dolata, J., Moore, H., et al. (2021). A retrospective review of communication evaluation practices of young Latinx children. *Journal of Early Intervention*, *43*(4), 295–313.

Individuals with Disabilities Education Act. Pub. L. No. 108-446, 118 Stat. 2647 (2004).

Karasik, L. B., & Robinson, S. R. (2022). Milestones or millstones: How standard assessments mask cultural variation and misinform policies aimed at early childhood development. *Federations of Associations in Behavioral and Brain Science*, 9(1), 57–64.

Linder, T. (2008). *Transdisciplinary Play-Based Assessment (TPBA-2)* (2nd ed.). Brookes.

Lipkin, P. H., Macias, M. M., Chen, B. B., Coury, D., Gottschlich, E. A., Hyman, S. L., et al. (2020). Trends in pediatricians' developmental screening: 2002–2016. *Pediatrics, 145*(4), e20190851.

Lord, C., Rutter, M., DiLavore, P. C., Risi, S., Gotham, K., & Bishop, S. (2012). *Autism Diagnostic Observation Schedule* (2nd ed.). Western Psychological Services.

Lovett M. W., Frijters J. C., Wolf, M., Steinbach K. A., Sevcik R. A., & Morris R. D. (2017). Early intervention for children at risk for reading disabilities: The impact of grade at intervention and individual differences on intervention outcomes. *Journal of Educational Psychology, 109*, 889–914.

Macy, M., Marks, K., & Towle, A. (2014). Missed, misused, or mismanaged: Improving early detection systems to optimize child outcomes. *Topics in Early Childhood Special Education*, *34*(2), 94–105.

Morgan, P. L., Farkas, G., Hillemeier, M. M., & Maczuga, S. (2012). Are minority children disproportionately represented in early intervention and early childhood special education? *Educational Researcher, 41*(9), 339–351.

Morse, W. C. (1993). Ecological approaches. In T. R. Kratochwill & R. J. Morris (Eds.), *Handbook of psychotherapy with children and adolescents* (pp. 320–355). Allyn & Bacon.

National Association of School Psychologists. (2023). *Early childhood services promoting positive outcomes for all young children* [Position statement]. *www.nasponline.org/assets/Documents/Research%20and%20Policy/Position%20Statements/PS_EarlyChildhoodServices.pdf*

National Research Council (2000). *From neurons to neighborhoods: The science of early childhood development*. National Academies Press.

Neisworth, J. T., & Bagnato, S. J. (2004). The MisMeasure of young children: The authentic assessment alternative. *Infants and Young Children, 17*(3), 198–212.

Newborg, J. (2020). *Batelle Developmental Inventory (BDI-3)* (3rd ed.). Riverside Insights.

Pizur-Barnekow, K., Erickson, S., Johnston, M., Bass, T., Lucinski, L., & Bleuel, D. (2010). Early identification of developmental delays through surveillance, screening, and diagnostic evaluation. *Infants & Young Children, 23*(4), 323–330.

Pretti-Frontczak, K., Grisham-Brown, J., & Sullivan, L. (2023). *Assessing young children in inclusive settings: The blended practices approach* (2nd ed.). Brookes.

Quebles, I., Perrigo, J. L., Bravo, R., Patel Gera, M., Poulsen, M. K., Wheeler, B. Y., & Williams, M. E. (2022). Latinx mothers' experiences with linkage to early intervention. *Infants and Young Children, 35*(3), 189–204.

Radecki, L., Sand-Loud, N., O'Connor, K. G., Sharp, S., & Olson, L. M. (2011). Trends in the use of standardized tools for developmental screening in early childhood: 2002–2009. *Pediatrics, 128*(1), 14–19.

Reynolds, C. R., & Kamphaus, R.W. (2015). *Behavioral Assessment System for Children (BASC-3)* (3rd ed.). Pearson.

Rispoli, K. M., Norman, M. Z., & Hicks, E. (2021). Early childhood educators' knowledge and attitudes about developmental screening for autism spectrum disorder. *Journal of Early Childhood Teacher Education, 43*(2), 291–306.

Robins, D. L., Barton, M., & Fein, D. (2009). *Modified Checklist for Autism in Toddlers, Revised with Follow-Up (M-CHAT-R/F)*. *www.mchatscreen.com*

Saletta, M., & Windsor, J. (2019). Communication disorders in infants and toddlers. In C. H. Zeanah (Ed.), *Handbook of infant mental health* (4th ed., pp. 345–357). Guilford Press.

Sandler, A. D. (2019). Value-driven care in developmental-behavioral pediatrics, Part 1: The value proposition of developmental behavioral pediatrics. *Journal of Developmental and Behavioral Pediatrics*, 40(6), 472–478.

Sansavini A., Favilla M. E., Guasti M. T., Marini A., Millepiedi S., Di Martino M. V., et al. (2021). Developmental language disorder: Early predictors, age for the diagnosis, and diagnostic tools. A scoping review. *Brain Sciences, 11*, 654.

Sapiets, S. J., Totsika, V., & Hastings, R. P. (2021). Factors influencing access to early intervention for families of children with developmental disabilities: A narrative review. *Journal of Applied Research in Intellectual Disabilities*, *34*(3), 695–711.

Shahidullah, J., Forman, S., Norton, A., Harris, J., Palejwala, M., & Chaudhuri, A. (2020). Implementation of developmental screening by childcare providers. *Infants and Young Children*, *33*(1), 21–34.

Squires, J., Bricker, D., & Twombly, E. (2002). *Ages & Stages Questionnaires®: Social-Emotional (ASQ:SE-2)* (2nd ed.). *https://agesandstages.com*

Squires, J., & Bricker, D. (2009). *Ages & Stages Questionnaires® (ASQ-3™)* (3rd ed.). *https://agesandstages.com*

Steed, E. A., Stein, R., Burke, H., & Charlifue-Smith, R. (2023). Early childhood professionals' reported use of culturally and linguistically responsive practices during initial evaluations: A mixed methods study. *Topics in Early Childhood Special Education*, *43*(3), 214–226.

Stein, R., & Albritton, K. (2022). Early childhood-focused training in school psychology. *Training and Education in Professional Psychology*, *16*(1), 36–43.

Stein, R., & Steed, E. A. (2023). Initial evaluation practices to identify young children with delays and disabilities. *Contemporary School Psychology*, *28*, 316–327.

Thomas, K. C., Ellis, A. R., McLaurin, C., Daniels, J., & Morrissey, J. P. (2007). Access to care for autism-related services. *Journal of Autism and Developmental Disorders*, *37*(10), 1902–1912.

Vasileva, M., Graf, R. K., Reinelt, T., Petermann, U., & Petermann, F. (2021). Research review: A meta-analysis of the international prevalence and comorbidity of mental disorders in children between 1 and 7 years. *Journal of Child Psychology and Psychiatry*, *62*(4), 372–381.

Voress, J. K., Maddox, T., & Hammill, D. D. (2012). *Developmental Assessment of Young Children (DAYC-2)* (2nd ed.). Pearson.

Wechsler, D. (2012). *Wechsler Preschool and Primary Scale of Intelligence (WPPSI-IV)* (4th ed.). Pearson.

CHAPTER 27

Behavioral Threat Assessment and Management in Schools

Dewey Cornell and Jordan Kerere

Following a series of high-profile school shootings in the 1990s, the public became deeply concerned about the potential for student violence. Prompted by the Gun-Free Schools Act of 1994, school authorities began to rely heavily on a zero-tolerance approach to automatically remove students from school for any statement or behavior, regardless of context, that suggested violence (Johnson & Johnson, 2023). Over the next 30 years, zero-tolerance discipline expanded beyond threats of violence to become a widely accepted response to student misbehavior, despite studies finding that school removal was ineffective as a disciplinary measure. A large body of research indicated that the use of exclusionary discipline was associated with lower academic achievement, higher dropout rates, and subsequent delinquency and criminal offending (Gerlinger et al., 2021; Noltemeyer et al., 2015). As the use of suspension and expulsion increased nationwide, students of color and students with disabilities were punished at disproportionately high rates (Ryberg et al., 2021). As a result of the ineffectiveness and inequity of exclusionary discipline, school authorities need alternatives to zero tolerance and the associated practice of exclusionary discipline. One alternative is the use of behavioral threat assessment and management (BTAM, or "threat assessment") when there is concern about a student's potential for violence. This chapter describes how BTAM can provide school authorities with a more flexible, culturally sensitive, and effective response to student threats of violence.

Based on studies of school shootings, violence prevention experts first recommended the use of BTAM more than two decades ago (Fein et al., 2004; O'Toole, 2000). Although threat assessment is primarily a violence prevention strategy rather than a disciplinary process, it allows school authorities who make disciplinary decisions to consider the context and seriousness of a student's behavior rather than take an inflexible zero-tolerance approach. The use of threat assessment can lead school authorities to be more flexible and to make use of alternative interventions such as school counseling, mental health services, and restorative practices. This chapter describes the BTAM process, components of BTAM that promote a culturally sensitive approach, and evidence of its effectiveness. Of particular interest are studies indicating that BTAM reduces both the overall use of exclusionary discipline and the disparities typically observed across race and disability status (e.g., Cornell & Lovegrove, 2015).

BEHAVIORAL THREAT ASSESSMENT AND MANAGEMENT

BTAM was originally developed by the U.S. Secret Service to protect public officials from targeted violence (Fein & Vossekuil, 1998). *Targeted violence* refers to a premeditated attempt to inflict physical injury on specific individuals or groups. However, the process has been adapted to prevent targeted violence in workplaces, communities, and schools (Borum et al., 1999; Meloy & Hoffmann, 2021). Threat assessment seemed appropriate for K-12 schools because studies revealed that most of the students who committed mass school shootings had engaged in threatening statements or behavior that aroused concern by others well in advance of their attack (Cybersecurity and Infrastructure Security Agency & U.S. Secret Service, 2023; Federal Bureau of Investigation, 2017; National Threat Assessment Center [NTAC], 2019, 2021; Pollack et al., 2008). Consequently, several groups have developed threat assessment protocols or systems for K-12 schools (Jackson & Viljoen, 2024).

By 2024, approximately 85% of U.S. schools reported having an established threat assessment team, with even higher prevalence rates in urban areas (National Center for Education Statistics, 2024). At least 39 states require or support the use of threat assessment teams in schools, including large states like Florida, Illinois, Texas, Ohio, Pennsylvania, Virginia, and Washington (National Association of State Boards of Education, n.d.). In 2024, the National Center for School Safety released the School Threat Assessment Toolkit (Cornell & Maeng, 2024) to meet the nationwide need for guidance on training, implementation, and evaluation of threat assessment teams.

Threat assessment is a systematic process of carefully assessing an individual and considering their intentions and the context for their behavior in deciding whether they pose a serious threat of violence (Meloy & Hoffman, 2021). Threat assessment is not designed to *predict* whether someone is violent, but to *prevent* violence by identifying a distressed individual and providing support to de-escalate a conflict or problem. Threat assessment follows a public health model of multi-tiered efforts to reduce the risk of violence rather than label and predict violence in individuals (Cornell & Maeng, 2024). The initial assessment leads to a management plan intended to reduce the risk of violence by responding to the individual's needs, problems, or concerns. Consequently, a properly conducted threat assessment requires school authorities to consider the student's intentions and needs for supportive interventions (Cornell & Maeng, 2024).

Threat assessments are conducted by school-based multidisciplinary teams, typically comprised of an administrator, one or more mental health professionals, and a school resource officer (SRO; Cornell & Maeng, 2024). Schools need an administrator on the team in order to inform disciplinary decisions and to facilitate decisions about services and other actions taken in response to the threat. School-based mental health professionals, such as school counselors, school psychologists, and school social workers, bring expertise in assessing students and providing supportive interventions (National Association of School Psychologists [NASP], 2020). An SRO can provide consultation and initiate a law enforcement investigation in the most serious cases (Canady, 2018; Cornell & Maeng, 2024). Schools may draw on other professionals, such as teachers and nurses, depending on their staff composition, as well as state requirements. For example, Virginia requires that each team include persons with expertise in counseling, instruction, school administration, and law enforcement.

The use of a multidisciplinary team is important to help assure a more comprehensive and culturally sensitive decision-making process. Teams bring broader expertise and more diverse perspectives and can provide a check on individual biases (American Psychological Association, n.d.; NASP, 2017). Well-trained teams take a fact-based, investigative approach that aims to understand the context and meaning of the student's behavior. Additionally, having a team in the school means that team members will know the student body and the school environment better than an outsider.

Threat assessment has three stages: (1) identification of a student who has made a threatening statement or engaged in behavior raising concern about potential violence; (2) assessment of the student's intentions and capabilities; and (3) management of the threat case to reduce the risk of violence through interventions for any needs, problems, or concerns identified in the assessment.

The threat assessment process begins when a threat or threatening behavior is identified and reported; therefore, the use of threat assessment in schools is dependent on the ability and willingness of students to come forward with information about threats (Pollack et al., 2008). Ideally, a student might approach a trusted adult in a school to report concerns about a classmate (Crichlow-Ball & Cornell, 2021; NTAC, 2018). However, students might be reluctant to report a threat because it would be considered snitching and/or lead to retaliation (Crichlow-Ball & Cornell, 2021; Payne et al., 2024). Some schools have implemented anonymous reporting systems to combat this code of silence among students. One study found that 83% of middle school students would anonymously report a peer for engaging in dangerous behavior, compared to just 70% of students if their identities were linked to the report (Brank et al., 2007). Adults in the school community, such as principals, parents, and other school personnel, generally agree that tip lines are an effective way to prevent school violence (Espelage et al., 2021; Planty et al., 2020; Schwartz et al., 2016). Students can use multiple avenues for reporting threats of violence. One study found that about half of secondary schools used phone, website, email, text, or app threat-reporting methods (Planty et al., 2020). Another found that 75% of threats were reported via apps, 25% online, and less than 3% via phone call (Office of the Attorney General, n.d.). Regardless of the reporting system, research suggests that student willingness to report threats and positive school climate are reliable predictors of threat reporting (Crichlow-Ball & Cornell, 2021; Payne et al., 2024).

The Comprehensive School Threat Assessment Guidelines

The Comprehensive School Threat Assessment Guidelines (CSTAG; Cornell, 2018) were developed in 2001 by Dewey Cornell and a research team at the University of Virginia.[1] A workgroup of school professionals advising the research team pointed out that student threats could range across a wide continuum of severity. Many seemingly threatening statements or behaviors are nothing more than ill-advised jokes or pranks. Some threats are rhetorical expressions of anger and attempts to gain attention or frighten someone. Still other threats are communications of serious lethal intent. The workgroup stressed that school teams needed a practical, straightforward approach that would quickly resolve threats that were not serious and concentrate efforts on the truly serious cases. The overarching goal would be to help students who have made threats rather than punish them for misbehavior, and to reduce risk factors rather than make predictions of violence.

The CSTAG model was created to allow teams to break away from an inflexible zero-tolerance approach and consider the individual circumstances of a student's behavior through a systematic process of gathering information concerning the student's motives, intentions, and capabilities. Not only does zero tolerance fail to make schools safer, but it also has been shown to be overly punitive to students with minoritized identities. Black children are substantially more likely to be referred to the office for defiant behavior than children of other races (Liu, 2023; Welsh & Little, 2018). Defiance and disrespect are much more subjective than a serious offense, like carrying a weapon on school property, and therefore these referrals are more reliant on teacher judgment. Once referred, Black children are significantly more likely to be suspended or expelled than White children for similar infractions (Cruz et al., 2021; Riddle & Sinclair, 2019). Overall, Black students are perceived as more problematic and subsequently punished more harshly than their White peers who commit similar offenses (Amemiya et al., 2020; Riddle & Sinclair, 2019).

CSTAG teams take a problem-solving approach to threats, based on the idea that most students make threats of violence because they are frustrated about a problem or conflict that they are unable to solve. The team focuses on helping the student solve the problem through interventions and supports such as conflict resolution, social skills training, social–emotional learning, and special education services. When necessary, the team will take protective actions, such as increasing the monitoring of a student, searching for weapons, consulting with parents, and conferring with threatened individuals. The team might recommend a brief suspension from the classroom to a supervised setting (including parental supervision at home) to assure safety while the team devises a safety plan.

The CSTAG model was designed to give schools a triage approach in which teams would use guided professional judgment to consider the context and meaning of the student's threat in order to distinguish serious (substantive) threats from threats that are not serious (transient). To accomplish this task, CSTAG teams use a five-step decision tree (see Figure 27.1) and a detailed,

[1] Dewey Cornell discloses that he has a financial interest as the developer of the Comprehensive School Threat Assessment Guidelines.

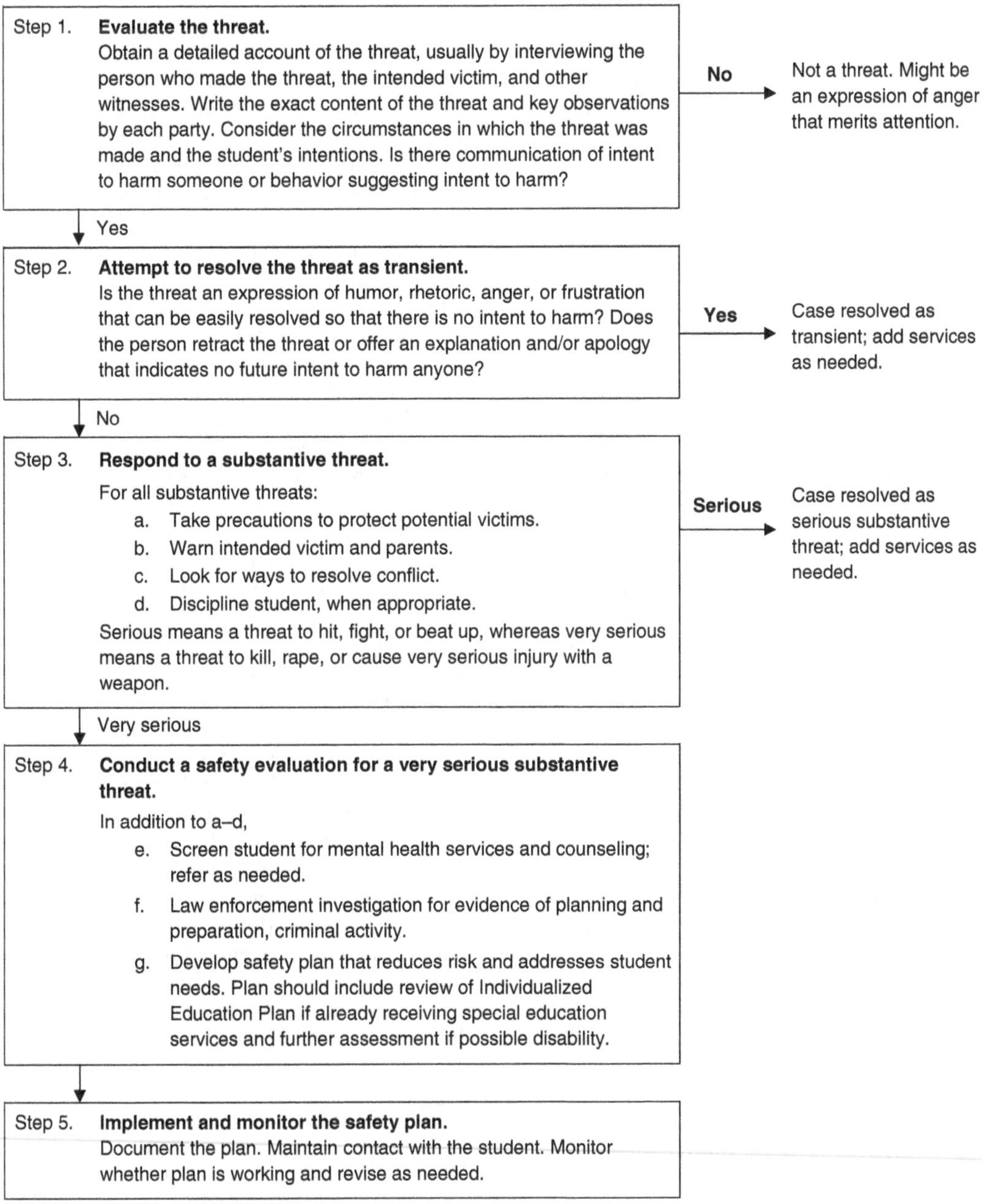

FIGURE 27.1. School threat assessment decision tree. Reprinted with permission from Cornell (2024). Copyright © 2024 School Threat Assessment Consultants.

180-page manual (Cornell, 2024) to gather information about a reported threat and, based on their assessment, undertake appropriately calibrated responses. The idea is that knowing the student as an individual reduces the likelihood of making a stereotypic or biased judgment (Fein et al., 2004; O'Toole, 2000).

This model is designed to help teams avoid overreacting to threats that are not serious and to focus attention on serious threats that merit protective action, supportive interventions, and monitoring (Burnette et al., 2018). There are four possible threat categories: (1) not a threat; (2) a transient threat, meaning there is no serious intent; (3) a serious substantive threat, meaning there is serious intent to assault or fight someone; and (4) a very serious substantive threat, meaning there is serious intent to kill, shoot, stab or in some other way inflict severe or life-threatening injury. Threat classification is determined through a five-step decision tree, reviewed in the following.

Step 1

At Step 1, the team conducts brief interviews to assess whether a student's behavior or communication expresses a serious threat. The team would likely interview the person(s) who reported a concern, the student who allegedly made the threat, and the target of the possible threat. There is a standard interview used with the student of concern and similar interviews for other witnesses. This interview is designed to be simple; there are six open-ended and nonleading questions to elicit information concerning the seriousness of the threat. Although the interview can be modified according to the circumstances of the threat and the student's age and level of functioning, in most cases, the following questions can be used:

1. What happened today when you were [place of incident]?
2. What exactly did you say? And what exactly did you do?
3. What did you mean when you said or did that?
4. How do you think [person who was threatened] feels about what you said or did? (Probe to see if the subject believes it frightened or intimidated the person.)
5. What was the reason you said or did that? (Probe to find out if there is a prior conflict or history to this threat.)
6. What are you going to do now?

In about 10% of cases, the reported behavior might be nothing more than a rumor or misunderstanding that did not constitute a threat (Maeng et al., 2024). For example, a student overheard talking about "killing" someone was referring to a video game. Such cases are classified as "not a threat" and resolved at the first step.

Step 2

The team uses all available information at Step 2 to judge the credibility and seriousness of the threat. A threat is considered transient if it is reasonably apparent that the student has no intent to carry out the threat. For example, a student might have been angry and threatened someone, but their statement was a rhetorical expression of frustration (e.g., "I'm going to kill you!"). Typically, a threat is classified as transient when the student has provided a convincing explanation, often with a spontaneous apology, and other sources of information show no indication that the student has serious intentions to harm someone. Transient threats do not require protective action or security efforts because the student who *made* a threat does not *pose* a threat.

Although the threat might be resolved as transient, the team might identify a problem or concern that needs attention. For example, a student might have made an angry threat because of problems getting along with others or difficulty with anger. There might also be some form of bullying taking place. An important preventive aspect of threat assessment is to identify these sorts of problems and take action to resolve them so that a relatively small problem does not escalate over time.

Several studies have found that approximately three-fourths of student threats can be resolved as transient (Burnette et al., 2018; Maeng et al., 2024). Transient threats can often be managed by a few team members without a full team assessment. On the other hand, if the team is unable to resolve the threat or if they are unsure about the threat's seriousness, then the decision tree directs them to move to Step 3 and respond to the case as a substantive threat. In contrast to transient threats, substantive threats pose a serious risk of harm to others and require protective action. One example is a student who threatened to beat up a classmate and refused to consider mediation for the conflict.

Step 3

Teams respond to a substantive threat at Step 3 with four actions (see Figure 27.1). The fundamental requirement of a substantive threat is that the team takes protective action to prevent the threat from being carried out. The kind of protective action depends on the circumstances of the threat and how it might be carried out. At a minimum, protective action includes notifying the intended victim (and parents, if the target is a student), as well as contacting the parents of the student who made the threat. Protective action also involves increased monitoring or supervision of the student of concern. The team then considers what kind of intervention (such as counseling or conflict mediation) would be appropriate to resolve the problem underlying the threat. The school administration may consider appropriate disciplinary consequences, informed by the team's understanding of the threat and how the student responded to intervention efforts.

There are two levels of substantive threats: serious and very serious. Threats involving a simple assault or a fight are examples of serious substantive threats, whereas a threat to kill, use a lethal weapon, or inflict severe injury on someone is classified as a very serious substantive threat. Serious substantive threats are resolved at Step 3, whereas very serious substantive threats require the additional actions specified for Steps 4 and 5.

Serious substantive threats are basically threats to hit someone or engage in a fight, which is a fairly common situation in schools, especially in the middle school grades. Approximately one in five threat referrals is classified as a serious substantive threat (Maeng et al., 2024). As school counselors and psychologists can attest, threats to fight can usually be resolved with counseling to mediate and resolve the conflict. Schools are free to use the methods that seem most appropriate to the individual case. If no major disciplinary violation has taken place, serious substantive threats can be resolved without exclusionary discipline.

Step 4

Approximately 5% of referrals for a threat assessment are classified as very serious substantive and reach Step 4 (Maeng et al., 2024). At Step 4, the school team takes three additional actions beyond the protective actions represented in Step 3 (see *e*, *f*, and *g* in Figure 27.1). In a nutshell, these actions include: (1) conducting a safety evaluation consisting primarily of more comprehensive interviews with the student of concern and the student's parents; (2) a law enforcement investigation conducted by the SRO; and (3) a synthesis of the interviews, law enforcement investigation, and any other available sources of information (such as school records and consultation with teachers) into a formal safety plan. A safety evaluation could take several days to complete, and during this time the student should be carefully supervised. As a safety precaution, the student might attend school in a supervised location such as a school suspension center or another well-supervised alternative site. If the student is sent home on suspension or placed on homebound instruction, there should be a clear understanding that the student will be supervised and monitored by parents or other responsible parties.

As part of the safety evaluation, one or more team members will conduct a more extensive safety interview with the student. The safety interview with the student is more extensive than the initial interview and will examine the reasons for the threat in more depth.

The interviewer (often a mental health professional on the team, such as a school counselor, psychologist, or social worker) will screen the student for possible mental health needs that could lead to a referral for services. This component of the safety evaluation is comparable to an evaluation of a student who is suicidal, because it is concerned with assessing risk factors and identifying strategies to reduce the risk of violence. The safety interview covers many of the factors that are considered in a suicide risk assessment, such as whether the student has a plan, serious intent, and a means of carrying out the threat. In addition to interviewing the student, a team member will interview other sources such as parents, teachers, and mental health service providers, as well as review educational and mental health records. There is a comprehensive list of topics and questions for the student interview in the CSTAG manual (Cornell, 2024).

The safety evaluation is not an evaluation for special education services, but it may indicate the need for a referral to the school's special education program. If the student is already receiving special education services, data from the threat assessment will provide the special education staff with information that can be used to review the student's special education program (such as an Individualized Education Plan or 504 Plan). Because students with disabilities make up about one-third of threat assessment referrals (Cornell, Kerere, et al., 2025; Maeng et al., 2024), it is recommended that at least one team member has special education expertise and can facilitate communication with the special education professionals at the school.

The two primary goals of the safety interview are to assess whether the student needs mental health services (or some other services) and to determine what conflict or problem underlies the threat. Both goals serve the ultimate purpose of preventing violence by identifying risk factors for intervention. A safety interview covers a wide range of topics that are summarized briefly here:

1. The interview should review the student's motivation in making the threat, and their understanding of the potential consequences of carrying it out. The interviewer should inquire about the student's relationship with the intended victim or victims and gain an under-

standing of the student's grievance. This information is used to develop a safety plan that includes helping the student resolve the conflict or problem underlying the threat.

2. Beyond the circumstances of the threat, the interview should cover other sources of stress in the student's life. Students making a very serious substantive threat often have multiple sources of stress that may be unrelated to the threat situation but have burdened the student and made it more difficult to cope with the conflict or problem underlying the threat. A comprehensive plan might include efforts to relieve these additional sources of stress. The interviewer should keep in mind that a student's response to a current stress could be influenced by previous trauma or loss that continues to have an impact on the student's adjustment. The student's cultural background, socioeconomic status, living situation, and other relevant factors should be considered.
3. The interviewer will examine the student's mental status and screen for symptoms of a mental disorder. There are standard questions about the student's mood and cognition, as well as symptoms of depression, anxiety, and disordered thinking, in the CSTAG manual (Cornell, 2024).
4. An interviewer will also want to inquire about a student's history of aggressive and delinquent behavior, as well as exposure to prior violence. For example, a student might reside in a neighborhood with high levels of violent crime or gang activity that makes travel to and from school stressful. Another student might be an immigrant who has witnessed violent incidents prior to coming to the United States. There may also be a history of domestic violence in the student's home.
5. More broadly, the interviewer will cover topics such as the student's friendships and romantic relationships, any involvement with gangs or negative peer groups, and any experiences of harassment or bullying. In covering these topics, the threat assessment team will gain insight into the student's social and cultural background and strive to understand the threat incident in an appropriate context.

The second action taken at Step 4 is a law enforcement investigation. Law enforcement officers will have their own agency procedures for investigation and take actions based on the circumstances of the case. An initial focus might be to determine whether a crime has been committed that would justify arrest or charges (e.g., if the student has brought a firearm to school). Arrests occur in less than 1% of threat assessment cases (Maeng et al., 2024). The officer will also investigate for evidence of planning and preparation and may conduct searches for weapons. Based on the nature of the threat and the level of concern in the school, law enforcement authorities might increase security measures.

The third team action is to integrate findings from the safety interviews and law enforcement investigation into a safety plan. A multidisciplinary team will strive to integrate multiple perspectives on the case and reach consensus on a plan that both reduces the risk of violence and addresses the student's needs or problems. Typically, the safety plan establishes the conditions under which the student can return to school or have a change in placement. For example, there might be a behavioral intervention plan and regular check-ins with a designated team member.

The plan should also include provisions for supporting individuals targeted by the threat and giving them information to reassure them about their safety. Sometimes schools are reluctant to share information because of concerns about confidentiality, but school authorities can seek permission from parents to share appropriate information that would facilitate their student returning to school. For example, in one case a student with an autism spectrum diagnosis had become angry and made a threatening statement when he misunderstood why a classmate was laughing. The student's parents agreed that school authorities could explain to the classmate and her parents that he had a disability that affected his understanding of social interactions. The team facilitated a meeting between the student who made the threat and his classmate to resolve his misunderstanding and clarify that he had no intentions to harm her.

Step 5

At Step 5, the team implements and monitors the safety plan formulated at Step 4. There might be a team member who serves as the case manager in documenting the plan, which should specify what interventions will be undertaken and who will provide them. The case manager will monitor the student's well-being and initiate a review to make any necessary changes to the plan.

Supporting Research

The first field test of CSTAG (initially known as the Virginia Student Threat Assessment Guidelines) was conducted in 2001 and found that teams could resolve threats safely and efficiently, with relatively few students suspended or removed from school (Cornell et al., 2004). Over the next 20 years, the University of Virginia research team conducted seven controlled studies in Virginia (Cornell et al., 2009, 2011, 2012; Gregory et al., 2010; JustChildren & Cornell, 2013; Maeng et al., 2020; Nekvasil & Cornell, 2015); studies of CSTAG training and implementation (Allen et al., 2008; Burnette et al., 2018; Cornell & Lovegrove, 2015; Maeng et al., 2020, 2024; Stohlman & Cornell, 2019; Stohlman et al., 2020); and separate statewide assessments in Virginia (Cornell & Maeng, 2020) and Florida public schools (Maeng et al., 2024). Across all studies, thousands of school threats were resolved peacefully, with relatively few acts of violence (e.g., primarily fights without serious injury). In the largest study conducted to date (Kerere et al., 2025; Maeng et al., 2024), less than one-half of 1% of 14,126 cases resulted in very serious injuries (defined as requiring hospital treatment). Selected findings relevant to the fairness and equity of the threat assessment process are summarized here.

A CSTAG professional development program was developed and refined over a period of years. Multidisciplinary school teams learn to use the CSTAG model in a full-day workshop using a standard curriculum that includes didactic material, small-group interaction, case studies, and team exercises. Seven studies of this workshop used a pre- and post-assessment to measure participant attitudes and knowledge (Allen et al., 2008; Cornell et al., 2004, 2009, 2011, 2012; Strong & Cornell, 2008; Stohlman et al., 2020). In brief, these studies found that across workshops with different trainers, participants demonstrated gains in knowledge of threat assessment and an ability to classify cases reliably. Notably, they also showed a decrease in fears of school shootings and markedly reduced support for zero tolerance and school exclusion. Because threat assessment is a multidisciplinary process, it was important to find that there were comparably large effects across groups of school administrators, counselors, psychologists, social workers, and SROs.

CSTAG teams are trained to consider most threats as an indication that the student is experiencing a problem or conflict that they cannot resolve. This problem-solving approach was reflected in the Florida statewide study (Maeng et al., 2024). In many cases, the problem was readily resolved, such as a threatening statement made in jest that resulted in a clarification and apology. In about 75% of cases, there was a referral for some kind of support service, such as short-term counseling, conflict resolution, mental health services, or special education. Approximately 90% of students continued in their original school, with some students transferring to a different school, moving to an alternative program, or receiving some other kind of service. Fewer than 2% of students were expelled.

Threat assessment teams do not make disciplinary decisions, but their findings are intended to influence administrative decisions regarding whether to suspend a student. Therefore, CSTAG studies have examined disciplinary outcomes resulting in school suspension or expulsion. In brief, these studies found that schools using threat assessment markedly decreased their use of out-of-school suspension (e.g., Cornell et al., 2011, 2012; Maeng et al., 2020) and that racial disparities in suspension were either reduced or eliminated (Cornell & Lovegrove, 2015; JustChildren & Cornell, 2013; Maeng et al., 2023). In the most recent study of Florida public schools using CSTAG, the suspension rate for White students (25.9%) was only slightly different from the suspension rates for Black (27.0%) and Hispanic (24.8%) students (Maeng et al., 2024). Suspension rates for students with disabilities (29.8%) were lower than for students without disabilities (30.4%). A Bayesian analysis directly tested the equity of disciplinary outcomes for 19,000 students receiving a threat assessment in 1,700 Florida public schools (Cornell, Maeng, et al., 2025a). This study found largely equitable rates of suspension, expulsion, and placement change for student groups defined by race/ethnicity, family income, and disability status. There were a few small differences in suspension that were much smaller than those typically found in the same schools for students not receiving a threat assessment.

Another important concern is whether the involvement of law enforcement officers in threat assessment would result in the criminalization of students for relatively minor misbehaviors. The CSTAG model helps to mitigate this concern by distinguishing transient threats from substantive threats and taking appropriately calibrated actions. In the Florida statewide sample, 82% of cases were resolved as non-threats or transient threats, with only 18% deemed to be substantive (Maeng et al., 2024). Law enforcement officers were required by state law to be on all threat assessment teams and to participate in all cases, but their role would vary depending on the nature of the case. Officers would most likely be involved in the investigation of the most serious threats, searches for weapons, and other protective actions. However, fewer than 1% of students were arrested, and fewer than 2% received court charges. A Bayesian analysis of 18,411 students in 1,646 Florida schools found that law enforcement actions (arrest, charges, and incarceration) were most strongly associated with student grade level and seriousness of the threat, and they were equitably distributed across student groups defined by race/ethnicity, family income, and disability status (Cornell, Maeng, et al., 2025b).

Although CSTAG research has found positive results across multiple studies, more research is needed on how those results are achieved and what features of the model (e.g., the use of a multidisciplinary team, a decision tree, a problem-solving approach) are most important. Most of the studies are archival, due to the logistical challenges and confidentiality of threat assessment cases. There is little research on the team's decision-making process, the success of different kinds of interventions with different students, and what happens to students over a longer period of time after a threat assessment. More research is needed on the qualities necessary to achieve consistency and fidelity of implementation and how outcomes generalize across schools in different regions and under different social and educational conditions. Finally, there is little research on other threat assessment models or how they compare to CSTAG in training, implementation, or outcomes (Jackson & Viljoen, 2024).

CULTURALLY RELEVANT PRACTICE CONSIDERATIONS

In light of the evidence that school staff refer students of color and students with disabilities for disciplinary violations at highly disproportionate rates (Liu, 2023; Welsh & Little, 2018), it is not surprising that there is similar (albeit less pronounced) disproportionality in referrals for a threat assessment (Cornell et al., 2018; Cornell, Kerere, et al., 2025; Maeng et al., 2023). However, if schools use a threat assessment process as a diversion from a disciplinary referral, cases that would otherwise lead to disproportionate use of school exclusion can result in outcomes that are fairer and more equitable. When referred for a threat assessment, students across demographic groups are less likely to be excluded from school, and disproportionalities in disciplinary outcomes are greatly reduced or eliminated (Cornell et al., 2018; Cornell, Maeng, et al., 2025a; Maeng et al., 2023, 2024).

The CSTAG model tries to minimize potential biases by using a multidisciplinary team approach so that decisions are not based on the perspective of a single individual or discipline. Teams must be sensitive to the possibility of implicit biases (American Psychological Association, n.d.). Teams are trained to consider the context and circumstances surrounding the threat rather than follow a zero-tolerance approach. Therefore, when a threat is reported, the team follows a systematic, semi-structured process with a five-step decision tree to gather information from multiple sources to gain a more complete understanding of the situation. They take a fact-based approach to gather evidence regarding a student rather than rely on profiling, and must repeatedly consider whether their decisions are based on objective evidence rather than supposition or assumption.

One of the most important protections against bias is that CSTAG teams take a problem-solving approach that considers what problem, conflict, or grievance underlies the threat. From this perspective, the team considers ways to help the student achieve a more appropriate, prosocial resolution. Understanding the student's perspective, their motivations and intentions, can help the team members view the student with empathy and understanding, and select interventions that will be supportive and facilitative. This approach is intended to achieve the ultimate goals of reducing the risk of violence and helping the student to be more successful in school.

For further guidance, the National Center for School Safety has released a School Threat Assessment Toolkit (Cornell & Maeng, 2024) that is intended to provide schools with a guide for developing a threat assessment program. Based on input from nearly 200 threat assessment experts and a comprehensive review of the school threat assessment literature, including key guidance from the NTAC (2018), the toolkit presents basic concepts of school threat assessment and key guidance on threat assessment programs. The toolkit has chapters on the selection and training of threat assessment teams, the implementation and functioning of teams, and how the program should be evaluated for both fidelity of implementation and student outcomes. The toolkit places a major emphasis on the protection of student rights and making sure that outcomes are fair and equitable for students of diverse backgrounds, including students with disabilities and students of color. It is essential that schools adhere to evidence-based practices and high standards of fidelity in carrying out a threat assessment program.

REFERENCES

Allen, K., Cornell, D., Lorek, E., & Sheras, P. (2008). Response of school personnel to student threat assessment training. *School Effectiveness and School Improvement, 19*, 319–332.

Amemiya, J., Mortenson, E., & Wang, M. (2020). Minor infractions are not minor: School infractions for minor misconduct may increase adolescents' defiant behavior and contribute to racial disparities in school discipline. *American Psychologist, 75*(1), 23–36.

American Psychological Association. (n.d.). *Implicit bias*. Author. *www.apa.org/topics/implicit-bias*

Borum, R., Fein, R., Vossekuil, B., & Berglund, J. (1999). Threat assessment: Defining an approach for evaluating risk of targeted violence. *Behavioral Sciences and the Law, 17*, 323–337.

Brank, E., M., Woolard, J. L., Brown, V. E., Fondacaro, M., Luescher, J. L., Chinn, R. G., & Miller, S. A. (2007). Will they tell? Weapons reporting by middle-school youth. *Youth Violence and Juvenile Justice, 5*(2), 125–146.

Burnette, A. G., Datta, P., & Cornell, D. (2018). The distinction between transient and substantive student threats. *Journal of Threat Assessment and Management, 5*(1), 4–20.

Canady, M. (2018). *Standards and best practices for school resource officers*. National Association of School Resource Officers. *www.nasro.org/clientuploads/About-Mission/NASRO-Standards-and-Best-Practices.pdf*

Cornell, D. (2024). *Comprehensive school threat assessment guidelines: Intervention and support to prevent violence* (2nd ed.). School Threat Assessment Consultants.

Cornell, D., Allen, K., & Fan, X. (2012). A randomized controlled study of the Virginia Student Threat Assessment Guidelines in grades K–12. *School Psychology Review, 41*, 100–115.

Cornell, D., Gregory, A., & Fan, X. (2011). Reductions in long-term suspensions following adoption of the Virginia Threat Assessment Guidelines. *Bulletin of the National Association of Secondary School Principals, 95*, 175–194.

Cornell, D., & Lovegrove, P. (2015). Student threat assessment as a method for reducing student suspensions. In D. Losen (Ed.), *Closing the school discipline gap: Research for policymakers* (pp. 180–191). Teachers College Press.

Cornell, D., & Maeng, J. (2020). *Student threat assessment as a safe and supportive prevention strategy: Final technical report*. School of Education and Human Development, University of Virginia.

Cornell, D., & Maeng, J. (2024). *School threat assessment toolkit*. National Center for School Safety. *www.nc2s.org/resource/school-threat-assessment-toolkit*

Cornell, D., Maeng, J., Huang, F., Shukla, K., & Konold, T. (2018). Racial/ethnic parity in disciplinary consequences using student threat assessment. *School Psychology Review, 47*(2), 183–195.

Cornell, D., Maeng, J., Winter, S., Huang, F., Konold, T., Kerere, J., Afolabi, K., & Cowley, D. (2025a). Behavioral threat assessment and equity in exclusionary school discipline. *School Psychology Review*. Advance online publication. *https://doi.org/10.1080/2372966X.2025.2457006*

Cornell, D., Maeng, J., Winter, S., Huang, F., Konold, T., Kerere, J., Afolabi, K., & Cowley, D. (2025b). Equity in law enforcement actions following a school threat assessment. *Law and Human Behavior, 49*, 338–352.

Cornell, D., Sheras, P., Gregory, A., & Fan, X. (2009). A retrospective study of school safety conditions in high schools using the Virginia Threat Assessment Guidelines versus alternative approaches. *School Psychology Quarterly, 24*, 119–129.

Cornell, D., Sheras, P., Kaplan, S., McConville, D., Douglass, J., Elkon, A., et al. (2004). Guidelines for student threat assessment: Field-test findings. *School Psychology Review, 33*, 527–546.

Cornell, D. G., Kerere, J., Konold, T., Maeng, J., Afolabi, K., Huang, F., & Cowley, D. (2025). Referral rates for school threat assessment. *Psychology in the Schools, 62*(4), 1294–1305.

Crichlow-Ball, C., & Cornell, D. (2021). Association of school climate with student willingness to report threats of violence. *Journal of Threat Assessment and Management, 8*(3), 77–93.

Cruz, R. A., Kulkarni, S. S., & Firestone, A. R. (2021). A quantcrit analysis of context, discipline, special education, and disproportionality. *AERA Open, 7*.

Cybersecurity and Infrastructure Security Agency & U.S. Secret Service. (2023). *Improving school safety through bystander reporting: A toolkit for strengthening K-12 reporting programs*. U.S. Department of Homeland Security, Cybersecurity and Infrastructure Security Agency, U.S. Secret Service.

Espelage, D. L., Robinson, L. E., Woolweaver, A., Valido, A., Davis, A., Hunt, K., et al. (2021). Implementation of tiplines and reporting apps for school safety: A qualitative analysis of parent and school personnel perspectives. *Journal of School Violence, 20*(3), 336–350.

Federal Bureau of Investigation. (2017). *Making prevention a reality: Identifying, assessing, and managing the threat of targeted attacks*. U.S. Department of Justice,

Federal Bureau of Investigation, National Center for the Analysis of Violent Crime, Behavioral Analysis Unit.

Fein, R. A., & Vossekuil, B. (1998). *Protective intelligence and threat assessment investigations: A guide for state and local law enforcement officials*. U.S. Department of Justice, Office of Justice Programs, National Institute of Justice.

Fein, R. A., Vossekuil, B., Pollack, W. S., Borum, R., Modzeleski, W., & Reddy, M. (2004). *Threat assessment in schools: A guide to managing threatening situations and to creating safe school climates. Revised*. U.S. Department of Education and U.S. Secret Service, National Threat Assessment Center. *https://eric.ed.gov/?id=ED515943*

Gerlinger, J., Viano, S., Gardella, J. H., Fisher, B. W., Curran, F. C., & Higgins, E. M. (2021). Exclusionary school discipline and delinquent outcomes: A meta-analysis. *Journal of Youth and Adolescence, 50*(8), 1493–1509.

Gregory, A., Cornell, D., Fan, X., Sheras, P., Shih, T., & Huang, F. (2010). Authoritative school discipline: High school practices associated with lower student bullying and victimization. *Journal of Educational Psychology, 102*, 483–496.

Jackson, J. R., & Viljoen, J. L. (2024). Preventing school violence: A review of school threat assessment models. *Journal of Threat Assessment and Management, 11*(1), 48–65.

Johnson, N. N., & Johnson, T. L. (2023). Zero tolerance policy analysis: A look at 30 years of school-based ZT policies in practice in the United States of America. *Cogent Education, 10*(1).

JustChildren & Cornell, D. (2013). *Prevention v. punishment: Threat assessment, school suspensions, and racial disparities*. *https://education.virginia.edu/documents/yvpthreat-assessment-reduces-school-suspension-and-racial-disproportionality2018-09-26.pdf*

Kerere, J., Cornell, D., Maeng, J., & Huang, F. (2025). Student attacks following a school threat assessment: Statewide trends in student and case characteristics. *Journal of Threat Assessment and Management*. Advance online publication. *https://doi.org/10.1037/tam0000249*

Liu, J. (2023). *Disciplinary referrals, teachers, and the source of racial disciplinary disproportionalities*. Brown Center Chalkboard, Brookings. *www.brookings.edu/articles/disciplinary-referrals-teachers-and-the-sources-of-racial-disciplinary-disproportionalities/#:~:text=In%20the%20first%20study%20of,the%20frequency%20of%20disciplinary%20referrals*

Maeng, J. L., Cornell, D. G., & Edwards, K. D. (2023). Threat assessment and disparities in school discipline. *Journal of Threat Assessment and Management,11*(3), 186–196.

Maeng, J. L., Cornell, D. G., & Huang, F. (2020). Student threat assessment as an alternative to exclusionary discipline. *Journal of School Violence, 19*(3), 377–388.

Maeng, J. L., Cornell, D. G., Kerere, J., Huang, F. Konold, T., Afolabi, A., & Cowley, D. (2024). *Statewide implementation of school threat assessment in Florida: Final technical report*. School of Education and Human Development, University of Virginia.

Meloy, J. R., & Hoffman, J. (Eds.). (2021). *International handbook of threat assessment* (2nd ed.). Oxford University Press.

National Association of School Psychologists. (2017). *Implicit bias: A foundation for school psychologists. www.nasponline.org/resources-and-publications/resources-and-podcasts/diversity-and-social-justice/social-justice/implicit-bias-a-foundation-for-school-psychologists*

National Association of School Psychologists. (2020). *The professional standards of the National Association of School Psychologists. www.nasponline.org/assets/documents/Standards%20and%20Certification/Standards/2020_Professional_Standards_Web.pdf*

National Association of State Boards of Education. (n.d.). *Threat assessment*. State Policy Database. *https://statepolicies.nasbe.org/health/categories/physical-environment/threat-assessment*

National Center for Education Statistics. (2024). *School pulse panel: Responses to the pandemic and efforts to recovery*. U.S. Department of Education. *https://nces.ed.gov/surveys/spp/results.asp#sc-safety-apr24-chart-5*

National Threat Assessment Center. (2018). *Enhancing school safety using a threat assessment model: An operational guide for preventing targeted school violence*. U.S. Department of Homeland Security, U.S. Secret Service, National Threat Assessment Center.

National Threat Assessment Center. (2019). *Averting targeted school violence: A U.S. Secret Service analysis of plots against schools*. U.S. Department of Homeland Security, U.S. Secret Service.

National Threat Assessment Center. (2021). *Protecting America's schools: A U.S. Secret Service analysis of targeted school violence*. U.S. Department of Homeland Security, U.S. Secret Service.

Nekvasil, E. K., & Cornell, D. G. (2015). Student threat assessment associated with safety in middle schools. *Journal of Threat Assessment and Management, 2*(2), 98–113.

Noltemeyer, A. L., Ward, R. M., & McLoughlin, C. (2015). Relationship between school suspension and student outcomes: A meta-analysis. *School Psychology Review, 44*(2), 224–240.

Office of the Attorney General. (n.d.). *Special report on student mental health. www.attorneygeneral.gov/wp-content/uploads/2022/04/oag_special_report_on_student_mental_health.pdf*

O'Toole, M. E. (2000). *The school shooter: A threat assessment perspective*. Critical Incident Response Group, National Center for the Analysis of Violence Crime, FBI Academy.

Payne, C., Cornell, D., & Konold, T. (2024). Anonymous reporting systems, school climate, and student threat reporting. *Journal of Threat Assessment and Management, 11*(3), 133–148.

Planty, M., Banks, D., Lindquist, C., Cartwright, J., & Witwer, A. (2020). *Tip lines for school safety: A national portrait of tip line use*. RTI International.

Pollack, W. S., Modzeleski, W., & Rooney, G. (2008). *Prior knowledge of potential school-based violence: Information students learn may prevent a targeted attack*. U.S. Department of Education.

Riddle, T., & Sinclair, S. (2019). Racial disparities in school-based disciplinary actions are associated with county-level rates of racial bias. *Proceedings of the National Academy of Sciences of the United States of America, 116*(17), 8255–8260.

Ryberg, R., Her, S., Temkin, D., & Harper, K. (2021). Despite reductions since 2011–12, Black students and students with disabilities remain more likely to experience suspension. *Child Trends. www.childtrends.org/publications/despite-reductions-black-students-and-students-with-disabilities-remain-more-likely-to-experience-suspension*

Schwartz, H. L., Ramchand, R., Barnes-Proby, D., Grant, S., Jackson, B. A., Leuschner, K. J., et al. (2016). *The role of technology in improving K–12 school safety*. Rand Corporation.

Stohlman, S., & Cornell, D. (2019). An online educational program to increase student understanding of threat assessment. *Journal of School Health, 89*(11), 899–906.

Stohlman, S., Konold, T., & Cornell, D. (2020). Evaluation of threat assessment training for school personnel. *Journal of Threat Assessment and Management, 7*, 29–40.

Strong, K., & Cornell, D. (2008). Student threat assessment in Memphis city schools: A descriptive report. *Behavioral Disorders, 34*(1), 42–54.

Welsh, R. O., & Little, S. (2018). The school discipline dilemma: A comprehensive review of disparities and alternative approaches. *Review of Educational Research, 88*(5), 752–794.

CHAPTER 28

Suicide Risk Assessment

Erik J. Reinbergs

> The pain and turmoil are hard to describe. How do you adequately convey what it is like to be in hell? You can't. You can only feel it, experience it. And I did. I felt this inside myself, and I didn't want to go on living anymore.
>
> —MARSHA M. LINEHAN (2019)

Youth suicide is a "wicked problem"—it is complex, ever-changing, both the result of and cause of other problems, without a singular formulation or solution, and with only partial answers that in turn give rise to new questions (Rittel & Webber, 1973). Indeed, despite the efforts of countless professionals, families, and organizations, the overall youth suicide rate for the 10- to 24-year-old age group in the United States has steadily increased over 56% between 2001–2021 (Centers for Disease Control and Prevention [CDC], 2024). Increases among certain groups of marginalized youth have been even greater. For example, the suicide rate among Black youth increased over 80% between 2001–2020 for the same age range (CDC, 2024). Deaths, however, are the tip of the iceberg of the suffering associated with suicidality. In 2021, 22% of high school students reported seriously considering suicide within the past year and 10% reported making at least one suicide attempt within the past year (CDC, 2023). Subgroup disparities are again substantial. Over 46% of lesbian, gay, and bisexual (LGB) youth reported seriously considering suicide in the past year (compared to 14.5% of heterosexual youth) and over 23% of LGB youth made a suicide attempt in the prior year (compared to 6.4% of their heterosexual peers) (Ivey-Stephenson et al., 2020). In the last 20 years, over 111,000 youth (10- to 24-year-olds) have died by suicide, representing over 5 million years of potential life lost (CDC, 2024).

The assessment of youth suicide risk is a dynamic task that can involve considerable stakes. Arguably, any youth encountering a mental health professional in either an assessment or treatment context should minimally be screened for suicidality—regardless of the reason for the visit or type of setting. A positive screening should trigger a comprehensive assessment of suicide risk. When done skillfully, an effective suicide assessment can promote hope, increase safety, reduce isolation, and provide information useful for intervention. This chapter outlines the essential ingredients of suicide risk assessment with youth. Overarching values-based stances of effective approaches are reviewed, followed by the assessment of several important domains of information, concluding with a discussion of integrating the information gathered during the assessment into a defensible risk formulation that can drive effective intervention with an emphasis on culturally relevant practice considerations. Legal and ethical issues, especially related to standard of care and documentation, are also briefly reviewed. The task of suicide risk assessment, when done collaboratively and therapeutically, can help put some understanding to the indescribable psychological pain Marsha Linehan mentions in the opening quote of this chapter.

BACKGROUND

Many licensed mental health professionals feel underprepared to work with suicidal individuals (Dexter-Mazza & Freeman, 2003; Jahn et al., 2016; Schmitz et al., 2012; Silva et al., 2016). Mental health professionals also report avoiding or being unwilling to work with suicidal individuals (Groth & Boccio, 2018). The lack of training requirements in suicidology for licensed mental health clinicians has been called "an egregious, enduring oversight by the mental health disciplines" (Schmitz et al., 2012, p. 297). Gaining the basic competency to assess youth suicide risk is an ethical imperative for all mental health professionals, as is managing their own reactions to potential suicide risk to prioritize the needs of the client. Recommended core competencies for working with this population are available elsewhere (e.g., Cramer et al., 2013). Providers' own emotional reactions during risk assessment can influence their recommendations to a greater extent than actual client risk (Barzilay et al., 2022).

One aspect that contributes to anxiety when working with suicidal individuals is the assumption that it is within the professionals' ability to predict suicide. Predicting suicide at the individual level, however, is a near statistical impossibility. The base rate of youth suicide (ages 10–24) is about 10.77/100,000 (CDC, 2024). This relatively low base rate precludes accurate prediction. Even if an assessment had a sensitivity of 99% and a specificity of 99%, it would only correctly predict a true positive 1% of the time for an outcome with a base rate of 10/100,000 (Pokorny, 1983). Thus, predicting suicide is arguably not the task of a risk assessment. That is, formulating risk is not analogous to predicting suicide. It is important that both clients and clinicians do not come away with unrealistic beliefs about risk assessments. Arguably, the key tasks of a risk assessment are to form an alliance with the youth and their family, gather key details on the youth's past and present suicidality to understand their risk, and gather information relevant to making effective intervention recommendations.

Ethical and Legal Considerations

Encountering suicidal youth can raise provider fears of malpractice litigation. Although more complete guidance is available elsewhere (e.g., Jobes, 2023; Stanley et al., 2019), several key issues are relevant to mention here. Three guideposts can help avoid malpractice rulings: (1) actively conveying genuine care and concern to both the youth and their caregivers throughout every contact, (2) adhering to standards of care, and (3) thoroughly documenting the information gathered during the risk assessment and one's decision making in consideration of that information. Consulting with another professional (and documenting this consultation) regarding high-risk youth can also help safeguard the provider by helping ensure quality care and by demonstrating diligence.

At a minimum, a defensible risk assessment includes gathering information about: (1) current and past suicidal ideation and related behaviors such as planning, degree of intent, preparatory activities, rehearsal behaviors, aborted or interrupted attempts, and attempts—considering the onset, duration, and intensity/severity of the ideation and behaviors—and the potential lethality of the plans and/or behaviors; (2) risk and protective factors, both static and malleable; (3) the youth's mental status; (4) past and present psychopathology and substance use; (5) antecedents or drivers of the youth's past and/or present suicidality; (6) mental health treatment history, including current medications; (7) access to lethal means, particularly firearms; (8) collateral information from the youth's caregiver(s); (9) the provision of a crisis plan if indicated, including emergency contact numbers and steps toward lethal means safety; and (10) documentation of the above information and the provider's decision-making process regarding degree of risk and actions taken.

The standard of care, however, is not synonymous with expert practice or expert recommendations. The standard of care is generally defined as what a reasonable provider with a similar patient in a similar situation would do (Jobes, 2023). Further, for malpractice to be substantiated, there must be a duty to the patient, a breach of this duty, an injury/harm of the patient, and the breach must have caused the injury (Jobes, 2023; Sher, 2015).

RISK ASSESSMENT AS A THERAPEUTIC INTERVENTION

As noted earlier, providers can experience anxiety and a range of challenging emotions when working with a suicidal young person. Because of this, providers may inadvertently jump into a legalistic risk management mode driven by provider reactions rather than remaining in a therapeutic stance that prioritizes the experience of the young person. A therapeutic stance is essential to competent risk assessment as abrupt changes in provider demeanor can discourage youth from speaking honestly about their suicidality. Instead, the best risk assessments are themselves therapeutic interactions where the young person feels validated, understood, and supported—rather than like a liability (Hawton et al., 2022). Except in the most unusual circumstances, the provider should prioritize a calm, level-headed, unhurried assessment versus quick action.

Evidence-based treatments for suicidality, most notably dialectical behavior therapy (DBT; Linehan, 1993, 2025a, 2025b) and the Collaborative Assessment and Management of Suicidality (CAMS; Jobes, 2023), likewise emphasize the importance of the therapeutic stance in working with those at risk for suicide. In DBT, a key aspect of this stance is that the provider must actively practice the skill of radical acceptance—of the client, of their own reactions, and of the reality that the person in front of them might indeed kill themselves (Linehan, 1993, 2025a, 2025b). CAMS emphasizes four pillars in its treatment philosophy: empathy, collaboration, honesty, and a suicide-focus (Jobes, 2023). Keeping these four principles in mind is essential to an effective suicide risk assessment.

Clinical Interviewing

The clinical interview remains a core tool of suicide risk assessment (Rudd & Bryan, 2022). Providers should have comfort conducting general clinical interviews with young people and their caregivers, including with adolescents who may be reluctant to share their experiences (McConaughy & Whitcomb, 2022). Keeping in mind the therapeutic stance discussed in the previous section, providers should convey a willingness to unflinchingly discuss suicide and an honest desire to understand the young person's experience. The provider may wish to start with a narrative approach, letting the young person tell the story of their suicidality by asking open-ended questions (Freedenthal, 2018). This approach has two distinct advantages in that it avoids immediately jumping into a formulaic risk assessment process and that it allows substantial amounts of critical information to be gathered. Within this narrative approach, the provider should be listening not only for information critical to the risk assessment but also for opportunities to validate the youth's experience. Although finding the kernel of truth to validate is at times challenging, it is essential (Linehan, 1997). The provider must also keep in mind that one can effectively validate the experience of suicidality without validating suicide as a solution to the experience. Throughout the narrative process, there will likely be natural points in which the provider can ask clarifying questions and obtain information relevant to the youth's risk.

Following the narrative section, the provider can ask to transition to more specific questions to gather any key information that was not already disclosed. This includes several aspects of the 10 pieces of suicide risk assessment discussed earlier. Information not already collected about past and present ideation, planning, intent, and behaviors (along with their onset, duration, and intensity/severity) are gathered here, in addition to information about risk and protective factors, access to lethal means, treatment history, the presence of psychopathology, and mental status information.

Although considering risk and protective factors is essential, there are no universal combinations of factors that accurately predict risk (Franklin et al., 2017). The role of risk and protective factors must be considered within the unique context of the individual. For example, a client may have multiple risk factors typically considered to be associated with increased risk in group research, but these risk factors might not be very relevant to the individual and their specific concerns. On the other hand, a person may only have one identified risk factor, but this risk factor is considered extreme and unbearable to the person. Within these two examples, someone with only one risk factor may be at greater risk than someone with multiple risk factors. Thus, simple actuarial or checklist approaches to risk factors can be misleading. Risk factors may also differentially contribute to chronic risk (e.g., distant past attempt) versus acute risk (e.g., current crisis and ready access to lethal means). Similarly, the level of risk conferred by risk factors is not static. An identified risk factor could contribute mild risk one day for a client and contribute extreme risk the next day.

Last, the provider and youth should collaboratively attempt to clarify the "drivers" of the youth's suicidality. Drivers are the self-identified reasons (e.g., thoughts, feelings, situations, problems) that lead the youth to seriously consider suicide (Jobes, 2023). Too often, unskilled risk assessments miss this essential step. Identifying drivers is key to (1) a true understanding of the youth's perspective, (2) developing actionable treatment targets, and (3) conveying hope that a more livable life is possible and that treatment can help them get there. Drivers and risk factors may sometimes overlap; however, drivers are conceptualized as modifiable concerns rather than intrinsic traits.

Extending the Clinical Interview: Chain Analysis

Chain analysis (more broadly referred to as functional assessment) is the nonexperimental process of understanding the vulnerability factors (motivating operations), pre-cursers (antecedents), specific behaviors (behavioral topography), and consequences (both short term and long term) of a target behavior such as a suicide attempt or episode of intense suicidal ideation (Linehan, 1993; Rizvi & Ritschel, 2014). Chain analyses typically go beyond overt behaviors to include thoughts, emotions, sensations, and urges present at each link of the chain. This can allow the provider to identify situations that may precipitate increases in suicidality, what interventions (i.e., skills) may be more effective at various points of the chain for the youth, and to form a hypothesis about the function and maintaining consequences of the behaviors. This is invaluable information for effective intervention. If time allows and the youth is willing, conducting a chain analysis as part of the risk assessment can enhance the provider's understanding of risk and how to modify their response accordingly. It also may help the youth have a way of understanding their suicidality, de-pathologize the experience, and begin to understand that changing behavioral patterns is possible. This can be especially relevant if the risk assessment is being conducted because the youth recently engaged in a concerning suicide-related behavior.

Assessment Tools

Assessment tools and psychometric measures can be useful components of a risk assessment. However, as in any assessment, the clinician should drive the assessment instead of the measure. A score on a psychometric measure is a datapoint in a risk assessment and is not in and of itself a risk assessment. A measure should also not get in the way of the therapeutic stance adopted by the provider. Too often risk assessments look like the provider pulling out and reading verbatim from a standardized assessment when a young person mentions suicide. This has the potential to hinder the information the provider can gather if the youth experiences this as invalidating and as if they are a liability to be managed. Another pitfall is that providers sometimes use risk *screeners* as full assessment measures rather than using it as only the starting point for additional information gathering. Two common and well-supported suicide risk screening measures are the Ask Screening Questions (ASQ; Horowitz et al., 2012) and the Columbia-Suicide Severity Rating Scale Screener (C-SSRS Screener; Bjureberg et al., 2022). However, these are not sufficient tools for a comprehensive risk assessment.

Three commonly used assessment tools for more comprehensive assessment include the full version of the C-SSRS (Posner et al., 2011), the CAMS Suicide Status Form (CAMS SSF; Jobes, 2023), and the Linehan Risk Assessment and Management Protocol (LRAMP; Linehan et al., 2012). For most practitioners and across most settings, the CAMS SSF will likely be the most easily implemented due to its collaborative design, inclusion of driver identification and treatment planning, emphasis on safety planning, and its ability to be used as legally defensible risk documentation. A strength of the LRAMP, due to the DBT emphasis on keeping clients out of the hospital, is its checklist of alternative actions taken when hospitalization is not warranted. It also asks the provider to specify why the risk assessment was (or was not) conducted in a specific instance. Other tools that may be relevant include the Suicide Ideation Questionnaire (SIQ; Reynolds, 1991) and Suicide Ideation Questionnaire—Junior (SIQ-JR; Reynolds & Mazza, 1999), the Reasons for Living Inventory for Adolescents (RFL-A; Gutierrez et al., 2000), the Beck Hopelessness Scale (Beck et al., 1974; Granö et al., 2017), and the Beck Scale for Suicide Ideation (Beck et al., 1979; Holi et al., 2005).

Given that measures cannot predict suicide at an individual level, it should be noted that national entities such as the National Institute for Health and Care Excellence (NICE) in the United Kingdom explicitly recommend *against* using risk assessment tools and scales (NICE, 2022)—largely for the reasons described earlier. These tools may falsely give the impression that risk is static rather than dynamic (NICE, 2022). They also recommend that these scales not be used to determine intervention access (or intervention discharge) (NICE, 2022).

Collateral Information

Although the inclusion of collateral information generally benefits all risk assessments, it is essential in youth suicide risk assessment. Caregivers can supply information about the youth's history, current behaviors, and changes in functioning that a young person may be unwilling or unable to accurately provide. Although often unavailable during the actual risk assessment, requesting records releases from previous treatment providers can also be useful in obtaining information about past behaviors and treatment history. In general, interviews with the youth and parent should be conducted separately when possible—although it is often wise to bring all parties together to discuss the risk formulation and next steps at the end of the risk assessment. When feasible, gathering information from a school staff member familiar with the student (e.g., a teacher, school counselor, school psychologist) can also provide important contextual information.

FORMULATING RISK

Traditionally, suicide risk assessments conclude with a clinical judgement about whether the client's suicide risk is low, moderate, high, or imminent. Imminent risk generally requires the initiation of emergency procedures in accordance with state law. Although definitions may vary by state, imminent risk is generally thought of as a level of risk in which serious injury or death is likely in the very near future if immediate intervention is not provided. A judgement of imminent risk, however, is a rare outcome of a risk assessment. Most clients will not require emergency detention or hospitalization. Beyond imminent risk, which has its own definitional uncertainties, there are no agreed-on definitions of low, moderate, or high risk (Berman & Silverman, 2014). To further complicate this judgement, a person may be a low chronic risk but high acute risk or vice versa.

Some have argued that risk stratification following a suicide risk assessment is too inaccurate to be useful and may cause harm (Carter & Spittal, 2018; NICE, 2022). Indeed, the literature on risk stratification demonstrates that the practice is of questionable validity (Berman & Silverman, 2014; Carter & Spittal, 2018). The NICE guidelines support this claim, explicitly recommending *against* using global risk stratification (NICE, 2022). However, the use of risk stratification is still arguably the standard of care within the United States. If continuing to use risk stratifications for legal reasons, the provider may wish to furnish documentation explaining their use and awareness of this limitation. A middle ground may be the approach adopted on the latest CAMS SSF, which asks the provider to rate their concern about the client's relative *stability* (i.e., rather than risk) by marking either none, mild, moderate, serious, or extreme (Jobes, 2023). This approach focuses the assessment on what is needed to stabilize a person's safety, rather than assigning interventions based on risk stratification.

This chapter previously discussed that prediction is not the goal of risk formulation. This information also calls into question whether the goal of formulating "risk" is similarly problematized. Although risk should be considered in decision making, it should not be the only factor. NICE (2022) frames this consideration as follows:

> Assessment of a person's needs, vulnerabilities, and safety should be a part of every assessment and that 'risk' should not be used to determine care management in isolation of other factors. . . . [M]ental health staff should conduct a risk formulation to place the person's safety considerations in context with their strengths and difficulties. (p. 57)

The NICE guidelines emphasize that using arbitrary risk thresholds to determine access to care could be harmful (NICE, 2022).

Disposition

Despite these concerns, the overarching goal of risk formulation is to collaboratively determine an appropriate course of action for the client—that is, to conduct an assessment for effective intervention. This decision will be informed by best-practice evidence, client/family preferences, the availability of resources, and the setting in which the risk assessment is conducted. Intervention recommendations should be tailored to increase safety and address client-identified drivers. Without engaging in assessment with the goal of effective intervention, it is difficult to have enough information to develop actionable care recommendations instead of global risk judgements. There is no one-size-fits-all care pathway for suicidal youth. Several suicide-specific interventions should likely be considered, however. Youth with identified risk should be engaged to collaboratively develop a safety plan (also called a crisis response plan or a stabilization plan) and their guardians should be engaged in supporting this plan (Bryan & Rudd, 2018; Jobes, 2023; Stanley & Brown, 2012). Youth and their families should receive lethal means counseling, particularly regarding firearm access, and part of their safety plan should involve reducing access to lethal means (Bandealy et al., 2020; Jobes, 2023; Stanley et al., 2020). The intervention with the strongest evidence for suicidal youth is DBT for adolescents (DBT-A; McCauley et al., 2018; Miller et al., 2017; Rathus & Miller, 2014). However, DBT-A is resource intensive and may not be readily available in many areas. Other best-practice treatments include CAMS (Jobes, 2023) or cognitive-behavioral therapy (CBT) specifically adapted to suicide, such as brief CBT for suicide prevention (BCBT-SP; Bryan, 2015). Each of these treatments are designed to target suicidal thoughts and behaviors directly, rather than treating an identified disorder (such as depression) to indirectly reduce suicidality. Adaptations of these treatments for adolescents typically involve the family in a support role in the youth's care through learning about suicide, helping to reduce access to lethal means and increase parental monitoring, supporting treatment engagement, improving communication with their child, and/or coaching adaptive use of skills learned in therapy. Cases in which family disfunction is severe and is an identified driver of the youth's suicidality may need special consideration regarding the degree of family involvement or whether a referral to family therapy is needed in addition to the suicide-specific treatment.

As noted earlier, referral to emergency services (e.g., police, emergency medical services, emergency rooms) or hospitalization should be reserved for cases where imminent risk is identified and is not able to be reduced with less restrictive interventions. There is nonexperimental evidence in adult literature that hospitalization for suicidality may be iatrogenic (Ross et al., 2023; Ward-Ciesielski & Rizvi, 2021). The treatments with the best evidence of reducing suicidality were developed as outpatient treatments (e.g., DBT, CAMS, BCBT-SP). However, hospitalization may be considered when any level of suicide risk is present in addition to a concern that warrants hospital treatment such as acute intoxication, severe akathisia or agitation, a manic episode, acute psychosis, or extremely severe depression.

CULTURALLY RELEVANT PRACTICE CONSIDERATIONS

Suicide is culturally situated, and suicide rates vary greatly across demographics and locations. Critical suicidology prioritizes an analysis of power relations at the individual, group, and societal levels in how suicide is theorized, how suicide is experienced/embodied, and in the formation and maintenance of disparities related to suicide (Chandler et al., 2022). The stigmas, meanings, and practices of suicide vary substantially across time and cultures. Even in cursory reviews of Western history, suicide has been considered an honorable/noble response, a spiritual malady, a crime against God, a crime against the state, an intellectual or romantic response to an unfeeling world, the result of the sociological organization of society, or an individualized medical concern, to name a few (Alvarez, 1990; Kushner, 1991). Whether a person has a legal right to suicide is also still contested (Stefan, 2016). The complexity of suicide in society is perhaps messier than many providers consider. There are, in the end, many reasons to choose death. Indeed, Camus wrote, "There is but one truly serious philosophical problem, and that is suicide. Judging whether life is or is not worth living amounts to answering the fundamental question of philosophy" (Camus, 1955/1991, p. 3). For example, suicide prevention in early U.S. history was, in part, used to ensure enslaved Black people were kept alive on forced labor camps for the financial (and sexual) gain of White enslavers (Snyder, 2015). In a society where some lives are valued more than others, where the assertion that Black lives matter receives violent backlash, providers need to be deeply attuned to the profound degree to which their clients' lives may be devalued by society and, unfortunately, other health care providers.

For many marginalized groups, seeking health care is fraught with risk. This is especially true in seeking care for suicidality, which often evokes stigma and fear of involuntary detention (which in turn may lead to cascading fears regarding police involvement, job loss, bankruptcy, and forced separation from children/family). These fears are not distributed equally. For example, the experience of being transported to the emergency room by the police can be experienced vastly differently by Black clients than by White clients due to the history of police violence in Black communities. This is yet another reason why emergency hospitalization procedures should only be used in situations of last resort. When clients do seek care for suicide, there is little guarantee that providers are using evidence-based and culturally responsive approaches.

A culturally responsive risk assessment adheres to best practices while considering client and provider experiences that arise during the encounter and are situated in larger societal structures. In addition to being aware of cultural influences, providers should have knowledge of the power dynamics of the social systems that influence clients' lives (e.g., the immigration system, the health care system, the prison-industrial complex, the education system, neoliberal policy). Such an approach has been termed *structural competency* within the medical literature (Metzl & Hansen, 2014). Both individual experiences and structural systems heavily influence suicide and related behaviors, stigma, and help-seeking behaviors among racially marginalized adolescents (Goldston et al., 2008). The following quote exemplifies the spirit of structural competency: "No one has a right to work with poor people unless they have a real analysis of why people are poor" (Morris et al., 2009, pp. 113–114; Neff et al., 2019).

A structural competency approach asks providers not only to help clients build lives worth living but also to build communities and societies worth living in. There are myriad societal factors that are associated with increased risk of suicide. For example, both institutional and interpersonal discrimination are associated with increased risk (Wang et al., 2021). Increases in minimum wage are associated with decreases in the suicide rate (Gertner et al., 2019). Neighborhood poverty is associated with increased suicidal ideation and attempts among adolescents in Canada (Dupéré et al., 2009). Increases in temperatures due to climate change have been associated with increased suicide rates in the United States and Mexico (Burke et al., 2018). Insufficient school funding appears associated with the rate of attempted suicide among adolescent males (Fang, 2018). Laws, such as marriage equality laws and gun safety laws, affect differences in adolescent suicide rates across states (Knopov et al., 2019; Raifman et al., 2017).

Attempts to psychometrically capture aspects of cultural differences as they relate to suicide, such as with the Cultural Assessment of Risk for Suicide measure (CARS; Chu et al., 2013), have measured domains of the cultural theory and model of suicide, including social discord, minority stress, idioms of distress, and cultural sanctions (Chu et al., 2010). While many researchers are actively pursuing research on suicide in marginalized youth populations (e.g. *www.youthsuicideresearch.org*), most existing randomized controlled trials of suicide and self-harm related treatments consist of majority White, non-Hispanic, and straight participants from North American or European countries (Maria Guzmán et al., 2024). This is especially concerning given that most suicides occur in middle- and low-income countries (World Health Organization, 2014). Further, bilingually trained mental health providers remain rare in the United States (Delgado-Romero et al., 2018).

However, there is emerging evidence of the effectiveness of culturally adapting suicide-specific treatments such as DBT to marginalized groups (see Haft et al., 2022, for a review of DBT adaptations). Many types of adaptation have been used, including language, persons, metaphors, content, concepts, goals, methods, and context. For example, concept adaptations are ways of include relating or presenting the concepts in DBT in ways that better match the client's culture and salient experiences, such as including *dichos* (sayings) and the concept of *familismo* (prioritizing family) with Spanish-speaking clients (Mercado & Hinojosa, 2017), or incorporating ideas of social harmony and elder respect into interpersonal effectiveness skills with a Chinese client (Cheng & Merrick, 2017). DBT adaptations particularly relevant for assessment include accounting for how acculturative stress, cultural differences, and/or discrimination interferes with effective skill use, focusing on somatic expressions of emotions in chain analyses, and examining how the stigma of suicide or of receiving mental health treatment affect the client (Haft et al., 2022).

Demographic Disparities

A full review of suicide-related disparities is beyond the scope of this risk assessment chapter. However, a basic understanding of key demographic differences in suicide may help the provider understand patterns that may arise over the course of many risk assessments and provide information about a client's chronic risk—and make clear the social structures that inequitably distribute risk. Native youth typically have the highest suicide rate, followed by White youth (CDC, 2024). While Black youth have historically had lower suicide rates than White youth, the suicide rate for Black youth is increasing faster when compared to White youth (CDC, 2024). Concerningly, Black youth are most likely to skip questions related to suicide attempts on the Youth Risk Behavior Survey (YRBS; Baiden et al., 2023). While female adolescents are more likely to attempt suicide, male adolescents are more likely to die by suicide (Rhodes et al., 2014). Sexual minority adolescents are particular at risk, with nearly 1 in 2 reporting seriously considering suicide in the past year and approximately 1 in 4 reporting attempting suicide in the year prior (Ivey-Stephenson et al., 2020). Although data quality are more limited, trans and gender-nonconforming youth are at even greater risk (Kirakosian et al., 2023; Toomey et al., 2018). Common risk factors appear to be more highly associated with suicide risk in some groups of racially marginalized youth than with others (Lee & Wong, 2020). For example, mental health problems were the most common antecedent of suicide among White women, but for other groups interpersonal problems were the most common antecedent: Latinx decedents had a greater likelihood of intimate partner problems; Native American decedents were more likely to have experienced a loss by suicide that preceded their death; and Black youth decedents were less likely to have a prior attempt (Lee & Wong, 2020).

FUTURE DIRECTIONS

Multiple efforts are needed to make progress on the "wicked problem" of youth suicide (Rittel & Webber, 1973). Improving risk assessments for youth is an important aspect of these efforts. As reviewed earlier, many mental health providers feel woefully untrained in working with suicidal individuals and many actively avoid serving this population. Youth mental health providers must adopt a paradigm shift in which training for the leading cause of death in their field is prioritized, valued, and doggedly pursued in a rigorous, compassionate, and culturally responsive fashion. Jobes (2023) explains the problem this way:

> Refusing to see or work with suicidal risk is akin to a primary care doctor who is unwilling to evaluate or treat symptoms of heart disease, which is the #1 killer in the world. Granted a cardiologist may be needed in more severe cases, but the vast majority of patients with symptoms of heart disease are effectively treated by general practitioners with no particular need for a specialist. (p. 100)

This thinking represents a major shift for the youth mental health workforce. Inherent in this shift is that skillful, therapeutic assessment of suicide risk reduces the need to refer for hospitalization or emergency room assessment for any youth that expresses suicide risk. Discrimination, microaggressions, and careless misunderstandings severely curtail the likelihood that the risk assessment encounter will be therapeutic. The benefits of this shift will be most strongly felt by marginalized youth. How to best inculcate this shift in new providers and in the existing workforce is an open question.

Rather than developing psychometric measures for risk prediction, future research exploring how assessment tools can be created and delivered in such a way to support the therapeutic approach described throughout this chapter is needed. The CAMS SSF is an excellent example of this idea as the tool itself is designed to foster both best-practice risk assessment and a collaborative stance between provider and client. Similarly, additional research on the most effective ways to involve parents in risk assessments is needed. This is especially true for parents who hold stigmatized views of suicide and of mental healthcare. Here again, the CAMS protocol now includes a stabilization support plan designed to help guide guardians and other caregivers in helping to ensure safety. Approaches that emphasize values clarification and listening for family strengths may be promising avenues.

Brief interventions such as safety planning and lethal means counseling are now standard aspects of working with suicidal youth and their families. These are often delivered within the same encounter as the suicide risk assessment. Additional research is needed on adopting these practices across nonclinical settings (e.g., schools) and whether there are additional brief interventions that can increase the therapeutic aspects of suicide risk assessment. How to extend risk assessment follow-up/monitoring most effectively when the provider is not working in an ongoing therapeutic role with the youth is also a complex question needing study across settings. One example of a middle ground intervention—interventions more intensive than a one session brief intervention but less intensive than typical outpatient therapy—is the Coping with Long Term Active Suicide Program (CLASP), which focuses on gaining connection to care, securing collateral supports, and pursuing values-based actions (Miller et al., 2022; Yen et al., 2019). Additional applications of middle ground

TABLE 28.1. Resources for Further Study

Resource	Description
Brief Cognitive Behavioral Therapy for Suicide Prevention (2018) by Craig Bryan and David Rudd	A CBT manual for working with suicidal clients, including assessment.
Child and Adolescent Suicidal Behavior: School-based Prevention, Assessment, and Intervention (2nd ed.) (2021) by David Miller	Reviews working with suicidal youth (including assessment), with a focus on school settings.
Counseling on Access to Lethal Means	An award-winning free online course for providers on lethal means counseling techniques, with substantial coverage of decreasing access to firearms. Available at *https://zerosuicide.edc.org/resources/trainings-courses/CALM-course*
DBT manuals for adolescents • *Dialectical Behavior Therapy with Suicidal Adolescents* (2017) by Alec Miller, Jill Rathus, and Marsha Linehan • *DBT Skills Manual for Adolescents* (2014) by Jill Rathus and Alec Miller	The adolescent adaptation of DBT, including adaptation of the skills materials. They also review how, when, and why to involve parents of suicidal adolescents.
DBT manuals • *Cognitive-behavioral Treatment for Borderline Personality Disorder* (1993) by Marsha Linehan • *DBT Skills Training Manual (rev. ed.)* (2025a) by Marsha Linehan • *DBT Skills Training Handouts and Worksheets (rev. ed.)* (2025b) by Marsha Linehan	The canonical DBT treatment materials by Marsha Linehan. The first describes the overall treatment philosophy, goals, and strategies. The second is a teaching manual for the DBT skills groups. The third has handouts and worksheets for client use in skills groups. Formal, official trainings in DBT are conducted through the Behavior Tech Institute at *https://behavioraltech.org*
Helping the Suicidal Person: Tips and Techniques for Professionals (2018) by Stacey Freedenthal	A collection of tips, techniques, and considerations in working with suicidal clients from assessment to treatment.
Managing Suicidal Risk: A Collaborative Approach (3rd ed.) (2023) by David Jobes	The treatment manual for the Collaborative Assessment and Management of Suicidality (CAMS), including the Suicide Status Form (CAMS SSF). The latest edition more extensively covers adolescent adaptation and parent involvement. Formal, official training is offered through *https://cams-care.com*
Suicide in Schools: A Practitioner's Guide to Multi-level Prevention, Assessment, Intervention, and Postvention (2nd ed.) (2024) by Terri Erbacher, Jonathan Singer, and Scott Poland	Covers best-practice school-based suicide prevention strategies, including assessment.

Note. Full citations are listed in the References section. Resources are listed alphabetically with no order of quality implied.

interventions could be tested in diverse settings such as schools.

More research, especially qualitative research, is needed to better understand potential harms of suicide risk assessment with young people. Although research has demonstrated that asking about suicide does not increase suicide risk (Dazzi et al., 2014; Gould et al., 2005; Harris & Goh, 2017), there may be other harms associated with the assessment—many of which have been mentioned throughout this chapter. The study of these harms could be further broken down by setting (e.g., primary care offices, hospital, school, specialty mental health clinics) and by type of harm (e.g., privacy, financial, relational, education, mental health, cultural invalidation/discrimination). It is likely that these nodes of potential harms may influence each other in complex ways and may be well-suited to be studied with network analysis techniques. How these harms are experienced across identity and social location is important information that could be used to improve current suicide risk assessment practice.

In addition, more research is needed on the processes and treatment options that follow risk assessment. The efficacy of assessment for effective intervention relies on the assumption that effective intervention is available. This is not always the case, particularly in low-income communities. Racially marginalized youth, for example, are more likely than their White peers to receive mental health services in schools due to lower access barriers in the school setting (Green et al., 2020). However, comparatively few suicide-specific individual level interventions have been experimentally tested in schools. Indeed, the relative lack of experimental trials of suicide-specific psychotherapy for youth does not match the need. Despite being the second leading cause of death for the 10- to 18-year-old age group, DBT-A is the only adolescent suicide psychotherapy with two independent randomized controlled trials supporting its use (McCauley et al., 2018). Several factors contribute to this lack of research including funding constraints, the regulatory/legal complexities of research trials with suicidal youth, and stigma. More intervention research is needed in both clinical settings and in alternate settings such as schools. Best-practice guidance for working with suicidal students in school settings is available (see Erbacher et al., 2024; Miller, 2021). More research is also needed on how to best implement existing evidence-based practices for youth suicide into routine practice across settings.

This chapter provides foundational awareness of evidence-based and culturally responsive youth suicide risk assessment. Readers are encouraged to continue to build competency with this population, as they are often in great need of services but encounter providers untrained or unwilling to treat them. Brief descriptions of additional resources for providers to obtain further education and training on this topic are provided in Table 28.1.

REFERENCES

Alvarez, A. (1990). *The savage god: A study of suicide.* Norton.

Baiden, P., Onyeaka, H. K., Aneni, K., Wood, B. M., LaBrenz, C. A., Hagedorn, A., et al. (2023). Racial/ethnic differences in adolescents' non-response to suicide attempt: Findings from the Youth Risk Behavior Survey, 2015–2019. *Journal of Psychiatric Research, 166*, 115–121.

Bandealy, A., Herrera, N., Weissman, M., & Scheidt, P. (2020). Use of lethal means restriction counseling for suicide prevention in pediatric primary care. *Preventive Medicine, 130*, 105855.

Barzilay, S., Gagnon, A., Yaseen, Z. S., Chennapragada, L., Lloveras, L., Bloch-Elkouby, S., & Galynker, I. (2022). Associations between clinicians' emotion regulation, treatment recommendations, and patient suicidal ideation. *Suicide and Life-Threatening Behavior, 52*(2), 329–340.

Beck, A. T., Kovacs, M., & Weissman, A. (1979). Assessment of suicidal intention: The Scale for Suicide Ideation. *Journal of Consulting and Clinical Psychology, 47*(2), 343–352.

Beck, A. T., Weissman, A., Lester, D., & Trexler, L. (1974). The measurement of pessimism: The Hopelessness Scale. *Journal of Consulting and Clinical Psychology, 42*(6), 861–865.

Berman, A. L., & Silverman, M. M. (2014). Suicide risk assessment and risk formulation part ii: Suicide risk formulation and the determination of levels of risk. *Suicide and Life-Threatening Behavior, 44*(4), 432–443.

Bjureberg, J., Dahlin, M., Carlborg, A., Edberg, H., Haglund, A., & Runeson, B. (2022). Columbia-Suicide Severity Rating Scale Screen Version: Initial screening for suicide risk in a psychiatric emergency department. *Psychological Medicine, 52*(16), 3904–3912.

Bryan, C. J. (Ed.). (2015). *Cognitive-behavioral therapy for preventing suicide attempts: A guide to brief treatments across clinical settings.* Routledge/Taylor & Francis Group.

Bryan, C. J., & Rudd, M. D. (2018). *Brief cognitive-behavioral therapy for suicide prevention.* Guilford Press.

Burke, M., González, F., Baylis, P., Heft-Neal, S., Baysan, C., Basu, S., & Hsiang, S. (2018). Higher temperatures increase suicide rates in the United States and Mexico. *Nature Climate Change, 8*(8), 723–729.

Camus, A. (1991). *The myth of Sisyphus and other essays* (J. O'Brien, Trans.; 1st Vintage international ed). Vintage Books. (Original work published 1955)

Carter, G., & Spittal, M. J. (2018). Suicide risk assessment: Risk stratification is not accurate enough to be clinically useful and alternative approaches are needed. *Crisis, 39*(4), 229–234.

Centers for Disease Control and Prevention (CDC). (2023). *2021 YRBS data user's guide* (Youth Risk Behavior Surveillance System). *www.cdc.gov/healthyyouth/data/yrbs/pdf/2021/2021_YRBS_Data_Users_Guide_508.pdf*

Centers for Disease Control and Prevention (CDC). (2024). *Web-Based Injury Statistics Query and Reporting Systems (WISQARS). www.cdc.gov/injury/wisqars/index.html*

Chandler, A., Cover, R., & Fitzpatrick, S. J. (2022). Critical suicide studies, between methodology and ethics: Introduction. *Health: An Interdisciplinary*

Journal for the Social Study of Health, Illness and Medicine, 26(1), 3–9.

Cheng, P.-H., & Merrick, E. (2017). Cultural adaptation of dialectical behavior therapy for a Chinese international student with eating disorder and depression. *Clinical Case Studies, 16*(1), 42–57.

Chu, J., Floyd, R., Diep, H., Pardo, S., Goldblum, P., & Bongar, B. (2013). A tool for the culturally competent assessment of suicide: The Cultural Assessment of Risk for Suicide (CARS) Measure. *Psychological Assessment, 25*(2), 424–434.

Chu, J. P., Goldblum, P., Floyd, R., & Bongar, B. (2010). The cultural theory and model of suicide. *Applied and Preventive Psychology, 14*(1–4), 25–40.

Cramer, R. J., Johnson, S. M., McLaughlin, J., Rausch, E. M., & Conroy, M. A. (2013). Suicide risk assessment training for psychology doctoral programs: Core competencies and a framework for training. *Training and Education in Professional Psychology, 7*(1), 1–11.

Dazzi, T., Gribble, R., Wessely, S., & Fear, N. T. (2014). Does asking about suicide and related behaviours induce suicidal ideation? What is the evidence? *Psychological Medicine, 44*(16), 3361–3363.

Delgado-Romero, E. A., De Los Santos, J., Raman, V. S., Merrifield, J. N., Vazquez, M. S., Monroig, M. M., et al. (2018). Caught in the middle: Spanish-speaking bilingual mental health counselors as language brokers. *Journal of Mental Health Counseling, 40*(4), 341–352.

Dexter-Mazza, E. T., & Freeman, K. A. (2003). Graduate training and the treatment of suicidal clients: The students' perspective. *Suicide and Life-Threatening Behavior, 33*(2), 211–218.

Dupéré, V., Leventhal, T., & Lacourse, É. (2009). Neighborhood poverty and suicidal thoughts and attempts in late adolescence. *Psychological Medicine, 39*(8), 1295–1306.

Erbacher, T. A., Singer, J. B., & Poland, S. (2024). *Suicide in schools: A practitioner's guide to multi-level prevention, assessment, intervention, and postvention* (2nd ed.). Routledge/Taylor & Francis Group.

Fang, M. (2018). School poverty and the risk of attempted suicide among adolescents. *Social Psychiatry and Psychiatric Epidemiology, 53*(9), 955–967.

Franklin, J. C., Ribeiro, J. D., Fox, K. R., Bentley, K. H., Kleiman, E. M., Huang, X., et al. (2017). Risk factors for suicidal thoughts and behaviors: A meta-analysis of 50 years of research. *Psychological Bulletin, 143*(2), 187–232.

Freedenthal, S. (2018). *Helping the suicidal person: Tips and techniques for professionals.* Routledge/Taylor & Francis Group.

Gertner, A. K., Rotter, J. S., & Shafer, P. R. (2019). Association between state minimum wages and suicide rates in the U.S. *American Journal of Preventive Medicine, 56*(5), 648–654.

Goldston, D. B., Molock, S. D., Whitbeck, L. B., Murakami, J. L., Zayas, L. H., & Hall, G. C. N. (2008). Cultural considerations in adolescent suicide prevention and psychosocial treatment. *American Psychologist, 63*(1), 14–31.

Gould, M. S., Marrocco, F. A., Kleinman, M., Thomas, J. G., Mostkoff, K., Cote, J., & Davies, M. (2005). Evaluating iatrogenic risk of youth suicide screening programs: A randomized controlled trial. *JAMA, 293*(13), 1635.

Granö, N., Oksanen, J., Kallionpää, S., & Roine, M. (2017). Specificity and sensitivity of the Beck Hopelessness Scale for suicidal ideation among adolescents entering early intervention service. *Nordic Journal of Psychiatry, 71*(1), 72–76.

Green, J. G., McLaughlin, K. A., Alegría, M., Bettini, E., Gruber, M., Hoagwood, K., et al. (2020). Associations of sociodemographic factors and psychiatric disorders with type of school-based mental health services received by youth. *Journal of Adolescent Health, 67*(3), 392–400.

Groth, T., & Boccio, D. E. (2018). Psychologists' willingness to provide services to individuals at risk of suicide. *Suicide and Life-Threatening Behavior, 49*(5), 1241–1254.

Gutierrez, P. M., Osman, A., Kopper, B. A., & Barrios, F. X. (2000). Why young people do not kill themselves: The Reasons for Living Inventory for Adolescents. *Journal of Clinical Child Psychology, 29*(2), 177–187.

Haft, S. L., O'Grady, S. M., Shaller, E. A. L., & Liu, N. H. (2022). Cultural adaptations of dialectical behavior therapy: A systematic review. *Journal of Consulting and Clinical Psychology, 90*(10), 787–801.

Harris, K. M., & Goh, M. T.-T. (2017). Is suicide assessment harmful to participants? Findings from a randomized controlled trial. *International Journal of Mental Health Nursing, 26*(2), 181–190.

Hawton, K., Lascelles, K., Pitman, A., Gilbert, S., & Silverman, M. (2022). Assessment of suicide risk in mental health practice: Shifting from prediction to therapeutic assessment, formulation, and risk management. *The Lancet Psychiatry, 9*(11), 922–928.

Holi, M. M., Pelkonen, M., Karlsson, L., Kiviruusu, O., Ruuttu, T., Heilä, H., et al. (2005). Psychometric properties and clinical utility of the Scale for Suicidal Ideation (SSI) in adolescents. *BMC Psychiatry, 5*(1), 8.

Horowitz, L. M., Bridge, J. A., Teach, S. J., Ballard, E., Klima, J., Rosenstein, D. L., et al. (2012). Ask Suicide-Screening Questions (ASQ): A brief instrument for the pediatric emergency department. *Archives of Pediatrics & Adolescent Medicine, 166*(12), 1170.

Ivey-Stephenson, A. Z., Demissie, Z., Crosby, A. E., Stone, D. M., Gaylor, E., Wilkins, N., et al. (2020). Suicidal ideation and behaviors among high school students—Youth Risk Behavior Survey, United States, 2019. *MMWR Supplements, 69*(1), 47–55.

Jahn, D. R., Quinnett, P., & Ries, R. (2016). The influence of training and experience on mental health practitioners' comfort working with suicidal individuals. *Professional Psychology: Research and Practice, 47*(2), 130–138.

Jobes, D. A. (2023). *Managing suicidal risk: A collaborative approach* (3rd ed.). Guilford Press.

Kirakosian, N., Stanton, A. M., McKetchnie, S. M., King, D., Dolotina, B., O'Cleirigh, C., et al. (2023). Suicidal ideation disparities among transgender and gender diverse compared to cisgender community health patients. *Journal of General Internal Medicine, 38*, 1357–1365.

Knopov, A., Sherman, R. J., Raifman, J. R., Larson, E., & Siegel, M. B. (2019). Household gun ownership and youth suicide rates at the state level, 2005–2015. *American Journal of Preventive Medicine, 56*(3), 335–342.

Kushner, H. I. (1991). *American suicide: A psychocultural exploration*. Rutgers University Press.

Lee, C. S., & Wong, Y. J. (2020). Racial/ethnic and gender differences in the antecedents of youth suicide. *Cultural Diversity and Ethnic Minority Psychology, 26*(4), 532–543.

Linehan, M. M. (1993). *Cognitive-behavioral treatment of borderline personality disorder*. Guilford Press.

Linehan, M. M. (1997). Validation and psychotherapy. In A. C. Bohart & L. S. Greenberg (Eds.), *Empathy reconsidered: New directions in psychotherapy*. (pp. 353–392). American Psychological Association.

Linehan, M. M. (2019, December 30). How Marsha Linehan developed the central feature of dialectical behavior therapy. *Psychology Today*. *www.psychologytoday.com/us/articles/201912/how-marsha-linehan-developed-the-central-feature-dialectical-behavior-therapy*

Linehan, M. M. (2025a). *DBT skills training manual* (rev. ed.). Guilford Press.

Linehan, M. M. (2025b). *DBT skills training handouts and worksheets* (rev. ed.) Guilford Press.

Linehan, M. M., Comtois, K. A., & Ward-Ciesielski, E. F. (2012). Assessing and managing risk with suicidal individuals. *Cognitive and Behavioral Practice, 19*(2), 218–232.

Maria Guzmán, E. M., LeDuc, M. K., Cha, C. B., Goger, P., Ng, M. Y., Huang, X., et al. (2024). Accounting for diversity in the treatment of suicide and self-injury: A systematic review of the past 50 years of randomized controlled trials. *Suicide and Life-Threatening Behavior, 54*(2), 250–262.

McCauley, E., Berk, M. S., Asarnow, J. R., Adrian, M., Cohen, J., Korslund, K., et al. (2018). Efficacy of Dialectical Behavior Therapy for adolescents at high risk for suicide: A randomized clinical trial. *JAMA Psychiatry, 75*(8), 777–785.

McConaughy, S. H., & Whitcomb, S. A. (2022). *Clinical interviews for children and adolescents: Assessment to intervention* (3rd ed.). Guilford Press.

Mercado, A., & Hinojosa, Y. (2017). Culturally adapted dialectical behavior therapy in an underserved community mental health setting: A Latina adult case study. *Practice Innovations, 2*(2), 80–93.

Metzl, J. M., & Hansen, H. (2014). Structural competency: Theorizing a new medical engagement with stigma and inequality. *Social Science & Medicine, 103*, 126–133.

Miller, A. L., Rathus, J. H., & Linehan, M. (2017). *Dialectical behavior therapy with suicidal adolescents*. Guilford Press.

Miller, D. N. (2021). *Child and adolescent suicidal behavior: School-based prevention, assessment, and intervention* (2nd ed.). Guilford Press.

Miller, I. W., Gaudiano, B. A., & Weinstock, L. M. (2022). *The Coping Long-Term with Active Suicide Program (CLASP): A multi-modal intervention for suicide prevention: Clinician guide*. Oxford University Press.

Morris, L. T., Roush, C., & Spencer, L. E. (2009). *The arc of the universe is long: Unitarian Universalists, antiracism, and the journey from Calgary*. Skinner House Books.

National Institute for Health and Care Excellence (NICE). (2022). *Self-harm: Assessment, management and preventing recurrence* (NICE Guideline NG225). *www.nice.org.uk/guidance/ng225*

Neff, J., Holmes, S. M., Strong, S., Chin, G., De Avila, J., Dubal, S., et al. (2019). The structural competency working group: Lessons from iterative, interdisciplinary development of a structural competency training module. In H. Hansen & J. M. Metzl (Eds.), *Structural Competency in Mental Health and Medicine* (pp. 53–74). Springer International Publishing.

Pokorny, A. D. (1983). Prediction of suicide in psychiatric patients: Report of a prospective study. *Archives of General Psychiatry, 40*(3), 249.

Posner, K., Brown, G. K., Stanley, B., Brent, D. A., Yershova, K. V., Oquendo, M. A., et al. (2011). The Columbia–Suicide Severity Rating Scale: Initial validity and internal consistency findings from three multisite studies with adolescents and adults. *American Journal of Psychiatry, 168*(12), 1266–1277.

Raifman, J., Moscoe, E., Austin, S. B., & McConnell, M. (2017). Difference-in-differences analysis of the association between state same-sex marriage policies and adolescent suicide attempts. *JAMA Pediatrics, 171*(4), 350.

Rathus, J. H., & Miller, A. L. (2014). *DBT skills manual for adolescents*. Guilford Press.

Reynolds, W. M. (1991). Psychometric characteristics of the adult Suicidal Ideation Questionnaire in college students. *Journal of Personality Assessment, 56*(2), 289–307.

Reynolds, W. M., & Mazza, J. J. (1999). Assessment of suicidal ideation in inner-city children and young adolescents: Reliability and validity of the Suicidal Ideation Questionnaire-JR. *School Psychology Review, 28*(1), 17–30.

Rhodes, A. E., Boyle, M. H, Bridge, J. A, Sinyor, M., Links, P. S, Tonmyr, L., et al. (2014). Antecedents and sex/gender differences in youth suicidal behavior. *World Journal of Psychiatry, 4*(4), 120–132.

Rittel, H., & Webber, M. (1973). Dilemmas in a general theory of planning. *Policy Sciences, 4*(2), 155–169.

Rizvi, S. L., & Ritschel, L. A. (2014). Mastering the art of chain analysis in dialectical behavior therapy. *Cognitive and Behavioral Practice, 21*(3), 335–349.

Ross, E. L., Bossarte, R. M., Dobscha, S. K., Gildea, S. M., Hwang, I., Kennedy, C. J., et al. (2023). Estimated average treatment effect of psychiatric hospitalization in patients with suicidal behaviors: A precision treatment analysis. *JAMA Psychiatry*.

Rudd, M. D., & Bryan, C. J. (2022). Finding effective and efficient ways to integrate research advances into the clinical suicide risk assessment interview. *Frontiers in Psychiatry, 13*, 846244.

Schmitz, W. M., Allen, M. H., Feldman, B. N., Gutin, N. J., Jahn, D. R., Kleespies, P. M., et al. (2012). Preventing suicide through improved training in suicide risk assessment and care: An American Association of Suicidology task force report addressing serious gaps in U.S. mental health training. *Suicide and Life-Threatening Behavior, 42*(3), 292–304.

Sher, L. (2015). Suicide medical malpractice: An educational overview. *International Journal of Adolescent Medicine and Health, 27*(2), 203–206.

Silva, C., Smith, A. R., Dodd, D. R., Covington, D. W., & Joiner, T. E. (2016). Suicide-related knowledge and confidence among behavioral health care staff in seven states. *Psychiatric Services, 67*(11), 1240–1245.

Snyder, T. L. (2015). *The power to die: Slavery and suicide in British North America*. The University of Chicago Press.

Stanley, B., & Brown, G. K. (2012). Safety planning intervention: A brief intervention to mitigate suicide risk. *Cognitive and Behavioral Practice, 19*(2), 256–264.

Stanley, I. H., Hom, M. A., Sachs-Ericsson, N. J., Gallyer, A. J., & Joiner, T. E. (2020). A pilot randomized clinical trial of a lethal means safety intervention for young adults with firearm familiarity at risk for suicide. *Journal of Consulting and Clinical Psychology, 88*(4), 372–383.

Stanley, I. H., Simpson, S., Wortzel, H. S., & Joiner, T. E. (2019). Documenting suicide risk assessments and proportionate clinical actions to improve patient safety and mitigate legal risk. *Behavioral Sciences & the Law, 37*(3), 304–312.

Stefan, S. (2016). *Rational suicide, irrational laws: Examining current approaches to suicide in policy and law*. Oxford University Press.

Toomey, R. B., Syvertsen, A. K., & Shramko, M. (2018). Transgender adolescent suicide behavior. *Pediatrics, 142*(4), e20174218.

Wang, L., Lin, H.-C., & Wong, Y. J. (2021). Perceived racial discrimination on the change of suicide risk among ethnic minorities in the United States. *Ethnicity & Health, 26*(5), 631–645.

Ward-Ciesielski, E. F., & Rizvi, S. L. (2021). The potential iatrogenic effects of psychiatric hospitalization for suicidal behavior: A critical review and recommendations for research. *Clinical Psychology: Science and Practice, 28*.

World Health Organization. (2014). *Preventing suicide: A global imperative. www.who.int/publications/i/item/9789241564779*

Yen, S., Spirito, A., Weinstock, L. M., Tezanos, K., Kolobaric, A., & Miller, I. (2019). Coping long term with active suicide in adolescents: Results from a pilot randomized controlled trial. *Clinical Child Psychology and Psychiatry, 24*(4), 847–859.

CHAPTER 29

Assessment of Emotional and Behavioral Disorder

Stacy-Ann A. January, Zelda Fleming, Bailey Braunstein, Kary Zarate, and Matthew C. Lambert

OVERVIEW

The Individuals with Disabilities Education Improvement Act (IDEIA; 2004) defines *emotional disturbance* (ED) as a condition that adversely affects a child's educational performance and is characterized by one or more of the following over an extended period: (1) an inability to learn that cannot be explained by intellectual, sensory, or health factors; (2) an inability to build or maintain satisfactory interpersonal relationships with peers and teachers; (3) inappropriate types of behavior or feelings under normal circumstances; (4) a general pervasive mood of unhappiness or depression; and (5) tendency to develop physical symptoms or fears associated with personal or school problems. The definition includes children with schizophrenia but excludes socially maladjusted children unless they have an ED. Federal law has maintained the same definition and assessment practices for ED since the Education for All Handicapped Children Act of 1975. There are, however, differences in the terminology and definition of ED.

Acknowledging the differences in terminology between federal, state, and clinical diagnostic purposes is important as it guides identification and eligibility for special education services. States can determine their own definitions and terminology independently of the federal IDEIA language and definition. According to a recent study, nine different terms are used across states with the federal term being most often used (48% of states; Sallese et al., 2024). Other common terms reported included emotional disability, emotional and/or behavioral disorder, and emotional behavioral disabilities (Sallese et al., 2024). For the purposes of this chapter, we will use the term emotional and behavioral disorder (EBD), as it includes students with externalizing and internalizing behaviors.

There is no direct equivalent of EBD outside of the public school system, as most health agencies in the United States utilize the American Psychiatric Association's (2022) *Diagnostic and Statistical Manual of Mental Disorders* (DSM) as the standard classification system of mental health disorders. The diagnoses in the DSM-5 fifth edition text revision (DSM-5-TR) that may share symptomology and characteristics with the EBD label include neurodevelopmental disorders (e.g., attention-deficit/hyperactivity disorder), bipolar and related disorders, depressive disorders, anxiety disorders, obsessive–compulsive and related disorders, trauma- and stressor-related disorders, and disruptive impulse-control and conduct disorders (Substance Abuse and Mental Health Services Administration [SAMSHA], 2014). SAMHSA continues to utilize the term *serious emotional disturbance* (SED) and publishes the *Federal Register* notice for national and state estimations of SED to guide grant allocations for community mental health services. The *Federal Register* notice defines children with SED as those who have a diagnosable mental, behavioral, or emotional disorder of sufficient duration to meet diagnostic criteria specified within DSM-5-TR and that resulted in functional impairment, which substantially interferes with or limits the child's role or functioning in family, school, or community activities (SAMHSA, 1993).

These definitions of ED, SED, and EBD are subjective and ambiguous, especially concerning the socially maladjusted (SM) exclusionary clause. The U.S. Department of Education did not define SM, which left states to determine what emotions or behaviors comprise social maladjustment in children (unless they have an ED). For decades there has been ongoing debate among scholars and practitioners about how to distinguish between ED and SM when determining eligibility and need for special education and if they can be reliably distinguished (Sullivan & Sadeh, 2014). One potential definition is that SM is "a pattern of engagement in purposive antisocial, destructive, and delinquent behavior" (Merrell & Walker, 2004, p. 901). Ultimately, if a student meets eligibility criteria for EBD (even if they are determined to also be "socially maladjusted"), that enables them to receive specially designed instruction and services under the EBD eligibility.

OBJECTIVES OF THIS CHAPTER

The purpose of this chapter is to provide the reader with some of the foundational knowledge needed to engage in culturally relevant and appropriate assessment for students with or at risk of EBD. One concept that is tantamount to developing the knowledge, skills, and practices necessary to engage in the approaches in this chapter is an understanding and embracement of cultural humility (see Pham et al., 2022). *Cultural humility* is a process of lifelong learning, reflexivity, and concomitant actions one engages in to work toward dismantling oppressive structures and uplifting marginalized communities (Pham et al., 2022). One important step is reflection on one's identities, their association with power and privilege in the larger societal context, and ongoing growth in moving toward anti-oppressive actions. We believe that a strong commitment to cultural humility is a foundation toward engaging in culturally responsive, relevant, and appropriate practices with the students, families, and communities we serve.

There are several marginalized groups within the U.S. context. In this chapter we will focus primarily on students who are marginalized due to race, ethnicity, disability, and gender (e.g., Cruz et al., 2021). Our focus on the intersection between race, ethnicity, disability, and gender is because these are the identities most prevalent in existing research, are the identities usually over or underrepresented in practice (e.g., in the number of disciplinary removals), and the students holding these intersectional identities have unique experiences compared to peers who may not. We acknowledge that there are students with other marginalized identities that have the EBD label and that students with the identities we are focusing on in this chapter may have other intersecting marginalized identities that are salient to their experiences. We encourage readers to explore other sources to learn more about the experiences of students who identify with communities who are marginalized due to sexual orientation or gender diversity.

In the next subsection, we will discuss the relevance of assessing for EBD to the field and disability critical race theory (DisCrit; Annamma et al., 2013), which grounds this chapter. In the section after that, we will discuss culturally relevant and appropriate assessment practices for students with or suspected to have an EBD. Following that we will review practices for using assessment to inform intervention and decision making. Last, we will discuss future directions for the field. Note that we will integrate culturally relevant and appropriate practice considerations throughout this chapter.

RELEVANCE TO THE FIELD

Students identified with an EBD often have difficulties with social–emotional functioning and are likely to experience academic challenges. In accordance with IDEIA (2004), every student with a disability is entitled to a free and appropriate education and entitled to receive services that are designed to meet their unique needs. Their education should be designed so they can prepare for future endeavors, whether this be future employment, independent living, and/or furthering their education. For students with disabilities eligible under EBD to receive these services, the first step is to identify them using a comprehensive and culturally appropriate assessment. Thus, it is essential to assess students who appear to have an educational impact from symptoms consistent with EBD within the school setting. Historically, this task has proven to be quite complex due to disproportionate outcomes among those who are typically identified under this category and disproportionate outcomes among achievement rates of students served within this category.

In general, it is hypothesized that we are currently underserving and under-identifying students with EBD within the public school systems (Wiley et al., 2013). As of 2022–2023, students with disabilities ages 3–21 accounted for around 15% of students enrolled in public schools (National Center for Education Statistics [NCES], 2024). Around 4% of these students with disabilities are identified as students with EBD (NCES, 2024). When examining who is typically served under this category, the disproportionality is evident. Indeed, most of these students are identified as being male: around 72% of those being identified as EBD were boys and 27% were girls (de Brey et al., 2019). This is not surprising because girls are generally underrepresented in all IDEIA categories, with boys representing 66% of all students currently receiving services and girls representing only 34% of students being served under IDEIA (de Brey et al., 2019). As these data do not accurately capture students who are nonbinary, trans, or gender nonconforming, these data may not be representative of all students. When examining race, Black or African American students are more likely than other students to be identified as having an EBD label, whereas Hispanic or Latine students tend to be underrepresented within this category (U.S. Department of Education, 2020; Wiley et al., 2013).

With the current and historic disproportionality among students who are racially and ethnically minoritized, this brings to light systemic issues including whether students are being adequately and appropriately assessed for this category (Wiley et al., 2013). Misidentification occurs in both directions, whereby students are being both over- and under-identified. Misidentification could be occurring as the result of various factors; some of the noted hypotheses for this occurrence are biased interpretations of minoritized students' behavior and achievement, dysfunctional interactions between schools and marginalized families, and inadequate access to quality instruction in general education (Artiles & Trent, 1994; Skiba et al., 2008). An alternative hypothesis is that racially minoritized students are over-represented in this category because they are differentially exposed to risk factors associated with the disability (Coutinho & Oswald, 2000; Wiley et al., 2013). Although these hypotheses help understand the phenomena occurring, they may not completely capture the discrepancies in identifying students with EBD, and they do not explain the under-identification of students.

In this chapter, we suggest that when assessing students for a potential EBD label, practitioners engage in an ecological approach to assessing students. To help practitioners do this, we suggest assessing students with EBD through the lens of DisCrit (Annamma et al., 2013). As an intersectional critical theory, DisCrit emphasizes that both racism and ableism intersect to marginalize specific individuals further and uphold the notion of what is considered normal. Although a detailed discussion is beyond the scope of this chapter, readers are strongly encouraged to learn more about DisCrit (see Annamma et al., 2013). The seven tenets of DisCrit will be integrated throughout this chapter. We will use DisCrit as a lens to discuss considerations to improve the cultural appropriateness of assessment practices for EBD.

There are seven key tenets of DisCrit. Tenet 1 "focuses on ways that the forces of racism and ableism circulate interdependently" to uphold notions of Whiteness and ability as normal (Annamma et al., 2013, p. 11). Tenet 2 emphasizes the importance of valuing multidimensional identities instead of viewing race, disability, class, or gender as separate and single identities. Tenet 3 emphasizes that race and ability are social constructions; that is, race is not biologically or genetically determined. Further, being disabled or with a racially minoritized identity sets one outside of the Western and White cultural norms. Tenet 4 aims to uplift and center voices of marginalized populations. Tenet 5 considers legal and historical aspects of disability and race and how both have been used separately and together to deny the rights of citizens with those identities. Tenet 6 recognizes that Whiteness and ability as property and that gains for racially minoritized people labeled with disabilities have largely been made as the result of interest convergence of White, middle-class citizens. Last, Tenet 7 encourages activism and supports all forms of resistance.

When assessing students for any special education category, including EBD, it is crucial that we do so to support students and not as another form of marginalization through a classification system. In this chapter, we provide information about conducting the initial eligibility assessments for students in the EBD category and how to conduct progress monitoring assessments and conduct this assessment with goals or provide interventions and accommodations that will benefit these students. It has also been noted that children with EBD have been more likely to not complete school than other students with disabilities for a wide variety of reasons. For example, in 2018, the percentage of students with disabilities who did not complete school was 16%; however, the percentage of students within that group with the EBD label was double—32% (de Brey et al., 2019). Further, students receiving services under the EBD label are also more likely to be suspended or expelled from school than all other students with disabilities (de Brey et al., 2019). These disproportionate outcomes should not be taken as a reflection of the students; rather, they show how much work there is to be done to improve outcomes for these students. Knowing this, it is essential that we use assessments in culturally appropriate ways to disrupt disproportionality in EBD eligibility and to help improve academic, behavioral, and socio-emotional outcomes for these students.

ASSESSMENT OF STUDENTS WITH EBD

Potential Bias in EBD Assessment

It is important that practitioners understand the bias fueled by racism and ableism that underlie the assessment of EBD and perceptions about behaviors that may be associated with EBD. This can be understood through the lens of DisCrit. As noted earlier, one key tenet of DisCrit is that race and disability intersect to create interlocking systems of oppression that privileges White and able-bodied individuals as "normal" (Annamma et al., 2013). As such, individuals with marginalized identities (e.g., Black or African American people) and who have a disability are othered or treated as less than others without those identities. This can be observed through the persistent and long-standing deficit-based lens that is enacted when working with youth with marginalized identities with an EBD label.

It is important to note that these systems of oppression permeate all systems in the United States, especially education where students and professionals are socialized with these ideas. It is up to individuals and communities to recognize and actively work to dismantle these systems of oppression. The over- and under-representation of youth with marginalized identities (U.S. Department of Education, 2020) provides evidence that the criteria are not applied or interpreted equally across groups of students, and/or how we assess for potential EBD eligibility in a systematic way. Using the lens of DisCrit, we can interrogate the assessment of EBD eligibility and understand potential bias in the perceptions of behaviors associated with the EBD label.

Another way that potential bias in the assessment of EBD can arise is related to perceptions of behaviors that are associated with EBD. Indeed, there is subjectivity in the interpretation of the criteria, which are not well-defined. For instance, what is determined to be "inappropriate types of behavior or feelings" or "satisfactory interpersonal relationships" is interpreted within the context of Eurocentric, middle class, cis-gender, and monolingual norms about what are "appropriate" behaviors and feelings. Individuals who do not fit these norms are othered and may be wrongfully found to meet EBD eligibility criteria. Second, the definitions of EBD often do not consider the real and pervasive nature of racism and other systems of oppression that may be reflected in a child or adolescent's behaviors, feelings, or thoughts. What may be labeled as "aggressive" or "inappropriate" may be an expected response to systemic racism, disproportionate exposure to trauma event, or other symptoms of systemic oppression. Similarly, the EBD criteria may not include a consideration of other environmental factors, such as the impact of living under impoverished conditions. Indeed, evidence suggests there is a higher prevalence of mental health conditions for youth who are living in impoverished communities (Kirkbride et al., 2024), not because of inherently higher risks within those youth, but rather due to factors such as the persistent underfunding and under-resourcing of those communities.

Assessment to Understand Emotional and Behavioral Needs

We contend that one of the primary purposes of assessment for EBD is to contribute to our understanding of the unique emotional and behavioral needs of the students we serve (January, 2023). Specifically, EBD assessment helps inform eligibility for evaluation, which ultimately guides the appropriate identification of disability, access to services and resources, and methods of progress monitoring to facilitate each student's success. To ensure that we accurately identify a student with an EBD, we must take a culturally considerate lens that centers on DisCrit and each student's unique identity, background, and traits throughout the entirety of the assessment process, including before we conduct EBD assessments, during assessment procedures, and while interpreting assessment data.

Before Conducting Assessment

Culturally considerate assessment begins with an ecological perspective (Bronfenbrenner, 1977) grounded in the embracement of cultural humility as a lifelong process (Pham et al., 2022). We must use a contextual assessment approach that evaluates culturally relevant considerations within the student's school environment and considers what changes in the environment could better support the child. As opposed to suggesting that the child is responsible for emotional or behavioral concerns that do not match the expectations of that environment, from an ecological perspective, we instead must evaluate the environment in its role of facilitating the emotional and behavioral needs of our students. This includes examining our beliefs and the students' identities and considering how the environment can support our students' emotional and behavioral needs from an ecological perspective.

An essential first step before conducting EBD assessments is to begin by self-reflecting and evaluating our identities, beliefs, and biases and being aware of those implications on assessment procedures (Hays, 2022). Furthermore, we can consider the ADDRESSING model as a framework that helps recognize and understand the complexities of individual identity and privilege (see Hays, 2022). Specifically, we must consider Age, Developmental disabilities, acquired Disabilities, Religion, Ethnicity, Sexual orientation, Socioeconomic status, Indigenous group membership, Nationality, and Gender and their intersection to gain a more comprehensive understanding of our own privilege and identity and a student's cultural identity. In other words, learning who a student is, their values, background, and unique experiences under an empathetic and ecological lens is critical in providing educational support and services to all students. Through the process of self-reflecting and learning about our students wholistically, we may come to see how differences in values, cultures, and privilege shape our perceptions and may assist us in taking a less biased approach.

We must evaluate the environment and its impact on emotional and behavioral student outcomes from an ecological perspective. The term *environment* encompasses any element within a student's school, community, or home that either facilitate their academic success or impede it. For example, ask, "What environmental factors may impact a student's academic performance?" Environmental factors may include school, family, economic, and community factors such as the presence of peers, the presence of an adult, the noise level of the classroom, chaotic hallways, and a space at home for completing homework. Home and community factors can also play a role in a child's emotional and behavioral characteristics; we should assess the assets of the environment and if the child is facing adversity, has access to food and clothing, and is getting sufficient sleep. Environmental factors must also consider the curriculum, access to instruction, and the associated task demands.

Once assessment is used to inform intervention and the skills to be targeted, a next step is to decide how progress will be monitored. Despite the growth in assessment options of emotional and behavioral strengths and needs within the past few decades, there remains a dearth of measures available and with psychometric evidence for progress monitoring (Lane, 2022). Nonetheless, monitoring students' progress in their emotional and behavioral skills is an important task for educators. Planning for progress monitoring should occur prior to implementing intervention or specially designed instruction and related services.

When planning assessments, educators should look for measures producing scores that have demonstrated reliability and validity for the purpose they are being used (assessment for eligibility, monitoring progress; January, 2023). That is, psychometric evidence for use of the measure should include students with an EBD label and with a socio-demographic background that is similar to the students being monitored. As with assessment data to determine eligibility, the student's age, cultural background, gender, ethnicity, race, and ability should be represented in the research supporting the use of the progress monitoring measure. Given the limited number of options at the time of this writing, it may not be possible to use a different tool. If this is the case, then the best available assessment tool should be used with the note and caveat that the psychometric evidence may not be ideal.

Assessment Procedures

Culturally responsive assessments should consider culturally specific challenges while taking a strengths-based approach and focusing on the positive aspects of the student's self, culture, interpersonal support, and environment. Most common practices suggest that case background and pre-evaluation data are primarily measured by assessing the child's observable behavior and emotional concerns. In other words, after a problem or student concern is identified, it is common to assess a child primarily from a within-child deficit lens, in which professionals aim to collect data on the child's emotional and behavioral problems. However, assessment data must incorporate the child's observed area of concern *in combination with* environmental factors, student strengths, and culturally appropriate assessment.

First, it is important to consider environmental factors that may explain or contribute to any observed or perceived room for emotional or behavioral growth. Evaluators should try to get detailed information on the student's social history. For example, whether the student has experienced a recent transition or sudden emotional experience (e.g., the loss of a family member, recent move to the United States, experienced trauma) would be critical to know during the evaluation process. The next assessment should assess which interventions have been attempted, whether they were culturally considerate, and whether interventions have been executed with fidelity. Specific interventions to consider while assessing children with EBD may include school-based counseling or a referral for emotional or behavioral support, classwide reinforcement systems, whether there has been a class schedule or teacher change to meet the children's needs better, and the presence of a positive behavior support plan. Further, we must consider the child's relationships and see if the child has been provided opportunities to learn and practice social skills, has a social support system, and has had opportunities to form developmentally appropriate relationships with peers and teachers. Additionally, we must assess the child's academic characteristics and consider whether there is a relationship between the child's emotions and behaviors and their academic needs. It is important to consider the curriculum and the associated task demands influence on the child and to ensure that the child is being provided high-quality instruction and a tiered system of academic support to ensure that they are not facing barriers to learning.

We first have to carefully consider the child's unique culture, background, and strengths; their school, home, and community environment; and their past intervention supports, relationships, and academic characteristics and supports. Last, we assess the child's emotional and behavioral characteristics with the primary goal of identifying ways to support the student's success. Emotional and behavioral characteristics may include internalizing signs of withdrawal, depression, anxiety, obsessions, compulsions, and associated physical symptoms of fear. Externalizing signs may include aggression, acting out, and noncompliant behaviors. Through assessing emotional and behavioral characteristics, we must acknowledge that emotional and behavioral expectations can be subjective and are culturally influenced. Therefore, it is important to incorporate multi-informant perspectives, including centering the perspective and voice of the child and their family. One potential consideration is that the student and/or their caregivers may best communicate in a language that is not English. Evaluators should make a concerted effort to gather information from the child and their family through means such as including a bilingual evaluator, use of forms in the preferred language (if literacy in their preferred language matches the language used on the rating form), and the school district's interpreter.

EBD Assessment Considerations

Recall the ambiguous language of the SM clause. Practitioners may wonder how to approach assessment of EBD within the context of the SM clause. First, remember that a child can be eligible for EBD *and* be "socially maladjusted." Therefore, determining whether a child is socially maladjusted may not be relevant for an EBD evaluation. Perhaps it is only most relevant if they do not meet the criteria for EBD. Within the context of an evaluation for EBD, there are some assessments that may be used as part of a body of evidence to determine the potential presence of social maladjustment, including Emotional Disturbance Decision Tree (EDDT), Scales for Assessing Emotional Disturbance, Second Edition (SAED-2), Conners 4, and the Differential Scales of Social Maladjustment and Emotional Disturbance (DSSMED). Overall, assessment data should be used as an equitable and culturally informed tool that centers student strengths while using assessment data to inform instruction and intervention. It is important that we do not withhold access to services because a student is "socially maladjusted" if they meet eligibility for EBD.

Assessment to Inform Intervention and Decision Making

Tenet 3 of DisCrit emphasizes that race and ability are social constructions. However, it recognizes the impacts of being labeled with a minoritized race or as disabled will set one outside of the Western, Eurocentric cultural norms. While recognizing that race and ability are social constructs, we must acknowledge that by giving these students an EBD label, we are in a way marginalizing them through our classification. If we are going to categorize these students, the benefit of doing so should outweigh the harm. In addition to assessing youth for classification, we should be assessing youth to develop interventions that can be used to support them. The goal of evaluating youth with EBD should be to provide support that helps them succeed and achieve their goals. Students that are provided with services under the EBD category struggle so significantly with socio-emotional and behavioral health challenges that their learning is impeded and academic progress is affected. Thus, common interventions utilized for students under the EBD category often involve improving social skills, behaviors, and academic achievement. A critical component in evidence-based interventions is ensuring that interventions developed are based on the student's evaluative data. In this section, we will discuss using assessment to create interventions that promote academic, behavioral, and social–emotional success for students receiving services under the EBD category and approaches for monitoring their progress.

Before Conducting Assessment

Before conducting any new assessments to create interventions, the evaluation team needs to review any previous assessments and interventions attempted with the student. Reviewing this information can provide more background knowledge on current areas of concern for the student. Evaluators should review any previously provided Tier 1 and Tier 2 services, including counseling, academic, or behavioral support services, and should consider the effectiveness of the interventions previously attempted. Following that review, the next set of assessments should be conducted to identify areas of growth to target for intervention. There should be a clear relationship between the assessment information process and the intervention planning process (January, 2023).

Additionally, it is helpful to work under an ecological framework when assessing and informing intervention for students under the EBD category (Bronfenbrenner, 1977). Evaluators should consider not only the student and their behavior but also the environment—the school, the classroom, the teachers, and the student's family and culture should be taken into consideration. Multiple methods of assessment should be used to assess a variety of perspectives. Further, both direct and indirect methods should be utilized. This can include direct observations where ideally two or more evaluators observe the same behavior simultaneously and agree on the occurrence and nonoccurrence of the behavior of interest (Gresham, 2003). This can also include the use of rating scales. The evaluator should always use multiple informants (Gresham, 1986). In addition to using multiple informants, it may also be beneficial to engage school staff raters in professional development that discusses implicit biases and their impact on our perceptions of behavior and performances (Pickens, 2022). It has been illustrated that when teachers are incongruently matched by race, they tend to rate behaviors as being more severe than they are; further, there is a tendency to underestimate academic abilities (Warren, 2015; Whitford & Emerson, 2019). As there is currently disproportionality, evaluators should take extra precautions to reduce bias when using assessments and create interventions that will ensure that they will be beneficial and effective for the students. Further, ensuring that the student's voice is centered throughout this process is essential. In addition to having adults who know the student well rate their strengths and areas for growth, have the student (as appropriate for their age and developmental level) rate their own emotional, social, and behavioral strengths and needs. Several rating scales also include a student self-report form that could be used in addition to interviewing the student. With these data, the evaluator can examine how aware the student may be of their strengths and needs, as well as gain a better understanding of differences across raters.

Functional Behavior Assessment to Develop Interventions and Monitor Progress

When designing an intervention to address a challenging or interfering behavior, the first step in creating interventions for students typically involves conducting a functional behavior assessment (FBA). The FBA aims to identify environmental conditions associated with the occurrence or nonoccurrence of challenging behaviors. A comprehensive definition of and procedures for an FBA can be found in Chapter 23 (this volume). Once the function of behavior is determined, this information can be used to design interventions to reduce problem behaviors and to increase more appropriate positive replacement behaviors (O'Neill et al., 1997; Witt et al., 2000). Interventions will also typically involve the use of positive or negative reinforcement. FBAs can be beneficial components in creating effective interventions.

In addition to the potential benefits of FBA, there are some limitations and important considerations of FBAs and their implications for crafting interventions. Practitioners should be aware of the use of the indirect measures sometimes included within the FBA. The indirect measures within the FBA often include rating scales and interviews. However, rating scales and interviews are subjective to the individual filling them out. Further, an important consideration when conducting FBAs is how the culture of the student and evaluator can impact or skew the results of the FBA. Implicit bias can impact the results of an FBA. For example, if a teacher labels a student's neutral behaviors as aggressive or disrespectful because of a preconceived notion they hold about students from that cultural group, this will likely impact the results of the FBA (Gopalan & Nelson, 2019; Miller et al., 2019). As there is a disproportionate number of Black students served under the EBD label, it should also be noted that often teachers, particularly White teachers, may perceive behaviors by Black or African American students as being more hostile, warranting more severe consequences even when Black or African American students' behavior is topographically like White students (Enders et al., 2022; Okonofua & Eberhardt, 2015). This can result in biased actions that may serve as relevant antecedents or consequences to that student's behavior. The perceptions of behaviors and understandings of function may all be impacted by, and rooted in, specific cultural values or norms, specifically Western norms (Enders et al., 2022). Thus, it is essential to remember that hypotheses drawn from conducting FBAs are just that and should not be taken to be a fact or prognosis about the student of interest.

Additionally, it is important to note that evaluators should weigh the risks of labeling student behaviors. Under the FBA, there are four functions of behavior: escape, attention, sensory, and access to tangibles. Labeling student behavior as "attention seeking" or "escape" can have potential drawbacks if the evaluator stops at just labeling. Additionally, the use of "attention seeking" has a negative connotation. One possible reframe for the function of attention is "connection seeking," where we may better understand the student's needs and what their behavior is trying to communicate. Evaluators should also aim to seek why the student may be seeking "attention" or trying to "escape" and create interventions to decrease the behaviors and the need for those behaviors, such as which skills might be areas for growth.

Assessing Social and Emotional Skills to Develop Interventions and Monitor Progress

Social and emotional skills can be thought of as the child or student's ability to "integrate thinking, feeling, and behaving to achieve important life tasks" (Zins et al., 2007, p. 184). Further, it pertains to children's ability to form close and secure relationships and regulate and express emotions in socially and culturally appropriate ways (Yates et al., 2008). Social and emotional skills are typically divided into five basic components: self-awareness, self-management/self-regulation, social awareness, relationship skills, and decision-making and social problem-solving skills (Collaborative for Social, Emotional, and Academic Learning, 2017). Students with more positive social interactions and relationships with their peers typically have higher academic achievement levels (Gresham, 2015). As students identified as EBD often struggle with peer relationships, social and emotional skills are often a targeted area of intervention. In addition to helping students enhance their peer relationships, developing these skills also aids in supporting students to build positive classroom behaviors such as cooperation, following rules, and getting along with others during collaborative work assignments (Gresham, 2015).

Social skills-based interventions are a commonly targeted area for students identified with EBD. It has been suggested that youth with a higher level of social skills typically have higher overall well-being and lower levels of depression, anxiety, conduct disorders, and conflict (Sancassiani et al., 2015). Further, students who get along well with their peers socially tend to have better academic achievement and engagement (Gresham, 2015).

Part of designing social skills interventions is appropriately assessing and targeting social areas for growth. Social skills broadly can be thought of as a specific class of behaviors to complete social tasks successfully. Social tasks could include peer conversations, making friends, playing games with peers, and working collaboratively with peers (Gresham, 2015).

Assessing Social Skills to Develop Interventions and Monitor Progress

Direct observations can be used to assess a child's social skills. Observations should be conducted across multiple settings, including the classroom (high and low preferred classes) and during special activities (recess or free period). Social skills can also be evaluated indirectly by using relevant judgments of the individuals' social behaviors, such as self-ratings, peer ratings, teacher ratings, and parent ratings. It should be noted, however, that indirect methods of assessment are subject to rater effects, which is when there is a variance in scores due to the rater and not due to the actual behaviors of the student (Anthony et al., 2022). Teachers sometimes tend to rate students classified under the EBD category more harshly than other students (Krämer & Zimmermann, 2022). In addition, it has been noted that teachers also may more harshly rate students from minoritized backgrounds (Minkos et al., 2017). As previously mentioned, when using rating scales to assess social skills, the evaluator should ensure the use of multiple informants (Gresham, 1986). When utilizing rating scales, the evaluator will want to use scales that ask the rater to evaluate the student's interpersonal skills, communication, cooperation, assertion, and empathy. Additionally, the evaluator will want to use scales that examine the student's engagement, self-control, responsibility, and behaviors that may be competing with social skills. Social skills interventions would then be designed and created to help strengthen areas of growth for students. Another way to evaluate social skills is to assess social performance relative to a normative standard using standardized social skills rating scales (Gresham, 1986). Social skills might also be assessed by evaluating pre-established explicit criteria, like the number of steps completed to conclude a social task (Gresham, 1986).

Traditionally, it has been said that when assessing social skills to develop an evidence-based intervention, it is important to distinguish between performance needs and skill needs (Gresham, 1981). One assessment that has often been used to help quantify this distinction between the two is the SSRS Social Skills Improvement System—Rating Scales (SSIS-RS) (Gresham & Elliott, 2008). Although this approach has been used in the past and has helped in creating interventions, it should be noted that social skills can often be much more complicated than being attributed to performance or skill "deficits." Environmental and cultural factors will play a significant role not only in the social skills the student possesses but also in the perception of their social skills. Recent research suggests that a sense of community or connection within one's school will also significantly impact the social skills exhibited by the student (Bateman, 2002; Prati et al., 2018). This is particularly important as students identified under the EBD label often report feeling low levels of connection to their school communities (Marsh et al., 2019). Another consideration regarding the assessment of social skills is the culture of the student, their school, and their evaluators. Currently, a high number of students served under the EBD classification are ethnically and racially minoritized (de Brey et al., 2019; Wiley et al., 2013). Further, someone's culture and cultural norms can also have a significant impact on the student's manifestation of their social skills, and the evaluator's culture could impact how they are perceived (An & Eggum-Wilkens, 2019; Zahra et al., 2021). Thus, evaluators should ensure they assess the student's environment and account for cultural differences when assessing social skills. This will be the most effective way to create successful interventions for students with EBD with room for growth in social skills.

In addition to assessment to inform interventions, it is important to identify appropriate assessments for the purposes of monitoring students' progress. Progress monitoring assessments should be directly linked to the intervention and the skills being targeted (January, 2023). As such, it is most useful to think about how progress will be monitored when instruction and intervention are planned. Structured options for monitoring the social, emotional, and behavioral skills of students with EBD are limited. Common approaches include direct observations and Direct Behavior Ratings (DBR; Cook et al., 2014). Direct observations can be helpful because they are direct (versus indirect) measures of behavior; however, they are time and resource intensive. DBRs are observation-based assessments in which a student or teacher rates the student's behavior on a scale, often 0–10 or 0–100%. DBRs are psychometrically sound and sensitive to change (Owens & Evans, 2018) yet are not as time-consuming as direct observations. Although typically used to monitor externalizing behaviors, they can be used to monitor internalizing behaviors as well (Dart et al., 2019).

Incorporating Strengths to Design Interventions

Strength-based assessments have been noted to contribute to an increase in youth functioning (Lambert et al., 2021). It is essential to take a balanced approach when using assessments to create interventions for youth receiving support under the EBD category. Evidence indicates that youth are more likely to succeed when we give them tools and curricula based not only on their interests but also on their strengths (Merrell et al., 2011). In addition to the use of a strength-based assessment being vital in building an effective intervention, it is also helpful in determining areas of growth for students. The presence of positive attributes, like strengths, can be considered assets for students. Thus, we should work not only on interventions to address gaps or deficits but also on interventions to build student strengths (Benner et al., 2008). One tool that can be utilized is the Behavioral Emotional Rating Scale (BERS; Epstein & Sharma, 1998). This scale assesses child strengths within the dimensions of interpersonal capacity, family involvement, intrapersonal competence, school functioning, and affective ability (Cox, 2006; Epstein & Sharma, 1998).

CONCLUSION

School personnel have been assessing children for EBD for decades and methods have changed over time. In this chapter, we reviewed approaches for engaging in culturally responsive assessment of EBD. Research in this area is active and there are several emerging trends in the field. In this section, we highlight potential gaps and future directions in adopting cultural humility into policy, practice, and research, and ways to authentically center the voices of students with EBD and their families.

One important emerging trend and potential for future developments in the assessment of EBD is the adoption of cultural humility into practice, research, and policy (Pham et al., 2022). As noted previously, cultural humility refers to process and commitment to continuous learning and growing, and engaging in reflexivity and actions to understand, identify, and combat systems of oppressions while elevating students and families who have been marginalized (Pham et al., 2022). Readers may be familiar with the idea of cultural competence. The idea of cultural competence implicitly suggests that it is a thing that can be achieved, and that once it has occurred, additional learning is not needed. Additionally, cultural competence does not fully address the importance of using an intersectional lens as a context for understanding the perspectives and experiences of students with EBD and their families. Cultural humility extends the concept of cultural competence in an acknowledgment that an individually cannot "become" culturally competent; there is a lifetime commitment and work that should occur. Researchers, practitioners, and policymakers who adopt and embody a strong commitment to cultural humility in addition to applying critical theories will likely have a foundation on which to build culturally appropriate assessment practices, culturally relevant and sustaining interventions, and other actions that push the field toward social justice.

It is important to authentically center and uplift the voices of students with EBD. This is consistent with the fourth tenet of DisCrit. Historically and currently, the voices, experiences, and perspectives of students with EBD (most of whom are students of color) have been intentionally and unintentionally silenced, erased, and marginalized. Centering the voices of these youth and their families is one way in which practitioners and researchers can disrupt the status quo and continue working toward social justice goals. It is particularly important that this work is done authentically and with cultural humility so that it does not have unintended effects such as causing more harm and marginalization. Examples can include conducting meaningful interviews with students and their families, involving students and families in every step of the assessment process, and creating ways that they can meaningfully contribute to decision making about themselves and their child.

REFERENCES

American Psychiatric Association. (2022). *Diagnostic and statistical manual of mental disorders* (5th ed., text rev.).

An, D., & Eggum-Wilkens, N. D. (2019). Do cultural orientations moderate the relation between Chinese adolescents' shyness and depressive symptoms? It depends on their academic achievement. *Social Development, 28*(4), 908–926.

Annamma, S. A., Connor, D., & Ferri, B. (2013). Dis/ability critical race studies (DisCrit): Theorizing at the intersections of race and dis/ability. *Race Ethnicity and Education, 16*(1), 1–31.

Anthony, C. J., Styck, K. M., Cooke, E., Martel, J. R., & Frye, K. E. (2022). Evaluating the impact of rater effects on behavior rating scale score validity and utility. *School Psychology Review, 51*(1), 25–39.

Artiles, A. J., & Trent, S. C. (1994). Overrepresentation of minority students in special education: A continuing debate. *The Journal of Special Education, 27*(4), 410–437.

Bateman, H. V. (2002). Sense of community in the school: Listening to students' voices. In *Psychological sense of community: Research, applications, and implications* (pp. 161–179). Springer.

Benner, G. J., Beaudoin, K., Mooney, P., Uhing, B. M., & Pierce, C. D. (2008). Convergent validity with the BERS-2 teacher Rating Scale and the Achenbach teacher's report form: A replication and extension. *Journal of Child and Family Studies, 17,* 427–436.

Bronfenbrenner, U. (1977). Toward an experimental ecology of human development. *American Psychologist, 32*(7), 513–531.

Collaborative for Social, Emotional, and Academic Learning. (2017). Core SEL competencies. Author. *www.casel.org/core-competencies*

Cook, C. R., Volpe, R. J., & Delport, J. (2014). Systematic progress monitoring of students with emotional and behavioral disorders: The promise of change-sensitive brief behavior rating scales. In H. M. Walker & F. M. Gresham (Eds.), *Handbook of evidence-based practices for emotional and behavioral disorders: Applications in schools* (pp. 211–228). Guilford.

Coutinho, M. J., & Oswald, D. P. (2000). Disproportionate representation in special education: A synthesis and recommendations. *Journal of Child and Family Studies,* 9, 135–156.

Cox, K. F. (2006). Investigating the impact of strength-based assessment on youth with emotional or behavioral disorders. *Journal of Child and Family Studies, 15*(3), 278–292.

Cruz, R. A., Kulkarni, S. S., & Firestone, A. R. (2021). A QuantCrit analysis of context, discipline, special education, and disproportionality. *AERA Open,* 7(1), 1–16.

Dart, E. H., Arora, P. G., Collins, T. A., & Doll, B. (2019). Progress monitoring measures for internalizing symptoms: A systematic review of the peer-reviewed literature. *School Mental Health, 11*(2), 265–275.

de Brey, C., Musu, L., McFarland, J., Wilkinson-Flicker, S., Diliberti, M., Zhang, A., et al. (2019). *Status and trends in the education of racial and ethnic groups 2018* (NCES 2019-038). U.S. Department of Education, National Center for Education Statistics.

Enders, O. G., Buonomo, K., & Robertson, R. (2022). Addressing race and implicit bias in the functional behavior assessment process: A pilot study of preservice teacher training modules. *Multiple Voices for Ethnically Diverse Exceptional Learners, 22*(1), 6–23.

Epstein, M. H., & Sharma, J. M. (1998). *Behavioral and emotional rating scale.* Pro-Ed.

Gopalan, M., & Nelson, A. A. (2019). Understanding the racial discipline gap in schools. *AERA Open,* 5(2), 1–26.

Gresham F. M. (1981). Social skills training with handicapped children: A review. *Review of Educational Research, 51,* 139–176.

Gresham, F. M. (1986). Conceptual and definitional issues in the assessment of children's social skills: Implications for classifications and training. *Journal of Clinical Child Psychology, 15*(1), 3–15.

Gresham, F. M. (2003). Establishing the technical adequacy of functional behavioral assessment: Conceptual and measurement challenges. *Behavioral Disorders, 28,* 282–298.

Gresham, F. M. (2015). Evidence-based social skills interventions for students at risk for EBD. *Remedial and Special Education, 36*(2), 100–104.

Gresham, F. M., & Elliott, S. N. (2008). Social Skills Improvement System: Rating Scales. Pearson.

Hays, P. A. (2022). *Addressing cultural complexities in counseling and clinical practice: An intersectional approach.* American Psychological Association.

Individuals with Disabilities Education Improvement Act. (2004). Public Law 108–446.

January, S.-A. A. (2023). Best practices in improving data-based decision making in schools. In P. L. Harrison, S. L. Proctor, & A. Thomas (Eds.), *Best practices in school psychology: Vol. 1. Data-based and collaborative decision making* (7th ed., pp. 77–89). National Association of School Psychologists.

Kirkbride, J. B., Anglin, D. M., Colman, I., Dykxhoorn, J., Jones, P. B., Patalay, P., et al. (2024). The social determinants of mental health and disorder: Evidence, prevention and recommendations. *World Psychiatry, 23*(1), 58–90.

Krämer, S., & Zimmermann, F. (2022). Students with emotional and behavioral disorder and teachers' stereotypes—effects on teacher judgments. *The Journal of Experimental Education, 91*(3), 450–471.

Lambert, M. C., January, S.-A. A., Gonzalez, J. E., Epstein, M. H., & Martin, J. (2021). Comparing behavioral and emotional strengths of students with and without emotional disturbance. *Journal of Psychoeducational Assessment, 39*(8), 999–1014.

Lane, K. L. (2022). Social, emotional, and behavioral assessment within tiered decision-making frameworks:

A closing commentary—looking back to move forward. *School Psychology Review, 51*(1), 63–66.

Marsh, R. J., Higgins, K., Morgan, J., Cumming, T. M., Brown, M., & McCreery, M. (2019). Evaluating school connectedness of students with emotional and behavioral disorders. *Children & Schools, 41*(3), 153–160.

Merrell, K. W., Felver-Gant, J. C., & Tom, K. M. (2011). Development and validation of a parent report measure for assessing social–emotional competencies of children and adolescents. *Journal of Child and Family Studies, 20*, 529–540.

Merrell, K. W., & Walker, H. M. (2004). Deconstructing a definition: Social maladjustment versus emotional disturbance and moving the EBD field forward. *Psychology in the Schools, 41*(8), 899–910.

Miller, K. L., Re Cruz, A., & Ala'i-Rosales, S. (2019). Inherent tensions and possibilities: Behavior analysis and cultural responsiveness. *Behavior & Social Issues, 28*(1), 16–36.

Minkos, M. L., Sassu, K. A., Gregory, J. L., Patwa, S. S., Theodore, L. A., & Femc-Bagwell, M. (2017). Culturally responsive practice and the role of school administrators. *Psychology in the Schools, 54*(10), 1260–1266.

National Center for Education Statistics (NCES). (2023). Students With Disabilities. *Condition of Education*. U.S. Department of Education, Institute of Education Sciences. *https://nces.ed.gov/programs/coe/indicator/cgg*

Okonofua, J. A., & Eberhardt, J. L. (2015). Two strikes race and the disciplining of young students. *Psychological Science, 26*(5), 617–624.

O'Neill, R., Horner, R., Albin, R., Storey, K., & Sprague, J. (1997). *Functional assessment and program development for behavior problems*. Brooks/Cole.

Owens, J. S., & Evans, S. W. (2018). Progress monitoring change in children's social, emotional, and behavioral functioning: Advancing the state of the science. *Assessment for Effective Intervention, 43*(2), 67–70.

Pham, A. V., Goforth, A. N., Aguilar, L. N., Burt, I., Bastian, R., & Diaków, D. M. (2022). Dismantling systemic inequities in school psychology: Cultural humility as a foundational approach to social justice. *School Psychology Review, 51*(6), 692–709.

Pickens, I. B. (2022). Integrating a culturally responsive lens into social, emotional, and behavioral assessment within tiered decision-making frameworks. *School Psychology Review, 51*(1), 55–58.

Prati, G., Cicognani, E., & Albanesi, C. (2018). The impact of sense of community in the school, social skills, and exposure to aggression and victimization on students' well-being. *Social Indicators Research, 140*(2), 637–651.

Sallese, M. R., Garwood, J. D., Vannest, K. J., Kolbe, T., & Carlson, A. (2024). Definitions of and evaluation procedures for emotional disturbance: A tale of 50 states. *Behavioral Disorders, 49*(2), 106–115.

Sancassiani, F., Pintus, E., Holte, A., Paulus, P., Moro, M. F., Cossu, G., et al. (2015). Enhancing the emotional and social skills of the youth to promote their wellbeing and positive development: A systematic review of universal school-based randomized controlled trials. *Clinical Practice and Epidemiology in Mental Health, 11*(Suppl 1 M2), 21–40.

Skiba, R. J., Simmons, A. B., Ritter, S., Gibb, A. C., Rausch, M. K., Cuadrado, J., & Chung, C. G. (2008). Achieving equity in special education: History, status, and current challenges. *Exceptional Children, 74*(3), 264-288.

Substance Abuse and Mental Health Services Administration, Center for Mental Health Services (SAMHSA). (1993). Defining serious emotional disturbance in children: Final notice. *Federal Register, 58*(96), 29422–29425.

Substance Abuse and Mental Health Services Administration (SAMHSA). (2014). *Serious emotional disturbance expert panel meetings* [Summary of panel discussions and recommendations]. *www.samhsa.gov/data/sites/default/files/SED%20Expert%20Panels%20Summary%20Report.pdf*

Sullivan, A. L., & Sadeh, S. S. (2014). Differentiating social maladjustment from emotional disturbance: An analysis of case law. *School Psychology Review, 43*(4), 450–471.

U.S. Department of Education, Office of Special Education and Rehabilitative Services, Office of Special Education Programs. (2020). *42nd annual report to Congress on the implementation of the Individuals with Disabilities Education Act, 2020.*

Warren, C. A. (2015). Conflicts and contradictions: Conceptions of empathy and the work of good-intentioned early career white female teachers. *Urban Education, 50*(5), 572–600.

Whitford, D. K., & Emerson, A. M. (2019). Empathy intervention to reduce implicit bias in pre service teachers. *Psychological Reports, 122*(2), 670–688.

Wiley, A. L., Brigham, F. J., Kauffman, J. M., & Bogan, J. E. (2013). Disproportionate poverty, conservatism, and the disproportionate identification of minority students with emotional and behavioral disorders. *Education and Treatment of Children, 36*(4), 29–50.

Witt, J. C., Daly, E., & Noell, G. H. (2000). *Functional assessments: A step by-step guide to solving academic and behavior problems*. Sopris West.

Yates, T., Ostrosky, M. M., Cheatham, G. A., Fettig, A., Shaffer, L., & Santos, R. M. (2008). Research synthesis on screening and assessing social-emotional competence. *The Center on the Social and Emotional Foundations for Early Learning*, 1–19.

Zahra, S. T., Saleem, S., Subhan, S., & Mahmood, Z. (2021). Interpersonal skills scale: Development and validation in urbanized sample of adolescents. *Social Development, 30*(1), 23–37.

Zins, J. E., Bloodworth, M. R., Weissberg, R. P., & Walberg, H. J. (2007). The scientific basis linking social and emotional learning to school success. *Journal of Educational and Psychological Consultation, 17*(2 & 3), 191–210.

Index

Page numbers in *italics* refer to tables and figures.